Best Books for High School Readers

Recent Titles in the
Children's and Young Adult Literature Reference Series
Catherine Barr, Series Editor

A to Zoo: Subject Access to Children's Picture Books
Carolyn W. Lima and John A. Lima

Best Books for Children: Preschool Through Grade 6
Catherine Barr and John T. Gillespie

Best Books for Middle School and Junior High Readers,
Supplement to the First Edition
John T. Gillespie and Catherine Barr

Books Kids Will Sit Still For 3
Judy Freeman

Classic Teenplots
John T. Gillespie and Corinne J. Naden

The Newbery/Printz Companion
John T. Gillespie and Corinne J. Naden

Best Books for High School Readers

Grades 9-12,

Supplement to the First Edition

John T. Gillespie

Catherine Barr

Children's and Young Adult Literature Reference Series
Catherine Barr, Series Editor

LIBRARIES UNLIMITED

U N L I M I T E D

A Member of the Greenwood Publishing Group

Westport, Connecticut • London

Library of Congress Cataloging-in-Publication Data

Gillespie, John Thomas, 1928–
  Best books for high school readers : grades 9–12. Supplement to the first edition /
by John T. Gillespie and Catherine Barr.
     p. cm. — (Children's and young adult literature reference)
  Includes bibliographical references and indexes.
  ISBN 1-59158-410-8 (alk. paper)
  1. Young adult literature—Bibliography. 2. High school libraries—United States—Book lists.
3. Teenagers—Books and reading—United States. I. Barr, Catherine, 1951– II. Title.
Z1037.G4816 2004 Suppl.
011.62—dc22   2006031663

British Library Cataloguing in Publication Data is available.

Library of Congress Catalog Card Number: 2006031663
ISBN: 1-59158-410-8

Libraries Unlimited, 88 Post Road West, Westport, CT 06881
A Member of the Greenwood Publishing Group, Inc.
www.lu.com

Printed in the United States of America

The paper used in this book complies with the
Permanent Paper Standard issued by the National
Information Standards Organization (Z39.48–1984).

10   9   8   7   6   5   4   3   2   1

Contents

JUN   2007

History and Geography

Philosophy and Religion

vii

Society and the Individual

Guidance and Personal Development

ix

Recreation and Sports

Major Subjects Arranged Alphabetically

Preface

Best Books for High School Readers supplies information on books recommended for readers in grades 9 through 12 or roughly ages 15 through 18. The companion volumes *Best Books for Children* and *Best Books for Middle School and Junior High Readers* contain books recommended for preschool through grade 6 and grades 6 through 9, respectively.

As every librarian knows, reading levels are elastic. There is no such thing, for example, as a tenth-grade book. Instead there are only tenth-grade readers who, in their diversity, can represent a wide range of reading abilities and interests. This bibliography contains a liberal selection of entries that, one hopes, will accommodate readers in these four grades and make allowance for their great range of tastes and reading competencies. By the ninth grade, a percentage of the books read should be at the adult level. Keeping this in mind, about a quarter of the entries in this volume are adult books suitable for young adult readers (they are designated by a reading level of usually 10–12 within the entries and by S–Adult in the subject index). At the other end of the spectrum, there are also many titles that are suitable for younger readers (indicated by grade level designations such as 5–10, 6–10, 7–10, and so forth).

In selecting books for inclusion, deciding on their arrangement, and collecting the information supplied on each, it was the editors' intention to reflect the current needs and interests of young readers while keeping in mind the latest trends and curricular emphases in today's schools.

General Scope and Criteria for Inclusion

This supplement covers a two-year period, picking up from *Best Books for High School Readers,* which was published in 2004, and including recommended titles published through mid-2006. Of the 2,659 titles listed in this supplement, 2,538 are individually numbered entries and 121 are cited within the annotations as additional recommended titles by the same author.

For most fiction and nonfiction, a minimum of two recommendations were required from the current reviewing sources consulted for a title to be considered for listing. However, there were a number of necessary exceptions. For example, in some reviewing journals only a few representative titles from extensive nonfiction series are reviewed even though others in the series will also be recommended. In such cases a single favorable review was enough for inclusion. This also held true for some of the adult titles suitable for young adult readers where, it has been found, reviewing journals tend to be less inclusive than with juvenile titles. Again, depending on the strength of the review, a single positive one was sufficient for inclusion. As well as favorable reviews, additional criteria such as availability, up-to-dateness, accuracy, usefulness, and relevance were considered.

Excluded from this bibliography are general reference works, such as dictionaries and encyclopedias, except for a few single-volume works that are so heavily illustrated and attractive that they can also be used in the general circulation collection. Also excluded are professional books for librarians and teachers and mass market series books.

The graphic novels section includes contemporary graphic novels, many with elements of fantasy and/or science fiction. However, books presenting classics in a graphic novel format will be found in the appropriate location for that classic.

Arrangement

In the Table of Contents, subjects are arranged by the order in which they appear in the book. Following the Table of Contents is a listing of Major Subjects Arranged Alphabetically, which provides entry numbers as well as page numbers for easy access. Following the main body of the text, there are three indexes. The Author Index cites authors and editors, titles, and entry numbers (joint authors and editors are listed separately). The Title Index gives the book's entry number. Works of fiction in both of these indexes are indicated by (F) following the entry number. Finally, an extensive Subject/Grade Level Index lists entry numbers under hundreds of subject headings with specific grade-level suitability given for each entry. The following codes are used to identify general grade levels:

JS   (Junior–Senior High) suitable for junior high and senior high (grades 7 and up)

S   (Senior High) suitable usually only for senior high grades (grades 10–12)

S–Adult (Senior High–Adult) written for an adult audience but suitable for high school collections (usually grades 10–12)

Books that contain material that might be objectionable to some readers (scenes of graphic sex, for example) usually include a note in the annotation indicating that the book is suitable for mature readers and may be restricted to grades 11 and 12.

Entries

A typical entry contains the following information where applicable: (1) author, joint author, or editor; (2) title and subtitle; (3) specific grade levels given in parentheses; (4) adapter or translator; (5) indication of illustrations; (6) series title; (7) publication date; (8) publisher and price of hardbound edition (LB = library binding); (9) International Standard Book Number (ISBN) of hardbound edition; (10) paperback publisher (paper) and price (if no publisher is listed it is the same as the hardbound edition); (11) ISBN of paperback edition; (12) number of pages; (13) annotation; (14) review citations; (15) Dewey Decimal classification number.

Review Citations

Review citations guide you to more-detailed information about each of the books listed. The periodical sources identified are:

Booklist (BL)
Bulletin of the Center for Children's Books (BCCB)
Horn Book (HB)
Horn Book Guide (HBG)
Library Media Connection (LMC)
School Library Journal (SLJ)
VOYA (Voice of Youth Advocates) (VOYA)

Acknowledgments

Many thanks to Barbara Ittner of Libraries Unlimited and to Don Amerman, Christine McNaull, and Julie Miller for all their help with this volume.

John Gillespie
Catherine Barr

Literary Forms

Fiction

Adventure and Survival Stories

1 Bowler, Tim. *Apocalypse* (10–12). 2005, Simon & Schuster $16.95 (1-4169-0370-4). 240pp. Kit and his parents, forced to ground their sinking boat on an unknown island, find themselves among primitive villagers who regard Kit as a figure of evil. (Rev: BL 9/15/05; SLJ 10/05; VOYA 8/05)

2 Hart, J. V. *Capt. Hook: The Adventures of a Notorious Youth* (7–10). 2005, HarperCollins LB $16.89 (0-06-000221-2). 352pp. The story of Captain Hook's youth follows his lonely childhood, time at Eton, difficult life aboard a slave ship, and dreams of a Neverland. (Rev: BL 7/05; SLJ 10/05)

3 MacPhail, Catherine. *Underworld* (7–10). 2005, Bloomsbury $16.95 (1-58234-997-5). 288pp. Five British teens with very different personalities find themselves trapped in a cave on a remote Scottish island; adding to their predicament is their fear of a giant worm reputed to inhabit the caves. (Rev: BL 7/05; SLJ 7/05; VOYA 8/05)

4 Meyer, L. A. *Under the Jolly Roger: Being an Account of the Further Nautical Adventures of Jacky Faber* (7–10). 2005, Harcourt $17.00 (0-15-205345-X). 528pp. In this volume full of adventure, plucky 15-year-old Jacky Faber — last seen in *Bloody Jack* (2002) and *Curse of the Blue Tattoo* (2004) — travels from Boston to England in 1804 in search of her true love but ends up taking control of a British warship. (Rev: BL 8/05; SLJ 9/05; VOYA 8/05)

5 Murray, Yxta Maya. *The Queen Jade* (11–12). Illus. 2005, HarperCollins $23.95 (0-06-058264-2). 352pp. When Lola Sanchez's archaeologist mother goes missing in the Guatemalan jungle, Lola enlists an unlikely ally in the search — Erik, her mother's

professional archrival; for mature teens. (Rev: BL 1/1–15/05)

6 Paulsen, Gary. *Brian's Hunt* (6–10). Series: Brian's Saga. 2003, Random LB $17.99 (0-385-90882-2). 144pp. Brian rescues a wounded dog and embarks on a hunt for a rogue bear that has savagely killed and partially eaten two of Brian's Cree friends. (Rev: BCCB 2/04; BL 1/1–15/04; SLJ 12/03)

Classics

Europe

GREAT BRITAIN AND IRELAND

7 Stevenson, Robert Louis. *Graphic Classics: Robert Louis Stevenson* (9–12). Series: Graphic Classics. 2004, Eureka paper $9.95 (0-9746648-0-4). 144pp. Six of Robert Louis Stevenson's most famous works, including *Kidnapped* and *The Strange Case of Dr. Jekyll and Mr. Hyde*, are presented in graphic novel format. (Rev: BL 9/15/04; VOYA 2/05)

8 Willard, Nancy, and John Milton. *The Tale of Paradise Lost: Based on the Poem by John Milton* (6–12). 2004, Simon & Schuster $17.95 (0-689-85097-2). 160pp. This prose retelling of Milton's immortal "Paradise Lost" traces the story of Adam and Eve's expulsion from the Garden of Eden and the fall of Satan from God's grace. (Rev: BL 10/1/04; HB 11/12/04; SLJ 1/05)

United States

9 Poe, Edgar Allan. *Edgar Allan Poe's Tales of Mystery and Madness* (7–12). Trans. by Stephen Soenkson. 2004, Simon & Schuster $17.95 (0-689-

84837-4). 144pp. Striking artwork brings to life four of Edgar Allan Poe's classic mystery tales, presented here in abridged form. (Rev: BL 10/15/04*; SLJ 10/04)

10 Twain, Mark. *Graphic Classics: Mark Twain* (7–10). Illus. Series: Graphic Classics. 2004, Eureka paper $9.95 (0-9712464-8-3). 144pp. Various artists offer diverse graphic novel treatments of Twain stories including "A Ghost Story," "Advice to Little Girls," and "The Mysterious Stranger." (Rev: SLJ 3/04)

Contemporary Life and Problems

General and Miscellaneous

11 Addonizio, Kim. *Little Beauties* (11–12). 2005, Simon & Schuster $23.00 (0-7432-7182-3). 256pp. Diana, a compulsive washer, is conflicted when unwed 17-year-old Jamie needs a place to stay with her new baby. (Rev: BL 7/05)

12 Anderson, Jodi Lynn. *Peaches* (8–11). 2005, HarperCollins LB $16.89 (0-06-073306-3). 320pp. Three teenage girls from diverse backgrounds forge lasting bonds during a summer picking peaches in a Georgia orchard. (Rev: BL 10/1/05; SLJ 8/05; VOYA 2/06)

13 Ashton, Victoria. *Confessions of a Teen Nanny* (8–12). 2005, HarperCollins LB $16.89 (0-06-077524-6). 198pp. Hired as a temporary nanny for an 8-year-old child prodigy, 16-year-old Adrienne finds herself being manipulated by her charge's older sister. (Rev: BL 8/05; SLJ 7/05)

14 Auster, Paul. *Auggie Wren's Christmas Story* (9–12). 2004, Holt $17.50 (0-8050-7723-5). 48pp. Auggie, a New York smoke-shop owner, tells a heartwarming Christmas fable. (Rev: BL 9/15/04)

15 Bates, Shelley. *Pocketful of Pearls* (9–12). 2005, Warner paper $12.99 (0-446-69491-6). 269pp. Former college professor Matthew Nicholas takes a job as handyman for Dinah Traynell, a woman caught in the vise-like grip of a religious cult, in a compelling story of unhappiness and newfound trust. (Rev: BL 10/1/05)

16 Bodett, Tom. *Norman Tuttle on the Last Frontier: A Novel in Stories* (8–10). 2004, Knopf LB $17.99 (0-679-99031-3). 208pp. In this coming-of-age story presented in interconnected episodes, klutzy Alaskan teenager Norman Tuttle experiences many firsts — first job, first date, first hunting expedition — and his relationship with his father evolves. (Rev: BL 12/1/04; SLJ 12/04; VOYA 12/04)

17 Brian, Kate. *Megan Meade's Guide to the McGowan Boys* (8–11). 2005, Simon & Schuster $14.95 (1-4169-0030-6). 272pp. Megan does not want to move to South Korea with her military parents and chooses instead to stay with the McGowans, a family with seven sons, requiring adjustments all round. (Rev: BL 9/15/05; SLJ 11/05; VOYA 12/05)

18 Brugman, Alyssa. *Finding Grace* (6–12). 2004, Dell LB $17.99 (0-385-90142-9). 240pp. College-bound Rachel is hired to care for a brain-injured woman named Grace and in the process learns some valuable lessons about both Grace and herself. (Rev: BL 9/15/04; SLJ 11/04; VOYA 12/04)

19 Cabot, Meg. *Teen Idol* (7–11). 2004, HarperCollins LB $16.89 (0-06-009617-9). 304pp. Jenny Greenley, a junior at an Indiana high school, acts as a student guide for teen idol Luke Striker who comes to the school to do undercover research for an upcoming role. (Rev: BL 10/1/04; SLJ 8/04; VOYA 10/04)

20 Caletti, Deb. *Wild Roses* (7–10). 2005, Simon & Schuster $15.95 (0-689-86766-2). 296pp. Seventeen-year-old Cassie finds life with her stepfather — an unstable violinist and composer — difficult at the best of times, but things go from bad to worse when she falls for one of his music students. (Rev: BCCB 10/05; BL 10/1/05; SLJ 11/05*; VOYA 12/05)

21 Cirrone, Dorian. *Dancing in Red Shoes Will Kill You* (9–12). 2005, HarperCollins LB $16.89 (0-06-055702-8). 224pp. Sixteen-year-old Kayla, a talented ballet student at Florida Arts High School, known by its students as "Farts," considers breast reduction surgery because she feels her over-ample bosom is keeping her from winning lead roles in school ballets. (Rev: BL 1/1–15/05; SLJ 2/05; VOYA 6/05)

22 Cole, Stephen. *Thieves Like Us* (8–11). 2006, Bloomsbury $16.95 (1-58234-653-4). 352pp. Jonah Wish, a member of a gang of teenage thieves, finds himself questioning the morality of certain activities. (Rev: BL 4/1/06)

23 Collins, Yvonne, and Sandy Rideout. *Introducing Vivien Leigh Reid: Daughter of the Diva* (7–10). 2005, St. Martin's $11.95 (0-312-33837-6). 240pp. Sent to Ireland to spend the summer on the set of her actress mother's latest film, 15-year-old Leigh Reid wins a bit part in the movie, develops a crush on a costar, and finally begins to build a meaningful relationship with her mom. (Rev: BL 6/1–15/05; SLJ 9/05)

24 Collins, Yvonne, and Sandy Rideout. *Now Starring Vivien Leigh Reid: Diva in Training* (8–12). 2006, Griffin paper $9.95 (0-312-33839-2). 242pp. In this sequel to the witty *Introducing Vivien Leigh Reid: Daughter of the Diva* (2005), 16-year-old Leigh lands a role in a soap opera and initially adopts a prima donna attitude that threatens her friendships and her job. (Rev: SLJ 1/06; VOYA 4/06)

25 Craft, Elizabeth, and Sarah Fein. *Bass Ackwards and Belly Up* (8–11). 2006, Little, Brown $16.99 (0-316-05793-2). 416pp. Harper starts a trend among her friends when she pretends she has rejected college (it was the other way round) to stay home and write; the novel follows the four girls through their adventures as aspiring author, aspiring actress, backpacking European tourist, and college freshman/aspiring ski champion. (Rev: BL 4/1/06)

26 Cunningham, Michael. *Specimen Days* (11–12). 2005, Farrar $24.00 (0-374-29962-5). 288pp. Channeling Walt Whitman, Cunningham weaves together three inventive and genre-rich stories of New York City, set in the mid-1800s, the 1920s, and the future; for mature teens. (Rev: BL 5/1/05; SLJ 10/05)

27 Czech, Jan M. *Grace Happens* (8–11). 2005, Viking $15.99 (0-670-05962-5). 160pp. Grace, 15-year-old daughter of movie star Constance Meredith, looks forward to a quiet summer on Martha's Vineyard, away from the buzz that usually surrounds her mom, but it turns out to be a much more rewarding summer than she imagined and she discovers not only her father but her grandmother. (Rev: BL 5/1/05; SLJ 7/05)

28 Dean, Zoey. *Girls on Film* (9–12). Series: The A-List. 2004, Little, Brown paper $8.99 (0-316-73475-6). 228pp. A fast-paced novel of wealth, shopping, intrigue, and gossip in Beverly Hills, with Anna Percy having to decide between the unsuitable but attractive Ben and the suitable but less stimulating Adam, as well as coping with her recovering-addict sister Susan's arrival on the West Coast; a sequel to *The A-List* (2003). (Rev: SLJ 5/04)

29 Dellin, Genell. *Montana Blue* (11–12). 2005, HQN paper $5.99 (0-373-77044-8). 384pp. Blue blames Gordon Campbell for his sister's drug addiction and his mother's death; now he must decide whether to help Gordon's stepdaughter with her addicted son Shane; for mature teens. (Rev: BL 9/15/05)

30 D'Erasmo, Stacey. *A Seahorse Year* (11–12). 2004, Houghton $24.00 (0-618-43923-4). 368pp. A complex story in which Christopher, a 16-year-old schizophrenic, disappears from his San Francisco home, causing much consternation to his parents, who are both gay; for mature readers. (Rev: BL 6/1–15/04)

31 DuPrau, Jeanne. *Car Trouble* (7–10). 2005, Greenwillow LB $16.89 (0-06-073674-7). 288pp. Seventeen-year-old Duff Pringle has various car and people adventures on the road from Virginia to a promised job in California. (Rev: BL 8/05; SLJ 10/05; VOYA 10/05)

32 Evans, Diana. *26a* (9–12). 2005, Morrow $23.95 (0-06-082091-8). 240pp. As twins Bessi and Georgia Hunter — daughters of a Nigerian mother and

English father — grow older, their closeness comes under increasing strain. (Rev: BL 8/05; SLJ 1/06)

33 Fitzgerald, Kitty. *Pigtopia* (11–12). 2005, Hyperion $22.95 (1-4013-5251-0). 256pp. Jack, so badly disfigured that he lives among pigs in what he calls "the Pig Palace," finds a friend — and temporary happiness — in loner Holly, a neighboring teen; for mature teens. (Rev: BL 9/1/05)

34 Fredericks, Mariah. *Crunch Time* (8–11). 2006, Simon & Schuster $15.95 (0-689-86938-X). 336pp. Four members of a private SAT study group — who have formed emotional attachments as they study — find themselves under suspicion of cheating. (Rev: BL 1/1–15/06; SLJ 1/06; VOYA 12/05)

35 Friesen, Gayle. *The Isabel Factor* (7–10). 2005, Kids Can $16.95 (1-55337-737-0). 256pp. Anna's best friend Zoe breaks her arm and, for the first time in years, Anna finds herself running her own life. (Rev: BL 9/1/05; SLJ 11/05)

36 Gallo, Donald R. *First Crossing: Stories About Teen Immigrants* (7–10). 2005, Candlewick $16.99 (0-7636-2249-4). 240pp. A collection of compelling and diverse stories about contemporary immigration to the United States and the situations of newly arrived teens. (Rev: BL 11/15/04; SLJ 10/04)

37 Gattis, Ryan. *Kung Fu High School* (11–12). Illus. 2005, Harcourt paper $13.00 (0-15-603036-5). 288pp. Full of strong language and extreme violence, this is the story of a school that has been taken over by gangs, drug dealers, and martial arts experts. (Rev: BL 8/05; VOYA 2/06)

38 Gonzalez, Julie. *Wings* (8–11). 2005, Delacorte LB $17.99 (0-385-90253-0). 176pp. A suspenseful story in which Ben is convinced he will someday sprout wings and take to the sky despite evidence to the contrary. (Rev: BCCB 4/05; BL 3/15/05; SLJ 8/05; VOYA 4/05)

39 Gore, Kristin. *Sammy's Hill* (9–12). 2004, Hyperion $23.95 (1-4013-5219-7). 400pp. An entertaining story about the trials and tribulations of a young innocent on Capitol Hill, by the daughter of the former vice president. (Rev: BL 8/04)

40 Hannah, Kristin. *Magic Hour* (11–12). 2006, Ballantine $23.95 (0-345-46752-3). 400pp. Disgraced in the eyes of her patients although exonerated by the courts, child psychiatrist Julia Cates returns to her small hometown in Washington state where she and her sister try to help a young girl who is believed to have been raised by wolves; for mature teens. (Rev: BL 12/15/05)

41 Henry, Patti Callahan. *Where the River Runs* (11–12). 2005, NAL paper $12.95 (0-451-21505-2). 256pp. Meridy must revisit a tragedy in her youth in this novel set in South Carolina's Low Country; for mature teens. (Rev: BL 5/1/05)

42 Hogan, Mary. *The Serious Kiss* (7–10). 2005, HarperCollins LB $16.89 (0-06-072207-X). 256pp. Fourteen-year-old Libby's life seems to be in the hands of others — her alcoholic father, her fat mother, the unkind kids at her new school. (Rev: BCCB 3/05; BL 2/1/05; SLJ 1/05; VOYA 2/05)

43 Homes, A. M. *This Book Will Save Your Life* (11–12). 2006, Viking $24.95 (0-670-03493-2). 372pp. For advanced readers, this is an entertaining story about lonely wealthy Richard, an LA money maker who finds his life turned around by a health scare and a sinkhole. (Rev: BL 3/1/06)

44 Houston, Pam. *Sight Hound* (11–12). 2005, Norton $23.95 (0-393-05817-4). 288pp. Playwright Rae and her menagerie of pets are taken by surprise by a marriage proposal in this novel written from many points of view, including a dog's. (Rev: BL 11/15/04; SLJ 5/05)

45 Hurwin, Davida Wills. *Circle the Soul Softly* (7–12). 2006, HarperCollins LB $16.89 (0-06-077506-8). 169pp. Only as 10th-grader Katie becomes more attached to David does she come to realize that her difficulties adapting to "normal" life stem from abuse by her now-deceased father. (Rev: BCCB 4/06; SLJ 3/06)

46 Hyland, M. J. *Carry Me Down* (9–12). 2006, Canongate $23.00 (1-84195-740-2). 352pp. John Egan is a study in confusion — he is only 11 but he's nearly 6 feet tall and has a deep voice; he considers himself a good liar but can't understand why his father needs to tell lies — and his first-person narrative explains the threats of the adult world. (Rev: BL 2/15/06)

47 Jacobson, Jennifer. *Stained* (9–12). 2005, Simon & Schuster $16.95 (0-689-86745-X). 208pp. A multilayered novel in which the disappearance of a young man who was sexually involved with a Roman Catholic priest is the most thought-provoking aspect. (Rev: BCCB 2/05; BL 4/1/05; HB 3–4/05; SLJ 3/05; VOYA 4/05)

48 Jensen, Liz. *The Ninth Life of Louis Drax* (10–12). 2005, Bloomsbury $23.95 (1-58234-517-1). 240pp. Louis, a French boy in a coma after the ninth accident of his young life, narrates this compelling novel along with his doctor, who is falling in love with Louis's mother. (Rev: BL 11/15/04)

49 Johnson, Angela. *Bird* (6–10). 2004, Penguin $15.99 (0-8037-2847-6). 144pp. Heartbroken when her stepfather abandons the family, 13-year-old Bird travels from Cleveland to Alabama to find him and bring him home and instead finds unexpected friendship. (Rev: BL 9/1/04; SLJ 9/04; VOYA 2/05)

50 Johnson, Catherine. *Face Value* (9–12). 2006, Walker $16.95 (0-8027-8920-X). 288pp. Lauren, 15, is pleased to have a modeling career ahead of her and is unaware that her guardian's anxiety stems from her worry that Lauren will follow the down- ward path of her dead mother, who was also a model. (Rev: BL 4/1/06)

51 Johnson, Maureen. *13 Little Blue Envelopes* (8–11). 2005, HarperCollins LB $16.89 (0-06-054142-3). 336pp. On a trip through Europe following instructions left to her in 13 letters written by her Aunt Peg before her death, 17-year-old Ginny learns about Peg's past and about herself. (Rev: BL 9/15/05; SLJ 10/05; VOYA 10/05)

52 Jones, Patrick. *Nailed* (9–12). 2006, Walker $16.95 (0-8027-8077-6). 224pp. Bret's unconventional interests in music and theater cause difficulties for him both at home and at school. (Rev: BL 2/15/06; VOYA 4/06)

53 Kaye, Amy. *The Real Deal: Unscripted* (7–12). 2004, Dorchester paper $5.99 (0-8439-5315-2). 208pp. Claire juggles a potential Broadway career, a romance with a teen star, and the needs of her newfound half-sister, all under the glare of reality TV cameras. (Rev: SLJ 5/04)

54 Klass, David. *Dark Angel* (8–11). 2005, Farrar $17.00 (0-374-39950-6). 320pp. Seventeen-year-old Jeff's family has hidden the existence of his older brother, a murderer who has been in jail; when Troy is released and comes home to live, Jeff's life is turned upside down. (Rev: BL 9/15/05; SLJ 10/05; VOYA 10/05)

55 Koertge, Ron. *Margaux with an X* (9–12). 2005, Candlewick $15.99 (0-7636-2401-2). 176pp. Drawn together by their unhappiness at home, gorgeous Margaux and geeky Danny strike up an unlikely alliance. (Rev: BL 9/15/04; SLJ 9/04)

56 Korman, Gordon. *Born to Rock* (7–10). 2006, Hyperion $15.99 (0-7868-0920-5). 272pp. Leo, a Young Republican with traditional values, finds himself in a totally different world when he discovers his biological father is a punk singer and joins his band in hope of getting tuition money. (Rev: BL 3/1/06)

57 Korman, Gordon. *Son of the Mob: Hollywood Hustle* (9–12). 2004, Hyperion $15.99 (0-7868-0918-3). 272pp. Eighteen-year-old Vince Luca, son of a New York crime boss, hopes to escape the taint of his family ties by going to college in Southern California, but it soon becomes clear that he can't escape the past so easily; a sequel to *Son of the Mob* (2002). (Rev: BL 10/1/04; SLJ 9/04)

58 Koss, Amy Goldman. *Poison Ivy* (7–10). 2006, Roaring Brook $16.95 (1-59643-118-0). 176pp. Multiple voices tell the story of the mock trial of the three bullies who have been making unpopular Ivy's life a misery. (Rev: BL 2/15/06; SLJ 3/06; VOYA 4/06)

59 Krauss, Nicole. *The History of Love* (11–12). 2005, Norton $23.95 (0-393-06034-9). 252pp. The stories of Leo Gurski, a retired locksmith who once wrote a book about his love for Alma back in pre-

Nazi Poland, and of lonely 14-year-old Alma intersect in this rich novel full of twists. (Rev: BL 3/15/05)

60 Krulik, Nancy. *Love and Sk8* (7–12). 2004, Simon & Schuster paper $5.99 (0-689-87076-0). 315pp. Eighteen-year-old Angie has three passions — skateboarding, art, and getting out of her Pennsylvania mill town — until she meets Carter, grandson of the mill owner, and her class preconceptions are turned upside down. (Rev: SLJ 10/04)

61 Lasky, Kathryn. *Blood Secret* (6–10). 2004, HarperCollins LB $16.89 (0-06-000065-1). 256pp. Silent since the sudden disappearance of her mother eight years earlier, 14-year-old Jerry Luna goes to live with a great-aunt where a trunk draws her into the time of the Spanish Inquisition and long-hidden secrets about her ancestors. (Rev: BL 10/1/04; SLJ 8/04; VOYA 10/04)

62 Levithan, David. *Are We There Yet?* (10–12). 2005, Knopf LB $17.99 (0-375-92846-4). 224pp. Brothers Elijah and Danny have little in common except their parents, who decide a vacation in Italy may help bring their sons back together again. (Rev: BCCB 7–8/05; BL 5/15/05; SLJ 7/05; VOYA 8/05)

63 Lockhart, E. *Fly on the Wall: How One Girl Saw Everything* (7–10). 2006, Delacorte LB $17.99 (0-385-90299-9). 184pp. Gretchen Yee's wish to be a fly on the wall of the boys' locker room comes true and in the process she gains confidence and learns a lot about boys and friendship. (Rev: BCCB 4/06; BL 7/06; HB 3–4/06; SLJ 3/06)

64 Lynch, Chris. *Inexcusable* (9–12). 2005, Simon & Schuster $16.95 (0-689-84789-0). 176pp. Keir, a senior in high school and football player, prides himself on being a "lovable rogue" and is used to rationalizing some of his less lovable activities, but can he convince himself of his innocence when he rapes Gigi? (Rev: BL 9/15/05*; SLJ 11/05*; VOYA 12/05)

65 McCouch, Hannah. *Mountain Betty* (11–12). 2005, Villard paper $12.95 (0-8129-6841-7). 240pp. Fired from her first post-college job, Betty heads west to try life as a ski bum; exhausted by two jobs and exasperated with her wayward, pot-smoking boyfriend, she returns to Connecticut to help her ill mother and reevaluate; for mature teens. (Rev: BL 12/15/04)

66 McNicoll, Sylvia. *A Different Kind of Beauty* (7–10). 2004, Fitzhenry & Whiteside $15.95 (1-55005-059-1); paper $8.95 (1-55005-060-5). 208pp. Elizabeth, who is training a puppy as a guide dog, and Kyle, whose diabetes has left him blind, attend the same high school without knowing each other. (Rev: SLJ 8/04; VOYA 8/04)

67 Marks, Graham. *Radio Radio* (8–11). 2004, Bloomsbury paper $11.99 (0-7475-5939-2). 220pp. A group of London club kids goes up against both the government and some unsavory competitors when they set up a pirate radio station. (Rev: BL 1/1–15/05; SLJ 1/05)

68 Mehran, Marsha. *Pomegranate Soup* (11–12). 2005, Random $24.95 (1-4000-6241-1). 240pp. Three Iranian sisters escape the violence in their country and make their way to Ireland where they open the Babylon Cafe in this novel full of food and romance suitable for mature teens. (Rev: BL 7/05)

69 Mitchard, Jacquelyn. *Cage of Stars* (9–12). 2006, Warner $24.95 (0-446-57875-4). 294pp. When her younger sisters are murdered, 12-year-old Veronica finds it impossible to follow her Mormon parents' example and forgive the perpetrator. (Rev: BL 2/15/06)

70 Na, An. *Wait for Me* (8–11). 2006, Penguin $15.99 (0-399-24275-9). 176pp. Unable to meet her mother's expectations, Korean American high school senior Mina resorts to lies and plans for escape, but when Ysrael, with whom she has fallen in love, is blamed for Mina's actions she must make a difficult choice. (Rev: BL 3/15/06*)

71 Nelson, Blake. *Prom Anonymous* (9–12). 2006, Viking $16.99 (0-670-05945-5). 272pp. Three friends, under the guidance of highly efficient Laura, learn some truths about themselves as they plan every last detail for the forthcoming prom. (Rev: BL 4/1/06; SLJ 3/06)

72 Nelson, D.-L. *The Card* (9–12). 2005, Five Star $26.95 (1-59414-417-6). 308pp. On the same recycled Christmas card that they exchange each year, longtime friends Diana and Jane each jot down a single sentence to summarize what the past year has brought. (Rev: BL 10/15/05)

73 Nields, Nerissa. *Plastic Angel* (7–10). 2005, Scholastic $17.95 (0-439-70913-X). 208pp. Thirteen-year-olds Randi and Gellie become friends despite their differences and form a band called Plastic Angel. (Rev: BL 8/05; SLJ 9/05; VOYA 2/06)

74 Nilsson, Per. *You and You and You* (9–12). Trans. by Tara Chase. 2005, Front Street $16.95 (1-932425-19-5). 250pp. Three characters — 12-year-old Anon, who believes his father is a god; 17-year-old Zarah, who is in a lonely and abusive relationship; and 20-year-old Nils, who is obsessed by death — are at the center of this offbeat, graphically sexual but compelling novel. (Rev: BL 7/05*; SLJ 8/05*)

75 O'Connell, Tyne. *Pulling Princes* (7–10). 2004, Bloomsbury $16.95 (1-58234-957-6). 221pp. Calypso Kelly, a 15-year-old from LA, finds it difficult to fit in at her posh English boarding school. (Rev: SLJ 12/04; VOYA 4/05)

76 Pollack, Jenny. *Klepto: Best Friends, First Love, and Shoplifting* (8–11). 2006, Viking $16.99 (0-670-06061-5). 288pp. In the early 1980s, Julie Prodsky, a 14-year-old drama major at New York's High

School of Performing Arts, meets cool Julie Braverman and sets out on a career of "getting" rather than buying. (Rev: BL 2/15/06; SLJ 4/06)

77 Prose, Francine. *A Changed Man* (9–12). 2005, HarperCollins $24.95 (0-06-019674-2). 416pp. An Ecstasy-fueled epiphany results in Vincent's renunciation of his neo-Nazi lifestyle; volunteering at a human rights organization, he's taken in by Bonnie, the center's altruistic assistant and single mom to two teenage sons. (Rev: BL 12/1/04)

78 Rallison, Janette. *Fame, Glory, and Other Things on My To-Do List* (7–10). 2005, Walker $16.95 (0-8027-8991-9). 192pp. Sixteen-year-old Jessica dreams of Hollywood stardom, but things don't look promising till Jordan, the good-looking son of an actor, moves to town. (Rev: BL 10/15/05; SLJ 11/05)

79 Rosoff, Meg. *How I Live Now* (8–11). 2004, Random LB $18.99 (0-385-90908-X). 208pp. In this riveting futuristic novel, 15-year-old New York City resident Daisy, desperate to escape her evil stepmother, goes to England to stay on her aunt's farm; there she finds friendship and a sexual relationship, but war soon intervenes. Printz Award, 2005. (Rev: BL 9/1/04*; SLJ 9/04; VOYA 12/04)

80 Rosten, Carrie. *Chloe Leiberman (Sometimes Wong)* (7–10). 2005, Delacorte LB $17.99 (0-385-90271-9). 224pp. Half Chinese and half Jewish, 17-year-old Chloe Leiberman lives for fashion, but she's not really sure what the future holds for her until she meets La Contessa, a neighbor who finally helps to give the privileged teenager's life some direction. (Rev: BL 11/15/05; SLJ 12/05)

81 Sambrook, Clare. *Hide and Seek* (9–12). 2005, Canongate $24.00 (1-84195-653-8). 288pp. Nine-year-old Harry's life falls apart after his younger brother Daniel disappears. (Rev: BL 7/05)

82 Scanlan, Patricia. *Two for Joy* (11–12). 2004, St. Martin's $25.95 (0-312-32895-8). 480pp. Three female Irish cousins experience different aspects of life — one is newly married, the others enjoying independence in Dublin; for mature readers. (Rev: BL 6/1–15/04)

83 Schrefer, Eliot. *Glamorous Disasters* (9–12). 2006, Simon & Schuster $23.95 (0-7432-8167-5). 330pp. After graduating from Princeton, Noah earns large sums tutoring the spoiled teenage children of wealthy New Yorkers and finds himself facing heavy ethical questions. (Rev: BL 3/15/06)

84 Schwartz, Lynne Sharon. *The Writing on the Wall* (11–12). 2005, Counterpoint $24.00 (1-58243-299-6). 304pp. The shocking events of September 11, 2001, have particular impact on Renata, a New York librarian who has tried to bury her own tragic past; for mature teens. (Rev: BL 5/1/05)

85 Shapiro, Anna. *Living on Air* (10–12). 2006, Soho $22.00 (1-56947-431-1). 272pp. In the 1960s,

14-year-old Maude faces a dichotomy between her artistic home life in middle-class Levittown and the wealth of her friends at the privileged Bay Farm School. (Rev: BL 4/1/06)

86 Sharp, Adrienne. *First Love* (11–12). 2005, Riverhead $23.95 (1-57322-310-7). 352pp. Adam and Sandra, young ballet dancers, are in love and must struggle against competing demands on their loyalties and time in this novel set in the 1980s and featuring a fictional George Balanchine. (Rev: BL 6/1–15/05)

87 Sheldon, Dyan. *Planet Janet in Orbit* (7–10). 2005, Candlewick $15.99 (0-7636-2755-0). 304pp. Janet, a live-wire British teen first seen in *Planet Janet* (2003), has a whirlwind year involving romance, friendship, family problems, driving lessons, and school adventures, all confided to her diary. (Rev: BL 10/1/05; SLJ 11/05)

88 Shulman, Polly. *Enthusiasm* (7–10). 2006, Penguin $15.99 (0-399-24389-5). 208pp. A romantic comedy of errors featuring Jane and Ashleigh, both fans of Jane Austen, who get roles in a play at the local boys' prep school. (Rev: BL 1/1–15/06*; SLJ 3/06; VOYA 4/06)

89 Shute, Jenefer. *User I.D.* (9–12). 2005, Houghton $23.00 (0-618-53906-9). 272pp. The stories of an identity thief and her victim are told from alternating viewpoints. (Rev: BL 8/05)

90 Siddons, Anne Rivers. *Sweetwater Creek* (10–12). 2005, HarperCollins $24.95 (0-06-621335-5). 368pp. Twelve-year-old Emily Parmenter finds solace in her work with hunting dogs after her brother's death and her mother's departure, but then the glamorous Lulu arrives and disrupts her carefully constructed life. (Rev: BL 7/05; SLJ 12/05)

91 Sittenfeld, Curtis. *The Man of My Dreams* (11–12). 2006, Random $22.95 (1-4000-6476-7). 288pp. Hannah's upbringing and her parents' breakup when she was 14 leave her ill-equipped to form lasting relationships with boyfriends. (Rev: BL 2/15/06)

92 Staples, Suzanne Fisher. *Under the Persimmon Tree* (7–10). 2005, Farrar $17.00 (0-374-38025-2). 288pp. The stories of Najmal, a brave young Afghani refugee, and Nusrat, an American woman helping with a refugee school, intersect as they wait for news of their loved ones in the chaos of the 2001 Afghan War. (Rev: BL 7/05*; SLJ 7/05; VOYA 10/05)

93 Stewart, Leah. *The Myth of You and Me* (9–12). 2005, Crown $22.00 (1-4000-9806-8). 288pp. Long after they left high school and their friendship came to an end, Cameron Wilson finds herself searching for former classmate Sonia. (Rev: BL 7/05; SLJ 3/06)

94 Sutherland, Regina Hale. *The Red Hat Society's Acting Their Age* (11–12). 2005, Warner paper

$5.99 (0-446-61674-5). 288pp. Members of the Red Hat Society (women over 50) offer sanctuary to a teenager who's run away from an abusive foster home; a humorous novel suitable for mature teens. (Rev: BL 12/15/05)

95 Sutherland, Tui T. *This Must Be Love* (7–10). 2004, HarperCollins LB $16.89 (0-06-056476-8). 256pp. Shakespearean plots are interwoven in this tale of Helena and Hermia, best friends in a modern New Jersey high school, and the comedy of errors that is their romantic life. (Rev: BCCB 1/05; SLJ 9/04)

96 Tanner, Mike. *Resurrection Blues* (10–12). 2005, Annick $19.95 (1-55037-897-X); paper $9.95 (1-55037-896-1). 250pp. Rock and roll beckons to 18-year-old Flynn and he drops out of school to go on the road with a traveling band. (Rev: BL 8/05; SLJ 8/05; VOYA 10/05)

97 Tracey, Rhian. *When Isla Meets Luke Meets Isla* (8–10). 2004, Bloomsbury paper $9.95 (0-7475-6344-6). 159pp. Told from alternating points of view, this is the story of troubled teens Isla and Luke — a Scottish girl who has just moved to England and a son of a newly divorced, obsessive mother — and the support and affection they give to each other. (Rev: SLJ 2/04)

98 Trembath, Don. *Rooster* (9–12). 2005, Orca paper $7.95 (1-55143-261-7). 200pp. Rooster risks failing to graduate from high school until he is persuaded to coach a bowling team of special-needs adults; the death of one of these bowlers is the catalyst that pushes him to succeed. (Rev: SLJ 1/06; VOYA 10/05)

99 Trevanian. *The Crazyladies of Pearl Street* (9–12). 2005, Crown paper $13.95 (1-4000-8037-1). 384pp. In 1936, Ruby moves 6-year-old Jean-Luc LaPointe and 3-year-old Anne-Marie to Albany, New York, to be with the father who is supposed to be getting out of jail but never turns up; they find a home on Pearl Street in a depressed Irish neighborhood and for the following years, Jean-Luc dreams of a better life. (Rev: BL 3/15/05)

100 Vernon, Olympia. *A Killing in This Town* (11–12). 2006, Grove $22.00 (0-8021-1813-5). 256pp. Bullock, Mississippi, is a sick town — made ill by industry-created lung disease and by prejudice involving appallingly violent acts by Klansmen against black residents; for mature teens. (Rev: BL 1/1–15/06)

101 Vrettos, Adrienne Maria. *Skin* (8–11). 2006, Simon & Schuster $16.95 (1-4169-0655-X). 240pp. Fourteen-year-old Donnie tells the story of his parents' unhappy marriage and his older sister's death from anorexia. (Rev: BL 3/1/06)

102 Waite, Judy. *Forbidden* (8–11). 2006, Simon & Schuster $16.95 (0-689-87642-4). 249pp. As one of the Chosen girls in the True Cause cult led by Howard, 16-year-old Elinor does not question her life until Outsider Jaime appears. (Rev: BCCB 2/06; BL 4/15/06; SLJ 3/06)

103 Wells, Rebecca. *Ya-Yas in Bloom* (11–12). 2005, HarperCollins $24.95 (0-06-019534-7). 272pp. This follow-up to *The Divine Secrets of the Ya-Ya Sisterhood* (1996) collects vignettes about the origins and exploits of the sisterhood and introduces the next two generations of Ya-Yas; for mature teens. (Rev: BL 1/1–15/05; VOYA 10/05)

104 Wesley, Valerie Wilson. *Playing My Mother's Blues* (9–12). 2005, Morrow $23.95 (0-06-018882-0). 240pp. An African American mother seeks to reconnect with the two now-adult daughters she abandoned years earlier. (Rev: SLJ 7/05)

105 Whitney, Kim Ablon. *The Perfect Distance* (7–10). 2005, Knopf LB $17.99 (0-375-93243-7). 256pp. Her riding ambitions and social, monetary, and romantic pressures all come to bear on Francie Martinez, daughter of a Mexican immigrant. (Rev: BL 9/1/05; SLJ 11/05)

106 Wiggs, Susan. *Table for Five* (11–12). 2005, MIRA $19.95 (0-7783-2167-3). 400pp. When their parents are killed, Cameron, Charlie, and Ashley all have problems that tax their co-caretakers — their uncle Sean and their teacher, Lily — but also draw them together; for mature teens. (Rev: BL 4/15/05)

107 Winston, Sherri. *Acting: A Novel* (9–12). 2004, Marshall Cavendish $15.95 (0-7614-5173-0). 256pp. Sixteen-year-old Eve struggles with her own sexual feelings amid the family upheaval when her twin sister announces her pregnancy. (Rev: BL 10/1/04; VOYA 6/05)

108 Winterson, Jeanette. *Lighthousekeeping* (11–12). 2005, Harcourt $23.00 (0-15-101117-6). 240pp. An orphan girl taken in by a blind Scottish lighthouse keeper learns that powerful stories can save — and destroy — lives; for mature teens. (Rev: BL 2/1/05)

109 Wright, Vinita Hampton. *Dwelling Places* (10–12). 2006, HarperSanFrancisco $23.95 (0-06-079080-6). 352pp. A family's emotional, spiritual, and physical well-being suffers through the father's efforts to hold onto his family farm in Iowa. (Rev: BL 1/1–15/06)

110 Wyeth, Sharon Dennis. *Orphea Proud* (7–12). 2004, Dell $15.95 (0-385-32497-9). 208pp. Seventeen-year-old Orphea, an orphan and aspiring poet, interweaves recitations of her poetry with the story of her love for Lissa, who died in a car accident only a day after their first kiss. (Rev: BL 11/1/04; SLJ 12/04; VOYA 12/04)

111 Wynne-Jones, Tim. *A Thief in the House of Memory* (7–10). 2005, Farrar $17.00 (0-374-37478-3). 224pp. Sixteen-year-old Dec can barely recall the events surrounding his mother's sudden disappearance six years earlier until the death of an intruder in the family home reawakens forgotten memories. (Rev: BCCB 5/05; BL 3/1/05; HB 5–6/05; SLJ 4/05; VOYA 6/05)

112 Young, Karen Romano. *Cobwebs* (9–12). 2004, Greenwillow $15.99 (0-06-029761-1). 400pp. In this unusual story of modern urban blending, 16-year-old Nancy, who seems to have inherited none of her Scottish-Italian and Jamaican parents' unusual spidery talents, finds comfort in her growing friendship with Dion, who is mysterious in his own way. (Rev: BL 1/1–15/05; SLJ 1/05; VOYA 2/05)

Ethnic Groups and Problems

113 Alegría, Malín. *Estrella's Quinceañera* (7–10). 2006, Simon & Schuster $14.95 (0-689-87809-5). 272pp. Planning for her fifteenth birthday celebration, Mexican American Estrella finds herself balancing her hopes against reality. (Rev: BL 2/15/06; SLJ 4/06)

114 Alvarez, Julia. *Finding Miracles* (8–11). 2004, Knopf LB $17.99 (0-375-82760-9). 272pp. Sixteen-year-old Milly Kaufman, rescued as a child from a strife-torn Latin American nation, is encouraged to return to her native country and learn more about her family roots. (Rev: BL 10/15/04; SLJ 10/04; VOYA 12/04)

115 Bates, Judy Fong. *Midnight at the Dragon Café* (11–12). 2005, Counterpoint paper $14.00 (1-58243-189-2). 326pp. Through deceptively simple narration, a Chinese girl tells of her immigration to Canada in the 1950s and her family's painful, hidden secrets; for mature teens. (Rev: BL 2/1/05)

116 Daswani, Kavita. *The Village Bride of Beverly Hills* (9–12). 2004, Penguin $23.95 (0-399-15214-8). 288pp. Priya's first year of marriage — in Los Angeles — is made difficult by her traditional Indian in-laws, who would disapprove if they knew of her job as a journalist at a *People*-like tabloid. (Rev: BL 8/04)

117 de la Cruz, Melissa. *Fresh off the Boat* (9–12). 2005, HarperCollins LB $16.89 (0-06-054541-0). 256pp. A recent immigrant from the Philippines, 14-year-old Vicenza finds it difficult as a scholarship student to fit in at the exclusive girls' school she attends in San Francisco. (Rev: BCCB 9/05; BL 4/15/05; SLJ 4/05; VOYA 8/05)

118 Flinn, Alex. *Fade to Black* (7–10). 2005, HarperCollins LB $17.89 (0-06-056841-0). 192pp. In alternating passages, an attack on an HIV-positive Hispanic teen is recounted from the viewpoints of three principals: the victim, the alleged attacker, and a witness. (Rev: BCCB 5/05; BL 4/15/05; SLJ 5/05; VOYA 4/05)

119 Griffis, Molly Levite. *Simon Says* (6–12). 2004, Eakin Press $22.95 (1-57168-836-6). It's 1942, and 11-year-old Jewish refugee Simon, shipped from Poland to live with an American family five years

earlier, is remembering his past amid signs of rising anti-Semitism in his adopted Oklahoma home; a sequel to *The Rachel Resistance* (2001) and *The Feester Filibuster* (2002). (Rev: BL 11/1/04; SLJ 1/05)

120 Kaldas, Pauline, and Khaled Mattawa, eds. *Dinarzad's Children: An Anthology of Contemporary Arab American Fiction* (9–12). 2004, Univ. of Arkansas paper $24.95 (1-55728-781-3). 336pp. Stories about what it is like to be an Arab in today's America, by Arab Americans from around the country. (Rev: BL 11/15/04)

121 Keltner, Kim Wong. *Buddha Baby* (11–12). 2005, Avon paper $12.95 (0-06-075322-6). 304pp. Chinese American Lindsey Owyang has become curious about her heritage — and, despite her permanent boyfriend, about what it would be like to date a Chinese guy — in this rich and entertaining novel in which she recalls her childhood worries about being different. (Rev: BL 8/05)

122 Lee, Marie Myung-Ok. *Somebody's Daughter* (11–12). 2005, Beacon $23.95 (0-8070-8388-7). 288pp. Raised in a stern adoptive midwestern family, 19-year-old Sarah travels to Korea, her birth land, intent on discovering the truth of her past. (Rev: BL 2/15/05; SLJ 4/05; VOYA 8/05)

123 McDonald, Janet. *Brother Hood* (7–12). 2004, Farrar $16.00 (0-374-30995-7). 176pp. Nate Whitely, a 16-year-old student at a prestigious boarding school, finds himself straddling two very different cultures as he seeks to remain loyal to his Harlem roots. (Rev: BL 9/1/04; SLJ 11/04; VOYA 2/05)

124 Myers, Walter Dean. *Autobiography of My Dead Brother* (8–11). 2005, HarperCollins LB $16.89 (0-06-058292-8). 224pp. In this compelling novel of teenage life in contemporary Harlem, Jessie watches helplessly as his friend Rise drifts away from him, dragged down in a whirlpool of drugs and crime. (Rev: BL 6/1–15/05; SLJ 8/05; VOYA 10/05)

125 Pagliarulo, Antonio. *A Different Kind of Heat* (7–10). 2006, Delacorte LB $9.99 (0-385-90319-7); paper $7.50 (0-385-73298-8). 192pp. Luz Cordero's anger about life in general and her brother's violent death in particular begins to abate when she finds friendship at the St. Therese Home for Boys and Girls and faces the truth. (Rev: BL 4/1/06)

126 Rose, Isabel. *The J. A. P. Chronicles* (11–12). 2005, Doubleday $22.95 (0-385-51286-4). 336pp. Seven Jewish women with varying adult problems look back at the year they were bunkmates in summer camp; for mature teens. (Rev: BL 4/1/05)

127 Roth, Matthue. *Never Mind the Goldbergs* (9–12). 2005, Scholastic $16.95 (0-439-69188-5). 361pp. Hava Aaronson, a somewhat unconventional Orthodox Jewish girl from New York City, is selected to star in a television sitcom caricaturing a modern Orthodox Jewish family and must reexamine her own beliefs. (Rev: BCCB 4/05; SLJ 6/05)

128 Saenz, Benjamin Alire. *Sammy and Juliana in Hollywood* (9–12). 2004, Cinco Puntos $19.95 (0-938317-81-4). 240pp. In the late 1960s in a tough barrio called Hollywood in Las Cruces, New Mexico, Sammy Santos faces problems ranging from the death of his girlfriend, poverty, racism, and the Vietnam War to unpopular dress codes. (Rev: BL 10/1/04; SLJ 9/04)

129 Singer, Marilyn, ed. *Face Relations: 11 Stories About Seeing Beyond Color* (7–12). 2004, Simon & Schuster $17.95 (0-689-85637-7). 240pp. This collection of 11 original short stories by well-known authors explores the issues of racial identity and race relations in American high schools. (Rev: BL 8/04*; SLJ 6/04; VOYA 8/04)

130 Vaught, Susan. *Stormwitch* (7–10). 2005, Bloomsbury $16.95 (1-58234-952-5). 200pp. Sixteen-year-old Ruba Cleo, transplanted in 1969 to a Mississippi Gulf Coast town from Haiti, wants to strike back at the racism and hostility she encounters by calling on the voodoo skills she learned in her native land. (Rev: BCCB 3/05; BL 2/15/05; SLJ 5/05; VOYA 2/05)

Family Life and Problems

131 Adoff, Jaime. *Jimi and Me* (8–11). 2005, Hyperion $15.99 (0-7868-5214-3). 330pp. Struggling to recover from the shock of his father's brutal murder, Keith, a biracial teen who loves the music of Hendrix, moves from Brooklyn to Ohio and discovers that his father had another son, named Jimi. (Rev: BL 10/1/05; SLJ 9/05)

132 Amateau, Gigi. *Claiming Georgia Tate* (8–12). 2005, Candlewick $15.99 (0-7636-2339-3). 196pp. When her beloved and protective grandmother dies, 12-year-old Georgia Tate finds herself at the mercy of her sexually abusive father in this novel set in the 1970s. (Rev: SLJ 6/05; VOYA 6/05)

133 Amidon, Stephen. *Human Capital* (9–12). 2004, Farrar $25.00 (0-374-17350-8). 384pp. A desperate father uses his daughter's romance as a stepping-stone to financial recovery in this indictment of modern morality. (Rev: BL 9/1/04)

134 Armstrong, Sarah. *Salt Rain* (11–12). 2006, MacAdam $22.00 (1-59692-173-0). 220pp. Spending time at the family farm in northern Australia after her mother commits suicide, 14-year-old Allie tries to find the truth about her father. (Rev: BL 3/15/06)

135 Auseon, Andrew. *Funny Little Monkey* (9–12). 2005, Harcourt $17.00 (0-15-205334-4). 304pp. Diminutive but smart Arty Moore is the fraternal twin of the tall but troubled Kurt; it takes a crisis to

bring the two closer together. (Rev: BCCB 7–8/05; BL 4/15/05; SLJ 6/05; VOYA 6/05)

136 Beauman, Sally. *The Sisters Mortland* (11–12). 2006, Warner $24.95 (0-446-57819-3). 433pp. A tragic accident during the summer of 1967 changes forever the lives of the three Mortland sisters; the first part of the book is narrated by 13-year-old Maisie; a compelling, complex novel suitable for mature teens. (Rev: BL 11/1/05)

137 Bohjalian, Chris. *Before You Know Kindness* (9–12). 2004, Crown $25.00 (1-4000-4745-5). 448pp. Young Charlotte accidentally shoots her father, an animal-rights activist, with her uncle's gun, leaving him disabled and causing injury to the rest of her family as well. (Rev: BL 8/04)

138 Braff, Joshua. *Unthinkable Thoughts of Jacob Green* (11–12). 2004, Algonquin $22.95 (1-56512-420-0). 259pp. In a wry and often funny first-person narrative, Jacob Green, son of a perfectionist Jewish father, describes his inner conflicts and ways of coping; for mature teens. (Rev: BL 7/04; SLJ 12/04; VOYA 2/05)

139 Bretton, Barbara. *Someone Like You* (11–12). 2005, Berkley paper $7.99 (0-425-20388-3). 336pp. When folk singer Mark Doyle disappears one day, he leaves behind his wife and two young daughters, affecting their lives for decades to come. (Rev: BL 7/05)

140 Burks, Cris. *Neecey's Lullaby* (11–12). 2006, Broadway paper $12.95 (0-7679-1983-1). 224pp. In this bleak coming-of-age story set in Chicago's poverty-stricken South Side in the 1950s, Neecey tries desperately to protect her younger siblings from her mother's abuse and neglect; for mature teens. (Rev: BL 12/15/05)

141 Carlson, Melody. *Just Ask* (8–12). Series: Diary of a Teenage Girl. 2005, Multnomah paper $12.99 (1-59052-321-0). 183pp. A family tragedy shakes the faith of 16-year-old Kim, who's been struggling to live a Christian life. (Rev: SLJ 12/05)

142 Chapman, Karen B. *The Marino Mission: One Girl, One Mission, One Thousand Words* (9–12). 2005, Wiley paper $12.99 (0-7645-7831-6). 326pp. Alexa reluctantly joins her marine biologist mother on a summer trip to Nicaragua, where she joins forces with a local boy to investigate the fate of a baby dolphin in this novel that introduces 1,000 SAT vocabulary words. (Rev: SLJ 7/05)

143 Corrigan, Eireann. *Splintering* (9–12). 2004, Scholastic $16.95 (0-439-53597-2). 192pp. In a gripping free-verse novel, siblings Paulie and Jeremy give voice to their feelings about an attack on their family by a drug-crazed intruder. (Rev: BCCB 4/04; BL 4/1/04; SLJ 7/04; VOYA 8/04)

144 Dalton, Annie, and Maria Dalton. *Invisible Threads* (8–11). 2006, Delacorte LB $17.99 (0-385-90303-0). 208pp. In alternating chapters, Carrie

Ann describes her need to find her birth mother and Naomi, the birth mother, talks about her pregnancy and the decision to give her baby up. (Rev: BL 4/1/06; SLJ 4/06)

145 Dermansky, Marcy. *Twins* (11–12). 2005, Morrow $21.95 (0-06-075978-X). 304pp. Identical twin sisters have increasing difficulties as they go through high school; for mature teens. (Rev: BL 8/05)

146 Deuker, Carl. *Runner* (7–10). 2005, Houghton $16.00 (0-618-54298-1). 224pp. Living on a weather-beaten sailboat on Puget Sound with his alcoholic father, high school senior Chance Taylor gets mixed up in some shady dealings to help pay the family bills. (Rev: BL 6/1–15/05; SLJ 6/05; VOYA 8/05)

147 Dewar, Isla. *Dancing in a Distant Place* (9–12). 2006, St. Martin's $23.95 (0-312-34946-7). 320pp. After her husband's death and the discovery that he gambled away all their money, Iris moves herself and her teenage children to a tiny village in Scotland, where they all have difficulties adjusting. (Rev: BL 2/15/06)

148 Finn, Melanie. *Away from You* (11–12). 2005, St. Martin's paper $12.95 (0-312-34146-6). 224pp. Estranged from her father since she was 10 years old, Ellie Cameron returns to her childhood home in Kenya after his death and attempts to unravel a mystery concerning his alleged involvement in a suspicious death; for mature teens. (Rev: BL 11/15/05)

149 Fletcher, Susan. *Eve Green* (11–12). 2004, Norton $23.95 (0-393-05988-X). 287pp. Eve Green, adopted more than 20 years earlier by her Welsh grandparents, is still struggling to come to grips with her mother's suicide when Eve was only 8 years old. (Rev: SLJ 2/05)

150 Flock, Elizabeth. *Me and Emma* (11–12). 2005, MIRA $17.95 (0-7783-2082-0). 304pp. This powerful novel explores the theme of family abuse through the narration of likable 8-year-old Carrie; for mature teens. (Rev: BL 2/1/05)

151 Forster, Gwynne. *If You Walked in My Shoes* (11–12). 2004, Kensington paper $14.00 (0-7582-0652-6). 304pp. For Coreen, who as a teenager was a rape victim, and Frieda, the daughter who was a result of that rape and who was herself abused, a reunion causes anger and pain; for mature teens. (Rev: BL 11/15/04)

152 Freymann-Weyr, Garret. *Stay with Me* (10–12). 2006, Houghton $16.00 (0-618-60571-1). 320pp. Sixteen-year-old Leila, who has always been uncertain in her relationships with her older stepsisters, decides to investigate when one of them kills herself in this complex and well-written novel. (Rev: BL 3/1/06*; SLJ 4/06)

153 Fusco, Kimberly Newton. *Tending to Grace* (7–10). 2004, Knopf LB $16.99 (0-375-92862-6).

176pp. Left with an eccentric great-aunt when her mother runs off with a boyfriend, 14-year-old Cornelia realizes in time that she and her aunt are both outcasts but together can help each other grow stronger. (Rev: BL 8/04*; SLJ 5/04; VOYA 6/04)

154 Gayle, Mike. *Dinner for Two* (9–12). 2004, Pocket paper $13.00 (0-7434-7766-9). 352pp. Dave learns he is 13-year-old Nicola's father in this breezy novel about complex relationships. (Rev: BL 6/1–15/04)

155 Halpin, Brendan. *Donorboy* (9–12). 2004, Villard $22.95 (1-4000-6277-2). 224pp. Rosalind moves in with her sperm-donor father, whom she had never met, after her lesbian mothers are killed in a car crash. (Rev: BL 7/04; SLJ 4/05)

156 Hart, Beth Webb. *Grace at Low Tide* (10–12). 2005, West Bow paper $13.99 (1-5955-4026-1). 320pp. Forced to retrench after a financial reverse, the DeLoach family trades its posh Charleston home for a modest cottage on South Carolina's Edisto Island; the faith of teenage daughter DeVeaux helps to lift family spirits as matters go from bad to worse. (Rev: BL 10/1/05)

157 Hrdlitschka, Shelley. *Kat's Fall* (9–12). 2004, Orca paper $7.95 (1-55143-312-5). 168pp. The news that his mother is going to be released from prison causes 15-year-old Darcy to revisit the incident in which his baby sister was dropped from a balcony. (Rev: SLJ 8/04; VOYA 12/04)

158 Jen, Gish. *The Love Wife* (11–12). 2004, Knopf $25.00 (1-4000-4213-5). 400pp. Carnegie, an Asian American, and his wife, a white woman named Blondie, find their lives turned upside down when Mama Wong dies and Lan arrives from China; for mature teens. (Rev: BL 7/04; SLJ 12/04)

159 Johnson, Maureen G. *The Key to the Golden Firebird* (7–10). 2004, HarperCollins LB $16.89 (0-06-054139-3). 304pp. Devastated by the sudden death of their father, three sisters struggle to cope with their feelings about their father, each other, and the meaning of life. (Rev: BL 9/1/04*; SLJ 6/04; VOYA 6/04)

160 Kantor, Melissa. *If I Have a Wicked Stepmother, Where's My Prince?* (8–12). 2005, Hyperion $15.99 (0-7868-0960-4). 283pp. In this modern variation on the Cinderella story with lots of interesting twists, high-schooler Lucy Norton must move to New York and coexist with her stepmother and twin stepsisters. (Rev: SLJ 9/05)

161 Kearney, Meg. *The Secret of Me* (7–10). 2005, Persea Bks. $17.95 (0-89255-322-7). 136pp. Lizzie, 14, is disappointed that her family won't discuss her adoption with her and her obsession with this secret affects her whole life; a novel told in verse. (Rev: BCCB 1/06; SLJ 1/06)

162 King, Lily. *The English Teacher* (11–12). 2005, Grove $24.00 (0-87113-897-2). 256pp. English teacher Vida's marriage to widower Tom appears to have been ill-advised, affecting both her son and Tom's children; but the story of her son's conception needs to be told before she can be happy; for mature teens. (Rev: BL 7/05; SLJ 4/06)

163 Kogler, Jennifer Anne. *Ruby Tuesday* (8–10). 2005, HarperCollins LB $16.89 (0-06-073957-6). 307pp. The world of 13-year-old Ruby Tuesday Sweet is turned upside down when her father is arrested for the murder of a bookie. (Rev: BCCB 5/05; SLJ 4/05; VOYA 8/05)

164 Kwasney, Michelle D. *Baby Blue* (6–10). 2004, Holt $16.95 (0-8050-7050-8). 208pp. In this poignant first novel, 13-year-old Blue, not yet fully recovered from the death of her father, is dealt yet another blow when her older sister runs away to escape beatings at the hands of their abusive stepfather. (Rev: BCCB 4/04; BL 4/1/04; SLJ 3/04; VOYA 4/04)

165 Lansens, Lori. *The Girls* (10–12). 2006, Little, Brown $23.95 (0-316-06903-5). 384pp. Rose and Ruby, 29-year-old conjoined twins, tell the stories of their lives in this novel suitable for mature teens. (Rev: BL 2/15/06)

166 Long, Kate. *The Bad Mother's Handbook* (9–12). 2005, Ballantine $21.95 (0-345-47965-3). 368pp. Unplanned pregnancy and its effects unite, and entangle, a mother and daughter in this heartwarming story. (Rev: BL 3/1/05; SLJ 8/05)

167 McCormick, Patricia. *My Brother's Keeper* (7–10). 2005, Hyperion $15.99 (0-7868-5173-2). 192pp. Thirteen-year-old Toby Malone idolizes his older brother Jake, but he feels powerless to help as he sees Jake falling under the spell of drugs. (Rev: BL 6/1–15/05; SLJ 8/05; VOYA 6/05)

168 MacCullough, Carolyn. *Stealing Henry* (9–12). 2005, Roaring Brook $16.95 (1-59643-045-1). 208pp. Unable to tolerate her drunken stepfather's abuse, 17-year-old Savannah knocks him out with a frying pan and takes off with her 8-year-old half brother. (Rev: BCCB 3/05; BL 4/1/05*; SLJ 4/05; VOYA 4/05)

169 McInerney, Monica. *The Alphabet Sisters* (11–12). 2005, Ballantine paper $13.95 (0-345-47953-X). 432pp. Three sisters return to Clare Valley, Australia, for their grandmother's 80th birthday and find themselves forced to get along; for mature teens. (Rev: BL 5/15/05)

170 McKenzie, Elizabeth. *Stop That Girl: A Novel in Stories* (9–12). 2005, Random $22.95 (1-4000-6224-1). 256pp. Spanning childhood, college, and a troubled marriage, nine wry, linked stories examine Ann's life with her reclusive mother and eccentric grandmother. (Rev: BL 12/15/04; SLJ 7/05)

171 Marchetta, Melina. *Saving Francesca* (8–10). 2004, Knopf LB $17.99 (0-375-92982-7). 256pp. Unhappy with life at her new Australian high

school, Francesca desperately needs the help and support of her mother, who is struggling with her own battle against depression. (Rev: BL 10/1/04; SLJ 9/04; VOYA 10/04)

172 Markey, Judy. *Just Trust Me* (10–12). 2004, MIRA $23.95 (0-7783-2062-6). 320pp. Danny is confused when he starts to unravel his mother's lies about her trip to Rome with her ex-husband. (Rev: BL 8/04)

173 Minter, J. *Pass It On: An Insiders Novel* (9–12). Series: Insiders. 2004, Bloomsbury paper $8.95 (1-58234-954-1). 346pp. In volume two of the series, Jonathan feels overwhelmed by all the secrets that have been entrusted to him, not the least of which is the fact that his father has cheated his friends' parents out of large sums of money. (Rev: SLJ 2/05; VOYA 4/05)

174 Murphy, Rita. *Looking for Lucy Buick* (8–11). 2005, Delacorte LB $17.99 (0-385-90176-3). 176pp. Adopted by the Sandoni family when she was found as an infant in the backseat of a Buick, 18-year-old Lucy sets off on a search for her true identity. (Rev: BL 10/15/05*; SLJ 11/05; VOYA 12/05)

175 Olsen, Sylvia. *White Girl* (7–10). 2005, Sono Nis paper $8.95 (1-55039-147-X). 240pp. When her mother marries a native Canadian, 15-year-old Josie feels anger at being moved to a reservation where she is taunted for being different, but she eventually works past her resentment and begins to appreciate the larger family of which she is now a part. (Rev: BCCB 9/05; BL 4/15/05*; SLJ 7/05; VOYA 6/05)

176 Page, Jean Reynold. *Accidental Happiness* (11–12). 2005, Ballantine $22.95 (0-345-46217-3). 336pp. Three months after Gina's young husband dies, his ex-wife appears with her 7-year-old daughter, forcing Gina to confront her grief and return to life; for mature teens. (Rev: BL 1/1–15/05)

177 Pearson, Mary E. *A Room on Lorelei Street* (9–12). 2005, Holt $16.95 (0-8050-7667-0). 272pp. Overcome by the burden of caring for her alcoholic mother, troubled 17-year-old Zoe moves into a rented room and struggles to find some peace. (Rev: BL 6/1–15/05; SLJ 8/05; VOYA 6/05)

178 Peters, Julie Anne. *Between Mom and Jo* (8–11). 2006, Little, Brown $16.99 (0-316-73906-5). 256pp. At the age of 14, Nick, the only student in his class to have gay parents, reviews his life with his two mothers and makes difficult decisions when they separate. (Rev: BL 3/1/06; SLJ 4/06*; VOYA 2/06)

179 Piccoult, Jodi, and Dustin Weaver. *The Tenth Circle* (11–12). Illus. 2006, Atria $26.00 (0-7434-9670-1). 400pp. Despite his troubled teenage years in Alaska, graphic artist Daniel Stone enjoys a quiet life in Maine with his wife and teenage daughter until his daughter accuses her ex-boyfriend of rape; for mature readers. (Rev: BL 12/1/05)

180 Ponders, Kim. *The Art of Uncontrolled Flight* (11–12). 2005, HarperCollins $19.95 (0-06-078608-6). 180pp. This compelling first novel follows the journey of Annie Shaw from her girlhood obsession with her pilot father and aviation to her deployment as a combat pilot in the Gulf War. (Rev: BL 8/05; SLJ 6/05)

181 Pritchett, Laura. *Sky Bridge* (11–12). 2005, Milkweed $22.00 (1-57131-046-0). 220pp. At the age of 22, Libby persuades her younger sister not to have an abortion, offering to raise the baby herself, a decision that is challenging on many levels; for mature teens. (Rev: BL 4/15/05; SLJ 5/05)

182 Reinhardt, Dana. *A Brief Chapter in My Impossible Life* (9–12). 2006, Random LB $17.99 (0-385-90940-3). 228pp. The identity of her birth mother has not been important to Simone, 16, and it comes as a shock when Rivka gets in touch and turns out to be dying of cancer. (Rev: BCCB 2/06; BL 1/1–15/06; SLJ 3/06*)

183 Reynolds, Sheri. *Firefly Cloak* (9–12). 2006, Crown $23.00 (0-609-61008-2). 304pp. Tessa Lee, now a teenager, is determined to find the mother who abandoned her and her younger brother in a campsite years before; the reunion is not what she had hoped. (Rev: BL 2/15/06; SLJ 4/06)

184 Rice, Luanne. *Summers Child* (11–12). 2005, Bantam paper $7.50 (0-553-58762-5). 400pp. Lily and her daughter Rose, who has a congenital heart defect, live in Nova Scotia under the shadow of continuing fear that Lily's abusive husband will find them; for mature teens. (Rev: BL 6/1–15/05)

185 Ryan, Darlene. *Rules for Life* (7–12). 2004, Orca paper $7.95 (1-55143-350-8). 163pp. Sixteen-year-old Izzy, whose mother died two years earlier, has difficulty coming to terms with her father's decision to remarry; suitable for reluctant readers. (Rev: BCCB 2/05; SLJ 3/05; VOYA 6/05)

186 Shamsie, Kamila. *Broken Verses* (10–12). 2005, Harcourt paper $14.00 (0-15-603053-5). 352pp. A 31-year-old Pakistani woman is pulled into a web of intrigue when she reads letters written in a code known only to her long-absent mother and her mother's lover, a poet believed to be dead. (Rev: BL 3/1/05; SLJ 6/05)

187 Shepherd, Paul. *More Like Not Running Away* (11–12). 2005, Sarabande paper $14.95 (1-932511-28-8). 248pp. In this prize-winning first novel, 12-year-old Levi Revel idolizes his often-violent father and is driven to the edge of madness by the endless murmur of voices only he can hear. (Rev: BL 10/1/05)

188 Shreve, Anita. *Light on Snow* (9–12). 2004, Little, Brown $25.95 (0-316-78148-7). 304pp. Twelve-year-old Nicky and his father discover an abandoned baby, forcing them to confront their grief over the loss of Nicky's mother and little sister. (Rev: BL 8/04; SLJ 12/04)

189 Slezak, Ellen. *All These Girls* (11–12). 2004, Hyperion $23.95 (0-7868-6742-6). 384pp. After the death of Candy's mother, Candy, her aunt, and her great-aunt retreat to a remote corner of Michigan; a family drama for mature teens. (Rev: BL 8/04)

190 Smith, Ali. *The Accidental* (11–12). 2006, Pantheon $22.95 (0-375-42225-0). 320pp. Amber, a late-night arrival at the summer home of the Smart family in the English countryside, touches the lives of all those who dwell within; for mature readers. (Rev: BL 12/1/05)

191 Sparks, Beatrice, ed. *Finding Katie: The Diary of Anonymous, a Teenager in Foster Care* (7–10). 2005, Avon paper $5.99 (0-06-050721-7). 181pp. In this angst-filled fictional diary, Katie, a teenager living on a California estate, makes it clear that money and privilege do nothing to ensure a happy life. (Rev: SLJ 10/05)

192 Strause, Brian. *Maybe a Miracle* (9–12). 2005, Ballantine $21.95 (1-4000-6464-3). 368pp. When Monroe's sister Annika slips into a coma after nearly drowning, miraculous events begin to occur; for mature teens. (Rev: BL 9/1/05)

193 Swanson, Julie A. *Going for the Record* (7–12). 2004, Eerdmans paper $8.00 (0-8028-5273-4). 223pp. High school soccer star Leah Weiczynkowski finds herself torn between family responsibilities and her sports aspirations when her father is diagnosed with terminal cancer. (Rev: BL 9/1/04*; SLJ 8/04; VOYA 10/04)

194 Trueman, Terry. *Cruise Control* (7–10). 2004, HarperCollins LB $16.89 (0-06-623961-3). 160pp. High school senior Paul McDaniel is a star athlete, but he's filled with rage over his brother's disabilities and his father's desertion; a companion to *Stuck in Neutral* (2000). (Rev: BCCB 11/04; BL 3/15/05; VOYA 10/04)

195 Willard, Katie. *Raising Hope* (11–12). 2005, Warner $23.95 (0-446-57687-5). 312pp. Twelve-year-old Hope, who has been raised by two women who are unlikely friends, seeks a clearer sense of identity and to know more about her father. (Rev: BL 3/15/05)

196 Wingate, Lisa. *The Language of Sycamores* (9–12). 2005, NAL paper $12.95 (0-451-21392-0). 304pp. Grappling with both job loss and the possible recurrence of her cancer, Karen Sommerfield returns to Missouri for a family reunion; there she rediscovers lost pleasures and connects with a neighbor child through music. (Rev: BL 12/1/04)

197 Witt, Martha. *Broken as Things Are* (11–12). 2004, Holt $23.00 (0-8050-7595-X). 304pp. Morgan Lee's adolescence is more turbulent than most, with a disturbed brother who is determined to protect her from the outside world, in this powerful and sexually charged story for mature readers. (Rev: BL 7/04)

198 Wolitzer, Meg. *The Position* (11–12). 2005, Scribner $24.00 (0-7432-6178-X). 320pp. This wicked satire follows the four Mellow children, scarred for life in 1975 after their parents first publish a detailed celebration of their sex life as a couple, then split up; for mature teens. (Rev: BL 12/15/04)

Physical and Emotional Problems

199 Antieau, Kim. *Mercy, Unbound* (9–12). 2006, Simon & Schuster paper $6.99 (1-4169-0893-5). 176pp. Fifteen-year-old Mercy's denial of her anorexia extends to a fantasy that she is an angel and has no need for nourishment. (Rev: BL 4/1/06)

200 Beard, Philip. *Dear Zoe* (9–12). 2005, Viking $21.95 (0-670-03401-0). 198pp. Tess, 15, deals with a year of grief and change by writing cathartic letters to her little sister after her death. (Rev: BL 2/1/05; SLJ 10/05)

201 Campbell, Bebe Moore. *72 Hour Hold* (11–12). 2005, Knopf $24.95 (1-4000-4074-4). 319pp. As her 18-year-old daughter's bipolar disorder renders her increasingly violent and unstable, Keri is prepared to try the most radical solutions; for mature teens. (Rev: BL 4/1/05)

202 Coburn, Jake. *Lovesick* (9–12). 2005, Dutton $16.99 (0-525-47383-1). 288pp. In their first year at college, recovering alcoholic and scholarship student Ted and wealthy bulimic Erica are thrown together and fall in love. (Rev: BL 9/15/05; SLJ 12/05; VOYA 12/05)

203 Diersch, Sandra. *Ceiling Stars* (7–12). Series: SideStreets. 2004, Lorimer paper $4.99 (1-55028-834-2). 141pp. The close friendship of two high school girls is put to the test when one falls victim to mental illness and begins acting strangely; suitable for reluctant readers. (Rev: SLJ 1/05)

204 Edwards, Johanna. *The Next Big Thing* (8–12). 2005, Berkley paper $13.00 (0-425-20028-0). Kat, determined to lose weight to win the heart of her online boyfriend, lands a spot on a reality TV makeover show but finds in the end that she likes herself just the way she is. (Rev: SLJ 11/05)

205 Forde, Catherine. *Fat Boy Swim* (6–10). 2004, Dell $15.95 (0-385-73205-8). 240pp. Fourteen-year-old Jimmy Kelly, taunted by his Glasgow schoolmates for his obesity, persuades a sympathetic soccer coach to teach him how to swim. (Rev: BL 9/1/04; SLJ 9/04)

206 Frank, E. R. *Wrecked* (9–12). 2005, Simon & Schuster $15.95 (0-689-87383-2). 256pp. Sixteen-year-old Anna is haunted by grief and guilt after the accident that leaves her brother's girlfriend dead, an accident that affects all members of her family. (Rev: BCCB 10/05; BL 12/1/05; HB 1–2/06; SLJ 11/05; VOYA 12/05)

207 Griffin, Adele. *Where I Want to Be* (7–10). 2005, Penguin $15.99 (0-399-23783-6). 160pp. In alternating chapters, teenage sisters Lily and Jane tell about their relationship and the mental illness that led to Jane's tragic death. (Rev: BCCB 3/05; BL 2/15/05*; HB 3–4/05; SLJ 4/05; VOYA 4/05)

208 Hautman, Pete. *Invisible* (7–10). 2005, Simon & Schuster $15.95 (0-689-86800-6). 160pp. It's clear to the reader from the beginning that there's something odd about the friendship between 17-year-old Doug Hanson and his only friend Andy, and the mystery unravels as Doug's state of mind deteriorates through the course of the book. (Rev: BL 6/1–15/05; SLJ 6/05; VOYA 8/05)

209 Moix, Ana Maria. *Julia* (11–12). Trans. by Sandra Kingery. 2004, Univ. of Nebraska $55.00 (0-8032-3235-7); paper $20.00 (0-8032-8291-5). 176pp. A disturbed young woman attempts suicide in hopes of eradicating her tortured past; for mature teens. (Rev: BL 9/1/04)

210 Myers, Edward. *Ice* (9–12). 2005, Montemayor $12.95 (0-9674477-9-8). 222pp. In this haunting novel, New Jersey teenagers Seth and Jenna struggle to come to grips with the loss of Frannie — Seth's girlfriend and Jenna's sister — in a car accident. (Rev: BL 12/1/05)

211 Noel, Katharine. *Halfway House* (11–12). 2006, Grove $24.00 (0-87113-934-0). 368pp. Seventeen-year-old Angie Voorster, an intelligent and athletic high school senior, suffers a mental meltdown that dramatically transforms her life and that of her family; for mature teens. (Rev: BL 12/1/05)

212 Perez, Marlene. *Unexpected Development* (7–12). 2004, Roaring Brook $16.95 (1-59643-006-0). 176pp. In a series of journal entries, high school senior Megan waxes eloquent on the drawbacks of having an overdeveloped bosom. (Rev: BL 11/15/04; SLJ 10/04; VOYA 12/04)

213 Peters, Julie Anne. *Luna* (8–12). 2004, Little, Brown $16.95 (0-316-73369-5). 256pp. Regan makes great sacrifices to protect her transgender brother Liam from discovery but has reservations when Liam decides he wants to make a permanent sex change. (Rev: BL 7/04; HB 7–8/04; SLJ 5/04; VOYA 6/04)

214 Rapp, Adam. *Under the Wolf, Under the Dog* (10–12). 2005, Candlewick $16.99 (0-7636-1818-7). 304pp. Deeply shaken by the loss of his mother to cancer and his brother to suicide, 16-year-old Steve Nugent recounts, in often-humorous journal entries, the chain of events that ended in his commitment to a facility for suicidal and drug-addicted teens. (Rev: BL 11/15/04; SLJ 10/04; VOYA 12/04)

215 Tokio, Mamelle. *More Than You Can Chew* (8–10). 2003, Tundra paper $9.95 (0-88776-639-0). 240pp. Anorexic 17-year-old Marty Black faces an uphill struggle as she begins treatment for her eating disorder but tackles it with some humor. (Rev: BL 1/1–15/04; SLJ 6/04; VOYA 8/04)

216 Trueman, Terry. *No Right Turn* (8–11). 2006, HarperCollins LB $16.89 (0-06-057492-5). 176pp. Only when his mother gets a boyfriend with a '76 Corvette does Jordan begin to emerge from the isolation caused by his father's suicide. (Rev: BL 2/1/06; SLJ 3/06; VOYA 2/06)

Personal Problems and Growing into Maturity

217 Acito, Marc. *How I Paid for College: A Novel of Sex, Theft, Friendship and Musical Theater* (11–12). 2004, Broadway $21.95 (0-7679-1841-X). 240pp. High school senior Edward and his friends will try just about anything to help the talented Edward pay for Juilliard in this offbeat, funny, and poignant novel set in the 1980s and featuring young men exploring their sexual identities; suitable for mature teens. (Rev: BL 8/04; SLJ 9/04)

218 Allen, M. E. *Gotta Get Some Bish Bash Bosh* (7–10). 2005, HarperCollins LB $16.89 (0-06-073201-6). 208pp. When he's dumped by his girlfriend Sandi, the 14-year-old narrator resolves to cultivate a brand-new image in this entertaining novel set in Britain. (Rev: BL 1/1–15/05; SLJ 4/05; VOYA 2/05)

219 Anderson, Laurie Halse. *Prom* (9–12). 2005, Viking $16.99 (0-670-05974-9). 224pp. High school senior Ashley couldn't care less about the upcoming prom, but she responds to her best friend's plea for help after the big event is jeopardized by an embezzling math teacher. (Rev: BL 1/1–15/05*; SLJ 2/05; VOYA 4/05)

220 Angel, Jodi. *The History of Vegas* (11–12). 2005, Chronicle $19.95 (0-8118-4625-3). 192pp. Ten short matter-of-fact stories feature West Coast teens in unhappy situations — violence, drugs and alcohol use, eating and disorders, and so forth. (Rev: BL 7/05)

221 Barbieri, Heather. *Snow in July* (11–12). 2004, Soho $24.00 (1-56947-384-6). 272pp. Eighteen-year-old Erin tries to hold things together for her older sister Meghan, who is a drug addict with two children, in this story set in Montana; for mature teens. (Rev: BL 9/15/04)

222 Beede, John R. *Climb On! Dynamic Strategies for Teen Success* (9–12). 2005, Sierra Nevada paper $12.95 (0-9765697-0-1). 126pp. A motivational novel in which troubled 16-year-old Anna joins a rock climbing group and learns skills including endurance and persistence and about the value of

positive change; hints are highlighted throughout. (Rev: SLJ 1/06)

223 Bellows, Melina Gerosa. *Wish* (9–12). 2005, NAL paper $12.95 (0-451-21653-9). 304pp. Haunted by her twin brother's autism, Bella Grandelli searches across several decades for a sense of fulfillment; for mature readers. (Rev: BL 10/15/05)

224 Bezos, MacKenzie. *The Testing of Luther Albright* (11–12). 2005, HarperCollins $23.95 (0-06-075141-X). 256pp. Teenage Elliot resorts to sabotage in his efforts to attract his father's full attention. (Rev: BL 6/1–15/05)

225 Brashares, Ann. *Girls in Pants: The Third Summer of the Sisterhood* (8–12). Series: Sisterhood of the Traveling Pants. 2005, Delacorte LB $18.99 (0-385-90919-5). 304pp. It's summer again for the four friends and they manage to get together for a weekend before they leave for separate colleges; the pants continue their travels. (Rev: BL 12/15/04*; SLJ 1/05; VOYA 2/05)

226 Brian, Kate. *The V Club* (9–12). 2004, Simon & Schuster $14.95 (0-689-86704-6). 288pp. Four members of the V (for Virginity) Club — formed by girls anxious to win a scholarship that will go to a candidate who exemplifies purity of soul, spirit, and body — confide their innermost thoughts as the competition intensifies. The paperback edition (2005) is titled *The Virginity Club*. (Rev: BCCB 6/04; BL 6/1–15/04; VOYA 8/04)

227 Brooks, Kevin. *Candy* (9–12). 2005, Scholastic $16.95 (0-439-68327-0). 368pp. Joe, a fairly ordinary London teenager, finds himself drawn into a dark, new world after he loses his heart to a 16-year-old, drug-addicted prostitute named Candy. (Rev: BCCB 2/05; BL 2/1/05; SLJ 3/05; VOYA 4/05)

228 Burchill, Julie. *Sugar Rush* (10–12). 2005, HarperCollins LB $17.89 (0-06-077620-X). 288pp. It is with trepidation that Kim leaves her privileged English school for a local one, but there she finds herself falling in love with Maria Sweet, a girl who wants to experience everything. (Rev: BL 9/1/05; SLJ 10/05; VOYA 6/05)

229 Burgess, Melvin. *Doing It* (10–12). 2004, Holt $15.95 (0-8050-7565-8). 336pp. Three sex-obsessed teenage boys — Ben, Dino, and Jonathan — share with one another the joys, confusion, and heartbreak of their sexual exploits. (Rev: BL 6/1–15/04; HB 7–8/04; SLJ 6/04; VOYA 6/04)

230 Butcher, Nancy. *Beauty* (7–12). 2005, Simon & Schuster paper $6.99 (0-689-86235-0). 166pp. A light read about Princess Tatiana Anatolia — 16-year-old daughter of an exceedingly vain queen — who finally stands up to her mother when she learns of the queen's plan to rid the kingdom of other beautiful women. (Rev: BCCB 3/05; SLJ 3/05)

231 Cann, Kate. *Shacked Up* (10–12). Series: Hard Cash Trilogy. 2004, Simon & Schuster paper $5.99 (0-689-85906-6). 345pp. In the second volume of this trilogy set in London, Rich is living rent-free, going to college, making money, and lusting after the gorgeous Portia when his old friend Bonny needs a place to stay and a shoulder to lean on. (Rev: SLJ 7/04)

232 Castellucci, Cecil. *Boy Proof* (7–10). 2005, Candlewick $15.99 (0-7636-2333-4). 208pp. Sixteen-year-old Victoria, who prefers to be known as Egg, is smart, cool, and totally in control until Max Carter enters her life and breaks the shell. (Rev: BCCB 2/05; BL 2/15/05; HB 5–6/05; SLJ 4/05; VOYA 4/05)

233 Castellucci, Cecil. *The Queen of Cool* (10–12). 2006, Candlewick $15.99 (0-7636-2720-8). 176pp. At the age of 16, Libby suddenly finds she's bored with her life and her many friends and she signs up for an internship at the Los Angeles Zoo. (Rev: BL 2/15/06; SLJ 3/06)

234 Cheshire, Simon. *Kissing Vanessa* (6–10). 2004, Delacorte LB $17.99 (0-385-90242-5). 144pp. Kevin is foolish enough to heed his friend's advice on attracting the opposite sex in this humorous novel set in Britain. (Rev: BCCB 1/05; SLJ 10/04)

235 Clairday, Robynn. *Confessions of a Boyfriend Stealer* (8–11). 2005, Delacorte LB $9.99 (0-385-90267-0); paper $7.95 (0-385-73242-2). 240pp. In entries from a blog, 16-year-old Gen, high school junior and aspiring documentary filmmaker, describes her growing disillusion with her best friends CJ and Tasha. (Rev: BL 9/15/05; SLJ 9/05)

236 Clark, Catherine. *The Alison Rules* (7–12). 2004, HarperCollins LB $16.89 (0-06-055981-0). 272pp. Reeling from her mother's death, high school sophomore Alison retreats into herself and creates sets of rules to help her cope; the arrival of a new student called Patrick finally brings her out of her shell. (Rev: BL 10/15/04; SLJ 8/04; VOYA 12/04)

237 Cohn, Rachel. *Pop Princess* (8–12). 2004, Simon & Schuster $15.95 (0-689-85205-3). 320pp. Sixteen-year-old Wonder Blake has a wry understanding of the changes affecting her life when she is offered a recording contract. (Rev: BCCB 4/04; BL 1/1–15/04; SLJ 3/04; VOYA 8/04)

238 Cohn, Rachel. *Shrimp* (9–12). 2005, Simon & Schuster $15.95 (0-689-86612-7). 288pp. In this entertaining sequel to *Gingerbread* (2002), Cyd Charisse, just back in San Francisco after an exciting summer in New York City, determines to rekindle the romance with Shrimp, her former boyfriend and an avid surfer. (Rev: BCCB 2/05; BL 5/1/05; HB 3–4/05; SLJ 2/05; VOYA 6/05)

239 Coleman, Michael. *On the Run* (8–12). 2004, Dutton $15.99 (0-525-47318-1). 208pp. When 15-year-old Luke Reid runs afoul of the law once again, he's assigned to serve as a guide for a blind runner who's training for part of the annual London Marathon. (Rev: BL 6/1–15/04; SLJ 6/04; VOYA 8/04)

240 Colgan, Jenny. *The Boy I Loved Before* (11–12). 2005, St. Martin's paper $13.95 (0-312-33198-3). 320pp. After wishing, at her best friend's wedding, the she could remake her life, 32-year-old Flora awakens the next day as a 16-year-old, with one month to make fresh choices — or revert to her adult life. (Rev: BL 2/15/05)

241 Cramer, W. Dale. *Levi's Will* (9–12). 2005, Bethany House paper $13.99 (0-7642-2995-8). 281pp. Will Mullet, a young Amish man rejected by his father, leaves his Ohio home in 1943 and heads out on his own. (Rev: BL 6/1–15/05)

242 Crane, Elizabeth. *All This Heavenly Glory* (11–12). 2005, Little, Brown $22.95 (0-316-00089-2). 224pp. Linked stories describe the coming of age of Charlotte Anne Byers, a thoughtful New York girl trying to cope with family and social problems. (Rev: BL 3/15/05)

243 Crutcher, Chris. *The Sledding Hill* (7–12). 2005, HarperCollins LB $16.89 (0-06-050244-4). 230pp. Not even death can separate teenage friends Billy Bartholomew and Eddie Proffit in this thought-provoking novel that not only features author Crutcher but also a controversial novel called *Warren Peace*. (Rev: SLJ 6/05; VOYA 6/05)

244 Davidson, Dana. *Played* (9–12). 2005, Hyperion $16.99 (0-7868-3690-3). 288pp. Ian Striver, a student at Cross High School, is challenged to get Kylie Winship to surrender her virginity and declare her love for him in three weeks or less. (Rev: BL 12/15/05)

245 Dayton, Anne, and May Vanderbilt. *Emily Ever After* (9–12). 2005, WaterBrook paper $11.95 (1-4000-7042-2). 311pp. Emily Hinton struggles to remain true to her Christian faith after she lands a job at a prestigious publishing company in New York City. (Rev: BL 5/1/05; SLJ 11/05)

246 de la Cruz, Melissa. *The Au Pairs* (9–12). 2004, Simon & Schuster $14.95 (0-689-87066-3). 288pp. Three girls from very different backgrounds spend their summer working as au pairs in New York's tony Hamptons, an experience that changes all three for the better. (Rev: BL 7/04; SLJ 6/04; VOYA 10/04)

247 de la Cruz, Melissa. *Skinny-Dipping* (9–12). Series: The Au Pairs. 2005, Simon & Schuster $14.95 (1-4169-0382-8). 291pp. In this sequel to the exploits of the three young ladies who like to party, *The Au Pairs* (2004), Mara is having second thoughts about dumping Ryan, who is now dating Eliza. (Rev: SLJ 7/05)

248 Delaney, Mark. *Pepperland* (8–12). 2004, Peachtree $14.95 (1-56145-317-X). 160pp. In this poignant coming-of-age novel set in 1980, 16-year-old Pamela Jean tries to cope with the pain of her mother's death from cancer. (Rev: BL 12/1/04; SLJ 11/04; VOYA 10/04)

249 de Oliveira, Eddie. *Lucky* (8–12). 2004, Scholastic paper $6.99 (0-439-54655-9). 256pp. Sam, a 19-year-old British university student, finds himself attracted to both boys and girls and struggles to discover where he fits into the overall scheme of things sexually. (Rev: BL 6/1–15/04; SLJ 6/04; VOYA 10/04)

250 Dessen, Sarah. *Just Listen* (8–11). 2006, Viking $17.99 (0-670-06105-0). 384pp. Annabel is shunned by her friends after being seen in a compromising situation with her best friend's boyfriend. (Rev: BL 3/15/06; VOYA 4/06)

251 Dierbeck, Lisa. *One Pill Makes You Smaller* (11–12). 2003, Farrar $24.00 (0-374-22649-0). 312pp. Alice, abandoned by her parents, is only 11 but must deal with a prematurely voluptuous body in this novel of drugs, dissolute art camp, and seduction set in the 1970s; for mature teens. (Rev: SLJ 1/04)

252 Dorfman, Ariel, and Joaquin Dorfman. *Burning City* (10–12). 2005, Random LB $17.95 (0-375-93203-8). 272pp. During a summer heat wave in New York City, 16-year-old bike messenger Heller Highland falls in love with a young waitress named Silvia. (Rev: BCCB 9/05; BL 4/15/05; HB 5–6/05; SLJ 1/06; VOYA 6/05)

253 Douglas, Lola. *True Confessions of a Hollywood Starlet* (8–10). 2005, Penguin $16.99 (1-59514-035-2). 260pp. Teen movie star Morgan Carter, on the mend from a drug overdose in Hollywood, adopts a new identity when she is sent to a midwestern high school in this credible and amusing novel. (Rev: BCCB 2/06; SLJ 12/05; VOYA 4/06)

254 Dower, Laura. *Rewind* (10–12). 2006, Scholastic paper $8.99 (0-439-70340-9). 264pp. This novel starts with Cady's amazement when she sees Lucas slap Hope at the prom; complex flashbacks reveal more about the events of the previous six months and the underlying problems. (Rev: BL 2/15/06)

255 Earls, Nick. *48 Shades of Brown* (10–12). 2004, Graphia paper $6.99 (0-618-45295-8). 288pp. Smart and sensitive 16-year-old Dan, left in Australia in the care of his 22-year-old aunt when his parents move to Switzerland, finds himself increasingly obsessed with his aunt's roommate, Naomi. (Rev: BCCB 7–8/04; BL 7/04; HB 9–10/04; SLJ 6/04; VOYA 4/04)

256 Elliot, Jessie. *Girls Dinner Club* (11–12). 2005, HarperCollins LB $16.89 (0-06-059540-X). 256pp. Three ethnically diverse Brooklyn high school students — Junie, Celia, and Danielle — get together weekly to cook dinner and discuss their latest romantic adventures; for mature readers. (Rev: BCCB 10/05; BL 3/1/05; SLJ 6/05; VOYA 10/05)

257 Erian, Alicia. *Towelhead* (11–12). 2005, Simon & Schuster $22.00 (0-7432-4494-X). 318pp. When her mother discovers that her boyfriend is abusing 13-year-old Jasira, she's sent to live with her Lebanese father, who seems repulsed by her puberty; when a neighbor sexually assaults her, she has nowhere to turn. For mature readers. (Rev: BL 2/15/05)

258 Ferri, Linda. *Enchantments* (10–12). Trans. by John Casey. 2005, Knopf $18.95 (1-4000-4069-8). 160pp. In a fictional, impressionistic memoir presented in a series of vignettes, a preteen Italian girl portrays her privileged life in late-60s Paris and the Italian countryside; it is mostly happy life but with dark foreshadows. (Rev: BL 2/1/05; SLJ 6/05)

259 Fletcher, Christine. *Tallulah Falls* (8–11). 2006, Bloomsbury $16.95 (1-58234-662-3). 304pp. At the age of 17, unhappy Tallulah (formerly known as Debbie) runs away from home looking for her older friend Maeve, who has bipolar disease and has left Oregon for Florida; on the way, Tallulah becomes stranded in Tennessee and finds a haven working in a veterinary clinic. (Rev: BL 4/1/06)

260 Foer, Jonathan Safran. *Extremely Loud and Incredibly Close* (10–12). 2005, Houghton $24.95 (0-618-32970-6). 368pp. Delightful New Yorker Oskar, 9, inventively grapples with the 9/11 loss of his father while an intersecting story details his grandparents' survival of World War II Dresden, culminating in a novel celebrating triumph over great loss. (Rev: BL 2/1/05; SLJ 7/05)

261 Francis, Brian. *Fruit* (11–12). 2004, MacAdam $23.00 (1-931561-76-1). 284pp. Peter, a young teen, struggles with body image (including mysteriously growing huge nipples) and his sexual identity before coming out of the closet in this appealing book suitable for mature readers. (Rev: BL 8/04)

262 Frank, Hillary. *I Can't Tell You* (9–12). 2004, Houghton $16.00 (0-618-41202-6); paper $6.99 (0-618-49491-X). 208pp. Jake swears off speaking after alienating his college roommate and best friend Sean in an argument about a girl, but he jots down his thoughts about life, love, and the agonies of adolescence on napkins and other scraps of paper. (Rev: BL 9/15/04; SLJ 12/04; VOYA 2/05)

263 Fredericks, Mariah. *Head Games* (7–10). 2004, Simon & Schuster $15.95 (0-689-85532-X). 272pp. After a rift with her best friend, 15-year-old Judith retreats into the world of online gaming, assuming a new identity as a male. (Rev: BL 9/15/04; SLJ 10/04; VOYA 4/05)

264 Garfinkle, D. L. *Storky: How I Lost My Nickname and Won the Girl* (8–11). 2005, Penguin

$16.99 (0-399-24284-8). 192pp. In journal entries, 14-year-old Mike Pomerantz chronicles the troubles and unexpected joys of his first year in high school. (Rev: BCCB 5/05; BL 3/15/05; SLJ 3/05)

265 Gehrman, Jody. *Summer in the Land of Skin* (9–12). 2004, Harlequin paper $12.95 (0-373-25066-5). 320pp. Anna travels to Seattle hoping to find the truth about her father, who recently committed suicide, and befriends a charismatic couple. (Rev: BL 8/04)

266 Giffin, Emily. *Something Blue* (9–12). 2005, St. Martin's $22.95 (0-312-32385-9). 352pp. Darcy's opinions of what's important in life change when she ends up pregnant and lonely. (Rev: BL 5/15/05)

267 Giles, Gail. *Playing in Traffic* (8–12). 2004, Roaring Brook $16.95 (1-59643-005-2). 176pp. Seventeen-year-old Matt Lathrop, a shy and geekish high school senior, is flattered when he's picked up by sexy Goth girl Skye Colby, but he soon learns she has ulterior motives; a gripping psychological thriller. (Rev: BL 9/1/04; SLJ 12/04; VOYA 12/04)

268 Goldstein, Jan. *All That Matters* (9–12). 2004, Hyperion $17.95 (1-4013-0110-X). 208pp. After surviving a suicide attempt, Jennifer learns about life from her dying grandmother Gabby. (Rev: BL 9/1/04)

269 Gonzalez, Gabriela, and Gaby Triana. *Backstage Pass* (6–12). 2004, HarperCollins LB $16.89 (0-06-056018-5). 224pp. Desert McGraw, 16-year-old daughter of an aging rock star, moves to Miami and longs more than anything for normalcy in her life. (Rev: BL 7/04; SLJ 8/04)

270 Goodman, Eric. *Child of My Right Hand* (10–12). 2004, Sourcebooks paper $14.00 (1-4022-0306-3). 320pp. Young Simon, who is gay and is accepted by his family but bullied at school, travels to San Francisco to meet his gay grandfather and his partner in this novel that includes discussion of the theory that homosexuality is hereditary. (Rev: BL 9/1/04)

271 Graham, Rosemary. *Thou Shalt Not Dump the Skater Dude and Other Commandments I Have Broken* (7–10). 2005, Viking $16.99 (0-670-06017-8). 224pp. When high school freshman Kelsey Wilcox breaks up with skateboarding champion C. J. Logan, her jilted boyfriend starts spreading lies about her. (Rev: BL 10/15/05; SLJ 1/06)

272 Grant, Vicki. *Dead-End Job* (7–12). 2005, Orca paper $7.95 (1-55143-378-8). 104pp. Frances finds her life coming apart at the seams after she meets an emotionally disturbed loner named Devin; suitable for reluctant readers. (Rev: SLJ 11/05)

273 Green, John. *Looking for Alaska* (9–12). 2005, Dutton $15.99 (0-525-47506-0). 237pp. Sixteen-year-old Miles Halter leaves his home in Florida to attend an Alabama boarding school and is promptly entranced by a sexy but self-destructive girl named Alaska. Printz Award, 2006. (Rev: BCCB 2/05*; HB 3–4/05; SLJ 2/05; VOYA 4/05)

274 Greenway, Alice. *White Ghost Girls* (9–12). 2006, Grove paper $13.00 (0-8021-7018-8). 176pp. Follows the sometimes dangerous activities of two teenage American sisters — Frankie and Kate, daughters of a war photographer who spends most of his time in Vietnam and of a mother who is absorbed in her painting — living in Hong Kong in 1967. (Rev: BL 11/15/05; SLJ 5/06)

275 Griffin, Adele. *My Almost Epic Summer* (7–10). 2006, Penguin $15.99 (0-399-23784-4). 176pp. Irene, 14, who is spending the summer babysitting, learns about friendship when she takes up with the beautiful and manipulative Starla. (Rev: BL 2/15/06; SLJ 4/06; VOYA 4/06)

276 Hall, Sarah. *The Electric Michelangelo* (9–12). 2005, HarperCollins paper $13.95 (0-06-081724-0). 368pp. Trained as a tattoo artist in an English seaside town, Cyril Parks travels to America, sets up shop in Coney Island, and begins an unusual relationship with an enigmatic circus performer named Grace; for mature readers. (Rev: BL 10/15/05)

277 Harper, Rachel M. *Brass Ankle Blues* (9–12). 2006, Simon & Schuster $23.00 (0-7432-7680-9). 304pp. In this poignant coming-of-age novel, 17-year-old Nellie — part white, part African American, and part Native American and with a strong feeling she doesn't fit in anywhere — spends a summer in Minnesota dealing with family problems, friendships, and potential romance. (Rev: BL 11/15/05)

278 Hart, Lenore. *Ordinary Springs* (9–12). 2005, Berkley paper $14.00 (0-425-20005-1). 384pp. In 1950s Florida, Dory's life changes forever when her widower father begins a passionate affair. (Rev: BL 1/1–15/05)

279 Hartinger, Brent. *The Order of the Poison Oak* (7–10). 2005, HarperCollins LB $16.89 (0-06-056731-7). 240pp. Anxious to escape the "gay kid" label, 16-year-old Russel Middlebrook and two of his friends sign up to be counselors at a summer camp for young burn victims; a sequel to *Geography Club* (2003). (Rev: BCCB 3/05; BL 1/1–15/05; SLJ 4/05; VOYA 4/05)

280 Haworth-Attard, Barbara. *Theories of Relativity* (8–11). 2005, Holt $16.95 (0-8050-7790-1). 240pp. When his mother sends him packing to make room for her latest boyfriend, 16-year-old Dylan Wallace struggles to survive on the streets without resorting to a life of crime. (Rev: BL 11/1/05; SLJ 11/05; VOYA 2/06)

281 Headley, Jason. *Small Town Odds* (10–12). 2004, Chronicle $23.95 (0-8118-4536-2). 341pp. Eric is forced to change his college plans when he becomes a father and must stay in the small West Virginia town where he grew up. (Rev: BL 9/15/04)

282 Hemphill, Stephanie. *Things Left Unsaid* (8–12). 2005, Hyperion $16.99 (0-7868-1850-6). 272pp. In this powerful free-verse novel, good girl Sarah Lewis becomes bored with her predictable life and adopts defiant Robin's bad habits, until Robin attempts suicide and Sarah must review her priorities. (Rev: BCCB 7–8/05; BL 5/1/05; HB 5–6/05; SLJ 2/05; VOYA 10/04)

283 Hobbs, Valerie. *Letting Go of Bobby James, Or How I Found My Self of Steam* (9–12). 2004, Farrar $16.00 (0-374-34384-5). 144pp. Abandoned by her husband at a Florida gas station, 16-year-old Jody takes a job at a nearby diner and tries to make a better life for herself. (Rev: BL 7/04; SLJ 9/04)

284 Iversen, Jeremy. *21* (10–12). 2005, Simon & Schuster paper $6.99 (0-689-87623-8). 272pp. Bret recounts the excesses of his 21st birthday party — held at his fraternity — and details of his adolescent soul searching; for mature teens. (Rev: BCCB 4/05; BL 4/1/05; SLJ 4/05)

285 James, Brian. *A Perfect World* (7–10). 2004, Scholastic $16.95 (0-439-67364-X). 192pp. Haunted by the suicide of her father, Lacie Johnson follows mindlessly in the footsteps of her best friend Jenna, but when she meets Benji and falls in love, she realizes that Jenna is not a real friend at all. (Rev: BL 1/1–15/05; SLJ 1/05)

286 Johnson, Maureen. *The Bermudez Triangle* (9–12). 2004, Penguin $16.99 (1-59514-019-0). 384pp. Three high school girls' longtime friendship is shattered when two of them fall in love with each other. (Rev: BL 11/1/04; SLJ 11/04)

287 Jonsberg, Barry. *The Crimes and Punishments of Miss Payne* (9–12). 2005, Knopf LB $17.99 (0-375-93240-2). 272pp. Calma Harrison and Jaryd Kiffing, a good student and a bad one, launch a campaign of harassment against Miss Payne, their strict new English teacher in this Australian novel about teens losing control. (Rev: BCCB 9/05; BL 5/15/05; SLJ 7/05; VOYA 10/05)

288 Juby, Susan. *Alice MacLeod, Realist at Last* (8–11). 2005, HarperCollins LB $16.89 (0-06-051550-3). 320pp. It's an eventful summer for unconventional 16-year-old Alice McLeod, who breaks up with her boyfriend, gets and loses jobs, attracts three new male admirers, and sees her activist mom packed off to jail — all with dark good humor. (Rev: BL 4/15/05; HB 9–10/05; SLJ 9/05)

289 Kincaid, Nanci. *As Hot as It Was You Ought to Thank Me* (9–12). 2005, Little, Brown paper $12.95 (0-316-00914-8). 336pp. When Berry Jackson's father vanishes from Pinetta, Florida, one searing summer, her very identity as "the principal's daughter" seems endangered; Berry's wry narration reveals strong, quirky characters and her own resilience. (Rev: BL 12/15/04)

290 Koertge, Ron. *Boy Girl Boy* (8–11). 2005, Harcourt $16.00 (0-15-205325-5). 176pp. Longtime friends Elliot, Teresa, and Larry find that their lives and their relationships change dramatically with high school graduation. (Rev: BL 9/1/05*; VOYA 12/05)

291 Koja, Kathe. *Talk* (8–11). 2005, Farrar $16.00 (0-374-37382-5). 144pp. Kit is used to acting — he is pretending to be straight, after all — and he wins the male lead in the high school play, opposite the popular Lindsay Walsh, who promptly falls for Kit. (Rev: BCCB 3/05; BL 3/15/05; HB 3–4/05; SLJ 3/05; VOYA 4/05)

292 Krinsky, Natalie. *Chloe Does Yale* (11–12). 2005, Hyperion $19.95 (1-4013-0107-X). 272pp. Based on the author's personal experiences, this novel introduces Chloe Carrington, a Yale senior who writes a sex advice column for the school newspaper; for mature teens. (Rev: BL 2/1/05)

293 Kyi, Tanya L. *My Time as Caz Hazard* (8–12). 2004, Orca paper $7.95 (1-55143-319-2). 103pp. Caz Hazard — who faces problems at home and at school — strikes up a friendship with Amanda and is drawn into a series of antisocial activities, one of which leads to the suicide of a classmate. (Rev: SLJ 3/05; VOYA 2/05)

294 Lane, Dakota. *The Orpheus Obsession* (10–12). 2005, HarperCollins LB $17.89 (0-06-074174-0). 288pp. Anooshka Stargirl, who leads a pretty bleak life in a small New York town with her unstable mother, becomes obsessed with a 21-year-old singer named Orpheus. (Rev: BL 9/15/05; SLJ 9/05; VOYA 10/05)

295 LaRochelle, David. *Absolutely, Positively Not* (7–10). 2005, Scholastic $16.95 (0-439-59109-0). 224pp. A funny and sensitive first-person portrayal of a 16-year-old's efforts to deny his homosexuality. (Rev: BL 7/05*; SLJ 9/05; VOYA 10/05)

296 Leitch, Will. *Catch* (9–12). 2005, Razorbill paper $7.99 (1-59514-069-7). 288pp. For Tim Temples, the summer after high school graduation — featuring a boring job, a romance with an older woman, and his older brother's mysterious decline — turns out to be a time for rethinking his future. (Rev: BCCB 11/05; BL 12/1/05; SLJ 11/05; VOYA 12/05)

297 Les Becquets, Diane. *Love, Cajun Style* (8–11). 2005, Bloomsbury $16.95 (1-58234-674-7). 300pp. Romance seems to be in the air in Lucy Beauregard's Louisiana town, spicing her interest in Dewey, son of the artist who has just opened an art gallery. (Rev: BL 9/15/05*; SLJ 10/05; VOYA 10/05)

298 Levithan, David. *Marly's Ghost* (7–10). 2006, Dial $14.99 (0-8037-3063-2). 112pp. In this contemporary spin on Dickens's *A Christmas Carol*, Ben, a teenager grieving over the loss of his girlfriend to cancer, is visited by her ghost and three other spirits on the eve of Valentine's Day. (Rev: BL 11/15/05)

299 Levithan, David. *The Realm of Possibility* (9–12). 2004, Random LB $17.99 (0-375-82845-1). 224pp. In this appealing but challenging free-verse novel, students at the same high school tell of their relationships, heartaches, goals, and triumphs in a series of interconnected stories. (Rev: BL 9/1/04; SLJ 9/04; VOYA 8/04)

300 Lion, Melissa. *Swollen* (8–12). 2004, Random LB $17.99 (0-385-90876-8). 192pp. Lonely San Diego high school student Samantha, who calls herself "invisible," runs track but never wins and indulges in casual sex. (Rev: BL 10/15/04; SLJ 8/04)

301 Lion, Melissa. *Upstream* (9–12). 2005, Random LB $17.99 (0-385-70877-6). 180pp. Amid the rich natural beauty of her home in Alaska, Marty has been blinded to almost everything by the death of her boyfriend, but a new friendship with Katherine helps Marty to confront the truth about the tragedy. (Rev: BL 6/1–15/05; SLJ 7/05; VOYA 6/05)

302 Lockhart, E. *The Boyfriend List* (8–11). 2005, Delacorte LB $17.99 (0-385-90238-7). 240pp. After her disastrous social life triggers a series of panic attacks, 15-year-old Ruby consults a psychiatrist. (Rev: BCCB 3/05; BL 4/1/05; SLJ 4/05)

303 Lubar, David. *Sleeping Freshmen Never Lie* (8–11). 2005, Dutton $15.99 (0-525-47311-4). 256pp. Aspiring writer Scott Hudson chronicles the highs and lows of his freshman year in high school. (Rev: BCCB 10/05; BL 5/15/05; SLJ 7/05*; VOYA 6/05)

304 Mac, Carrie. *The Beckoners* (9–12). 2004, Orca $16.95 (1-55143-309-5). 192pp. Fifteen-year-old Zoe Anderson, the new girl in school, agrees to join a brutal, bullying girls' gang, if only to protect herself from becoming one of its victims; as the gang's misdeeds become progressively more outrageous, Zoe is finally forced to take a stand against it. (Rev: BL 11/15/04; SLJ 12/04; VOYA 2/05)

305 McCafferty, Megan. *Charmed Thirds* (11–12). 2006, Crown $21.00 (1-4000-8042-8). 400pp. This third volume in the series — after *Sloppy Firsts* (2001) and *Second Helpings* (2003) — sees witty Jessica Darling through her academic and social adventures at Columbia University; for mature teens. (Rev: BL 3/15/06)

306 Mackler, Carolyn. *Vegan Virgin Valentine* (8–12). 2004, Candlewick $16.99 (0-7636-2155-2). 256pp. High school senior Mara Valentine, a classic overachiever, is right on schedule with her short-term goals for her future when Vivian comes to live with Mara's family. (Rev: BL 6/1–15/04; SLJ 8/04; VOYA 10/04)

307 McWilliams, Kelly. *Doormat* (6–10). 2004, Delacorte LB $17.99 (0-385-90204-2). 144pp. For much of her young life, 15-year-old Jaime has felt like a doormat, but things begin to look up when she finds a new beau, wins the lead in a school play, and helps her best friend deal with the discovery that she is pregnant. (Rev: BL 12/1/04; SLJ 9/04; VOYA 12/04)

308 Maillard, Keith. *Running* (9–12). 2005, Brindle & Glass paper $11.95 (1-897142-06-4). 154pp. In the 1950s John Dupre is a student at a military academy, loves life and running, and hopes to become a writer; John is also conflicted about his sexual identity and calls himself a "boy-girl." (Rev: BL 9/15/05)

309 Manning, Sarra. *Pretty Things* (10–12). 2005, Dutton $15.99 (0-525-47522-2). 256pp. While participating in a summer drama workshop, four British teens are caught in a tangled web of love affairs, some gay, in this story told in alternating narratives. (Rev: BCCB 10/05; BL 5/1/05*; SLJ 6/05; VOYA 10/05)

310 Marino, Peter. *Dough Boy* (7–10). 2005, Holiday House $16.95 (0-8234-1873-1). 221pp. Fifteen-year-old Tristan, a child of divorce, is unfazed by his weight until Kelly, the health-obsessed daughter of his mother's boyfriend, starts picking on him. (Rev: BL 11/15/05; SLJ 11/05; VOYA 2/06)

311 Matthews, Andrew. *A Winter Night's Dream* (7–10). 2004, Delacorte $15.95 (0-385-73097-7). 160pp. Heeding their English teacher's advice to "go out and fall in love with someone," high school freshman Casey and senior Stewart soon have reason to question their romantic choices; a funny novel featuring fast repartee. (Rev: BL 9/1/04; SLJ 8/04; VOYA 12/04)

312 Mayall, Beth. *Mermaid Park* (8–11). 2005, Penguin $16.99 (1-59514-029-8). 256pp. To escape family turmoil, 16-year-old Amy spends the summer with a family friend in a New Jersey shore town and dreams of becoming an underwater performer at nearby Mermaid Park. (Rev: BL 10/1/05; SLJ 9/05; VOYA 8/05)

313 Mazetti, Katarina. *God and I Broke Up* (9–12). 2004, Douglas & McIntyre $15.95 (0-88899-584-9). 160pp. In this poignant Swedish import, 16-year-old Linnea reflects on her short but rewarding friendship with Pia, who has committed suicide. (Rev: BCCB 1/05; BL 2/1/05; SLJ 3/05)

314 Mechling, Lauren, and Laura Moser. *The Rise and Fall of a 10th Grade Social Climber* (9–12). 2005, Houghton paper $7.99 (0-618-55519-6). 304pp. Newly transplanted to New York after her parents separate, 15-year-old Mimi Shulman bets a longtime friend that she can get the most popular girls in her 10th-grade class to accept her. (Rev: BCCB 5/05; BL 4/15/05; SLJ 6/05; VOYA 6/05)

315 Meno, Joe. *Hairstyles of the Damned* (11–12). 2004, Akashic paper $14.95 (1-888451-70-2). 290pp. Two teenagers — Brian and Gretchen — bond through punk rock and their anger at the world in this novel written in the first person and set in Chicago in 1990; strong language restricts this to mature teens. (Rev: BL 9/15/04)

316 Miller, Mary Beth. *On the Head of a Pin* (9–12). 2006, Button $16.99 (0-525-47736-5). 288pp. A prom queen is accidentally shot at a party, and the resulting cover-up exposes the characters of the three boys involved. (Rev: BL 2/15/06*; SLJ 4/06; VOYA 4/06)

317 Miller, Sarah. *Inside the Mind of Gideon Rayburn* (9–12). 2006, St. Martin's $16.95 (0-312-33375-7). 304pp. A female narrator, whose identity is revealed at the end of the book, reveals all the thoughts and feelings of 15-year-old New England prep school student Gideon Rayburn. (Rev: BL 4/1/06)

318 Mitchell, David. *Black Swan Green* (9–12). 2006, Random $24.95 (1-4000-6379-5). 304pp. Thirteen-year-old Jason Taylor narrates incidents in his life — avoiding stammering, trying to keep his parents from arguing, dealing with schoolmates — over the period a year in the early 1980s in a small village in Worcestershire, England. (Rev: BL 2/15/06)

319 Moore, Peter. *Caught in the Act* (8–11). 2005, Viking $16.99 (0-670-05990-0). 256pp. Honor student Ethan Lederer is having trouble keeping his grades up and his problems multiply when he falls for Lydia, a Goth-type who turns out to be alarmingly manipulative. (Rev: BCCB 6/05; BL 3/1/05; HB 3–4/05; SLJ 5/05; VOYA 4/05)

320 Moriarty, Jaclyn. *The Year of Secret Assignments* (8–12). 2004, Scholastic $16.95 (0-439-49881-3). 352pp. A rollicking year in the lives of three Australian high school girls — Lydia, Emily, and Cassie — is chronicled in their correspondence with male pen pals at a rival school. (Rev: BCCB 4/04; BL 1/1–15/04; HB 3–4/04; SLJ 3/04; VOYA 6/04)

321 Myracle, Lauren. *ttfn* (10–12). 2006, Abrams $15.95 (0-8109-5971-2). 224pp. Angela, Zoe, and Madigan, now 16, continue to be friends and to share details of their lives through text messages in this sequel to *ttyl* (2004). (Rev: BL 4/1/06; SLJ 3/06)

322 Naylor, Phyllis Reynolds. *Alice on Her Way* (7–10). 2005, Simon & Schuster $15.95 (0-689-87090-6). 336pp. Alice, now almost 16 and hoping to get her driver's license, protests the idea of attending a sex class at church, but finds to her surprise that it's interesting and informative. (Rev: BL 7/05; SLJ 5/05; VOYA 8/05)

323 Nelson, Blake. *Rock Star, Superstar* (9–12). 2004, Penguin $16.99 (0-670-05933-1). 240pp. As his rock music career begins to heat up, 16-year-old Pete fears that his newfound fame will jeopardize his budding romance with Margaret. (Rev: BL 11/1/04; SLJ 10/04)

324 Nelson, R. A. *Teach Me* (9–12). 2005, Penguin $16.99 (1-59514-084-0). 272pp. Carolina, a high school senior known as "Nine," becomes sexually involved with her English teacher and is devastated when he abruptly ends the affair. (Rev: BCCB 9/05; BL 11/15/05; HB 11–12/05; SLJ 10/05; VOYA 12/05)

325 Newman, Leslea. *Jailbait* (10–12). 2005, Delacorte LB $17.99 (0-385-90230-1). 224pp. Overweight and very much alone, 15-year-old Andi Kaplan turns out to be easy prey for an unscrupulous 30-year-old drifter named Frank. (Rev: BL 6/1–15/05; SLJ 6/05; VOYA 6/05)

326 Noël, Alyson. *Art Geeks and Prom Queens* (9–12). 2005, St. Martin's paper $8.95 (0-312-33636-5). 240pp. No one is more surprised than geekish 16-year-old Rio when she's befriended by cheerleader Kristi, the most popular girl at Rio's new school, but she soon learns that friendships like Kristi's can be very fleeting. (Rev: BL 10/1/05; SLJ 11/05)

327 Noël, Alyson. *Faking 19* (9–12). 2005, St. Martin's paper $8.95 (0-312-33633-0). 210pp. Seventeen-year-old Alex reevaluates her life and her friendship with M. when she realizes she needs to pave the way for a meaningful future. (Rev: SLJ 9/05; VOYA 10/05)

328 Nothomb, Amelie. *The Book of Proper Names* (9–12). Trans. by Shaun Whiteside. 2004, St. Martin's $19.95 (0-312-32055-8). 128pp. Orphan Plectrude receives a baptism by fire at the Paris Opera Ballet School, where cruelty and eating disorders are the norm. (Rev: BL 7/04)

329 Oates, Joyce Carol. *Sexy* (9–12). 2005, HarperCollins LB $17.89 (0-06-054150-4). 272pp. Darren Flynn, a 16-year-old star athlete who is shy about his good looks and sex appeal, faces a dilemma when a teacher rumored to be gay asks for his help. (Rev: BCCB 3/05; BL 2/1/05; HB 3–4/05; SLJ 4/05; VOYA 4/05)

330 O'Connell, Tyne. *Dueling Princes* (7–10). Series: Calypso Chronicles. 2005, Bloomsbury $16.95 (1-58234-658-5). 250pp. In the third volume of the series, Calypso Kelly, an American student attending a British boarding school, is dating Prince Freddie and stands an excellent chance of winning a spot on Britain's national fencing team. (Rev: BL 12/1/05; SLJ 1/06; VOYA 2/06)

331 Palmer, Liza. *Conversations with the Fat Girl* (9–12). 2005, Warner paper $12.95 (0-446-69395-2). 328pp. Maggie's self-image is not improved when best friend and fellow traveler Olivia slims down and bags a neat fiancé. (Rev: BL 8/05)

332 Papademetriou, Lisa, and Christopher Tebbetts. *M or F?* (9–12). 2005, Penguin $16.99 (1-59514-034-4). 304pp. In this delightful contemporary variation on the Cyrano de Bergerac theme, Marcus, a gay teen, helps his friend Frannie build an online relationship with Jeff but finds he's developing feelings for him as well. (Rev: BL 10/15/05; SLJ 1/06; VOYA 12/05)

333 Pascal, Francine. *The Ruling Class* (8–11). 2004, Simon & Schuster $14.95 (0-689-87332-8). 192pp. Brutally harassed by bullies at her new high school in Dallas, 16-year-old Twyla Gay briefly considers dropping out but decides instead to seek revenge. (Rev: BCCB 12/04; BL 1/1–15/05; SLJ 12/04)

334 Perkins, Mitali. *Monsoon Summer* (7–12). 2004, Delacorte LB $17.99 (0-385-90147-X). 272pp. Fifteen-year-old Jazz reluctantly accompanies her mother to India for the summer, where Jazz learns some valuable lessons about her heritage and herself. (Rev: BL 6/1–15/04; SLJ 9/04)

335 Peters, Julie Anne. *Far from Xanadu* (9–12). 2005, Little, Brown $16.99 (0-316-15881-X). 282pp. Tough girl Mike falls in love with new-girl-in-town Xanadu, who is straight and uninterested. (Rev: BL 9/1/05; SLJ 6/05; VOYA 6/05)

336 Prue, Sally. *The Devil's Toenail* (7–10). 2004, Scholastic $16.95 (0-439-48634-3). 224pp. Thirteen-year-old Stevie Saunders, still trying to recover from a brutal bullying incident that left him scarred, enters a new school determined to endear himself. (Rev: BCCB 9/04; BL 4/15/04; SLJ 8/04)

337 Qualey, Marsha. *Just Like That* (9–12). 2005, Dial $16.99 (0-8037-2840-9). 240pp. Hanna, 18, feels guilty about the death of two teens; after she meets and becomes romantically and sexually involved with Will, who also is connected to the tragedy, she is distressed to discover that he is only 14. (Rev: BL 8/05; SLJ 5/05; VOYA 6/05)

338 Rivers, Karen. *The Healing Time of Hickeys* (9–12). 2004, Raincoast paper $6.95 (1-55192-600-8). 304pp. Haley Andromeda Harmony, a 16-year-old hypochondriac, expects wonders from her senior year in high school but instead encounters a seemingly endless series of disasters and illnesses that she relates to her diary with wry wit. (Rev: BL 8/04; SLJ 6/04; VOYA 8/04)

339 Robbins, Maggie. *Suzy Zeus Gets Organized* (11–12). 2005, Bloomsbury $17.95 (1-58234-535-X). 160pp. An inventive novella in verse about saucy, sexy Suzy Zeus, newly arrived in New York from Indiana and full of zest for life until romance goes wrong; for mature readers. (Rev: BL 3/1/05)

340 Roberts, Laura Peyton. *The Queen of Second Place* (7–10). 2005, Delacorte LB $17.99 (0-385-

90200-X). 256pp. High school student Cassie's efforts to attract hunky Kevin Matthews do not show her in a good light, but her friends and family have the sense to see her through this folly. (Rev: BL 6/1–15/05; SLJ 9/05; VOYA 12/05)

341 Sanchez, Alex. *Rainbow Road* (9–12). 2005, Simon & Schuster $16.95 (0-689-86565-1). 256pp. Gay teens Jason, Kyle, and Nelson take a road trip to LA where Jason will speak at the opening of a high school for gay and lesbian teens, encountering a variety of interesting individuals along the way. The final novel in a trilogy. (Rev: BL 9/1/05; SLJ 10/05)

342 Sandoval, Lynda. *Who's Your Daddy?* (7–10). 2004, Simon & Schuster paper $6.99 (0-689-86440-X). 318pp. Sixteen-year-old Lila Moreno and her two closest friends find their search for romance hampered by the jobs their fathers hold. (Rev: SLJ 1/05; VOYA 2/05)

343 Scott, Kieran. *I Was a Non-Blonde Cheerleader* (7–10). 2005, Penguin $15.99 (0-399-24279-1). 256pp. As a brunette, Annisa has a hard time fitting in at her new high school where almost everybody else is blond. (Rev: BL 1/1–15/05; SLJ 1/05; VOYA 4/05)

344 Selvadurai, Shyam. *Swimming in the Monsoon Sea* (8–11). 2005, Tundra $18.95 (0-88776-735-4). 224pp. In Sri Lanka in 1980, Amrith's expected quiet summer is enlivened by the arrival from Canada of his cousin Niresh, a boy with whom he soon falls in love but who does not share his feelings. (Rev: BL 9/15/05*; SLJ 11/05)

345 Shaw, Tucker. *Confessions of a Backup Dancer* (8–12). 2004, Simon & Schuster paper $8.99 (0-689-87075-2). 272pp. Seventeen-year-old Kelly Kimball, a talented dancer, suddenly finds herself thrust into a close relationship with pop diva Darcy Barnes; in this journal-like novel, Kelly dishes the dirt on Darcy and the diva's entourage. (Rev: BL 9/15/04; SLJ 8/04)

346 Sherrill, Martha. *The Ruins of California* (9–12). 2006, Penguin $24.95 (1-59420-080-7). 318pp. In this engaging coming-of-age story set in California in the 1970s, teenage Inez Garcia Ruin struggles to find her identity as she shuttles between the homes of her divorced, and very different, parents. (Rev: BL 11/15/05)

347 Siegel, Lee. *Who Wrote the Book of Love?* (11–12). 2005, Univ. of Chicago $24.00 (0-226-75700-5). 536pp. A humorous look at the sexual ambitions of a young male narrator in the 1950s; for mature teens. (Rev: BL 5/1/05)

348 Sittenfeld, Curtis. *Prep* (11–12). 2005, Random $24.95 (1-4000-6231-4). 400pp. A scholarship student at an exclusive Eastern prep school, self-absorbed Lee sacrifices academics for a misguided love affair and an embittered quest for popularity; for mature teens. (Rev: BL 12/15/04; SLJ 5/05)

349 Smith, D. James. *My Brother's Passion* (11–12). 2005, Permanent $22.00 (1-57962-107-4). 128pp. Dave, a Korean American preteen, comes of age in the 70s and during and after his adored brother's tour in Vietnam witnesses shocking small-town cruelties that culminate in tragedy. (Rev: BL 2/15/05; SLJ 7/05)

350 Soto, Gary. *Accidental Love* (7–10). 2006, Harcourt $16.00 (0-15-205497-9). 192pp. Something clicks when 14-year-old Marisa meets wimpy Rene and she is inspired to transfer to his school, where, despite complications, she finds herself blossoming socially and academically — and enjoying her first love. (Rev: BL 1/1–15/06; SLJ 1/06; VOYA 2/06)

351 Standiford, Natalie. *The Dating Game* (9–12). Series: Dating Game. 2005, Little, Brown $9.99 (0-316-11040-X). 224pp. High school sophomores Madison, Holly, and Lina set up a popular Web site — it includes a sex quiz and dating program — as a class project. (Rev: BL 3/15/05; SLJ 8/05)

352 Steinhofel, Andreas. *The Center of the World* (10–12). Trans. by Alisa Jaffa. 2005, Delacorte LB $18.99 (0-385-90266-2). 480pp. Phil, 17 and gay, is from an unconventional family that is not wholly accepted in the conservative German town where they live; a challenging but rewarding story. (Rev: BCCB 6/05; BL 4/1/05*; HB 3–4/05; SLJ 9/05)

353 Stone, Tanya Lee. *A Bad Boy Can Be Good for a Girl* (10–12). 2006, Random LB $16.99 (0-385-90946-2). 240pp. Three high school girls relate their experiences with a sexy senior who loves them and leaves them. (Rev: BL 1/1–15/06; SLJ 1/06)

354 Strauss, Peggy Guthart. *Getting the Boot* (8–12). Series: Students Across the Seven Seas. 2005, Penguin paper $6.99 (0-14-240414-4). 224pp. A light story about popular high school junior Kelly Brandt's summer as an exchange student in Italy. (Rev: BL 5/15/05; SLJ 8/05)

355 Summer, Jane. *Not the Only One: Lesbian and Gay Fiction for Teens* (7–12). 2004, Alyson paper $13.95 (1-55583-834-0). 224pp. This revised edition includes 10 new stories featuring gay and lesbian teens. (Rev: BL 12/15/04; VOYA 2/05)

356 Taylor, Michelle. *What's Happily Ever After, Anyway?* (9–12). 2004, Brown Barn paper $10.95 (0-9746481-3-2). 178pp. Sixteen-year-old Miranda and her boyfriend, Keith, face a tough decision when she discovers that she is pregnant. (Rev: SLJ 2/05)

357 Thomson, Sarah L. *The Manny* (7–10). 2005, Dutton $15.99 (0-525-47413-7). 181pp. Sixteen-year-old Justin Blakewell looks forward to a summer of sun and fun when he lands a job as a male nanny for the 4-year-old son of a wealthy couple in the Hamptons. (Rev: BCCB 9/05; SLJ 6/05; VOYA 8/05)

358 Toews, Miriam. *A Complicated Kindness: A Novel* (10–12). 2004, Counterpoint $23.00 (1-58243-321-6). 246pp. Sixteen-year-old Nomi Nichol, increasingly uncomfortable living in a repressive Mennonite community in Canada, tries to lose herself in drugs and dreams of escape to New York City. (Rev: BL 9/15/04; SLJ 4/05)

359 Townley, Roderick. *Sky: A Novel in 3 Sets and an Encore* (7–10). 2004, Simon & Schuster $16.95 (0-689-85712-8). 272pp. Angered by his father's opposition to his interest in jazz, 15-year-old Sky runs away from home and moves in with the blind jazz pianist whose life he saved. (Rev: BL 8/04; SLJ 7/04)

360 Triana, Gaby. *Cubanita* (9–12). 2005, HarperCollins LB $16.89 (0-06-056021-5). 208pp. Funny first-person narrative relates 17-year-old Cuban American Isabel Diaz's disagreements with her family about culture and her unsuitable boyfriend. (Rev: BCCB 10/05; BL 5/15/05*; SLJ 8/05)

361 Tullson, Diane. *Blue Highway* (9–12). 2004, Fitzhenry & Whiteside (1-55005-124-5). 276pp. High school student Truth is bound to her friend Skye by a traumatic childhood incident, and together the two slip deeper into an alcoholic haze until Truth wakes up to what's happening to her life. (Rev: BL 11/15/04; SLJ 12/04; VOYA 2/05)

362 Tussing, Justin. *The Best People in the World* (11–12). 2006, HarperCollins $24.95 (0-06-081533-7). 352pp. In this appealing coming-of-age novel suitable for mature teens, 17-year-old Thomas falls in love with his 23-year-old teacher in Paducah, Kentucky, and the two escape the town's disapproval by moving to the Vermont mountains with a drifter named Shiloh. (Rev: BL 12/15/05)

363 Vail, Rachel. *If We Kiss* (7–10). 2005, HarperCollins LB $16.89 (0-06-056915-8). 272pp. Fourteen-year-old Charlie struggles with feelings of guilt after she kisses Kevin, who just happens to be her best friend's steady. (Rev: BCCB 5/05; BL 3/15/05; HB 7–8/05; SLJ 5/05)

364 Volponi, Paul. *Black and White* (9–12). 2005, Viking $15.99 (0-670-06006-2). 181pp. Marcus and Eddie — best friends, stars of their high school basketball team, and African American and white respectively — find their friendship put to the test when they commit a robbery and only one of them is caught. (Rev: BCCB 6/05; BL 9/1/05*; SLJ 6/05)

365 Von Ziegesar, Cecily. *Because I'm Worth It* (10–12). Series: Gossip Girl. 2003, Little, Brown paper $8.99 (0-316-90968-8). 232pp. The soap opera continues as Dan, Vanessa, and Serena all have successes but Nat is caught using drugs and Blair is still trying to get into Yale and risks becoming entangled with an older man. (Rev: SLJ 2/04)

366 Von Ziegesar, Cecily. *Nothing Can Keep Us Together* (10–12). Series: Gossip Girl. 2005, Little, Brown $9.99 (0-316-73509-4). 222pp. In the eighth volume of this series, the regular cast of characters prepares for high school graduation and what lies beyond. (Rev: BL 12/1/05)

367 Wasserman, Robin. *Lust* (8–11). Series: Seven Deadly Sins. 2005, Simon & Schuster paper $7.99 (0-689-87782-X). 240pp. In an entertaining opening volume of a soap-opera-like series, several sex-obsessed high school seniors in a small California town ruthlessly scheme to win the girl or guy of their dreams. (Rev: BL 12/1/05; SLJ 1/06)

368 Weaver, Will. *Full Service* (7–10). 2005, Farrar $17.00 (0-374-32485-9). 240pp. Paul, a sheltered Christian 15-year-old, discovers hippies, alcohol, and sex when he takes a job at a gas station in the summer of 1965. (Rev: BL 9/1/05; SLJ 11/05; VOYA 10/05)

369 Withrow, Sarah. *What Gloria Wants* (7–10). 2005, Groundwood $15.95 (0-88899-628-4); paper $6.95 (0-88899-692-6). 176pp. Gloria always seems to be a step behind her best friend Shawna, so Gloria initially exults when she is first to land a boyfriend. (Rev: BCCB 11/05; BL 12/1/05; HB 1–2/06; SLJ 2/06; VOYA 12/05)

370 Wittlinger, Ellen. *Heart on My Sleeve* (9–12). 2004, Simon & Schuster $16.95 (0-689-84997-4). 224pp. The growing long-distance relationship between Chloe and Julian — two college-bound high school graduates — is documented through their correspondence with each other and their siblings. (Rev: BL 7/04; SLJ 8/04; VOYA 8/04)

371 Wittlinger, Ellen. *Sandpiper* (8–12). 2005, Simon & Schuster $16.95 (0-689-86802-2). 240pp. Her promiscuous past has severely tarnished 16-year-old Sandpiper's reputation, but when she develops a friendship with Walker, both troubled teens begin to make some important discoveries about the ways in which the past is shaping their future. (Rev: BL 6/1–15/05; SLJ 7/05; VOYA 8/05)

372 Yardley, Cathy. *Couch World* (11–12). 2005, Harlequin paper $12.95 (0-373-89509-7). 304pp. PJ, a couch-surfing substitute DJ, finds her itinerant lifestyle morphing when a famous manager, an opportunistic stylist, and a meddling investigative reporter step in; for mature teens. (Rev: BL 12/15/04)

373 Zeises, Lara M. *Anyone But You* (10–12). 2005, Delacorte LB $17.99 (0-385-90177-1). 256pp. The close relationship of teenage skateboarders Seattle and Critter, raised pretty much like sister and brother, undergoes some major changes when each of them falls in love; for mature teens. (Rev: BCCB 3/06; BL 12/15/05; SLJ 1/06; VOYA 12/05)

374 Zephaniah, Benjamin. *Gangsta Rap* (9–12). 2004, Bloomsbury paper $7.95 (1-58234-886-3). 336pp. Expelled from his London school, 15-year-old Ray is given one last chance to redeem himself when he teams up with friends Prem and Tyrone to form a rap music group that, against all odds, wins a lucrative recording contract. (Rev: BL 6/1–15/04; HB 7–8/04; SLJ 2/05; VOYA 2/05)

375 Zusak, Markus. *I Am the Messenger* (9–12). 2005, Knopf LB $18.99 (0-375-83099-X). 368pp. For most of his 19 years, Ed has been wandering aimlessly through life, barely connecting with those around him, but after he thwarts a bank robbery, his life begins to undergo a startling transformation. (Rev: BL 1/1–15/05*; SLJ 2/05; VOYA 2/05)

World Affairs and Contemporary Problems

376 Adams, Lorraine. *Harbor* (11–12). 2004, Knopf $23.95 (1-4000-4233-X). 304pp. Aziz Arkoun's life is only more complicated after he flees Algeria to live the hard life of an illegal alien in the United States; for mature teens. (Rev: BL 7/04)

377 Adoff, Jaime. *Names Will Never Hurt Me* (7–10). 2004, Dutton $15.99 (0-525-47175-8). 144pp. As their high school marks the first anniversary of the shooting death of a fellow student, four very different teenagers express their feelings about school, their classmates, and themselves. (Rev: BCCB 4/04; BL 4/1/04; HB 7–8/04; SLJ 4/04; VOYA 4/04)

378 Babcock, Joe. *The Tragedy of Miss Geneva Flowers* (11–12). 2005, Carroll & Graf paper $13.95 (0-7867-1520-0). 352pp. Erick Taylor, an unhappy 16-year-old, is enchanted by the persona and life of a drag queen; unfortunately the lure of crystal meth is even stronger than that of the stage; for mature teens. (Rev: BL 4/15/05)

379 Benaïssa, Slimane. *The Last Night of a Damned Soul* (11–12). Trans. by Janice and Daniel Gross. 2004, Grove $24.00 (0-8021-1780-5). 272pp. After his father's death, Arab American Raouf is drawn into the world of Muslim fundamentalism and terrorism. (Rev: BL 9/15/04)

380 Bryher. *Visa for Avalon* (11–12). 2004, Paris paper $15.00 (1-930464-07-X). 192pp. First published in 1965, this story of a couple hoping to escape to a land called Avalon when "the Movement" forces them out of their home mirrors the predicament faced by many during World War II. (Rev: BL 10/15/04)

381 Budhos, Marina. *Ask Me No Questions* (7–10). 2006, Simon & Schuster $16.95 (1-4169-0351-8). 176pp. Fourteen-year-old Nadira describes the legal and emotional upheavals her family faces as Bangladeshis living illegally in the United States. (Rev: BCCB 3/06; BL 12/15/05*; HB 3–4/06; SLJ 4/06; VOYA 2/06)

382 Burstyn, Varda. *Water Inc* (9–12). 2004, Verso $25.00 (1-85984-596-7). 294pp. A plot to control the United States' water supply is foiled by a plucky team of environmentalists. (Rev: BL 8/04)

383 Carlson, Melody. *Crystal Lies* (9–12). 2004, WaterBrook paper $12.99 (1-57856-840-4). 352pp. Glennis's life is turned upside down when her son becomes addicted to crystal methamphetamine. (Rev: BL 10/1/04)

384 Divakaruni, Chitra Banerjee. *Queen of Dreams* (11–12). 2004, Doubleday $21.95 (0-385-50682-1). 352pp. Rakhi, a Californian with Indian roots, fears for the well-being of herself, her daughter, her friends and her tea house in the aftermath of 9/11; for mature readers. (Rev: BL 7/04)

385 Flake, Sharon G. *Bang!* (9–12). 2005, Hyperion $16.99 (0-7868-1844-1). 304pp. Fearful of losing another son to urban violence, Mann's father abandons teenage Mann and a friend at a remote campsite in imitation of an African coming-of-age ritual. (Rev: BL 7/05; SLJ 10/05; VOYA 12/05)

386 Hopkins, Ellen. *Crank* (8–12). 2004, Simon & Schuster paper $6.99 (0-689-86519-8). 544pp. In this debut novel written in verse, Hopkins introduces readers to Kristina Snow and how the high school junior became addicted to crystal meth. (Rev: BL 11/15/04; SLJ 11/04; VOYA 2/05)

387 Kass, Pnina Moed. *Real Time* (9–12). 2004, Clarion $15.00 (0-618-44203-0). 192pp. This chilling story of a suicide bomb attack on an Israeli bus is told from the viewpoints of bus passengers and their friends and loved ones. (Rev: BL 2/1/05; HB 1–2/05; SLJ 10/04; VOYA 2/05)

388 Lalami, Laila. *Hope and Other Dangerous Pursuits* (10–12). 2005, Algonquin $21.95 (1-56512-493-6). 208pp. Stories of four Moroccans who risk their lives to get across the Strait of Gibraltar to Spain reveal much about the circumstances in Morocco and the individuals' often unreasonable expectations of their destinations. (Rev: BL 8/05; SLJ 12/05)

389 Lewis, Richard. *The Flame Tree* (8–12). 2004, Simon & Schuster $16.95 (0-689-86333-0). 276pp. Isaac, 12-year-old son of American missionary doctors in Java, Indonesia, finds himself held hostage by Muslim fundamentalists in the days following September 11, 2001. (Rev: SLJ 10/04)

390 Lynch, Janet Nichols. *Peace Is a Four-Letter Word* (7–10). 2005, Heyday paper $9.95 (1-59714-014-7). 168pp. The carefully ordered life of high school cheerleader Emily Rankin is shattered when a history teacher inspires her to get involved in the peace movement on the eve of the Gulf War. (Rev: BL 10/1/05; SLJ 10/05)

391 Lynn, Tracy. *Rx* (9–12). 2006, Simon & Schuster paper $6.99 (1-4169-1155-3). 272pp. From stealing an initial bottle of Ritalin, Thyme's familiarity with prescription drugs increases until she is supply-ing many classmates with their chosen medications. (Rev: BL 3/1/06)

392 Matthews, Tom. *Like We Care* (11–12). 2004, Bancroft $23.95 (1-890862-36-3). 272pp. High-schoolers Todd and Joel head a boycott of everything marketed to teenagers — candy, cigarettes, even TV — putting them in the center of a media frenzy in this satirical novel suitable for mature teens. (Rev: BL 8/04; SLJ 11/04; VOYA 12/04)

393 Meyer, Adam. *The Last Domino* (10–12). 2005, Penguin $16.99 (0-399-24332-1). 240pp. A frightening story of school violence in which manipulative Daniel exploits Travis's unhappiness about his older brother's suicide. (Rev: BL 9/1/05; SLJ 11/05; VOYA 8/05)

394 Nye, Naomi Shihab. *Going Going* (7–10). 2005, Greenwillow LB $16.89 (0-06-029366-7). 233pp. Angered by the exodus of small businesses from her hometown, 16-year-old Florrie launches a grassroots campaign against the giant chain stores that she believes are responsible. (Rev: BCCB 7–8/05; BL 4/1/05; HB 7–8/05; SLJ 5/05; VOYA 10/05)

395 Simon, Scott. *Pretty Birds* (11–12). 2005, Random $24.95 (1-4000-6310-8). 368pp. Irena, a high school basketball star in Sarajevo, takes on a new role as a sniper when the war there overwhelms the populace; for mature teens. (Rev: BL 4/15/05)

396 Stein, Tammar. *Light Years: A Novel* (8–12). 2005, Knopf $15.95 (0-375-83023-5). 272pp. Twenty-year-old Maya leaves her native Israel to attend college in Virginia, but her memories of the death of her boyfriend, killed by a suicide bomber, intrude on her new life. (Rev: BL 12/1/04; SLJ 1/05; VOYA 6/05)

397 Stine, Catherine. *Refugees* (9–12). 2005, Delacorte LB $17.99 (0-385-90216-6). 288pp. Set against the backdrop of the September 11, 2001, terrorist attacks, this novel chronicles the long-distance relationship between Dawn, a 16-year-old runaway living in New York, and Johar, an Afghani teen who fled his native country for the safety of Pakistan. (Rev: BCCB 4/05; BL 3/1/05; SLJ 3/05; VOYA 2/05)

398 Updike, John. *Terrorist* (11–12). 2006, Knopf $25.00 (0-307-26465-3). 310pp. Eighteen-year-old Ahmad's obsession with Islam draws him inexorably into a tangled and dangerous web. (Rev: BL 3/15/06)

399 Woods, Brenda. *Emako Blue* (7–10). 2004, Penguin $15.99 (0-399-24006-3). 128pp. After Emako, a talented singer, is mistakenly killed in a drive-by shooting in Los Angeles, her surviving friends — Eddie, Jamal, and Monterey — share their thoughts about what she meant to them. (Rev: BL 7/04; SLJ 7/04)

Fantasy

400 Adlington, L. J. *The Diary of Pelly D* (8–12). 2005, Greenwillow LB $16.89 (0-06-076616-6). 288pp. While working on an excavation crew in the ruins of City Five, Tony V finds the journal of a girl named Pelly D, and her story of wide-scale ethnic cleansing causes the young worker to reexamine his own beliefs. (Rev: BCCB 5/05; BL 5/1/05*; HB 7–8/05; SLJ 5/05)

401 Anthony, Piers. *Currant Events* (9–12). Series: Xanth. 2004, Tor $24.95 (0-765-30407-4). 336pp. Clio goes on a dragon-saving quest and falls in love in this installment full of the usual wordplay. (Rev: BL 10/1/04)

402 Ash, Sarah. *Children of the Serpent Gate* (9–12). Series: Tears of Artamon. 2005, Bantam $23.00 (0-553-38212-8). 528pp. In the final book of the trilogy, the children of the kingdom are threatened by daemon-dragons and it is up to Kiukiu to save them from the Realm of Shadows. (Rev: BL 9/1/05)

403 Ash, Sarah. *Prisoner of the Iron Tower* (9–12). 2004, Bantam $23.00 (0-553-38211-X). 467pp. While Gavril gives up his powers, Eugene gains more power than he needs or wants in this engaging fantasy. (Rev: BL 8/04)

404 Asprin, Robert, and Eric Del Carlo. *Wartorn Resurrection* (9–12). 2005, Berkley paper $6.99 (0-441-01235-3). 304pp. Emperor Matokin sends his army, led by Lord Weisel, to claim to the isthmus separating his North realm from the South. Weisel, possessed by the spirit of Dardas, a legendary, ruthless militarist, wreaks havoc, engendering a resistance movement of fighters and sorcerers. (Rev: BL 12/15/04)

405 Baker, Kage. *Mother Aegypt and Other Stories* (11–12). 2004, Night Shade $27.00 (1-892389-75-4). 256pp. An engrossing collection of 13 engaging fantasy stories for strong, mature teen readers. (Rev: BL 7/04)

406 Barker, Clive. *Days of Magic, Nights of War* (7–12). Series: Abarat. 2004, HarperCollins $24.99 (0-06-029170-2). 512pp. In the second installment in the series, Candy Quackenbush makes discoveries about herself and the islands of Abarat as she tries to stay one step ahead of the Lord of Midnight. (Rev: BL 9/1/04; SLJ 11/04)

407 Barron, T. A. *The Great Tree of Avalon* (6–12). Series: Great Tree of Avalon. 2004, Penguin $19.99 (0-399-23763-1). 448pp. The fate of Avalon, which the Lady of the Lake has prophesied will be destroyed by the Dark Child, rests in the hands of two 17-year-old boys: Tamwyn and Scree. (Rev: BL 9/1/04*; SLJ 10/04)

408 Barron, T. A. *Shadows on the Stars* (7–10). Series: Great Tree of Avalon. 2005, Philomel $19.99 (0-399-23764-X). 448pp. In the year 1002 Tamwyn, Elli, and Scree set off on separate quests to conquer the evil Rhita Gawr and save Avalon in this sequel to *Child of the Dark Prophecy* (2004). (Rev: BL 9/15/05; SLJ 12/05)

409 Benjamin, Curt. *Lords of Grass and Thunder* (9–12). 2005, DAW $24.95 (0-7564-0197-6). 464pp. Prince Tayy must achieve certain goals before taking over leadership of the Qubal clans. (Rev: BL 4/15/05)

410 Berman, Judith. *Bear Daughter* (10–12). 2005, Ace paper $15.00 (0-441-01322-8). 432pp. Once a bear, now a girl, Cloud must run from her evil stepfather, King Rumble, and help save the world along the way in this rich mixture of myth and folktale. (Rev: BL 9/1/05; VOYA 2/06)

411 Black, Holly. *Valiant: A Modern Tale of Faerie* (8–11). 2005, Simon & Schuster $16.95 (0-689-86822-7). 320pp. In this dark fantasy featuring drugs and homeless teens in New York City, 17-year-old Val becomes involved with trolls and faeries. (Rev: BL 7/05; SLJ 6/05)

412 Blackman, Malorie. *Naughts and Crosses* (8–11). 2005, Simon & Schuster $15.95 (1-4169-0016-0). 400pp. Callum, a 15-year-old, pale-skinned Naught in a world dominated by the dark-skinned Crosses, falls in love with Sephy, daughter of the Cross politician for whom Callum's mother works. (Rev: BL 6/1–15/05*; SLJ 6/05; VOYA 8/05)

413 Blumlein, Michael. *The Healer* (9–12). 2005, Prometheus $25.00 (1-59102-314-9). 344pp. Fourteen-year-old Payne has unique healing powers in a world in which beings known as grotesques are considered inferior to humans. (Rev: BL 7/05; SLJ 10/05)

414 Bray, Libba. *A Great and Terrible Beauty* (8–12). 2003, Delacorte $16.95 (0-385-73028-4); paper $17.99 (0-385-90161-5). 403pp. In 1895 England, 16-year-old Gemma, attending a boarding school after her mother's death in India, learns to control her visions and enter a sinister world called the Realms. (Rev: BCCB 5/04; BL 3/15/04; SLJ 2/04; VOYA 4/04)

415 Bray, Libba. *Rebel Angels* (9–12). 2005, Delacorte LB $18.99 (0-385-90257-3). 560pp. In this appealing sequel to *A Great and Terrible Beauty* (2003), 17-year-old Gemma Doyle journeys with two friends to the magical Realms to ferret out the meaning of a nightmarish vision that keeps haunting her. (Rev: BL 10/1/05; VOYA 8/05)

416 Brom. *The Plucker* (9–12). Illus. 2005, Abrams $24.95 (0-8109-5792-2). 142pp. In a riveting blend of horror and fairy tale, spirits inhabiting a young boy's toys do battle for the soul of the child. (Rev: BL 10/15/05; SLJ 2/06)

417 Brooks, Terry. *Straken: High Druid of Shannara* (9–12). Series: High Druid of Shannara. 2005, Del Rey $26.95 (0-345-45112-0). 384pp. In the final volume in this complex trilogy, Druids take from Pen Ohmsford the darkwand that he acquired in *Tanequil* (2004). (Rev: BL 6/1–15/05; VOYA 2/06)

418 Browne, N. M. *The Story of Stone* (9–12). 2005, Bloomsbury $17.95 (1-58234-655-0). 336pp. Nela, an archaeologist, discovers a mysterious black stone that allows her to look into the distant past and observe the interaction between two very different clans. (Rev: BL 10/15/05; SLJ 11/05; VOYA 10/05)

419 Bruchac, Josephine. *Wabi: A Hero's Tale* (7–10). 2006, Dial $16.99 (0-8037-3098-5). 192pp. A white great horned owl named Wabi has the power to transform himself into a human being and falls in love with an Abenaki girl named Dojihla. (Rev: BL 2/15/06; SLJ 4/06*; VOYA 4/06)

420 Buffie, Margaret. *The Finder* (6–10). Series: The Watcher's Quest. 2004, Kids Can $16.95 (1-55337-671-4). 416pp. In the final volume of the trilogy, shape-changing heroine Emma Sweeny defies her training master and passes through a magical portal where she must get to four hidden power wands before they're found by the evil Eefa. (Rev: BL 10/15/04; SLJ 1/05; VOYA 2/05)

421 Bujold, Lois McMaster. *The Hallowed Hunt* (9–12). 2005, HarperCollins $24.95 (0-06-057462-3). 480pp. In the same world as *The Curse of Chalion* (2001) and *Paladin of Souls* (2003), Lord Ingrey kin Wolfcliff finds himself attracted to the young woman accused of killing Prince Bolesco. (Rev: BL 6/1–15/05)

422 Bunting, Eve. *The Lambkins* (7–10). 2005, HarperCollins LB $16.89 (0-06-059907-3). 192pp. Kyle's offer to help a woman with a flat tire goes awry when she kidnaps him and shrinks him to the size of a Coke bottle. (Rev: BL 8/05; SLJ 8/05)

423 Butcher, Jim. *Academ's Fury* (9–12). Series: Codex Alera. 2005, Ace $24.95 (0-441-01283-3). 480pp. In the action-packed sequel to *Furies of Calderon* (2004), assassins are only one of the problems young Tavi faces as he battles to save the realm. (Rev: BL 7/05)

424 Butcher, Jim. *Furies of Calderon* (9–12). Series: Codex Alera. 2004, Berkley $23.95 (0-441-01199-3). 448pp. Tavi is caught up in the war raging in his homeland, Aliera, whose people have special powers over the elements. (Rev: BL 10/1/04)

425 Card, Orson Scott. *Magic Street* (9–12). 2005, Del Rey $24.95 (0-345-41689-9). 400pp. A well-written contemporary fantasy about an African American boy known as Mack Street, who was found in a grocery sack and lives with his adopted

parents in Los Angeles; his ability to dream others' dreams is a dubious attribute. (Rev: BL 4/15/05; VOYA 12/05)

426 Cash, Steve. *The Meq* (11–12). 2005, Del Rey paper $13.95 (0-345-47092-3). 416pp. When Z turns 12 in 1881, he learns of his heritage and fate as a Meq, a race living among humans; Z works to defeat the evil Fleur-du-Mal against a backdrop of richly detailed historical events at the turn of the 20th century; for mature teens. (Rev: BL 12/15/04)

427 Chapman, Janet. *Tempting the Highlander* (11–12). Series: Highlander. 2004, Pocket paper $6.99 (0-7434-8630-7). 384pp. Catherine, an abused wife and mother of two, finds herself falling in love with Robbie, who happens to be a time traveler from 13th-century Scotland; for mature teens. (Rev: BL 9/1/04)

428 Clarke, Susanna. *Jonathan Strange and Mr. Norrell: A Novel* (9–12). 2004, Bloomsbury $27.95 (1-58234-416-7). 782pp. In this sweeping novel set in early-19th-century England, two magicians — Gilbert Norrell and his pupil Jonathan Strange — set out to return magic to its former glory but soon clash over how to pull it off. (Rev: BL 7/04; SLJ 1/05)

429 Coe, David B. *Bonds of Vengeance* (11–12). Series: Winds of the Forelands. 2005, Tor $24.95 (0-312-87809-5). 416pp. In a new entry in the series, peace between the magical Qirsi and the neighboring Eandi is disrupted when the mysterious Weaver compellingly preaches rebellion. (Rev: BL 2/1/05)

430 Coe, David B. *Shapers of Darkness* (10–12). Series: Winds of the Forelands. 2005, Tor $25.95 (0-312-87810-9). 416pp. In the fourth volume of the Winds of the Forelands series, Prince Tavis joins forces with Qirsi shaper Grinsa jal Arriet to find out the true identity of the evil Weaver. (Rev: BL 12/1/05)

431 Constable, Kate. *The Tenth Power* (7–10). Series: Chanters of Tremaris. 2006, Scholastic $16.99 (0-439-55482-9). 306pp. Mourning the loss of her nine powers of chantment, 18-year-old Calwyn returns to Antaris to discover she must go in search of the key to the mysterious tenth, healing, power. (Rev: BL 3/15/06; SLJ 3/06)

432 Constable, Kate. *The Waterless Sea* (8–11). Series: Chanters of Tremaris. 2005, Scholastic $16.95 (0-439-55480-2). 320pp. In the second volume of the trilogy, Calwyn and her friends travel to the desolate Merithuran Empire on a mission to rescue some children with magical powers. (Rev: BL 5/15/05; SLJ 8/05; VOYA 8/05)

433 Cornish, D. M. *Foundling* (7–10). Illus. Series: Monster Blood Tattoo. 2006, Penguin $18.99 (0-399-24638-X). 434pp. Rossamund Bookchild, a foundling boy with a girl's name, sets off from the orphanage to his new job as a lamplighter and finds himself in a perilous world (called Half-Continent) full of monsters. (Rev: BL 4/1/06*)

434 Croggon, Alison. *The Naming* (7–10). 2005, Candlewick $17.99 (0-7636-2639-2). 528pp. The life of 16-year-old Maerad, a slave, changes dramatically after she meets Cadvan, who tells her of her epic destiny. (Rev: BCCB 9/05; BL 5/1/05; SLJ 10/05*; VOYA 8/05)

435 Del Vecchio, Gene. *The Pearl of Anton* (7–10). 2004, Pelican $16.95 (1-58980-172-5). 256pp. In this complex, gripping fantasy, Jason inherits the Wizard's Stone when he turns 15, but the stone's powers cannot be realized until it is joined with the Pearl of Anton, which is hidden in a mountain cave and guarded by two fearsome beasts. (Rev: BL 6/1–15/04*; VOYA 10/04)

436 de Lint, Charles. *Widdershins* (9–12). 2006, Tor $27.95 (0-765-31285-9). 560pp. An intricate addition to de Lint's urban fantasies set in Newford, in which Lizzie Mahone finds her way into the spirit world and meets characters from previous books including Jilly Coppercorn and Geordie Riddell. (Rev: BL 3/15/06)

437 Dickinson, John. *The Cup of the World* (9–12). 2004, Random LB $17.99 (0-385-75025-0). 432pp. Sixteen-year-old Phaedra, the willful daughter of a widowed baron, rejects a number of noble would-be suitors and instead weds a mysterious knight, setting off a clash between good and evil. (Rev: BL 10/15/04; SLJ 9/04; VOYA 2/05)

438 Dickinson, John. *The Widow and the King* (9–12). 2005, Random LB $20.99 (0-385-75085-4). 624pp. More than 10 years after the events of *The Cup of the World* (2004), Ambrose — son of the dead king — is in danger from the evil "undercraft" and must flee for his life. (Rev: BL 7/05; SLJ 7/05; VOYA 6/05)

439 DiTocco, Robyn, and Tony DiTocco. *Atlas' Revenge: Another Mad Myth Mystery* (7–12). 2005, Brainstorm $19.95 (0-9723429-2-3); paper $11.95 (0-9723429-3-1). 234pp. PJ Allen, a carefree college senior, is called upon to travel to the world of mythology to complete the legendary Twelve Labors of Hercules and solve a cryptic riddle in this fast-paced novel full of legendary characters and literary references. (Rev: SLJ 6/05)

440 Douglass, Sara. *Sinner* (11–12). Series: Wayfarer Redemption. 2004, Tor $26.95 (0-312-87046-9). 464pp. Trouble is brewing once again in Tencendor among the humans, the bird people, and the Avar; for mature teens. (Rev: BL 9/15/04)

441 *Dr. Ernest Drake's Dragonology: The Complete Book of Dragons* (5–12). Illus. 2003, Candlewick $18.99 (0-7636-2329-6). Presented as the recently discovered research of a 19th-century scientist, this richly illustrated volume presents a very realistic

encyclopedia of dragon facts and figures. (Rev: BL 4/15/04; SLJ 4/04)

442 Dunkle, Clare B. *In the Coils of the Snake* (7–10). Series: Hollow Kingdom. 2005, Holt $16.95 (0-8050-7747-2). 240pp. When human girl Miranda learns she will not after all marry the new goblin king, she flees from the kingdom; this final volume in the trilogy is set 30 years after *Close Kin* (2004). (Rev: BL 1/1–15/06*; SLJ 10/05; VOYA 10/05)

443 Ewing, Lynne. *Barbarian* (8–12). Series: Sons of the Dark. 2004, Hyperion $9.99 (0-7868-1811-5). 264pp. Four gorgeous and immortal teens with magical powers escape slavery in the parallel universe of Nefandus and must deal with life in modern Los Angeles before fulfilling their destinies. (Rev: SLJ 10/04; VOYA 2/05)

444 Ewing, Lynne. *Outcast* (9–12). Series: Sons of the Dark. 2005, Hyperion $9.99 (0-7868-1813-1). 257pp. The third volume in the series about four young aliens trying to fit in to contemporary America. (Rev: SLJ 6/05)

445 Fallon, Jennifer. *Treason Keep* (9–12). Series: Hythrun Chronicles. 2004, Tor $25.95 (0-765-30987-4). 496pp. Medalon is under attack by the gods and must rely on the Hythruns for help in this sequel to *Medalon*. (Rev: BL 11/15/04; VOYA 6/05)

446 Farley, Terri. *Seven Tears into the Sea* (7–10). 2005, Simon & Schuster paper $6.99 (0-689-86442-6). 288pp. Working at her clairvoyant grandmother's seaside inn for the summer, 17-year-old Gwen becomes attracted to Jesse, a strange boy with secrets. (Rev: BCCB 4/05; BL 4/1/05; SLJ 6/05; VOYA 6/05)

447 Farrell, S. L. *Heir of Stone* (9–12). Series: Cloudmages. 2005, DAW $23.95 (0-7564-0254-9). 464pp. In the third volume of the Cloudmages Celtic fantasy series, twins Sevai and Kayne come of age while defending their clan — from assault by the bestial Arruk, and treachery by Doyle, their grandmother's stepbrother. (Rev: BL 1/1–15/05; VOYA 6/05)

448 Fawcett, Bill, and Brian Thomsen, eds. *Masters of Fantasy* (9–12). 2004, Baen $25.00 (0-7434-8822-9). 384pp. A collection of stories by well-known fantasy writers — Alan Dean Foster, Mercedes Lackey, and Andre Norton, to name only three. (Rev: SLJ 12/04)

449 Federici, Debbie, and Susan Vaught. *L.O.S.T* (8–12). 2004, Llewellyn paper $9.95 (0-7387-0561-6). 321pp. Fantasy and romance are intertwined in this fast-paced story about 17-year-old Bren, who is kidnapped by Jazz, 16-year-old Queen of the Witches, because she believes he is the long-prophesied Shadowalker. (Rev: SLJ 1/05)

450 Fisher, Jude. *The Rose of the World* (11–12). Series: Fool's Gold. 2005, DAW $23.95 (0-7564-

0187-9). 512pp. In this complex, riveting conclusion to the series, three deities, separated by a powerful mage, reunite and attempt to staunch the carnage wracking the land of Elda. (Rev: BL 2/1/05; VOYA 8/05)

451 Fisk, Pauline. *The Red Judge* (7–10). 2005, Bloomsbury $16.95 (1-58234-942-8). 208pp. Haunted by grief and guilt over his involvement in his sister's accident, Zed Fitztalbot is sent to live in the Welsh home of his recently deceased grandmother in this stand-alone companion to *The Secret of Sabrina Fludde* (2002) that combines fantasy, mythology, and typical teen problems. (Rev: BL 12/1/05; SLJ 3/06)

452 Foon, Dennis. *The Dirt Eaters* (5–10). Series: Longlight Legacy Trilogy. 2003, Annick $19.95 (1-55037-807-4); paper $9.95 (1-55037-806-6). 320pp. In this well-written first installment of a trilogy, 15-year-old Roan finds himself torn between the peaceful ways of his upbringing and a desire to avenge a murderous attack on his village. (Rev: SLJ 1/04; VOYA 2/04)

453 Gaiman, Neil. *Anansi Boys* (9–12). 2005, Morrow $26.95 (0-06-051518-X). 368pp. To his surprise, Fat Charlie Nancy discovers that his father was Anansi, the West African trickster, and that he has a brother called Spider. (Rev: BL 8/05; SLJ 1/06)

454 Gandolfi, Silvana. *Aldabra, or the Tortoise Who Loved Shakespeare* (6–12). 2004, Scholastic $16.95 (0-439-49741-8). 160pp. In this whimsical tale set in Venice, 10-year-old Elisa faces some daunting challenges when her beloved grandmother is magically transformed into a giant tortoise. (Rev: BCCB 7–8/04; BL 4/1/04; SLJ 8/04; VOYA 8/04)

455 Gardner, Sally. *I, Coriander* (7–10). 2005, Dial $16.99 (0-8037-3099-3). 288pp. In a fantasy full of the atmosphere of 17th-century England, Coriander is the daughter of a human father and a fairy princess. (Rev: BL 8/05; SLJ 9/05; VOYA 10/05)

456 Gelder, Gordon Van, ed. *In Lands That Never Were* (9–12). 2004, Thunder's Mouth paper $16.95 (1-56858-314-1). 416pp. A collection of fantasy stories from the *Magazine of Fantasy and Science Fiction*. (Rev: BL 9/1/04)

457 Gemmell, David. *Troy: Lord of the Silver Bow* (9–12). 2005, Del Rey $24.95 (0-345-45835-4). 496pp. The first volume in a trilogy about the Trojan War, this alternate history features Aeneas in the person of a Trojan ally called Helikaon who is in love with Hector's fiancée Andromache. (Rev: BL 9/1/05)

458 Golden, Christopher, and Thomas E. Sniegoski. *The Nimble Man* (11–12). 2004, Berkley paper $6.99 (0-441-01215-9). 352pp. Sir Arthur Conan Doyle is a sorcerer fighting the Night People with

the help of a vampire in this first book in a series. (Rev: BL 10/15/04)

459 Hale, Shannon. *Enna Burning* (8–11). 2004, Bloomsbury $17.95 (1-58234-889-8). 336pp. In this companion to *The Goose Girl*, Enna returns to her home in the forest and learns to wield the power of fire, but she must struggle to use that power wisely without risking her life or those of her people. (Rev: BL 9/15/04; SLJ 9/04; VOYA 12/04)

460 Harrison, M. John. *Viriconium* (9–12). 2005, Bantam paper $16.00 (0-553-38315-9). 480pp. A collection of four classic novels and several stories set in the richly imagined mythical post-apocalyptic city of Viriconium and straddling the genres of fantasy and science fiction. (Rev: BL 9/15/05)

461 Harrison, Mette. *Mira, Mirror* (7–10). 2004, Penguin $17.99 (0-670-05923-4). 320pp. Transformed into a mirror by her adopted sister, Mira seeks help from a peasant girl in her quest to regain human form. (Rev: BL 9/1/04; SLJ 9/04; VOYA 10/04)

462 Haydon, Elizabeth. *Elegy for a Lost Star* (9–12). Series: Symphony of Ages. 2004, Tor $27.95 (0-312-87883-4). 318pp. War and conflict continue in this fifth installment in the series that started with *Rhapsody: Child of Blood* (1999). (Rev: BL 8/04)

463 Hearn, Julie. *Sign of the Raven* (7–10). 2005, Simon & Schuster $16.95 (0-689-85734-9). 328pp. Living with his grandmother in London while his mother recovers from cancer, 12-year-old Tom finds a portal into an 18th-century world far different from his own. (Rev: BCCB 12/05; HB 1–2/06; SLJ 11/05; VOYA 10/05)

464 Hemingway, Amanda. *The Greenstone Grail* (9–12). 2005, Ballantine $16.95 (0-345-46078-2). 368pp. In a contemporary England with traditional and fantasy elements, young Nathan becomes convinced he is destined for something different; the first installment in a trilogy. (Rev: BL 3/15/05; VOYA 10/05)

465 Hemingway, Amanda. *The Sword of Straw* (9–12). 2006, Del Rey paper $12.95 (0-345-46080-4). 336pp. Nathan Ward, a 14-year-old whose dreams take him to other worlds, wants to save a princess he sees trapped in a ruined city; a sequel to *The Greenstone Grail* (2005). (Rev: BL 3/15/06)

466 Hendee, Barb, and J. C. Hendee. *Sister of the Dead* (11–12). 2005, NAL $7.50 (0-451-46009-X). 400pp. In this sequel to *Thief of Lives* (2004) suitable for mature teens, Magiere, half-human and half-vampire, journeys with her half-elf friend Leesil in search of answers about their parentage. (Rev: BL 1/1–15/05)

467 Hetley, James A. *The Winter Oak* (9–12). 2004, Berkley paper $14.00 (0-441-01201-9). 304pp. Sisters Maureen and Jo Pierce fight witches and dragons in this sequel to *The Summer Country* (2002). (Rev: BL 11/15/04)

468 Hill, Laban Carrick. *Casa Azul: An Encounter with Frida Kahlo* (7–10). 2005, Watson-Guptill $15.95 (0-8230-0411-2). 150pp. In this appealing novel, two country children roaming the streets of Mexico City in search of their mother are befriended by artist Frida Kahlo and introduced to the magical world in which she dwells. (Rev: BL 10/1/05; SLJ 9/05)

469 Hill, Stuart. *The Cry of the Icemark* (8–11). 2005, Scholastic $19.95 (0-439-68626-1). 496pp. In this sprawling military fantasy, 13-year-old Thirrin succeeds her fallen father as ruler of Icemark and sets off to forge alliances with werewolves, vampires, and talking snow leopards to help her defend her tiny country. (Rev: BCCB 4/05; BL 2/15/05; SLJ 5/05; VOYA 6/05)

470 Hoffman, Alice. *The Foretelling* (7–10). 2005, Little, Brown $16.99 (0-316-01018-9). 167pp. Rain, the daughter of an unaffectionate Amazon queen, questions the tribe's beliefs and customs. (Rev: BL 7/05; SLJ 10/05; VOYA 12/05)

471 Hoffman, Mary. *Stravaganza: City of Flowers* (7–10). Series: Stravaganza. 2005, Bloomsbury $17.95 (1-58234-887-1). 496pp. In the final volume of the trilogy, Sky Meadows, a 17-year-old biracial Londoner, travels back in time to 16th-century Talia, where many of the characters become involved in multilayered intrigue. (Rev: BL 3/1/05; SLJ 5/05)

472 Hoving, Isabel. *The Dream Merchant* (8–12). Trans. from Dutch by Hester Velmans. 2005, Candlewick $17.99 (0-7636-2880-8). 630pp. An action-packed, intricately plotted adventure involving three young people in time travel and a world of collective dreams called *umaya*. (Rev: SLJ 1/06; VOYA 12/05)

473 Isaak, Elaine. *The Singer's Crown* (9–12). 2005, Eos paper $14.95 (0-06-078253-6). 480pp. Kattanan duRhys, the only member of his royal family to survive a deadly attack by his uncle, is castrated and trained to sing, but years later he embarks on a fight to reclaim the family kingdom. (Rev: BL 10/15/05)

474 Johnson, Kathleen Jeffrie. *A Fast and Brutal Wing* (8–11). 2004, Roaring Brook $16.95 (1-59643-013-3). 192pp. In a series of e-mails, journal entries, and newspaper stories, three teens recount the mysterious and fantastic events that led to a Halloween disappearance. (Rev: BL 12/15/04; SLJ 12/04; VOYA 12/04)

475 Jones, Diana Wynne. *Unexpected Magic: Collected Stories* (5–10). 2004, Greenwillow $16.99 (0-06-055533-5). An exciting anthology of 16 tales of mystery and magic by a master of fantasy. (Rev: BL 4/15/04; SLJ 9/04)

476 Jubert, Hervé. *Dance of the Assassins* (9–12). Trans. from French by Anthea Bell. Series: Devil's Dances. 2005, HarperCollins LB $17.89 (0-06-077718-4). 396pp. In the opening volume of this trilogy, sorceress Roberta Morgenstern and rookie cop Clement Martineau travel to a series of virtual-reality theme parks modeled after historic cities in their quest to unravel a murder mystery. (Rev: BCCB 9/05; SLJ 12/05; VOYA 10/05)

477 Kearney, Paul. *The Mark of Ran* (9–12). 2005, Bantam paper $12.00 (0-553-38361-2). 320pp. In the opening volume of the Sea Beggars series, 15-year-old Rol Cortishane, accused of witchcraft and driven from his village, takes refuge in the tower sanctuary of family friend Michal Psellos. (Rev: BL 11/15/05)

478 Keyes, Greg. *The Charnel Prince* (11–12). 2004, Del Rey $23.95 (0-345-44067-6). 560pp. In this sequel to *The Briar King* (2003), Crotheny is in the throes of a battle between good and evil forces, and the future of the monarchy is in danger. (Rev: BL 8/04)

479 Klause, Annette. *Freaks: Alive on the Inside!* (10–12). 2006, Simon & Schuster $16.95 (0-689-87037-X). 336pp. Brought up at Faeryland, a resort displaying people with "oddities" such as missing limbs and extra hair, normal 17-year-old Abel tries unsuccessfully to escape this life; set in the late 1890s, this is a mix of fantasy and reality. (Rev: BL 2/1/06*; SLJ 1/06; VOYA 12/05)

480 Knox, Elizabeth. *Dreamhunter: Book One of the Dreamhunter Duet* (9–12). 2006, Farrar $19.00 (0-374-31853-0). 384pp. Laura, a retiring 15-year-old, has inherited her father's gift as a dreamhunter, but her father has disappeared and she must draw on new reserves to continue his mission. (Rev: BL 4/1/06*; SLJ 3/06)

481 Lackey, Mercedes. *Sanctuary* (9–12). Series: The Dragon Jousters. 2005, DAW $25.95 (0-7564-0246-8). 320pp. In the final volume of the trilogy that started with *Joust* (2003) and *Alta* (2004), Kiron and his fellow jousters and dragons seek refuge from the evil Magi in the abandoned city called Sanctuary. (Rev: BL 5/1/05)

482 Lackey, Mercedes. *The Wizard of London* (10–12). Series: Elemental Masters. 2005, DAW $25.95 (0-7564-0174-7). 400pp. In Victorian England, Lord Alderscroft, head of the British Elemental Masters Council, is reunited with a former lover who needs his help in a struggle to rescue two girls. (Rev: BL 10/15/05)

483 Lanagan, Marge. *Black Juice* (9–12). 2005, HarperCollins LB $16.89 (0-06-074391-3). 208pp. A collection of 10 diverse literary fantasy stories. (Rev: BCCB 3/05; BL 4/15/05; HB 5–6/05; SLJ 3/05; VOYA 4/05)

484 Larbalestier, Justine. *Magic or Madness* (8–11). 2005, Penguin $16.99 (1-59514-022-0). 288pp. Australian 15-year-old Reason resists the idea of magic until she is transported from her grandmother's home to New York City and finds herself tackling new realities. (Rev: BCCB 3/05; BL 3/15/05*; SLJ 3/05; VOYA 2/05)

485 Lawrence, Michael. *A Crack in the Line* (8–12). 2004, HarperCollins $15.99 (0-06-072477-3). 336pp. Still mourning his mother's death, 16-year-old Alaric discovers how to travel to an alternate reality where his mother is still alive. (Rev: BL 6/1–15/04*; SLJ 8/04)

486 Lawrence, Michael. *Small Eternities* (9–12). 2005, Greenwillow $15.99 (0-06-072480-3). 336pp. Two years after his mother's tragic, accidental death, 16-year-old Alaric finds himself transported to an alternate reality where his mother is still alive in this sequel to *A Crack in the Line* (2004). (Rev: BL 11/1/05; SLJ 3/06; VOYA 12/05)

487 Le Guin, Ursula K. *Gifts* (6–10). 2004, Harcourt $17.00 (0-15-205123-6). 288pp. In this engaging fantasy, Gry and Orrec, two Uplanders with supernatural abilities, are hesitant to use their awesome powers for fear that they will cause more harm than good. (Rev: BL 8/04*; SLJ 9/04; VOYA 12/04)

488 London, Dena. *Shapeshifter's Quest* (7–10). 2005, Dutton $16.99 (0-525-47310-6). 192pp. Syanthe, a shape-shifting teenager, ventures outside the forest that has always been her home on a mission to unravel the secret of the king's black magic. (Rev: BL 10/1/05; SLJ 10/05; VOYA 8/05)

489 McCaffrey, Todd. *Dragonsblood* (9–12). Series: Dragonriders of Pern. 2005, Del Rey $24.95 (0-345-44124-9). 448pp. The dragons of Pern are threatened and only Wind Blossom can save them in this novel by the son of the creator of the series. (Rev: BL 11/1/04)

490 McGann, Oisín. *The Gods and Their Machines* (8–11). 2004, Tor $19.95 (0-765-31159-3). 240pp. Fantasy and allegory are blended in this story about Chamus, a teenage Altiman fighter pilot trainee, whose denigration of the people of nearby Bartokhrin as ignorant religious fanatics is revised when a Bartokhrin girl helps him after his plane is forced to land near her home. (Rev: BL 12/15/04)

491 McKiernan, Dennis L. *Once Upon an Autumn Eve* (11–12). 2006, Roc $23.95 (0-451-46069-3). 352pp. Liaze, princess of the Autumnwood, is a strong-willed young lady determined to rescue her true love Luc from an evil witch in this romantic fairy tale suitable for older teens. (Rev: BL 4/1/06)

492 McKillip, Patricia A. *Harrowing the Dragon* (8–12). 2005, Ace $23.95 (0-441-01360-0). 320pp. A collection of fantasy short stories featuring dragons, princesses in distress, sorcerers, shape-shifters, and more. (Rev: BL 11/1/05; SLJ 3/06)

493 McKillip, Patricia A. *Od Magic* (9–12). 2005, Ace $22.95 (0-441-01248-5). 320pp. The great magician Od, savior of the land of Numis, where all magic is controlled, invites the talented Brenden Vetch to a position in her school of wizardry. (Rev: BL 5/1/05; VOYA 10/05)

494 Magrs, Paul. *The Good, the Bat, and the Ugly* (6–10). 2004, Simon & Schuster $15.95 (0-689-87019-1). 247pp. Thirteen-year-old Jason's father is suspected of murdering some puppets in this dark but humorous fantasy set in England. (Rev: BCCB 7–8/04; SLJ 7/04)

495 Maguire, Gregory. *Son of a Witch* (9–12). 2005, Regan $26.95 (0-06-054893-2). 352pp. Liir, 14, faces many mysteries — was the witch Elphaba his mother? does he have magical powers? how did he come to be in the Cloister of St. Glinda, wounded and amnesiac? — in this multilayered sequel to *Wicked* (1995). (Rev: BL 9/15/05; SLJ 3/06)

496 Marillier, Juliet. *Foxmask* (9–12). 2004, Tor $27.95 (0-765-30674-3). 464pp. Creidhe is threatened by the Long Knife people but in love with their leader-to-be, Thorvald, in this romantic and thrilling fantasy. (Rev: BL 7/04; VOYA 8/04)

497 Marley, Louise. *Singer in the Snow* (8–11). 2005, Viking $16.99 (0-670-05965-X). 304pp. Mreen and Emle, two gifted young Singers from the ice planet of Nevya, are sent to a remote outpost where together they complement one another's powers in this follow-up to the Singers of Nevya trilogy. (Rev: BL 12/15/05; SLJ 1/06; VOYA 12/05)

498 Melling, O. R. *The Hunter's Moon* (8–11). 2005, Abrams $16.95 (0-8109-5857-0). 260pp. Gwen, an American, travels to Ireland to spend a fun-packed vacation with her cousin Findabhair but soon finds herself leading a rescue effort after Findabhair is abducted by the King of the Faeries. (Rev: BCCB 4/05; BL 4/15/05*; SLJ 4/05; VOYA 6/05)

499 Micklem, Sarah. *Firethorn* (9–12). 2004, Scribner $25.00 (0-7432-4794-9). 400pp. This feminist fantasy finds the healer Firethorn torn between her love for Sir Galan and her desire for self-reliance. (Rev: BL 6/1–15/04)

500 Modesitt, L. E. *Ordermaster* (9–12). Series: Recluce. 2005, Tor $27.95 (0-765-31213-1). 480pp. Lord Kharl nobly strives to maintain harmony in both his adoptive land and his homeland in this entry in the series. (Rev: BL 1/1–15/05)

501 Moorcock, Michael. *The White Wolf's Son* (9–12). 2005, Warner $24.95 (0-446-57702-2). 288pp. Oonaugh, the Dreamthief's granddaughter, must find White Wolf's son in order to avert a takeover of the Multiverse in this action-packed epic fantasy. (Rev: BL 6/1–15/05; SLJ 11/05)

502 Newcomb, Robert. *Savage Messiah* (9–12). Series: Destinies of Blood and Stone. 2005, Ballantine $26.95 (0-345-47707-3). 592pp. In the opening volume of a trilogy that follows the Chronicles of Blood and Stone, Prince Tristan and Wizard Wigg take desperate measures to heal the failing Orb of Vigors, from which all magic flows. (Rev: BL 12/15/05)

503 Niffenegger, Audrey. *The Three Incestuous Sisters* (11–12). Illus. 2005, Abrams $27.95 (0-8109-5927-5). 176pp. For mature teens, this dark fairy tale about three sisters and the love affair that tears them apart is presented in a "novel in pictures." (Rev: BL 8/05) [813]

504 Odom, Mel. *The Destruction of the Books* (9–12). 2004, Tor $25.95 (0-765-30723-5). 384pp. This sequel to *The Rover* finds Jugh, Edgewick Lamplighter's apprentice, fighting goblins and other evil beings in order to save the Vault of All Known Knowledge. (Rev: BL 7/04; VOYA 2/05)

505 Paolini, Christopher. *Eldest* (8–11). Series: Inheritance. 2005, Knopf LB $24.99 (0-375-92670-4). 704pp. Eragon continues his training as a Dragon Rider while his cousin Roran is under threat in this second installment in the trilogy. (Rev: BL 8/05; SLJ 10/05; VOYA 12/05)

506 Park, Paul. *A Princess of Roumania* (9–12). 2005, Tor $24.95 (0-765-31096-1). 368pp. Miranda, a princess of an alternate Romania, is sent by her aunt Aegypt to grow up in safety in contemporary Massachusetts, but the evil Baroness Ceaucescu's pursuit does not end and Miranda must travel through time and confront danger. (Rev: BL 7/05)

507 Peck, Dale. *The Drift House: The First Voyage* (8–11). 2005, Bloomsbury $16.95 (1-58234-969-X). 350pp. The Oakenfield siblings are sent to live with their Uncle Farley in Canada, and when their uncle's ship-like home is swept away in a flood, they enjoy a magical journey on the Sea of Time. (Rev: BL 10/1/05; SLJ 11/05; VOYA 10/05)

508 Pierce, Tamora. *Trickster's Queen* (7–12). 2004, Random LB $19.99 (0-375-81467-1). 480pp. In this thrilling sequel to *Trickster's Choice*, Aly must call upon her magical powers to protect the Balitang children and ensure that one of them — Dove — ascends to the throne of the Copper Isles. (Rev: BCCB 10/04; BL 10/1/04; SLJ 9/04; VOYA 2/05)

509 Pierce, Tamora. *The Will of the Empress* (8–11). 2005, Scholastic $17.99 (0-439-44171-4). 550pp. Bowing to the will of the Empress of Namorn, Sandry, accompanied by her mage friends from the Winding Circle, embarks on a perilous journey to visit her cousin, the empress; this stand-alone novel comes after the Circle of Magic and The Circle Opens quartets. (Rev: BCCB 1/06; BL 11/15/05*; HB 11–12/05; SLJ 11/05; VOYA 10/05)

510 Pini, Wendy, and Richard Pini. *ElfQuest: Wolfrider*, Vol.1 (9–12). Illus. Series: ElfQuest. 2003, DC Comics paper $9.95 (1-4012-0131-8). A collec-

tion of earlier published episodes, with various artists, about the Wolfrider tribe of elves and their struggles against humans. (Rev: SLJ 1/04)

511 Pratchett, Terry. *Going Postal* (8–12). Series: Discworld. 2004, HarperCollins $24.95 (0-06-001313-3). 377pp. In this humorous and inventive 29th Discworld novel, career criminal Moist von Lipwig escapes hanging by accepting the job of postmaster for Ankh-Morpork, a job he intends to leave far behind as soon as he can. (Rev: BL 9/1/04; SLJ 2/05)

512 Pratchett, Terry. *A Hat Full of Sky* (6–10). 2004, HarperCollins $16.99 (0-06-058660-5). 288pp. Witch-in-training Tiffany Aching battles a monster with help from the wee men and head witch Granny Weatherwax in the sequel to *The Wee Free Men*. (Rev: BCCB 5/04; BL 4/15/04; HB 7–8/04; SLJ 7/04; VOYA 6/04)

513 Pratchett, Terry. *Thud!* (9–12). Series: Discworld. 2005, HarperCollins $24.95 (0-06-081522-1). 384pp. As the anniversary of the battle between trolls and dwarfs at Koom Valley nears, Commander Sam Vimes must solve the murder of a dwarf to forestall mayhem in Ankh-Morpork. (Rev: BL 9/1/05)

514 Priest, Cherie. *Four and Twenty Blackbirds* (10–12). 2005, Tor paper $13.95 (0-765-31308-1). 288pp. In this chilling contemporary spin on the southern gothic novel, Eden, a girl of mixed race, leaves the Tennessee mountains where she's lived with her aunt and uncle and sets off on a journey to learn more about her familial roots. (Rev: BL 10/1/05)

515 Putney, M. J. *Stolen Magic* (11–12). 2005, Ballantine $23.95 (0-345-47689-1). 352pp. Romance and fantasy are interwoven as Simon Malmain, Lord Falconer and one of the Guardians who protects those who do not possess magic, attempts to foil the evil Lord Drayton and in the process comes to know a young woman named Meg; for mature teens. (Rev: BL 5/1/05; VOYA 12/05)

516 Rabe, Jean. *The Finest Creation* (9–12). 2004, Tor $24.95 (0-765-30820-7). 320pp. Gallant-Stallion, a human-like horse, carries young Meven and Kalantha to a mountain hideaway to escape the violence engulfing their land since the death of their prince. (Rev: BL 11/1/04)

517 Reichert, Mickey Zucker. *The Return of Nightfall* (9–12). Series: Nightfall. 2004, DAW $24.95 (0-7564-0201-8). 464pp. This fast-paced sequel to *The Legend of Nightfall* (1993), full of sorcery and treachery, finds Sudian assuming his Nightfall disguise in order to fight forces of evil and rescue King Edward. (Rev: BL 9/1/04)

518 Rowling, J. K. *Harry Potter and the Half-Blood Prince* (5–12). 2005, Scholastic LB $34.99 (0-439-78677-0). 672pp. In this sixth and penultimate volume, Harry, now 16, begins mapping a strategy to defeat the evil Lord Voldemort. (Rev: BL 8/05*; SLJ 9/05; VOYA 10/05)

519 Russon, Penni. *Undine* (9–12). 2006, Greenwillow LB $16.89 (0-06-079390-2). 256pp. Not only does 16-year-old Undine have strange powers but she receives strange messages; with her friend Trout, she finds a link with *The Tempest* and sets off for the sea to find answers to her questions. (Rev: BL 2/15/06; SLJ 2/06*; VOYA 2/06)

520 Sabin, E. Rose. *When the Beast Ravens* (7–12). 2005, Tor $23.95 (0-765-30858-4). 288pp. In the conclusion of the trilogy set at a school for gifted sorcerers (preceding volumes are *A School for Sorcery*, 2002, and *A Perilous Power*, 2004), students and faculty struggle to solve murders on campus and drive away demons from the Dire Realm. (Rev: BL 1/1–15/05; SLJ 7/05; VOYA 8/05)

521 Salvatore, R. A. *Promise of the Witch-King* (9–12). 2005, Wizards of the Coast $27.95 (1-7869-3823-4). 352pp. In this sequel to *Servant of the Shard*, Jarlaxle Baenre, a dark elf, and Artemis Entreri, a human assassin wielding a vampire sword, team up to search for the source of the power of the Witch-King Zhengyi. (Rev: BL 10/15/05)

522 Sarrantonio, Al, ed. *Flights: Extreme Visions of Fantasy* (9–12). 2004, NAL $24.95 (0-451-45977-6). 560pp. A collection of fantasy writing, some disturbing, frightening, or both, by well-known authors. (Rev: BL 6/1–15/04)

523 Shinn, Sharon. *Mystic and Rider* (9–12). Series: Twelve Houses. 2005, Ace $23.95 (0-441-01246-9). 448pp. At the king's bidding, a band of warriors and magicians investigates possible rebellion. This first volume in the series combines fantasy, strong characterization, and a bit of romance. (Rev: BL 3/1/05; VOYA 10/05)

524 Shinn, Sharon. *The Truth-Teller's Tale* (7–10). 2005, Viking $16.99 (0-670-06000-3). 288pp. Twin sisters Eleda and Adele are mirror images — Eleda can neither tell nor hear a lie, while Adele can be trusted to keep secret anything she is told. (Rev: BCCB 9/05; BL 4/15/05*; SLJ 7/05; VOYA 8/05)

525 Shusterman, Neal. *Duckling Ugly* (7–10). Series: Dark Fusion. 2006, Dutton $15.99 (0-525-47585-0). 176pp. Apart from her ability to spell, Cara DeFido has no known attributes until she finds herself in a magic kingdom; her successes there prompt her to return home, however. (Rev: BL 2/1/06)

526 Smith, Jeff. *Bone* (9–12). Illus. 2004, Cartoon paper $39.95 (1-888963-14-X). 1,344pp. A massive volume containing the complete, and very popular, Bone fantasy saga. (Rev: BL 10/15/04)

527 Spiegler, Louise. *The Amethyst Road* (8–11). 2005, Clarion $16.00 (0-618-48572-4). 336pp. In this cautionary futuristic novel, siblings Serena and Willow, half-Gorgio and half-Yulang, struggle to survive the violence of their urban neighborhood and the ostracism caused by their mixed blood. (Rev: BL 12/1/05; SLJ 11/05; VOYA 2/06)

528 Stackpole, Michael. *A Secret Atlas* (10–12). 2005, Bantam paper $15.00 (0-553-38237-3). 462pp. The family of the powerful Royal Cartographer of Nalenyr explores uncharted, sometimes magical lands, and defends against intrigue and sabotage at home, in the first of a series. (Rev: BL 3/1/05)

529 Steiber, Ellen. *A Rumor of Gems* (10–12). 2005, Tor $25.95 (0-312-85879-5). 496pp. In the city of Arcato, four lives are changed by the influence of gemstones with strange powers. (Rev: BL 6/1–15/05; VOYA 8/05)

530 Stemple, Adam. *Singer of Souls* (10–12). 2005, Tor $22.95 (0-765-31170-4). 288pp. Planning to abandon his drug habit for ever, busker Douglas Stewart goes to stay with his grandmother in Edinburgh, where a slip with a white powder has an expected effect — allowing him to see fairies, who are not all peaceable. (Rev: BL 8/05; SLJ 10/05; VOYA 10/05)

531 Stross, Charles. *The Family Trade* (9–12). 2004, Tor $24.95 (0-765-30929-7). 304pp. A magical locket carries Miriam to the world of Gruinmarkt, a world being rocked by conflict among six families. (Rev: BL 11/15/04)

532 Stroud, Jonathan. *The Golem's Eye* (7–12). Series: The Bartimaeus Trilogy. 2004, Miramax $17.95 (0-7868-1860-3). 574pp. In this sequel to *The Amulet of Samarkand*, 14-year-old Nathaniel, a magician's apprentice, joins forces with the mischievous djinni Bartimaeus to foil the evil plot of a golem. (Rev: BL 8/04; SLJ 10/04)

533 Taylor, G. P. *Tersias the Oracle* (8–11). 2006, Penguin $17.99 (0-399-24258-9). 272pp. Tersias, a 12-year-old blind boy, and Jonah, a young thief, become embroiled in a struggle for power in this multilayered novel. (Rev: BL 3/15/06)

534 Tiernan, Cate. *A Chalice of Wind* (8–11). Series: Balefire. 2005, Penguin paper $5.99 (1-59514-045-X). 256pp. Thais discovers that she has a twin — and that she is a witch — when her father dies and she is sent to live in New Orleans. (Rev: BL 9/1/05; SLJ 8/05)

535 Tiernan, Cate. *Night's Child* (7–12). Series: Sweep. 2003, Penguin paper $6.99 (0-14-250119-0). 318pp. In this 15th installment — a double-length, stand-alone novel — Moira, 15-year-old daughter of the powerful blood witch Morgan, learns about her heritage and tackles faces danger and treachery as well as romance. (Rev: SLJ 2/04)

536 Tiffany, Grace. *Ariel* (9–12). 2005, HarperCollins LB $17.89 (0-06-075328-5). 240pp. A fanciful imagining of the events leading up to Shakespeare's

The Tempest, centered on Ariel, the spirit whom Sycorax imprisoned in a tree. (Rev: BL 9/1/05*; SLJ 10/05; VOYA 10/05)

537 Touré. *Soul City* (9–12). 2004, Little, Brown $23.95 (0-316-74158-2). 208pp. When he visits Soul City, populated by the descendants of slaves who flew there to escape their owners, Cadillac Jackson finds himself falling in love with Mahogany Sunshine. (Rev: BL 9/1/04)

538 Troop, Alan F. *A Host of Dragons* (11–12). Series: Dragon DelaSangre. 2006, Roc paper $7.99 (0-451-46061-8). 352pp. Peter DelaSangre faces dragon-related problems with his wife and his business in this fourth installment; for mature teens. (Rev: BL 1/1–15/06)

539 Troop, Alan F. *The Seadragon's Daughter* (9–12). 2004, NAL paper $6.99 (0-451-46007-3). 304pp. In this fast-paced sequel to *The Dragon DelaSangre* (2002) and *Dragon Moon* (2003), dragon hero Peter DelaSangre returns to defend his island — and himself — against attacks by the resurgent seadragons, who need male dragons to repopulate. (Rev: BL 12/15/04)

540 Turtledove, Harry. *In High Places* (10–12). Series: Crosstime Traffic. 2006, Tor $22.95 (0-765-30696-4). 272pp. Annette Klein, an 18-year-old Californian who travels with her family between alternate worlds, is captured by bandits and separated from her parents, making it doubtful she'll be able to return to her normal world. (Rev: BL 12/1/05)

541 Turtledove, Harry. *Return Engagements* (11–12). Series: Settling Accounts. 2004, Del Rey $26.95 (0-345-45723-4). 640pp. The first volume in an alternate U.S. history trilogy related to The Great War and American Empire cycles; the later volumes are *Drive to the East* (2005) and *The Grapple* (2006). (Rev: BL 7/04)

542 Tuttle, Lisa. *The Silver Bough* (10–12). 2006, Bantam $22.00 (0-553-38297-7). 336pp. The small town of Appleton, Scotland, suffered a decline after its orchards were removed but now an earthquake isolates it and the town's magic is allowed to reappear. (Rev: BL 4/1/06)

543 Vaughan, Brian K., et al. *Girl on Girl*, Vol. 6 (9–12). Illus. Series: Y: The Last Man. 2005, DC Comics paper $12.99 (1-4012-0501-1). 128pp. In the sixth volume of Y: The Last Man collection, Yorick Brown, the last surviving human male on Earth, and his female escorts go in search of Ampersand, Brown's pet monkey that was abducted by a Japanese mercenary. (Rev: BL 1/1–15/06)

544 Ward, James M. *Midshipwizard Halcyon Blithe* (10–12). 2005, Tor $24.95 (0-765-31253-0). 288pp. Fantasy combines with seamanship aboard the *Sanguine*, a magical ship on the back of a sea dragon. (Rev: BL 9/1/05; SLJ 2/06)

545 Weis, Margaret. *The Dragon's Son* (9–12). Series: Dragonvald. 2004, Tor $25.95 (0-765-30469-4). 384pp. Two boys (twins, although one has a dragon for a father) become pawns in the struggle that runs through the trilogy of which this is the middle volume. (Rev: BL 7/04)

546 Witcover, Paul. *Tumbling After* (11–12). 2005, HarperCollins $24.95 (0-06-105285-X). 336pp. Twins Jack and Jilly find themselves swept up in a dangerous and frightening galactic battle in this rich and sometimes violent fantasy featuring mutant races and parallel worlds. (Rev: BL 3/15/05; SLJ 7/05)

547 Wooding, Chris. *The Haunting of Alaizabel Cray* (9–12). 2004, Scholastic $16.95 (0-439-54656-7). 304pp. In this fantasy thriller set in an alternate Victorian London, 17-year-old Thaniel Fox, a wych-hunter, joins forces with guardian Cathaline and a haunted young woman named Alaizabel to combat the forces of evil. (Rev: BL 8/04*; SLJ 8/04)

548 Yancey, Rick. *The Extraordinary Adventures of Alfred Kropp* (9–12). 2005, Bloomsbury $16.95 (1-58234-693-3). 300pp. Excalibur, King Arthur's legendary sword, ends up in the hands of 15-year-old Alfred Kropp, changing his life in many action-packed and often violent ways. (Rev: BL 8/05; SLJ 10/05)

549 Zahn, Timothy. *Dragon and Soldier: The Second Dragonback Adventure* (7–10). Series: Dragonback Adventure. 2004, Tor $17.95 (0-765-30125-3). 304pp. Jack Morgan, the 14-year-old symbiotic human host for a dragon warrior named Draycos, tries to find out who's behind a plot to annihilate all the members of Draycos's race; a sequel to *Dragon and Soldier* (2003). (Rev: BL 8/04)

550 Zevin, Gabrielle. *Elsewhere* (7–10). 2005, Farrar $16.00 (0-374-32091-8). 288pp. After dying of a head injury, 15-year-old Liz Hall does not adapt easily to afterlife in Elsewhere and at first spends a lot of time watching what's going on on Earth. (Rev: BL 8/05*; SLJ 10/05*)

Graphic Novels

551 Aida, Yu. *Gunslinger Girl*, Vol. 2 (10–12). Trans. from Japanese by Eiko McGregor. Series: Gunslinger Girl. 2005, ADV paper $9.99 (1-4139-0233-2). 135pp. The continuing manga adventures of a band of murderous young female cyborgs who are highly trained but have not totally forgotten their humanity. (Rev: SLJ 11/05)

552 Akane, Kazuki, and Satelight Akane. *Heat Guy J*, Vol. 1 (10–12). Trans. from Japanese by Beni Axia Hirayama. 2005, TokyoPop paper $9.99 (1-

59182-777-9). 218pp. Special Service agent Daisuke Aurora and his trusty android partner, Heat Guy J, try to keep the peace in the metropolis of Jewde, but the local mob boss is determined to keep them from interfering in his nefarious business dealings. (Rev: SLJ 11/05)

553 *All Star Comics: Archives*, Vol. 11 (7–12). Series: Archive Editions. 2005, DC Comics $49.95 (1-4012-0403-1). 272pp. The final volume of the Archive Editions series continues the adventures of the Justice Society of America, a band of comic book superheroes that includes the Green Lantern, Flash, Wonder Woman, Atom, and Hawkman. (Rev: BL 7/05; SLJ 9/05)

554 Allie, Scott, ed. *The Dark Horse Book of Witchcraft* (9–12). Illus. 2004, Dark Horse $14.95 (1-59307-108-6). 96pp. This appealing blend of fact and fiction, presented in graphic novel format, explores various aspects of witchcraft. (Rev: BL 11/1/04)

555 Asakura, George. *A Perfect Day for Love Letters*, Vol. 1 (10–12). Adapted by David Walsh and Eriko Walsh. 2005, Del Rey paper $10.95 (0-345-48266-2). The five love stories in this manga collection are loosely connected by the unifying love letters theme. (Rev: SLJ 9/05)

556 Austen, Chuck. *Superman: The Wrath of Gog* (5–12). 2005, DC Comics paper $14.99 (1-4012-0450-3). Superman is gravely injured in a battle with Gog and returns to his boyhood home to recuperate. (Rev: SLJ 9/05)

557 Azzarello, Brian, et al. *For Tomorrow*, Vol. 2 (9–12). Illus. 2005, DC Comics $24.99 (1-4012-0715-4). 128pp. In the second volume of the Superman: For Tomorrow series, the superhero continues to search for the truth behind the cataclysmic event that resulted in the disappearance of millions of people from Earth. (Rev: BL 10/15/05)

558 Baker, Kyle. *Plastic Man: On the Lam!* (8–12). Series: Plastic Man. 2005, DC Comics paper $14.95 (1-4012-0343-4). Plastic Man's original (1940s) zany disregard for superhero conventions is revived here as the elastic hero faces his own past and the FBI amid much play with words and slapstick humor. (Rev: BL 9/15/04; SLJ 7/05)

559 Baker, Kyle. *Rubber Bandits: Plastic Man 2* (9–12). Illus. 2006, DC Comics paper $14.99 (1-4012-0729-4). 144pp. Comic book artist Kyle Baker successfully revives the popular 1940s character Plastic Man. (Rev: BL 2/15/06)

560 Baron, Mike, and Steve Rude. *Nexus*, Vol. 1 (10–12). Illus. Series: Nexus. 2005, Dark Horse $49.95 (1-59307-398-4). 216pp. The first volume in the series collects the early exploits of the unhappy superhero. (Rev: BL 12/15/05)

561 Bennett, Ian. *Leap Years* (10–12). Illus. 2005, Candle Light paper $17.95 (0-9743147-9-X).

212pp. This amusing and thoughtful graphic novel tells how the life of high school sophomore Jake is transformed after he strikes up a friendship with an imaginary frog that's 6 feet tall. (Rev: BL 11/1/05)

562 Bishop, Debbie. *Black Tide: Awakening of the Key* (6–10). 2004, Angel Gate paper $19.99 (1-93243-100-4). 208pp. In this gripping graphic novel, which collects the first eight issues of an ongoing comic book series, past and present collide when Justin Braddock embarks on a mission to solve a series of international murders. (Rev: BL 4/15/04)

563 Boyd, Andrew, and Ryan Yount. *Scurvy Dogs: Rags to Riches* (11–12). Illus. 2005, Ait paper $12.95 (1-932051-27-9). 160pp. This volume collects all five published issues of the offbeat, independent comic book and adds commentary, character profiles, and interviews with the creators; for mature readers. (Rev: BL 4/15/05)

564 Busiek, Kurt. *Local Heroes* (9–12). Series: Astro City. 2005, Wildstorm paper $17.99 (1-4012-0284-5). 255pp. Nine engaging vignettes about the ordinary people and superheroes of Astro City. (Rev: SLJ 1/06)

565 Busiek, Kurt. *Shockrockets* (9–12). Illus. 2004, Dark Horse paper $14.95 (1-59307-129-9). 160pp. In this futuristic fantasy, the Shockrockets — elite fighter pilots who work against crime, rebellions, and natural disasters — accept outsider Alejandro Cruz to help them fend off the threat of takeover by a military genius who's gone mad. (Rev: BL 11/1/04; SLJ 3/05)

566 Cadigan, Glen. *Titans Companion* (9–12). Illus. 2005, TwoMorrows paper $24.95 (1-893905-50-0). 224pp. Published to mark the 25th anniversary of the New Teen Titans, superhero sidekick successors to the Teen Titans of the 1960s, this retrospective goes back to the very beginning. (Rev: BL 3/15/06)

567 Cammuso, Frank. *Max Hamm, Fairy Tale Detective*, Vol. 1 (8–12). Illus. Series: Fairy Tale Detectives. 2005, Nite Owl paper $14.95 (0-9720061-4-1). 208pp. Max Hamm, a pig, is also a private eye in a cycle of pulp-novel-style stories involving fairy tale characters and much clever wordplay. (Rev: BL 8/05; SLJ 11/05)

568 Campbell, Bruce, et al. *Man with the Screaming Brain* (9–12). Illus. 2005, Dark Horse paper $13.95 (1-59307-397-6). 104pp. In this graphic novel adaptation of Campbell's film of the same name, American industrialist William Cole goes behind the Iron Curtain on business but gets into serious trouble when he encounters a beautiful woman named Tatoya. (Rev: BL 11/15/05)

569 Carey, Mike. *John Constantine: Hellblazer — All His Engines* (10–12). 2005, DC Comics $24.95 (1-4012-0316-7). 128pp. Hellblazer squares off against demonic forces who've been stealing children's souls to provide them with energy. (Rev: SLJ 7/05)

570 Carey, Mike. *My Faith in Frankie* (9–12). Illus. 2004, DC Comics paper $6.95 (1-4012-0390-6). 112pp. In this engaging graphic novel, 17-year-old Frankie finds herself torn between the god Jeriven, a jealous deity who's watched over her since infancy, and stunningly handsome Dean, who may be hiding a dark secret. (Rev: BL 1/1–15/05)

571 Cassaday, John, et al. *Mike Mignola's Hellboy*, Vol. 2 (10–12). Illus. Series: Weird Tales. 2004, Dark Horse paper $17.95 (1-56971-953-5). 144pp. The second volume of the Weird Tales series collects 13 short stories about Hellboy and his investigations into paranormal phenomena. (Rev: BL 11/15/04; SLJ 7/05)

572 Cavalieri, Joey, ed. *Bizarro World* (10–12). Illus. 2005, DC Comics $29.95 (1-4012-0656-5). Underground and alternative comic book artists offer their twisted take on the comic book world's superheroes in this sequel to *Bizarro Comics*, published in 2001. (Rev: SLJ 7/05)

573 Chadwick, Paul. *Fragile Creature: Concrete 3* (9–12). Illus. Series: Concrete. 2006, Dark Horse paper $12.95 (1-59307-464-6). 208pp. In volume three of the Concrete series, the title character faces daunting new challenges when he is hired to perform special effects for a blockbuster sci fi movie. (Rev: BL 4/1/06)

574 Chan, Queenie. *The Dreaming* (9–12). Illus. Series: Dreaming. 2005, TokyoPop paper $9.99 (1-59816-382-5). 192pp. Identical twins Amber and Jeanie are thrilled to be accepted into an exclusive Australian boarding school, but they soon find themselves swept into a mystery when students begin to disappear; the first volume in a manga trilogy. (Rev: BL 12/1/05)

575 Christin, Pierre, and Enki Bilal. *Townscapes* (9–12). Trans. by Justin Kelly. Illus. 2004, DC Comics paper $17.95 (1-4012-0361-2). 176pp. In this trio of graphic novel tales from Europe, small towns fight back against the depredations of big business. (Rev: BL 11/1/04)

576 Clamp. *Tsubasa: Reservoir Chronicle*, Vol.1 (9–12). Trans. from Japanese by Anthony Gerard. Series: Tsubasa: Reservoir Chronicle. 2004, Del Rey paper $10.95 (0-345-47057-5). 209pp. Characters from other CLAMP manga series return in this story of teenage Sakura, princess of Clow and endowed with a mysterious power, and Syaoran, with whom she is in love; together the two set out on a quest to retrieve Sakura's dispersed memories. (Rev: SLJ 10/04)

577 Cole, Jack. *The Plastic Man: Archives*, Vol. 7 (9–12). Illus. 2005, DC Comics $49.99 (1-4012-0410-4). 200pp. The seventh volume of the Plastic

Man series collects issues of the popular comic book from 1947. (Rev: BL 2/1/06)

578 Colline, Max Allan, et al. *Detour 2004* (10–12). Illus. Series: Road to Perdition. 2004, DC Comics paper $7.95 (1-4012-0174-1). 94pp. In the final volume of the trilogy, Michael O'Sullivan and his son continue their pursuit of Connor Looney, the man responsible for killing the rest of the O'Sullivan family. (Rev: BL 9/1/04)

579 Cooke, Darwyn, and Dave Stewart. *DC: The New Frontier*, Vol. 2 (9–12). Illus. Series: DC: The New Frontier. 2005, DC Comics paper $19.99 (1-4012-0461-9). 208pp. Contemporary adventures of superheroes including Green Lantern and the Martian Manhunter. (Rev: BL 5/15/05; SLJ 9/05)

580 Diggle, Andy, and Enrique Breccia. *Swamp Thing: Bad Seed* (11–12). Illus. 2005, DC Comics paper $9.95 (1-4012-0421-X). 144pp. Swamp Thing is back with new creators, vowing to restore the balance between flora and fauna, putting humankind at jeopardy; for mature readers. (Rev: BL 2/15/05)

581 Dini, Paul, et al. *Paul Dini's Jingle Belle* (9–12). Illus. 2005, Dark Horse paper $12.95 (1-59307-382-8). 96pp. Jingle Belle, Santa's teenage daughter, tries a number of schemes to increase her visibility. (Rev: BL 11/15/05)

582 Dixon, Chuck. *Nightwing: On the Razor's Edge* (8–12). 2005, DC Comics paper $14.99 (1-4012-0437-6). 182pp. Robin, Batman's former sidekick, now takes on the superhero identity of Nightwing and must defend himself against his foes. (Rev: SLJ 11/05)

583 Doyle, Arthur Conan. *Graphic Classics: Arthur Conan Doyle* (8–11). Ed. by Tom Pomplun. 2d ed. Illus. Series: Graphic Classics. 2005, Eureka paper $11.95 (0-9746648-5-5). 144pp. This revised edition adds several non-Holmes stories to the collection. (Rev: BL 9/15/05; SLJ 11/05; VOYA 4/06)

584 Eisner, Will. *The Best of the Spirit* (9–12). Illus. 2005, DC Comics paper $14.99 (1-4012-0755-3). 192pp. Highlights from Eisner's The Spirit comic book series, which was published off and on between 1939 and 1952, are collected in this single paperback volume. (Rev: BL 2/1/06)

585 Eisner, Will. *Fagin the Jew* (10–12). 2003, Doubleday paper $15.95 (0-385-51009-8). 128pp. Eisner takes the character from *Oliver Twist* and envisions his youth. (Rev: BL 9/1/03; SLJ 1/04)

586 Eisner, Will. *Will Eisner's The Spirit Archives*, Vol. 17 (9–12). Illus. 2005, DC Comics $49.99 (1-4012-0417-1). 196pp. The 17th volume of the Spirit series showcases a dozen of the most celebrated stories from the 12-year run of Will Eisner's popular comic book. (Rev: BL 3/1/06)

587 Eldred, Tim. *Grease Monkey* (9–12). Illus. 2006, Tor $27.95 (0-765-31325-1). 352pp. In this long sci fi graphic novel with elements of comedy and romance, Robin Plotnick, a young space cadet, is apprenticed to ace mechanic Mac Gimbensky, a talking gorilla, aboard the spaceship Fist of Earth. (Rev: BL 3/15/06)

588 Ellis, Warren, et al. *Ocean* (9–12). Illus. 2005, DC Comics paper $14.99 (1-4012-0849-5). 168pp. In this graphic novel science fiction thriller, UN weapons inspector Nathan Kane journeys to a distant space station to investigate an alarming discovery. (Rev: BL 1/1–15/06)

589 Endo, Hiroki. *Eden: It's an Endless World*, Vol. 1 (11–12). Trans. by Kumar Sivasubramanian. Illus. 2005, Dark Horse paper $12.95 (1-59307-406-9). 216pp. In this futuristic graphic novel fantasy, a small band of survivors of a worldwide plague that has killed billions encounters intrigues and perils in its travels; for mature readers. (Rev: BL 1/1–15/06)

590 Endo, Hiroki. *Eden: It's an Endless World! 2* (9–12). Trans. by Kumar Sivasubramanian. Illus. Series: Eden: It's an Endless World! 2006, Dark Horse paper $12.95 (1-59307-454-9). 208pp. There's graphic gore and violence aplenty in volume two of this post-apocalyptic manga. (Rev: BL 3/15/06)

591 Espinosa, Rod. *Neotopia Color Manga* (6–12). Series: Neotopia. 2004, Antarctic paper $9.99 (1-932453-57-1). 168pp. In the opening volume of the graphic novel series, Nalyn, a servant girl, takes over her spoiled mistress's responsibilities as grand duchess of Mathenia, but the going gets tough when Mathenia comes under attack from the evil empire of Krossos. (Rev: BL 12/1/04)

592 Fujita, Maki. *Kids Joker*, Vol. 1 (9–12). Trans. from Japanese by Kay Bertrand. 2005, ADV paper $9.99 (1-4139-0162-X). 190pp. Hotaru Yanagawa, a high school student, is determined to tag along with Yui, a young man who's part of a secret organization. (Rev: SLJ 7/05)

593 Gallagher, Fred. *Megatokyo*, Vol. 3 (9–12). Illus. Series: Megatokyo. 2005, Dark Horse paper $9.95 (1-59307-305-4). 224pp. In the third volume of the manga series, romantic Piro and gamer geek Largo, stuck in Japan, continue to stir up trouble every way they turn. (Rev: BL 3/15/05)

594 Gerber, Steve, and Brian Hurtt. *Hard Time: 50 to Life* (11–12). Illus. 2004, DC Comics paper $9.95 (1-4012-0471-6). 144pp. In this graphic novel jailhouse thriller, 15-year-old Ethan Harrow struggles to survive behind bars after he's sentenced to 50 years in the state penitentiary; for mature teens. (Rev: BL 12/15/04)

595 Gibbons, Dave. *The Originals* (11–12). Illus. 2004, DC Comics $24.95 (1-4012-0355-8). 160pp. In this futuristic graphic novel reminiscent of the "mod" 1960s in Britain, teens Lel and Bok soon

find there's a downside to being a part of the "in" group; for mature readers. (Rev: BL 11/1/04)

596 Giffen, Keith, et al. *I Can't Believe It's Not the Justice League* (9–12). Illus. 2005, DC Comics paper $12.99 (1-4012-0478-3). 144pp. The zany antics of such second-string superheroes as Mary Marvel, Blue Beetle, and the Elongated Man. (Rev: BL 1/1–15/06)

597 Gross, Allan. *Cryptozoo Crew*, Vol.1 (7–12). 2005, NBM paper $9.95 (1-56163-437-9). Wacky, pun-filled adventures starring cryptozoologist Tork Darwyn and his smart and luscious wife Tara. (Rev: BL 9/15/05; SLJ 1/06)

598 Gross, Milt. *He Done Her Wrong* (9–12). Illus. 2006, Fantagraphics paper $16.95 (1-56097-694-2). 256pp. Milt Gross's wordless graphic novel from the early 1930s — one of the comics masterpieces of the 20th century — is presented anew in this attractive paperback edition. (Rev: BL 2/15/06)

599 Harris, James S. *Shades of Blue*, Vol.1 (9–12). Illus. 2005, Devil's Due paper $10.95 (1-932796-26-6). 144pp. In this humor-filled superhero send-up, Heidi Page lives the life of an average teenager until she wakes one morning to discover she has blue hair and unusual powers. (Rev: BL 6/1–15/05; SLJ 9/05)

600 Holkins, Jerry, and Mike Krahulik. *Attack of the Bacon Robots! Penny Arcade 1* (11–12). Illus. Series: Penny Arcade. 2006, Dark Horse paper $12.95 (1-59307-444-1). 168pp. Collects some of the zany — sometimes violent — adventures from the popular online comic strip for gamers. (Rev: BL 2/1/06)

601 Huddleston, Courtney, et al. *Decoy: Menagerie, Part 1* (9–12). Illus. 2005, Penny Farthing $19.95 (0-9719012-3-6). 144pp. A collection of seven stories about an alien named Decoy who is locked in a symbiotic relationship with a wounded rookie cop, Bobby Luck, and their efforts to solve crimes in Dolphin City. (Rev: BL 11/1/05)

602 Hurd, Damon, and Tatiana Gill. *A Strange Day* (8–12). Illus. 2005, Alternative Comics paper $3.95 (1-891867-74-1). 48pp. This appealing graphic novella tells a story of instant attraction between two teens who share the same tastes in music. (Rev: BL 5/1/05)

603 Ikezawa, Satomi. *Guru Guru Pon-Chan*, Vol. 1 (5–12). Trans. from Japanese by Douglas Varenas. 2005, Del Rey paper $10.95 (0-345-48095-3). 171pp. In this whimsical shape-changing story, Ponta, a Labrador retriever puppy, nibbles on a newly invented "chit-chat" bone and turns into a human girl who comically retains doggy behavior. (Rev: SLJ 11/05)

604 Ikezawa, Satomi. *Othello*, Vol. 3 (10–12). Trans. from Japanese by William Flanagan. 2005, Del Rey paper $10.95 (0-345-47998-X). 192pp.

Frequent appearances by her alter ego — the polar opposite of her primary personality — are complicating life for Yaya. (Rev: SLJ 9/05)

605 Johns, Geoff. *The Flash: The Secret of Barry Allen* (9–12). 2005, DC Comics paper $19.99 (1-4012-0723-5). Wally West regains his memory of being the Flash in this volume and must make difficult choices about who to trust with his identity, and about information he receives in a letter from his dead predecessor, Barry Allen. (Rev: SLJ 3/06)

606 Johns, Geoff. *Hawkman: Wings of Fury*, Vol. 3 (10–12). 2005, DC Comics paper $17.99 (1-4012-0467-8). 180pp. In volume three of the Hawkman series, the title character teams up with Kendra Saunders to fight the villainous Headhunter. (Rev: SLJ 9/05)

607 Johns, Geoff. *JSA: Black Reign* (7–12). 2005, DC Comics paper $12.99 (1-4012-0480-5). In a setting reminiscent of present-day Iraq, superhero Black Adam fights for an unpopular cause and faces strong opposition from the people he's trying to help. (Rev: SLJ 11/05)

608 Johns, Geoff, et al. *Ignition* (8–12). Illus. Series: Flash. 2005, DC Comics paper $14.95 (1-4012-0463-5). 144pp. In volume five of the series, police mechanic Wally West slowly but surely remembers — and regains — his superhuman powers as the Flash. (Rev: BL 5/15/05)

609 Johns, Geoff, et al. *Rebirth: Green Lantern* (9–12). Illus. 2005, DC Comics $24.99 (1-4012-0710-3). 176pp. The return of longtime character Hal Jordan (after his untimely demise in 1994) is chronicled in these stories. (Rev: BL 12/1/05)

610 Johnson, Kim "Howard," et al. *Superman: True Brit* (8–12). Illus. 2004, DC Comics $24.95 (1-4012-0022-2). 96pp. In this British variation on the Superman legend coauthored by John Cleese, young Colin Clark, raised on an English farm, struggles to conceal his superhuman abilities. (Rev: BL 12/1/04)

611 Johnson, R. *Kikuo. Night Fisher* (9–12). Illus. 2005, Fantagraphics paper $12.95 (1-56097-719-1). 144pp. This affecting coming-of-age graphic novel features Loren Foster, a boy who finds his new life in Hawaii challenging. (Rev: BL 11/1/05)

612 Kawasaki, Anton, ed. *Batman Begins: The Movie and Other Tales of the Dark Knight* (8–12). Illus. 2005, DC Comics paper $12.99 (1-4012-0440-6). 160pp. Based on the plot of the 2005 film of the same name, this graphic novel explores the origins of Batman, specifically the tragic events in Bruce Wayne's childhood that led him to become the masked crusader. (Rev: BL 9/1/05; SLJ 1/06)

613 Kelly, Joe. *Justice League Elite*, Vol. 1 (8–12). 2005, DC Comics paper $19.99 (1-4012-0481-3). Superman and other members of the Justice League clash with the rival Justice League Elite over strate-

gies for dealing with evildoers. (Rev: BL 10/1/05; SLJ 11/05)

614 Kelly, Joe, and Michael Turner. *Godfall* (9–12). Illus. Series: Superman. 2005, DC Comics paper $9.99 (1-4012-0236-5). 128pp. The superhero is temporarily taken out of action when his memory is erased and he's trapped in the miniaturized city of Kandor. (Rev: BL 9/15/05)

615 Kennedy, Mike. *Superman: Infinite City* (5–12). 2005, DC Comics $24.99 (1-4012-0067-2). 96pp. Superman and Lois become enmeshed in a power struggle in an alternate world known as Infinite City. (Rev: SLJ 9/05)

616 Kibuishi, Kazu, ed. *Flight*, Vol. 2 (7–12). Illus. 2005, Image Comics paper $24.95 (1-58240-477-1). 432pp. Volume two of the Flight anthology series features original stories by promising young artists from the world of comic books and graphic novels. (Rev: BL 6/1–15/05)

617 Kieth, Sam. *The Maxx*, Vol. 4 (11–12). Illus. 2005, DC Comics paper $17.95 (1-4012-0613-1). 144pp. Volume four of the Maxx series collects seven issues and provides clues to the origin of the title character, a purple homeless man who fancies himself a superhero; for mature teens. (Rev: BL 3/15/05)

618 Kindt, Matt. *2 Sisters* (8–12). Illus. 2004, Top Shelf paper $19.95 (1-891830-58-9). 336pp. In this graphic novel thriller, set in Europe during World War II, Elle, a volunteer ambulance driver, is recruited as a spy and dispatched on perilous missions behind enemy lines. (Rev: BL 11/1/04)

619 Klein, Grady. *The Snodgrass Conspiracy* (10–12). Illus. Series: Lost Colony. 2006, Roaring Brook paper $14.95 (1-59643-097-4). 120pp. The opening volume in a series introduces readers to the 19th-century inhabitants of a mysterious island unknown to the rest of the world but full of aspects that may seem strangely familiar. (Rev: BL 3/15/06)

620 Knaak, Richard A. *Dragon Hunt* (7–10). Series: Warcraft Sunwell. 2005, TokyoPop paper $9.99 (1-59532-712-6). 192pp. In the first volume of a graphic novel trilogy, Kalec, a shape-changing dragon, and Anveena race to reach the all-powerful Sunwell before the villainous Dar'khan can get to it. (Rev: BL 6/1–15/05; SLJ 7/05)

621 Kubert, Joe. *Edgar Rice Burroughs' Tarzan: The Joe Kubert Years*, Vol. 1 (9–12). Illus. 2005, Dark Horse $49.95 (1-59307-404-2). 200pp. This volume collects the first eight issues of *Tarzan* from DC Comics, as drawn by artist Joe Kubert. (Rev: BL 11/15/05)

622 Kubert, Joe. *Edgar Rice Burroughs' Tarzan: The Joe Kubert Years*, Vol. 2 (9–12). Illus. Series: Tarzan: The Joe Kubert Years. 2006, Dark Horse $49.95 (1-59307-416-6). 208pp. Volume two in the Tarzan: The Joe Kubert Years series collects ten issues of the popular comic book from the early 1970s. (Rev: BL 3/15/06)

623 Lee, Na Hyeon. *Traveler of the Moon*, Vol. 1 (7–12). Trans. from Korean by Je-wa Jeong. 2005, Infinity paper $9.95 (1-59697-061-8). 176pp. In this appealing Korean manwha, Yuh-Ur, a human girl, develops a close friendship with a vampire boy named Ida. (Rev: SLJ 7/05)

624 Lee, So-Young. *Arcana*, Vol. 1 (10–12). Trans. from Japanese by Youngju Ryu. 2005, TokyoPop paper $9.99 (1-59532-481-X). 204pp. In the opening volume of this fantasy manga, a young girl with magical powers roams the countryside with her wizard grandfather. (Rev: SLJ 11/05)

625 Loeb, Jeph. *Superman Batman: Absolute Power*, Vol. 3 (10–12). 2005, DC Comics $19.99 (1-4012-0447-3). In volume three of the Superman/Batman series, the two comic book heroes fall under the spell of evil super beings. (Rev: SLJ 11/05)

626 Loeb, Jeph, et al. *Public Enemies* (9–12). Illus. Series: Superman/Batman. 2004, DC Comics $19.95 (1-4012-0323-X). 160pp. Superman and Batman team up to unseat the villainous Lex Luthor from the presidency of the United States. (Rev: BL 9/1/04)

627 Love, Courtney, and D. J. Milky. *Princess Ai: Lumination*, Vol. 2 (7–12). Trans. from Japanese by Kimiko Fujikawa and Yuki N. Johnson. 2005, TokyoPop paper $9.99 (1-59182-670-5). 185pp. In volume two of the Princess Ai series, the title character, an aspiring rock star, turns ever more angelic as her music career begins to take off. (Rev: SLJ 11/05)

628 McGreal, Pat, et al. *Chiaroscuro: The Private Lives of Leonardo da Vinci* (11–12). Illus. 2005, DC Comics paper $24.99 (1-4012-0498-8). 264pp. This fictionalized account, presented in graphic novel format, traces the meteoric rise of Leonardo da Vinci's career, as seen through the eyes of Salai, a youth adopted by the Renaissance artist; for mature readers. (Rev: BL 12/1/05)

629 Manabe, Shohei. *Smuggler* (10–12). Illus. 2006, TokyoPop paper $9.99 (1-59532-150-0). 192pp. In this gritty manga title, Kinuta turns to the underworld to survive after his attempts to break into acting fail. (Rev: BL 3/15/06)

630 Masamune, Shirow. *Man-Machine Interface: Ghost in the Shell 2* (9–12). Trans. by Frederik L. Schodt and Toren Smith. Illus. 2005, Dark Horse paper $24.95 (1-59307-204-X). 312pp. Manga artist Masamune Shirow delivers the long-awaited sequel to the first volume. (Rev: BL 3/15/05)

631 Medley, Linda. *Castle Waiting* (9–12). Illus. 2006, Fantagraphics $29.95 (1-56097-747-7). 456pp. In the castle home of Sleeping Beauty after she and her handsome prince have decamped for Happily-Ever-After, the princess's former ladies in waiting and new arrivals at the castle each recount fascinating stories of their own. (Rev: BL 3/15/06*)

632 Mignola, Mike, and Guy Davis. *B.P.R.D.: Plague of Frogs* (9–12). Illus. Series: B.P.R.D. 2005, Dark Horse paper $17.95 (1-59307-288-0). 144pp. Abe Sapien's amphibious origins come to light as the Bureau for Paranormal Research and Defense confronts a plague of frog-monsters. (Rev: BL 2/15/05)

633 Mignola, Mike, et al. *The Dead: B.P.R.D.*, Vol. 4 (9–12). Illus. 2005, Dark Horse paper $17.95 (1-59307-380-1). 152pp. Mike Mignola, creator of Hellboy, teams with coauthor John Arcudi and artist Guy Davis for the fourth volume of the B.P.R.D. series, in which the Bureau for Paranormal Research and Defense makes an interesting discovery while moving into its new headquarters. (Rev: BL 10/15/05)

634 Mignola, Mike, et al. *The Soul of Venice and Other Stories* (9–12). Ed. by Scott Allie. Illus. 2004, Dark Horse paper $17.95 (1-59307-132-9). 128pp. In the second volume of the B.P.R.D. series, Hellboy's colleagues from the Bureau of Paranormal Research and Defense do battle with assorted evildoers in five different stories. (Rev: BL 9/1/04)

635 Millar, Mark, and Peter Gross. *Chosen* (11–12). Illus. 2005, Dark Horse paper $9.95 (1-59307-213-9). 72pp. Twelve-year-old Jodie Christianson recovers from a devastating accident to find that he now possesses miraculous powers, leading the boy to believe that he is the returned Jesus Christ. (Rev: BL 11/1/05)

636 Millionaire, Tony. *Billy Hazelnuts* (9–12). Illus. 2006, Fantagraphics $19.95 (1-56097-701-9). 100pp. The creator of the Sock Monkey and Maakies comic characters makes his graphic novel debut with this offbeat tale about Becky, a girl scientist, and her friend, Billy, a creature fashioned by mice out of garbage. (Rev: BL 2/1/06)

637 Monroe, Kevin. *El Zombo Fantasma* (7–10). Illus. 2005, Dark Horse paper $9.95 (1-59307-284-8). 88pp. In this eye-popping superhero graphic novel, Mexican wrestler El Zombo Fantasma, murdered for throwing a match, seeks to avoid eternal damnation by becoming guardian angel to a feisty 10-year-old and tracking down his own killer. (Rev: BL 3/15/05; VOYA 8/05)

638 Moore, Alan, et al. *Tom Strong: Book 4* (9–12). Illus. Series: Tom Strong. 2005, DC Comics $24.95 (1-4012-0571-2). 160pp. Volume four of the Tom Strong series is highlighted by a tale of parallel worlds. (Rev: BL 1/1–15/05)

639 Moore, Alan, et al. *Tom Strong Collected Edition*, Vol. 3 (8–12). Illus. 2004, DC Comics $24.95 (1-4012-0282-9). 144pp. Superhero Tom Strong, the creation of legendary comic book artist Alan Moore, tackles a number of new challenges in the third volume of the Tom Strong series. (Rev: BL 9/1/04)

640 Moore, Alan, et al. *Tom Strong's Terrific Tales: Book 1* (9–12). Illus. Series: Tom Strong. 2005, DC Comics $24.95 (1-4012-0030-3). 176pp. The opening volume of the Tom Strong series looks back at the comic book superhero's childhood on the island of Attaban Teru. (Rev: BL 1/1–15/05)

641 Morrison, Grant, et al. *Seven Soldiers of Victory*, Vol. 1 (9–12). Illus. 2006, DC Comics paper $14.99 (1-4012-0925-4). 208pp. In the first of three volumes, comic book artist Grant Morrison offers his vision of four second-string characters from the DC Comics stable. (Rev: BL 3/1/06)

642 Morrison, Grant, and Duncan Fegredo. *Kid Eternity* (10–12). Illus. 2006, DC Comics paper $14.99 (1-4012-0933-5). 144pp. This volume collects all three issues of Grant Morrison's comic book miniseries of 1991. (Rev: BL 4/1/06)

643 Morrison, Grant, and Frank Quitely. *WE3* (11–12). Illus. 2005, DC Comics paper $12.99 (1-4012-0495-3). 104pp. Three former household pets, reprogrammed by the government into experimental weapons, escape their human captors and try to make their way home; violent, moving, and thought-provoking, this is for mature teens. (Rev: BL 7/05; SLJ 11/05)

644 Mowll, Joshua. *Operation Red Jericho* (8–11). Illus. Series: Guild Trilogy. 2005, Candlewick $15.99 (0-7636-2634-1). 288pp. In this first volume of a graphic novel trilogy set in the early 20th century, teens Becca and Doug MacKenzie search for their parents, who disappeared in China, and document their exciting adventures. (Rev: BL 11/15/05; SLJ 12/05)

645 Murakami, Maki. *Kanpai!* Vol. 1 (8–12). Trans. from Japanese by Christine Schilling. 2005, TokyoPop paper $9.99 (1-59532-317-1). 209pp. Yamada finds himself torn between his rigid training to be a monster guardian and his infatuation with attractive Taino Municipal Middle School classmate Nao. (Rev: SLJ 1/06)

646 Nicieza, Fabian, et al. *A Stake to the Heart* (8–12). Illus. 2004, Dark Horse paper $12.95 (1-59307-012-8). 104pp. Angel's efforts to help Buffy and Dawn cope with their parents' problems backfire in this graphic novel that precedes the events of the TV show. (Rev: BL 6/1–15/04)

647 Nightow, Yasuhiro. *Trigun Anime Manga*, Vol.1 (9–12). Illus. 2005, Dark Horse paper $14.95 (1-59307-105-1). 160pp. In the first volume of a new graphic novel series set in a post-apocalyptic world and based on a Japanese television series, two insurance agents are dispatched to contact the outlaw known as Vash the Stampede and hopefully stem the flood of claims that seem to follow wherever he goes. (Rev: BL 5/1/05)

648 Niles, Steve, and Kelley Jones. *Last Train to Deadsville* (11–12). Illus. 2005, Dark Horse paper $14.95 (1-59307-107-8). 144pp. In this action-packed graphic novel for mature teens, supernatural detective Cal McDonald and sidekick Mo'lock try to rid a California town of demonic forces. (Rev: BL 5/1/05)

649 No, Yee-Jung. *Visitor*, Vol. 1 (7–10). Trans. from Japanese by Jennifer Hahm. 2005, TokyoPop paper $9.99 (1-59532-342-2). 175pp. On her first day at a new school, Hyo-Bin attracts a number of admirers, but she rebuffs them all, fearful that they could be harmed by the magical powers she's not yet learned to control. (Rev: SLJ 9/05)

650 Park, Sang-Sun. *The Tarot Café*, Vol. 1 (11–12). Trans. by Sukhee Ryu. Illus. 2005, TokyoPop paper $9.99 (1-59182-555-7). 192pp. The opening volume in the series introduces Pamela, a tarot card reader who offers help to a handful of supernatural beings that dwell in the human world; for mature teens. (Rev: BL 3/15/05)

651 Park, Young-Ha. *BamBi*, Vol. 1 (8–12). Trans. from Korean by Je-wa Jeong. 2005, Infinity paper $9.95 (1-59697-011-1). 164pp. This Korean manwha, similar to Japanese manga, recounts the forbidden romance between a girl with amnesia and a handsome young man who has a swan's wing where one of his arms should be. (Rev: SLJ 7/05)

652 Pini, Wendy. *Elfquest: The Searcher and the Sword* (9–12). 2004, DC Comics $24.95 (1-4012-0183-0). 96pp. Shuna, a human girl adopted by the elfin Wolfriders, seeks to bridge the gap between members of her race and the elves who've cared for her. (Rev: BL 8/04)

653 Porcellino, John. *Diary of a Mosquito Abatement Man* (11–12). Illus. 2005, La Mano paper $12.00 (0-9765255-0-X). 106pp. A fascinating memoir that follows on the events of *Perfect Example* (2001); for older teens. (Rev: BL 8/05)

654 Powell, Eric, and Thomas Lennon. *Virtue and the Grim Consequences Thereof: The Goon 4* (9–12). Illus. 2006, Dark Horse paper $16.95 (1-59307-456-5). 144pp. Volume four of the Goon series chronicles five high-octane adventures starring the title character. (Rev: BL 2/1/06)

655 Raymond, Alex. *Alex Raymond's Flash Gordon*, Vol. 4 (9–12). Illus. Series: Flash Gordon. 2005, Checker paper $19.95 (1-933160-26-8). 100pp. Volume four of the Flash Gordon series collects comic strips that first appeared in Sunday newspapers in the late 1930s and 1940. (Rev: BL 9/15/05)

656 Raymond, Alex, and Don Moore. *Alex Raymond's Flash Gordon*, Vol. 2 (8–12). Illus. 2004, Checker paper $19.95 (0-9741664-6-4). 96pp. The second volume of the Flash Gordon series collects comic strips that first appeared in 1935 and 1936. (Rev: BL 10/1/04)

657 Reger, Rob, et al. *Emily the Strange: The Boring Issue*, Vol. 1 (9–12). Series: Emily the Strange.

2005, Dark Horse paper $7.95 (1-59307-323-2). 48pp. Emily is a mysterious girl with dark hair, talking cats, an unusual slant on life, and a strong sense of humor. (Rev: BL 9/15/05)

658 Robinson, James, and Peter Snejbjerg. *Grand Guignol* (9–12). Illus. Series: Starman. 2004, DC Comics paper $19.95 (1-4012-0257-8). 296pp. In volume nine of the Starman series, Jack Knight returns from a lengthy expedition in space to find his beloved Opal City under attack by evil forces led by the villainous Shade. The final volume in the series is *Sons of the Father* (2005). (Rev: BL 12/1/04)

659 Rodi, Rob. *Crossovers* (5–12). Illus. 2003, CrossGeneration paper $15.95 (1-931484-85-6). 160pp. This graphic novel is an entertaining look at a suburban family whose members possess a unique power. (Rev: BL 2/1/04)

660 Ru, Lee. *Witch Class*, Vol. 1 (8–12). Trans. from Korean by Je-wa Jeong. 2005, Infinity paper $9.95 (1-59697-081-2). 174pp. The opening volume in the series introduces readers to Dorothy, a young girl who agrees to become a witch. (Rev: SLJ 9/05)

661 Rucka, Greg, et al. *Bitter Rivals* (9–12). Illus. 2005, DC Comics paper $12.95 (1-4012-0462-7). 128pp. In this brightly illustrated title from the Wonder Woman series, the comic book heroine seeks help from Batman in solving the murder of the leader of an anti-Wonder Woman protest group. (Rev: BL 3/15/05)

662 Rucka, Greg, et al. *Eyes of the Gorgon: Wonder Woman* (9–12). Illus. Series: Wonder Woman. 2005, DC Comics paper $19.99 (1-4012-0797-9). 192pp. In this riveting thriller, the Amazon heroine faces off against the deadly Medousa and her allies, who include Circe and Dr. Veronica Cale. (Rev: BL 3/15/06)

663 Rucka, Greg, et al. *Land of the Dead: Wonder Woman* (9–12). Illus. 2006, DC Comics paper $12.99 (1-4012-0938-6). 128pp. Wonder Woman (Diana) faces problems new and old: her longtime enemy Medousa plus complications from her island home's new location near the U.S. coast. (Rev: BL 3/15/06)

664 Rucka, Greg, et al. *Wonder Woman: Down to Earth 2004* (9–12). Illus. 2004, DC Comics paper $14.95 (1-4012-0226-8). 160pp. Wonder Woman, now serving as ambassador from the Amazon island of Themyscria, seeks to promote the ideals of gender equality and peace. (Rev: BL 10/15/04)

665 Rucka, Greg, and Michael Lark. *Gotham Central: Half a Life* (11–12). Illus. 2005, DC Comics paper $14.99 (1-4012-0438-4). 168pp. Volume two in this Batman spin-off focuses on the public outing and then framing of Renee Montoya, a lesbian police detective in Gotham City. (Rev: BL 8/05; SLJ 11/05)

666 Rugg, Jim, and Brian Maruca. *Street Angel: The Princess of Poverty*, Vol. 1 (11–12). Illus. Series: Street Angel. 2005, SLG paper $14.95 (1-59362-012-8). 208pp. The opening volume in this entertaining series introduces its title character, a 12-year-old Hispanic American girl who fights foes ranging from ninjas to evil geologists using her skateboard and her knowledge of martial arts; for mature teens. (Rev: BL 9/1/05)

667 Russell, P. Craig. *Conan and the Jewels of Gwahlur* (9–12). Illus. 2005, Dark Horse $13.95 (1-59307-491-3). 88pp. Comic book artist P. Craig Russell offers his interpretation of one of author Robert E. Howard's stories about Conan the Barbarian. (Rev: BL 2/1/06)

668 Sabatini, Rafael. *Graphic Classics: Rafael Sabatini* (9–12). Ed. by Tom Pomplun. Illus. Series: Graphic Classics. 2006, Eureka paper $11.95 (0-974664-86-3). 144pp. Graphic novel adaptations of eight stories by Sabatini, author of *Captain Blood* and *Scaramouche*. (Rev: BL 3/15/06)

669 Sacks, Adam. *Salmon Doubts* (7–10). Illus. 2004, Alternative Comics paper $14.95 (1-891867-71-7). 128pp. In this allegorical graphic novel, two young salmon — Geoff and Henry — struggle to figure out their place in the overall scheme of things. (Rev: BL 1/1–15/05; SLJ 12/04)

670 Sakai, Stan. *Usagi Yojimbo: Volume 18: Travels with Jotaro* (8–12). 2004, Dark Horse paper $15.95 (1-59307-220-1). 208pp. In the 18th volume of the series, the title character, a rabbit samurai in feudal Japan, encounters a series of adventures while traveling with Jotaro, who is Usagi's son but doesn't know it. (Rev: BL 9/15/04; SLJ 10/04)

671 Sakuishi, Harold. *Beck: Mongolian Chop Squad*, Vol. 1 (11–12). Trans. from Japanese by Stephen Paul. 2005, TokyoPop paper $9.99 (1-59532-770-3). 214pp. In this appealing manga, Yukio Tanaka, a 14-year-old nerd, finds his horizons broadened when the lovely Izumi and the exciting Ryusuke introduce him to the world of rock music. (Rev: SLJ 11/05)

672 Sakura, Tsukuba. *Land of the Blindfolded* (8–11). Illus. 2004, DC Comics paper $9.95 (1-4012-0524-0). 208pp. This manga designed primarily for girls tells of two Japanese high school friends (boy and girl) who become close as they decide how to use their conflicting super powers. (Rev: BL 2/15/05)

673 Sala, Richard. *Mad Night* (10–12). Illus. 2005, Fantagraphics paper $16.95 (1-56097-681-0). 232pp. Bodies, scares, and general silliness abound as coed detective Judy Drood and pal Kasper Keene investigate mysterious goings-on at Lone Mountain College. (Rev: BL 11/1/05)

674 Schultz, Mark, et al. *Tom Strong: Book 5* (10–12). Illus. 2005, DC Comics $24.99 (1-4012-

0624-7). 144pp. The later adventures of comic book hero Tom Strong, created by Alan Moore but later taken over by a series of other artists, are collected in this fifth volume. (Rev: BL 11/15/05)

675 Schulz, Charles M. *The Complete Peanuts: 1953 to 1954* (9–12). Illus. Series: Peanuts. 2004, Fantagraphics $28.95 (1-56097-614-4). 344pp. The second volume in the Peanuts series collects strips that first appeared in newspapers during 1953 and 1954. Also recommended are volumes with the same title covering 1955 to 1956 and 1957 to 1958 (both 2005). (Rev: BL 10/15/04)

676 Seagle, Steven T., and Justin Norman. *Solstice* (9–12). Illus. 2005, Active Images paper $12.95 (0-9766761-1-7). 116pp. In this striking graphic novel adventure tale, multimillionaire Russell Waterhouse and his son embark on a perilous journey to find the fountain of youth. (Rev: BL 10/1/05)

677 Sfar, Joann. *The Rabbi's Cat* (8–12). Illus. 2005, Pantheon $21.95 (0-375-42281-1). 152pp. The entertaining and sophisticated adventures of a talking cat who lives with a rabbi and his daughter in 1930s Algeria. (Rev: BL 7/05; SLJ 3/06)

678 Sfar, Joann. *Vampire Loves* (10–12). Trans. by Alexis Siegel. Illus. 2006, Roaring Brook paper $16.95 (1-59643-093-1). 188pp. In this entertaining graphic novel, Ferdinand is a romantic and gentle young vampire from Lithuania. (Rev: BL 3/15/06)

679 Shanower, Eric. *Sacrifice* (8–12). 2004, Image Comics $29.95 (1-58240-360-0). 224pp. In this second volume of the graphic novel series, Shanower picks up his epic retelling of the Trojan War with the return of Paris and Helen to Troy. (Rev: BL 10/15/04; SLJ 10/04) [741.5]

680 Shimizu, Aki. *Qwan*, Vol. 1 (7–12). Trans. from Japanese by Mike Kief. 2005, TokyoPop paper $9.99 (1-59532-534-4). 178pp. This compelling graphic novel follows Qwan and his friend as they embark on a magical journey to uncover Qwan's destiny. (Rev: SLJ 7/05)

681 Shurei, Kouyo. *Alichino*, Vol. 2 (9–12). Trans. from Japanese by Amy Forsyth. 2005, TokyoPop paper $9.99 (1-59532-479-8). 144pp. This exquisitely drawn manga, volume two of the Alichino series, explores the relationship of the Alichino with the Kusabi. (Rev: SLJ 11/05)

682 Siegel, Jerry, et al. *Superman in the Forties* (9–12). Illus. 2005, DC Comics paper $19.99 (1-4012-0457-0). 192pp. A selection of stories from the first decade of Superman's comic book existence. (Rev: BL 12/1/05; SLJ 3/06)

683 Spears, Rick. *Dead West* (11–12). Illus. 2005, Gigantic paper $14.95 (0-9763038-1-7). 144pp. This offbeat graphic novel blends the best of the horror and western genres in its tale of an ill-fated town that was built on the site of a Native American village. (Rev: BL 9/15/05; SLJ 11/05)

684 Spears, Rick. *Teenagers from Mars* (10–12). 2005, Gigantic paper $19.95 (0-9763038-0-9). 255pp. Three teenage comic book lovers in the small town of Mars declare war on the town's adults who've decided to rid their community of all vestiges of comics. (Rev: SLJ 9/05)

685 Stanley, John, and Irving Tripp. *Letters to Santa* (9–12). Illus. Series: Little Lulu. 2005, Dark Horse paper $9.95 (1-59307-386-0). 248pp. The attractions of Little Lulu, the girl with the curly black locks, have lasted more than 50 years; this sixth volume includes five issues dealing with the winter holidays. Also recommended are *Sunday Afternoon* (the fourth volume, 2004) and *Lulu's Umbrella Service* (the seventh volume, 2005). (Rev: BL 12/15/05)

686 Stanley, John, and Irving Tripp. *Lulu Takes a Trip* (9–12). Illus. Series: Little Lulu. 2005, Dark Horse paper $9.95 (1-59307-317-8). 200pp. Volume two of the Little Lulu series collects early stories from the classic comic strip. (Rev: BL 4/15/05)

687 Stassen, Jean-Philippe. *Deogratias: A Tale of Rwanda* (11–12). Trans. by Alexis Siegel. Illus. 2006, Roaring Brook paper $16.95 (1-59643-103-2). 96pp. The unspeakable horrors of the Rwandan genocide of the early 1990s are revisited in this heartrending graphic novel. (Rev: BL 3/15/06)

688 Sugisaki, Yukiro. *Rizelmine* (8–12). Trans. from Japanese by Alethea Nibley and Athena Nibley. 2005, TokyoPop paper $9.99 (1-59532-901-3). 136pp. Fifteen-year-old Iwaki Tomonori rejects the advances of robot-like Rizel, who's become his bride by government decree. (Rev: SLJ 11/05)

689 Tajima, Sho-U, and Eiji Otsuka. *Madara*, Vol. 1 (11–12). Illus. 2004, DC Comics paper $9.95 (1-4012-0529-1). 198pp. In this fantasy manga, the title character, badly maimed as a child, learns to function using mechanical limbs crafted by the villagers who rescue him; for mature teens only. (Rev: BL 2/1/05)

690 Thompson, Jill. *The Dead Boy Detectives* (9–12). Illus. 2005, DC Comics paper $9.99 (1-4012-0313-2). 120pp. Ghost detectives Edwin Paine and Charles Rowland investigate the disappearance of a student from a girls' boarding school in Chicago. (Rev: BL 8/05)

691 Toyoda, Minoru. *Love Roma*, Vol. 1 (8–11). Illus. 2005, Del Rey paper $10.95 (0-345-48262-X). 208pp. This delightful manga chronicles the budding romance of teenagers Hoshino and Negishi. (Rev: BL 10/15/05; SLJ 1/06)

692 Trondheim, Lewis. *Dungeon* (9–12). 2004, NBM paper $14.95 (1-56163-401-8). 96pp. In this French graphic novel import, a compelling blend of horror and heroic fantasy, Herbert the Duck is suddenly elevated from lowly messenger to the awesome responsibility of defending the Dungeon from outside attack. (Rev: BL 12/1/04)

693 Trondheim, Lewis, and Manu Larcenet. *Astronauts of the Future*, Vol. 1 (9–12). Trans. by Joe Johnson. Illus. Series: Astronauts of the Future. 2004, NBM paper $14.95 (1-56163-407-7). 96pp. Talented and isolated young friends Gil and Martina find themselves facing off against the rest of the world, which is made up of either aliens or robots depending on the point of view. (Rev: BL 1/1–15/05)

694 Tsukiji, Toshihiko. *Maburaho*, Vol. 1 (8–12). Trans. from Japanese by Kay Bertrand. 2005, ADV paper $9.99 (1-4139-0293-6). 161pp. Kazuki, a hapless magician-in-training, is pursued by three female students who know that he is destined to father a child who'll become a powerful wizard. (Rev: SLJ 7/05)

695 Tucci, Billy, and JC Vaughan. *Ju-Nen: Shi* (9–12). Illus. 2006, Dark Horse paper $12.95 (1-59307-451-4). 104pp. Ana Ishikawa returns to Japan in hopes of finding respite from earlier adventures, but she soon finds herself caught up in a deadly confrontation between rival monk warriors from Kyoto and Nara. (Rev: BL 4/1/06)

696 Vaughan, Brian, et al. *Tag: Ex Machina, Book 2* (11–12). Illus. 2005, DC Comics paper $12.99 (1-4012-0626-3). 128pp. In the second volume of Vaughan's Ex Machina graphic novel series, Mitchell Hundred, who possesses extraordinary powers, quits the police force to run for mayor of New York City; for mature readers. (Rev: BL 10/15/05)

697 Vaughan, Brian K., et al. *Safeword* (11–12). Illus. Series: Y: The Last Man. 2004, DC Comics paper $12.95 (1-4012-0232-2). 144pp. Volume four of the series collects issues 18 to 23 of the post-apocalyptic road story. (Rev: BL 1/1–15/05)

698 Veitch, Rick, and Alfredo Alcala. *Spontaneous Generation: Swamp Thing 8* (9–12). Illus. 2006, DC Comics paper $19.99 (1-4012-0793-6). 160pp. The eighth volume of the Swamp Thing series contains some of the early issues created by Rick Veitch, who took over the comic from its original creator Alan Moore. (Rev: BL 2/1/06)

699 Verheiden, Mark. *The American* (9–12). Illus. 2005, Dark Horse paper $14.95 (1-59307-419-0). 360pp. Collected in this volume are several issues of the late-1980s comic book series featuring The American, a cynical government creation designed to foster the illusion of U.S. military invincibility. (Rev: BL 2/1/06)

700 Von Sholly, Pete. *Dead But Not Out! Pete Von Sholly's Morbid 2* (7–12). Illus. 2005, Dark Horse paper $14.95 (1-59307-289-9). 96pp. Cheap horror movies are the target of this entertaining parody. (Rev: BL 3/15/05)

701 Wagner, Matt. *Trinity* (10–12). Illus. 2004, DC Comics $24.95 (1-4012-0309-4). 208pp. Superman and Wonder Woman join Batman to thwart the evil plot of one of the Caped Crusader's longtime enemies. (Rev: BL 9/1/04)

702 Waid, Mark. *Legion of Super-Heroes: Teenage Revolution* (8–11). 2005, DC Comics paper $14.99 (1-4012-0482-1). 200pp. In this comic book vision of the future, teenage superheroes rebel against their parents' utopian government. (Rev: BL 1/1–15/06; SLJ 3/06)

703 Whedon, Joss, and John Cassaday. *Astonishing X-Men: Gifted* (9–12). Illus. 2005, Marvel paper $14.99 (0-7851-1531-5). 152pp. The opening volume of a new series featuring a struggle between good (a team of handsome young outcasts) and evil (a homicidal alien). (Rev: BL 3/15/05)

704 Whedon, Joss, et al. *Tales of the Vampires* (9–12). Illus. 2004, Dark Horse paper $15.95 (1-56971-749-4). 144pp. Screenwriter Joss Whedon, creator of *Buffy the Vampire Slayer*, weaves together an anthology of original vampire stories with a unifying tale of young vampire slayers in training. (Rev: BL 1/1–15/05)

705 Whedon, Joss, et al. *Those Left Behind: Serenity 1* (9–12). Illus. 2006, Dark Horse paper $9.95 (1-59307-449-2). 104pp. In this adventure, the captain and crew of the *Serenity* take on a scavenger mission that turns out to be not at all what it first seemed. (Rev: BL 2/1/06)

706 Willingham, Bill, et al. *Fables: March of the Wooden Soldiers* (11–12). Illus. 2004, DC Comics paper $17.95 (1-4012-0222-5). 240pp. In this fourth volume in the series, Boy Blue's romantic hopes soar when he encounters a grown-up Red Riding Hood, but doubts soon arise; for mature teens. Also recommended is the sixth volume, *Homelands* (2006). (Rev: BL 2/15/05)

707 Willingham, Bill, et al. *Fables: Storybook Love* (11–12). Illus. 2004, DC Comics paper $14.95 (1-4012-0256-X). 192pp. The third volume of the Fables series contains four more stories about fairy-tale characters who live in a section of New York City called Fabletown; for mature readers. (Rev: BL 7/04)

708 Windsor-Smith, Barry. *The Freebooters* (9–12). Illus. 2005, Fantagraphics $29.95 (1-56097-662-4). 184pp. Gripping and humorous tales feature the ancient Freebooters, who first appeared in the short-lived *Storyteller* magazine. (Rev: BL 11/15/05)

709 Winick, Judd. *Outsiders: Wanted* (10–12). Illus. 2005, DC Comics paper $14.99 (1-4012-0460-0). 192pp. In volume three of the Outsiders graphic novel series, Nightwing, the leader of the team and a protégé of Batman, seems headed for a confrontation with his former mentor. (Rev: BL 1/1–15/06; SLJ 3/06)

Historical Fiction and Foreign Lands

Prehistory

710 Levin, Betty. *Thorn* (7–10). 2005, Front Street $16.95 (1-932425-46-2). 168pp. Thorn, a young boy with an atrophied leg, is befriended by Willow but still feels uncomfortable and plans his escape. (Rev: BL 12/15/05; SLJ 1/06)

Ancient and Medieval History

GENERAL AND MISCELLANEOUS

711 Holland, Cecelia. *The Serpent Dreamer* (9–12). 2005, Forge $24.95 (0-765-30557-7). 336pp. In the concluding volume of Cecelia Holland's trilogy on life in 10th-century Vinland, Corban, shunned by most tribe members, is taken in by the Wolf Clan and finds love with Epashti. (Rev: BL 11/1/05)

712 McCaughrean, Geraldine. *Not the End of the World* (7–10). 2005, HarperCollins LB $17.89 (0-06-076031-1). 256pp. A harrowing but thought-provoking story of what it was really like aboard Noah's ark, with terrified animals and humans unhinged by their circumstances. (Rev: BL 8/05; SLJ 8/05*; VOYA 8/05)

713 Rice, Anne. *Christ the Lord: Out of Egypt* (9–12). 2005, Knopf $25.95 (0-375-41201-8). 336pp. Told from the point of view of a 7-year-old Jesus, this novel chronicles the events of his early life. (Rev: BL 11/1/05; SLJ 12/05)

GREECE AND ROME

714 Davis, Lindsey. *Scandal Takes a Holiday* (10–12). 2004, Mysterious $24.95 (0-89296-812-5). 332pp. Ancient Roman detective Falco tackles his sixteenth case, investigating the disappearance of a muckraking gossip columnist with the *Daily Gazette*. (Rev: BL 9/1/04; SLJ 4/05)

715 Durham, David Anthony. *Pride of Carthage* (11–12). 2005, Doubleday $26.95 (0-385-50603-1). 656pp. This sweeping epic depicts Hannibal's ultimately disastrous march on Rome in the third century B.C.; violent content limits this to mature teens. (Rev: BL 1/1–15/05)

716 Iggulden, Conn. *Emperor: The Field of Swords* (11–12). Series: Emperor. 2005, Delacorte $25.00 (0-385-33663-2). 467pp. The projected penultimate volume in the series that started with *Emperor: The Gates of Rome* (2003), this focuses on Julius Caesar's political maneuverings and successful conquest of Britain. (Rev: BL 2/15/05)

717 Rao, Sirish, and Gita Wolf. *Sophocles' Oedipus the King* (7–10). 2004, Getty $18.95 (0-89236-764-4). 29pp. This retelling of Sophocles' tragic tale of Oedipus is highlighted by the striking illustrations of Indrapromit Roy. (Rev: BL 1/1–15/05)

MIDDLE AGES

718 Cadnum, Michael. *The Dragon Throne* (7–10). 2005, Viking $16.99 (0-670-03631-5). 224pp. Edmund and Herbert, newly returned to England from the Crusades and just knighted, are ordered by Eleanor of Aquitaine to safeguard Lady Ester on a perilous pilgrimage to Rome; the third volume in a trilogy that includes *The Book of the Lion* (2000) and *The Leopard Sword* (2002). (Rev: BL 6/1–15/05; SLJ 6/05; VOYA 10/05)

719 Garland, Nicole. *The Fool's Tale* (9–12). 2005, Morrow $25.95 (0-06-072150-2). 544pp. The king's fool, Gwirion, comes between King Maelgwyn and Isabel, who were married for political reasons in this novel set in Wales in 1198. (Rev: BL 11/15/04)

720 Jinks, Catherine. *Pagan's Scribe* (9–12). Series: Pagan Chronicles. 2005, Candlewick $16.99 (0-7636-2022-X). 368pp. Twenty years after the events of *Pagan's Vows* (2004), Pagan Kidrouk, now Archdeacon of Carcassonne, mentors a young clerk named Isidore. (Rev: BCCB 4/05; BL 3/1/05; HB 3–4/05; SLJ 4/05)

721 Jinks, Catherine. *Pagan's Vows* (8–10). 2005, Candlewick $16.99 (0-7636-2021-1). 336pp. Seventeen-year-old Pagan Kidrouk, squire to Lord Roland, joins his master at the Abbey of St. Martin where they are to begin training as monks, but Pagan soon finds that he has trouble adjusting to all the rules of his new life. (Rev: BL 10/1/04; SLJ 9/04; VOYA 10/04)

722 Newman, Sharan. *The Witch in the Well* (9–12). 2004, Forge $24.95 (0-765-30881-9). 352pp. With her family's castle well running dry — foretelling murderous doom — stalwart Catherine LeVendeur seeks answers in this mystery set in 12th-century France. (Rev: BL 12/15/04)

723 Thal, Lilli. *Mimus* (8–11). Trans. by John Brownjohn. 2005, Annick $19.95 (1-55037-925-9); paper $9.95 (1-55037-924-0). 398pp. Prince Florin is taken captive and made a jester when the kingdom of Vinland overpowers Moltovia in this novel of the Middle Ages. (Rev: BL 9/1/05*; SLJ 12/05*; VOYA 2/06)

724 Tingle, Rebecca. *Far Traveler* (7–10). 2005, Penguin $17.99 (0-399-23890-5). 240pp. In this historical novel set in 10th-century England, 16-year-old Aelfwyn flees when her uncle, West Saxon King Edward, tells her she must marry one of his allies or enter a convent. (Rev: BCCB 3/05; BL 2/1/05; SLJ 2/05; VOYA 8/05)

Africa

725 Atta, Sefi. *Everything Good Will Come* (11–12). 2005, Interlink $24.95 (1-56656-570-7). 336pp. Two girlfriends come of age in Nigeria in 1971, struggling in a society that oppresses women. (Rev: BL 3/1/05)

726 Courtenay, Bryce. *The Power of One* (9–12). 2005, Delacorte LB $17.99 (0-385-90274-3). 320pp. In South Africa during World War II, a white boy named Peekay finds the strength to survive a grim boarding school and go on to become a successful boxer, getting help from diverse individuals along the way and giving help to African chaingang prisoners. (Rev: BL 9/1/05; SLJ 11/05; VOYA 12/05)

727 Glass, Linzi Alex. *The Year the Gypsies Came* (8–11). 2006, Holt $16.95 (0-8050-7999-8). 260pp. An elderly Zulu watchman turns out to be young Emily's strongest anchor in this moving story about a 12-year-old in 1960s Johannesburg, whose life is changed when a family of Australian vagabonds arrives, bringing additional tensions. (Rev: BL 3/1/06)

728 Stolz, Joelle. *The Shadows of Ghadames* (6–10). 2004, Random LB $17.99 (0-385-73104-3). 128pp. In late-19th-century Libya, Malika dreads the restricted life her 12th birthday will bring, but her father's two wives defy convention and nurse a wounded man back to health within the women's community, opening new horizons for Malika. (Rev: BL 12/1/04*; SLJ 11/04)

729 Stratton, Allan. *Chanda's Secrets* (9–12). 2004, Annick $8.95 (1-55037-835-X). 200pp. The devastating impact of AIDS in sub-Saharan Africa is poignantly conveyed in the gripping first-person story of 16-year-old Chanda, whose life is crumbling around her as the insidious disease spreads through her village and family. (Rev: BCCB 10/04; BL 7/04; SLJ 7/04) [813.54]

730 Wein, Elizabeth E. *The Sunbird* (7–12). Series: The Winter Prince. 2004, Viking $16.99 (0-670-03691-9). 224pp. Telemakos, grandson of noblemen, undertakes a perilous journey to the African kingdom of Aksum to find those responsible for allowing the plague to enter the kingdom in this third volume in the saga. (Rev: BL 6/1–15/04; HB 3–4/04; SLJ 5/04; VOYA 4/04)

Asia and the Pacific

731 Dumbleton, Mike. *Watch Out for Jamie Joel* (9–12). 2004, Allen & Unwin paper $7.95 (1-86508-532-4). 139pp. Craig Eliot, the new deputy principal at an urban Australian high school, tries to help Jamie Joel, an intelligent but troubled girl. (Rev: SLJ 6/04; VOYA 8/04)

732 Hartnett, Sonya. *Stripes of the Sidestep Wolf* (10–12). 2005, Candlewick $16.99 (0-7636-2644-9). 208pp. Stuck in a dying Australian town, 23-year-old Satchel O'Rye sees hope for reversing the town's fortunes when he spots what he believes to be an animal long thought to be extinct. (Rev: BCCB 3/05; BL 3/1/05; SLJ 3/05; VOYA 6/05)

733 Herrick, Steven. *The Simple Gift* (8–10). 2004, Simon Pulse paper $14.95 (0-689-86867-7). 205pp. In this compelling free-verse novel told in three voices, Australian 16-year-old Billy escapes an unhappy family life and takes up residence in an abandoned freight car where he finds both friendship and love. (Rev: BL 8/04; SLJ 9/04; VOYA 2/05)

734 Jeans, Peter. *Stoker's Bay* (8–12). 2003, Cygnet paper $13.50 (1-876268-97-2). 222pp. In Australia after World War II, Angus McCrea adjusts to life at high school, makes a friend called Kes, and falls in love with Kate, whose continuing sexual harassment by Charlie leads to tragedy. (Rev: SLJ 4/04)

735 Rees, Douglas. *Smoking Mirror: An Encounter with Paul Gauguin* (9–12). Series: Art Encounters. 2005, Watson-Guptill $15.95 (0-8230-4863-2). 176pp. Joe Sloan, a 15-year-old Mexican American, travels to Tahiti in the 1890s and develops a friendship with French artist Paul Gauguin in this compelling story that interweaves fact and fiction. (Rev: BL 3/15/05; SLJ 3/05)

736 Sa, Shan. *The Girl Who Played Go* (10–12). Trans. from Japanese by Adriana Hunter. 2003, Knopf $22.95 (1-4000-4025-6). 230pp. A 16-year-old Chinese girl and a Japanese soldier in disguise fall in love as they play go against the backdrop of the Japanese invasion of Manchuria; an intense and tragic story for strong readers. (Rev: SLJ 1/04)

737 See, Lisa. *Snow Flower and the Secret Fan* (11–12). 2005, Random $21.95 (1-4000-6028-1). 264pp. In 19th-century China, two women from different backgrounds who were friends as young people start to drift apart when each gets married. (Rev: BL 7/05)

738 Sheth, Mashmira. *Koyal Dark, Mango Sweet* (8–11). 2006, Hyperion $15.99 (0-7868-3857-4). 224pp. At the age of 16, Jeeta, who lives in Mumbai (formerly Bombay), finds many of the traditions that preoccupy her mother to be old-fashioned and inappropriate. (Rev: BL 4/1/06; SLJ 4/06)

739 Xinran. *Sky Burial* (11–12). Trans. by Julia Lovell and Esther Tyldesley. 2005, Doubleday $18.95 (0-385-51548-0). 224pp. Wen, a young Chinese widow, travels to Tibet to find out more about her husband Kejun's death in this story of differing cultures in the mid-20th century. (Rev: BL 7/05)

Europe and the Middle East

740 Bajoria, Paul. *The Printer's Devil* (7–10). 2005, Little, Brown $16.99 (0-316-01090-1). 382pp. Mog Winter, a 12-year-old orphan in Victorian London, is working as a printer's apprentice when a case of mistaken identity sends the boy headlong into the violent underworld of the English capital. (Rev: BL 12/1/05; SLJ 10/05; VOYA 10/05)

741 Barlow, John. *Eating Mammals: Three Novellas* (10–12). 2004, Perennial paper $12.95 (0-06-059175-7). 272pp. Three novellas give readers a fascinating — and sometimes dark — view of life in rural Yorkshire during the Victorian era. (Rev: BL 8/04; SLJ 1/05)

742 Byrd, Nicole. *Beauty in Black* (10–12). 2004, Berkley paper $6.99 (0-425-19683-6). 336pp. In this complex and entertaining Regency romance, Louisa is angered when the man she's set her sights on is attracted instead to her chaperone. (Rev: SLJ 3/05)

743 Cook, Gloria. *Pengarron Rivalry* (11–12). Series: Pengarron. 2004, Severn $28.95 (0-7278-6075-5). 288pp. Kelynen and her brother Luke clash over their family's estate, and Kelynen finds herself falling in love with Sir Rafe in this novel set in 1780. (Rev: BL 11/15/04)

744 Darnton, John. *The Darwin Conspiracy* (9–12). 2005, Knopf $25.00 (1-4000-4137-6). 320pp. A fast-paced and dramatic story that blends facts about Darwin's life and theory of evolution with the mysteries that surrounded him; his daughter Lizzie and two contemporary Darwin scholars also play key roles. (Rev: BL 8/05)

745 Dines, Carol. *The Queen's Soprano* (9–12). 2006, Harcourt $17.00 (0-15-205477-4). 336pp. Based on a real 17th-century character, this story features 17-year-old Angelica Voglia, a girl with a wonderful voice who faces numerous obstacles in conservative Rome. (Rev: BL 2/15/06)

746 Donn, Linda. *The Little Balloonist* (10–12). 2006, Dutton $21.95 (0-525-94928-3). 208pp. This compelling historical novel chronicles the life — and love — of Sophie Blanchard, one of the first woman balloonists in Napoleonic France. (Rev: BL 12/15/05)

747 Essex, Karen. *Leonardo's Swans* (11–12). 2006, Doubleday $21.95 (0-385-51706-8). 352pp. At the heart of this rich historical novel set in Renaissance Italy is the rivalry between ambitious sisters Isabella and Beatrice d'Este; for mature teens. (Rev: BL 11/15/05)

748 Garcia y Robertson, R. *White Rose* (9–12). 2004, Forge $25.95 (0-312-86994-0). 400pp. Following *Lady Robyn* (2001) and *Knight Errant* (2002), this entertaining trip through time has Robyn caught up in the War of the Roses and pregnant with the child of the future King Edward IV; for mature teens. (Rev: BL 10/1/04; VOYA 4/05)

749 Gavin, Jamila. *The Blood Stone* (7–10). 2005, Farrar $18.00 (0-374-30846-2). 352pp. In this sprawling historical fantasy set in the 17th century, 12-year-old Filipo Veroneo makes a dangerous journey from Venice to Hindustan to rescue the father he has never met, and finds help in strange quarters. (Rev: BL 12/15/05; SLJ 12/05; VOYA 12/05)

750 Harris, Robert, and Jane Yolen. *Prince Across the Water* (6–10). 2004, Penguin $18.99 (0-399-23897-2). 320pp. Thirteen-year-old Duncan shares his countrymen's pride at Bonnie Prince Charlie's struggle to reclaim the crown of England and Scotland from German-born George II, but when the boy runs away from home to join the battle, he discovers the true horrors of war. (Rev: BL 11/15/04; SLJ 12/04; VOYA 10/04)

751 Hawes, Louise. *The Vanishing Point* (8–10). 2004, Houghton $17.00 (0-618-43423-2). 256pp. In this appealing historical novel that imagines the adolescence of Italian Renaissance artist Lavinia Fontana, young Vini resorts to subterfuge to get her father to let her paint in his studio. (Rev: BL 11/1/04; SLJ 12/04; VOYA 12/04)

752 Hearn, Julie. *The Minister's Daughter* (7–10). 2005, Simon & Schuster $16.95 (0-689-87690-4). 272pp. In this historical novel set against the backdrop of the English Civil Wars, a Puritan minister's daughter tries to blame her pregnancy on spells cast by the granddaughter of the village's healer. (Rev: BL 5/15/05; SLJ 6/05)

753 Heuston, Kimberley. *Dante's Daughter* (10–12). 2003, Front Street $16.95 (1-886910-97-9). 312pp. In early-14th-century Italy, Antonia Alighieri, daughter of the controversial poet Dante, struggles to establish herself as an artist despite the instability in her life. (Rev: BCCB 3/04; BL 1/1–15/04; SLJ 2/04; VOYA 4/04)

754 Holub, Josef. *An Innocent Soldier* (8–11). Trans. by Michael Gofmann. 2005, Scholastic $16.99 (0-439-62771-0). 240pp. Pressed into Napoleon's army for the ill-fated Russian campaign, Adam, a teenage farmhand, is selected as a personal servant by Konrad, an officer from a wealthy family, and the two develop a strong friendship. (Rev: BL 11/15/05; SLJ 12/05; VOYA 2/06)

755 Japin, Arthur. *In Lucia's Eyes* (11–12). Trans. by David Colmer. 2005, Knopf $24.00 (1-4000-4464-2). 272pp. In this compelling historical novel suitable for mature teens, Lucia, the first love of legendary seducer Casanova, falls ill with smallpox and flees rather than reveal the true nature of her illness to her lover. (Rev: BL 11/15/05)

756 Lawrence, Iain. *The Convicts* (7–10). 2005, Delacorte LB $17.99 (0-385-90109-7). 224pp. In early-19th-century London, 14-year-old Tom is cast into the streets after his father is hauled away to debtor's prison and has various adventures including being transported to Australia. (Rev: BCCB 4/05; BL 3/15/05; HB 3–4/05; SLJ 7/05)

757 Le Clezio, J. M. G. *Wandering Star* (11–12). Trans. by C. Dickson. 2004, Curbstone paper $15.00 (1-931896-11-9). 320pp. A young woman who has survived the Holocaust and made her way to Jerusalem meets a Palestinian girl who is being displaced by the Jews. (Rev: BL 9/15/04)

758 Llywelyn, Morgan. *1972: A Novel of Ireland's Unfinished Revolution* (11–12). 2005, Forge $24.95 (0-312-87857-5). 368pp. This novel in a series chronicling Irish history follows Barry as he joins the IRA, culminating in the events of Bloody Sunday in Derry. (Rev: BL 2/15/05)

759 MacKall, Dandi Daley. *Eva Underground* (8–11). 2006, Harcourt $17.00 (0-15-205462-6). 256pp. In 1978, Eva Lott's father moves her from her high school life in Chicago to Communist Poland, where she initially rebels but later meets a young political activist named Tomek and develops a strong affection for him and an understanding of the oppression he is fighting. (Rev: BL 3/1/06)

760 Malone, Patricia. *Lady Ilena: Way of the Warrior* (7–10). 2005, Delacorte LB $17.99 (0-385-90251-4). 224pp. In this engaging sequel to *The Legend of Lady Ilena* (2002) set in Britain in the Dark Ages, the title character triggers a war when she refuses to accept the marriage proposal of a warrior from Dun Struan. (Rev: BL 12/1/05; SLJ 12/05)

761 Morgan, Nicola. *Fleshmarket* (8–12). 2004, Delacorte LB $17.99 (0-385-90192-5). 208pp. In early 19th-century Edinburgh, Robbie nurtures a hatred for the doctor who operated on his dying mother as Robbie and his sister struggle to survive. (Rev: BCCB 10/04; HB 7–8/04; SLJ 9/04; VOYA 2/05)

762 Ortiz, Michael J. *Swan Town: The Secret Journal of Susanna Shakespeare* (7–10). 2006, HarperCollins LB $16.89 (0-06-058127-1). 208pp. Shakespeare's teenage daughter Susanna writes in her diary about her current circumstances and her literary and acting ambitions, revealing much about Elizabethan life. (Rev: BL 2/15/06; SLJ 3/06; VOYA 2/06)

763 Rees, Elizabeth M. *The Wedding: An Encounter with Jan van Eyck* (8–11). Series: Art Encounters. 2005, Watson-Guptill $15.95 (0-8230-0407-4). 144pp. In this novel set in 15th-century Bruges and channeling Jan van Eyck's *The Arnolfini Portrait*, 14-year-old Giovanna falls in love with a troubador called Angelo even as her father plans her marriage to a wealthy man. (Rev: BL 9/15/05; SLJ 9/05)

764 Shaw, Rebecca. *A Country Affair* (10–12). Series: Barleybridge. 2006, Three Rivers paper

$12.95 (1-4000-9820-3). 288pp. In the hills of Yorkshire, 19-year-old Kate accepts her poor exam results and instead of studying to be a vet works instead as a receptionist in a vet's office. (Rev: BL 2/15/06)

765 Vande Velde, Vivian. *The Book of Mordred* (8–11). 2005, Houghton $18.00 (0-618-50754-X). 352pp. A multilayered account of Mordred's acts, seen through the eyes of three women who know him well. (Rev: BL 9/15/05; SLJ 10/05; VOYA 10/05)

766 Wallace, Karen. *Wendy* (7–10). 2004, Simon & Schuster $16.95 (0-689-86769-7). 208pp. In this engaging story set before the events of *Peter Pan*, life in the Darling household is less than idyllic for 9-year-old Wendy and her brothers. (Rev: BCCB 3/04; BL 1/1–15/04; HB 3–4/04; SLJ 3/04; VOYA 4/04)

767 Wyatt, Melissa. *Raising the Griffin* (8–12). 2004, Random LB $18.99 (0-385-90115-1). 288pp. When the people of Rovenia vote to restore their monarchy, 16-year-old Alex Varenhoff leaves Britain with his family so his father can ascend to the throne of his homeland, but the teen finds life as a prince is not all it's cracked up to be. (Rev: BCCB 2/04; BL 1/1–15/04; SLJ 2/04)

Latin America and Canada

768 Jocelyn, Marthe. *Mable Riley: A Reliable Record of Humdrum, Peril, and Romance* (5–10). Illus. 2004, Candlewick $15.99 (0-7636-2120-X). 288pp. This is a charming, humorous diary set in 1901 by a 14-year-old girl who accompanies her sister when she becomes a teacher in Stratford, Ontario. (Rev: BL 3/1/04; HB 5–6/04; SLJ 3/04; VOYA 6/04)

769 Kositsky, Lynne. *Claire by Moonlight* (7–10). 2005, Tundra paper $9.95 (0-88776-659-5). 272pp. History and romance are interwoven in this story of 15-year-old Claire's struggle to return to Acadia with her brother and sister after their deportation in the 1750s. (Rev: BL 7/05; SLJ 10/05)

770 Noël, Michel. *Good for Nothing* (8–11). 2004, Douglas & McIntyre $18.95 (0-88899-478-8). 256pp. In this powerful coming-of-age novel set in northern Quebec in the late 1950s and early 1960s, 15-year-old Nipishish, part Algonquin and part white, struggles to find his own identity. (Rev: BL 1/1–15/05; SLJ 1/05; VOYA 2/05)

771 Razzell, Mary. *Snow Apples* (9–12). 2006, Groundwood $15.95 (0-88899-741-8). 210pp. In the mid-1940s in rural British Columbia, 16-year-old Sheila Bray is in constant conflict with her mother and must turn elsewhere when she finds herself pregnant. (Rev: BL 3/15/06*)

772 Whyman, Matt. *Boy Kills Man* (9–12). 2005, HarperCollins LB $16.89 (0-06-074664-5). 160pp. Thirteen-year-old Sonny, a school dropout, aspires to live the high life in Medellin, Colombia, by carrying out paid assassinations for a local drug lord. (Rev: BCCB 3/05; BL 3/1/05; SLJ 3/05; VOYA 6/05)

United States

NATIVE AMERICANS

773 Anaya, Rudolfo. *Serafina's Stories* (9–12). 2004, Univ. of New Mexico $22.95 (0-8263-3569-1). 202pp. In a story reminiscent of the Arabian Nights, 15-year-old Serafina, a Pueblo Indian held captive by the Spaniards who control 17th-century New Mexico, tells stories to the Spanish governor in exchange for the release of her fellow captives. (Rev: SLJ 3/05)

774 Bruchac, Joseph. *Geronimo* (7–10). 2006, Scholastic $16.99 (0-439-35360-2). 384pp. Geronimo's fictional adopted grandson narrates the tragic story of Geronimo's final surrender and the subsequent treatment of his people in this well-researched novel. (Rev: BL 3/15/06; SLJ 4/06)

775 Carvell, Marlene. *Sweetgrass Basket* (7–10). 2005, Dutton $15.99 (0-525-47547-8). 160pp. Mohawk sisters Mattie and Sarah describe the abuse they endure at the Carlisle Indian Industrial School at the turn of the 20th century. (Rev: BL 8/05*; SLJ 12/05)

776 Creel, Ann Howard. *Under a Stand Still Moon* (6–10). 2005, Brown Barn paper $8.95 (0-9746481-8-3). 192pp. In this captivating story set among the ancient Anasazi of the American Southwest, a young girl uses her magical powers to preserve her people's way of life. (Rev: SLJ 11/05)

777 Spooner, Michael. *Last Child* (8–11). 2005, Holt $16.95 (0-8050-7739-1). 256pp. Rosalie, who is part Mandan and part Scottish American, is caught up in the conflicts between the Native Americans and the whites in 1837 North Dakota. (Rev: BL 9/1/05; SLJ 11/05; VOYA 8/05)

COLONIAL PERIOD AND FRENCH AND INDIAN WARS

778 Noyes, Deborah. *Angel and Apostle* (11–12). 2005, Unbridled $24.95 (1-932961-10-0). 304pp. This promising first novel suitable for mature readers tells the story of Pearl, the illegitimate daughter of Hester Prynne of Nathaniel Hawthorne's *The Scarlet Letter*. (Rev: BL 10/15/05)

779 Rinaldi, Ann. *The Color of Fire* (7–10). 2005, Hyperion $15.99 (0-7868-0938-8). 208pp. Based on a little-known historical event, this compelling novel chronicles what happens when false accusa-

tions unleash a storm of violence toward black people in mid-18th-century New York City. (Rev: BCCB 4/05; BL 2/1/05; SLJ 5/05; VOYA 4/05)

REVOLUTIONARY PERIOD AND THE YOUNG NATION (1775–1809)

780 Ernst, Kathleen. *Betrayal at Cross Creek* (5–10). 2004, Pleasant $10.95 (1-58485-879-6). 178pp. During the Revolutionary War, a young Scottish refugee and her grandparents are torn by conflicting loyalties. (Rev: BL 3/1/04; SLJ 5/04)

NINETEENTH CENTURY TO THE CIVIL WAR (1809–1861)

781 Allende, Isabel. *Zorro* (11–12). 2005, HarperCollins $25.95 (0-06-077897-0). 400pp. Allende retells the legend of Zorro as the complex story of a Spanish-Shoshone boy who becomes a champion of the oppressed in 18th-century California. (Rev: BL 2/15/05*)

782 Bass, Rick. *The Diezmo* (11–12). 2005, Houghton $22.00 (0-395-92617-3). 224pp. Based on the story of the Mier Expedition, this compelling novel tells about two young men who join Sam Houston's militia patrolling the Mexican border and find themselves amid appalling violence and political intrigue. (Rev: BL 3/1/05)

783 Bittner, Rosanne. *Into the Prairie: The Pioneers* (11–12). Series: Westward America! 2004, Forge $23.95 (0-765-30980-7). 256pp. In the third book in this series suitable for mature teens, Jonah Wilde and his wife and child settle in the Indiana Territory but are soon attacked by Potawatomi Indians. (Rev: BL 7/04)

784 Draper, Sharon. *Copper Sun* (9–12). 2006, Simon & Schuster $16.95 (0-689-82181-6). 320pp. A moving story — full of historical detail — of the sufferings of Amari, captured in her village in Africa and taken to America, where she is bought as a gift for a plantation owner's son, and of her eventual bid for freedom. (Rev: BL 2/1/06*; SLJ 1/06*; VOYA 2/06)

785 Moses, Shelia P. *I, Dred Scott* (8–11). 2005, Simon & Schuster $16.95 (0-689-85975-9). 112pp. In this fictionalized account, Dred Scott, born a slave, chronicles the ultimately unsuccessful 11-year legal battle to win his freedom. (Rev: BCCB 4/05; BL 3/15/05; SLJ 2/05; VOYA 4/05)

786 Rawles, Nancy. *My Jim* (11–12). 2005, Crown $19.95 (1-4000-5400-1). 192pp. The wife of *Huckleberry Finn*'s Jim tells her side of their story, recalling their separation when she was sold and Jim's attempt to find her. (Rev: BL 11/15/04; SLJ 5/05)

787 Wilson, Diane Lee. *Black Storm Comin'* (7–10). 2005, Simon & Schuster $16.95 (0-689-87137-6).

304pp. Son of a white father and a freed-slave mother, 12-year-old Colton Westcott joins the Pony Express in an effort to make sure his mother and siblings finally make it to the West Coast. (Rev: BL 8/05*; SLJ 7/05; VOYA 10/05)

THE CIVIL WAR (1861–1865)

788 Brooks, Geraldine. *March* (9–12). 2005, Viking $24.95 (0-670-03335-9). 280pp. Styled like a 19th-century novel, this explores the imagined life of Captain March, the father in Alcott's *Little Women*. (Rev: BL 2/1/05; SLJ 7/05)

789 Elliott, Laura Malone. *Annie, Between the States* (7–11). 2004, HarperCollins LB $16.89 (0-06-001211-0). 496pp. As the Civil War rages around her northern Virginia home, 15-year-old Annie finds her feelings about the North-South conflict evolving. (Rev: BL 12/1/04; SLJ 11/04)

790 Myers, Anna. *Assassin* (7–12). 2005, Walker $16.95 (0-8027-8989-7). 212pp. The events surrounding the assassination of Abraham Lincoln are explored in this fictionalized account, narrated in alternating chapters by a teenage White House seamstress and assassin John Wilkes Booth. (Rev: SLJ 12/05; VOYA 10/05)

791 Turtledove, Harry. *Fort Pillow* (10–12). 2006, St. Martin's $24.95 (0-312-35520-3). 336pp. The controversial events of the attack on the Union garrison at Fort Pillow, Tennessee, in April 1864 are the subject of this harrowing novel. (Rev: BL 4/1/06)

WESTWARD EXPANSION AND PIONEER LIFE

792 Carbone, Elisa. *Last Dance on Holladay Street* (8–11). 2005, Knopf LB $17.99 (0-375-92896-0). 208pp. After the deaths of her black foster parents, 13-year-old Eva sets off to search for her birth mother and discovers she is a white prostitute; set in the late 19th century. (Rev: BCCB 6/05; BL 2/1/05; SLJ 4/05; VOYA 4/05)

793 Crew, Linda. *A Heart for Any Fate: Westward to Oregon, 1845* (9–12). 2005, Oregon Historical Society $21.95 (0-87595-291-7). 239pp. A fictionalized account of a Missouri family's journey from its home in the Midwest to Oregon. (Rev: SLJ 10/05)

794 Doig, Ivan. *The Whistling Season* (11–12). 2006, Harcourt $25.00 (0-15-101237-7). 352pp. Paul Milliron, in charge of schools in late 1950s Montana, looks back on his own 7th grade in a one-room school in 1910, the year in which Halley's Comet came and his motherless family got a housekeeper. (Rev: BL 12/15/05)

795 Leigh, Ana. *The Lawman Said "I Do"* (11–12). 2006, Pocket paper $6.99 (0-7434-6996-8). 384pp. In this compelling western romance suitable for mature teens, Colt Fraser, a former Confederate soldier bound for California, foils a stagecoach robbery, wins a temporary job as deputy in a small New Mexico town, and falls in love with the sheriff's daughter. (Rev: BL 12/1/05)

796 Overholser, Stephen. *Chasing Destiny* (9–12). 2005, Five Star $25.95 (1-59414-124-X). 217pp. Michael and a dog named Boy join Destiny in the search for her father and are secretly followed by a shady frontiersman who might be her father's murderer in this western novel. (Rev: BL 2/15/05)

797 Parnham, I. J. *Miss Dempsey's School for Gunslingers* (9–12). 2005, Avalon $21.95 (0-8034-9690-7). 192pp. Con games and corruption abound in Destiny, a frontier town where even the contest for Miss Destiny's hand is crooked. (Rev: BL 1/1–15/05)

798 Turner, Nancy E. *Sarah's Quilt: The Diary of Sarah Agnes Prine, 1906* (11–12). 2005, St. Martin's $24.95 (0-312-33262-9). 416pp. The determined, twice-widowed Sarah deals with drought and thievery as she struggles to hold onto her Arizona ranch. (Rev: BL 3/1/05)

799 Wolf, Allan. *New Found Land: Lewis and Clark's Voyage of Discovery* (7–12). 2004, Candlewick $18.99 (0-7636-2113-7). 500pp. Seaman the dog, here called Oolum, is the primary narrator of this verse account of the famous expedition that draws heavily on such primary source documents as letters and journals. (Rev: BL 9/04; SLJ 9/04)

RECONSTRUCTION TO WORLD WAR I (1865–1914)

800 Lavender, William. *Aftershocks* (9–12). 2006, Harcourt $17.00 (0-15-205882-6). 352pp. In San Francisco in 1906, 14-year-old Jessie faces upheavals — an argument with her father over her wish to become a doctor, the discovery that her father has impregnated their Chinese maid, and a major earthquake. (Rev: BL 3/1/06; VOYA 4/06)

801 Lerangis, Peter. *Smiler's Bones* (7–10). 2005, Scholastic $16.95 (0-439-34485-9). 160pp. Lerangis brings alive the sad story, based on truth, of an Inuit boy named Minik, who, with his father and four others, was brought to New York City in the late 19th century by explorer Robert Peary. (Rev: BCCB 6/05; BL 4/1/05; SLJ 6/05; VOYA 8/05)

802 Tal, Eve. *Double Crossing: A Jewish Immigration Story* (7–10). 2005, Cinco Puntos $16.95 (0-938317-94-6). 216pp. At the beginning of the 20th century, young Raizel and her Orthodox Jewish grandfather travel from Europe to New York only to find they are rejected by immigration officials. (Rev: BL 8/05*; SLJ 10/05; VOYA 4/06)

803 Taylor, Kim. *Bowery Girl* (8–11). 2006, Viking $16.99 (0-670-05966-8). 288pp. A realistic story about orphaned teen girls who resort to picking pockets and prostitution to survive in late-19th-century New York City. (Rev: BL 3/1/06; SLJ 3/06; VOYA 4/06)

BETWEEN THE WARS AND THE GREAT DEPRESSION (1919–1941)

804 Fergus, Jim. *The Wild Girl: The Notebooks of Ned Giles, 1932* (9–12). 2005, Hyperion $23.95 (1-4013-0054-5). 368pp. In 1932, 17-year-old orphan Ned Giles joins an expedition to rescue a boy kidnapped by Apaches, and finds himself attracted to a wild Apache girl they find in a Mexican jail. (Rev: BL 4/15/05)

805 Ingold, Jeanette. *Hitch* (8–11). 2005, Harcourt $17.00 (0-13-204747-6). 271pp. When he loses his job during the Great Depression, 17-year-old Moss Trawnley leaves home in search of his father and ends up in an interesting job with the Civilian Conservation Corps. (Rev: BCCB 9/05; BL 5/15/05; SLJ 8/05)

806 Kerr, M. E. *Your Eyes in Stars* (9–12). 2006, HarperCollins LB $16.89 (0-06-075683-7). 240pp. In a story that starts in upstate New York during the Depression and looks at prejudices, 14-year-old Jessica develops a strong friendship with Elisa, daughter of a German professor who's been hired to teach at nearby Cornell University. (Rev: BL 12/1/05*; SLJ 1/06)

807 Morris, Mary McGarry. *The Lost Mother* (11–12). 2005, Viking $23.95 (0-670-03389-8). 276pp. In Depression-era Vermont, Thomas and his younger sister Margaret, abandoned by their mother, struggle profoundly with their father's neglect, dire poverty, and exploitation by various adults; for mature teens. (Rev: BL 12/1/04; SLJ 9/05)

POST WORLD WAR II UNITED STATES (1945–)

808 Devoto, Pat Cunningham. *The Summer We Got Saved* (10–12). 2005, Warner $23.95 (0-446-57696-4). 416pp. Told from three points of view, this is a complex story of 1960s Alabama, the civil rights movement, and young women coming of age in a time of turmoil. (Rev: BL 4/15/05; SLJ 11/05)

809 Feldman, Ellen. *The Boy Who Loved Anne Frank* (9–12). 2005, Norton $23.95 (0-393-05944-8). 288pp. Peter Van Pels hid with Anne Frank and died in the camps before liberation; Feldman reimagines him as a survivor and immigrant to the United States, who denies his Jewish past until the edited *Diary*, play, and movie cause his new life to crumble. (Rev: BL 2/15/05)

810 Godwin, Gail. *Queen of the Underworld* (11–12). 2006, Random $24.95 (0-345-48318-9). 336pp. It's 1959, and brand-new journalist Emma Gant, eager

to make her mark on the *Miami Star* finds herself embroiled in the world of Cuban refugees; for mature teens. (Rev: BL 9/15/05)

811 Haigh, Jennifer. *Baker Towers* (10–12). 2005, Morrow $24.95 (0-06-050941-4). 352pp. The five Novak children, of Italian and Polish heritage, grow up and leave their Pennsylvania home in the years after World War II — some enjoying more success than others — but the mining town still calls to them. (Rev: BL 11/1/04; SLJ 5/05)

812 Houston, Julian. *New Boy* (8–11). 2005, Houghton $16.00 (0-618-43253-1). 256pp. In the late 1950s, Rob Garrett, an African American teen from Virginia, is the first black student at a tony Connecticut prep school, where he learns about different forms of prejudice and watches civil rights developments in the South. (Rev: BL 11/15/05*; SLJ 3/06; VOYA 2/06)

813 Joseph, Frank S. *To Love Mercy* (10–12). 2006, Mid-Atlantic Highlands paper $14.95 (0-9744785-3-9). 260pp. In 1940s Chicago, a white boy and an African American boy form an unlikely friendship that reveals the racial tensions of the time. (Rev: BL 4/1/06)

814 Kadohata, Cynthia. *Kira-Kira* (6–12). 2004, Simon & Schuster $15.95 (0-689-85639-3). 256pp. Poverty, exploitation, and racial prejudice form a backdrop to this moving story of two Japanese American sisters growing up in a small Georgia town in the late 1950s and facing the older sister's death from lymphoma. Newbery Medal, 2005. (Rev: BCCB 1/04; BL 1/1–15/04; HB 3–4/04; SLJ 3/04; VOYA 8/04)

815 Stephenson, Lynda. *Dancing with Elvis* (9–12). 2005, Eerdmans $17.00 (0-8028-5293-9). 320pp. In a Texas town during the late 1950s made turbulent by racial tensions, feisty 15-year-old Frankilee Baxter has trouble getting along with her foster sister Angel; realistic language may be a problem for some readers. (Rev: BL 11/15/05; SLJ 1/06; VOYA 4/06)

816 Zafris, Nancy. *Lucky Strike* (10–12). 2005, Unbridled $23.95 (1-932961-04-6). 352pp. In 1950s Utah quirky characters including young siblings Beth and Charlie stake their fortunes on discovering uranium. (Rev: BL 3/1/05)

Twentieth-Century Wars

WORLD WAR I

817 Morpurgo, Michael. *Private Peaceful* (7–12). 2004, Scholastic $16.95 (0-439-63648-5). 176pp. Fifteen-year-old Thomas, who lied about his age to follow his beloved older brother into combat in World War I, reflects on the life he left behind in England and the horrors of life on the front lines. (Rev: BL 10/1/04*; SLJ 11/04; VOYA 12/04)

818 Sedgwick, Marcus. *The Foreshadowing* (8–11). 2006, Random LB $18.99 (0-385-90881-4). 288pp. Plagued by premonitions about her brother, 17-year-old Sasha signs up as a nurse so that she can look for him on the grim battlefields of World War I France. (Rev: BL 4/1/06*)

819 Spillebeen, Geert. *Kipling's Choice* (7–10). Trans. by Terese Edelstein. 2005, Houghton $16.00 (0-618-43124-1). 160pp. In this fictionalized biography of John Kipling, the son of the world-famous British author uses his father's influence to get into the army despite his poor eyesight, giving the teen a chance to do battle with the "barbaric Huns" in World War I. (Rev: BCCB 6/05; BL 5/15/05; SLJ 6/05; VOYA 12/05)

WORLD WAR II AND THE HOLOCAUST

820 Charlesworth, Monique. *The Children's War* (11–12). 2004, Knopf $24.95 (1-4000-4009-4). 384pp. Ilse, a German girl whose father is Jewish, fights for survival in Africa and France during World War II, while Nicolai, a boy from a wealthy Nazi family whose nanny is Ilse's mother, enjoys a life of privilege but comes to question his own position in this multilayered novel suitable for mature teens. (Rev: BL 8/04; SLJ 3/05)

821 Friedman, D. Dina. *Escaping into the Night* (7–10). 2006, Simon & Schuster $14.95 (1-4169-0258-9). 208pp. Based on true events, this is the story of Halina Rudowski's escape into the forest during a Nazi roundup of Jews, and her subsequent efforts to survive. (Rev: BL 1/1–15/06; SLJ 3/06; VOYA 4/06)

822 Goyer, Tricia. *Night Song* (9–12). 2004, Moody paper $12.99 (0-8024-1555-5). 400pp. The fates of a Jewish prisoner, a Nazi musician, an American doctor, and an Austrian woman come together at the Mauthausen concentration camp. (Rev: BL 9/1/04)

823 Graber, Janet. *Resistance* (7–10). 2005, Marshall Cavendish $15.95 (0-7614-5214-1). 144pp. In this suspenseful World War II novel, 15-year-old Marianne reluctantly joins her mother and brother in fighting for the French Resistance despite her fears that they will be found out by the German soldier billeted in their home. (Rev: BCCB 6/05; BL 5/15/05; SLJ 8/05)

824 Hamamura, John Hideyo. *Color of the Sea* (10–12). 2006, St. Martin's $24.95 (0-312-34073-7). 320pp. A poignant story of Japanese Americans in the turmoil after the bombing of Pearl Harbor, featuring young lovers Sam and Keiko who are separated by events. (Rev: BL 3/15/06)

825 Hunter, Bernice Thurman. *The Girls They Left Behind* (7–10). 2005, Fitzhenry & Whiteside paper $9.95 (1-55041-927-7). 192pp. This coming-of-age novel, set in Toronto against the backdrop of World War II, paints a vivid portrait of what life was like for the teenage girls left behind on the home front. (Rev: BCCB 7–8/05; BL 5/15/05; SLJ 8/05; VOYA 8/05)

826 Kositsky, Lynne. *The Thought of High Windows* (8–12). 2004, Kids Can $16.95 (1-55337-621-8). 175pp. A Jewish refugee named Esther describes her experiences in France during World War II — lice and other discomforts, loneliness, longing for her family, her differences from the other refugees — and her involvement in the Resistance in this affecting novel based on true events. (Rev: HB 5–6/04; SLJ 5/04)

827 Lawrence, Iain. *B for Buster* (7–12). 2004, Delacorte LB $17.99 (0-385-90108-9). 336pp. To escape his abusive parents, 16-year-old Kak lies about his age and joins the Canadian Air Force in 1943; he soon finds himself part of a crew flying nighttime bombing raids over Germany. (Rev: BL 6/1–15/04; SLJ 7/04; VOYA 8/04)

828 Mazer, Harry. *Heroes Don't Run: A Novel of the Pacific War* (7–10). 2005, Simon & Schuster $15.95 (0-689-85534-6). 128pp. In this gripping sequel to *A Boy at War* (2001) and *A Boy No More* (2004), 17-year-old Adam Pelko lies about his age to join the U.S. Marines and fights in a climactic battle with the Japanese on Okinawa. (Rev: BL 5/15/05; SLJ 8/05; VOYA 8/05)

829 Orgel, Doris. *Daniel, Half Human: And the Good Nazi* (7–12). 2004, Simon & Schuster $17.95 (0-689-85747-0). 304pp. Daniel and Armin, best friends in Germany in the early 1930s, both admire Hitler, but their friendship is tested when Daniel learns that he is half-Jewish. (Rev: BL 9/15/04; SLJ 12/04)

830 Patneaude, David. *Thin Wood Walls* (6–10). 2004, Houghton $16.00 (0-618-34290-7). 240pp. In this poignant tale set against the backdrop of an America reeling from the Japanese attack on Pearl Harbor, Joe Hanada and his Japanese American family feel the rising tide of prejudice and are eventually sent to an internment camp in California. (Rev: BL 9/15/04; SLJ 10/04; VOYA 12/04)

831 Ross, Catherine. *Last Light* (10–12). 2005, Severn $28.95 (0-7278-6254-5). 256pp. In England in 1943, three young women working on an air force base get used to the rules imposed by bureaucracy, enjoy the company of the male pilots, and worry about them when they leave for raids on Europe. (Rev: BL 9/15/05)

832 Roth, Philip. *The Plot Against America: A Novel* (10–12). 2004, Houghton $26.00 (0-618-50928-3). 400pp. A chilling alternate history in which the ascent to the presidency in 1940 of Hitler sympathizer Charles Lindbergh strikes fear into the heart of the young Jewish narrator. (Rev: BL 8/04; SLJ 11/04)

833 Salisbury, Graham. *Eyes of the Emperor* (7–10). 2005, Random LB $17.99 (0-385-90874-1). 240pp. Sixteen-year-old Eddie Okubo, a Japanese American from Hawaii, lies about his age to join the U.S. Army but is subjected to suspicion and harassment after the Japanese attack Pearl Harbor only weeks later. (Rev: BCCB 9/05; BL 5/15/05*; HB 7–8/05; SLJ 9/05; VOYA 8/05)

834 Turtledove, Harry. *Days of Infamy* (9–12). 2004, NAL $24.95 (0-451-21307-6). 464pp. An alternate history taking the bombing of Pearl Harbor a step further into an invasion, with the point of view of the Japanese soldiers fully explored. (Rev: BL 9/15/04)

835 Turtledove, Harry. *End of the Beginning* (9–12). 2005, NAL $25.95 (0-451-21668-7). 448pp. The Japanese who have occupied Hawaii are now awaiting the inevitable attack from the U.S. mainland in this alternate-history sequel to *Days of Infamy* (2004). (Rev: BL 9/1/05)

KOREAN, VIETNAM, AND OTHER WARS

836 Couloumbis, Audrey. *Summer's End* (7–10). 2005, Penguin $16.99 (0-399-23555-8). 192pp. Grace finds solace at her grandmother's farm after her brother burns his draft card and sparks a family feud in this thought-provoking novel set during the Vietnam War. (Rev: BL 7/05*; SLJ 6/05)

837 Hughes, Dean. *Search and Destroy* (7–10). 2006, Simon & Schuster $16.95 (0-689-87023-X). 224pp. Rick Ward, who joined the army during the Vietnam War to escape his home life, returns from a tour of duty unable to adjust to normal life. (Rev: BL 2/1/06; SLJ 1/06; VOYA 2/06)

838 Lee, Edward Jae-Suk. *The Good Man: A Novel* (10–12). 2005, BridgeWorks $21.95 (1-882593-94-4). 248pp. Still haunted by sketchy memories of his war experiences, aging Korean War veteran Gabriel Guttman returns to his boyhood home in Montana. (Rev: BL 11/15/04; SLJ 7/05)

839 Maraniss, David. *They Marched into Sunlight: War and Peace Vietnam and America October 1967* (10–12). 2003, Simon & Schuster $29.95 (0-7432-1780-2). 572pp. In the same month in 1967 a U.S. Army battalion walks into a bloody ambush in Vietnam and a student demonstration in Wisconsin ends in a battle with police. (Rev: BL 9/1/03; SLJ 1/04)

Horror Stories and the Supernatural

840 Benson, Amber, and Christopher Golden. *Accursed* (11–12). 2005, Del Rey paper $13.95 (0-345-47130-X). 400pp. Charged with defending the soul of England as Protectors of Albion, siblings William and Tamara Swift call on ghostly allies when dark forces threaten; set in Victorian England and suitable for mature teens. (Rev: BL 11/15/05)

841 Butler, Octavia E. *Fledgling* (11–12). 2005, Seven Stories $24.95 (1-58322-690-7). 320pp. After awakening from traumatic injuries to find that she is a 53-year-old vampire trapped in the body of a young girl, Shori Matthews struggles to learn what has happened to her; for mature readers. (Rev: BL 10/15/05)

842 Cabot, Meg. *Twilight* (7–10). Series: The Mediator. 2005, HarperCollins LB $16.89 (0-06-072468-4). 241pp. Suze, deeply in love with a ghost named Jesse, faces a real dilemma when she discovers a way to give Jesse back his life that would mean losing him as a boyfriend; the sixth installment in the series. (Rev: SLJ 2/05)

843 Cary, Kate. *Bloodline* (7–10). 2005, Penguin $16.99 (1-59514-012-3). 336pp. When Quincey Harker takes John Shaw's sister, Lily, to Transylvania to be his bride, John and his fiancée Mary realize they must save Lily from a terrible fate. (Rev: BL 9/1/05; SLJ 9/05)

844 Casey, Joe, and Steve Parkhouse. *The Milkman Murders* (11–12). Illus. 2005, Dark Horse paper $12.95 (I-59307-080-2). 104pp. In this horror graphic novel, for mature readers only, Barbara, a housewife dealing with a particularly difficult family, is pushed over the edge when she is assaulted by a milkman. (Rev: BL 4/15/05)

845 Clegg, Douglas. *The Priest of Blood* (9–12). Series: Vampyricon. 2005, Ace $19.95 (0-441-01327-9). 320pp. In this opening volume of the Vampyricon series, Aleric, a young peasant chosen to train hunting birds for the local baron, runs afoul of his master when he falls in love with his daughter. (Rev: BL 10/15/05)

846 Connor, Gina. *Dead on Town Line* (8–11). 2005, Dial $15.99 (0-8037-3021-7). 144pp. In free-verse poems, Cassie reveals the circumstances of her own murder and her relationship with other ghosts. (Rev: BL 7/05; SLJ 7/05; VOYA 6/05)

847 de Lint, Charles. *The Blue Girl* (8–11). 2004, Penguin $17.99 (0-670-05924-2). 384pp. Imogene, determined to turn over a new leaf at her new high school, strikes up an alliance with loner Maxine and meets the ghost of a former pupil, foreshadowing a struggle between an evil underworld and an inhospitable reality. (Rev: BL 11/15/04; SLJ 11/04; VOYA 12/04)

848 Fox, Andrew. *Bride of the Fat White Vampire* (9–12). 2004, Ballantine paper $14.95 (0-345-46408-7). 448pp. The entertaining sequel to *Fat White Vampire Blues* finds vampire Jules back together again (after changing himself into 187 rats) and trying to get to the bottom of a mystery involving black vampires. (Rev: BL 8/04)

849 Golden, Christopher. *The Shell Collector* (10–12). Illus. 2006, Cemetery Dance $30.00 (1-58767-114-X). 120pp. A brief and suspenseful horror story set in a Massachusetts fishing town. (Rev: BL 3/15/06)

850 Golden, Christopher. *Wildwood Road* (11–12). 2005, Bantam paper $12.00 (0-553-38208-X). 315pp. For mature teens, this is a spooky horror story about a mysterious child whose constant appearances threaten to ruin a couple's lives. (Rev: BL 4/15/05)

851 Harris, Charlaine. *Dead as a Doornail* (11–12). 2005, Ace $22.95 (0-441-01279-5). 304pp. Sookie, last seen in *Dead to the World* (2004), continues to lead a dangerous life — this time with the Were-people; for mature teens. (Rev: BL 5/1/05)

852 Harris, Charlaine. *Grave Sight* (10–12). 2005, Berkley $23.95 (0-425-20568-1). 272pp. Hit by lightning and imbued with the magical power to find dead bodies and discern the cause of death, Harper Connolly travels to Arkansas to help find the body of a missing teenage girl. (Rev: BL 10/1/05)

853 Jenkins, A. M. *Beating Heart: A Ghost Story* (9–12). 2006, HarperCollins LB $16.89 (0-06-054608-5). 244pp. Dreams begin to affect reality — and his relationship with Carrie — as 17-year-old Evan is haunted by a spirit named Cora who lived in his house 100 years before. (Rev: BCCB 2/06; SLJ 3/06)

854 Jordan, River. *The Messenger of Magnolia Street* (9–12). 2006, HarperSanFrancisco $22.95 (0-06-084176-1). 256pp. Nehemiah Trust enjoys a successful career in Washington, D.C., but he heads south when dark forces threaten his Alabama hometown of Shibboleth. (Rev: BL 10/15/05)

855 King, Stephen. *Cell* (9–12). 2006, Scribner $26.95 (0-7432-9233-2). 384pp. In a world rendered mad by a single cell phone call, Clay Riddell, accompanied by 15-year-old Alice and bright 12-year-old Tom, seeks to survive and to set things to rights. (Rev: BL 1/1–15/06)

856 King, Stephen. *The Dark Tower* (9–12). Illus. Series: Dark Tower. 2004, Scribner $35.00 (1-880418-62-2). 864pp. A suspenseful finale to the long-running saga about the last gunslinger in the world. (Rev: BL 9/1/04)

857 Koontz, Dean. *Forever Odd* (10–12). 2005, Bantam $27.00 (0-553-80416-2). 416pp. In this sequel to *Odd Thomas* (2003), the appealing protagonist who can communicate with ghosts is drawn into a trap as he investigates the disappearance of a friend. (Rev: BL 11/15/05)

858 Koontz, Dean. *Life Expectancy* (8–12). 2004, Bantam $27.00 (0-553-80414-6). 401pp. Jimmy is stalked by a mad clown from the moment of his birth in this novel that spoofs cinematic and literary conventions. (Rev: BL 11/1/04)

859 Koontz, Dean, and Kevin J. Anderson. *Prodigal Son* (11–12). 2005, Bantam paper $7.99 (0-553-58788-9). 477pp. With Victor Frankenstein, now in biotechnology in 21st-century New Orleans, secretly striving to create a perfect "New Race," his first monster, Deucalion, seeks to thwart him; for mature teens. (Rev: BL 1/1–15/05)

860 Lucas, Tim. *The Book of Renfield: A Gospel of Dracula* (11–12). 2005, Touchstone paper $14.00 (0-7432-4354-4). 416pp. Dr. Seward's study of Renfield, a minor character in Stoker's *Dracula*, forms the core of this documentary-like novel. (Rev: BL 6/1–15/05)

861 Martinez, A. Lee. *Gil's All Fright Diner* (10–12). 2005, Tor $23.95 (0-765-31143-7); paper $12.95 (0-765-31471-1). 288pp. Teenage Tammy — aka Mistress Lilith, Queen of the Night — is not pleased when her zombies are driven off by the arrival of vampire Earl and werewolf Duke in this comic supernatural story. (Rev: BL 5/15/05; SLJ 8/05)

862 Meyer, Stephanie. *Twilight* (9–12). 2005, Little, Brown $17.99 (0-316-16017-2). 499pp. Seventeen-year-old Bella Swan, a new arrival in the rain-soaked city of Forks, Washington, falls quickly for fellow student Edward Cullen only to find he has dark secrets. (Rev: BL 11/15/05*; SLJ 10/05*; VOYA 10/05)

863 Myracle, Lauren. *Rhymes with Witches* (8–11). 2005, Abrams $16.95 (0-8109-5859-7). 208pp. Invited to join a super-popular clique at her high school, Jane is at first flattered but soon discovers that she's involved in something sinister. (Rev: BCCB 5/05; BL 3/15/05; SLJ 4/05)

864 Noyes, Deborah. *Gothic! Ten Original Dark Tales* (7–10). 2005, Candlewick $15.99 (0-7636-2243-5). 256pp. Ten Gothic tales by contemporary authors embody the dark fantasy and the fairy tale aspects of the genre as well as offering supernatural horror plus humor. (Rev: BL 10/15/04; SLJ 1/05)

865 Olin, Sean. *Killing Britney* (10–12). 2005, Simon & Schuster paper $8.99 (0-689-87778-1). 234pp. Britney Johnson finds her life turned upside down when someone starts killing those she loves; for mature readers. (Rev: BCCB 9/05; SLJ 7/05)

866 Page, Jan. *Rewind* (7–10). 2005, Walker $16.95 (0-8027-8995-1). 224pp. When he is injured in an accident while playing drums onstage, Liam finds himself back in time watching his parents as teenagers, when they had a band whose drummer was killed. (Rev: BL 9/1/05; SLJ 11/05; VOYA 10/05)

867 Richardson, E. E. *Devil's Footsteps* (8–11). 2005, Delacorte LB $17.99 (0-385-90279-4). 128pp. Still troubled by his brother's disappearance at the hands of the Dark Man five years earlier, 15-year-old Bryan meets two other teens struggling with the effects of similar attacks. (Rev: BCCB 10/05; BL 5/1/05; SLJ 1/06)

868 Rock, Peter. *The Bewildered* (11–12). 2005, MacAdam $23.00 (1-59692-112-9). 300pp. Teens hired to steal copper wire discover an eerie zombie-like cult seemingly addicted to electricity; for mature teens. (Rev: BL 2/1/05)

869 Shan, Darren. *Lord Loss* (9–12). Series: Demonata. 2005, Little, Brown $15.99 (0-316-11499-5). 240pp. A teenager witnesses the brutal murder of his family by demons in the opening volume of a new Shan series. (Rev: BL 11/1/05; SLJ 11/05; VOYA 10/05)

870 Sleator, William. *The Boy Who Couldn't Die* (7–10). 2004, Abrams $16.95 (0-8109-4824-9). 176pp. After his best friend dies in a plane crash, 16-year-old Ken visits a voodoo princess and has his soul removed to keep him safe — with consequences he at first enjoys but later comes to rue. (Rev: BCCB 4/04; SLJ 4/04; VOYA 6/04)

871 Sosnowski, David. *Vamped* (9–12). 2004, Free Press $24.00 (0-7432-6253-0). 352pp. In a future where regular humans are rare, vampire Martin takes in a young girl, Isuzu Trooper Cassidy, and finds himself coming to care about her. (Rev: BL 8/04)

872 Stahler, David. *A Gathering of Shades* (7–10). 2005, HarperCollins LB $16.89 (0-06-052295-X). 304pp. Sixteen-year-old Aidan, who moves to rural Vermont with his mother after his father's death, discovers that his grandmother is secretly feeding ghosts with a mixture of her own blood and spring water. (Rev: BCCB 5/05; BL 5/1/05; SLJ 8/05)

873 Stine, R. L. *The Taste of Night* (6–12). Series: Dangerous Girls. 2004, HarperCollins LB $15.89 (0-06-059617-1). 240pp. Livvy, who has chosen life as a vampire, tries to bring her twin sister Destiny over to the dark side, while her twin works with equal intensity to return Livvy to human form as their father works to rid the town of vampires. (Rev: BL 9/1/04; SLJ 8/04)

874 Stoker, Bram. *Dracula* (7–12). Adapted by Gary Reed. Series: Puffin Graphics. 2006, Puffin paper $9.99 (0-14-240572-8). 176pp. A compelling graphic novel version of the famous vampire story. (Rev: SLJ 3/06)

875 Thurlo, David, and Aimée Thurlo. *Blood Retribution* (11–12). Series: Lee Nez. 2004, Tor $23.95 (0-765-30442-2). 272pp. This sequel to *Second Sunrise* finds Lee Nez, who is half vampire, being stalked by an assassin while on the trail of shape-shifting smugglers; for mature teens. (Rev: BL 9/1/04)

876 Thurlo, David, and Aimée Thurlo. *Pale Death* (9–12). Series: Lee Nez. 2005, Forge $23.95 (0-765-31385-5). 264pp. In the third installment of the Lee Nez series, the title character, a New Mexico

state trooper who is Navajo and half-vampire, joins forces with FBI agent Diane Lopez to track down an evil vampire named Stewart Tanner. (Rev: BL 10/15/05)

877 Wellington, David. *Monster Island* (11–12). 2006, Thunder's Mouth paper $13.95 (1-56025-850-0). 288pp. In the aftermath of a global disaster that has rendered most humans zombies, a band of teenage girl soldiers and a former UN arms inspector arrive in New York seeking medicine and ready for battle. (Rev: BL 3/15/06)

878 Westerfeld, Scott. *Peeps* (9–12). 2005, Penguin $16.99 (1-59514-031-X). 320pp. Soon after he arrived in New York from Texas, college freshman Cal lost his virginity and in the process became the carrier of a parasite that causes vampirism; now he is in a key position to save the whole city. (Rev: BL 8/05; SLJ 10/05*)

879 Westerfeld, Scott. *The Secret Hour* (6–10). Series: Midnighters. 2004, HarperCollins LB $16.89 (0-06-051952-5). 297pp. In this exciting first volume, 15-year-old Jessica Day discovers that — like several others — she has special abilities to battle supernatural creatures. (Rev: SLJ 6/04; VOYA 4/04)

880 Westerfeld, Scott. *Touching Darkness* (6–10). Illus. Series: Midnighters. 2005, HarperCollins LB $16.89 (0-06-051955-X). 330pp. In volume two of the Midnighters series, five teens born at the stroke of midnight learn about the hidden past of their Oklahoma hometown and a frightening conspiracy that threatens them all. (Rev: SLJ 3/05)

881 Whedon, Joss. *Fray* (10–12). 2003, Dark Horse paper $19.95 (1-56971-751-6). Melaka Fray, a vampire-fighting street kid in a grim, future Manhattan, finds herself leading a fight to save mankind. (Rev: SLJ 5/04)

882 Whitcomb, Laura. *A Certain Slant of Light* (9–12). 2005, Houghton paper $8.99 (0-618-58532-X). 288pp. In this truly haunting romance, Helen — dead for 130 years — continues to exist in spirit form, but it's not until James comes along that anyone has been able to truly see her. (Rev: BL 11/15/05; HB 11–12/05; SLJ 9/05; VOYA 2/06)

Humor

883 Acampora, Paul. *Defining Dulcie* (7–10). 2006, Dial $16.99 (0-8037-3046-2). 176pp. Dulcie may only be 16 but she knows her own mind, and when her mother moves her to California following her janitor father's death, Dulcie drives home to Connecticut and lives with her janitor grandfather. (Rev: BL 4/1/06*; SLJ 4/06*; VOYA 4/06)

884 Bacus, K. C. *Calamity Jayne* (11–12). 2006, Dorchester paper $5.99 (0-505-52665-4). 352pp. Followed by trouble wherever she goes, Tressa Jayne Turner gets involved in some serious difficulties when she accidentally takes someone else's car and discovers a large amount of cash and a corpse in its trunk; entertaining fare for mature teens. (Rev: BL 12/15/05)

885 Bradley, Alex. *24 Girls in 7 Days* (8–11). 2005, Dutton $15.99 (0-525-47369-6). 272pp. Dateless only two weeks before the senior prom, Jack is desperate, so desperate that two of his friends run a personal ad in the school paper in an effort to get Jack a date. (Rev: BL 1/1–15/05; SLJ 3/05; VOYA 2/05)

886 Burnham, Niki. *Spin Control* (8–10). 2005, Simon & Schuster paper $5.99 (0-689-86669-0). 245pp. Valerie is desperately unhappy when she's forced to leave Schwerinborg and her prince boyfriend and return to Virginia, but a reunion with an old boyfriend soon eases her pain in this sequel to *Royally Jacked* (2004). (Rev: SLJ 2/05)

887 Cabot, Meg. *Princess in Training* (7–10). 2005, HarperCollins $16.99 (0-06-009613-6). 288pp. Princess Mia's current worries range from English and geometry, running for student council president, and her college boyfriend's expectations, to her new baby brother and the ecology of the Bay of Genovia. (Rev: BL 8/05; SLJ 6/05; VOYA 8/05)

888 Cabot, Meg. *Ready or Not* (9–12). Series: All-American Girl. 2005, HarperCollins LB $16.89 (0-06-072451-X). 256pp. Samantha is still dating the president's son in this sequel to *All-American Girl* (2002) but she's conflicted about having sex with him. (Rev: BL 9/15/05; SLJ 10/05)

889 Dent, Grace. *LBD: Live and Fabulous!* (7–10). 2005, Penguin $15.99 (0-399-24188-4). 288pp. In this engaging sequel to *LBD: It's a Girl Thing*, Les Bambinos Dangereuses — Fleur, Ronnie, and Claude — land free tickets to a big musical festival. (Rev: BL 3/1/05; HB 3–4/05; SLJ 3/05)

890 Ehrenhaft, Daniel. *Tell It to Naomi* (7–12). 2004, Random LB $9.99 (0-385-73129-9). 208pp. In a convoluted scheme to win the heart of his secret crush, 15-year-old Dave Rosen covertly pens a high school advice column called "Dear Naomi." (Rev: BL 9/15/04; SLJ 8/04; VOYA 8/04)

891 Ehrenhaft, Daniel. *10 Things to Do Before I Die* (8–12). 2004, Random LB $17.99 (0-385-73007-1). 224pp. Sixteen-year-old Ted Burger believes he is dying and sets out to achieve the goals his friends had urged him to experience — losing his virginity, telling the truth, robbing a bank, and more. (Rev: BL 11/1/04; SLJ 11/04)

892 Gerber, Michael. *Freshman* (10–12). 2006, Hyperion $16.99 (0-7868-3850-7). 336pp. A satirical look at elite college admissions and campus life, in which Hart Fox accepts an assignment to look

after the local millionaire's son in exchange for free tuition. (Rev: BL 4/1/06; SLJ 4/06)

893 Greenland, Seth. *The Bones: A Novel* (10–12). 2005, Bloomsbury $24.95 (1-58234-550-3). 400pp. Frank Bones, a comedian who's temporarily down on his luck, gets a chance to break into television with his own sitcom, but he'll have to play a walrus-riding Eskimo. (Rev: SLJ 4/05)

894 Hautman, Pete. *Godless* (7–10). 2004, Simon & Schuster $15.95 (0-689-86278-4). 208pp. Rebelling against his devoutly Catholic father, 16-year-old Jason Block and his best friend Shin create a religion of their own with the town's water tower as the deity. (Rev: BL 6/1–15/04*; HB 7–8/04; SLJ 8/04; VOYA 10/04)

895 Howard, Heather H. *Chore Whore: Adventures of a Celebrity Personal Assistant* (11–12). 2005, HarperCollins $23.95 (0-06-072391-2). 288pp. Howard, a former personal assistant to celebrities, pens a fictionalized tell-all about a single mom who's had it with her Hollywood clients' demands; for mature teens. (Rev: BL 2/15/05)

896 Limb, Sue. *Girl, (Nearly) 16: Absolute Torture* (7–10). 2005, Delacorte LB $17.99 (0-385-90245-X). 224pp. In this appealing sequel to *Girl, 15, Charming But Insane*, Jess Jordan is taken on a two-week trip to visit her long-absent father just as her romance with Fred is beginning to intensify. (Rev: BL 10/1/05; SLJ 12/05; VOYA 10/05)

897 Liss, David. *The Ethical Assassin* (11–12). 2006, Ballantine $24.95 (1-4000-6421-X). 336pp. Lemuel Altick, a 17-year-old high school graduate who sells encyclopedias to help finance his college education, finds himself the unlikely ally of a wild-haired man who shot and killed two of Lem's prospective customers in this offbeat novel suitable for mature teens. (Rev: BL 12/1/05)

898 Maxwell, Katie. *They Wear What Under Their Kilts?* (8–11). 2004, Dorchester paper $5.99 (0-8439-5258-X). 208pp. Emily Williams, the 16-year-old American introduced in the riotous *The Year My Life Went Down the Loo*, is off to a Scottish sheep farm on a month-long work-study program. (Rev: BL 1/1–15/04)

899 Milligan, J. *Jack Fish: A Novel* (10–12). 2005, Soho $23.00 (1-56947-382-X). 224pp. Jack Fish, a denizen of the deep, is assigned by the Elders of Atlantis to handle a sensitive mission on dry land in this funny look at life in New York City. (Rev: SLJ 6/05)

900 Niederhoffer, Galt. *A Taxonomy of Barnacles* (11–12). 2006, St. Martin's $24.95 (0-312-33483-4). 384pp. When Barry Barnacle declares that he will leave his entire estate to the daughter who can find a way to immortalize the family name, the Barnacle girls — part of a wacky family full of fun and appetites — happily accept his challenge; for mature teens. (Rev: BL 11/15/05)

901 Parkhurst, Carolyn. *Lost and Found* (11–12). 2006, Little, Brown $23.95 (0-316-15638-8). 304pp. The diverse teams competing in a reality show called "Lost and Found" all find their relationships and aspirations challenged as the game proceeds; for mature teens. (Rev: BL 3/1/06)

902 Rennison, Louise. *Away Laughing on a Fast Camel: Even More Confessions of Georgia Nicolson* (7–10). 2004, HarperCollins $15.99 (0-06-058934-5). 288pp. Georgia finds that her interest in Robby the Sex God fades fast when he goes off to New Zealand. (Rev: BL 9/1/04; SLJ 11/04; VOYA 10/04)

903 Rennison, Louise. *Then He Ate My Boy Entrancers: More Mad, Marvy Confessions of Georgia Nicolson* (7–10). 2005, HarperCollins $15.99 (0-06-058937-X). 320pp. In her sixth volume of diaries, Georgia travels to and critiques the United States as well as cataloging her usual problems at home with friends, boyfriends, siblings, and cats. (Rev: BL 8/05; SLJ 8/05; VOYA 10/05)

904 Sheldon, Dyan. *Sophie Pitt-Turnbull Discovers America* (7–10). 2005, Candlewick $15.99 (0-7636-2740-2). 192pp. Privileged English teenager Sophie is totally unprepared for what awaits her when she spends the summer in Brooklyn. (Rev: BCCB 5/05; BL 4/1/05; SLJ 6/05)

905 Swendson, Shanna. *Enchanted, Inc* (9–12). 2005, Ballantine paper $12.95 (0-345-48125-9). 320pp. Katie Chandler is 26, living in a New York City full of fairies, elves, and other magical beings, and — it turns out — valuable for the fact that she does not have any special powers. (Rev: BL 5/15/05; SLJ 9/05)

906 Tropper, Jonathan. *Everything Changes* (11–12). 2005, Delacorte $20.00 (0-385-33807-4). 335pp. In his early 30s, Zach King has fiancée problems, a difficult father, a job he doesn't like, sad memories of a dead friend, and blood in his urine in this romantic comedy. (Rev: BL 3/15/05)

907 Vizzini, Ned. *Be More Chill: A Novel* (9–12). 2004, Hyperion $16.95 (0-7868-0995-7). 304pp. Desperate to become cool and accepted by the school's elite, high school geek Jeremy Heere swallows a pill-sized supercomputer that promises to help him achieve his goal but discovers that this quick fix has a downside; a funny novel that includes profanity and sex. (Rev: BL 8/04; SLJ 6/04; VOYA 6/04)

908 Wilkins, Rose. *So Super Stylish* (7–11). 2006, Dial $16.99 (0-8037-3064-0). 288pp. Privileged Octavia Clairbrook-Cleve, who transferred to the local school in *So Super Starry* (2004), is adjusting well to her new environment until her nemesis India Withers turns up, researching the school for her role

in a movie. (Rev: BL 2/15/06; SLJ 3/06; VOYA 4/06)

909 Wood, Maryrose. *Sex Kittens and Horn Dawgs Fall in Love* (7–10). 2006, Delacorte LB $17.99 (0-385-90296-4). 192pp. To get closer to Matthew, the object of her affection, 14-year-old Felicia suggests that the two of them work together on a science fair project investigating the workings of love's "X-factor." (Rev: BL 11/15/05; SLJ 2/06)

Mysteries, Thrillers, and Spy Stories

910 Abrahams, Peter. *Down the Rabbit Hole* (7–10). Series: Echo Falls. 2005, HarperCollins LB $16.89 (0-06-073702-6). 384pp. Thirteen-year-old Ingrid Levin-Hill takes a page from her idol Sherlock Holmes and sets out to track down the murderer of an eccentric townswoman. (Rev: BCCB 4/05; BL 5/1/05*; SLJ 5/05; VOYA 6/05)

911 Adamson, Isaac. *Kinki Lullaby* (9–12). 2004, HarperCollins paper $13.95 (0-06-051624-0). 368pp. In the fourth, colorful book in the series, Billy Chaka investigates a mystery and a murder in the Osaka district of Japan. (Rev: BL 9/1/04; SLJ 2/05)

912 Alphin, Elaine Marie. *The Perfect Shot* (8–12). 2005, Carolrhoda LB $16.95 (1-57505-862-6). 360pp. Brian, a high school basketball star, learns important lessons about justice, racial prejudice, and civic responsibility when his girlfriend's father is charged with the murder of his wife and two daughters and an African American teammate is arrested on trumped-up charges. (Rev: SLJ 10/05*; VOYA 12/05)

913 Altman, Steven-Elliot, et al. *The Irregulars: . . . In the Service of Sherlock Holmes* (7–12). Illus. 2005, Dark Horse paper $12.95 (1-59307-303-8). 128pp. In this suspenseful graphic novel, Holmes assigns the Baker Street Irregulars to find out who's responsible for a murder for which Dr. Watson has been charged. (Rev: BL 5/1/05)

914 Barr, Nevada. *High Country* (10–12). 2004, Penguin $24.95 (0-399-15144-3). 323pp. Ranger Anna Pigeon assumes the guise of a waitress to investigate the disappearance of four young Yosemite workers and, on a wilderness hike, she comes across some very dangerous villains. (Rev: BCCB 2/04; SLJ 6/04)

915 Barron, Stephanie. *Jane and His Lordship's Legacy* (10–12). 2005, Bantam $24.00 (0-553-80225-9). 304pp. Sleuth Jane Austen, mourning roguish Lord Harold's death, moves to Chawton Cottage with her mother and finds there is a body in the basement. (Rev: BL 2/15/05)

916 Beaton, M. C. *Death of a Poison Pen: A Hamish Macbeth Mystery* (10–12). 2004, Mysterious $23.95 (0-89296-788-9). 244pp. The independent-minded Constable Hamish Macbeth looks into a spate of unpleasant letters and a rash of murders and suicides in this mystery full of humor and romance, set in the Scottish Highlands. (Rev: SLJ 7/04)

917 Bone, Ian. *Sleep Rough Tonight* (8–12). 2005, Dutton $16.99 (0-525-47373-4). 276pp. Set in Australia, this is a harrowing story about Alex, who lacks self-confidence, and his submission to a bullying older boy who takes him on an urban survival trip. (Rev: BCCB 5/05; BL 4/15/05; SLJ 5/05; VOYA 4/05)

918 Brasme, Anne Sophie. *Breathe* (9–12). Trans. by Roy Mulholland. 2004, St. Martin's paper $9.95 (0-312-33153-3). 128pp. Charlene's obsession with Sarah leads to murder in this compelling novel. (Rev: BL 9/1/04)

919 Burke, Morgan. *Last Call* (9–12). Series: The Party Room. 2005, Simon & Schuster paper $5.99 (0-689-87227-5). 253pp. In the final volume of the trilogy, Kirsten Sawyer, now a student at NYU, looks into a student suicide that may really have been a murder. (Rev: SLJ 11/05)

920 Burt, Guy. *A Clock Without Hands* (11–12). 2004, Ballantine $24.95 (0-345-44656-9). 448pp. English artist Alex Carlisle returns to Italy, where as a child he and two friends made a decision that still haunts him; for mature teens. (Rev: BL 9/1/04; SLJ 1/05)

921 Chamberlain, Diane. *The Bay at Midnight* (11–12). 2005, MIRA $19.95 (0-7783-2146-0). 384pp. When new evidence suggests that the wrong man was convicted in the death of her teenaged sister 41 years before, writer Julie is plunged into real mystery — and romance; for mature teens. (Rev: BL 12/15/04)

922 Chan, Cassandra. *The Young Widow* (10–12). 2005, St. Martin's $23.95 (0-312-33748-5). 290pp. A police procedural in which Sgt. Jack Gibbons of New Scotland Yard and Philip Betancourt, an amateur detective, strive to solve a poisoning in which there are several suspects including the attractive widow Annette. (Rev: SLJ 1/06)

923 Coel, Margaret. *Killing Raven* (11–12). 2003, Prime $22.95 (0-425-19261-X). 288pp. As the murder of a white man and dissent over the new casino cause heightened tensions on and off the reservation, Arapaho lawyer Vicky Holden and her good friend Father John O'Malley investigate. (Rev: SLJ 5/04)

924 Conwell, Kent. *Skeletons of the Atchafalaya* (10–12). 2003, Avalon $19.95 (0-8034-9628-1). 192pp. A hurricane isolates private detective Tony Boudreaux in a house with a Louisiana family and

at least one murderer in this tense thriller. (Rev: SLJ 1/04)

925 Cree, Ronald. *Desert Blood 10pm/9c* (8–11). 2006, Simon & Schuster paper $7.99 (1-4169-1156-1). 320pp. It's not clear to Gus Gonzalez why TV star Nicolas Hernandez adopted him, and the mystery deepens as he starts to receive threats and friends begin to disappear. (Rev: BL 2/15/06; SLJ 4/06)

926 Crichton, Michael. *State of Fear* (9–12). 2005, HarperCollins $27.95 (0-06-621413-0). 606pp. In a scientific thriller presupposing that global warming's threat has been overblown, eco-terrorists in Antarctica plot to convince the world otherwise. (Rev: BL 1/1–15/05)

927 Cussler, Clive, and Paul Kemprecos. *Lost City: A Kurt Austin Adventure* (9–12). Series: NUMA Files. 2004, Penguin $26.95 (0-399-15177-X). 420pp. Kurt Austin, leader of the National Underwater Marine Agency's Special Assignments Team, is involved in an exciting adventure involving a life-prolonging enzyme found deep underwater. (Rev: BL 9/1/04; SLJ 11/04)

928 Dumas, Margaret. *Speak Now* (10–12). 2004, Poisoned Pen $24.95 (1-59058-121-0). 326pp. Charley Van Leeuwen, manager of a repertory theater company, returns from a yearlong working trip to London with a new husband, but things start to go terribly wrong when the couple finds a dead body in their hotel suite. (Rev: BL 9/1/04; SLJ 1/05)

929 Dyja, Thomas. *The Moon in Our Hands* (11–12). 2005, Carroll & Graf $25.00 (0-7867-1505-7). 362pp. A fictionalized account of Walter White, a light-skinned young African American recruited by the NAACP in 1918 to perform undercover investigations of lynching in the South; violence restricts this to mature teens. (Rev: BL 2/1/05)

930 Fackler, Elizabeth. *Endless River* (11–12). 2005, Five Star $25.95 (1-59414-270-X). 226pp. Spurned by Amy, sociopathic high schooler Zeb Mulroney, abetted by his wealthy family, concocts an elaborate plan to exact revenge; based on a true story. (Rev: BL 3/1/05)

931 Farris, John. *Phantom Nights* (11–12). 2005, Tor $24.95 (0-765-30778-2). 304pp. In 1952, a small-town sheriff reluctantly investigates a Tennessee politician for the rape and murder of Mally, an African American nurse whose ghost remains restless; for mature teens. (Rev: BL 2/1/05)

932 Fforde, Jasper. *The Big Over Easy* (11–12). 2005, Viking $24.95 (0-670-03423-1). 400pp. Detective Inspector Jack Spratt and Detective Sergeant Mary Mary of the Nursery Crime Division investigate the death of Humpty Dumpty in this mystery/fantasy for lovers of puns. (Rev: BL 6/1–15/05)

933 Fielding, Helen. *Olivia Joules and the Overactive Imagination* (11–12). 2004, Viking $24.95 (0-670-03333-2). 306pp. Olivia suspects that a man she meets while on assignment in Miami might be a terrorist in this entertaining novel for mature readers by the author of *Bridget Jones's Diary* (1998). (Rev: BL 7/04)

934 Galloway, Gregory. *As Simple as Snow* (9–12). 2005, Penguin $23.95 (0-399-15231-8). 320pp. The teen narrator of this meandering, ambiguous, and yet compelling novel decides to find out why his quirky Goth girlfriend has vanished. (Rev: BL 1/1–15/05; SLJ 5/05)

935 Gellis, Roberta. *Chains of Folly* (9–12). 2006, Five Star $25.95 (1-59414-472-9). 320pp. In 12th-century London, Magdalene la Batarde and Sir Bellamy investigate the death of a prostitute found in the Bishop of Winchester's room. (Rev: BL 3/1/06)

936 Golden, Christopher, and Rick Hautala. *Throat Culture* (8–11). Series: Body of Evidence. 2005, Simon & Schuster paper $5.99 (0-689-86527-9). 247pp. College sophomore Jenna Blake investigates the mysterious illness that has stricken her father's new bride. (Rev: BL 5/1/05; SLJ 7/05)

937 Goodman, Carol. *The Ghost Orchid* (9–12). 2006, Ballantine $24.95 (0-345-46213-0). 368pp. Fledgling writer Ellis Brooks comes to Bosco, a Victorian mansion in upstate New York that serves as an artist's colony, to write a book about the house's lurid and violent past; alarming events ensue. (Rev: BL 12/1/05)

938 Grant, Vicki. *Quid Pro Quo* (7–10). 2005, Orca $16.95 (1-55143-394-X); paper $7.95 (1-55143-370-2). 168pp. When his mother — newly graduated from law school — suddenly disappears, 13-year-old Cyril Floyd MacIntyre tries to unravel the mystery surrounding her disappearance. (Rev: SLJ 6/05)

939 Gross, Philip. *Turn to Stone* (7–10). 2005, Dial $16.99 (0-8037-3005-5). 224pp. Nick, a 16-year-old runaway, and Swan, a street performer who specializes in posing as a statue, are selected to join a special school for immobilists, but they soon realize that the school harbors some dark secrets. (Rev: BCCB 3/05; BL 4/15/05; SLJ 8/05; VOYA 4/05)

940 Hartinger, Brent. *The Last Chance Texaco* (6–10). 2004, HarperCollins LB $16.89 (0-06-050913-9). 240pp. When authorities threaten to close down a group foster home for troubled teens because they suspect one of its residents is responsible for a series of car fires, 15-year-old Lucy Pitt decides to track down the real culprit. (Rev: BCCB 3/04; BL 1/1–15/04; SLJ 3/04; VOYA 2/04)

941 Hillerman, Tony. *Skeleton Man* (9–12). 2004, HarperCollins $25.95 (0-06-056344-3). 256pp. Joe Leaphorn, a retired Navajo Tribal Police lieutenant, tries to track down diamonds that went to the bottom of the Grand Canyon in a 1956 airplane crash. (Rev: BL 9/15/04; SLJ 2/05)

942 Hillerman, Tony, and Rosemary Herbert, eds. *A New Omnibus of Crime* (10–12). 2005, Oxford $30.00 (0-195-18214-6). 464pp. This anthology of short-form crime fiction shows how this popular genre has evolved from the 1930s through the present. (Rev: BL 10/15/05)

943 Holder, Nancy. *Pretty Little Devils* (9–12). 2006, Penguin $14.99 (1-59514-030-1). 256pp. A tense story about a close-knit clique of high school girls and the violence that surfaces around it. (Rev: BL 2/15/06; SLJ 2/06)

944 Horowitz, Anthony. *Scorpia* (8–11). Series: Alex Rider Adventure. 2005, Penguin $17.99 (0-399-24151-5). 320pp. Teenage spy Alex Rider infiltrates a terrorist organization called Scorpia. (Rev: BL 2/1/05; SLJ 3/05; VOYA 4/05)

945 Jaffe, Michele. *Bad Kitty* (9–12). 2006, HarperCollins LB $17.89 (0-06-078109-2). 288pp. A funny first-person narrative recounting 17-year-old Jasmine's participation in the investigation of a mystery in Las Vegas. (Rev: BL 1/1–15/06; SLJ 2/06; VOYA 2/06)

946 Johansen, Iris. *Blind Alley* (11–12). 2004, Bantam $25.00 (0-553-80341-7). 336pp. Jane's face, which echoes that of a woman who died long ago, is putting her life in danger and Joe Quinn is on the case in this international thriller suitable for mature teens. (Rev: BL 8/04)

947 Johansen, Iris. *Countdown* (11–12). 2005, Bantam $25.00 (0-553-80342-5). 416pp. Jane MacGuire, who bears an uncanny resemblance to an ancient Roman woman called Cira, faces dangerous terrorists in this third book about the plucky young lady with a difficult background; for mature teens. (Rev: BL 4/15/05)

948 Kaminsky, Stuart M. *Now You See It* (10–12). 2004, Carroll & Graf $25.00 (0-7867-1423-9). 240pp. A mystery set in 1940s Hollywood in which a famous magician finds his life and his illusions in danger. (Rev: BL 10/1/04)

949 Kane, Andrea. *Wrong Place, Wrong Time* (11–12). 2006, Morrow $21.95 (0-06-074132-5). 336pp. In this action-packed romantic thriller suitable for mature teens, veterinarian Devon Montgomery vows to find out who killed her mother's friend but finds herself strongly attracted to the man who is at the top of the suspect list. (Rev: BL 12/1/05)

950 Koontz, Dean. *Velocity* (11–12). 2005, Bantam $27.00 (0-553-80415-4). 401pp. A tense thriller in which a serial killer targets a bartender called Willy, selecting people Willy knows as his victims and planting evidence implicating Willy in the crimes; for mature teens. (Rev: BL 5/1/05; SLJ 9/05)

951 Lowell, Elizabeth. *Always Time to Die* (11–12). 2005, Morrow $24.95 (0-06-050415-3). 352pp. Carly May, an orphan who specializes in genealogy, finds herself in danger as she investigates a prominent New Mexico family; for mature teens. (Rev: BL 6/1–15/05)

952 Lupica, Mike. *Too Far* (9–12). 2005, Penguin $24.95 (0-399-15210-5). 304pp. Ben Mitchell comes out of retirement from journalism to investigate suspicious happenings on the South Fork High School basketball team. (Rev: BL 11/15/04)

953 McGown, Jill. *Unlucky for Some: A Novel of Suspense* (9–12). 2005, Ballantine $22.95 (0-345-47655-7). 368pp. Detectives Danny Lloyd and Judy Hill, with help from journalist Tony Baker, investigate a suspicious death that may be the work of a serial killer. (Rev: SLJ 7/05)

954 McNab, Andy, and Robert Rigby. *Traitor* (10–12). 2005, Penguin $15.99 (0-399-24464-6). 288pp. Orphan Danny Watts sets out to discover the truth about his grandfather in this British adventure story. (Rev: BL 10/15/05; SLJ 1/06; VOYA 4/06)

955 Madison, Bennett. *Lulu Dark Can See Through Walls* (7–10). 2005, Penguin $9.99 (1-59514-010-7). 256pp. Lulu Dark, a junior at an exclusive high school, turns detective after the theft of her purse leads to a case of stolen identity in this lighthearted mystery. (Rev: BCCB 6/05; BL 5/1/05; SLJ 6/05; VOYA 8/05)

956 Marks, Graham. *Zoo* (8–11). 2005, Bloomsbury paper $8.95 (1-58234-991-6). 272pp. A complex and suspenseful adventure story in which 17-year-old Cam escapes from kidnappers only to find that he has a mysterious chip in his arm and his parents may have been involved in his capture. (Rev: BL 9/15/05; SLJ 10/05; VOYA 8/05)

957 Michaels, Kasey. *High Heels and Homicide* (11–12). 2005, Kensington paper $14.00 (0-7582-0880-4). 288pp. Regency romance author Maggie Kelly gets more than she bargained for when she heads to England to watch one of her books made into a film in this funny critique of the movie making; for mature teens. (Rev: BL 11/1/05)

958 Miller, Linda Lael. *One Last Look* (11–12). 2005, Pocket paper $13.00 (0-7374-7050-8). 320pp. Longing for some peace and quiet (and pregnant with his child), trouble-attracting attorney Clare Westbrook follows her fiancé, detective Tony Sonterra, to a new job in a small Arizona town; the last volume in a romantic suspense trilogy suitable for mature readers. (Rev: BL 10/1/05)

959 Moloney, James. *Black Taxi* (8–11). 2005, HarperCollins LB $16.89 (0-06-055938-1). 272pp. When her grandfather is sent to jail for six months, 16-year-old Rosie Sinclair is appointed caretaker of his eye-catching black Mercedes; she enlists the help of her friends — one an attractive young man

— when she starts getting threatening phone calls. (Rev: BCCB 5/05; BL 3/1/05; SLJ 3/05; VOYA 8/05)

960 Morgenroth, Kate. *Jude* (9–12). 2004, Simon & Schuster $16.95 (0-689-86479-5). 288pp. Still in shock from witnessing the murder of his drug-dealing father, 15-year-old Jude is tricked into pleading guilty to a crime he didn't commit to help advance his mother's political career. (Rev: BL 11/15/04; SLJ 11/04)

961 Mortman, Doris. *Shades of Red* (11–12). 2005, St. Martin's $24.95 (0-312-27558-7). 368pp. Vera Hunt, a character very similar to the real-life Martha Stewart, finds her life in danger and her daughters in conflict with each other. (Rev: BL 11/15/04)

962 Nelscott, Kris. *War at Home* (10–12). 2005, St. Martin's $24.95 (0-312-32527-4). 368pp. In the fifth mystery featuring African American PI Smokey Dalton, the search for a missing Yale student leads him to New Haven and New York during the turbulence of 1969. (Rev: BL 2/15/05)

963 Pascal, Francine. *Fearless FBI: Kill Game* (8–11). Series: Fearless FBI. 2005, Simon & Schuster paper $7.99 (0-689-87821-4). 240pp. Despite her unreliability, the FBI invites intrepid Gaia — of the earlier Fearless series — to try their boot camp training program. (Rev: BL 8/05; SLJ 6/05)

964 Poirier, Mark Jude. *Modern Ranch Living* (11–12). 2004, Hyperion $23.95 (1-4013-0042-1). 304pp. Sixteen-year-old fitness fanatic Kendra, her older brother, and a neighbor Merv find themselves working together to solve a mystery one hot Tucson summer; for mature teens. (Rev: BL 9/1/04)

965 Reed, Terry. *The Full Cleveland* (11–12). 2005, Simon & Schuster $22.00 (0-7432-6273-5). 256pp. Cleveland P.I. Milan Jacovich investigates ad sales — some made to the Mob — by a shady magazine "publisher" whose staffers are being murdered; for mature teens. (Rev: BL 1/1–15/05)

966 Riccio, Dolores Stewart. *The Divine Circle of Ladies Making Mischief* (11–12). 2005, Kensington paper $14.00 (0-7582-0986-X). 320pp. A group of Wiccan crime fighters returns for a humorous third caper, led by Cass, a feisty entrepreneur who chats telepathically with her dog Scruffy. (Rev: BL 2/15/05)

967 Riccio, Dolores Stewart. *Ladies Courting Trouble* (11–12). 2006, Kensington paper $14.00 (0-7582-0987-8). 320pp. The five Wiccan women featured in *Circle of Five* (2003) must teach the minister's wife some arcane skills when the minister is a potential target. (Rev: BL 3/1/06)

968 Richards, Linda L. *Mad Money* (11–12). Series: Madeline Carter. 2004, MIRA paper $6.50 (0-7783-2103-7). 384pp. Madeline's stockbroker ex gives her a bad tip then turns up missing in this fast-paced corporate murder mystery/thriller/romance. (Rev: BL 11/15/04)

969 Robards, Karen. *Bait* (11–12). 2004, Penguin $24.95 (0-399-15202-4). 352pp. FBI agent Sam McCabe finds love — and a new canine friend — while chasing down a serial killer in this gripping and suspenseful mystery; for mature readers. (Rev: BL 6/1–15/04)

970 Rose, Malcolm. *Framed!* (7–10). Series: Traces. 2005, Kingfisher paper $5.95 (0-7534-5829-2). 232pp. In this futuristic mystery novel, 16-year-old Luke Harding, newly graduated from forensics training, is assigned to investigate the murder of a classmate. (Rev: BL 5/1/05; SLJ 7/05)

971 Russell, Kirk. *Dead Game* (10–12). 2005, Chronicle $23.95 (0-8118-5078-1). 320pp. Marquez, the Fish and Game warden, is on the track of sturgeon poachers and kidnappers in this gripping ecothriller. (Rev: BL 8/05)

972 Russell, Kirk. *Night Game* (11–12). 2004, Chronicle $23.95 (0-8118-4112-X). 368pp. Department of Fish and Game officer John Marquez, introduced in *Shell Games* (2003), tracks down a murderous bear-poaching ring. (Rev: BL 9/15/04)

973 Saylor, Steven. *A Gladiator Dies Only Once: The Further Investigations of Gordianus the Finder* (9–12). 2005, St. Martin's $23.95 (0-312-27120-4). 288pp. Nine compelling stories about Gordianus the Finder's early successes in solving mysteries convey a lot of information about life in ancient Rome. (Rev: BL 4/1/05)

974 Schmidt, Gary. *First Boy* (7–10). 2005, Holt $16.95 (0-8050-7859-2). 208pp. With the help of kind neighbors, 14-year-old Cooper hopes to be able to live alone on his grandparents' farm, but questions about his missing parents seem linked to politics and the presidential elections. (Rev: BCCB 2/06; BL 9/15/05; HB 9–10/05; SLJ 10/05; VOYA 4/06)

975 Scrimger, Richard. *From Charlie's Point of View* (7–10). 2005, Dutton $10.99 (0-525-47374-2). 288pp. Fourteen-year-old Charlie is blind, but best friend Bernadette acts as his eyes, and together they set out to prove that Charlie's dad had nothing to do with a series of neighborhood ATM thefts. (Rev: BCCB 9/05; BL 5/1/05; SLJ 8/05)

976 Simmons, Michael. *Finding Lubchenko* (7–10). 2005, Penguin paper $16.99 (1-59514-021-2). 281pp. Evan Macalister, a 16-year-old slacker, steals high-value computer equipment from his father's business and sells it for spending cash, but he faces a moral dilemma when he discovers evidence that could clear his father of murder charges on a laptop he's stolen; a funny, offbeat novel. (Rev: BCCB 7–8/05; SLJ 6/05; VOYA 12/04)

977 Sloan, Kay. *The Patron Saint of Red Chevys: A Novel* (11–12). 2004, Permanent $21.95 (1-57962-

104-X). 221pp. Years after her mother was murdered in Mississippi, daughter Jubilee Starling, who has made a new life for herself in California, looks back and decides to investigate. (Rev: BL 6/1–15/04; SLJ 12/04)

978 Soos, Troy. *Burning Bridges* (9–12). 2004, Kensington paper $6.99 (0-7582-0624-0). 320pp. In late 19th-century New York, passions run high regarding merging Manhattan and Brooklyn — even to the point of murder? (Rev: SLJ 12/04)

979 Sorrells, Walter. *Club Dread* (8–11). 2006, Dutton paper $10.99 (0-525-47618-0). 256pp. In this thrilling, action-packed sequel to *Fake I.D.* (2004), 16-year-old Chass has formed a band in San Francisco but witnesses a murder and becomes drawn into the investigation. (Rev: BL 1/1–15/06; SLJ 3/06)

980 Sorrells, Walter. *Fake I.D.* (8–11). 2005, Dutton $10.99 (0-525-47514-1). 256pp. On the run with her mother since she was a baby, 16-year-old Chastity Pureheart has only six days to find out what happened to her mother or face placement in foster care. (Rev: BL 5/1/05*; SLJ 6/05)

981 Speart, Jessica. *Restless Waters* (11–12). 2005, Severn $28.95 (0-7278-6274-X). 300pp. Now working in Hawaii, Fish and Wildlife agent Rachel Porter uncovers illegal animal trading in a fast-paced novel suitable for mature teens. (Rev: BL 7/05)

982 Stabenow, Dana. *Blindfold Game* (10–12). 2006, St. Martin's $23.95 (0-312-34323-X). 272pp. In this gripping thriller suitable for mature teens, Hugh Rincon, an Alaskan native working for the CIA far from home, learns of plans for a terrorist attack in Alaska and must warn his wife, Sara, who works for the Coast Guard in Alaskan waters. (Rev: BL 11/1/05)

983 Stewart, Sean. *Perfect Circle* (9–12). 2004, Small Beer $24.00 (1-931520-07-0); paper $15.00 (1-931520-11-9). 248pp. DK, a down-on-his-luck father who communicates with the dead, finds himself in the middle of a ghostly murder mystery. (Rev: BL 6/1–15/04)

984 Sturman, Jennifer. *The Jinx* (10–12). 2005, Red Dress Ink paper $12.95 (0-373-89540-2). 320pp. In this sequel to *The Pact* (2004), investment banker Rachel Benjamin's trip to Boston to do a little business and visit her boyfriend does not go as she expected. (Rev: BL 12/15/05)

985 Thomas, John Ira, and Jeremy Smith. *The Fairer Sex: A Tale of Shades and Angels*, Vol. 1 (11–12). Illus. 2004, Candle Light paper $13.95 (0-9743147-5-7). 136pp. In this gripping graphic novel mystery, homicide detectives Tom and Fred try to track down the woman responsible for gunning down multiple victims in a shooting at the local mall; for mature readers. (Rev: BL 10/1/04)

986 Truman, Margaret. *Murder at Union Station* (9–12). Series: Capital Crime. 2004, Ballantine $24.95 (0-345-44490-6). 336pp. A murder in Washington, D.C., has politicians, journalists, and others jockeying for power. (Rev: BL 9/1/04; SLJ 3/05)

987 Updale, Eleanor. *Montmorency and the Assassins* (7–10). 2006, Scholastic $16.99 (0-439-68343-2). 416pp. Montmorency and Lord George Selwyn-Fox, plus some teen helpers, investigate bomb-planting anarchists in this Victorian mystery that ranges from London to Florence to New Jersey. (Rev: BL 3/15/06; VOYA 2/06)

988 Walker, Sue. *The Reunion* (11–12). 2004, Morrow $24.95 (0-06-072609-1). 320pp. A horrifying camping trip for disturbed teenagers leads to death and violence years later; for mature teens. (Rev: BL 8/04)

989 Wan, Michelle. *Deadly Slipper* (11–12). 2005, Doubleday $23.95 (0-385-51457-3). 320pp. After discovering a camera with shots of wild orchids in the Dordogne, a woman sets out to find out more about the disappearance of her twin sister nearly 20 years before; for mature teens. (Rev: BL 5/1/05)

990 Ward, Liza. *Outside Valentine* (11–12). 2004, Holt $23.00 (0-8050-7598-4). 304pp. A moving, multilayered novel based on the murderous rampage of Charles Starkweather and his 14-year-old girlfriend in the 1950s; suitable for mature teens. (Rev: BL 8/04; SLJ 2/05)

991 Wesley, Valerie Wilson. *Dying in the Dark* (10–12). 2004, Ballantine $22.95 (0-345-46806-6). 240pp. When an old high school friend with a complicated past is murdered, Tamara takes on the case, revisiting her old stomping grounds in New Jersey. (Rev: BL 9/1/04)

992 Westerfeld, Scott. *So Yesterday* (7–12). 2004, Penguin $16.99 (1-59514-000-X). 240pp. Two teenagers who help big companies identify coming trends in the consumer marketplace find themselves caught up in a mystery when their boss disappears. (Rev: BL 9/15/04; SLJ 10/04; VOYA 10/04)

993 Wilde, Lori. *You Only Love Twice* (11–12). 2006, Warner paper $6.50 (0-446-61516-1). 360pp. Adventure, suspense, and romance are combined in this action-packed tale about a female cartoonist whose government conspiracy plots enrage some readers and the Naval Intelligence agent assigned to protect her; for mature teens. (Rev: BL 2/15/06)

994 Wootson, Alice. *Aloha Love* (11–12). 2005, BET paper $6.99 (1-58314-538-9). 320pp. In a novel laced with romance and government intrigue, Hawaiian helicopter pilot Jeanine Stewart survives a suspicious crash along with her interesting passenger, but is later troubled by a mysterious federal agent; for mature teens. (Rev: BL 1/1–15/05)

Romances

995 Ahern, Cecelia. *Rosie Dunne* (9–12). 2005, Hyperion $22.95 (1-4013-0091-X). 448pp. Four decades of correspondence between Alex and his best friend Rosie reveal the pitfalls and triumphs of their intense relationship. (Rev: BL 1/1–15/05)

996 Anderson, Catherine. *My Sunshine* (11–12). 2005, Signet paper $6.99 (0-451-21380-7). 432pp. Laura, living with brain damage from a swimming accident, accepts a job as a kennel keeper and her joie de vivre and skill with animals intrigue her boss, vet Isaiah Coulter; a warm novel suitable for mature teens. (Rev: BL 1/1–15/05)

997 Ashton, Victoria. *Rich Girls: A Novel* (9–12). Series: Confessions of a Teen Nanny. 2006, HarperCollins LB $16.89 (0-06-077525-4). 208pp. Romantic intrigue is at the center of this light and fast-paced second volume about the antics of the wealthy. (Rev: SLJ 3/06; VOYA 2/06)

998 Baer, Judy. *The Whitney Chronicles* (9–12). 2004, Steeple Hill paper $12.95 (0-373-78526-7). 336pp. Whitney sets out to find Mr. Right in this amusing Christian romance. (Rev: BL 9/1/04)

999 Bennett, Cherie, and Jeff Gottesfeld. *A Heart Divided* (6–10). 2004, Delacorte LB $17.99 (0-385-90039-2). 320pp. Tensions over their Tennessee high school's symbol — the Confederate flag — intrude into the romance between new student Kate from New Jersey and Jack, whose family is proud of its southern tradition. (Rev: BCCB 5/04; BL 1/1–15/04; SLJ 5/04; VOYA 4/04)

1000 Blayney, Mary. *The Captain's Mermaid* (9–12). 2004, Zebra paper $4.99 (0-8217-7507-3). 256pp. Captain William Chartwell allows his next-door neighbor Lavinia to tutor his young charge, Angus, and soon finds himself falling in love with her in this Regency romance. (Rev: BL 9/1/04)

1001 Bodwell, Teresa. *Loving Miranda* (11–12). Series: Zebra Historical Romance. 2005, Zebra paper $5.99 (0-8217-7816-1). 352pp. The quiet ranch life of Mercy and Thaddeus is shattered by the sudden appearance of Mercy's sister, Miranda, and Benjamin Lansing. (Rev: BL 10/1/05)

1002 Bretton, Barbara. *Chances Are* (11–12). 2004, Berkley paper $6.99 (0-425-19796-4). 336pp. Maddy Bainbridge and Aidan O'Malley, who met in *Shore Lights* (2003), are getting married, an occasion involving their extended families, some of whom have secrets. (Rev: BL 10/1/04)

1003 Cabot, Meg. *Every Boy's Got One* (10–12). 2005, Avon paper $12.95 (0-06-008546-0). 352pp. When Jane is asked to fly to Italy to serve as maid of honor for her best friend, Holly, she gladly agrees, only to discover that her chemistry with the best man is less than ideal in this fast-paced novel that relies on e-mails, blogs, and journal entries to tell much of the story. (Rev: BL 11/15/04; SLJ 4/05)

1004 Cabot, Meg. *Size 12 Is Not Fat* (10–12). 2005, Avon paper $12.95 (0-06-052511-8). 368pp. Heather Wells, former teen idol, turns detective after a number of coeds are found dead at the college where she works part-time as a residence hall director; for mature teens. (Rev: BL 11/15/05)

1005 Caldwell, Linda. *The Year of Living Famously* (9–12). 2004, Harlequin paper $12.95 (0-373-25075-4). 336pp. Kyra marries an Irish movie star and finds out that fame is not all it's cracked up to be. (Rev: BL 10/1/04)

1006 Camp, Candace. *An Independent Woman* (11–12). 2006, HQN paper $6.99 (0-373-77097-9). 384pp. A Regency romance mixed with intrigue featuring newly impoverished Juliana, who now works as a lady's companion, and Nicholas, an heir who offers her a marriage of convenience. (Rev: BL 3/15/06)

1007 Clark, Catherine. *Maine Squeeze* (9–12). 2004, HarperCollins paper $5.99 (0-06-056725-2). 349pp. College-bound Colleen struggles to keep to her parents' 10 rules while her parents are away for the summer. (Rev: SLJ 8/04)

1008 Coffey, Jan. *Tropical Kiss* (8–11). 2005, HarperCollins paper $5.99 (0-06-076003-6). 338pp. Morgan's summer on Aruba with her father turns out to be more fun than she expected, but the discovery that her dad may be in trouble casts a cloud over her enjoyment of a new friend and boyfriend. (Rev: SLJ 8/05)

1009 Cohen, Paula Marantz. *Jane Austen in Scarsdale: Or Love, Death, and the SATs* (11–12). 2006, St. Martin's $23.95 (0-312-32502-9). 304pp. This romantic comedy echoing Austen's *Persuasion* features Anne Ehrlich, a guidance counselor who regrets following her wealthy family's wishes at age 21 and rejecting the attentions of penniless Ben Cutler, who has now reappeared in her life. (Rev: BL 4/1/06)

1010 Cohn, Rachel, and David Levithan. *Nick and Norah's Infinite Playlist* (10–12). 2006, Knopf LB $18.99 (0-375-93531-2). 192pp. Nick asks Norah to pretend to be his girlfriend just for a few minutes, but that brief start turns into a long night of discovery in this romance between two intelligent and funny teens who enjoy the same music. (Rev: BL 4/1/06)

1011 Crane, Caprice. *Stupid and Contagious* (9–12). 2006, Warner paper $12.95 (0-446-69572-6). 336pp. A funny romantic comedy full of band references, featuring two 20-somethings whose initial

animosity turns to something closer on a road trip across the country. (Rev: BL 3/15/06)

1012 Davenport, Kiana. *House of Many Gods* (11–12). 2006, Ballantine $24.95 (0-345-48150-X). 352pp. Determined to break away from the dysfunction of her extended Hawaiian family, Ana Kapakahi falls in love with a visiting documentary filmmaker from Russia; suitable for mature teens, this novel includes rich descriptions of Hawaii and Russia. (Rev: BL 12/15/05; SLJ 4/06)

1013 Davidson, Dana. *Jason and Kyra* (7–12). 2004, Hyperion $16.99 (0-7868-1851-4). 336pp. Brainiac Kyra and basketball star Jason come from sharply different African American worlds, but when they're teamed up by for a research project, the two find they have much more in common than they could have imagined. (Rev: BL 6/1–15/04; SLJ 7/04; VOYA 6/04)

1014 de Oliveira, Eddie. *Johnny Hazzard* (10–12). 2005, Scholastic $16.95 (0-439-67361-5). 333pp. At the age of 15, Texan Johnny finds new value in his usual summer in London with his father when he falls in love with an older British girl. (Rev: BL 9/15/05; SLJ 9/05; VOYA 2/06)

1015 Dokey, Cameron. *How Not to Spend Your Senior Year* (9–12). 2004, Simon & Schuster paper $5.99 (0-689-86703-4). 293pp. Used to moving because she and her father are in the witness protection program, Jo usually keeps a low profile at school, but in her first day at a Seattle high school she attracts the attention of Alex Crawford in this light romantic comedy. (Rev: SLJ 3/04)

1016 Earls, Nick. *After Summer* (10–12). 2005, Houghton paper $6.99 (0-618-45781-X). 240pp. A love story set in the Australian summer as Alex Delaney waits to hear if he has been accepted at university. (Rev: BL 7/05; SLJ 7/05; VOYA 10/05)

1017 Elmer, Robert. *The Celebrity* (9–12). 2004, WaterBrook paper $12.99. (1-57856-741-6). 304pp. Crooner Jamie Lane, realizing he's unhappy despite his success, returns incognito to his Oregon hometown, where he falls for a young woman recovering from brain damage; will his deception prove too much for her? (Rev: BL 5/15/05)

1018 Evanovich, Janet, and Charlotte Hughes. *Full Bloom* (11–12). 2005, St. Martin's paper $7.99 (0-312-93430-0). 352pp. A fast-paced, funny story of Annie Fortenberry's Peach Tree Bed and Breakfast, its offbeat residents, a dead body, and an attractive man named Wes Bridges. (Rev: BL 3/15/05)

1019 Evans, Richard Paul. *The Sunflower* (10–12). 2005, Simon & Schuster $19.95 (0-7432-8701-0). 368pp. In Peru to do charity work after her engagement is broken off, dental hygienist Christine falls for Paul, a handsome former ER doctor now running an orphanage. (Rev: BL 9/1/05)

1020 Feather, Jane. *Almost a Bride* (11–12). 2005, Bantam paper $6.99 (0-553-58755-2). 448pp. Gambler Jack Fortescu, Duke of St. Jules, wins all the possessions of Frederick Lacey in a card game and hopes also to acquire his beautiful sister Arabella; a Regency romance with a strong heroine. (Rev: BL 3/15/05)

1021 Friedman, Aimee. *A Novel Idea* (7–11). 2006, Simon & Schuster paper $5.99 (1-416-90785-8). 234pp. A light romantic comedy in which Norah's focus switches from her college resumé to the attractive James. (Rev: SLJ 2/06)

1022 Henry, Patti Callahan. *When Light Breaks* (11–12). 2006, NAL paper $12.95 (0-451-21834-5). 304pp. Almost on the eve of her wedding to Peyton, Kara Larson listens to an elderly woman telling a story of love lost and remembers her own passion for Jack, a passion that will soon be resurrected by his reappearance; for mature teens. (Rev: BL 4/1/06)

1023 Jacobs, Holly. *Pickup Lines* (8–12). 2005, Avalon $21.95 (0-8034-9704-0). 192pp. A comic romance in which teacher Mary Rosenthal and businessman Ethan Westbrook vie to win a pickup truck. (Rev: BL 4/1/05)

1024 Jeffries, Sabrina. *Never Seduce a Scoundrel* (11–12). 2006, Pocket paper $6.99 (1-4165-1608-5). 384pp. In Regency London, the unconventional Lady Amelia Plume and American soldier Lucas Winter maneuver around a secret that might harm her family; for mature teens. (Rev: BL 3/1/06)

1025 Johnson, Kathleen Jeffrie. *Dumb Love* (8–11). 2005, Roaring Brook $16.95 (1-59643-062-1). 160pp. A funny romance in which high school student Carlotta aspires both to win the heart of Pete and to write a novel. (Rev: BL 9/15/05; SLJ 11/05)

1026 Kantor, Melissa. *Confessions of a Not It Girl* (7–12). 2004, Hyperion $15.99 (0-7868-1837-9). 256pp. Jan Miller has high hopes that love will come her way during her senior year in high school, but it's soon obvious that it won't be easy in this entertaining, true-to-life romantic comedy. (Rev: BL 6/1–15/04; HB 7–8/04; SLJ 4/04; VOYA 6/04)

1027 Kendrick, Beth. *Fashionably Late* (10–12). 2006, Pocket paper $13.00 (0-7434-9959-X). 320pp. Bored with her humdrum life and humdrum boyfriend in Phoenix, Becca Davis sets out for Los Angeles, where she's determined to make a name for herself in the world of fashion. (Rev: BL 11/15/05)

1028 King, Valerie. *Wicked and Wonderful* (9–12). 2005, Zebra paper $4.99 (0-8217-7847-1). 224pp. A single kiss is enough to convince the Earl of Kelthorne that he wants to spend more time with the clever and independent-minded Judith Lovington,

who is traveling with a troupe of actors in this Regency romance. (Rev: BL 9/15/05)

1029 Kirkwood, Gwen. *Children of the Glens* (10–12). 2004, Severn $28.95 (0-7278-6122-0). 304pp. The farm is threatened by an unwise marriage in this third installment in the series about the Maxwell family's Scottish dairy farm, set in the early 1960s. (Rev: BL 11/1/04)

1030 Kitt, Sandra. *Southern Comfort* (11–12). Series: Sizzling Sands. 2004, BET paper $6.99 (1-58314-548-6). 320pp. Rachel receives a beach house as an inheritance but it comes with a catch — in the form of Lucas, the son of the woman who left her the house; for mature readers. (Rev: BL 7/04)

1031 Kraft, Bridget. *Fields of Gold* (11–12). 2005, Five Star $26.95 (1-59414-362-5). 278pp. In the early 1880s, developer Kellen O'Roarke woos Guinevere Talbot, who controls a piece of northern California land he needs to build his hot springs resort; for mature teens. (Rev: BL 11/15/05)

1032 Krentz, Jayne Ann. *Falling Awake* (11–12). 2004, Penguin $24.95 (0-399-15222-9). 432pp. Isabel, a dream analyst, is offered a "dream job" by the dreamy Ellis Cutler. (Rev: BL 10/1/04)

1033 Krovatin, Christopher. *Heavy Metal and You* (10–12). 2005, Scholastic $16.95 (0-439-73648-X). 186pp. Sam, who attends a classy prep school in New York City, faces a difficult decision when girlfriend Melissa objects to his passion for heavy metal music. (Rev: BL 8/05*; SLJ 10/05; VOYA 10/05)

1034 Krulik, Nancy. *Ripped at the Seams* (9–12). 2004, Simon & Schuster paper $5.99 (0-689-86771-9). 326pp. A romantic comedy series featuring a Minnesota 18-year-old named Sami who soon realizes that her dreams of immediate success in New York City were unrealistic. (Rev: SLJ 7/04)

1035 Love, Kathy. *Wanting Something More* (11–12). 2005, Zebra paper $5.99 (0-8217-7614-2). 352pp. Marty recalls high school, where she and her sisters Abby and Ellie were not social successes, when she returns to her Maine hometown and finds she has attracted the attention of Nathaniel Peck; the final volume in a trilogy suitable for mature teens. (Rev: BL 7/05)

1036 Love, Kathy. *Wanting What You Get* (11–12). Series: Stepp Sisters. 2004, Zebra paper $5.99 (0-8217-7613-4). 352pp. Ellie, a librarian lacking in self-confidence, and Mason, the popular and flirtatious town mayor, find themselves thrown together at a wedding; the second installment in a trilogy. (Rev: BL 11/1/04)

1037 Mallery, Susan. *Falling for Gracie* (9–12). 2005, Harlequin paper $6.99 (0-373-77034-0). 384pp. At 14, Gracie had such an obsessive crush on 18-year-old Riley that her family shipped her off to live with relatives; a successful wedding cake designer at 28, she returns home to work on her demanding sister's wedding and discovers that Riley's running for mayor; for mature teens. (Rev: BL 2/15/05)

1038 Mason, Sarah. *Party Girl* (11–12). 2005, Ballantine paper $12.95 (0-345-46956-9). 336pp. Isabel Serranti, a British party planner, is reunited with a childhood tormentor when she's given the job of setting up a circus-themed gala at his family's estate; for mature teens. (Rev: BL 11/1/05)

1039 Metzger, Barbara. *Love, Louisa* (11–12). 2004, Five Star $26.95 (1-4104-0198-7). 284pp. Louisa holes up in her parents' summer cottage after being jilted by her fiancé and finds herself falling in love with her neighbor Dante. (Rev: BL 6/1–15/04)

1040 Metzger, Barbara. *A Perfect Gentleman* (11–12). 2004, NAL paper $6.99 (0-451-21041-7). 352pp. Stony, a handsome viscount who is paid to escort ladies to balls, falls in love with his latest assignment, Ellianne Kane, in this amusing Regency romance. (Rev: BL 10/1/04)

1041 Michael, Judith. *The Real Mother* (9–12). 2005, Morrow $24.95 (0-06-059929-4). 304pp. Sara is raising her three stepsiblings and dealing with her shiftless brother when she meets the mysterious Reuben. (Rev: BL 11/15/04)

1042 Michaels, Kasey. *A Gentleman by Any Other Name* (11–12). 2006, HQN paper $6.99 (0-373-77100-2). 384pp. Smuggling is at the heart of this romance set in the time of Napoleon and featuring the young, beautiful, and intelligent Julia Carruthers and Chance Becket, whose child she looks after and who is trying to guard family secrets; for mature teens. (Rev: BL 4/1/06)

1043 Michaels, Kasey. *Shall We Dance?* (11–12). 2005, Harlequin paper $6.99 (0-373-77038-3). 384pp. Competition for succession to the English throne drives the subterfuge and seduction in this Regency romance. (Rev: BL 3/1/05)

1044 Montefiore, Santa. *Last Voyage of the Valentina* (10–12). 2006, Simon & Schuster paper $15.00 (0-7432-7686-8). 416pp. Half-Italian and half-British, Alba, whose mother died soon after her birth, decides to travel to Italy in search of her family there in this novel that blends mystery and romance and alternates between wartime Italy and 1970s London. (Rev: BL 4/1/06)

1045 Moore, Laurie. *Constable's Wedding* (11–12). 2005, Five Star $26.95 (1-59414-249-1). 361pp. Jinx Porter, constable of Tarrant County, Texas, tries to win back the heart of Raven, his deputy and former flame, only days before her scheduled wedding to Tommy, who's missing in action; for mature readers. (Rev: BL 10/15/05)

1046 Morren, Ruth Axtell. *Wild Rose* (9–12). 2004, Steeple Hill paper $12.95 (0-373-78527-5). 368pp. A romance between an orphan and a disgraced sea

captain, set on the seaside in 1873. (Rev: BL 10/1/04)

1047 Murray, J. J. *Original Love* (11–12). 2005, Kensington paper $15.00 (0-7582-1164-3). 336pp. Peter Underhill, a 40-year-old white writer down on his luck, sets out to find his first love, an African American woman named Ebony Mills. (Rev: BL 10/1/05)

1048 Nance, Kathleen. *Jigsaw* (11–12). 2005, Leisure paper $6.99 (0-8439-5491-4). 384pp. Romance, high technology, and terrorism are intertwined in this exciting story about Bella, who has created an artificial intelligence, and Daniel, who works for the National Security Agency; for mature teens. (Rev: BL 4/1/05)

1049 Nathan, Melissa. *Persuading Annie* (10–12). 2004, Avon paper $12.95 (0-06-059580-9). 352pp. Annie is still drawn to her ex, Jake, but the failing family business keeps getting in the way. (Rev: BL 7/04)

1050 Neale, Naomi. *Calendar Girl* (11–12). 2005, Dorchester paper $12.95 (0-8439-5470-1). 336pp. Nan, disappointed in love and adrift, listens to sympathetic friends and takes steps to effect her own happiness in this humorous and realistic novel suitable for mature teens. (Rev: BL 1/1–15/05)

1051 Norfleet, Celeste O. *The Fine Art of Love* (11–12). 2005, BET paper $6.99 (1-58314-673-3). 320pp. Kennedy Evan, a young, attractive museum curator, is high on the suspect list when valuable items from one of her exhibits disappear, but FBI agent Juwan Mason finds his interest in her is not altogether professional; for mature teens. (Rev: BL 11/1/05)

1052 Owens, Sharon. *The Ballroom on Magnolia Street* (11–12). 2005, Penguin paper $15.00 (0-399-15286-5). 368pp. When Shirley and Declan get engaged, older sister Kate is determined to find herself a husband fast in this entertaining novel featuring modern Belfast nightlife. (Rev: BL 7/05)

1053 Parra, Nancy J. *The Bettin' Kind* (11–12). 2005, Avalon $21.95 (0-8034-9736-9). 192pp. Devastated when her brother loses her beloved horse to a professional gambler, Amelia Morgan is swept into a hasty marriage in an effort to remain close to the animal; for mature readers. (Rev: BL 10/1/05)

1054 Parra, Nancy J. *The Marryin' Kind* (9–12). 2005, Avalon $21.95 (0-8034-9694-X). 192pp. When her father insists that her marriage must precede any courting of her younger sisters, Maddie Morgan and her brother concoct a (temporary) solution in this historical romance. (Rev: BL 2/1/05)

1055 Petersen, P. J., and Ivy Ruckman. *Rob and Sara.com* (7–11). 2004, Dell $15.95 (0-385-73164-7). 224pp. Rob and Sara conduct an online relationship that is always tinged with the question of whether each is really the person claimed. (Rev: BL 10/15/04; SLJ 12/04)

1056 Plumley, Lisa. *Josie Day Is Coming Home* (11–12). 2005, Zebra paper $6.50 (0-8217-7696-7). 352pp. Las Vegas showgirl Josie Day saves a celebrity's life and receives a mansion in gratitude; the ramshackle place is in her Arizona hometown, where everyone believes rumors that she's a stripper. (Rev: BL 2/15/05)

1057 Plumley, Lisa. *Perfect Switch* (11–12). 2004, Zebra paper $5.99 (0-8217-7342-9). 352pp. When ordinary Meredith poses as her twin, movie star Marley, hilarity ensues in this sequel to *Perfect Together* (2003); for mature readers. (Rev: BL 6/1–15/04)

1058 Quick, Amanda. *Lie by Moonlight* (11–12). 2005, Penguin $24.95 (0-399-15288-1). 400pp. In Victorian England, plucky Concordia Glade and her four teen charges escape from an isolated castle with the aid of private investigator Ambrose Wells; for mature teens. (Rev: BL 4/15/05)

1059 Quick, Amanda. *Second Sight* (11–12). 2006, Penguin $24.95 (0-399-15352-7). 400pp. A romantic thriller set in Victorian England and featuring Venetia Milton, a photographer in need of a husband. (Rev: BL 2/15/06)

1060 Rice, Luanne. *Beach Girls* (9–12). 2004, Bantam paper $7.50 (0-553-58724-2). 464pp. When Stevie's childhood friend Emma dies, Emma's daughter Nell looks to Stevie for guidance — and Emma's husband looks to her for comfort — in this romance suitable for mature teens, set at the seashore. (Rev: BL 8/04)

1061 Rice, Luanne. *Silver Bells* (11–12). 2004, Bantam $15.00 (0-553-80411-1). 224pp. A heart-warming Christmas tale in which a father and runaway son are reunited and a new romance is fulfilled. (Rev: BL 10/15/04)

1062 Richardson, Evelyn. *A Lady of Talent* (9–12). 2005, Signet paper $4.99 (0-451-21009-3). 224pp. Sebastian once fell in love with the portrait of a lady, but was unsuccessful in identifying her; now taking his fiancée to sit for a portrait, he finds that artist C. A. Manners is not only a woman, but the very one in the painting. (Rev: BL 2/15/05)

1063 Roberts, Nora. *Blue Dahlia* (11–12). 2004, Berkley paper $7.99 (0-515-13855-X). 384pp. Stella's life — and her job at a plant nursery — is complicated by her handsome coworker Logan and the ghost that's haunting her house. (Rev: BL 11/1/04)

1064 Schindler, Nina. *An Order of Amelie, Hold the Fries* (9–12). 2004, Annick $18.95 (1-55037-861-9); paper $8.95 (1-55037-860-0). 112pp. This clever and funny novel, told in a series of e-mails, text messages, and letters, traces the growing relationship between Tim and Amelie, who turns out to be a

different girl than the one he thought she was. (Rev: BL 1/1–15/05; SLJ 1/05; VOYA 4/05)

1065 Shaw, Tucker. *The Hookup Artist* (8–12). 2006, HarperCollins LB $16.89 (0-06-075621-7). 200pp. Teens Cate and her best friend Lucas both fall for Derek when he arrives in town. (Rev: SLJ 2/06; VOYA 2/06)

1066 Shay, Kathryn. *Someone to Believe In* (11–12). 2005, Berkley paper $7.99 (0-425-20530-4). 368pp. Bailey O'Neil, a woman working to keep teens out of gangs, and Clay Wainwright, a senator who has blocked her funding, feel sparks between them despite their different beliefs; for mature teens. (Rev: BL 9/1/05)

1067 Sneed, Tamara. *The Way He Makes Me Feel* (11–12). 2005, St. Martin's paper $6.99 (0-312-98731-5). 320pp. On a bet, Dunston sets out to seduce Claire but then finds he's genuinely fond of her in this sexy romance suitable for mature teens. (Rev: BL 6/1–15/05)

1068 Sparks, Nicholas. *At First Sight* (11–12). 2005, Warner $24.95 (0-446-53242-8). 278pp. In this compelling and melodramatic sequel to *True Believer* (2005), the relationship between Jeremy Marsh and Lexie Darnell is threatened when seeds of doubt are planted; for mature readers. (Rev: BL 10/1/05)

1069 Tan, Maureen. *A Perfect Cover* (11–12). 2004, Harlequin paper $5.50 (0-373-51323-2). 304pp. A mystery set in the Little Vietnam section of New Orleans, with a spunky female detective of Afro Asian heritage who goes undercover and finds unexpected love; for mature teens. (Rev: BL 9/15/04)

1070 Tanner, Janet. *Forgotten Destiny* (11–12). 2004, Severn $28.95 (0-7278-6095-X). 288pp. A gothic romance involving a heroine with amnesia who is forced into a loveless and dangerous marriage. (Rev: BL 10/1/04)

1071 Taylor, Janelle. *Dying to Marry* (11–12). 2004, Zebra paper $6.99 (0-8217-7464-6). 304pp. When Lizbeth, a "Down Hill" girl, becomes engaged to Dylan, from "Up Hill," her very life is threatened and she must rely on Detective Lake for protection. (Rev: BL 10/15/04)

1072 Thompson, Colleen. *Fatal Error* (11–12). 2004, Leisure paper $6.99 (0-8439-5421-3). 384pp. Susan must enlist the help of former flame (and brother-in-law) Luke after her husband skips town. (Rev: BL 11/15/04)

1073 Wingate, Lisa. *Over the Moon at the Big Lizard Diner* (9–12). 2005, NAL paper $13.95 (0-451-21664-4). 320pp. While in Texas working on an undercover mission involving dinosaur tracks, paleontologist Lindsey Atwood, a divorcee with an 8-year-old daughter, meets and falls in love with rancher Zach Truitt. (Rev: BL 10/15/05)

1074 Woodward, Rhonda. *Moonlight and Mischief* (9–12). 2004, Penguin paper $4.99 (0-451-21288-6). 222pp. Despite her best efforts, Mariah finds herself falling in love with the rakish Lord Haverstone. (Rev: BL 11/15/04)

1075 Wootson, Alice. *Perfect Wedding* (9–12). 2005, BET paper $6.99 (1-58314-684-9). 288pp. To fulfill her dream of a trip to Hawaii, 6th-grade teacher Dana Dillard searches frantically for a fiancé so they can compete on the *Perfect Wedding* reality TV show; for mature teens. (Rev: BL 12/1/05)

1076 Wright, Courtni. *Espresso for Two* (11–12). 2004, BET paper $6.99 (1-58314-556-7). 320pp. Brandi, a bookstore owner, falls for the man who owns the coffee shop next door, and together they fight the mega-bookstore that wants to put them both out of business; for mature teens. (Rev: BL 9/15/04)

Science Fiction

1077 Asaro, Catherine. *Sunrise Alley* (10–12). 2004, Baen $24.00 (0-7434-8840-7). 320pp. A fast-paced story in which biotech engineer Samantha Bryton agrees to help android Turner Pascal, who is on the run from the evil bioengineer Charon. (Rev: BL 8/04; SLJ 1/05)

1078 Baxter, Stephen. *Exultant* (9–12). 2004, Del Rey $25.95 (0-345-45788-9). 480pp. Humans, who have taken over much of the galaxy, attempt to assimilate the Xeelee people in this rich sequel to *Coalescent* (2003) that involves time travel and a black hole. (Rev: BL 11/15/04; SLJ 3/05)

1079 Bornes, John. *The Armies of Memory* (10–12). 2006, Tor $25.95 (0-765-30330-2). 432pp. Giraut Leone, Thousand Cultures secret agent, undertakes a dangerous last mission before retirement in which his life — and that of civilization — is at stake. (Rev: BL 4/1/06)

1080 Bova, Ben. *Titan* (9–12). 2006, Tor $24.95 (0-765-30413-9). 464pp. As a colony ship approaches Saturn's largest satellite in 2095, debates rage among the staff. (Rev: BL 3/1/06)

1081 Card, Orson Scott. *First Meetings: In the Enderverse* (6–12). 2003, Tor $17.95 (0-765-30873-8). 208pp. Contains the novella "Ender's Game," first published in 1977, and three other stories, one previously unpublished. (Rev: SLJ 1/04)

1082 Card, Orson Scott. *Shadow of the Giant* (10–12). Series: Ender's Saga. 2005, Tor $25.95 (0-312-85758-6). 384pp. In a continuation of the saga, Bean and his fellow Battle School graduates, some of whom rule their own kingdoms, must face and

work to resolve Earth's political turmoil. (Rev: BL 3/1/05)

1083 Collins, Paul. *The Skyborn* (8–11). 2005, Tor $17.95 (0-765-31273-5). 272pp. Accepted by the Earthborn after his ship *Colony* crashed on post-holocaust Earth, 14-year-old Welkin, born a Skyborn, learns the Earthborn are in danger from the Skyborn; a sequel to *The Earthborn* (2003). (Rev: BL 2/15/06)

1084 Dietz, William C. *Runner* (9–12). 2005, Ace $24.95 (0-441-01326-0). 432pp. Interstellar messenger Jak Rebo is assigned to escort a boy, who is believed to be the reincarnation of a spiritual leader, on a journey to the planet Thara. (Rev: BL 10/1/05)

1085 Drake, David, et al., eds. *The World Turned Upside Down* (9–12). 2005, Baen $24.00 (0-7434-9874-7). 752pp. This fiction collection anthologizes seminal science fiction stories and writers, including Arthur C. Clarke and Isaac Asimov. (Rev: BL 12/1/04)

1086 Faust, Minister. *The Coyote Kings of the Space Age Bachelor Pad* (11–12). 2004, Del Rey paper $13.95 (0-345-46635-7). 544pp. Two friends fight mysterious enemies for control of a power-giving device called a zodiascope; for mature teens. (Rev: BL 6/1–15/04)

1087 Foster, Alan Dean. *Lost and Found* (9–12). 2004, Del Rey $23.95 (0-345-46125-8). 256pp. Marc, along with beings from other planets, is abducted by aliens and may be sold as an oddity in outer space in this entertaining and imaginative start to a trilogy. (Rev: BL 6/1–15/04)

1088 Gerrold, David. *Child of Earth* (9–12). 2005, BenBella paper $14.95 (1-932100-47-4). 176pp. Twelve-year-old Kaer's family volunteers to migrate to the parallel world of Linna, where there are giant and beautiful horses — and unadvertised perils. (Rev: BL 6/1–15/05)

1089 Gould, Steven. *Reflex* (11–12). 2004, Tor $24.95 (0-312-86421-3). 384pp. In this years-later sequel to *Jumper* (1992), a sinister group entraps and exploits Davy Rice, who can teleport from place to place, leaving his wife, her own teleporting ability born of the crisis, to find and rescue Davy; for mature teens. (Rev: BL 12/15/04)

1090 Hayden, Patrick Nielsen, ed. *New Skies: An Anthology of Today's Science Fiction* (7–12). 2003, Tor $19.95 (0-7653-0010-8). 288pp. Short stories that were originally published in science fiction magazines include pieces by Orson Scott Card, Philip K. Dick, and Connie Willis. (Rev: BL 1/1–15/04)

1091 Herbert, Brian, and Kevin J. Anderson. *The Battle of Corrin* (9–12). Series: Dune. 2004, Tor $27.95 (0-765-30159-8). 624pp. This prequel to the classic *Dune* sets the stage on the planet Arrakis following a long battle between the Jihad and the machines. (Rev: BL 8/04)

1092 Hopkinson, Nalo, and Uppinder Mehan, eds. *So Long Been Dreaming: Postcolonial Science Fiction and Fantasy* (11–12). 2004, Arsenal Pulp paper $19.95 (1-55152-158-X). 270pp. Science fiction and fantasy stories dealing with colonialization, of both alien and Earth societies; sex and violence limit this to mature teens. (Rev: BL 9/1/04)

1093 Jeapes, Ben. *The New World Order* (9–12). 2005, Random LB $17.99 (0-385-75015-3). 448pp. In this historical science fiction novel, Jeapes weaves together an alien invasion and the bloody English Civil War of the mid-17th century. (Rev: BL 1/1–15/05; SLJ 4/05; VOYA 4/05)

1094 Kelly, James Patrick. *Burn* (9–12). 2005, Tachyon $19.95 (1-892391-27-9). 192pp. In this literary science fiction novel, injured firefighter Spur becomes involved in the fight for the soul of his planet, which is named Walden for its dedication to the simple way of life. (Rev: BL 12/15/05)

1095 Lackey, Mercedes, and Eric Flint. *The Wizard of Karres* (9–12). 2004, Baen $22.00 (0-7434-8839-3). 320pp. In this sequel to James Schmitz's *The Witches of Karres* (1966), Captain Pausert and his motley circus of a crew take the *Venture* on a new mission to save humanity. (Rev: BL 8/04; SLJ 11/04)

1096 Levitin, Sonia. *The Goodness Gene* (9–12). 2005, Dutton $16.99 (0-525-47397-1). 320pp. Cloning, euthanasia, and the environment are only three of the topics raised in this thought-provoking novel set in the year 2305 and featuring 16-year-old twins Will and Berk. (Rev: BL 9/1/05; SLJ 12/05; VOYA 10/05)

1097 Luceno, James. *Dark Lord: The Rise of Darth Vader* (8–12). 2005, Del Rey $25.95 (0-345-47732-4). 336pp. Chronicles the transformation of Anakin Skywalker from disaffected, young Jedi into the ruthless Darth Vader. (Rev: BL 11/15/05)

1098 Luceno, James. *Labyrinth of Evil* (9–12). 2005, Del Rey $25.95 (0-345-47572-0). 352pp. This prequel to the film *Revenge of the Sith* pits Jedi Knight Anakin Skywalker and Obi-Wan Kenobi against separatists, culminating in battle on the planet Coruscant. (Rev: BL 1/1–15/05)

1099 McCaffrey, Anne, and Elizabeth Ann Scarborough. *Changelings* (9–12). Series: Twins of Petaybee. 2005, Del Rey $19.95 (0-345-47002-8). 272pp. In the opening volume of the second Twins of Petaybee trilogy, shape-shifting twins Murel and Ronan are sent to live on a space station with a family friend. (Rev: BL 12/1/05)

1100 McDonald, Steven E. *Waystation* (9–12). 2004, Tor $24.95 (0-705-30485-6). 272pp. The crew of the *Andromeda* encounters trouble on the planet Kantar. (Rev: BL 7/04)

1101 Meluch, R. M. *The Myriad* (9–12). 2005, DAW $23.95 (0-7564-0279-4). 320pp. The space warship *Merrimack*, battling the Swarm, is blasted into a parallel universe in this series starter. (Rev: BL 1/1–15/05)

1102 Modesitt, L. E. *Flash* (10–12). 2004, Tor $25.95 (0-765-31128-3). 480pp. Set in the 24th century, this thriller imagines a world in which product placement, politics, and murder go hand-in-hand. (Rev: BL 9/1/04)

1103 Morvan, Jean David. *Wake*, Vol. 6/7 (9–12). 2005, NBM paper $14.95 (1-56163-420-4). 96pp. In this science fiction graphic novel, part of a multivolume series, a human girl named Navee faces daunting challenges. (Rev: BL 4/15/05; SLJ 7/05)

1104 Mosley, Walter. *47* (7–10). 2005, Little, Brown $16.99 (0-316-11035-3). 232pp. In this compelling blend of folklore, science fiction, and history, a slave named 47 is trained to take on new and important roles by a mysterious stranger who calls himself Tall John. (Rev: BCCB 6/05; BL 4/15/05; HB 7–8/05; SLJ 6/05; VOYA 6/05)

1105 Niven, Larry, and Brenda Cooper. *Building Harlequin's Moon* (10–12). 2005, Tor $25.95 (0-765-31266-2). 464pp. Rachel, a leader of the Moon Born, comes to realize that the Earth Born have been abusing her people. (Rev: BL 6/1–15/05; VOYA 8/05)

1106 Reed, Gary. *Mary Shelley's Frankenstein: The Graphic Novel* (7–10). Series: Puffin Graphics. 2005, Penguin paper $9.99 (0-14-240407-1). 176pp. This graphic novel adaptation accurately conveys the dominant themes of the classic. (Rev: BL 3/15/05; SLJ 9/05; VOYA 8/05)

1107 Reed, Kit. *Thinner Than Thou* (10–12). 2004, Tor $24.95 (0-765-30762-6). 336pp. Annie is an anorexic in a society that literally worships perfect bodies, and it gets her into trouble. (Rev: BL 6/1–15/04)

1108 Reeve, Philip. *Predator's Gold* (7–10). Series: The Hungry City Chronicles. 2004, Morrow $16.99 (0-06-072193-6). 336pp. In a future world where large cities move about and eat up smaller towns, Tom and Hester seek refuge in Anchorage, hopeful that the small city will make its way to the Dead Continent of America before it is caught and consumed by Arkangel; a sequel to *Mortal Engines* (2003). (Rev: BL 8/04; SLJ 9/04; VOYA 10/04)

1109 Sagan, Nick. *Edenborn* (10–12). 2004, Penguin $19.95 (0-399-15186-9). 320pp. Post-humans — the only survivors of the Black Ep plague — rely on virtual reality to survive in this complex sequel to *Idlewild* (2003). (Rev: BL 9/1/04)

1110 Sawyer, Robert J. *Iterations* (11–12). 2004, Red Deer paper $22.95 (0-88995-303-1). 306pp. Mind-bending short stories by a master of science fiction. (Rev: BL 10/1/04)

1111 Sherman, David, and Dan Cragg. *Flashfire* (9–12). Series: Starfist. 2006, Del Rey $19.95 (0-345-46054-5). 336pp. In this installment of the military science fiction series, the marines of the 34th FIST (Fleet Initial Strike Team) are dispatched to prevent civil war when the planet Ravenette and several of its neighbors secede from the Confederation. (Rev: BL 12/15/05)

1112 Skurzynski, Gloria. *The Revolt* (8–12). Series: The Virtual War Chronologs. 2005, Simon & Schuster $16.95 (0-689-84265-1). 247pp. In this action-packed third volume in the series, Corgan flees to Florida to put an end to his battle with Brigand but is soon followed there by his violent enemy. (Rev: SLJ 7/05)

1113 Steele, Allen. *Coyote Frontier* (10–12). 2005, Ace $24.95 (0-441-01331-7). 368pp. The future of the interstellar colony of Coyote hangs in the balance as survivors of its original settlers battle refugees from an ecologically bankrupt Earth. (Rev: BL 12/1/05)

1114 Stewart, Sean. *Dark Rendezvous* (9–12). 2004, Del Rey paper $7.50 (0-345-46309-9). 352pp. Prequeling the film *Revenge of the Sith*, this *Clone Wars* series entry pits Jedi Master Yoda and several Knights against former disciple Count Dooku, who has embraced the Dark Side. (Rev: BL 12/15/04)

1115 Varley, John. *Red Lightning* (11–12). 2006, Ace $23.95 (0-441-01364-3). 336pp. Ray Garcia-Strickland, son of a Martian explorer and entrepreneur, comes to Earth to rescue his grandmother after the U.S. East Coast is hit by an unidentified object, and finds himself embroiled in a battle for power. (Rev: BL 3/15/06)

1116 Westerfeld, Scott. *Pretties* (8–11). 2005, Simon & Schuster paper $6.99 (0-689-86539-2). 384pp. In the sequel to *Uglies* (2005), Tally enjoys her transformation into a Pretty and the accompanying hedonistic lifestyle until she is reminded of her underlying purpose and faces real danger. (Rev: BL 9/15/05; SLJ 12/05; VOYA 10/05)

1117 Westerfeld, Scott. *Uglies* (7–10). 2005, Simon & Schuster paper $6.99 (0-689-86538-4). 448pp. In a futuristic dystopia, 15-year-old Tally is counting the days until she turns 16 and is transformed from ugly to pretty but events threaten this happening on schedule; a thought-provoking novel about the importance of image and ethics. (Rev: BCCB 2/05; BL 3/15/05*; SLJ 3/05; VOYA 6/05)

1118 White, Andrea. *No Child's Game: Reality TV 2083* (7–10). 2005, HarperCollins LB $16.89 (0-06-055455-X). 336pp. In this chilling look at a future in which television is used to distract the populace from grim reality, five teens will live or die while reenacting a historic Antarctic expedition for the entertainment of the viewing audience. (Rev: BL 4/15/05; SLJ 7/05)

1119 Williams, Sean. *The Resurrected Man* (10–12). 2005, Prometheus $25.00 (1-59102-311-4). 425pp. Science fiction and mystery are blended in this late-21st-century thriller about detective Marylin Blaylock's efforts to track down a serial killer who's using flaws in the latest transportation technology to kidnap and murder victims. (Rev: SLJ 4/05)

1120 Zahn, Timothy. *Night Train to Rigel* (9–12). 2005, Tor $24.95 (0-765-30716-2). 352pp. In this riveting sci fi thriller, the Spiders hire former government investigator Frank Compton to find out who is trying to take over the Quadrail interstellar transport system. (Rev: BL 10/15/05)

Sports

1121 Averett, Edward. *The Rhyming Season* (9–12). 2005, Clarion $16.00 (0-618-46948-6). 224pp. Brenda's finding her last year at school difficult — her older brother has died, her parents have separated, her favorite coach has left, the town is economically depressed — but she and the new poetry-loving coach succeed in taking the basketball team to success. (Rev: BL 9/1/05; SLJ 11/05)

1122 Carter, Alden R. *Love, Football, and Other Contact Sports* (8–11). 2006, Holiday House $16.95 (0-82341-975-4). 261pp. The football team at Argyle West High School is at the center of these entertaining short stories. (Rev: BL 3/15/06*)

1123 Coy, John. *Crackback* (8–11). 2005, Scholastic $16.99 (0-439-69733-6). 208pp. High school football player Miles Manning faces many challenges including difficult relationships with his father and his coach, girl problems, and whether to join his teammates in using steroids. (Rev: BL 9/1/05*; SLJ 12/05; VOYA 12/05)

1124 Esckilsen, Erik E. *Offsides* (6–10). 2004, Houghton $15.00 (0-618-46284-8). 176pp. Tom Gray, a top-notch soccer player, is proud of his Mohawk heritage and when he moves to a new town where the school's mascot is an Indian, he refuses to play. (Rev: BL 9/1/04; SLJ 1/05; VOYA 12/04)

1125 Guest, Jacqueline. *Racing Fear* (7–10). Series: SideStreets. 2004, Lorimer paper $4.99 (1-55028-838-5). 158pp. Trent and Adam are best friends and car racing buddies until an accident puts a strain on their friendship; suitable for reluctant readers. (Rev: SLJ 1/05)

1126 Hughes, Pat. *Open Ice* (9–12). 2005, Random LB $17.99 (0-385-90906-3). 288pp. The game is everything for 16-year-old high school hockey star Nick Taglio, so he is devastated when he is sidelined by an injury and he finds many aspects of his life more difficult. (Rev: BL 11/1/05*; SLJ 12/05; VOYA 12/05)

1127 Martino, Alfred. *Pinned* (9–12). 2005, Harcourt $17.00 (0-15-205355-7). 320pp. Alternating chapters chronicle the lives of high school wrestlers Ivan Korske and Bobby Zane as they move toward a match against one another in the finals of the New Jersey State Wrestling Championship. (Rev: BCCB 4/05; BL 3/1/05; SLJ 2/05; VOYA 4/05)

1128 Mosher, Howard Frank. *Waiting for Teddy Williams* (9–12). 2004, Houghton $24.00 (0-618-19722-2). 288pp. Ethan Allen, a young Red Sox fan who longs to be a baseball star — and to know more about his long-departed father, hopes a stranger called Teddy Williams can make his Fenway Park dreams come true in this entertaining novel. (Rev: BL 8/04; SLJ 9/04)

1129 Peet, Mal. *Keeper* (9–12). 2005, Candlewick $15.99 (0-7636-2749-6). 240pp. Looking back on his life in an interview, World Cup soccer star El Gato describes his humble beginnings in the rain forest and the ghost that trained him. (Rev: BL 8/05; SLJ 9/05)

1130 Peña, Matt de la. *Ball Don't Lie* (9–12). 2005, Delacorte LB $18.99 (0-385-90258-1). 288pp. Seventeen-year-old Sticky, raised in a series of foster homes, pins his hopes for a better life on his ability to play basketball. (Rev: BL 11/15/05; SLJ 11/05*; VOYA 10/05)

1131 Stirling, S. M. *Dies the Fire* (9–12). 2004, NAL $23.95 (0-451-45979-2). 496pp. In an alternate reality in which modern technology has been disabled, only the strong and resourceful survive. (Rev: BL 8/04)

1132 Strasser, Todd. *Cut Back* (7–12). Series: Impact Zone. 2004, Simon & Schuster paper $5.99 (0-689-87030-2). 320pp. In this action-packed series installment, 15-year-old Kai faces off against his nemesis, Lucas Frank, in a surfing competition; a sequel is *Take Off* (2004). (Rev: BL 7/04; SLJ 8/04)

1133 Waltman, Kevin. *Learning the Game* (9–12). 2005, Scholastic $16.95 (0-439-73109-7). 224pp. Nate is talked into committing a crime with his basketball teammates and wrestles with his guilty conscience in this compelling multilayered novel. (Rev: BL 9/1/05; SLJ 12/05; VOYA 10/05)

Short Stories and General Anthologies

1134 Alarcón, Daniel. *War by Candlelight* (11–12). 2005, HarperCollins $23.95 (0-06-059478-0). 208pp. In nine stories set in Peru and New York,

Alarcón explores the effect of natural disasters, poverty, and political strife in the denigration of life. (Rev: BL 2/15/05)

1135 Almond, Steve. *The Evil B. B. Chow and Other Stories* (11–12). 2005, Algonquin $21.95 (1-56512-422-7). 256pp. Almond's edgy stories conjure love, lust, and a river trip on which Abraham Lincoln and Frederick Douglass get drunk together; for mature readers. (Rev: BL 2/15/05)

1136 Aspin, Diana. *Ordinary Miracles* (10–12). Series: Northern Lights Young Novels. 2003, Red Deer paper $7.95 (0-88995-277-9). 168pp. Thirteen compelling short stories about teens' coming-of-age concerns in small Sky Falls, Canada, are linked through the memories of an elderly man who came to the community decades before. (Rev: SLJ 4/04; VOYA 2/04)

1137 Banks, William H., ed. *Beloved Harlem: A Literary Tribute to Black America's Most Famous Neighborhood, from the Classics to the Contemporary* (11–12). 2005, Broadway paper $18.95 (0-7679-1478-3). 544pp. Harlem's role as a center of African American culture is documented through excerpts from works of literature; for mature teens. (Rev: BL 7/05) [810.8]

1138 Boyle, T. C. *The Human Fly and Other Stories* (10–12). 2005, Penguin $17.99 (0-670-06054-2); paper $9.99 (0-14-240363-6). 192pp. This collection of short stories — many previously published for adults — includes many realistic young adult characters and is full of humor and surprises as well as some shocks. (Rev: BL 11/1/05; SLJ 11/05)

1139 Bradbury, Ray. *The Cat's Pajamas: Stories* (10–12). 2004, Morrow $24.95 (0-06-058565-X). 234pp. Previously unpublished stories dating as far back as the 1940s are mixed in with recent pieces, offering a surprisingly consistent selection of science fiction and fantasy, plus an interesting author's introduction. (Rev: BL 7/04; SLJ 12/04)

1140 Brown, Charles N., and Jonathan Strahan, eds. *The Locus Awards: Thirty Years of the Best in Science Fiction and Fantasy* (11–12). 2004, HarperCollins paper $15.95 (0-06-059426-8). 512pp. Selected from past winners of the Locus Awards, the stories in this anthology represent the best in fantasy and science fiction writing over the past three decades; for mature teens. (Rev: BL 7/04; SLJ 3/05)

1141 Carlson, Lori Marie, ed. *Moccasin Thunder: American Indian Stories for Today* (8–11). 2005, HarperCollins LB $16.89 (0-06-623959-1). 176pp. Ten contemporary short stories feature Native American teens. (Rev: BL 8/05; SLJ 12/05*; VOYA 2/06)

1142 Cart, Michael, ed. *Face: A Journal of Contemporary Voices*, Vol. 3 (8–12). Illus. Series: Rush Hour. 2005, Delacorte LB $12.99 (0-385-90182-8);

paper $9.95 (0-385-73032-2). 211pp. Our images of ourselves and others are at the heart of this collection of stories and poems that tackle a wide variety of situations. (Rev: HB 5–6/05; SLJ 7/05)

1143 Datlow, Ellen, et al., eds. *The Year's Best Fantasy and Horror: Seventeenth Annual Collection* (9–12). 2004, St. Martin's $35.00 (0-312-32927-X); paper $19.95 (0-312-32928-8). 554pp. Stories by Adam Corbin Fusco, Dale Bailey, Brian Hodges, Lucius Shepard, and others. (Rev: BL 8/04)

1144 Didato, Thom, and Alexander Steele, eds. *The Gotham Writers' Workshop Fiction Gallery: Exceptional Short Stories Selected by New York's Acclaimed Creative Writing School* (10–12). 2004, Bloomsbury paper $14.95 (1-58234-462-0). 386pp. A collection of short stories by writers including Anton Chekhov, T. C. Boyle, and Daniel Orozco. (Rev: SLJ 11/04)

1145 Estevis, Anne. *Down Garrapata Road* (6–12). 2003, Arte Publico paper $12.95 (1-55885-397-9). 128pp. In this collection of closely linked short stories, Estevis paints an appealing portrait of life in a small Mexican American community in South Texas during the 1930s and 1940s. (Rev: BL 1/1–15/04)

1146 Finlay, Charles Coleman. *Wild Things* (9–12). 2005, Subterranean $25.00 (1-59606-030-1). 232pp. Fourteen inventive short stories display a wide range of styles and genres. (Rev: BL 8/05)

1147 Ford, Jeffrey. *The Empire of Ice Cream* (11–12). 2006, Golden Gryphon $24.95 (1-930846-39-8). 319pp. A wide-ranging collection of well-written stories that are followed by comments by the author. (Rev: BL 3/15/06)

1148 Fuguet, Alberto. *Shorts* (11–12). 2005, HarperCollins paper $12.95 (0-06-081714-3). 336pp. In this collection of short stories suitable for mature readers, Fuguet, a Chilean who spent much of his childhood in California, focuses on young people's search for cultural identity. (Rev: BL 12/1/05)

1149 Gilchrist, Ellen. *Nora Jane: A Life in Stories* (11–12). 2005, Little, Brown paper $14.95 (0-316-05838-6). 432pp. Gilchrist's stories about the likable Nora Jane and her life are gathered in a single volume; for mature teens. (Rev: BL 6/1–15/05)

1150 Gioia, Dana, and R. S. Gwynn, eds. *The Art of the Short Story* (9–12). 2005, Pearson paper $18.95 (0-321-33722-0). 926pp. This anthology of short fiction showcases the work of 52 great writers — including Margaret Atwood, Sandra Cisneros, Ha Jin, and Gustave Flaubert — and adds commentary and discussion of the elements of short fiction. (Rev: BL 4/15/05) [808.3]

1151 Hemmings, Kaui Hart. *House of Thieves* (9–12). 2005, Penguin $22.95 (1-59420-048-3). 242pp. Hawaii is the setting for a compelling collection of stories about family life that feature young people in diverse situations. (Rev: BL 4/15/05)

1152 Henríquez, Cristina. *Come Together, Fall Apart* (11–12). 2006, Riverhead $23.95 (1-59448-915-7). 340pp. Eight beautifully written short stories and a novella set in Panama feature young people confronting adversity. (Rev: BL 3/15/06)

1153 Kulka, John, and Natalie Danford, eds. *Best New American Voices 2005* (10–12). 2004, Harcourt paper $14.00 (0-15-602899-9). 380pp. This collection of diverse short stories introduces some of America's most promising new writers. (Rev: BL 9/15/04; SLJ 4/05)

1154 Kurtz, Jane, ed. *Memories of Sun: Stories of Africa and America* (6–10). 2004, Greenwillow LB $16.89 (0-06-051051-X). 160pp. In this appealing anthology of short stories and poems, contemporary African and African American authors write about their cultures. (Rev: BL 1/1–15/04; HB 1–2/04; SLJ 1/04; VOYA 2/04)

1155 Lapcharoensap, Rattawut. *Sightseeing* (11–12). 2005, Grove $22.00 (0-8021-1788-0). 224pp. Ironic and sharply observed, these short stories portray young people in modern Thailand; for mature teens. (Rev: BL 12/15/04; SLJ 5/05)

1156 Levithan, David, ed. *Where We Are, What We See: Poems, Stories, Essays, and Art from the Best Young Writers and Artists in America* (8–11). 2005, Scholastic paper $7.99 (0-439-73646-3). 272pp. Winning entries in the Scholastic Art and Writing Awards program. (Rev: BL 9/15/05; SLJ 1/06) [810]

1157 Lombardo, Billy. *The Logic of a Rose: Chicago Stories* (9–12). 2005, BkMk paper $15.95 (1-886157-50-2). 150pp. Short stories reveal sensitive young Petey's awareness of the world around him as he grows up in early 1970s Chicago. (Rev: BL 6/1–15/05)

1158 Marcus, Ben, ed. *The Anchor Book of New American Short Stories* (9–12). 2004, Anchor paper $13.00 (1-4000-3482-5). 320pp. Selections by Lydia Davis, Stephen Dixon, Jhumpa Lahiri, and many others. (Rev: BL 8/04)

1159 Meno, Joe. *Bluebirds Used to Croon in the Choir* (11–12). 2005, Northwestern Univ. $21.95 (0-8101-5167-7). 189pp. Seventeen offbeat short stories, many featuring young people in difficult situations; for mature teens. (Rev: BL 11/15/05)

1160 Mercado, Nancy, ed. *Every Man for Himself: Ten Short Stories About Being a Guy* (10–12). 2005, Dial $16.99 (0-8037-2896-4). 176pp. This collection includes a story told in comic book form, one about a boy's coming out, and others about triumphs, defeats, embarrassments, and other important experiences leading to adulthood. (Rev: BL 9/1/05; SLJ 9/05; VOYA 10/05)

1161 Monson, Ander. *Other Electricities* (11–12). 2005, Sarabande paper $14.95 (1-932511-15-6). 192pp. An interconnected collection of affecting and inventive stories set in a town on Michigan's Upper Peninsula and featuring many teen characters; for mature teens who are strong readers. (Rev: BL 5/1/05)

1162 Nix, Garth. *Across the Wall: A Tale of the Abhorsen and Other Stories* (7–10). 2005, Harper-Collins LB $17.89 (0-06-074714-5). 320pp. In this collection of short stories, Garth offers an eclectic mix of genres and settings — only the first is related to Abhorsen — suitable for a range of readers. (Rev: BL 6/1–15/05; SLJ 11/05; VOYA 10/05)

1163 November, Sharyn, ed. *Firebirds Rising: An Anthology of Original Science Fiction and Fantasy* (7–10). 2006, Penguin $19.99 (0-14-240549-3). 512pp. Contributors to this anthology of 16 original stories include Tamora Pierce, Charles de Lint, Patricia A. McKillip, Kara Dalkey, and Tanith Lee. (Rev: BL 4/1/06; SLJ 4/06; VOYA 4/06)

1164 Palmer, Diana, et al. *More Than Words* (11–12). 2004, Harlequin paper $12.95 (0-373-83619-8). 384pp. Five Harlequin authors write stories focusing on acts of kindness and charity. (Rev: BL 9/15/04)

1165 Peck, Richard. *Past Perfect, Present Tense* (5–12). 2004, Dial $16.99 (0-8037-2998-7). 192pp. This anthology includes 11 previously published stories and two new ones, with comments on each story's inspiration and tips on writing fiction. (Rev: BL 4/1/04; HB 3–4/04; SLJ 4/04; VOYA 6/04)

1166 Phillips, Holly. *In the Palace of Repose* (10–12). 2005, Prime $29.95 (1-894815-58-0). 208pp. Nine stories suitable for strong readers incorporate elements of fantasy, mystery, and the heroic. (Rev: BL 2/1/05)

1167 Pierce, Tamora, and Josepha Sherman, eds. *Young Warriors: Stories of Strength* (7–10). 2005, Random LB $19.99 (0-375-92962-2). 320pp. This collection of 15 short stories recounts the exploits of teenage warriors in such diverse settings as ancient Greece, colonial India, World War II, and the plains of Africa. (Rev: BL 10/1/05; SLJ 10/05; VOYA 10/05)

1168 Pomplun, Tom, ed. *Adventure Classics: Graphic Classics*, Vol. 12 (9–12). Illus. Series: Graphic Classics. 2005, Eureka paper $11.95 (0-9746648-4-7). 144pp. Comic book adaptations of adventure stories and poems by such well-known authors as Alexandre Dumas, Zane Grey, and Rudyard Kipling are accompanied by short biographies of the writers and artists. (Rev: BL 10/1/05; SLJ 1/06; VOYA 4/06) [745.1]

1169 Satchelle, Christen, and Natasha Tarpley, eds. *What I Know Is Me: Black Girls Write About Their World* (11–12). 2005, Broadway paper $10.95 (0-7679-1214-4). 256pp. In various formats — short stories, poems, rap lyrics — young black women talk about what is important in their lives. (Rev: BL 9/15/05) [305.235]

1170 Sawyers, June S., ed. *The Best in Rock Fiction* (11–12). 2005, Hal Leonard paper $16.95 (0-634-08028-8). 272pp. An anthology of short stories and novel excerpts exemplifying a "rock and roll sensibility," including work by T. C. Boyle, Sherman Alexie, Nick Hornby, and Don DeLillo. (Rev: BL 2/15/05)

1171 Scott, Whitney, ed. *Things That Go Bump in the Night: The Supernatural from the Horrific to the Hilarious* (11–12). Series: Black-and-White Anthology. 2004, Outrider paper $17.95 (0-9712903-1-8). 246pp. An entertaining collection of diverse contemporary tales of the supernatural; for mature readers. (Rev: BL 9/15/04) [398.2]

1172 Sedaris, David, ed. *Children Playing Before a Statue of Hercules* (9–12). 2005, Simon & Schuster paper $14.95 (0-7432-7394-X). 320pp. Sedaris's choices for this collection include short stories by Katherine Mansfield, Flannery O'Connor, Alice Munro, and Jhumpa Lahiri. (Rev: BL 5/1/05)

1173 Singer, Marilyn. *Make Me Over: 11 Original Stories About Transforming Ourselves* (7–10). 2005, Dutton $16.99 (0-525-47480-3). 272pp. Teenage transformations and the importance of relationships are themes of these stories by writers including Joseph Bruchac, Margaret Peterson Haddix, and Joyce Sweeney. (Rev: BL 9/15/05; SLJ 2/06)

1174 Singleton, George. *Why Dogs Chase Cars* (11–12). 2004, Algonquin paper $14.95 (1-56512-404-9). 336pp. For Mendal Dawes, growing up in South Carolina with an opinionated father can be funny, frustrating, and fortuitous; short stories for mature teens. (Rev: BL 8/04)

1175 Smiley, Jane, et al., eds. *Best New American Voices, 2006* (10–12). 2005, Harcourt paper $14.00 (0-15-602901-4). 324pp. This collection of 15 short stories showcases the work of some of America's most promising new writers. (Rev: BL 10/1/05)

1176 Solomon, Barbara H., and Eileen Panetta, eds. *Once Upon a Childhood: Stories and Memoirs of American Youth* (9–12). 2004, NAL paper $14.00 (0-451-21296-7). 352pp. This anthology of stories about growing up in America features the work of such well-known authors as Ernest Hemingway, F. Scott Fitzgerald, Mary McCarthy, Sandra Cisneros, T. C. Boyle, and Alice Hoffman. (Rev: BL 10/1/04) [810.8]

1177 Soto, Gary. *Help Wanted* (7–10). 2005, Harcourt $17.00 (0-15-205201-1). 224pp. In this collection of ten short stories, Soto explores the dreams and struggles of Mexican American teens living in central California. (Rev: BCCB 5/05; BL 5/1/05; HB 5–6/05; SLJ 5/05)

1178 *Twice Told: Original Stories Inspired by Original Artwork* (7–10). Illus. 2006, Dutton $19.99 (0-525-46818-8). 320pp. Nine charcoal drawings by Scott Hunt were provided as inspiration to pairs of popular YA writers; the resulting short stories cover a wide range of styles and themes. (Rev: BL 2/15/06*; SLJ 4/06)

1179 Van Pelt, James. *The Last of the O-Forms and Other Stories* (9–12). 2005, Fairwood paper $17.95 (0-9746573-5-2). 220pp. A diverse collection covering many genres including ghost stories, sports stories, and science fiction. (Rev: BL 8/05)

1180 Vreeland, Susan. *Life Studies* (11–12). 2005, Viking $24.95 (0-670-03177-1). 292pp. Small, imagined incidents in the lives of artists such as Van Gogh, Cezanne, and Monet inspire many of these stories, while others depict characters whose lives are enriched by encounters with art; for mature teens. (Rev: BL 12/1/04)

1181 *What a Song Can Do: 12 Riffs on the Power of Music* (8–10). 2004, Random LB $17.99 (0-375-92499-X). 208pp. The power of music to transform young lives is explored in this appealing collection of 12 short stories. (Rev: BL 8/04; SLJ 7/04)

1182 Williams, Joy. *Honored Guest* (11–12). 2004, Knopf $23.00 (0-679-44647-8). 213pp. A collection of disturbing literary short stories, with themes including death, abuse, mental illness, and misery; for mature teens. (Rev: BL 9/1/04)

1183 Wood, Brian, and Becky Cloonan. *Demo* (9–12). Illus. 2005, Ait paper $19.95 (1-932051-42-2). 288pp. Author Brian Wood and artist Becky Cloonan collaborate to present 12 stories of teenagers in conflict. (Rev: BL 2/1/06)

1184 Yolen, Jane, and Patrick Nielsen Hayden, eds. *The Year's Best Science Fiction and Fantasy for Teens* (9–12). 2005, Tor $17.95 (0-765-31383-9); paper $12.95 (0-765-31384-7). 288pp. A winning collection of 11 outstanding fantasy and science fiction stories representing many subgenres and appropriate for young adults. (Rev: BL 6/1–15/05; SLJ 7/05; VOYA 10/05)

Plays

General and Miscellaneous Collections

1185 Bansavage, Lisa, and L. E. McCullough, eds. *111 Shakespeare Monologues for Teens: The Ultimate Audition Book for Teens Volume V* (7–12). Series: Young Actors. 2003, Smith & Kraus paper $11.95 (1-57525-356-9). 192pp. Monologues ranging from 15 seconds to 2 minutes and chosen for the youthful speakers or topics of interest to young people are arranged in three sections: for female actors, for male actors, and for male or female; an introduction explains Shakespeare's language and rhythms. (Rev: SLJ 7/04) [808.82]

1186 Dabrowski, Kristen. *111 One-Minute Monologues* (9–12). 2004, Smith & Kraus $24.95 (1-57525-307-0). 116pp. Aspiring teenage actors will find a wealth of audition material in this collection of 111 one-page monologues. (Rev: BL 8/04; SLJ 3/05) [812]

1187 Dabrowski, Kristen. *Teens Speak, Boys Ages 16 to 18: Sixty Original Character Monologues* (7–12). Series: Kids Speak. 2005, Smith & Kraus paper $11.95 (1-57525-415-8). 71pp. A collection of brief, varied monologues for teenage boys from 16 to 18. Also in the series are *Teens Speak, Boys Ages 13 to 15: Sixty Original Character Monologues*, *Teens Speak, Girls Ages 16 to 18: Sixty Original Character Monologues*, and *Teens Speak, Girls Ages 13 to 15: Sixty Original Character Monologues* (all 2005). (Rev: SLJ 7/05) [808.82]

1188 Dabrowski, Kristen. *Twenty 10-Minute Plays for Teens*, Vol. 1 (9–12). Series: Young Actors. 2004, Smith & Kraus paper $14.95 (1-57525-405-0). 129pp. Twenty short plays with roles for multiple characters deal with issues of interest to teens, from school life and sports to drinking, dating, and sexual identity. (Rev: SLJ 1/05) [812]

1189 Krell-Oishi, Mary. *Scenes Keep Happening: More Real-Life Snapshots of Teen Lives* (9–12). 2005, Meriwether paper $15.95 (1-56608-108-4). 215pp. Fifty 5- to 10-minute acts featuring teens in diverse situations are grouped by girls, boys, and mixed casts. (Rev: SLJ 2/06) [812]

1190 Lane, Eric, and Nina Shengold, eds. *Under Thirty: Plays for a New Generation* (9–12). 2004, Vintage paper $17.00 (1-4000-7616-1). 639pp. This collection of plays will appeal to actors and audiences in their teens and twenties. (Rev: SLJ 4/05)

Geographical Regions

Europe

GREAT BRITAIN AND IRELAND

1191 McKeown, Adam, retel. *Macbeth* (5–10). Series: The Young Reader's Shakespeare. 2005, Sterling $14.95 (1-4027-1116-6). 96pp. This conversational prose retelling includes an introduction to the play and incorporates many of the important poetic passages. (Rev: BL 3/1/05; SLJ 5/05) [822.3]

1192 McKeown, Adam. *Romeo and Juliet: Young Reader's Shakespeare* (5–10). 2004, Sterling $14.95 (1-4027-0004-0). 96pp. Faithful to the original, this retelling uses finely crafted prose and interweaves many of the best-known poetic stanzas. (Rev: BL 8/04; SLJ 10/04) [822.3]

1193 *Othello* (9–12). 2005, Sourcebooks $19.95 (1-4022-0645-0); paper $14.95 (1-4022-0102-8). 400pp. An audio CD that features recordings of scenes performed by well-known actors is included in this annotated full-text edition of the play; among additional features are essays on Shakespeare, an analysis of the play in popular culture, and interviews with actors and actresses. (Rev: SLJ 11/05*) [822]

1194 *Romeo and Juliet* (9–12). Series: The Sourcebooks Shakespeare. 2005, Sourcebooks $19.95 (1-402-20644-5); paper $14.95 (1-4022-0101-X). 400pp. An audio CD that features recordings of scenes performed by well-known actors is included in this annotated full-text edition of the play; among additional features are essays on Shakespeare, an analysis of the play in popular culture, and inter-

views with actors and actresses. (Rev: SLJ 11/05*) [822]

United States

1195 Fleischman, Paul. *Zap* (9–12). 2005, Candlewick $16.99 (0-7636-2774-7). 96pp. Works by Shakespeare, Chekhov, Tennessee Williams, and Samuel Beckett are among those featured in this chaotic play in which the audience can "zap" any boring moments. (Rev: BL 9/15/05; SLJ 11/05) [812]

Poetry

General and Miscellaneous Collections

1196 Janeczko, Paul B., ed. *Blushing: Expressions of Love in Poems and Letters* (8–12). 2004, Scholastic $15.95 (0-439-53056-3). 112pp. All aspects of love — from the first blush of new love to the heartbreak that follows love gone wrong — are covered in this anthology that includes classic and contemporary works. (Rev: BL 1/1–15/04; SLJ 5/04; VOYA 4/04) [821.008]

1197 Jay, Peter, ed. *The Sea! The Sea!* (9–12). 2006, Anvil paper $13.95 (0-85646-379-5). 176pp. This anthology of varied poetry about the sea was published to mark the bicentennial of the Battle of Trafalgar. (Rev: BL 3/1/06) [808.81]

1198 Mark, Jan, ed. *A Jetblack Sunrise: Poems About War and Conflict* (7–10). 2005, Hodder paper $8.99 (0-340-89379-6). 160pp. This anthology of poems explores not only the barbarity and savagery of war but also the courage, selflessness, and valor that sometimes shine through. (Rev: BL 9/1/05) [808.9]

1199 Nye, Naomi Shihab. *A Maze Me: Poems for Girls* (8–11). 2005, Greenwillow LB $17.89 (0-06-058190-5). 128pp. In this collection of more than 70 original poems, Nye addresses a broad range of subjects that will resonate with teenage girls. (Rev: BL 1/1–15/05*; SLJ 3/05; VOYA 2/05) [811]

1200 Nye, Naomi Shihab. *You and Yours* (9–12). 2005, BOA $22.95 (1-929918-68-2); paper $15.50 (1-929918-69-0). 104pp. Nye's Palestinian American heritage informs this collection of poems that explores a wide array of topics and environments. (Rev: BL 8/05) [811]

1201 Parisi, Joseph, ed. *100 Essential Modern Poems* (9–12). 2005, Ivan R. Dee $24.95 (1-56663-612-4). 224pp. The former editor of *Poetry* magazine offers 100 of the greatest modern poems written in English, providing fascinating profiles of the authors. (Rev: BL 10/1/05) [821]

1202 Payne, Nina. *Summertime Waltz* (9–12). 2005, Farrar $16.00 (0-374-37291-8). 32pp. Swiatkowska's artwork beautifully complements Nina Payne's three-stanza poem celebrating the long summer days of childhood, presented in picture-book format. (Rev: BL 5/15/05; SLJ 7/05) [811]

1203 Rachel, T. Cole, and Rita D. Costello, eds. *Bend, Don't Shatter* (9–12). 2004, Soft Skull paper $11.95 (1-932360-17-4). 111pp. Nearly 60 poems explore the coming-of-age experiences of young people who are gay, lesbian, bisexual, or transgendered. (Rev: BCCB 7–8/04; SLJ 1/05) [811]

1204 Rosenberg, Liz, and Deena November, eds. *I Just Hope It's Lethal: Poems of Sadness, Madness and Joy* (9–12). 2005, Houghton paper $7.99 (0-618-56452-7). 176pp. Editors Rosenberg and November, who have both suffered from depression, have compiled a collection of poems on mental problems by a wide variety of writers. (Rev: BL 11/15/05; SLJ 12/05; VOYA 2/06) [811]

1205 Strand, Mark, ed. *100 Great Poems of the Twentieth Century* (8–12). 2005, Norton $24.95 (0-393-05894-8). 256pp. Pulitzer Prize-winning poet Strand offers his selection of the 100 best poems of the 20th century. (Rev: BL 5/15/05) [821]

Geographical Regions

Europe

GREAT BRITAIN AND IRELAND

1206 Noyes, Alfred. *The Highwayman* (7–10). Series: Visions in Poetry. 2005, Kids Can $16.95 (1-55337-425-8). 48pp. In this beautifully illustrated Art Deco version of Noyes's immortal poem, the title character is transformed into a motorcycle-riding thief who roams the streets of New York City, while his beloved Bess is now a voluptuous glamour girl. (Rev: BL 5/1/05; SLJ 8/05; VOYA 10/05) [821]

United States

1207 Carlson, Lori, ed. *Red Hot Salsa: Bilingual Poems on Being Young and Latino in the United States* (8–11). 2005, Holt $14.95 (0-8050-7616-6). Poems in Spanish and English voice issues important to teens and the joys and sorrows of straddling two cultures. (Rev: BL 8/05; SLJ 8/05*) [811]

1208 Carruth, Hayden. *Toward the Distant Islands* (10–12). Ed. by Sam Hamill. 2006, Copper Canyon paper $17.00 (1-55659-236-1). 181pp. This collection showcases many facets of Carruth's work. (Rev: BL 3/1/06) [811]

1209 Clifton, Lucille. *Mercy* (11–12). 2004, BOA $22.00 (1-929918-54-2); paper $14.95 (1-929918-55-0). 94pp. The African American poet explores such sensitive subjects as cancer, death, and the aftershocks from the 9/11 tragedy; for mature readers. (Rev: BL 9/15/04) [811]

1210 Coval, Kevin. *Slingshots: (A Hip-Hop Poetica)* (10–12). 2006, EM paper $15.00 (0-9708012-4-6). 94pp. The Chicago-based hip-hop poet explores questions of compassion and identity. (Rev: BL 3/15/06) [811]

1211 Cummings, E. E. *Love: Selected Poems* (9–12). 2005, Hyperion $16.99 (0-7868-0796-2). 48pp. Bright images full of magical realism complement the love poetry of e. e. cummings. (Rev: BL 11/15/05; SLJ 1/06) [811]

1212 DeDonato, Collete. *City of One: Young Writers Speak to the World* (7–12). 2004, Aunt Lute Books paper $10.95 (1-879960-69-9). 239pp. In this moving collection of poetry from San Francisco-based WritersCorps, scores of young people give voice to their feelings about peace and violence. (Rev: BL 8/04; SLJ 8/04; VOYA 10/04) [810.8]

1213 Hollander, John, ed. *American Poetry* (4–10). Series: Poetry for Young People. 2004, Sterling $14.95 (1-4027-0517-4). 48pp. A colorful celebration of American life, containing 26 poems by well-known poets including Robert Frost, Walt Whitman, Maya Angelou, and Langston Hughes. (Rev: SLJ 8/04) [811]

1214 Hudson, Wade, ed. *Poetry from the Masters: The Pioneers* (6–12). 2003, Just Us Bks. paper $9.95 (0-940975-96-3). 88pp. Two-page biographical profiles introduce 11 African Americans and their works; among them are Phillis Wheatley, Paul Laurence Dunbar, Countee Cullen, Langston Hughes, and Gwendolyn Brooks. (Rev: SLJ 2/04) [811]

1215 *Is This Forever, or What? Poems and Paintings from Texas* (9–12). 2004, HarperCollins $19.99 (0-06-051178-8). 176pp. The many faces of the Lone Star State are beautifully portrayed in this appealing collection of poems and paintings by Texans; some are bilingual and many refer to Mexican heritage. (Rev: BL 7/04; HB 7–8/04; SLJ 7/04) [811]

1216 Lauer, Brett Fletcher, and Aimee Kelley, eds. *Isn't It Romantic: 100 Love Poems by Younger American Poets* (10–12). 2004, Verse paper $19.95 (0-9746353-1-6). 180pp. Love poems by 100 American poets born after 1960 are collected in this appealing and diverse anthology. (Rev: BL 1/1–15/05) [811]

1217 Myers, Walter Dean. *Voices from Harlem: Poems in Many Voices* (7–10). 2004, Holiday House $16.95 (0-8234-1853-7). 96pp. In this appealing collection of 54 poems, modeled on Edgar Lee Masters's *Spoon River Anthology*, Myers speaks in the diverse voices of imagined Harlem residents from many walks of life. (Rev: BCCB 12/04; BL 11/1/04*; HB 1–2/05; SLJ 12/04; VOYA 2/05) [811]

1218 Nelson, Marilyn. *Fortune's Bones: The Manumission Requiem* (7–12). 2005, Front Street $16.95 (1-932425-12-8). 40pp. Six poems celebrate the life of Fortune, a slave who died in 1798 but continued to serve his master, who rendered his bones and used Fortune's skeleton to teach anatomy. (Rev: BCCB 2/05; BL 11/15/04; HB 1–2/05; SLJ 12/04) [811]

1219 Nelson, Marilyn. *A Wreath for Emmett Till* (9–12). 2005, Houghton $17.00 (0-618-39752-3). 48pp. In this collection of 15 connected sonnets — in the form known as a heroic crown — Nelson remembers the 1955 lynching and the impact this tragic event had on the evolution of race relations in the United States. (Rev: BL 2/1/05*; SLJ 5/05) [811]

1220 Plath, Sylvia. *Ariel: The Restored Edition: A Facsimile of Plath's Manuscript, Reinstating Her*

Original Selection and Arrangement (9–12). 2004, HarperCollins $24.95 (0-06-073259-8). 240pp. This original version shows how Plath intended *Ariel* to appear. (Rev: BL 10/15/04) [811]

1221 Rampersad, Arnold, and Hilary Herbold, eds. *The Oxford Anthology of African-American Poetry* (10–12). 2005, Oxford $30.00 (0-19-512563-0). 432pp. An impressive anthology of poetry by African Americans. (Rev: BL 9/1/05) [811]

1222 Rodriguez, Luis J. *My Nature Is Hunger: New and Selected Poems, 1989–2004* (9–12). 2005, Curbstone paper $14.95 (1-931896-24-0). 150pp. In this collection of poetry, Luis Rodriguez, the son of Mexican immigrants, gives voice to his frustrations, anger, and hopes. (Rev: BL 8/05) [811]

1223 Roessel, David, and Arnold Rampersad, eds. *Langston Hughes* (7–10). 2006, Sterling $14.95 (1-4027-1845-4). 48pp. An illustrated picture-book-format collection of 26 poems with a useful introduction, a biography, and notes. (Rev: BL 2/1/06*) [811]

1224 Rylant, Cynthia. *Boris* (7–10). 2005, Harcourt $16.00 (0-15-205412-X). 80pp. This collection of free-verse poems celebrates the life and times of Boris, a big, gray cat adopted from a humane shelter. (Rev: BCCB 4/05; BL 2/15/05; HB 5–6/05; SLJ 4/05; VOYA 4/05) [811]

1225 Tamblyn, Amber. *Free Stallion: Poems* (11–12). 2005, Simon & Schuster $14.95 (1-4169-0259-7). 79pp. For mature readers, this is a frank collection of poems musing on the joys and agonies of teenage years and the developing sexuality. (Rev: SLJ 12/05)

1226 Williams, Saul. *The Dead Emcee Scrolls: The Lost Teachings of Hip-Hop and Connected Writings* (9–12). 2006, Pocket paper $12.95 (1-4165-1632-8). 208pp. Performance poet Saul Williams fuses hip-hop and poetry in this powerful collection. (Rev: BL 2/1/06) [811]

Other Regions

1227 Achebe, Chinua. *Collected Poems* (10–12). 2004, Anchor paper $12.00 (1-4000-7658-7). 128pp. Nigerian-born novelist Achebe is also an accomplished poet, as this collection demonstrates. (Rev: BL 8/04) [821]

Folklore and Fairy Tales

General and Miscellaneous

1228 Dokey, Cameron. *Sunlight and Shadow* (6–10). Series: Once Upon a Time. 2004, Simon & Schuster paper $5.99 (0-689-86999-1). 192pp. Mina — daughter of Pamina, the Queen of the Night, and of Sarastro, the Mage of the Day — falls in love with a prince called Tern and together the two face obstacles in this reworking of "The Magic Flute." (Rev: SLJ 11/04; VOYA 12/04)

1229 MacDonald, Margaret Read. *Three Minute Tales: Stories from Around the World to Tell or Read When Time Is Short* (8–12). 2004, August House $24.95 (0-87483-728-6); paper $17.95 (0-87483-729-4). 160pp. Brief tales that are easy to learn come with notes about sources and tips about effective telling. (Rev: BL 9/15/04; SLJ 10/04) [398.2]

Geographical Regions

Africa

1230 McCall Smith, Alexander. *The Girl Who Married a Lion and Other Tales from Africa* (8–12). 2004, Pantheon $20.00 (0-375-42312-5). 208pp. Traditional tales feature characterful animals and humans. (Rev: BL 11/1/04) [398.2]

Asia and the Middle East

1231 Napoli, Donna Jo. *Bound* (7–12). 2004, Simon & Schuster $16.95 (0-689-86175-3). 192pp. In this multilayered and thought-provoking Cinderella tale that draws on traditional Chinese elements, Xing Xing is mistreated by her stepmother and stepsister after the death of the girl's beloved father, but she escapes the cruel foot binding inflicted on her stepsister. (Rev: BL 12/1/04*; SLJ 11/04; VOYA 2/05)

Europe

1232 Andersen, Hans Christian. *Fairy Tales* (8–12). Ed. by Jackie Wullschlager. Trans. by Tuna Nunnally. Illus. 2005, Viking $27.95 (0-670-03377-4). 438pp. A collection of new translations of 30 stories. (Rev: BL 3/15/05)

Mythology

General and Miscellaneous

1233 Ashkenazi, Michael. *Handbook of Japanese Mythology* (10–12). Series: Handbooks of World Mythology. 2003, ABC-CLIO $75.00 (1-57607-467-6). 375pp. After an extensive introduction to the nature of Shinto and Buddhist myths, more than 200 alphabetical entries explain major figures, themes, and concepts of Japanese mythology. (Rev: SLJ 4/04) [299]

1234 Berk, Ari. *The Runes of Elfland* (7–12). 2003, Abrams $25.00 (0-8109-4612-2). 111pp. Brief stories and wonderful art highlighting the rune's significance and associations accompany each of 24 runes. (Rev: SLJ 5/04; VOYA 2/04) [398.2]

1235 Bingham, Ann. *South and Meso-American Mythology A to Z* (6–12). Series: Mythology A to Z. 2004, Facts on File $35.00 (0-8160-4889-4). 142pp. A handsome and thorough guide to the legends and folklore of early civilizations in Central and South America. (Rev: BL 10/1/04; SLJ 2/05) [398.2]

1236 Lynch, Patricia Ann. *Native American Mythology A to Z* (6–12). Series: Mythology A to Z. 2004, Facts on File $35.00 (0-8160-4891-6). 130pp. A handsome and thorough guide to Native American legends and folklore. (Rev: BL 10/1/04; SLJ 2/05) [398.2]

1237 Philip, Neil. *Mythology of the World* (8–12). 2004, Houghton $24.95 (0-7534-5779-2). 160pp. An excellent and thorough overview of world mythology, introducing readers to the plots and characters of myth and legend and examining the historical, cultural, and spiritual aspects of mythology. (Rev: BL 12/1/04; SLJ 10/04) [398.2]

1238 Roberts, Jeremy. *Japanese Mythology A to Z* (6–12). Illus. Series: Mythology A to Z. 2003, Facts on File $35.00 (0-8160-4871-1). 136pp. An easy-to-use alphabetically arranged volume introducing important places, practices and rituals, people, creatures, and so forth, with guidance on pronunciation. (Rev: SLJ 4/04) [299]

Classical

1239 Daly, Kathleen N. *Greek and Roman Mythology A to Z*. Rev. ed. (6–12). Illus. Series: Mythology A to Z. 2003, Facts on File $35.00 (0-8160-5155-0). 146pp. A newly updated, easy-to-use volume containing more than 500 entries of differing lengths covering places, practices and rituals, people, creatures, and so forth. (Rev: BL 3/1/04; SLJ 4/04; VOYA 6/04) [292]

1240 Geras, Adele. *Ithaka* (10–12). 2006, Harcourt $17.00 (0-15-205603-3). 368pp. This colorful retelling of Homer's *Odyssey* uses the viewpoint of young protagonists to make the story accessible to a teen audience. (Rev: BL 12/15/05; SLJ 2/06; VOYA 2/06)

1241 Hovey, Kate. *Ancient Voices* (6–10). 2004, Simon & Schuster $18.95 (0-689-83342-3). 40pp.

Poems and dramatic illustrations introduce key characters of Greek myths, occasionally injecting contemporary realism. (Rev: BL 1/1–15/04; SLJ 3/04) [811]

1242 Spinner, Stephanie. *Quicksilver* (8–11). 2005, Knopf LB $17.99 (0-375-92638-0). 240pp. Hermes, son of Zeus and quite a character in this incarnation, describes his participation in various well-known myths. (Rev: BCCB 4/05; BL 4/15/05; HB 3–4/05; SLJ 9/05; VOYA 4/05)

Scandinavian

1243 Daly, Kathleen N. *Norse Mythology A to Z.* Rev. ed. (6–12). Illus. Series: Mythology A to Z. 2003, Facts on File $35.00 (0-8160-5156-9). 126pp. A newly updated, easy-to-use volume containing approximately 400 entries covering places, practices and rituals, people, creatures, and so forth. (Rev: BL 3/1/04; SLJ 4/04; VOYA 6/04) [292.1]

Humor and Satire

1244 Mash, Robert. *How to Keep Dinosaurs*. Rev. ed. (7–12). Illus. 2003, Weidenfeld & Nicolson $14.99 (0-297-84347-8). 96pp. A tongue-in-cheek cleverly illustrated guide to the selection and care of your own pet prehistoric animal. (Rev: SLJ 4/04; VOYA 8/04)

Speeches, Essays, and General Literary Works

1245 *The Best American Magazine Writing, 2005* (10–12). 2005, Columbia paper $16.95 (0-231-13781-8). 544pp. This anthology showcases 17 articles that won National Magazine awards in 2005. (Rev: BL 11/1/05) [818]

1246 Couturier, Lisa. *The Hopes of Snakes: And Other Tales from the Urban Landscape* (9–12). 2005, Beacon $23.00 (0-8070-8564-2). 159pp. In this collection of essays, Couturier celebrates encounters with nature in and around the cities of the northeastern United States. (Rev: BL 12/1/04; SLJ 6/05) [808]

1247 Eggers, Dave, ed. *The Best American Nonrequired Reading, 2005* (11–12). Series: Best American. 2005, Houghton $27.50 (0-618-57047-0); paper $14.00 (0-618-57048-9). 368pp. For mature readers, this mixed bag of short fiction, magazine articles, and comics includes contributions from Al Franken, George Saunders, and William T. Vollmann. (Rev: BL 10/15/05) [818]

1248 Herbert, Bob. *Promises Betrayed: Waking Up from the American Dream* (10–12). 2005, Holt $25.00 (0-8050-7864-9). 352pp. A collection of thought-provoking essays in which *New York Times* columnist Herbert voices concern over America's failure to fulfill its promise of fairness and justice for all. (Rev: BL 4/15/05) [306]

1249 Kerouac, Jack. *Book of Sketches, 1952–54* (9–12). 2006, Penguin paper $18.00 (0-14-200215-1). 496pp. Jack Kerouac's jottings from his years on the road offer valuable insights into the creative mind of the leader of America's Beat movement. (Rev: BL 3/15/06) [818]

1250 Menand, Louis, and Robert Atwan, eds. *The Best American Essays, 2004* (9–12). 2004, Houghton $27.50 (0-618-35706-8); paper $14.00 (0-618-35709-2). 352pp. Louis Menand, author of *The Metaphysical Club*, served as guest editor for this collection of essays by such diverse writers as James Agee, Laura Hillenbrand, Tennessee Williams, and Jonathan Franzen. (Rev: BL 10/15/04) [80]

1251 Orlean, Susan, and Robert Atwan, eds. *The Best American Essays, 2005* (11–12). Series: Best American. 2005, Houghton $27.50 (0-618-35712-2); paper $14.00 (0-618-35713-0). 320pp. Well-known writers represented in this volume for advanced readers include Jonathan Franzen, Ted Kooser, David Sedaris, and Cathleen Schine. (Rev: BL 10/1/05) [808]

1252 Sedaris, David. *Dress Your Family in Corduroy and Denim* (8–12). 2004, Little, Brown $24.95 (0-316-14346-4). 272pp. In this collection of 27 essays, David Sedaris mines humor from a series of incidents in his personal life, some of which were not at all funny when they happened. (Rev: SLJ 1/05) [813]

1253 Williams, Patricia. *Open House: Of Family, Friends, Food, Piano Lessons, and the Search for a Room of My Own* (10–12). 2004, Farrar $24.00 (0-374-11407-2). 272pp. Williams, an African American law professor, offers her thoughts on a wide array of topics, including race, family, personal identify, and politics. (Rev: BL 11/15/04) [070.92]

Literary History and Criticism

Fiction

General and Miscellaneous

1254 Haugen, David M., ed. *Comic Books* (9–12). Series: Examining Pop Culture. 2005, Gale $34.95 (0-7377-2545-1). 174pp. A scholarly analysis of comic books as a social and cultural phenomenon, with discussion of their essential elements and of their evolution over time. (Rev: SLJ 9/05) [306]

1255 Jones, Stephen, and Kim Newman, eds. *Horror: Another 100 Best Books* (9–12). 2005, Carroll & Graf paper $15.95 (0-7867-1577-4). 272pp. In this collection of 100 essays, writers and critics single out their horror favorites, using a broad definition of the term *horror*. (Rev: BL 9/15/05) [808.83]

Europe

Great Britain and Ireland

1256 Beahm, George. *Muggles and Magic: J. K. Rowling and the Harry Potter Phenomenon* (7–12). Illus. 2004, Hampton Roads paper $16.95 (1-57174-412-6). 393pp. An impressive collection of information about the boy-wizard, his world, and his creator, J. K. Rowling. (Rev: SLJ 2/05)

1257 Bloom, Harold, ed. *Elizabeth Bennet* (10–12). Series: Bloom's Major Literary Characters. 2004, Chelsea House LB $31.95 (0-7910-7672-5). 264pp. An analysis of the character and importance of the key figure in Jane Austen's *Pride and Prejudice*. (Rev: SLJ 9/04) [813]

1258 Bloom, Harold, ed. *Jane Austen* (10–12). Series: Bloom's Modern Critical Views. 2003, Chelsea House LB $37.95 (0-7910-7656-3). 300pp. Scholarly essays analyze Austen's key works, examining themes, characters, and social context. (Rev: SLJ 6/04) [813]

1259 Bloom, Harold, ed. *King Arthur* (10–12). Series: Bloom's Major Literary Characters. 2003, Chelsea House LB $31.95 (0-7910-7670-9). 252pp. Arthurian tales by Thomas Malory, Alfred Lord Tennyson, and T. H. White are dissected by scholars exploring such topics as spirituality, violence, treason, and the origins of the legends themselves. (Rev: SLJ 6/04) [813]

1260 Crusie, Jennifer, ed. *Flirting with Pride and Prejudice: Fresh Perspectives on the Original Chick-Lit Masterpiece* (9–12). 2005, BenBella paper $14.95 (1-932100-72-5). 248pp. This entertaining collection of thought-provoking essays explores various aspects of Jane Austen's *Pride and Prejudice*, including the suggestion that the classic novel provides a model for contemporary chick-lit fiction. (Rev: BL 10/1/05) [823]

1261 Dailey, Donna, and John Toniedi. *London* (9–12). Ed. by Harold Bloom. Series: Bloom's Literary Places. 2005, Chelsea House LB $31.95 (0-7910-7841-8). 231pp. This wide-ranging volume takes readers on a tour of London sites of literary significance, placing them in historical and social context. (Rev: SLJ 9/05) [823]

1262 Dickens, Charles. *The Annotated Christmas Carol: A Christmas Carol in Prose* (10–12). Ed. by Michael Patrick Hearn. Illus. 2003, Norton $29.95 (0-393-05158-7). 287pp. With many illustrations by a number of artists plus extensive quotations from many sources, this volume offers a biography of Dickens, discussion of the story's publication and reception, and the original text with many footnotes and supplementary facts. (Rev: SLJ 1/04) [823]

1263 Swisher, Clarice. *Understanding The Canterbury Tales* (8–12). Series: Understanding Great Literature. 2003, Gale LB $21.96 (1-56006-782-9).

128pp. Background on Chaucer and medieval life precedes discussion of the themes, characters, and literary devices found in the tales. (Rev: SLJ 1/04) [821]

1264 *Treasure Island and the Pirates of the 18th Century* (9–12). Illus. Series: Looking at Literature Through Primary Sources. 2004, Rosen LB $21.95 (0-8239-4507-3). 64pp. After a brief biography of Robert Louis Stevenson, there is a plot summary plus information on 19th-century pirates and seafaring that is tied to specific passages. (Rev: BL 11/15/04) [823]

United States

1265 Bernard, Catherine. *Understanding To Kill a Mockingbird* (7–10). Series: Understanding Great Literature. 2003, Gale LB $27.45 (1-56006-860-4). 112pp. Provides a biography of Harper Lee, historical background, and discussion of the plot and characters in addition to study questions and quotations from reviews and articles. (Rev: SLJ 3/04) [813]

1266 Bloom, Harold, ed. *George F. Babbitt* (10–12). Series: Bloom's Major Literary Characters. 2003, Chelsea House LB $31.95 (0-7910-7667-9). 124pp. In addition to essays by contributors (including H. L. Mencken and Gore Vidal) on Sinclair Lewis and his work, this volume includes a character profile and a bibliography. (Rev: SLJ 5/04)

1267 Bloom, Harold, ed. *Jay Gatsby* (10–12). Series: Bloom's Major Literary Characters. 2003, Chelsea House LB $31.95 (0-7910-7673-3). 160pp. In addition to essays by contributors (including Thomas H. Pauly and Edwin S. Fussell) on Fitzgerald and his work, this volume includes a character profile and a bibliography. (Rev: SLJ 5/04)

1268 Bloom, Harold, ed. *Truman Capote* (9–12). Series: Bloom's Modern Critical Views. 2003, Chelsea House LB $37.95 (0-7910-7397-1). 186pp. Eight scholarly essays analyze Capote's key works and explore the influences of his life and times. (Rev: SLJ 2/04) [813]

1269 Carlson, Julie. *Uncle Tom's Cabin and the Abolitionist Movement* (9–12). Illus. Series: Looking at Literature Through Primary Sources. 2004, Rosen LB $21.95 (0-8239-4508-1). 64pp. Biographical information on Harriet Beecher Stowe is accompanied by a summary of the plot and discussion of race relations and social structures. (Rev: BL 11/15/04; SLJ 11/04) [813]

1270 Diorio, Mary Ann L. *A Student's Guide to Nathaniel Hawthorne* (7–10). Series: Understanding Literature. 2004, Enslow LB $21.95 (0-7660-2283-

8). 160pp. The plot, characters, themes, and literary devices found in Hawthorne's works are discussed, and there are details of his life and major influences. (Rev: SLJ 6/04) [813]

1271 Newman, Gerald, and Eleanor Newman Layfield. *A Student's Guide to John Steinbeck* (8–12). Series: Understanding Literature. 2004, Enslow LB $27.93 (0-7660-2259-5). 176pp. This guide examines the writer's life as well as the characters, themes, and symbolism found in his novels. (Rev: SLJ 3/05) [813]

1272 Pennell, Melissa McFarland. *Student Companion to Edith Wharton* (10–12). Series: Student Companions to Classic Writers. 2003, Greenwood $40.00 (0-313-31715-1). 186pp. Introduces the life and works of the American writer, with critical analysis of her works, including *Ethan Frome* and *The Age of Innocence*. (Rev: SLJ 4/04) [8113]

1273 Phillips, Jerry, and Andrew Ladd. *Romanticism and Transcendentalism (1800–1860)* (9–12). Illus. Series: Background to American Literature. 2006, Facts on File LB $30.00 (0-8160-5668-4). 96pp. Emerson, Longfellow, and Thoreau are among the authors discussed in this overview of two important literary movements of the 19th century. (Rev: BL 4/1/06) [810.9]

1274 Pingelton, Timothy J. *A Student's Guide to Ernest Hemingway* (7–12). Series: Understanding Literature. 2005, Enslow LB $27.93 (0-7660-2431-8). 160pp. Introduces Hemingway's life and works, with analysis of some of his best-known writings. (Rev: SLJ 10/05) [813]

1275 Schultz, Jeffrey, and Luchen Li. *Critical Companion to John Steinbeck: A Literary Reference to His Life and Work* (9–12). 2005, Facts on File $65.00 (0-8160-4300-0). 406pp. This comprehensive volume offers a biography of Steinbeck, alphabetically arranged articles on his works, and information about people, places, and topics relating to his life and work. (Rev: BL 2/1/06; SLJ 2/06) [813]

1276 Vincent, Bev. *The Road to the Dark Tower: Exploring Stephen King's Magnum Opus* (9–12). 2004, NAL paper $14.95 (0-451-21304-1). 416pp. A useful companion to King's seven-volume Dark Tower series, with the story behind the writing of the series, a book-by-book analysis, and comments on links with other King novels. (Rev: BL 10/1/04) [813]

1277 Weisbrod, Eva. *A Student's Guide to F. Scott Fitzgerald* (9–12). Series: Understanding Literature. 2004, Enslow LB $21.95 (0-7660-2202-1). 160pp. A biography of Fitzgerald and a guide to his major works are combined in this useful volume. (Rev: BL 4/1/04; SLJ 6/04) [813]

Plays and Poetry

Shakespeare

1278 Bloom, Harold, ed. *Romeo and Juliet* (9–12). Series: Bloom's Guides. 2005, Chelsea House $23.95 (0-7910-8170-2). 140pp. A critical analysis of the tale about ill-fated teen lovers, with essays that examine the characters and such topics as Shakespeare's treatment of adolescents. (Rev: SLJ 7/05) [822.3]

1279 Page, Philip, and Marilyn Pettit, eds. *Romeo and Juliet* (8–11). Illus. Series: Picture This! Shakespeare. 2005, Barrons paper $7.95 (0-7641-3144-3). 64pp. This attractive title uses both straight text and cartoon characters to present not only the full text of Shakespeare's tragic romance but also notes on devices and related information. (Rev: BL 3/15/05; SLJ 9/05) [745.1]

1280 Woodford, Donna. *Understanding King Lear: A Student Casebook to Issues, Sources, and Historical Documents* (9–12). Series: Literature in Context. 2004, Greenwood $45.00 (0-313-31936-7). 183pp. This guide uses period documents and literature to help readers get the most from *King Lear*. (Rev: SLJ 3/05) [822.3]

United States

1281 Borus, Audrey. *A Student's Guide to Emily Dickinson* (7–12). Series: Understanding Literature. 2005, Enslow LB $27.93 (0-7660-2285-4). 152pp. Introduces Dickinson's life and poetry, with discussion of key themes, how to analyze the poems, and a glossary of terms. (Rev: SLJ 10/05) [813]

1282 Dunkleberger, Amy. *A Student's Guide to Arthur Miller* (7–12). Series: Understanding Literature. 2005, Enslow LB $27.93 (0-7660-2432-6). 160pp. Combines biographical information and discussion of Miller's key works. (Rev: SLJ 10/05) [813]

1283 Jimerson, M. N. *Understanding The Crucible* (7–10). Series: Understanding Great Literature. 2003, Gale LB $28.70 (1-56006-996-1). 112pp. A look at the characters, plot, and historical context of the classic play, with biographical information on Arthur Miller. (Rev: SLJ 2/04)

Language and Communication

Words and Languages

1284 Balistreri, Maggie. *Evasion-English Dictionary* (9–12). 2003, Melville House paper $12.95 (0-9718-6597-3). 87pp. A brief look at the real meanings of favorite teen words such as "like" and "whatever." (Rev: SLJ 1/04)

1285 Casagrande, June. *Grammar Snobs Are Great Big Meanies: A Guide to Language for Fun and Spite* (8–12). 2006, Penguin paper $14.00 (0-14-303683-1). 200pp. A lighthearted review of the rules of grammar, from prepositions and split infinitives to new conventions for e-mail and text messaging. (Rev: BL 4/1/06) [428]

1286 MacNeil, Robert, and William Cran. *Do You Speak American?* (10–12). 2005, Doubleday $23.95 (0-385-51198-1). 228pp. An entertaining exploration of the continuing evolution of English as spoken by Americans, as well as the many regional, racial, and ethnic variants of the language. (Rev: BL 12/1/04; SLJ 6/05) [427]

1287 Truss, Lynne. *Eats, Shoots and Leaves: The Zero Tolerance Approach to Punctuation* (9–12). 2004, Gotham $17.95 (1-59240-087-6). 240pp. A witty plea for proper punctuation. (Rev: BL 6/1–15/04; SLJ 8/04) [428.2]

Writing and the Media

General and Miscellaneous

1288 Baker, Nicholson, and Margaret Brentano. *The World on Sunday: Graphic Art in Joseph Pulitzer's Newspaper (1898–1911)* (9–12). Illus. 2005, Bulfinch $50.00 (0-8212-6193-2). 144pp. Baker and his wife present representative examples of the graphic art that appeared in the pages of the *Sunday World*, Joseph Pulitzer's groundbreaking New York City newspaper. (Rev: BL 10/15/05) [071]

1289 Boynton, Robert S. *The New New Journalism: Conversations with America's Best Nonfiction Writers on Their Craft* (9–12). 2005, Vintage paper $13.00 (1-4000-3356-X). 304pp. Some of today's leading literary journalists, including Jon Krakauer, Susan Orlean, Lawrence Weschler, and Jane Kramer, offer insights into how they do their job. (Rev: BL 2/15/05) [071]

1290 Currie, Stephen, ed. *Terrorism* (7–10). Illus. Series: Writing the Critical Essay. 2005, Gale LB $20.96 (0-7377-3206-7). 111pp. Opposing viewpoints on terrorism are combined with tips for writing a succinct essay on the subject. (Rev: BL 3/1/06) [363.32]

1291 Francis, Barbara. *Other People's Words: What Plagiarism Is and How to Avoid It* (6–12). Series: Issues in Focus Today. 2005, Enslow LB $31.93 (0-7660-2525-X). 112pp. Practical suggestions about avoiding plagiarism are accompanied by examples of plagiarism through history and current instances of "borrowing" ideas and words. (Rev: SLJ 12/05)

1292 Harper, Timothy, and Elizabeth Harper. *Your Name in Print: A Teen's Guide to Publishing for Fun, Profit and Academic Success* (8–12). 2005, St. Martin's paper $13.95 (0-312-33759-0). 186pp. The Harpers (father and daughter) offer alternating how-to advice on writing and getting published in a variety of formats. (Rev: BL 9/1/05; SLJ 11/05; VOYA 8/05) [808]

1293 Orr, Tamra. *Extraordinary Essays* (9–12). Illus. Series: F. W. Prep. 2005, Scholastic $30.50 (0-531-16761-5); paper $9.95 (0-531-17576-6). 128pp. From choosing a suitable topic to researching, writing, and revising, this is a practical and well-organized guide that also provides advice on preparing for the SAT essay. (Rev: BL 2/1/06; SLJ 1/06; VOYA 4/06) [808.4]

1294 Pilger, John, ed. *Tell Me No Lies: Investigative Journalism That Changed the World* (10–12). 2005, Thunders Mouth paper $18.95 (1-56025-786-5). 626pp. A collection of important pieces of investigative journalism, each preceded by biographical information and a note giving context. (Rev: BL 9/15/05) [071]

Books and Publishing

1295 Shaw, Mark. *Book Report: Publishing Strategies, Writing Tips, and 101 Literary Ideas for Aspiring Authors and Poets.* 4th ed. (9–12). 2004, Books for Life paper $17.95 (0-9717596-6-9). 264pp. A practical guide to writing, editing, and selling fiction and nonfiction. Also use *Grammar Report: Basic Writing Tools for Aspiring Authors and Poets* and *Poetry Report: Creative Ideas and Publishing Strategies for Aspiring Poets* (both 2004). (Rev: SLJ 2/05) [808]

Print and Other Media

1296 *Embedded in America: The Onion Ad Nauseam Complete News Archives*, Vol. 16 (10–12). Illus. 2005, Three Rivers paper $18.95 (1-4000-5456-7). 320pp. The 16th collection of the faux news in which the Onion specializes; for mature readers. (Rev: BL 11/15/05) [071]

1297 Fingeroth, Danny. *Superman on the Couch* (9–12). 2004, Continuum paper $19.95 (0-8264-1540-7). 192pp. A thoughtful, easy-to-read exploration of superheroes — male and female — and why they are popular and what they tell us about ourselves. (Rev: SLJ 8/04) [741.5]

1298 Mills, Eleanor, and Kira Cochrane, eds. *Journalistas: 100 Years of the Best Writing and Reporting by Women Journalists* (9–12). 2006, Carroll & Graf paper $14.95 (0-7867-1667-3). 384pp. A fascinating collection of the best in reporting by women over the past century, touching on many important subjects, including the need to choose between career and family. (Rev: BL 11/1/05) [071]

1299 Pilcher, Tim, and Brad Brooks. *The Essential Guide to World Comics* (9–12). Illus. 2006, Collins & Brown paper $19.95 (1-84340-300-5). 320pp. A survey of the best of the genre from around the globe. (Rev: BL 2/15/06) [741.5]

1300 Rollins, Prentis. *The Making of a Graphic Novel* (7–12). 2006, Watson-Guptill paper $19.95 (0-8230-3053-9). 168pp. One side of this "double-sided flip book" contains the text of a graphic novel called *The Resonator*; the other side holds a detailed account of the construction of this novel and the inspirations for the designs. (Rev: SLJ 3/06) [741.5]

1301 Voger, Mark. *The Dark Age: Grim, Great and Gimmicky Post-Modern Comics* (10–12). Illus. 2006, TwoMorrows paper $19.95 (1-893905-53-5). 168pp. An overview of the grittier and more violent comic books that began appearing in the mid-1980s. (Rev: BL 3/15/06)

Biography, Memoirs, Etc.

General and Miscellaneous

1302 Hatch, Robert, and William Hatch. *The Hero Project: How We Met Our Greatest Heroes and What We Learned from Them* (8–12). Illus. 2005, McGraw-Hill paper $14.95 (0-07-144904-3). 204pp. Fascinating interviews with such luminaries as Jackie Chan, Lance Armstrong, Orson Scott Card, Yo-Yo Ma, and Jimmy Carter result from the Hatch brothers' "hero project," which started when William was only 11 years old. (Rev: BL 9/15/05; SLJ 1/06) [920]

Adventurers and Explorers

Collective

1303 Fleming, Fergus. *Tales of Endurance and Exploration* (8–12). Illus. 2005, Grove $26.00 (0-87113-899-9). 560pp. From the well known — Marco Polo and Christopher Columbus, for example — to less-recognized adventurers, this celebration of the courage of 45 explorers is divided into three eras and accompanied by excellent black-and-white illustrations. (Rev: BL 6/1–15/05) [910]

Individual

CROCKETT, DAVY

1304 Groneman, William. *David Crockett: Hero of the Common Man* (10–12). 2005, Forge $19.95 (0-765-31067-8). 208pp. Groneman cuts through the haze of myth and folklore to present the real — and not always inspiring — story of the legendary frontiersman and Alamo defender. (Rev: BL 11/1/05) [973.5]

EARHART, AMELIA

1305 Van Pelt, Lori. *Amelia Earhart: The Sky's No Limit* (8–12). Series: American Heroes. 2005, Tor $21.95 (0-765-31061-9). 208pp. A brief but information-packed biography that gives lots of personal details as well as covering her passion for flying. (Rev: BL 3/1/05) [629.13]

MARTIN, JESSE

1306 Martin, Jesse. *Kijana: The Real Story* (9–12). 2005, Allen & Unwin paper $16.95 (1-74114-429-9). 241pp. Jesse Martin, who at 18 became the youngest person to sail alone around the world, chronicles a subsequent global tour he undertook with his brother and three friends. (Rev: BL 11/1/05) [910.41]

SHACKLETON, SIR ERNEST

1307 Riffenburgh, Beau. *Shackleton's Forgotten Expedition: The Voyage of the Nimrod* (8–12). 2004, Bloomsbury $25.95 (1-58234-488-4). 384pp. This story of Shackleton's first expedition to the Antarctic aboard the *Nimrod* underlines its significant scientific and exploratory achievements. (Rev: BL 10/15/04) [919.8]

Artists, Authors, Composers, and Entertainers

Collective

1308 Bostrom, Kathleen Long. *Winning Authors: Profiles of the Newbery Medalists* (5–10). Series: Popular Authors. 2003, Libraries Unlimited $52.00 (1-56308-877-0). 338pp. Report writers will find useful information on the authors who won this prestigious award, including quotations and material on experiences that relate to the winning books. (Rev: SLJ 6/04; VOYA 6/04) [920]

1309 De Angelis, Gina. *Motion Pictures: Making Cinema Magic* (6–10). Series: Innovators. 2004, Oliver LB $21.95 (1-881508-78-1). 144pp. Profiles eight inventors of motion picture technology, including Auguste and Louis Lumière, Lee de Forest, and Mike Todd. (Rev: BCCB 5/04; SLJ 9/04) [920]

1310 Farrington, Lisa E. *Creating Their Own Image: The History of African-American Women Artists* (9–12). Illus. 2005, Oxford $55.00 (0-19-516721-X). 368pp. Farrington profiles African American women artists, introduces their work, and discusses the challenges they faced. (Rev: BL 2/1/05) [704]

1311 Koopmans, Andy. *Filmmakers* (7–10). Illus. Series: History Makers. 2005, Gale LB $22.96 (1-59018-598-6). 112pp. Profiles five of the world's most influential filmmakers — Alfred Hitchcock, Stanley Kubrick, Francis Ford Coppola, Spike Lee, and Peter Jackson. (Rev: BL 6/1–15/05) [920]

1312 Tessitore, John. *Extraordinary American Writers* (6–12). 2004, Children's Pr. LB $39.00 (0-516-22656-8). 288pp. Writers profiled here "examined and analyzed American society in their works" and range from Benjamin Franklin to Philip Roth; biographical essays include information on important works and a brief excerpt. (Rev: SLJ 9/04) [920]

Artists and Architects

ADAMS, ARTHUR

1313 Khoury, George, and Eri Nolen-Weathington. *Arthur Adams: Modern Masters*, Vol. 6 (9–12). Illus. Series: Modern Masters. 2006, TwoMorrows paper $14.95 (1-893905-54-3). 128pp. A look at the life and art of Arthur Adams, the award-winning comic book creator who became known in the mid-1980s for his Longshot series. (Rev: BL 4/1/06) [741.5]

AUDUBON, JOHN JAMES

1314 Audubon, John James. *The Audubon Reader* (9–12). Ed. by Richard Rhodes. Illus. 2006, Everyman's Library $25.00 (1-4000-4369-7). 560pp. Excerpts from the author's lively letters, journals, and other writings document his wide-ranging travels and zest for life. (Rev: BL 3/15/06) [598]

1315 Souder, William. *Under a Wild Sky; John James Audubon and the Making of The Birds of America* (10–12). Illus. 2004, Farrar $25.00 (0-86547-671-3). 336pp. Souder delves into the center of this interesting artist and naturalist who was born in Haiti in the late 18th century. (Rev: BL 6/1–15/04) [598]

CATLETT, ELIZABETH

1316 Herzog, Melanie Anne. *Elizabeth Catlett: In the Image of the People* (9–12). Illus. 2005, Yale paper $9.95 (0-300-11612-8). 36pp. This brief biography of painter, sculptor, and printmaker Elizabeth Catlett focuses on the African American artist's commitment to social and political issues. (Rev: BL 2/1/06) [730]

COLAN, GENE

1317 Field, Tom. *Secrets in the Shadows: The Art and Life of Gene Colan* (9–12). Illus. 2005, TwoMorrows $44.95 (1-893905-46-2); paper $21.95 (1-893905-45-4). 192pp. This eye-catching retrospective chronicles the long career of comic book artist Gene Colan. (Rev: BL 10/15/05) [741.5]

GARCÍA-LÓPEZ, JOSÉ LUIS

1318 Weathington, Eric Nolen, ed. *José Luis García-López: Modern Masters*, Vol. 5 (9–12). Illus. Series: Modern Masters. 2005, TwoMorrows paper $14.95 (1-893905-44-6). 128pp. Chronicles the life and work of Argentine-born José Luis García-López, one of the world's greatest comic book artists. (Rev: BL 10/15/05) [741.5]

GEHRY, FRANK

1319 Lazo, Caroline Evensen. *Frank Gehry* (7–10). Series: A&E Biography. 2005, Twenty-First Century LB $27.93 (0-8225-2649-2); paper $7.95 (0-8225-3388-X). 112pp. Introduces the architect and his most famous structures, with full-color photos and reproductions. (Rev: SLJ 2/06) [921]

RIVERA, DIEGO

1320 Litwin, Laura Baskes. *Diego Rivera: Legendary Mexican Painter* (7–10). Illus. Series: Latino Biography. 2005, Enslow LB $23.95 (0-7660-2486-5). 128pp. The life, art, and controversial politics of Mexican artist Diego Rivera are explored in this attractive and readable title. (Rev: BL 11/1/05; SLJ 4/06) [759.972]

TIMM, BRUCE

1321 Weathington, Eric Nolen, ed. *Bruce Timm* (9–12). Illus. Series: Modern Masters. 2004, TwoMorrows paper $14.95 (1-893905-30-6). 120pp. Television animator/comic book artist Timm discusses the influences that helped to shape his distinctive style; this volume also includes a portfolio of his work. (Rev: BL 10/15/04) [741.5]

WARHOL, ANDY

1322 Greenberg, Jan, and Sandra Jordan. *Andy Warhol, Prince of Pop* (8–12). 2004, Random LB $18.99 (0-385-73056-X). 208pp. Warhol had a successful career in commercial art before rising to fame as a pop icon; this volume covers his youth, early career, love of celebrity, and early death as well as his art and its lasting influence. (Rev: BCCB 12/04; BL 6/1–15/04*; HB 1–2/05; SLJ 11/04; VOYA 10/04) [709]

WRIGHT, FRANK LLOYD

1323 Fandel, Jennifer. *Frank Lloyd Wright* (7–12). Series: Xtraordinary Artists. 2005, Creative Education LB $21.95 (1-58341-378-2). 48pp. This well-illustrated life of the visionary architect draws on comments from his students, contemporaries, and admirers. (Rev: SLJ 12/05)

Authors

ABU-JABER, DIANA

1324 Abu-Jaber, Diana. *The Language of Baklava* (9–12). 2005, Pantheon $23.00 (0-375-42304-4). 352pp. Novelist Abu-Jaber writes an absorbing account of growing up in upstate New York as the daughter of an American mother and a Jordanian father, remembering the challenges of the immigrant experience and the joys of the good food her household enjoyed. (Rev: BL 2/15/05; SLJ 9/05) [641.59]

AUSTEN, JANE

1325 Locke, Juliane. *England's Jane: The Story of Jane Austen* (8–11). Illus. 2006, Morgan Reynolds LB $26.95 (1-931798-82-6). 144pp. The parallels between Austen's life and novels are evident in this appealing biography. (Rev: BL 2/15/06; SLJ 2/06) [823]

1326 Wagner, Heather Lehr. *Jane Austen* (7–10). Series: Who Wrote That? 2003, Chelsea House LB $22.95 (0-7910-7623-7). 112pp. Details of Austen's family life and education and of the mores of the time give insight into her humorous attitude toward society and romance. (Rev: SLJ 6/04) [921]

BRADSTREET, ANNE DUDLEY

1327 Gordon, Charlotte. *Mistress Bradstreet: The Untold Life of America's First Poet* (10–12). Illus. 2005, Little, Brown $27.95 (0-316-16904-8). 304pp. The life and literary career of 17th-century Puritan poet Anne Dudley Bradstreet. (Rev: BL 3/1/05; SLJ 11/05) [811]

BRENNAN, CHRISTINE

1328 Brennan, Christine. *Best Seat in the House: A Father, a Daughter, a Journey Through Sports* (9–12). Illus. 2006, Scribner $26.00 (0-7432-5436-8). 352pp. A childhood and adolescence steeped in sports helped Brennan to realize her dream of a career in sports journalism. (Rev: BL 3/15/06) [070.4]

BROOKS, GWENDOLYN

1329 Hill, Christine M. *Gwendolyn Brooks: "Poetry Is Life Distilled"* (7–10). Illus. Series: African-American Biography Library. 2005, Enslow LB $23.95 (0-7660-2292-7). 128pp. Poet Gwendolyn Brooks, the first African American to win the Pulitzer Prize, is profiled in accessible text with lots of photos and background information. (Rev: BL 11/1/05; SLJ 11/05) [811]

CISNEROS, SANDRA

1330 Brackett, Virginia. *A Home in the Heart: The Story of Sandra Cisneros* (7–12). Series: World Writers. 2004, Morgan Reynolds LB $21.95 (1-931798-42-7). 128pp. The life and literary career of Mexican American author Sandra Cisneros. (Rev: BL 12/1/04; SLJ 3/05) [921]

DERY, DOMINIKA

1331 Dery, Dominika. *The Twelve Little Cakes* (9–12). 2004, Riverhead $24.95 (1-57322-283-6). 384pp. In this warmhearted memoir, Czech poet/playwright Dery looks back fondly on a childhood that not even the brutality of her country's Communist regime could dim. (Rev: BL 9/15/04) [891.8]

DICKENS, CHARLES

1332 Caravantes, Peggy. *Best of Times: The Story of Charles Dickens* (7–10). Illus. Series: Writers of Imagination. 2005, Morgan Reynolds LB $24.95 (1-931798-68-0). 160pp. Examines the events in the author's life that led to his literary preoccupation with social injustices. (Rev: BL 8/05; SLJ 12/05) [823]

DICKINSON, EMILY

1333 Herstek, Amy Paulson. *Emily Dickinson: Solitary and Celebrated Poet* (7–10). Series: Historical American Biographies. 2003, Enslow LB $20.95 (0-7660-1977-2). 128pp. A life of Dickinson, describing her childhood, the development of her beliefs, her love of nature, family, and friends, and her work. (Rev: SLJ 5/04; VOYA 4/04) [921]

1334 Meltzer, Milton. *Emily Dickinson* (8–11). Illus. Series: American Literary Greats. 2006, Lerner LB $31.93 (0-7613-2949-8). 128pp. Dickinson's life story is interwoven with quotes from her poetry and excerpts from primary sources including letters. (Rev: BL 2/15/06; VOYA 4/06) [811]

DINESEN, ISAK

1335 Leslie, Roger. *Isak Dinesen: Gothic Storyteller* (8–12). Illus. 2004, Morgan Reynolds LB $21.95 (1-931798-17-6). 128pp. Danish-born author Isak Dinesen, best known for *Out of Africa*, a memoir of her years spent in Kenya, is profiled in this engaging volume that emphasizes her battle with syphilis. (Rev: BL 4/1/04; SLJ 5/04) [921]

FITZGERALD, F. SCOTT

1336 Boon, Kevin Alexander. *F. Scott Fitzgerald* (7–10). Series: Writers and Their Works. 2005, Benchmark LB $25.95 (0-7614-1947-0). 142pp. *The Great Gatsby* is discussed in some detail in this overview of Fitzgerald's life and works. (Rev: SLJ 3/06) [921]

GILMAN, SUSAN JANE

1337 Gilman, Susan Jane. *Hypocrite in a Pouffy White Dress: Tales of Growing Up Groovy and Clueless* (10–12). 2004, Warner paper $12.95 (0-446-67949-6). 354pp. A funny and totally recognizable memoir, detailing Gilman's life from a Jewish childhood in New York City's Upper West Side in the late 1960s and early 1970s through adolescence, adulthood, and marriage; for mature readers. (Rev: BL 9/1/04; SLJ 9/05) [974.7]

HAKAKIAN, ROYA

1338 Hakakian, Roya. *Journey from the Land of No: A Girlhood Caught in Revolutionary Iran* (9–12). 2004, Crown $23.00 (1-4000-4611-4). 272pp. Poet and documentary filmmaker Hakakian writes about her childhood and adolescence as a Jew in Iran and the violent changes brought by the revolution in the late 1970s. (Rev: BL 7/04; SLJ 12/04) [955.05]

HUGHES, LANGSTON

1339 Rummel, Jack. *Langston Hughes: Poet*. Rev. ed. (7–12). Series: Black Americans of Achievement. 2005, Chelsea House LB $23.95 (0-7910-8250-4). 108pp. A revised edition of the highly readable and well illustrated biography of the African American poet and fiction writer, containing excerpts from his writings. (Rev: SLJ 11/05) [921]

KEROUAC, JACK

1340 Brinkley, Douglas, ed. *The Windblown World: The Journals of Jack Kerouac 1947–1954* (11–12). 2004, Viking $25.95 (0-670-03341-3). 387pp. The journals of Kerouac, an author and icon of the "Beat Generation," reveal much about his writing, reading, and social life while writing his first novel in his mid-20s; for mature readers. (Rev: BL 10/15/04; SLJ 3/05) [818]

KIDDER, TRACY

1341 Kidder, Tracy. *My Detachment* (11–12). 2005, Random $24.95 (0-375-50615-2). 208pp. Kidder, an award-winning writer, shares with humor and perception the story of his tour of duty as a young officer in Vietnam; for mature teens. (Rev: BL 7/05) [959.704]

KING, STEPHEN

1342 Whitelaw, Nancy. *Dark Dreams: The Story of Stephen King* (7–10). Illus. Series: World Writers. 2005, Morgan Reynolds $26.95 (1-931798-77-X). 128pp. An inviting introduction to King and to his writing, with lots of interesting anecdotes and snippets of his work. (Rev: BL 11/15/05; VOYA 2/06) [813]

LESTER, JULIUS

1343 Lester, Julius. *On Writing for Children and Other People* (9–12). 2004, Penguin $16.99 (0-8037-2867-0). 160pp. Award-winning African American children's author Lester writes engagingly about his life and his craft, talking in particular about his love of retelling folktales while retaining their original essence. (Rev: BCCB 10/04; BL 10/1/04; SLJ 10/04) [921]

MCCOURT, FRANK

1344 McCourt, Frank. *Teacher Man* (9–12). 2005, Scribner $26.00 (0-7432-4377-3). 352pp. With humor and eloquence, the author of *Angela's Ashes* (1996) recounts his experiences as a teacher in the public schools of New York City. (Rev: BL 9/15/05) [929]

MANZANO, JUAN FRANCISCO

1345 Engle, Margarita. *The Poet Slave of Cuba: A Biography of Juan Francisco Manzano* (7–10). 2006, Holt $16.95 (0-8050-7706-5). 184pp. This lyrical free-verse biography tells the story of the poet born into slavery in Cuba in 1797, describing his early talent with languages and how it helped him survived amazing brutality. (Rev: BL 2/15/06*; SLJ 4/06*) [811]

MELTZER, MILTON

1346 Meltzer, Milton. *Milton Meltzer: Writing Matters* (8–11). Illus. 2004, Watts LB $28.00 (0-531-12257-3). 160pp. Meltzer combines recollections of his childhood, adolescence, and working days with details of his progression as a writer. (Rev: BL 1/1–15/05; SLJ 4/05) [973.07]

MELVILLE, HERMAN

1347 Meltzer, Milton. *Herman Melville: A Biography* (8–12). Series: American Literary Greats. 2005, Twenty-First Century LB $31.93 (0-7613-2749-5). 128pp. Traces the writer's difficult life and links his

struggles to passages from his works, in particular *Moby Dick*. (Rev: SLJ 1/06) [921]

MILLER, ARTHUR

1348 Andersen, Richard. *Arthur Miller* (7–10). Series: Writers and Their Works. 2005, Benchmark LB $25.95 (0-7614-1946-2). 144pp. *The Crucible* and *Death of a Salesman* are discussed in some detail in this overview of Miller's life and works. (Rev: SLJ 3/06) [921]

MOEHRINGER, J. R.

1349 Moehringer, J. R. *The Tender Bar* (11–12). 2005, Hyperion $23.95 (1-4013-0064-2). 384pp. Pulitzer Prize-winning journalist Moehringer writes about growing up on Long Island and the male role models he found in a local bar; for mature teens. (Rev: BL 8/05) [070.92]

MORRISON, TONI

1350 Andersen, Richard. *Toni Morrison* (7–10). Series: Writers and Their Works. 2005, Benchmark LB $25.95 (0-7614-1945-4). 144pp. *Sula* and *The Bluest Eye* are discussed in some detail in this overview of Morrison's life and works. (Rev: SLJ 3/06) [921]

MYERS, WALTER DEAN

1351 Burshtein, Karen. *Walter Dean Myers* (7–10). Series: The Library of Author Biographies. 2004, Rosen LB $26.50 (0-8239-4020-9). 112pp. A look at the life and work of the well-known author, with many quotations. (Rev: SLJ 9/04) [921]

NASH, OGDEN

1352 Parker, Douglas M. *Ogden Nash: The Life and Work of America's Laureate of Light Verse* (10–12). 2005, Ivan R. Dee $27.50 (1-56663-637-X). 316pp. A readable profile of the playful poet. (Rev: SLJ 8/05) [921]

PECK, ROBERT

1353 Peck, Robert Newton. *Weeds in Bloom: Autobiography of an Ordinary Man* (8–11). 2005, Random LB $17.99 (0-375-92801-4). 224pp. In a series of essays, Peck looks back at his life and at various important incidents and people who played a part in it. (Rev: BL 4/15/05) [813]

PEKAR, HARVEY

1354 Pekar, Harvey. *The Quitter* (9–12). 2005, Vertigo $19.99 (1-4012-0399-X). Pekar tells the story of his troubled childhood and his tendency to quit anything in which he didn't excel. (Rev: BL 10/1/05; SLJ 3/06) [741.5]

POE, EDGAR ALLAN

1355 Schoell, William. *Mystery and Terror: The Story of Edgar Allan Poe* (7–12). Illus. Series: Writers of Imagination. 2004, Morgan Reynolds LB $21.95 (1-931798-39-7). 128pp. Poe's unhappy childhood, marriage, and alcoholism are among the personal aspects covered in this biography that also talks about his work and his continuing need to earn enough money. (Rev: BL 10/1/04; SLJ 12/04) [921]

PULLMAN, PHILIP

1356 Yuan, Margaret Speaker. *Philip Pullman* (7–10). Illus. Series: Who Wrote That? 2005, Chelsea House LB $30.00 (0-7910-8658-5). 120pp. In addition to profiling this author of award-winning books, this biography describes his writing methods. (Rev: BL 3/15/06) [823]

RAND, AYN

1357 Britting, Jeffrey. *Ayn Rand* (9–12). Illus. Series: Overlook Illustrated Lives. 2005, Overlook $19.95 (1-58567-406-0). 135pp. A useful introduction to the Russian-born writer's individualist beliefs and to her works. (Rev: SLJ 6/05) [921]

SANTIAGO, ESMERALDA

1358 Santiago, Esmeralda. *The Turkish Lover* (10–12). 2004, Da Capo $25.00 (0-7382-0820-5). 336pp. Santiago — who has shared earlier stages of her life in *When I Was Puerto Rican* (1993) and *Almost a Woman* (1999) — now describes her turbulent relationship with Turkish immigrant Ulvi Dogan. (Rev: BL 9/1/04; SLJ 2/05) [974.7]

WOOLF, VIRGINIA

1359 Brackett, Virginia. *Restless Genius: The Story of Virginia Woolf* (7–12). Series: Writers of Imagination. 2004, Morgan Reynolds LB $21.95 (1-931798-37-0). 144pp. Woolf's personal life — her relationship with Vita Sackville-West is touched on — and mental stability are the main focus of this brief, interesting biography that also discusses her writing and its influence. (Rev: BCCB 11/04; BL 10/1/04; SLJ 11/04) [921]

Composers

BACH, JOHANN SEBASTIAN

1360 Getzinger, Donna, and Daniel Felsenfeld. *Johann Sebastian Bach and the Art of Baroque Music* (6–12). Illus. Series: Classical Composers. 2004, Morgan Reynolds LB $23.95 (1-931798-22-2). 144pp. This biography reviews Bach's life and times, emphasizing in particular his musical education and commitment and his love for this family. (Rev: BL 6/1–15/04; SLJ 8/04) [780]

HANDEL, GEORGE FRIDERIC

1361 Getzinger, Donna, and Daniel Felsenfeld. *George Frideric Handel and Music for Voices* (6–10). Series: Classical Composers. 2004, Morgan Reynolds LB $23.95 (1-931798-23-0). 144pp. Handel's life and career are placed in historical context. (Rev: SLJ 11/04) [921]

WAGNER, RICHARD

1362 Getzinger, Donna, and Daniel Felsenfeld. *Richard Wagner and German Opera* (6–10). Series: Classical Composers. 2004, Morgan Reynolds LB $23.95 (1-931798-24-9). 144pp. A well-written, balanced biography that discusses Wagner's flaws as well as his great achievements. (Rev: SLJ 11/04) [921]

Performers and Media Personalities (Actors, Musicians, Directors, etc.)

AMOS, TORI

1363 Amos, Tori, and Ann Powers. *Tori Amos: Piece by Piece* (11–12). Illus. 2005, Broadway $23.95 (0-7679-1676-X). 368pp. Amos provides insights into her music and her life in this collection of conversations with journalist Ann Powers; for mature teens. (Rev: BL 2/15/05) [782.4]

BALANCHINE, GEORGE

1364 Gottlieb, Robert. *George Balanchine: The Ballet Maker* (8–12). 2004, HarperCollins $19.95 (0-06-075070-7). 224pp. Balanchine's ballet talent was recognized at a young age; this biography follows his progress from St. Petersburg to New York and worldwide fame. (Rev: BL 11/1/04) [792.8]

1365 Teachout, Terry. *All in the Dances: A Brief Life of George Balanchine* (9–12). Illus. 2004, Harcourt $22.00 (0-15-101088-9). 208pp. In this engaging biography, Teachout looks at the Russian-born choreographer's body of work and how it was received by the critics and public. (Rev: BL 11/1/04) [792.8]

BEASTIE BOYS (MUSICAL GROUP)

1366 Light, Alan. *The Skills to Pay the Bills: The Story of the Beastie Boys* (9–12). Illus. 2006, Three

Rivers paper $14.00 (0-609-60478-3). 224pp. The Beastie Boys, three white Jewish boys from New York City, and their unlikely climb to rap music stardom are profiled here. (Rev: BL 1/1–15/06) [782.42164]

BELUSHI, JOHN

1367 Pisano, Judith Belushi, and Tanner Colby. *Belushi* (9–12). Illus. 2005, RuggedLand $29.95 (1-59071-048-7). 288pp. The life and unique comedy talents of John Belushi are celebrated in this richly illustrated tribute from the comedian's widow, incorporating contributions from many show-biz personalities. (Rev: BL 10/15/05) [791.45]

BROWN, JAMES

1368 Brown, James. *I Feel Good: A Memoir of a Life of Soul* (9–12). 2005, New American Library $24.95 (0-451-21393-9). 266pp. James Brown looks back on his successful musical career and the ups and downs of his personal life, and reflects on people he has known and contemporary musical trends. (Rev: BL 12/1/04; SLJ 6/05) [921]

CHARLES, RAY

1369 Duggleby, John. *Uh Huh! The Story of Ray Charles* (6–12). 2005, Morgan Reynolds LB $26.95 (1-931798-65-6). 160pp. In addition to an account of Ray Charles's life and music, this volume reveals much about the social context of his times. (Rev: SLJ 10/05) [921]

DYLAN, BOB

1370 Roberts, Jeremy. *Bob Dylan: Voice of a Generation* (8–11). Illus. Series: Lerner Biographies. 2005, Lerner LB $27.93 (0-8225-1368-4). 128pp. This evenhanded biography chronicles the folk singer's transformation from Bobby Zimmerman in small-town Minnesota to cultural icon. (Rev: BL 6/1–15/05) [921]

EMERICK, GEOFF

1371 Emerick, Geoff, and Howard Massey. *Here, There and Everywhere: My Life Recording the Music of the Beatles* (9–12). 2006, Gotham $26.00 (1-592-40179-1). 304pp. Emerick, recording engineer on Beatles albums including *Sgt. Pepper's Lonely Hearts Club Band*, tells about the ups and downs of working with the group and later with

McCartney on solo and group productions. (Rev: BL 2/1/06) [782.42]

EMINEM (MARSHALL MATHERS)

1372 Lane, Stephanie. *Eminem* (9–12). Illus. Series: People in the News. 2004, Gale LB $21.96 (1-59018-449-1). 112pp. This is a frank profile of controversial rapper Eminem (born Marshall Mathers) and the violent and sexual images he favors in his lyrics. (Rev: BL 2/1/05) [782.4]

GRANDBERRY, OMARI

1373 Grandberry, Omari. *O* (9–12). Illus. 2005, Pocket paper $14.95 (1-4165-0328-5). 118pp. The former lead singer of B2K writes about his childhood in Los Angeles and his rise to prominence in the world of hip-hop music. (Rev: BL 2/15/05) [782.4]

HENDRIX, JIMI

1374 Cross, Charles R. *Room Full of Mirrors: A Biography of Jimi Hendrix* (11–12). Illus. 2005, Hyperion $24.95 (1-4013-0028-6). 400pp. Traces the brief life and career of rock guitarist Jimi Hendrix; for mature readers. (Rev: BL 6/1–15/05) [787.87]

KING, B. B.

1375 King, B. B., and Dick Waterman. *The B. B. King Treasures: Photos, Mementos and Music from B. B. King's Collection* (9–12). Illus. 2005, Bulfinch $40.00 (0-8212-5724-2). 160pp. Photos, biographical information, memorabilia, and a CD of recordings and interview excerpts celebrate the life and musical contributions of the legendary musician. (Rev: BL 9/1/05) [921]

LENNON, JOHN

1376 Henke, James. *Lennon Legend: An Illustrated Life of John Lennon* (10–12). Illus. 2003, Chronicle $40.00 (0-8118-3517-0). 62pp. Highly illustrated and with facsimiles of Lennon artifacts plus a CD that includes an interview, this is a very attractive celebration of the Beatle's life. (Rev: SLJ 5/04) [921]

1377 Partridge, Elizabeth. *John Lennon: All I Want Is the Truth* (9–12). Illus. 2005, Viking $24.99 (0-670-05954-4). 256pp. This appealing biography chronicles the late, great Beatle's life from his birth during a Nazi air raid over Liverpool in October

1940 to his assassination in New York City in December 1980. (Rev: BL 10/1/05*; SLJ 10/05; VOYA 10/05) [782.42166]

PETTY, TOM

1378 Zollo, Paul. *Conversations with Tom Petty* (9–12). Illus. 2005, Omnibus $24.95 (1-84449-815-8). 448pp. An in-depth look at the life and career of rock musician Tom Petty. (Rev: BL 10/15/05) [782.421]

Miscellaneous Artists

DISNEY, WALT

1379 Jackson, Kathy Merlock, ed. *Walt Disney: Conversations* (9–12). Illus. Series: Conversations with Comic Artists. 2006, Univ. Press of Mississippi $50.00 (1-57806-712-X); paper $20.00 (1-57806-713-8). 168pp. This collection of interviews and speeches offers useful insights into the man responsible for launching an empire. (Rev: BL 1/1–15/06) [791.43]

Contemporary and Historical Americans

Collective

1380 Angelo, Bonnie. *First Families: Their Lives in the White House* (8–12). Illus. 2005, Morrow $25.95 (0-06-056356-7). 352pp. A fascinating look at life in the White House for presidents and their family members. (Rev: BL 8/05) [973]

1381 Hutchinson, Kay Bailey. *American Heroines: The Spirited Women Who Shaped Our Country* (8–12). Illus. 2004, Morrow $24.95 (0-06-056635-3). 384pp. Hutchinson, U.S. senator from Texas, celebrates the lives of courageous American women from many walks of life, both in and out of the limelight. (Rev: BL 11/15/04) [920.72]

1382 Kallen, Stuart A. *Women of the Civil Rights Movement* (7–12). Series: Women in History. 2005, Gale LB $28.70 (1-59018-569-2). 112pp. Women who made important contributions to the U.S. civil rights movement are celebrated in chapters devoted to organizations, protests, education, voting rights, radicals, and so forth. (Rev: SLJ 11/05) [920]

1383 Rodriguez, Robert, and Tamra Orr. *Great Hispanic-Americans* (6–12). 2005, Publications Int'l LB $38.00 (1-4127-1148-7). 128pp. More than 50 Hispanic Americans from different walks of life are profiled in accessible text. (Rev: SLJ 1/06) [920]

1384 Schiff, Karenna Gore. *Lighting the Way: Nine Women Who Changed Modern America* (9–12). Illus. 2006, Hyperion $25.95 (1-4013-5218-9). 528pp. Schiff, daughter of Al Gore, profiles nine 20th-century women who helped to shape America's social and political history. (Rev: BL 12/15/05) [920]

1385 Shetterly, Robert. *Americans Who Tell the Truth* (9–12). Illus. 2005, Dutton $18.99 (0-525-47429-3). 48pp. With portraits, supplemented by quotes from his subjects, artist Robert Shetterly cel-

ebrates the lives of 50 Americans he deeply admires; included in his collection are such diverse figures as Chief Joseph, Mark Twain, Frederick Douglass, Rosa Parks, Noam Chomsky, and Cesar Chavez. (Rev: BL 4/1/05; SLJ 7/05) [920.073]

1386 Sullivan, Otha Richard. *African American Millionaires* (5–10). Series: Black Stars. 2004, Wiley $24.95 (0-471-46928-9). 158pp. Tyra Banks and Oprah Winfrey are included here, but so are many names that may be unfamiliar to readers, such as William Alexander Leidesdorff and Annie Turnbo Malone. (Rev: SLJ 5/05) [920]

Civil and Human Rights Leaders

BAKER, ELLA

1387 Bohannon, Lisa Frederiksen. *Freedom Cannot Rest: Ella Baker and the Civil Rights Movement* (7–12). Illus. Series: Civil Rights Leaders. 2005, Morgan Reynolds LB $24.95 (1-931798-71-0). 176pp. A well-illustrated and evenhanded introduction to the life and accomplishments of Ella Baker, a major — but often overlooked — player in the U.S. civil rights movement. (Rev: SLJ 12/05)

BATES, DAISY

1388 Fradin, Judith Bloom, and Dennis Brindell Fradin. *The Power of One: Daisy Bates and the Little Rock Nine* (8–11). Illus. 2004, Clarion $19.00 (0-618-31556-X). 178pp. A detailed profile of Daisy Bates, who as president of the Arkansas chapter of the NAACP played a pivotal role in the 1957 integration of Central High School in Little Rock. (Rev: BL 2/1/05; SLJ 4/05) [323]

BROWN, JOHN

1389 Reynolds, David S. *John Brown, Abolitionist: The Man Who Killed Slavery, Sparked the Civil War, and Seeded Civil Rights* (8–12). 2005, Knopf $30.00 (0-375-41188-7). 496pp. This insightful biography adds fuel to the continuing debate over what motivated the fiery abolitionist. (Rev: BL 2/1/05) [973.7]

DU BOIS, W. E. B.

1390 Hinman, Bonnie. *A Stranger in My Own House: The Story of W. E. B. Du Bois* (9–12). Illus. Series: Civil Rights Leaders. 2005, Morgan Reynolds LB $24.95 (1-931798-45-1). 176pp. The personal story of the scholar and controversial civil rights leader is placed in interesting social and historical context. (Rev: BL 3/15/05; SLJ 7/05) [305.896]

FRIEDAN, BETTY

1391 Bohannon, Lisa Frederiksen. *Woman's Work: The Story of Betty Friedan* (9–12). Illus. Series: Feminist Voices. 2004, Morgan Reynolds LB $21.95 (1-931798-41-9). 144pp. Friedan's life and contributions to the women's movement are placed in historical and cultural context. (Rev: BL 1/1–15/05; SLJ 11/04) [305.42]

HAMER, FANNIE LOU

1392 Fiorelli, June Estep. *Fannie Lou Hamer: A Voice for Freedom* (5–10). Series: Avisson Young Adult. 2005, Avisson paper $19.95 (1-888105-62-3). 117pp. Hamer's life, including her youth, are described and placed in the context of events in the United States at the time. (Rev: SLJ 2/06) [921]

HOUSE, CALLIE

1393 Berry, Mary Frances. *My Face Is Black Is True: Callie House and the Struggle for Ex-Slave Reparations* (10–12). Illus. 2005, Knopf $26.95 (1-4000-4003-5). 320pp. Callie House, a former slave herself, fought for decades to win pensions and aid for her counterparts and was imprisoned for her activities. (Rev: BL 7/05) [323]

KING, CORETTA SCOTT

1394 Rhodes, Lisa Renee. *Coretta Scott King: Civil Rights Activist* (7–12). Illus. Series: Black Americans of Achievement. 2005, Chelsea House LB $23.95 (0-79108-251-2). 136pp. This revised edition of King's life adds new photographs and information boxes to the description of her childhood, education, marriage, participation in the civil rights movement, and work after her husband's assassination. (Rev: SLJ 11/05) [921]

KING, MARTIN LUTHER, JR.

1395 Pastan, Amy. *Martin Luther King Jr.* (5–10). Illus. Series: DK Biography. 2004, DK LB $14.99 (0-7566-0491-5); paper $4.99 (0-7566-0342-0). 128pp. A heavily illustrated, attractive biography of King that offers broad historical background. (Rev: BL 6/1–15/04) [921]

1396 Schloredt, Valerie, and Pam Brown. *Martin Luther King Jr.* (5–10). Illus. Series: World Peacemakers. 2004, Gale LB $27.44 (1-56711-977-8). 64pp. A readable account of this civil rights leader and the times in which he lived. (Rev: BL 2/15/04; SLJ 2/94) [921]

NICHOLS, CLARINA

1397 Eickhoff, Diane. *Revolutionary Heart: The Life of Clarina Nichols and the Pioneering Crusade for Women's Rights* (10–12). Illus. 2006, Beagle Bay paper $14.95 (0-9764434-4-9). 288pp. The life and achievements of Clarina Nichols, a pioneer in the struggle for women's rights who has been largely overlooked in history books. (Rev: BL 2/15/06) [305.42]

RANDOLPH, A. PHILIP

1398 Miller, Calvin Craig. *A. Philip Randolph and the African-American Labor Movement* (7–10). Illus. Series: Civil Rights Leaders. 2005, Morgan Reynolds $24.95 (1-931798-50-8). 160pp. The life and achievements of the founding president of the Brotherhood of Sleeping Car Porters. (Rev: BL 2/15/05; SLJ 5/05) [323]

RUSTIN, BAYARD

1399 Miller, Calvin Craig. *No Easy Answers: Bayard Rustin and the Civil Rights Movement* (7–10). Illus. Series: Civil Rights Leaders. 2005, Morgan Reynolds LB $24.95 (1-931798-43-5). 160pp. Rustin's significant achievements in the field of civil rights are discussed along with his homosexuality, which was a large factor in his relative obscurity. (Rev: BL 2/1/05; SLJ 6/05; VOYA 8/05) [323]

STANTON, ELIZABETH CADY

1400 Gornick, Vivian. *The Solitude of Self: Thinking About Elizabeth Cady Stanton* (10–12). 2005, Farrar $17.00 (0-374-29954-4). 144pp. A thoughtful assessment of Stanton's importance to women's suffrage and to feminism as a whole, introducing both the woman herself and the social conditions of her time. (Rev: BL 9/1/05) [305.42]

WOODHULL, VICTORIA

1401 Brody, Miriam. *Victoria Woodhull: Free Spirit for Women's Rights* (7–12). Series: Oxford Portraits. 2004, Oxford LB $28.00 (0-19-514367-1). 159pp. Presenting historical and social context, this biography covers the American reformer's difficult childhood and complex adult life. (Rev: SLJ 2/05) [921]

Presidents and Their Families

CLINTON, BILL

1402 Warshaw, Shirley Ann. *The Clinton Years* (9–12). Series: Presidential Profiles. 2004, Facts on File $85.00 (0-8160-5333-2). 524pp. An overview of the major events of Bill Clinton's presidency is followed by more than 200 profiles of U.S. and world figures who played key roles during his administration. (Rev: SLJ 2/05) [921]

GRANT, ULYSSES S.

1403 Rice, Earle, Jr. *Ulysses S. Grant: Defender of the Union* (8–11). Illus. Series: Civil War Leaders. 2005, Morgan Reynolds LB $24.95 (1-931798-48-6). 176pp. A vivid portrait of Grant, who rose from humble beginnings in his native Ohio to achieve acclaim as a military leader and ascend to the highest office in the land. (Rev: BL 3/15/05; SLJ 11/05) [973.8]

HARRISON, BENJAMIN

1404 Calhoun, Charles W. *Benjamin Harrison* (9–12). Series: American Presidents. 2005, Holt $20.00 (0-8050-6952-6). 192pp. Calhoun casts light on Harrison's background and little-known accomplishments. (Rev: BL 5/15/05) [973.8]

JACKSON, ANDREW

1405 Marrin, Albert. *Old Hickory: Andrew Jackson and the American People* (6–12). 2004, Penguin $30.00 (0-525-47293-2). 240pp. The life and times of a colorful president are presented in a suitably vivid biography. (Rev: BL 12/1/04; SLJ 12/04; VOYA 6/05) [921]

1406 Wilentz, Sean. *Andrew Jackson* (11–12). 2006, Holt $20.00 (0-8050-6925-9). 224pp. This biography emphasizes the seventh U.S. president's unflagging support for the common man, offering new insight for advanced history students. (Rev: BL 12/15/05) [973.5]

JEFFERSON, THOMAS

1407 Bernstein, R. B. *Thomas Jefferson: The Revolution of Ideas* (9–12). Series: Oxford Portraits. 2004, Oxford LB $28.00 (0-19-514368-X). 251pp. An evenhanded portrayal of Jefferson's personal life, accomplishments, and legacy, with mention of controversial subjects such as his relationship with Sally Hemmings. (Rev: SLJ 9/04) [921]

1408 Hitchens, Christopher. *Thomas Jefferson: Author of America* (9–12). Series: Eminent Lives. 2005, HarperCollins $19.95 (0-06-059896-4). 160pp. A brief biography that succeeds in covering the essentials, highlighting Jefferson's contributions to the institution of democracy while admitting his weaknesses. (Rev: BL 4/15/05) [973.4]

KENNEDY, JOHN F.

1409 Kaplan, Howard S. *John F. Kennedy* (5–10). Illus. Series: DK Biography. 2004, DK paper $4.99 (0-7566-0340-4). 128pp. A heavily illustrated, attractive biography of Kennedy that offers broad historical background. (Rev: BL 6/1–15/04) [921]

1410 Siracusa, Joseph M. *The Kennedy Years* (9–12). Series: Presidential Profiles. 2004, Facts on File $85.00 (0-8160-5444-4). 616pp. Following a summary of the important events of Kennedy's presidency, more than 300 key individuals are profiled. (Rev: SLJ 2/05) [921]

LINCOLN, ABRAHAM

1411 Donald, David Herbert, and Harold Holzer, eds. *Lincoln in the Times: The Life of Abraham Lincoln as Originally Reported in the New York Times* (9–12). Illus. 2005, St. Martin's $29.95 (0-312-34919-X). 432pp. For advanced students, this volume offers lots of fodder for reports and discussion. (Rev: BL 10/15/05) [973.7]

1412 Stone, Tanya Lee. *Abraham Lincoln* (5–10). Illus. Series: DK Biography. 2005, DK $14.99 (0-7566-0833-3); paper $4.99 (0-7566-0834-1). 128pp. A heavily illustrated, attractive biography of Lincoln that offers broad historical background. (Rev: BL 6/1–15/04) [921]

MONROE, JAMES

1413 Hart, Gary. *James Monroe* (9–12). Series: American Presidents. 2005, Holt $20.00 (0-8050-6960-7). 192pp. Former U.S. Senator Gary Hart profiles America's fifth president, best remembered for his doctrine declaring the Western Hemisphere off-limits to European intervention. (Rev: BL 10/1/05) [973.5]

VAN BUREN, MARTIN

1414 Widmer, Ted. *Martin Van Buren* (9–12). Series: American Presidents. 2005, Holt $20.00 (0-8050-6922-4). 192pp. A lively, very readable account of Van Buren's life and achievements. (Rev: BL 12/1/04) [973.5]

WASHINGTON, GEORGE

1415 Ellis, Joseph J. *His Excellency: George Washington* (9–12). 2004, Knopf $26.95 (1-4000-4031-0). 352pp. Washington's complex character is the main focus of this biography that draws heavily on the president's correspondence. (Rev: BL 9/15/04; SLJ 3/05) [973.4]

1416 Hort, Lenny. *George Washington* (5–10). Illus. Series: DK Biography. 2005, DK $14.99 (0-7566-0832-5); paper $4.99 (0-7566-0835-X). 128pp. A heavily illustrated, attractive biography of the man born in Virginia. (Rev: BL 6/1–15/04) [921]

WASHINGTON, MARTHA

1417 Brady, Patricia. *Martha Washington: An American Life* (9–12). 2005, Viking $24.95 (0-670-03430-4). 264pp. Martha and George's marriage is shown as a strong partnership. (Rev: BL 5/15/05) [973.4]

WILSON, WOODROW

1418 Lukes, Bonnie L. *Woodrow Wilson and the Progressive Era* (6–10). Series: World Leaders. 2005, Morgan Reynolds LB $26.95 (1-931798-79-6). 192pp. A chronological survey of Wilson's life from birth in 1856 through his death in 1924, with discussion of his achievements in light of the global events of the time. (Rev: SLJ 2/06) [921]

Other Government and Public Figures

CLINTON, HILLARY RODHAM

1419 Gullo, Jim. *Hillary Rodham Clinton* (7–12). Series: The Importance Of. 2004, Gale LB $21.96 (1-59018-310-X). 112pp. Clinton's natural leadership abilities and achievements in office are the main focus of this balanced biography that also covers her youth, education, and law career. (Rev: SLJ 4/04) [921]

FRANKLIN, BENJAMIN

1420 Dash, Joan. *A Dangerous Engine: Benjamin Franklin, from Scientist to Diplomat* (6–10). 2006, Farrar $17.00 (0-374-30669-9). 246pp. Franklin's keen interest in science and the development of new technology is emphasized in this lively biography illustrated with pen-and-ink drawings. (Rev: BCCB 1/06; HB 3–4/06; SLJ 2/06) [921]

1421 Gaustad, Edwin S. *Benjamin Franklin* (9–12). Illus. Series: Lives and Legacies. 2006, Oxford $17.95 (0-19-530535-3). 160pp. Gaustad enumerates Franklin's many and wide-ranging accomplishments in this useful biography that also examines Franklin's character and beliefs. (Rev: BL 2/1/06) [973.3]

1422 Gaustad, Edwin S. *Benjamin Franklin: Inventing America* (7–10). Series: Oxford Portraits. 2004, Oxford LB $28.00 (0-19-515732-X). 143pp. The life and achievements of Benjamin Franklin are described using many quotations from Franklin's autobiography. (Rev: SLJ 2/05) [921]

1423 Wood, Gordon S. *The Americanization of Ben Franklin* (9–12). 2004, Penguin $25.95 (1-59420-019-X). 299pp. Traces the transformation of Benjamin Franklin from a loyal supporter of the British monarchy to a leadership position in the forces pushing for American independence. (Rev: SLJ 1/05) [921]

JACKSON, STONEWALL

1424 Brager, Bruce L. *There He Stands: The Story of Stonewall Jackson* (8–10). Illus. Series: Civil War Leaders. 2005, Morgan Reynolds LB $24.95 (1-931798-44-3). 176pp. The life and military career of Stonewall Jackson, one of the Civil War's most skilled tacticians; photographs, reproductions, and maps complement the well-written text. (Rev: SLJ 11/05) [921]

JOSEPH (NEZ PERCE CHIEF)

1425 Moulton, Candy. *Chief Joseph: Guardian of the People* (8–12). 2005, Tor $21.95 (0-765-31063-5). 240pp. The story of Chief Joseph's 1877 attempt to lead the Nez Percé tribe to safety in Canada. (Rev: BL 3/1/05) [979.50]

KERRY, JOHN

1426 Brager, Bruce L. *John Kerry: Senator from Massachusetts* (6–10). 2005, Morgan Reynolds LB $21.95 (1-931798-64-8). 128pp. Kerry's life and military service are presented along with his career in politics and unsuccessful bid for the presidency in 2004. (Rev: SLJ 8/05) [921]

LEE, ROBERT E.

1427 Rice, Earle, Jr. *Robert E. Lee: First Soldier of the Confederacy* (8–10). Illus. Series: Civil War Leaders. 2005, Morgan Reynolds LB $24.95 (1-931798-47-8). 176pp. Lee's childhood, adult life, and military career are covered; photographs, reproductions, and maps complement the well-written text. (Rev: SLJ 11/05) [921]

1428 Robertson, James I. *Robert E. Lee: Virginian Soldier, American Citizen* (7–10). Illus. 2005, Simon & Schuster $21.95 (0-689-85731-4). 176pp. A rich and even-handed portrait of Robert E. Lee, including a number of excerpts from such primary sources as letters and diaries. (Rev: BL 11/15/05; SLJ 1/06; VOYA 10/05) [973.7]

LITTLE CROW

1429 Swain, Gwenyth. *Little Crow: Leader of the Dakota* (6–12). 2004, Minnesota Historical Society $22.95 (0-87351-502-1). 112pp. Little Crow, who died in 1863, did all in his power to keep his people from war but joined them on the front lines when they chose to disregard his counsel. (Rev: BL 7/04; SLJ 7/04) [978.004]

MARSHALL, GEORGE C.

1430 Gimpel, Lee. *Fighting Wars, Planning for Peace: The Story of George C. Marshall* (9–12). Illus. Series: World Leaders. 2005, Morgan Reynolds LB $24.95 (1-931798-66-4). 176pp. A clear profile of the American soldier and diplomat and his importance to the world in the 20th century. (Rev: BL 1/1–15/06; SLJ 12/05) [973.918]

NORTON, ELEANOR HOLMES

1431 Marcovitz, Hal. *Eleanor Holmes Norton* (7–12). Series: African-American Leaders. 2003, Chelsea House LB $22.95 (0-7910-7682-2). 115pp. Profiles the woman representing Washington, D.C. in the House of Representatives, and discusses her work on sexual harassment in the workplace. (Rev: SLJ 4/04) [921]

PAINE, THOMAS

1432 Collins, Paul. *The Trouble with Tom: The Strange Afterlife and Times of Thomas Paine* (9–12). 2005, Bloomsbury $24.95 (1-58234-502-3). 256pp. A witty account of the author's research into Tom Paine's life and the strange tale of his lost remains. (Rev: SLJ 3/06) [921]

PATTON, GEORGE S.

1433 Axelrod, Alan. *Patton* (9–12). Illus. Series: Great Generals. 2006, Palgrave Macmillan $21.95 (1-4039-7139-0). 224pp. A no-holds-barred portrait of the life and wartime achievements of the controversial World War II general. (Rev: BL 2/1/06) [355]

Miscellaneous Persons

BUZZELL, COLBY

1434 Buzzell, Colby. *My War: Killing Time in Iraq* (10–12). 2005, Penguin $25.95 (0-399-15327-6). 416pp. In this gripping war memoir based on his blog, Buzzell recounts his experiences as a U.S. Army machine gunner in Iraq. (Rev: BL 10/15/05) [956.7044]

CARTER, ROBERT, III

1435 Levy, Andrew. *The First Emancipator: The Forgotten Story of Robert Carter, the Founding Father Who Freed His Slaves* (10–12). 2005, Random $25.95 (0-375-50865-1). 336pp. Robert Carter III was a wealthy Virginia planter who in 1791 freed all of his slaves, hoping to serve as an example to other slave holders. (Rev: BL 4/15/05) [973.3]

DIX, DOROTHEA

1436 Muckenhoupt, Margaret. *Dorothea Dix: Advocate for Mental Health Care* (9–12). Series: Oxford Portraits. 2004, Oxford LB $28.00 (0-19-512921-0). 127pp. Dix was a tireless advocate on behalf of the mentally ill; this volume also describes her work as a teacher and nurse. (Rev: SLJ 7/04) [921]

FENTON, PETER

1437 Fenton, Peter. *Eyeing the Flash: The Education of a Carnival Con Artist* (9–12). 2005, Simon & Schuster $23.00 (0-7432-5854-1). 256pp. In this humorous memoir, Fenton tells how his friendship with a boy from a family of carnies and con artists led him into a life on the midway. (Rev: SLJ 3/05) [021]

GATES, HENRY LOUIS, JR.

1438 Kjelle, Marylou Morano. *Henry Louis Gates, Jr.* (6–12). Series: African-American Leaders. 2003, Chelsea House LB $22.95 (0-7910-7687-3). 111pp. A life of the influential historian and author who teaches at Harvard. (Rev: SLJ 4/04) [921]

KELLER, HELEN

1439 Garrett, Leslie. *Helen Keller: Biography* (5–10). Series: DK Biography. 2004, DK paper $4.99 (0-7566-0339-0). 128pp. Keller's struggles to conquer her physical disabilities and her worldwide recognition as a political activist and public speaker are covered in the usual rich DK format. (Rev: BL 6/1–15/04) [921]

SLANGER, FRANCES

1440 Welch, Bob. *American Nightingale: The Story of Frances Slanger, Forgotten Heroine of Normandy* (10–12). 2004, Atria $22.00 (0-7434-7758-8). 320pp. Before her death, Frances Slanger — the first American Army nurse to die after the D-Day invasion of Normandy — wrote a moving letter about the soldiers' sufferings. (Rev: BL 6/1–15/04) [940.54]

WEST, CORNEL

1441 Morrison, John. *Cornel West* (7–12). Series: African-American Leaders. 2003, Chelsea House LB $22.95 (0-7910-7686-5). 120pp. West's commitment to populism and improved race relations is the focus of this biography of the African American Ivy League professor. (Rev: SLJ 4/04) [921]

YOUNG, CHARLES

1442 Shellum, Brian G. *Black Cadet in a White Bastion: Charles Young at West Point* (10–12). Illus. 2006, Univ. of Nebraska paper $16.95 (0-8032-9315-1). 235pp. The life and achievements of Charles Young, who was born into slavery but became the third African American to graduate from the U.S. Military Academy at West Point and went on to become a colonel. (Rev: BL 2/15/06) [355]

Science, Medicine, Industry, and Business Figures

Collective

1443 Aaseng, Nathan. *Business Builders in Broadcasting* (7–10). Series: Business Builders. 2005, Oliver LB $24.95 (1-881508-83-8). 160pp. From Morse and Marconi to Sarnoff and Rupert Murdoch, this is a useful overview of key figures in broadcasting. (Rev: SLJ 3/06) [920]

1444 Balchin, Jon. *Science: 100 Scientists Who Changed the World* (6–12). 2003, Enchanted Lion $18.95 (1-59270-017-9). 208pp. Two-page chapters introduce 100 scientists and their accomplishments, grouped by century. (Rev: SLJ 1/04) [920]

1445 Cullen, Katherine. *Science, Technology, and Society: The People Behind the Science* (8–11). Illus. Series: Pioneers in Science. 2006, Chelsea House $29.95 (0-8160-5468-1). 172pp. Pioneers whose biographies appear in this volume include Marie Curie, Louis Pasteur, Guglielmo Marconi, Rachel Carson, and J. Robert Oppenheimer. (Rev: BL 4/1/06) [509]

1446 De Angelis, Gina, and David J. Bianco. *Computers: Processing the Data* (7–10). Illus. Series: Innovators. 2005, Oliver LB $24.95 (1-881508-87-0). 144pp. Profiles of computer pioneers including Charles Babbage, Steve Wozniak, and Tim Berners-Lee are accompanied by explanations of the technology involved. (Rev: BL 12/1/05; SLJ 1/06) [004]

1447 Evans, Harold. *They Made America: From the Steam Engine to the Search Engine: Two Centuries of Innovators* (8–12). Illus. 2004, Little, Brown $40.00 (0-316-27766-5). 496pp. For both browsing and research, this is an interesting and information-packed celebration of American inventiveness, focusing as much on the entrepreneurs as on the products. (Rev: BL 10/1/04) [609.2]

1448 Holmes, Madelyn. *American Women Conservationists: Twelve Profiles* (9–12). Illus. 2004, McFarland paper $35.00 (0-7864-1783-8). 208pp. Profiles of 12 women who played a significant role in protecting America's natural resources include information on their youthful aspirations. (Rev: BL 9/1/04) [333.72]

1449 Leroy, Francis, ed. *A Century of Nobel Prize Recipients: Chemistry, Physics, and Medicine* (9–12). Illus. 2003, Marcel Dekker $150.00 (0-8247-0876-8). 380pp. Nobel laureates are presented chronologically by discipline, with portraits, key data, and essays on their contributions. (Rev: SLJ 2/04) [920]

1450 Marshall, David, and Bruce Harper. *Wild About Flying: Dreamers, Doers, and Daredevils* (8–12). 2003, Firefly $35.00 (1-55297-849-4). 232pp. Brief biographies of key figures in the history of aviation are grouped in three categories: Dreamers, Doers, and Daredevils. (Rev: SLJ 3/04; VOYA 6/04) [920]

1451 Shell, Barry. *Sensational Scientists: The Journeys and Discoveries of 24 Men and Women of Science* (8–11). Illus. 2006, Raincoast paper $15.95 (1-55192-727-6). 208pp. Profiles of 24 scientists associated with Canada cover a wide range of interests. (Rev: BL 2/15/06) [509]

1452 Stux, Erica. *The Achievers: Great Women in the Biological Sciences* (9–12). Series: Avisson Young Adult. 2005, Avisson paper $19.95 (1-888105-70-4). 148pp. Eight women who made significant contributions to the biological sciences are introduced with details of their careers and personalities. (Rev: BL 7/05) [570]

Science and Medicine

SAGAN, CARL

1453 Head, Tom, ed. *Conversations with Carl Sagan* (10–12). 2005, Univ. Press of Mississippi $50.00 (1-57806-735-9); paper $20.00 (1-57806-736-7). 194pp. Sixteen interviews — from such diverse sources as *Rolling Stone*, *Psychology Today*, and *The Charlie Rose Show* — reveal much about the popular astrophysicist. (Rev: BL 12/1/05) [520]

BOHR, NIELS

1454 Ottaviani, Jim, et al. *Suspended in Language: Niels Bohr's Life, Discoveries, and the Century He Shaped* (9–12). Illus. 2004, G. T. Labs paper $24.95 (0-9660106-5-5). 320pp. A strikingly designed graphic novel-format account of the life and accomplishments of Danish physicist Niels Bohr. (Rev: BL 8/04) [530.092]

BREAZEAL, CYNTHIA

1455 Brown, Jordan D. *Robo World: The Story of Robot Designer Cynthia Breazeal* (6–10). Series: Women's Adventures in Science. 2005, Watts LB $31.00 (0-531-16782-8). 108pp. An interesting biography that blends personal information with scientific facts. (Rev: SLJ 2/06) [921]

CARLSON, CHESTER

1456 Owen, David. *Copies in Seconds: How a Lone Inventor and an Unknown Company Created the Biggest Communication Breakthrough Since Gutenberg — Chester Carlson and the Birth of the Xerox Machine* (9–12). Illus. 2004, Simon & Schuster $24.00 (0-7432-5117-2). 320pp. Chester Carlson's invention of xerography, the modern copying process, was followed by 20 years of battles to bring the product to market. (Rev: BL 8/04) [686.4]

CHINN, MAY

1457 Haulsey, Kuwana. *Angel of Harlem* (9–12). 2004, Ballantine $19.95 (0-345-50870-8). 352pp. A fictional first-person biography of Dr. May Chinn, who overcame adversity to become the first African American woman doctor in New York City; includes many details about the Harlem Renaissance and personalities of the time. (Rev: BL 9/1/04)

COPERNICUS, NICOLAUS

1458 Gingerich, Owen, and James MacLachlan. *Nicolaus Copernicus: Making the Earth a Planet* (9–12). Illus. 2005, Oxford LB $28.00 (0-19-

516173-4). 128pp. A thorough and insightful profile of Copernicus, the Polish astronomer who revolutionized world thinking about the solar system. (Rev: BL 12/1/05) [520]

CRICK, FRANCIS

1459 Ridley, Matt. *Francis Crick: Discoverer of the Genetic Code* (9–12). Series: Eminent Lives. 2006, HarperCollins $19.95 (0-06-082333-X). 192pp. A clear explanation of the problems facing the discoverer of the double helix, plus personal details of Crick's life and working style. (Rev: BL 4/1/06) [576.5]

CURIE, MARIE

1460 Goldsmith, Barbara. *Obsessive Genius: The Inner World of Marie Curie* (8–12). Illus. 2004, Norton $23.95 (0-393-05137-4). 320pp. Curie's personal triumphs are also covered in this account of her scientific achievements. (Rev: BL 12/1/04) [540]

1461 McClafferty, Caria Killough. *Something Out of Nothing: Marie Curie and Radium* (7–10). Illus. 2006, Farrar $18.00 (0-374-38036-8). 144pp. This readable biography examines Curie's personal life and her valuable contributions to scientific knowledge. (Rev: BL 3/1/06) [540]

DARWIN, CHARLES

1462 Eldredge, Niles. *Darwin: Discovering the Tree of Life* (11–12). Illus. 2005, Norton $35.00 (0-393-05966-9). 288pp. Eldredge, a leading evolutionary theorist and curator at New York's American Museum of Natural History, celebrates the life and revolutionary ideas of Charles Darwin; a well-illustrated volume. (Rev: BL 11/1/05) [576.8]

EINSTEIN, ALBERT

1463 Hasday, Judy L. *Albert Einstein: The Giant of 20th Century Science* (7–12). Series: Nobel Prize–Winning Scientists. 2004, Enslow LB $20.95 (0-7660-2185-8). 128pp. Report writers will find this a useful source of material on Einstein's breakthrough achievements in physics. (Rev: SLJ 4/04) [921]

FERMI, ENRICO

1464 Stux, Erica. *Enrico Fermi: Trailblazer in Nuclear Physics* (7–12). Illus. Series: Nobel Prize–Winning Scientists. 2004, Enslow LB $20.95 (0-7660-2177-7). 128pp. This review of Fermi's achievements in nuclear physics offers good material for report writers. (Rev: BL 6/1–15/04; SLJ 4/04) [921]

FOSSEY, DIAN

1465 de la Bédoyère, Camilla, and Dian Fossey. *No One Loved Gorillas More: Dian Fossey, Letters from the Mist* (11–12). Illus. 2005, National Geographic $30.00 (0-7922-9344-4). 194pp. Photographs, biographical narrative, and letters by Fossey herself tell the story of her life among the mountain gorillas of Rwanda. (Rev: BL 2/15/05) [599.8]

FRANCE, DIANE

1466 Hopping, Lorraine Jean. *Bone Detective: The Story of Forensic Anthropologist Diane France* (7–10). Illus. Series: Women's Adventures in Science. 2005, Watts LB $31.00 (0-531-16776-3). 128pp. Part of the Women's Adventures in Science series, this compelling biography of Diane France traces the forensic anthropologist's life from her childhood in Colorado to her role in identifying victims of the 9/11 terrorist attacks. (Rev: BL 10/15/05; SLJ 2/06) [363.25]

FUNG, INEZ

1467 Skelton, Renee. *Forecast Earth: The Story of Climate Scientist Inez Fung* (6–10). Illus. Series: Women's Adventures in Science. 2005, Watts LB $31.00 (0-531-16777-1). 116pp. An interesting biography that blends personal information with scientific facts. (Rev: SLJ 2/06) [921]

GOODALL, JANE

1468 Greene, Meg. *Jane Goodall: A Biography* (9–12). Series: Greenwood Biographies. 2005, Greenwood LB $29.95 (0-313-33139-1). 146pp. Goodall's personality is highlighted in this appealing biography. (Rev: SLJ 3/06) [921]

HAMMEL, HEIDI

1469 Bortz, Fred. *Beyond Jupiter: The Story of Planetary Astronomer Heidi Hammel* (6–10). Illus. Series: Women's Adventures in Science. 2005, Watts LB $31.00 (0-531-16775-5). 110pp. An interesting biography that blends personal information with scientific facts. (Rev: SLJ 2/06) [921]

HORNEY, KAREN

1470 Hitchcock, Susan Tyler. *Karen Horney: Pioneer of Feminine Psychology* (9–12). Series: Women in Medicine. 2004, Chelsea House LB $22.95 (0-7910-8025-0). 116pp. A life of Karen Horney, an outspoken critic of Sigmund Freud's concentration on the male psyche. (Rev: SLJ 6/05) [921]

JONES, THOMAS D.

1471 Jones, Thomas D. *Sky Walking: An Astronaut's Memoir* (9–12). 2006, HarperCollins $26.95 (0-06-085152-X). 384pp. A frank and illuminating account of a career building to four flights on the space shuttle. (Rev: BL 1/1–15/06) [629.45]

KOEHL, MIMI

1472 Parks, Deborah. *Nature's Machines: The Story of Biomechanist Mimi Koehl* (6–10). Illus. Series: Women's Adventures in Science. 2005, Watts LB $31.00 (0-531-16780-1). 118pp. An interesting biography that blends personal information with scientific facts. (Rev: SLJ 2/06) [921]

KÜBLER-ROSS, ELISABETH

1473 Worth, Richard. *Elisabeth Kübler-Ross: Encountering Death and Dying* (9–12). Series: Women in Medicine. 2004, Chelsea House LB $22.95 (0-7910-8027-7). 116pp. The life and career of the psychiatrist who was a pioneer in the study of death and dying. (Rev: SLJ 6/05) [921]

LEAKEY FAMILY

1474 Bowman-Kruhm, Mary. *The Leakeys: A Biography* (9–12). Series: Greenwood Biographies. 2005, Greenwood LB $29.95 (0-313-32985-0). 150pp. Lays out the contributions of three generations of the Leakey family to the world of anthropology, with good coverage of the individuals' personalities. (Rev: SLJ 3/06) [921]

MULLANE, MIKE

1475 Mullane, Mike. *Riding Rockets: The Outrageous Tales of a Space Shuttle Astronaut* (9–12). 2006, Scribner $26.00 (0-7432-7682-5). 352pp. Mullane writes candidly about his life in the shuttle program, the three shuttle missions he flew between 1984 and 1990, and his concerns about NASA; some strong language. (Rev: BL 2/1/06) [629.4]

PAULING, LINUS

1476 Pasachoff, Naomi. *Linus Pauling: Advancing Science, Advocating Peace* (7–12). Illus. Series: Nobel Prize–Winning Scientists. 2004, Enslow LB $20.95 (0-7660-2130-0). 128pp. Pauling's scientific errors are not dismissed in this biography that relates the Nobel prize winner's achievements in science and his campaign against nuclear weapons. (Rev: BL 6/1–15/04) [921]

RUTHERFORD, ERNEST

1477 Pasachoff, Naomi. *Ernest Rutherford: Father of Nuclear Science* (6–12). Series: Great Minds of

Science. 2005, Enslow LB $26.60 (0-7660-2441-5). 128pp. The life and scientific career of the New Zealand-born physicist who helped to pave the way for the development of nuclear physics. (Rev: SLJ 8/05)

TESLA, NIKOLA

1478 Aldrich, Lisa J. *Nikola Tesla and the Taming of Electricity* (8–11). Illus. Series: Modern Scientists. 2005, Morgan Reynolds LB $24.95 (1-931798-46-X). 160pp. The life and many inventions — including radio — of the Croatian-born electrical engineer. (Rev: BL 5/1/05; SLJ 10/05; VOYA 10/05) [621.3]

TURING, ALAN

1479 Leavitt, David. *The Man Who Knew Too Much: Alan Turing and the Invention of the Computer* (9–12). 2005, Norton $22.95 (0-393-05236-2). 288pp. David Leavitt's unflinching biography of computer pioneer Alan Turing examines the British mathematician's accomplishments and also how his brilliant career and life were cut short by homophobia. (Rev: BL 10/15/05) [510]

WEXLER, NANCY

1480 Glimm, Adele. *Gene Hunter: The Story of Neuropsychologist Nancy Wexler* (6–10). Illus. Series: Women's Adventures in Science. 2005, Watts LB $31.00 (0-531-16778-X). 118pp. An interesting biography that blends personal information with scientific facts. (Rev: SLJ 2/06) [921]

Industry and Business

CARNEGIE, ANDREW

1481 Edge, Laura B. *Andrew Carnegie: Industrial Philanthropist* (7–10). Series: Lerner Biography. 2004, Lerner LB $25.26 (0-8225-4965-4). 128pp. The fascinating story of Carnegie's progress from poor Scottish immigrant to wealthy industrialist and generous philanthropist. (Rev: BL 6/1–15/04; SLJ 2/04) [936.2]

CHANEL, COCO

1482 Gaines, Ann. *Coco Chanel* (6–12). Series: Women in the Arts. 2003, Chelsea House LB $22.95 (0-7910-7455-2). 116pp. Introduces the life of the famous designer, attempting to distinguish between fact and Chanel's own fictions about herself. (Rev: SLJ 2/04) [921]

ORFALEA, PAUL

1483 Orfalea, Paul, and Ann Marsh. *Copy This! Lessons from a Hyperactive Dyslexic Who Turned a Bright Idea into One of America's Best Companies* (9–12). Illus. 2005, Workman $23.95 (0-7611-3777-7). 288pp. The founder of Kinko's describes in entertaining fashion how he overcame the challenges of dyslexia and hyperactivity and gives advice on life and business success. (Rev: SLJ 9/05) [921]

Sports Figures

Automobile Racing

ALLISON, BOBBY

1484 Golenbock, Peter. *The Miracle: Bobby Allison and the Saga of the Alabama Gang* (9–12). Illus. 2006, St. Martin's $24.95 (0-312-34001-X). 416pp. Golenbock describes the triumphs and tragedies that have followed the winning NASCAR driver throughout his career. (Rev: BL 12/15/05) [796.72]

Baseball

CLEMENTE, ROBERTO

1485 Maraniss, David. *Clemente: The Passion and Grace of Baseball's Last Hero* (9–12). Illus. 2006, Simon & Schuster $26.00 (0-7432-1781-0). 418pp. This compelling biography by Pulitzer Prize-winning author Maraniss chronicles Clemente's life and his legacy as both an athlete and a humanitarian. (Rev: BL 3/1/06) [796.357]

Basketball

AURIEMMA, GENO

1486 Auriemma, Geno, and Jackie MacMullan. *Geno: In Pursuit of Perfection* (9–12). Illus. 2006, Warner $25.95 (0-446-57764-2). 336pp. The coach of the phenomenally successful UConn women's basketball team tells of coming to America with his

parents at the age of 7 and of his lifelong struggle to succeed. (Rev: BL 1/1–15/06) [796.323]

HASKINS, DON

1487 Haskins, Don, and Dan Wetzel. *Glory Road: My Story of the 1966 NCAA Basketball Championship and How One Team Triumphed Against the Odds and Changed America Forever* (10–12). 2006, Hyperion paper $14.95 (1-4013-0791-4). 272pp. Haskins tells how he led the all-black Texas Western College basketball team to the NCAA championship in 1966. (Rev: BL 1/1–15/06) [796.323]

JORDAN, MICHAEL

1488 Leahy, Michael. *When Nothing Else Matters: Michael Jordan's Last Comeback* (9–12). 2004, Simon & Schuster $26.00 (0-7432-5426-0). 400pp. This unflinching portrait focuses on Jordan's years as president of — and occasional player with — the Washington Wizards. (Rev: BL 11/1/04) [796.3]

MING, YAO

1489 Ming, Yao, and Ric Bucher. *Yao: A Life in Two Worlds* (8–12). Illus. 2004, Miramax $22.95 (1-4013-5214-6). 272pp. Yao Ming writes of his success in the NBA and also of the sharp contrast between the culture of his native China and that of the United States. (Rev: BL 9/1/04) [796.323]

STARKS, JOHN

1490 Starks, John. *My Life: Don't Ever Give Up* (9–12). Illus. 2004, Sports Publishing $24.95 (1-58261-802-X). 233pp. The NBA basketball star describes how he escaped the mean streets of Tulsa, Oklahoma, to become a top player for the New York Knicks. (Rev: BL 10/15/04) [796.323]

Football

NGUYEN, DAT

1491 Nguyen, Dat, and Rusty Burson. *Dat: Tackling Life and the NFL* (9–12). Illus. 2005, Texas A & M Univ. $24.95 (1-58544-472-3). 224pp. Dat Nguyen, the only Vietnamese American in the NFL, writes about the long and difficult road he traveled to make his mark in professional football. (Rev: BL 9/15/05) [796.332]

TUAOLO, ESERA

1492 Tuaolo, Esera, and John Rosengren. *Alone in the Trenches: My Life as a Gay Player in the NFL* (11–12). Illus. 2006, Sourcebooks $24.95 (1-4022-0505-8). 304pp. Longtime NFL lineman Tuaolo Esera tells how he hid his homosexuality to protect his career in professional football; for mature readers. (Rev: BL 11/1/05) [796.332]

YOAST, BILL

1493 Yoast, Bill. *Remember This Titan: Lessons Learned from a Celebrated Coach's Journey* (9–12). Illus. 2005, Taylor $21.95 (1-58979-278-5). 192pp. Yoast, replaced by an African American as head football coach at T. C. Williams High School in Alexandria, Virginia, in 1972, recounts how he worked with his successor, Herman Boone, to lead the newly integrated team to the state championship. (Rev: BL 10/1/05) [796.332]

Tennis

GIBSON, ALTHEA

1494 Gray, Frances Clayton, and Yanick Rice Lamb. *Born to Win: The Authorized Biography of Althea Gibson* (9–12). Illus. 2004, Wiley $24.95 (0-471-47165-8). 256pp. The story of African American Gibson's remarkable achievements in tennis in the 1950s, a time when the sport was largely played by whites. (Rev: BL 9/1/04) [796.34]

Miscellaneous Sports

ARMSTRONG, LANCE

1495 Coyle, Daniel. *Lance Armstrong's War: One Man's Battle Against Fate, Fame, Love, Death, Scandal, and a Few Other Rivals on the Road to the Tour de France* (8–12). Illus. 2005, HarperCollins $25.95 (0-06-073794-3). 336pp. Traces Armstrong's winning 2004 season and reviews the daunting challenges the cyclist has had to overcome in his life. (Rev: BL 6/1–15/05) [796.6]

BECKHAM, DAVID

1496 Beckham, David. *Both Feet on the Ground: An Autobiography* (8–12). 2003, HarperCollins $24.95 (0-06-057093-8). 400pp. Full of illustrations, this biography traces Beckham's life from childhood through soccer stardom. (Rev: SLJ 1/04; VOYA 2/04) [921]

FERRERAS, PIPIN

1497 Ferreras, Pipin. *The Dive: A Story of Love and Obsession* (10–12). Illus. 2004, Regan $25.95 (0-06-056416-4). 288pp. A record-breaking free diver talks about his obsession with the sport and about his wife's death setting an earlier record. (Rev: BL 9/1/04) [797.2]

GARDNER, RULON

1498 Gardner, Rulon, and Bob Schaller. *Never Stop Pushing: My Life from a Wyoming Farm to the Olympic Medals Stand* (9–12). Illus. 2005, Carroll & Graf paper $14.95 (0-7867-1593-6). 304pp. The inspiring story of Rulon Gardner, who won an Olympic gold medal in wrestling after hypothermia caused him to lose part of each foot. (Rev: BL 9/1/05) [796.812]

HAWK, TONY

1499 Peterson, Todd. *Tony Hawk: Skateboarder and Businessman* (8–11). Illus. Series: Ferguson Career Biographies. 2005, Ferguson LB $25.00 (0-8160-5893-8). 122pp. Skateboarder Tony Hawk's childhood, skating career, and business achievements are all covered in this readable volume. (Rev: BL 9/1/05) [796.22]

MILLER, BODE

1500 Miller, Bode, and Jack McEnany. *Bode: Go Fast, Be Good, Have Fun* (9–12). Illus. 2005, Villard $24.95 (1-4000-6235-7). 256pp. The unusual childhood of the boy from rural New Hampshire who became a world skiing star. (Rev: BL 9/1/05) [921]

SCDORIS, RACHEL

1501 Scdoris, Rachel, and Rick Steber. *No End in Sight: My Life as a Blind Iditarod Racer.* Rev. ed. (9–12). Illus. 2006, St. Martin's $22.95 (0-312-35273-5). 288pp. Scdoris, who is legally blind, tells about her experiences raising and training sled-dog teams and her participation in the 2005 Iditarod race

across 1,050 miles of desolate Alaskan terrain. (Rev: BL 2/1/06; SLJ 4/06) [798.8]

THORPE, JIM

1502 Crawford, Bill. *All American: The Rise and Fall of Jim Thorpe* (8–12). Illus. 2004, Wiley $24.95 (0-471-55732-3). 288pp. An in-depth look at the tumultuous life of the Native American athlete who triumphed on the world's playing fields but ultimately died in relative obscurity. (Rev: BL 11/15/04) [796]

World Figures

Collective

1503 Bledsoe, Karen E. *Daredevils of the Air: Thrilling Tales of Pioneer Aviators* (7–12). Series: Avisson Young Adult. 2003, Avisson paper $19.95 (1-888105-58-5). 155pp. The Wright brothers, Eddie Rickenbacker, Bessie Coleman, and Beryl Markham are among the early flyers profiled in stories of exciting aerial exploits. (Rev: SLJ 1/04) [920]

1504 Cawthorne, Nigel. *Military Commanders: The 100 Greatest Throughout History* (6–12). 2004, Enchanted Lion $18.95 (1-59270-029-2). 208pp. This chronology identifies the greatest military battles in world history and the men who led their forces to victory in those battles. (Rev: BL 6/1–15/04; SLJ 4/04) [355]

1505 Coddon, Karin S., ed. *Black Women Activists* (9–12). Series: Profiles in History. 2004, Gale LB $26.96 (0-7377-2313-0). 220pp. Mary Church Terrell, Sojourner Truth, Rosa Parks, Fannie Lou Hamer, and Winnie Mandela are among the 11 women profiled in this volume. (Rev: SLJ 11/04) [920]

1506 Dunn, Jane. *Elizabeth and Mary: Cousins, Rivals, Queens* (11–12). 2004, Knopf $30.00 (0-375-40898-3). 453pp. For strong readers, this well-documented, well-illustrated, and well-written account of the two very different queens will be rewarding. (Rev: SLJ 5/04) [920]

1507 Hastings, Max. *Warriors: Portraits from the Battlefield* (9–12). Illus. 2006, Knopf $27.50 (1-4000-4441-3). 400pp. British military historian Hastings celebrates the warrior spirit in profiles of 14 men and one woman who fought for their countries during the 19th and 20th centuries. (Rev: BL 12/15/05) [355]

1508 Nardo, Don. *Ancient Philosophers* (7–12). Series: History Makers. 2004, Gale LB $21.96 (1-59018-281-2). 112pp. The lives and essential philosophies of Democritus, Plato, Aristotle, Buddha, and Confucius are laid out in clear text. (Rev: SLJ 6/04) [920]

1509 Phibbs, Cheryl Fisher, ed. *Pioneers of Human Rights* (8–11). Illus. Series: Profiles in History. 2005, Gale LB $27.96 (0-7377-2146-4). 240pp. Among the figures profiled in this volume are Mohandas Gandhi, Frederick Douglass, Nelson Mandela, and Eleanor Roosevelt. (Rev: BL 7/05) [323]

1510 Scandiffio, Laura. *Evil Masters: The Frightening World of Tyrants* (7–10). 2005, Annick $24.95 (1-55037-895-3); paper $12.95 (1-55037-894-5). 230pp. Nero, Ivan the Terrible, Hitler, Stalin, and Saddam Hussein are five of the seven rulers profiled; an introduction discusses personality traits and the reasons why such men are able to assume power. (Rev: SLJ 1/06) [920]

1511 Showalter, Dennis. *Patton and Rommel: Men of War in the Twentieth Century* (9–12). 2005, Berkley $22.95 (0-425-19346-2). 288pp. Showalter compares the lives and military careers of U.S. General George Patton and German Field Marshall Erwin Rommel, military leaders on opposing sides of the conflict. (Rev: BL 4/15/05) [940.54]

1512 Young, Mitchell, ed. *Terrorist Leaders* (11–12). Series: Profiles in History. 2004, Gale LB $33.70 (0-7377-2649-0). 224pp. After a section on Osama bin Laden, chapters organize biographies under state terrorists (Stalin, Pol Pot), liberation fighters (Menachem Begin, Yasir Arafat), and ideologists (the Unabomber, Timothy McVeigh). (Rev: SLJ 4/05) [920]

Africa

CLEOPATRA

1513 Nardo, Don. *Cleopatra: Egypt's Last Pharaoh* (6–10). Series: The Lucent Library of Historical Eras. 2005, Gale LB $28.70 (1-59018-660-5). 112pp. Presenting many quotations from ancient writings about Cleopatra, Nardo discusses their biases plus the importance of the Egyptian leader's relationships with Julius Caesar and Marc Antony. (Rev: SLJ 11/05) [921]

MANDELA, NELSON

1514 Pogrund, Benjamin. *Nelson Mandela* (5–10). Illus. Series: World Peacemakers. 2004, Gale LB $27.44 (1-56711-978-6). 64pp. As well as a fine biography of Mandela, this book gives a concise history of apartheid in South Africa. (Rev: BL 2/15/04; SLJ 5/04) [921]

Asia and the Middle East

BIN LADEN, OSAMA

1515 Loehfelm, Bill. *Osama bin Laden* (6–12). Illus. Series: History's Villains. 2004, Gale LB $21.96 (1-56711-760-0). 112pp. Osama bin Laden, nominal leader of al-Qaeda and arguably the world's most wanted man, is profiled here, with information on his wealthy family, his youth, and the factors that led him to terrorism. (Rev: BL 7/04) [958.104]

GANDHI, MAHATMA

1516 Nicholson, Michael. *Mahatma Gandhi* (6–12). Series: World Peacemakers. 2003, Gale LB $24.95 (1-56711-976-X). 64pp. Although Gandhi's peace-making activities are the emphasis of this slim, introductory biography, it also covers his youth. (Rev: SLJ 5/04) [921]

GENGHIS KHAN

1517 Rice, Earle, Jr. *Empire in the East: The Story of Genghis Khan* (7–11). Illus. Series: World Leaders. 2005, Morgan Reynolds LB $24.95 (1-931798-62-1). 160pp. A life of Genghis Khan, who rose from obscurity to become leader of the Great Mongol Nation and ruler of vast territories that stretched from the Adriatic to the Pacific. (Rev: BL 8/05; SLJ 8/05) [950]

HUSSEIN, SADDAM

1518 Stewart, Gail B. *Saddam Hussein* (8–12). Series: Heroes and Villains. 2004, Gale LB $21.96 (1-59018-350-9). 96pp. Ending before Saddam Hussein's capture by U.S. forces, this is a portrait of a ruthless dictator and his ascent to and maintenance of power. (Rev: SLJ 4/04) [921]

POL POT

1519 Koopmans, Andy. *Pol Pot* (8–12). Series: Heroes and Villains. 2005, Gale LB $28.70 (1-59018-596-X). 112pp. A readable biography of the leader of Cambodia's murderous Khmer Rouge guerrillas. (Rev: SLJ 9/05) [921]

RIZAL, JOSE

1520 Arruda, Suzanne Middendorf. *Freedom's Martyr: The Story of José Rizal, National Hero of the Philippines* (6–12). Series: Avisson Young Adult. 2003, Avisson paper $19.95 (1-888105-55-0). 106pp. A patriot and activist on behalf of the native peoples of the Philippines, Rizal was executed by the Spanish for treason in 1896 and remains the country's national hero. (Rev: SLJ 5/04) [921]

SUNG, KIM IL

1521 Ingram, Scott. *Kim Il Sung* (6–12). Illus. Series: History's Villains. 2004, Gale LB $21.96 (1-4103-0259-8). 112pp. Profiles North Korean dictator Kim Il Sung, who ruled his country with a brutal hand for more than 40 years. (Rev: BL 7/04; SLJ 5/04) [951.930]

Europe

ALEXANDER THE GREAT

1522 Cantor, Norman. *Alexander the Great: Journey to the End of the Earth* (10–12). 2005, HarperCollins $21.95 (0-06-057012-1). 192pp. The key events of the Macedonian ruler's brief life are placed in cultural and historical context. (Rev: BL 9/1/05) [921]

1523 Foreman, Laura. *Alexander the Conqueror* (9–12). Illus. 2004, Da Capo $35.00 (0-306-81293-2). 211pp. This richly illustrated biography traces the Macedonian leader's conquest of vast territories stretching from the Mediterranean on the west to India on the east, separating fact from legend. (Rev: SLJ 3/05) [921]

ATTILA THE HUN

1524 Oliver, Marilyn Tower. *Attila the Hun* (6–10). Series: Heroes and Villains. 2005, Gale LB $28.70 (1-59018-638-9). 112pp. The softer side of Attila is revealed in this balanced and well-documented account of his youth and later achievements. (Rev: SLJ 3/06) [921]

CATHERINE THE GREAT

1525 Whitelaw, Nancy. *Catherine the Great and the Enlightenment in Russia* (8–12). Illus. Series: European Queens. 2004, Morgan Reynolds LB $24.95 (1-931798-27-3). 160pp. The colorful life of the Russian empress from childhood in her native Germany to her pivotal role in leading her adopted country into full participation in the cultural and political life of Europe. (Rev: BL 12/15/04; SLJ 12/04) [921]

CHURCHILL, SIR WINSTON

1526 Addison, Paul. *Churchill: The Unexpected Hero* (9–12). Series: Lives and Legacies. 2005, Oxford $20.00 (0-19-927934-9). 208pp. Churchill's critics are the focus of this analysis of the British statesman's reputation. (Rev: BL 2/1/05) [941.084]

CLEISTHENES

1527 Parton, Sarah. *Cleisthenes: Founder of Athenian Democracy* (7–10). Series: Leaders of Ancient Greece. 2004, Rosen LB $31.95 (0-8239-3826-3). 110pp. Information about Cleisthenes and his times is carefully couched in discussion of the sources used and the ways in which this material has been gathered and analyzed. (Rev: SLJ 9/04) [921]

CROMWELL, OLIVER

1528 Gaunt, Peter. *Oliver Cromwell* (10–12). Illus. Series: British Library Historic Lives. 2004, New York Univ. $22.00 (0-8147-3164-3). 144pp. A compact, well-illustrated, and balanced profile of Cromwell, who altered the course of British history in the mid-17th century, clearly presenting historical and religious context. (Rev: BL 10/15/04; SLJ 4/05) [941.06]

DIDEROT, DENIS

1529 Stark, Sam. *Diderot: French Philosopher and Father of the Encyclopedia* (9–12). Illus. Series: Philosophers of the Enlightenment. 2005, Rosen LB $23.95 (1-4042-0418-0). 112pp. Presents the life and achievements of Diderot, focusing on the Frenchman's work on the Encyclopédie, one of the Enlightenment's most significant books. (Rev: BL 11/1/05) [034]

DRAKE, SIR FRANCIS

1530 Whitfield, Peter. *Sir Francis Drake* (8–12). Illus. Series: British Library Historic Lives. 2004, New York Univ. $22.00 (0-8147-9403-3). 160pp.

Drake's great naval accomplishments are balanced against less admirable activities. (Rev: BL 10/15/04) [942.05]

THE FRANK FAMILY

1531 Denenberg, Barry. *Shadow Life: A Portrait of Anne Frank and Her Family* (6–10). 2005, Scholastic $16.95 (0-439-41678-7). 240pp. In this engaging title from the Shadow Life series, author Barry Denenberg tells the complete story of Anne Frank and her family from their earlier life in Frankfurt to their eventual transport to Nazi concentration camps. (Rev: BL 2/1/05*; SLJ 4/05; VOYA 4/05) [940.53]

FRANK, ANNE

1532 Sawyer, Kem Knapp. *Anne Frank: A Photographic Story of a Life* (5–10). Illus. Series: DK Biography. 2004, DK LB $14.99 (0-7566-0341-2); paper $4.99 (0-7566-0490-7). 128pp. This richly illustrated biography draws on Anne's diary and accounts by her father and by Miep Gies. (Rev: BL 6/1–15/04) [921]

HIMMLER, HEINRICH

1533 Worth, Richard. *Heinrich Himmler: Murderous Architect of the Holocaust* (8–11). Illus. Series: Holocaust Heroes and Nazi Criminals. 2005, Enslow LB $20.95 (0-7660-2532-2). 160pp. A profile of the career of the architect of Nazi Germany's lethally effective campaign against the Jews and other victims of the Holocaust. (Rev: BL 10/15/05; SLJ 1/06) [940.53]

JOHN PAUL II, POPE

1534 Behnke, Alison. *Pope John Paul II* (7–10). Illus. Series: A&E Biography. 2005, Lerner LB $27.93 (0-8225-2798-7); paper $8.95 (0-8225-3387-1). 112pp. This very human portrait of Pope John Paul II traces his life and presents the views of his critics as well as his supporters. (Rev: BL 10/1/05; SLJ 9/05) [282]

LENIN, VLADIMIR ILICH

1535 Naden, Corinne J., and Rose Blue. *Lenin* (6–10). Series: Importance Of. 2005, Gale $27.45 (1-59018-233-2). 112pp. The life and political career of Vladimir Lenin, founder of the Russian Communist Party. (Rev: BL 6/1–15/04) [921]

MARIE ANTOINETTE

1536 Lotz, Nancy, and Carlene Phillips. *Marie Antoinette and the Decline of the French Monarchy* (8–12). Illus. Series: European Queens. 2004, Morgan Reynolds LB $24.95 (1-931798-28-1). 160pp. The turbulent life of Marie Antoinette from her birth in Vienna to her death on the guillotine in October 1793. (Rev: BL 12/15/04; SLJ 12/04) [921]

MENGELE, JOSEF

1537 Grabowski, John F. *Josef Mengele* (8–12). Series: Heroes and Villains. 2004, Gale LB $21.96 (1-59018-425-4). 112pp. A life of the Nazi who committed atrocities during World War II but escaped to South America. (Rev: SLJ 4/04) [921]

PUTIN, VLADIMIR

1538 Streissguth, Thomas. *Vladimir Putin* (7–10). Illus. Series: A&E Biography. 2005, Lerner LB $27.93 (0-8225-2374-4); paper $7.95 (0-8225-9630-X). 112pp. Putin's professional and political life take center stage in this biography that will be useful for report writers. (Rev: BL 9/1/05) [947.086]

SOLON

1539 Randall, Bernard. *Solon: The Lawmaker of Athens* (7–10). Series: Leaders of Ancient Greece. 2004, Rosen LB $31.95 (0-8239-3829-8). 112pp. Information about Solon and his times is carefully introduced with discussion of the sources used and the ways in which this material has been gathered and analyzed. (Rev: SLJ 9/04) [921]

THEMISTOCLES

1540 Morris, Ian Macgregor. *Themistocles: Defender of Greece* (7–10). Series: Leaders of Ancient Greece. 2004, Rosen LB $31.95 (0-8239-3830-1). 110pp. Information about Themistocles and his times is carefully couched in discussion of the sources used and the ways in which this material has been gathered and analyzed. (Rev: SLJ 9/04) [921]

Miscellaneous Interesting Lives

Collective

1541 Sjoholm, Barbara, ed. *Steady as She Goes: Women's Adventures at Sea* (10–12). 2003, Seal paper $15.95 (1-58005-094-8). 290pp. Women writers describe a variety of seagoing situations — some scary, some joyous, some athletic, some thought-provoking. (Rev: SLJ 5/04)

Individual

AKBAR, SAID HYDER

1542 Akbar, Said Hyder, and Susan Burton. *Come Back to Afghanistan: A California Teenager's Story* (9–12). 2005, Bloomsbury $24.95 (1-58234-520-1). 352pp. Said Hyder Akbar, son of Afghani immigrants to the United States, writes movingly about his visits to his parents' homeland in the wake of the fall of the Taliban government in late 2001. (Rev: BL 9/1/05; SLJ 12/05*) [958.104]

AMIRY, SUAD

1543 Amiry, Suad. *Sharon and My Mother-in-Law: Ramallah Diaries* (9–12). 2005, Pantheon $23.00 (0-375-42379-6). 224pp. With humor and pathos, Amiry describes life in the West Bank town of Ramallah during the Israeli occupation. (Rev: BL 9/1/05) [956.95]

ANDERS, GIGI

1544 Anders, Gigi. *Jubana! The Awkwardly True and Dazzling Adventures of a Jewish Cubana Goddess* (11–12). 2005, HarperCollins $23.95 (0-06-056369-9). 304pp. Anders's entertaining and poignant descriptions of her Jewish family's forced emigration from Cuba to the United States and her adjustment to life in suburban Washington, D.C., will fascinate older teens. (Rev: BL 6/1–15/05) [973]

APPELT, KATHI

1545 Appelt, Kathi. *My Father's Summers: A Daughter's Memoir* (6–12). 2004, Holt $15.95 (0-8050-7362-0). 208pp. In a series of prose poems, Appelt paints a poignant portrait of her life growing up in Houston and the pain caused by the extended absences of her father. (Rev: BCCB 7–8/04; BL 6/1–15/04; SLJ 6/04; VOYA 6/04) [813]

BARBER, CHARLES

1546 Barber, Charles. *Songs from the Black Chair: A Memoir of Mental Interiors* (11–12). 2005, Univ. of Nebraska $22.00 (0-8032-1298-4). 218pp. Barber writes movingly about how the suicide of a close friend and Barber's own struggles with obsessive-compulsive disorder led him to become a psychiatrist; for mature teens. (Rev: BL 3/1/05) [616.89]

BECHDEL, ALISON

1547 Bechdel, Alison. *Fun Home: A Family Tragicomic* (11–12). Illus. 2006, Houghton $19.95 (0-618-47794-2). 240pp. In this excellent and moving graphic memoir, Allison Bechdel writes candidly about her lesbianism and her relationship with her father, who she later learned was gay; for mature teens. (Rev: BL 3/15/06) [741.5]

BEN-ATAR, ROMA NUTKIEWICZ

1548 Ben-Atar, Roma Nutkiewicz, and Doron S. Ben-Atar. *What Time and Sadness Spared: Mother and Son Confront the Holocaust* (9–12). Illus. 2006, Univ. of Virginia $27.95 (0-8139-2513-4). 208pp.

In this searing Holocaust memoir co-written with her son, Roma Ben-Atar recalls the horrors of the Warsaw Ghetto and life in Nazi concentration camps. (Rev: BL 3/15/06) [940.53]

BITTON-JACKSON, LIVIA

1549 Bitton-Jackson, Livia. *Hello, America* (9–12). 2005, Simon & Schuster $16.95 (0-689-86755-7). 240pp. In the final installment of a trilogy about her life before, during, and after the Holocaust, the Czech-born author tells of her experiences as an 18-year-old immigrant to Brooklyn in 1951. (Rev: BL 1/1–15/05; SLJ 3/05; VOYA 4/05) [940.53]

BLOLAND, SUE ERIKSON

1550 Bloland, Sue Erikson. *In the Shadow of Fame: A Memoir by the Daughter of Erik H. Erikson* (9–12). 2005, Viking $24.95 (0-670-03374-X). 230pp. Bloland describes her unhappy childhood as the daughter of a widely acclaimed child psychologist. (Rev: BL 12/1/04) [150.19]

BOOTH, MARTIN

1551 Booth, Martin. *Golden Boy: Memories of a Hong Kong Childhood* (11–12). 2005, St. Martin's $24.95 (0-312-34817-7). 352pp. In this engaging memoir suitable for mature readers, Booth recounts what it was like growing up in Hong Kong more than 50 years ago. (Rev: BL 10/15/05) [828]

BRADLEY, ERNESTINE

1552 Bradley, Ernestine. *The Way Home: A German Childhood, an American Life* (11–12). 2005, Pantheon $24.00 (0-375-42279-X). 272pp. In this frank memoir, Ernestine Bradley writes of her childhood in war-torn Germany, immigration to the United States, marriage to former Senator Bill Bradley, and battle with breast cancer; for older readers. (Rev: BL 2/1/05) [382.73]

BRKIC, COURTNEY ANGELA

1553 Brkic, Courtney Angela. *The Stone Fields: An Epitaph for the Living* (11–12). 2004, Farrar $24.00 (0-374-20774-7). 304pp. Brkic intertwines her own experiences working with a UN team investigating genocide in Bosnia with the story of her grandmother's dangerous love for a Jew during World War II. (Rev: BL 8/04) [949.703]

CARROLL, LINDA

1554 Carroll, Linda. *Her Mother's Daughter: A Memoir of the Mother I Never Knew and of My Daughter, Courtney Love* (11–12). 2006, Doubleday $24.95 (0-385-51247-3). 320pp. The author, mother of singer/actor Courtney Love, tells of her own trou-

bled childhood with an adoptive family, her estrangement from her famous daughter, and the search for her biological mother; for mature teens. (Rev: BL 12/1/05) [616.89]

CHEEK, GENE

1555 Cheek, Gene. *The Color of Love: A Mother's Choice in the Jim Crow South* (9–12). 2005, Lyons $22.95 (1-59228-626-7). 272pp. Cheek describes how the courts took him away from his loving mother because of her forbidden love affair with an African American in early-1960s North Carolina. (Rev: BL 4/1/05) [305.896]

CHILDERS, MARY

1556 Childers, Mary. *Welfare Brat* (11–12). 2005, Bloomsbury $23.95 (1-58234-586-4). 272pp. In this inspiring memoir, Childers tells how education helped her to escape the bonds of poverty; for mature teens. (Rev: BL 4/1/05) [974.7]

CONLON-MCIVOR, MAURA

1557 Conlon-McIvor, Maura. *FBI Girl: How I Learned to Crack My Father's Code* (9–12). 2004, Warner $23.00 (0-446-53310-6). 306pp. In this engaging memoir going back to the 1960s, Conlon-McIvor writes about how she confused her father's unhappiness with his job. (Rev: BL 7/04) [363]

CORYAT, SONJA HEINZE

1558 Coryat, Sonja Heinze. *Sunny, Ward of the State: Calamity Strikes a Family During the Great Depression* (10–12). 2004, PublishAmerica paper $24.95 (1-4137-1523-0). 287pp. A poignant memoir of a harrowing childhood, much of it spent in institutions as a ward of the state. (Rev: SLJ 4/05) [921]

CRAVAN, ARTHUR

1559 Richardson, Mike, and Rick Geary. *Cravan* (10–12). Illus. 2005, Dark Horse $14.95 (1-59307-291-0). 72pp. In this graphic novel-format biography, Mike Richardson and Rick Geary chronicle the stranger-than-fiction life of Arthur Cravan, a self-confessed con artist, forger, and thief. (Rev: BL 11/15/05; VOYA 2/06) [741.5]

DORNSTEIN, KEN

1560 Dornstein, Ken. *The Boy Who Fell Out of the Sky* (11–12). Illus. 2006, Random $23.95 (0-375-50359-5). 320pp. In this moving memoir, Ken Dornstein recounts how he came to terms with the death of his older brother in the 1988 terrorist attack on Pan Am Flight 103; for mature readers. (Rev: BL 12/1/05) [973.91]

EDNEY, OLGA

1561 Williams, Stephanie. *Olga's Story: Three Continents, Two World Wars, and Revolution — One Woman's Epic Journey Through the Twentieth Century* (11–12). Illus. 2005, Doubleday $26.00 (0-385-50851-4). 352pp. Williams paints a sprawling portrait of her Russian-born grandmother's incredible life, including her flight to China during the Bolshevik Revolution and her eventual arrival in England; for mature readers. (Rev: BL 5/15/05) [909]

FEIG, PAUL

1562 Feig, Paul. *Superstud; or, How I Became a 24-Year-Old Virgin* (11–12). 2005, Three Rivers paper $13.95 (1-4000-5175-4). 320pp. The creator of the critically acclaimed *Freaks and Geeks* television program reveals the trials and tribulations of his early experiences with girls; for mature teens. (Rev: BL 6/1–15/05) [306.7]

FICK, NATHANIEL

1563 Fick, Nathaniel. *One Bullet Away: The Making of a Marine Officer* (11–12). Illus. 2005, Houghton $25.00 (0-618-55613-3). 384pp. In this riveting memoir suitable for mature readers, a classics major recounts his experiences as an elite Marine in Afghanistan and Iraq. (Rev: BL 10/15/05) [359.9]

GORDON, EMILY FOX

1564 Gordon, Emily Fox. *Are You Happy? A Childhood Remembered* (9–12). 2006, Riverhead $22.95 (1-59448-904-1). 208pp. In this poignant memoir, Emily Fox Gordon recounts her troubled childhood in Williamstown, Massachusetts. (Rev: BL 3/1/06) [974.4]

GREGORY, JULIE

1565 Gregory, Julie. *Sickened: The Memoir of a Munchausen by Proxy Childhood* (10–12). 2003, Bantam $24.95 (0-553-80307-7). 244pp. The troubling but compelling story of the abuse Gregory endured as the child of a mother who invented sickness in her daughter to attract attention to herself. (Rev: SLJ 4/04; VOYA 2/04) [616.85]

GURDON, MARTIN

1566 Gurdon, Martin. *Travels with My Chicken: A Man and His Companion Take to the Road* (9–12). Illus. 2005, Lyons paper $12.95 (1-59228-778-6). 176pp. The British author of *Hen and the Art of Chicken Maintenance* (2004) chronicles the unique book-promotion tour he undertook with a chicken named Tikka; offbeat humor and wry perceptions. (Rev: BL 11/15/05) [914.104]

HANCOCK, BILL

1567 Hancock, Bill. *Riding with the Blue Moth* (9–12). Illus. 2005, Sports Publishing $24.95 (1-59670-104-8). 252pp. In this poignant memoir, Bill Hancock, coordinator of the annual NCAA March Madness basketball tournament, tells how a cross-country bicycle trip helped him — and his wife — to deal with the heartbreak of their son's death in an airplane crash. (Rev: BL 9/1/05) [796.6]

HESTER, CHARLEY

1568 Hester, Charley. *The True Life Wild West Memoir of a Bush-Popping Cow Waddy* (9–12). Ed. by Kirby Ross. Illus. 2004, Univ. of Nebraska paper $13.95 (0-8032-7346-0). 142pp. A fascinating memoir of an exciting period in American history, by the great-great-grandfather of the editor. (Rev: BL 9/1/04) [978]

IACUZZO, TERRY

1569 Iacuzzo, Terry. *Small Mediums at Large: The True Tale of a Family of Psychics* (11–12). 2005, Penguin $22.95 (0-399-15235-0). 368pp. Stories of growing up in a Sicilian family in Buffalo provide plenty of drama; the fact that they are psychics just adds to the mix; for mature teens. (Rev: BL 12/1/04) [130]

JACOBS, A. J.

1570 Jacobs, A. J. *The Know-It-All: One Man's Humble Quest to Become the Smartest Person in the World* (10–12). 2004, Simon & Schuster $25.00 (0-7432-5060-5). 384pp. In this humorous alphabetically organized memoir, Jacobs tells how his mind was expanded — to the breaking point — by reading every volume of the *Encyclopaedia Britannica*; for mature readers. (Rev: BL 9/1/04; SLJ 2/05) [031]

JACOBS, MOLLY BRACE

1571 Jacobs, Molly Brace. *Secret Girl* (11–12). 2006, St. Martin's $22.95 (0-312-32094-9). 240pp. In this moving memoir suitable for mature readers, Jacobs writes about her difficult childhood and her decision as an adult to seek out the younger sister who had been declared mentally retarded at birth and committed to an institution. (Rev: BL 12/15/05) [362.196]

KARPEL, NINI

1572 Kaplan, Vivian Jeanette. *Ten Green Bottles: The True Story of One Family's Journey from War-Torn Austria to the Ghettos of Shanghai* (11–12). 2004, St. Martin's $24.95 (0-312-33054-5). 304pp. Kaplan recounts the story of her family's grueling experiences in World War II, escaping from Nazi-occupied Austria to China, one of the few countries accepting Jewish refugees during this troubled period; for mature readers. (Rev: BL 10/1/04) [940.53]

KATIN, MIRIAM

1573 Katin, Miriam. *We Are on Our Own* (11–12). Illus. 2006, Drawn & Quarterly $19.95 (1-896597-20-3). 136pp. In this gripping World War II memoir presented in graphic novel format, animator Katin tells the harrowing story of her escape from Budapest with her mother; for mature readers. (Rev: BL 3/15/06) [741.5]

KIMMEL, HAVEN

1574 Kimmel, Haven. *She Got Up off the Couch: And Other Heroic Acts from Mooreland, Indiana* (9–12). 2006, Free Press $24.00 (0-7432-8499-2). 288pp. In this appealing sequel to *A Girl Named Zippy* (2001), Kimmel describes the changes in her life as her mother transforms from couch potato to slim college student. (Rev: BL 12/1/05) [977.2]

LAWFORD, CHRISTOPHER KENNEDY

1575 Lawford, Christopher Kennedy. *Symptoms of Withdrawal: A Memoir of Snapshots of Redemption* (11–12). Illus. 2005, Morrow $25.95 (0-06-073248-2). 416pp. The son of actor Peter Lawford and Pat Kennedy writes movingly about his youthful excesses and abuse of drugs; for mature teens. (Rev: BL 8/05) [791.43]

LAWRENCE, CANDIDA

1576 Lawrence, Candida. *Fear Itself* (10–12). 2004, Unbridled $19.95 (1-932961-01-1). 224pp. In her third soul-baring memoir, Lawrence looks back at her first marriage and the terrible price she paid for her involvement in the early years of the atomic age. (Rev: BL 10/15/04) [362.19]

MACDONALD, WARREN

1577 Macdonald, Warren. *A Test of Will: One Man's Extraordinary Story of Survival* (8–12). 2004, Douglas & McIntyre paper $14.95 (1-55365-064-6). 208pp. The riveting story of Macdonald's survival after his legs were pinned under a massive rock on an island off Australia. (Rev: BL 9/15/04) [790.5]

MCGOUGH, MATTHEW

1578 McGough, Matthew. *Bat Boy: My True Life Adventures Coming of Age with the New York Yankees* (8–12). 2005, Doubleday $22.95 (0-385-51020-9). 240pp. McGough tells how a boyhood dream came true when he was selected to be a bat-boy for the New York Yankees. (Rev: BL 3/1/05; SLJ 11/05) [796.357]

MOAVENI, AZADEH

1579 Moaveni, Azadeh. *Lipstick Jihad: A Memoir of Growing Up Iranian in America and American in Iran* (9–12). 2005, PublicAffairs $25.00 (1-58648-193-2). 272pp. Moaveni, the American daughter of Iranian-born parents, offers an eye-opening look at life for young people in today's Iran as well as the problems faced by young Iranians in America. (Rev: BL 2/15/05; SLJ 6/05) [392.15]

MORTENSON, GREG

1580 Mortenson, Greg, and David Oliver Relin. *Three Cups of Tea: One Man's Mission to Fight Terrorism and Build Nations . . . One School at a Time* (9–12). 2006, Viking $25.95 (0-670-03482-7). 334pp. Mortenson relates his efforts to build a school for a Pakistani village whose inhabitants nursed him back to health while on a climbing trip. (Rev: BL 3/15/06) [371]

NEUFELD, JOSH

1581 Neufeld, Josh. *A Few Perfect Hours . . . and Other Stories from Southeast Asia and Central Europe* (11–12). Illus. 2004, Alternative Comics paper $12.95 (1-891867-79-2). 128pp. An interesting graphic treatment of a travel memoir, describing backpacking through Southeast Asia and Central Europe; for mature readers. (Rev: BL 9/15/04) [741.5]

OLIVER, ANNA CYPRA

1582 Oliver, Anna Cypra. *Assembling My Father: A Daughter's Detective Story* (9–12). Illus. 2004, Houghton $25.00 (0-618-34152-8). 368pp. Anna Cypra Oliver writes movingly of the search to learn more about her heritage. (Rev: BL 8/04) [362.28]

PARRADO, NANDO

1583 Parrado, Nando, and Vince Rause. *Miracles in the Andes: 72 Days on the Mountain and My Long Trek Home* (11–12). 2006, Crown $25.00 (1-4000-9767-3). 304pp. Parrado, a survivor of the 1972 Andean plane crash chronicled in *Alive*, recounts the harrowing tale of two months in the mountains and his 10-day journey in search of help; for mature teens. (Rev: BL 3/15/06) [982]

PAZIRA, NELOFER

1584 Pazira, Nelofer. *A Bed of Red Flowers: In Search of My Afghanistan* (11–12). Illus. 2005, Free Press paper $15.00 (0-7432-8133-0). 416pp. The star of the movie *Kandahar* writes about the turbulent political and social backdrop to her youth in Afghanistan; for mature teens. (Rev: BL 8/05) [958.104]

PRESS, EYAL

1585 Press, Eyal. *Absolute Convictions: My Father, a City, and the Conflict That Divided America*

(10–12). Illus. 2006, Holt $26.00 (0-8050-7731-6). 304pp. In this absorbing memoir, journalist Eyal Press writes about what it was like to grow up as the son of an abortionist during a time when the pro-life movement was becoming increasingly vocal and often violent. (Rev: BL 3/1/06) [363.4]

RALSTON, ARON

1586 Ralston, Aron. *Between a Rock and a Hard Place* (9–12). Illus. 2004, Atria $26.00 (0-7434-9281-1). 320pp. Trapped by a boulder in a remote canyon in Utah, Ralston amputated his arm and set off to hike to help. (Rev: BL 8/04; SLJ 2/05) [796.51]

ROSEN, CHRISTINE

1587 Rosen, Christine. *My Fundamentalist Education: A Memoir of a Divine Girlhood* (9–12). 2006, PublicAffairs $25.00 (1-58648-258-0). 186pp. In this compelling and humorous memoir, Rosen recalls her experiences while attending a fundamentalist Christian school in Florida during the 1970s and 1980s. (Rev: BL 10/1/05) [277.59]

RUNYAN, BRENT

1588 Runyon, Brent. *The Burn Journals* (8–12). 2004, Random LB $19.99 (0-375-82621-1). 384pp. In this powerful memoir, Runyon recounts his journey to recovery from life-threatening burns suffered in a teenage suicide attempt. (Rev: BL 6/1–15/04; SLJ 11/04) [362.28]

SAGINOR, JENNIFER

1589 Saginor, Jennifer. *Playground* (9–12). 2005, HarperCollins $24.95 (0-06-076156-3). 288pp. In this compelling memoir, suitable only for mature teens and young adults, Jennifer Saginor tells what it was like growing up in and around the Los Angeles Playboy Mansion, where her father, a friend of Hugh Hefner, lived full-time. (Rev: BL 6/1–15/05) [306.89]

SALBI, ZAINAB

1590 Salbi, Zainab, and Laurie Becklund. *Between Two Worlds: Escaping from Tyranny: Growing Up in the Shadow of Saddam* (11–12). 2005, Gotham $26.00 (1-592-40156-2). 272pp. Salbi, a member of a prominent Iraqi family, writes about growing up within Saddam Hussein's circle and marrying to escape it; for mature teens. (Rev: BL 9/1/05) [956.7]

SALEEM, HINER

1591 Saleem, Hiner. *My Father's Rifle: A Childhood in Kurdistan* (9–12). Trans. by Catherine Temerson. 2005, Farrar $17.00 (0-374-21693-2).

112pp. In this powerful coming-of-age memoir, recommended for mature teens and young adults only, Hiner Saleem tells about growing up as a Kurd in Iraq under the iron-fisted rule of Saddam Hussein. (Rev: BL 11/15/04) [956.7]

SARTOR, MARGARET

1592 Sartor, Margaret. *Miss American Pie: A Diary of Love, Secrets and Growing Up in the '70s* (11–12). 2006, Bloomsbury $19.95 (1-59691-200-6). 288pp. Race relations, religion, and typical teen problems all figure in this reminiscence of 1970s Louisiana; for mature readers. (Rev: BL 3/15/06) [305.235]

SATRAPI, MARJANE

1593 Satrapi, Marjane. *Persepolis 2: The Story of a Return* (10–12). Illus. 2004, Pantheon $17.95 (0-375-42288-9). 192pp. Picking up from the comic-strip memoir *Persepolis* (2003), Satrapi recounts her time at school in Vienna, far from her home in Tehran, and her difficulties adjusting to adolescence in a very foreign country. (Rev: BL 8/04; SLJ 12/04) [741.5]

SCHEERES, JULIA

1594 Scheeres, Julia. *Jesus Land* (11–12). 2005, Counterpoint $23.00 (1-58243-338-0). 288pp. In this harrowing coming-of-age memoir suitable for older readers, Scheeres recounts how she and her adopted black brother helped each other through a soul-scarring fundamentalist Christian childhood and a stay in a brutal reform school in the Dominican Republic. (Rev: BL 9/1/05) [811]

SCHOMAKER, ANNEMARIE REUTER

1595 Schomaker, Annemarie Reuter. *Out of the Ashes: Berlin 1930 to 1950* (10–12). 2003, Authorhouse paper $14.50 (1-4140-1733-2). 233pp. A compelling account of Schomaker's experiences as a young person in pre-World War II Germany and the hard times that followed, extending through the Berlin Airlift that brought much-needed food and supplies to the western sector of the city. (Rev: SLJ 5/04) [921]

SEATON, BILL

1596 Seaton, Bill. *My Seven Years in Captivity: Tails and Misadventures in the San Diego Zoo* (9–12). Illus. 2006, SP paper $19.95 (1-59025-902-5). 268pp. In this appealing memoir, Seaton describes his years working as public relations director of the world-famous San Diego Zoo. (Rev: BL 1/1–15/06) [636.088]

SMITH, TARA BRAY

1597 Smith, Tara Bray. *West of Then: A Mother, a Daughter, and a Journey Past Paradise* (11–12). 2004, Simon & Schuster $24.00 (0-7432-3679-3). 336pp. In this deeply moving memoir, Smith relates her search for her homeless, drug-addicted mother on the streets of Honolulu; for mature readers. (Rev: BL 9/1/04) [362.29]

STRINGER, LEE

1598 Stringer, Lee. *Sleepaway School: Stories from a Boy's Life* (10–12). 2004, Seven Stories $21.95 (1-58322-478-5). 240pp. In this moving memoir, Stringer, an African American, writes about the three years he spent at a "sleepaway school" for troubled boys and the events that led to his being sent there. (Rev: BL 6/1–15/04; SLJ 11/04) [649.153]

SWADOS, ELIZABETH

1599 Swados, Elizabeth. *My Depression: A Picture Book* (8–12). Illus. 2005, Hyperion $16.95 (1-4013-0789-2). 160pp. In a candid yet entertaining cartoon picture-book format, Swados reveals her struggles with severe depression. (Rev: BL 3/15/05) [818]

TRUSSONI, DANIELLE

1600 Trussoni, Danielle. *Falling Through the Earth* (11–12). 2006, Holt $23.00 (0-8050-7732-4). 256pp. Trussoni's memoir of growing up with her hard-drinking father will resonate with many young adults; for mature readers. (Rev: BL 1/1–15/06) [810]

UNG, LOUNG

1601 Ung, Loung. *Lucky Child: A Daughter of Cambodia Reunites with the Sister She Left Behind* (9–12). 2005, HarperCollins $24.95 (0-06-073394-2). 288pp. The author of *They Killed My Father* (2000) now writes movingly of her escape to America from war-torn Cambodia and of her eventual reunion with the older sister she left behind. (Rev: BL 2/15/05) [973]

VEGA, MARTA MORENO

1602 Vega, Marta Moreno. *When the Spirits Dance Mambo* (9–12). 2004, Three Rivers paper $13.00 (1-4000-4924-5). 288pp. Vega, of Puerto Rican heritage, writes fluently about coming of age in Spanish Harlem during the 1950s. (Rev: BL 11/15/04; SLJ 5/05) [974.7]

WARNER, ANDREA

1603 Warren, Andrea. *Escape from Saigon: How a Vietnam War Orphan Became an American Boy* (5–12). Illus. 2004, Farrar $17.00 (0-374-32224-4). 128pp. An inspiring account of a young Amerasian war orphan's long journey from Vietnam to a new and successful life in the United States. (Rev: BL 6/1–15/04*; SLJ 10/04) [959.704]

WEBBER, THOMAS L.

1604 Webber, Thomas L. *Flying over 96th Street: Memoir of an East Harlem White Boy* (10–12). 2004, Scribner $24.00 (0-7432-4750-7). 288pp. Webber writes about the problems of growing up a white boy on the predominantly black and Hispanic streets of East Harlem. (Rev: BL 8/04) [974.7]

WEINSTEIN, LAUREN

1605 Weinstein, Lauren. *Girl Stories* (7–10). Illus. 2006, Holt paper $16.95 (0-80507-863-0). 240pp. Episodic graphic novel-format vignettes paint a vivid portrait of the author's 8th- and 9th-grade years. (Rev: BL 3/15/06; VOYA 4/06) [741.5]

WHITE, SHANE

1606 White, Shane. *North Country* (9–12). Illus. 2005, NBM paper $13.95 (1-56163-435-2). 96pp. In graphic novel format, this compelling memoir realistically recounts a painful childhood growing up in an abusive home in the Great Lakes/St. Lawrence River region. (Rev: BL 10/1/05; SLJ 11/05; VOYA 4/06) [741.5]

WILKS, BURREL LEE

1607 Wilks, Burrel Lee. *Tattoos on My Soul: From the Ghetto to the Top of the World* (11–12). 2006, Burrell Streetwise $29.95 (0-9768736-0-5). 181pp. Wilks writes frankly about his past as a drug dealer and hustler and explains how he was able to turn away from crime and make something positive of his life; for mature teens. (Rev: BL 3/15/06) [332.6]

YU, CHUN

1608 Yu, Chun. *Little Green: Growing Up During the Chinese Cultural Revolution* (7–10). 2005, Simon & Schuster $15.95 (0-689-86943-6). 112pp. Chun Yu, who was born the year that China's Cultural Revolution began, recounts in poetry what life was like during one of the most tumultuous periods in Chinese history. (Rev: BL 1/1–15/05; SLJ 3/05; VOYA 10/05) [951.05]

ZENATTI, VALÉRIE

1609 Zenatti, Valérie. *When I Was a Soldier* (8–11). Trans. by Adriana Hunter. 2005, Bloomsbury $16.95 (1-58234-978-9). 250pp. In this compelling memoir, Valérie Zenatti, an immigrant to Israel from France, chronicles her two years of compulsory service in the Israeli army. (Rev: BCCB 7–8/05; BL 5/1/05*; SLJ 5/05) [921]

The Arts and Entertainment

General and Miscellaneous

1610 Chadwick, Paul. *Depths: Concrete*, Vol. 1 (9–12). Illus. Series: Concrete. 2005, Dark Horse paper $12.95 (1-59307-343-7). 208pp. Early strips about the laid-back comic strip character are reprinted here along with previously uncollected pieces. (Rev: BL 10/15/05) [741.5]

1611 Herriman, George. *"A Wild Warmth of Chromatic Gravy": Krazy and Ignatz, 1935–36* (9–12). Ed. by Bill Blackbeard. Illus. 2005, Fantagraphics paper $19.95 (1-56097-690-X). 120pp. Color arrives in this sixth volume of the collected Krazy Kat comic strip series, which showcases panels that first appeared in Sunday newspapers during the mid-1930s. (Rev: BL 10/15/05) [741.5]

1612 Ketcham, Hank. *Hank Ketcham's Complete Dennis the Menace: 1951–1952* (9–12). Illus. 2005, Fantagraphics $24.95 (1-560-97680-2). 600pp. This hefty volume collects the first two years of cartoonist Hank Ketcham's popular Dennis the Menace comic strip, which celebrates the antics of everybody's favorite neighborhood brat. (Rev: BL 10/1/05; SLJ 2/06) [741.5]

1613 Smith, Anna Deavere. *Letters to a Young Artist* (9–12). Illus. 2006, Vintage paper $13.00 (1-4000-3238-5). 192pp. Anna Deavere Smith, an author and actress, offers some sage advice to would-be artists of all stripes. (Rev: BL 1/1–15/06; SLJ 4/06) [700]

Architecture and Building

History of Architecture

1614 Nardo, Don. *Artistry in Stone: Great Structures of Ancient Egypt* (6–10). Illus. Series: The Lucent Library of Historical Eras. 2005, Gale LB $28.70 (1-59018-661-3). 112pp. Photographs, reproductions, and film and documentary stills illustrate this well-documented examination of massive ancient Egyptian structures such as the pyramids and the Sphinx. (Rev: SLJ 11/05) [932]

Various Types of Buildings

1615 Rense, Paige, ed. *Architectural Digest: Hollywood at Home* (9–12). Illus. 2005, Abrams $40.00 (0-8109-5929-1). 256pp. A fascinating peek inside the homes of stars from the earliest days of Hollywood to today's celebrities. (Rev: BL 11/1/05) [728.09]

Painting, Sculpture, and Photography

General and Miscellaneous

1616 Adamowicz, Adam, et al. *New Recruits*, Vol. 1 (9–12). Illus. 2006, Dark Horse paper $12.95 (1-59307-383-6). 128pp. In this volume, Dark Horse showcases the work of five promising new comic book artists. (Rev: BL 2/15/06) [741.5]

1617 Aldana, Patricia, ed. *Under the Spell of the Moon: Art for Children from the World's Great Illustrators* (6–12). Trans. by Stan Dragland. 2004, Groundwood $25.00 (0-88899-559-8). 72pp. Artwork by children's book illustrators from around the world celebrates children's literature and the work of the International Board on Books for Young People. (Rev: BL 12/15/04; SLJ 1/05) [741.6]

1618 *The Art of Reading: Forty Illustrators Celebrate RIF's 40th Anniversary* (7–10). Illus. 2005, Dutton $19.99 (0-525-47484-6). 96pp. To mark Reading Is Fundamental's 40th birthday, 40 illustrators choose a favorite children's book, talk about its importance, and create an image that captures the spirit of the book; a large, attractive volume. (Rev: BL 7/05; SLJ 8/05*) [745.6]

1619 Ditko, Steve, et al. *Marvel Visionaries: Steve Ditko* (9–12). Ed. by Mark D. Beazley. Illus. 2005, Marvel $29.99 (0-7851-1783-0). 344pp. The work of longtime comic book artist Steve Ditko, co-creator of Spider-Man, is showcased in this attractive volume. (Rev: BL 8/05) [741.5]

1620 Ganz, Nicholas. *Graffiti World: Street Art from Five Continents* (8–12). Ed. by Tristan Manco. Illus. 2004, Abrams $35.00 (0-8109-4979-2). 376pp. Graffiti from around the world is organized by continent and then by artist, with more than 2,000 color photos showing the common themes and wonderful inventiveness of these artists. (Rev: BL 1/1–15/05; SLJ 5/05) [751.7]

1621 Geisel, Theodor Seuss. *The Early Works of Dr. Seuss*, Vol. 1 (10–12). Illus. 2005, Checker paper $22.95 (0-9753808-9-3). 170pp. A look at Seuss's early works including political cartoons, advertising layouts, and art for government pamphlets. (Rev: BL 11/1/05) [741.5]

1622 Hand, John Oliver. *National Gallery of Art: Master Paintings from the Collection* (8–12). Illus. 2004, Abrams $60.00 (0-8109-5619-5). 480pp. Four hundred paintings from the National Gallery serve as the base for a satisfying review of European and American art. (Rev: BL 11/15/04) [750]

1623 Lehmann, Timothy R. *Manga: Masters of the Art* (11–12). Illus. 2005, Collins Design paper $24.95 (0-06-083331-2). 255pp. For mature manga fans, Lehmann offers interviews with 12 noted artists. (Rev: BL 12/15/05) [741.5]

1624 Moore, Alan. *DC Universe: The Stories of Alan Moore* (9–12). Illus. 2006, DC Comics paper $19.99 (1-4012-0927-0). 309pp. This volume showcases some of comic book artist Alan Moore's earlier work for DC Comics. (Rev: BL 3/1/06) [741.5]

1625 Rynck, Patrick De, ed. *How to Read a Painting: Lessons from the Old Masters* (8–12). Illus. 2004, Abrams $35.00 (0-8109-5576-8). 383pp. Introduces readers to the symbols, themes, and motifs that aid understanding of the great masters' art; two-page spreads display 150 paintings and frescoes. (Rev: BL 12/15/04) [753]

History of Art

1626 Little, Stephen. . . . *Isms: Understanding Art* (9–12). Illus. 2004, Universe $16.95 (0-7893-1209-3). 160pp. An introduction to the major movements that have shaped the world of art, covering more than 50 "isms" and profiling key artists and works. (Rev: BL 12/15/04) [709]

1627 Robinson, Shannon. *Cubism* (6–12). Series: Movements in Art. 2005, Creative Education LB $31.35 (1-58341-347-2). 48pp. A review of cubism from the works of Picasso and Braque through the movement's influence on sculpture and architecture, with large, clear reproductions. (Rev: SLJ 2/06)

Regions

Europe

1628 Impelluso, Lucia. *Nature and Its Symbols* (8–12). Trans. by Stephen Sartarelli. Illus. 2004, J. Paul Getty Museum paper $24.95 (0-89236-772-5). 384pp. A helpful guide to the symbols found in European painters' depictions of the natural world from the 14th through the 17th centuries. (Rev: BL 12/15/04) [704.9]

North America

UNITED STATES

1629 Amaki, Amalia K., ed. *A Century of African American Art: The Paul R. Jones Collection* (8–12). Illus. 2004, Rutgers paper $29.95 (0-8135-3457-7). 288pp. The work of 66 African American artists is showcased in this attractive volume that includes profiles and commentary. (Rev: BL 2/1/05) [704.03]

1630 Biel, Steven. *American Gothic: A Life of America's Most Famous Painting* (10–12). 2005, Norton $21.95 (0-393-05912-X). 160pp. The history and multiple meanings of "American Gothic," one of this country's most iconic paintings. (Rev: BL 5/1/05) [759.13]

1631 Brookman, Philip, ed. *Common Ground: Discovering Community in 150 Years of Art* (9–12). Illus. 2004, Merrell $49.95 (1-85894-265-9). 208pp. More than 160 items — drawings, paintings, photographs, and sculptures — from the collection of Julia J. Norell are organized under five themes: past and present; a sense of place; community; hope and belief; and memory and tribute. (Rev: BL 2/1/05) [709]

1632 Curtis, Edward S., and Christopher Cardozo. *Edward S. Curtis: The Women* (8–12). Illus. 2005, Bulfinch $35.00 (0-8212-2895-1). 128pp. This stunning volume showcases 100 of photographer Edward S. Curtis's portraits of Native American women. (Rev: BL 4/1/05) [779]

1633 Panchyk, Richard. *American Folk Art for Kids: With 21 Activities* (6–12). 2004, Chicago Review paper $16.95 (1-55652-499-4). 128pp. This historical survey of American folk art is supplemented by detailed instructions for projects that readers can make for themselves. (Rev: BL 11/1/04; SLJ 11/04) [745]

1634 Slowik, Theresa J. *America's Art: Smithsonian American Art Museum* (8–12). Illus. 2006, Abrams $65.00 (0-8109-5532-6). 324pp. An oversize volume showcasing some of the best-known works in the collection of the Smithsonian American Art Museum. (Rev: BL 3/15/06) [709]

1635 Smolan, Rick, and David Elliot Cohen. *America 24/7: 24 Hours, 7 Days: Extraordinary Images of One American Week* (9–12). 2003, DK $50.00 (0-7894-9975-4). 304pp. In a single week, more than 25,000 professional and amateur photographers took digital photographs of life in America; the 1,000+ images published here show the diversity of everyday life. (Rev: SLJ 4/04) [779]

Music

Jazz and Popular Music (Country, Rap, Rock, etc.)

1636 Brown, Ethan. *Queens Reigns Supreme* (11–12). Illus. 2005, Anchor paper $13.00 (1-4000-9523-9). 288pp. The music editor of *New York* magazine explores the links between the 1980s cocaine trade in Queens borough and the "gangsta" rap movement in popular music. (Rev: BL 12/1/05) [364.106]

1637 Cepeda, Raquel, ed. *And It Don't Stop* (11–12). 2004, Faber and Faber paper $15.00 (0-571-21159-3). 368pp. The best in media coverage of hip-hop music and culture is collected in this volume suitable for mature readers. (Rev: BL 9/1/04) [782.42]

1638 Chang, Jeff. *Can't Stop Won't Stop: The History of the Hip-Hop Generation* (11–12). Illus. 2005, St. Martin's $27.95 (0-312-30143-X). 560pp. A sweeping survey of the genre's growth since it was first introduced into the South Bronx in the mid-1970s. (Rev: BL 2/1/05; SLJ 10/05) [306.4]

1639 DeRogatis, Jim, and Carmel Carrillo, eds. *Kill Your Idols: A New Generation of Rock Writers Reconsiders the Classics* (9–12). Illus. 2004, Barricade paper $16.00 (1-56980-276-9). 320pp. In this collection of 35 essays, contemporary rock music critics pick apart some of the so-called classics of an earlier generation. (Rev: BL 6/1–15/04) [781.66]

1640 Gueraseva, Stacy. *Def Jam, Inc: Russell Simmons, Rick Rubin, and the Extraordinary Story of the World's Most Influential Hip-Hop Label* (11–12). Illus. 2005, Ballantine $23.95 (0-345-46804-X). 352pp. The story behind the founding, growth, and financial ups and downs of the record label Def Jam. (Rev: BL 8/05; SLJ 11/05) [782.4]

1641 Harris, John. *The Dark Side of the Moon: The Making of the Pink Floyd Masterpiece* (9–12). Illus. 2005, Da Capo $24.00 (0-306-81342-4). 208pp. A behind-the-scenes look at the making of one of the most influential rock albums in history. (Rev: BL 11/1/05) [782.4]

1642 Kot, Greg. *Wilco: Learning How to Die* (10–12). 2004, Broadway paper $14.00 (0-7679-1558-5). 256pp. The story of Wilco, an alt-country rock group that abandoned its record label to self-market the album it believed in. (Rev: BL 6/1–15/04; SLJ 10/04) [781.66]

1643 Marsalis, Wynton. *Jazz A B Z: An A to Z Collection of Jazz Portraits* (7–12). Illus. 2005, Candlewick $24.99 (0-7636-2135-8). 76pp. Arranged in alphabet-book format, this strikingly illustrated volume celebrates jazz and its best-known practitioners. (Rev: BL 1/1–15/06; SLJ 1/06*) [811]

1644 Oliver, Richard, and Tim Leffel. *Hip-Hop, Inc: Success Strategies of the Rap Moguls* (9–12). 2006, Thunder's Mouth paper $14.95 (1-56025-732-6). 240pp. Authors Richard Oliver and Tim Leffel chronicle the success stories of rap moguls Sean "Diddy" Combs, Percy "Master P" Millers, and Russell Simmons. (Rev: BL 3/1/06) [782.4]

1645 The Rza, and Chris Norris. *The Wu-Tang Manual* (YA). Illus. 2005, Riverhead paper $16.00 (1-59448-018-4). 243pp. Two members of the Wu-Tang Clan recount the story of the rap group's climb to success in the 1990s and also discuss its philosophy. (Rev: SLJ 7/05)

1646 Warren, Holly George, ed. *Farm Aid: A Celebration of the American Family Farm* (9–12). Illus. 2005, Rodale $35.00 (1-59486-285-0). 256pp. This overview of Farm Aid, a program launched by country and western singer Willie Nelson two decades ago, includes interviews with musician-directors Nelson, Neil Young, John Mellencamp, and Dave Matthews; poems and song lyrics about farming and farm life; and hundreds of photographs. (Rev: BL 9/1/05) [781.64]

1647 Willman, Chris. *Rednecks and Bluenecks: The Politics of Country Music* (10–12). Illus. 2005, New Press $25.95 (1-59558-017-4). 320pp. Willman, senior writer for *Entertainment Weekly*, explores the diversity of political views within the country music industry. (Rev: BL 11/1/05) [781.642]

Theater, Dance, and Other Performing Arts

General and Miscellaneous

1648 Babinski, Tony. *Cirque du Soleil: 20 Years Under the Sun* (9–12). Illus. 2004, Abrams $50.00 (0-8109-4636-X). 352pp. Cirque du Soleil's growth from a group of young street performers to an international concern is documented with beautiful photographs. (Rev: BL 1/1–15/05; SLJ 5/05) [791.3]

1649 Ellis, Roger. *The Complete Audition Book for Young Actors: A Comprehensive Guide to Winning by Enhancing Acting Skills* (9–12). 2004, Meriwether paper $17.95 (1-56608-088-6). 295pp. This practical, well-written guide covers the selection and preparation of material for an audition, cold readings, musical theater, and other more general aspects of a job search, with practical exercises and lists of resources. (Rev: SLJ 7/04) [792.02]

Dance (Ballet, Modern, etc.)

1650 Anderson, Janet. *Modern Dance* (7–12). Series: World of Dance. 2003, Chelsea House LB $22.95 (0-7910-7644-X). 115pp. Traces the history of modern dance, describing key personalities and innovations and looking at a modern dance class. (Rev: SLJ 3/04; VOYA 8/04) [792.8]

1651 Fishman, Katharine Davis. *Attitude! Eight Young Dancers Come of Age at the Ailey School* (10–12). 2004, Putnam $23.95 (1-58542-355-6). 304pp. For mature readers interested in dance, this is a revealing account of the work required of students at the prestigious Ailey School in New York City. (Rev: BL 10/1/04) [792.8]

1652 Rinaldi, Robin. *Ballet* (7–12). Series: World of Dance. 2003, Chelsea House LB $22.95 (0-7910-7640-7). 114pp. Traces the history of ballet, describing key personalities and innovations and looking at a modern ballet class. (Rev: SLJ 3/04; VOYA 8/04) [792.8]

Motion Pictures

1653 Brin, David, ed. *King Kong Is Back! An Unauthorized Look at One Humongous Ape!* (10–12). 2005, BenBella paper $17.95 (1-932100-64-4). 176pp. This collection of essays analyzes the cultural impact of King Kong, brought to the screen in three motion picture incarnations since 1933. (Rev: BL 11/1/05) [791.43]

1654 Clee, Paul. *Before Hollywood: From Shadow Play to the Silver Screen* (7–12). Illus. 2005, Clarion $22.00 (0-618-44533-1). 192pp. Early technologies and the reactions of early audiences are the focus of this fascinating account. (Rev: BCCB 7–8/05; HB 9–10/05; SLJ 7/05) [791.43]

1655 Harryhausen, Ray, and Tony Dalton. *The Art of Ray Harryhausen* (9–12). Illus. 2006, Billboard $50.00 (0-8230-8400-0). 230pp. Pioneering animator Harryhausen, best known for his fantasy films, offers readers a look at a representative collection of drawings, storyboards, and photographs of models from his archives. (Rev: BL 2/15/06) [791.43]

1656 Knoll, John. *Creating the Worlds of Star Wars: 365 Days* (10–12). 2005, Abrams $29.95 (0-8109-5936-4). 744pp. Knoll describes the techniques used in making the "365 Days" series, with photos of concept art and props, dazzling panoramic views of film sets, and a CD-ROM with 360-degree shots. (Rev: SLJ 2/06) [791.43]

1657 McCaig, Iain, et al. *Star Wars Visionaries* (7–10). Illus. 2005, Dark Horse paper $17.95 (1-

59307-311-9). 128pp. Artists who worked on *The Revenge of the Sith* showcase their individual artistic styles in this gallery of Star Wars scenarios. (Rev: BL 5/15/05; SLJ 11/05) [741.5]

1658 Miller, Frank, and Robert Rodriguez. *Frank Miller's Sin City: The Making of the Movie* (11–12). Ed. by Chris Roberson. Illus. 2005, Troublemaker $30.00 (1-933104-00-7). 272pp. A behind-the-scenes look at how Miller's graphic novel *Sin City* was made into a film; for mature teens. (Rev: BL 5/1/05) [791.43]

1659 Miller, Ron. *Special Effects: An Introduction to Movie Magic* (7–10). Illus. 2006, Lerner LB $26.60 (0-76132-918-8). 128pp. Covers both the history of special effects and the techniques used today; boxed features discuss key figures and offer career advice. (Rev: BL 3/15/06) [778.5]

1660 Morris, Mark, ed. *Cinema Macabre* (9–12). Illus. 2006, PS Publishing $45.00 (1-904619-44-4). 232pp. Fifty horror writers — mostly British and some very well known — discuss in entertaining fashion their favorite films in this genre. (Rev: BL 3/15/06) [791.43]

1661 Patmore, Chris. *Moviemaking Course: Principles, Practice, and Techniques: the Ultimate Guide for the Aspiring Filmmaker* (9–12). Illus. Series: Barron's Educational. 2005, Barron's paper $19.99 (0-7641-3191-5). 144pp. From preproduction through postproduction and on to marketing via film festivals and the Internet, this book explains the steps involved in making a short film in clear text with helpful color photographs. (Rev: SLJ 1/06) [791.43]

1662 Schwartz, Mark Evan. *How to Write: A Screenplay* (11–12). 2005, Continuum paper $14.95 (0-8264-1711-6). 141pp. Schwartz, who teaches screenwriting at Loyola Marymount University, uses a screenplay to demonstrate the fundamentals of the craft. (Rev: SLJ 8/05)

1663 Vankin, Jonathan, and John Whalen. *Based on a True Story: Fact and Fantasy in 100 Favorite Movies* (9–12). 2005, Chicago Review $18.95 (1-55652-559-1). 512pp. The facts behind many "true" stories are questioned in this interesting analysis of 100 movies. (Rev: SLJ 3/05) [791.43]

1664 Vaz, Mark Cotta, et al. *The Art of The Incredibles* (8–12). Illus. 2004, Chronicle $40.00 (0-8118-4433-1). 160pp. Many illustrations enhance this look at the making of the popular animated motion picture. (Rev: BL 10/15/04) [791.43]

Radio, Television, and Video

1665 Abbott, Stacey, ed. *Reading Angel: The TV Spin-Off with a Soul* (11–12). 2005, I. B. Tauris paper $14.95 (1-85043-839-0). 256pp. Fans of *Angel*, the spin-off from *Buffy the Vampire Slayer* that ran for five seasons on television, will enjoy this retrospective; for mature teens. (Rev: BL 8/05) [791.45]

1666 Schieffer, Bob. *Face the Nation: My Favorite Stories from the First 50 Years of the Award-Winning News Broadcast* (8–12). Illus. 2004, Simon & Schuster $26.95 (0-7432-6585-8). 240pp. Highlights from the first 50 years of CBS's popular *Face the Nation*. (Rev: BL 9/1/04) [791.45]

1667 Turner, Chris. *Planet Simpson: How a Cartoon Masterpiece Defined a Generation* (9–12). 2004, Da Capo $24.00 (0-306-81341-6). 464pp. The pop culture phenomenon of *The Simpsons* cartoon sitcom is lovingly analyzed by Canadian journalist Chris Turner. (Rev: BL 11/1/04) [791.45]

1668 Wilcox, Rhonda. *Why Buffy Matters: The Art of Buffy the Vampire Slayer* (11–12). 2005, I. B. Tauris paper $14.95 (1-84511-029-3). 256pp. A scholarly look at the themes, symbolism, and characters of television's long-running *Buffy the Vampire Slayer*; for mature readers. (Rev: BL 12/15/05) [791.45]

1669 Wild, David. *Friends . . . 'til the End* (10–12). Illus. 2004, Time Inc. $39.95 (1-932273-27-1); paper $24.95 (1-932273-19-0). 288pp. For fans of the popular *Friends* television series, this is a last look, full of photos and interviews with the show's primary cast members. (Rev: BL 6/1–15/04) [791.05]

Theater and Other Dramatic Forms

1670 Blumenthal, Eileen. *Puppetry: A World History* (9–12). Illus. 2005, Abrams $65.00 (0-8109-5587-3). 272pp. The colorful history of puppetry from ancient Asia and Africa to the Muppets and *The Lion King*. (Rev: BL 9/1/05) [791.5]

History and Geography

Paleontology

1671 Dixon, Dougal, and John Malam. *Dinosaur* (7–12). Illus. Series: DK/Google e.guides. 2004, DK $17.99 (0-7566-0761-2). 96pp. An attractive, highly illustrated yet informative overview of dinosaurs and dinosaur discoveries, with a link to a Web site that offers additional material. (Rev: BL 12/1/04) [567.9]

Anthropology and Evolution

1672 Gibbons, Ann. *The First Human: The Race to Discover Our Earliest Ancestors* (10–12). 2006, Doubleday $26.00 (0-385-51226-0). 288pp. Science writer Ann Gibbons explores the intense rivalry between competing teams of paleoanthropologists to learn more about human origins. (Rev: BL 4/1/06) [576.8]

1673 Naff, Clay Farris, ed. *Evolution* (7–12). Series: Exploring Science and Medical Discoveries. 2005, Gale LB $34.95 (0-7377-2823-X). 222pp. This collection of writings documents the history of theories about human origins from ancient Greece to the 20th century. (Rev: SLJ 12/05)

1674 Robertshaw, Peter, and Jill Rubalcaba. *The Early Human World* (8–12). Series: The World in Ancient Times. 2005, Oxford LB $32.95 (0-19-516157-2). 173pp. Using primary sources and good illustrations, this volume looks at the world's earliest hominids and the evidence that they evolved from more primitive primates. (Rev: SLJ 6/05; VOYA 8/04) [599]

World History and Geography

General

1675 Davis, James C. *The Human Story: Our History, from the Stone Age to Today* (9–12). Illus. 2004, HarperCollins $29.95 (0-06-051619-4). 480pp. An excellent overview of mankind's history, with references to pertinent background facts throughout. (Rev: BL 6/1–15/04) [909]

1676 De Porti, Andrea. *Explorers: The Most Exciting Voyages of Discovery — from the African Expeditions to the Lunar Landing* (8–12). Illus. 2005, Firefly $49.95 (1-55407-101-1). 174pp. Rare archival photos document the history of exploration over the past 150 years, telling 53 stories of discovery — some well-known and others more obscure. (Rev: BL 12/1/05) [910.92]

1677 Diamond, Jared. *Collapse: How Societies Choose to Fail or Succeed* (10–12). 2004, Viking $29.95 (0-670-03337-5). 576pp. Diamond examines the factors that led to the decline of past civilizations and threaten to do the same in the foreseeable future. (Rev: BL 11/1/04; SLJ 6/05) [973]

1678 Grant, Kevin Patrick. *Exploration in the Age of Empire, 1750–1953* (6–10). Series: Discovery and Exploration. 2004, Facts on File $35.00 (0-8160-5260-3). 166pp. A look at the exploration that took place during these two centuries and the underlying political and religious motivations, in clear, informative text plus photographs, illustrations, and excerpts from primary sources. (Rev: SLJ 12/04) [973]

1679 Helphand, Kenneth I. *Defiant Gardens: Making Gardens in Wartime* (9–12). Illus. 2006, Trinity Univ. $34.95 (1-59534-021-1). 320pp. A fascinating look at gardens created in the worst of circumstances. (Rev: BL 4/1/06) [635]

1680 Huff, Toby. *An Age of Science and Revolutions: 1600–1800* (7–10). Illus. Series: Medieval and Early Modern World. 2005, Oxford $32.95 (0-19-517724-X). 176pp. A sweeping overview of history in both the East and West from the beginning of the 17th century through the end of the 18th century, with color photographs, maps, profiles of key figures, and so forth. (Rev: BL 10/15/05) [909]

1681 Jenkins, Mark, ed. *Worlds to Explore: Classic Tales of Travel and Adventure from National Geographic* (9–12). 2006, National Geographic $23.00 (0-7922-5487-2). 480pp. This collection of *National Geographic* articles celebrates the wonders of travel in all the varied forms available from the 1890s to the 1950s. (Rev: BL 3/1/06) [910.9163]

1682 Johnston, Andrew K. *Earth from Space: Smithsonian National Air and Space Museum* (7–12). Illus. 2004, Firefly $49.95 (1-55297-820-6). 272pp. Breathtakingly detailed color images of Earth are organized into categories such as weather, geology, and human activity. (Rev: BL 12/1/04) [525]

1683 Middleton, Nick. *Extremes: Surviving the World's Harshest Environments* (8–12). 2005, St. Martin's $24.95 (0-312-34266-7). 272pp. Middleton, an Oxford geography professor, describes his experiences visiting — and trying to be more than a tourist in — some of the world's most extreme climates. (Rev: BL 4/1/05) [910.4]

1684 *One People: Many Journeys* (8–12). Illus. 2005, Lonely Planet $40.00 (1-74104-600-9). 288pp. Striking photographs from around the world capture the universality of the human experience and demonstrate the wide diversity of resources. (Rev: BL 1/1–15/06) [910]

1685 Whitfield, Peter. *Cities of the World: A History in Maps* (9–12). Illus. 2005, Univ. of California $39.95 (0-520-24725-6). 208pp. Maps dating from the Renaissance to the Victoria era show how some of the world's great cities have evolved over time and also provide clues to how those cities wanted to be perceived. (Rev: BL 12/1/05) [911.1]

1686 Wojtanik, Andrew. *Afghanistan to Zimbabwe: Country Facts That Helped Me Win the National Geographic Bee* (5–12). 2005, National Geographic LB $28.90 (0-7922-7442-3); paper $12.95 (0-7922-7981-6). 384pp. Facts and figures about the world's 192 independent countries are organized into three categories: Physical, Political, and Environmental/Economic. (Rev: SLJ 10/05; VOYA 8/05) [910]

Ancient History

General and Miscellaneous

1687 Bowman, John S., and Maurice Isserman, eds. *Exploration in the World of the Ancients* (6–10). Series: Discovery and Exploration. 2004, Facts on File $35.00 (0-8160-5257-3). 144pp. A look at the voyages and routes of explorers from prehistoric times to the beginning of the Middle Ages. (Rev: SLJ 12/04) [973]

1688 Fagan, Brian M., ed. *The Seventy Great Inventions of the Ancient World* (7–12). Illus. 2004, Thames & Hudson $40.00 (0-500-05130-5). 304pp. This photo-filled volume explores inventions in categories ranging from hunting and farming to artwork and communications. (Rev: BL 12/1/04) [609]

1689 Reinhard, Johan. *The Ice Maiden: Inca Mummies, Mountain Gods, and Sacred Sites in the Andes* (9–12). Illus. 2005, National Geographic $26.00 (0-7922-6838-5). 400pp. A compelling account of the 1995 discovery of the Ice Maiden and what it revealed about the ancient civilization of the Incas. (Rev: BL 3/15/05) [985]

Egypt and Mesopotamia

1690 Cline, Eric H., and Jill Rubalcaba. *The Ancient Egyptian World* (5–10). Series: The World in Ancient Times. 2005, Oxford LB $32.95 (0-19-517391-0). 190pp. An overview of ancient Egyptian history and culture, with chronologically arranged chapters covering religion, medicine, clothing, arts, and so forth and introducing key figures such as Hatshepsut, Tutankhamen, and Cleopatra. (Rev: SLJ 1/06) [932]

1691 Giblin, James Cross. *Secrets of the Sphinx* (7–12). 2004, Scholastic LB $17.95 (0-590-09847-0). 48pp. Full of interesting facts and details of archaeological discoveries, this is a handsome, well-illustrated picture-book-format account of the mysteries that still surround the Sphinx and the facts

that are known. (Rev: BL 9/15/04; HB 11–12/04; SLJ 11/04) [932]

1692 Hawass, Zahi. *Tutankhamun and the Golden Age of the Pharaohs* (8–12). Illus. 2005, National Geographic $35.00 (0-7922-3873-7). 256pp. Companion to a traveling exhibit, this volume highlights the importance of items retrieved from Tutankhamen's tomb. (Rev: BL 6/1–15/05) [932]

1693 Nardo, Don. *Arts, Leisure, and Sport in Ancient Egypt* (6–10). Illus. Series: The Lucent Library of Historical Eras. 2005, Gale LB $28.70 (1-59018-706-7). 112pp. Photographs, reproductions, and film and documentary stills illustrate this well-documented examination of the art and leisure activities of ancient Egyptians, from music and dance to hunting and fishing. Also use *Mummies, Myth, and Magic: Religion in Ancient Egypt* (2005). (Rev: SLJ 11/05) [932]

1694 Podany, Amanda H., and Marni McGee. *The Ancient Near Eastern World* (8–12). Series: The World in Ancient Times. 2005, Oxford LB $32.95 (0-19-516159-9). 174pp. Using primary sources and useful illustrations, this volume explores the ancient civilizations that flourished in the Fertile Crescent until the region was conquered by Alexander the Great in the 4th century B.C. (Rev: SLJ 6/05; VOYA 10/04) [935]

Greece

1695 Ackroyd, Peter. *Ancient Greece* (7–12). Illus. Series: Voyages Through Time. 2005, DK $19.99 (0-7566-1368-X). 144pp. With maps, photographs, and other illustrations, this introduction to ancient Greece and its geography, history, culture, most important institutions, and key figures will be a useful volume for report writers. (Rev: BL 10/1/05; SLJ 2/06) [938]

1696 Nardo, Don. *A History of the Ancient Greeks* (8–12). Illus. Series: The Lucent Library of Historical Eras. 2004, Gale LB $21.96 (1-59018-525-0). 112pp. An excellent overview of ancient Greek history. (Rev: SLJ 1/05) [938]

1697 Roberts, Jennifer T., and Tracy Barrett. *The Ancient Greek World* (7–10). Series: The World in Ancient Times. 2004, Oxford LB $32.95 (0-19-515696-X). 190pp. The authors take a lively and humorous approach to their carefully researched account of political and cultural life in ancient Greece. (Rev: SLJ 8/04) [938]

Rome

1698 Mellor, Ronald, and Marni McGee. *The Ancient Roman World* (7–10). Illus. Series: The World in Ancient Times. 2004, Oxford LB $32.95 (0-19-515380-4). 192pp. This attractive and accessible volume introduces readers to the history, people, and culture of ancient Rome, using many quotations and illustrations. (Rev: BL 4/1/04; SLJ 7/04) [937]

1699 Nardo, Don. *The Roman Army: Instrument of Power* (8–12). Illus. Series: The Lucent Library of Historical Eras. 2003, Gale LB $27.45 (1-59018-316-9). 112pp. An interesting survey of Roman military power and tactics, with comparisons to other systems of the time and helpful diagrams of famous battles. Also in this series are *Arts, Leisure, and Entertainment: Life of the Ancient Romans* and *From Founding to Fall: A History of Rome* (both 2003). (Rev: SLJ 5/04)

1700 Nardo, Don. *A Roman Gladiator* (6–10). Series: The Working Life. 2004, Gale LB $27.45 (1-59018-480-7). 112pp. Gladiators' recruitment, training, living conditions, and status are all covered here. (Rev: SLJ 1/05) [937]

Middle Ages Through the Renaissance (500–1700)

1701 Aronson, Marc. *John Winthrop, Oliver Cromwell, and the Land of Promise* (7–10). 2004, Houghton $20.00 (0-618-18177-6). 224pp. In this fascinating historical study, Aronson explores the interrelationship between John Winthrop, 17th-century governor of the Massachusetts Bay Colony, and Oliver Cromwell, who led the successful Puritan revolt against Britain's King Charles I. (Rev: BL 6/1–15/04; HB 7–8/04; SLJ 9/04) [974.4]

1702 Crompton, Samuel Willard. *The Third Crusade: Richard the Lionhearted vs. Saladin* (7–12). Series: Great Battles Through the Ages. 2003, Chelsea House LB $22.95 (0-7910-7437-4). 114pp. A useful survey of the First and Second Crusades is followed by details of the third campaign and portrayals of Richard and Saladin. (Rev: SLJ 5/04) [909.07]

1703 Lane, George. *Genghis Khan and Mongol Rule* (10–12). Series: Greenwood Guides to Historic Events of the Medieval World. 2004, Greenwood $45.00 (0-313-32528-6). 224pp. Lane argues that the Mongols, usually dismissed as bloodthirsty barbarians, made important contributions in the areas of religious tolerance, culture, and international commerce. (Rev: SLJ 1/05) [947]

1704 McKitterick, Rosamond. *Atlas of the Medieval World* (9–12). Illus. 2005, Oxford $45.00 (0-195-22158-3). 304pp. Chronicles developments on multiple fronts during the years between the fall of the Roman Empire and the 16th century, using detailed maps, diagrams, timelines, and other useful visual aids. (Rev: BL 9/1/05; SLJ 12/05)

1705 Nicholson, Helen. *The Crusades* (10–12). Series: Greenwood Guides to Historic Events of the Medieval World. 2004, Greenwood $45.00 (0-313-32685-1). 196pp. This broad overview of the Crusades explores all Christian campaigns during the medieval period that were directed against Muslims, pagans, and even other Christians who were judged guilty of heresy. (Rev: SLJ 1/05) [909.07]

1706 Ritchie, Robert. *Historical Atlas of the Renaissance* (8–12). Illus. Series: Historical Atlas. 2004, Facts on File $35.00 (0-8160-5731-1). 192pp. Art, culture, politics, literature, science, and key figures are all covered in this chronologically organized atlas. (Rev: SLJ 2/05)

1707 Thomson, Melissa, and Ruth Dean. *Women of the Renaissance* (7–12). Series: Women in History. 2004, Gale LB $27.45 (1-59018-473-4). 128pp. A look at women's lives during the Renaissance, covering such topics as work, religion, and art. (Rev: SLJ 3/05)

1708 White, Pamela. *Exploration in the World of the Middle Ages, 500–1500* (6–12). Illus. Series: Discovery and Exploration. 2005, Facts on File $40.00 (0-8160-5264-6). 176pp. The expeditions of Marco Polo, the Vikings, and other explorers of the Middle Ages are chronicled in clear, informative text plus maps, illustrations, and excerpts from primary sources. (Rev: SLJ 8/05) [973]

Eighteenth Through Nineteenth Centuries (1700–1900)

1709 Streissguth, Thomas. *The Napoleonic Wars: Defeat of the Grand Army* (9–12). Series: History's Great Defeats. 2003, Gale LB $21.96 (1-59018-065-8). 112pp. Napoleon's flaws — including a tendency to overestimate his own abilities and to underestimate those of his enemies — are underlined in this look at his defeats. (Rev: SLJ 1/04) [944.05]

Twentieth Century

General and Miscellaneous

1710 Bussey, Jennifer A. *1940–1960* (9–12). Illus. Series: Events That Changed the World. 2004, Gale LB $26.96 (0-7377-1756-4); paper $17.96 (0-7377-1757-2). 188pp. Introduces pivotal events during the turbulent decades between 1940 and 1960. (Rev: BL 4/1/04) [909.8]

1711 Zacharias, Gary. *1900–1920* (9–12). Illus. Series: Events That Changed the World. 2004, Gale LB $26.96 (0-7377-1752-1); paper $17.96 (0-7377-1753-X). 224pp. Introduces pivotal events in politics, science, and the arts during the first two decades of the 20th century. (Rev: BL 4/1/04) [909.82]

World War II and the Holocaust

1712 Altman, Linda J. *Crimes and Criminals of the Holocaust* (5–10). Illus. Series: Holocaust in History. 2004, Enslow LB $20.95 (0-7660-1995-0). 104pp. This book focuses on the end of World War II and the war crimes trials in Nuremberg as well as other cases such as that of Adolf Eichmann. (Rev: BL 5/1/04) [940.53]

1713 Altman, Linda J. *Impact of the Holocaust* (5–10). Illus. Series: Holocaust in History. 2004, Enslow LB $20.95 (0-7660-1996-9). 104pp. Discusses the Holocaust's influence in the creation of a homeland for the Jews and a Universal Declaration of Human Rights. (Rev: BL 5/1/04) [940.53]

1714 Clive, A. Lawton. *Hiroshima* (6–12). 2004, Candlewick $18.99 (0-7636-2271-0). 48pp. This powerful photoessay presents the history of the development and dropping of the first atom bomb, documenting with many quotations the misgivings of some of the key figures. (Rev: BL 7/04; SLJ 11/04) [940.54]

1715 Downing, David. *The Origins of the Holocaust* (7–10). Illus. Series: World Almanac Library of the Holocaust. 2005, World Almanac LB $22.50 (0-8368-5943-X). 48pp. Downing looks at the roots of anti-Semitism and the continuing persecution of the Jews over the centuries, connecting this history with the rise of the Nazi Party. (Rev: BL 10/15/05; SLJ 3/06) [940.53]

1716 Fountain, Nigel, ed. *WWII: The People's Story* (9–12). 2003, Reader's Digest $39.95 (0-7621-0376-0). 320pp. Using letters, diary entries, speeches, and interviews, this richly illustrated volume is a tribute to the men, women, and children who lived through World War II, providing insight into the lives of the ordinary people in several nations as well as key figures of the time; an accompanying CD contains firsthand accounts. (Rev: SLJ 4/04) [940.53]

1717 Fuller, William, and Jack James. *Reckless Courage: The True Story of a Norwegian Boy Under Nazi Rule* (8–11). 2005, Taber Hall paper $13.95 (0-9769252-0-6). 168pp. The true story of a Norwegian boy's participation in the resistance against his country's Nazi occupiers. (Rev: BL 9/15/05) [940.53]

1718 Hillman, Laura. *I Will Plant You a Lilac Tree: A Memoir of a Schindler's List Survivor* (8–11). 2005, Simon & Schuster $16.95 (0-689-86980-0). 256pp. In this inspiring true story of Holocaust survival, Hannelore escapes the Nazi gas chambers when her name is added to Schindler's list. (Rev:

BCCB 7–8/05; BL 5/1/05*; HB 7–8/05; SLJ 9/05; VOYA 8/05) [940.5]

1719 Marston, Daniel, ed. *The Pacific War Companion: From Pearl Harbor to Hiroshima* (9–12). Illus. 2005, Osprey $29.95 (1-84176-882-0). 272pp. This well-illustrated collection of accessible essays offers an excellent introduction to events and key figures in the Pacific theater of World War II. (Rev: BL 7/05) [940.54]

1720 Miller, Donald L. *D-Days in the Pacific* (8–12). Illus. 2005, Simon & Schuster paper $13.00 (0-7432-6929-2). 384pp. The Allied military offensives that finally brought an end to World War II in the Pacific are described in readable text with excellent illustrations. (Rev: BL 3/15/05) [940.54]

1721 O'Donnell, Joe. *Japan, 1945: A U.S. Marine's Photographs from Ground Zero* (8–12). Illus. 2005, Vanderbilt $39.95 (0-8265-1467-7). 120pp. Black-and-white photographs, long kept private by the Marine Corps photographer who took them and became ill from the radiation, reveal the devastation caused by the atomic bombs dropped on Japan in 1945. (Rev: BL 3/15/05) [779]

1722 Shapiro, Stephen, and Tina Forrester. *Hoodwinked: Deception and Resistance* (7–10). Series: Outwitting the Enemy: Stories from World War II. 2004, Annick LB $29.95 (1-55037-833-3); paper $14.95 (1-55037-832-5). 96pp. This compelling title explores some of the inventive deceptive strategies that Allied forces employed against the Axis powers. (Rev: BL 1/1–15/05; SLJ 1/05) [940.54]

1723 Stargardt, Nicholas. *Witnesses of War: Children's Lives Under the Nazis* (9–12). Illus. 2006, Knopf $30.00 (1-4000-4088-4). 528pp. The horrors of World War II for children are clearly demonstrated in this collection of first-person accounts culled from school papers, diaries, and letters. (Rev: BL 11/15/05) [940.53]

1724 Steinbacher, Sybille. *Auschwitz* (11–12). Trans. by Shaun Whiteside. 2005, HarperCollins $23.95 (0-06-082581-2). 128pp. Auschwitz's transformation into a concentration camp, its status after liberation, the trials of SS members, and today's prevalence of Holocaust deniers; for strong readers. (Rev: BL 6/1–15/05) [940.53]

1725 Tucker, Todd. *The Great Starvation Experiment: The Heroic Men Who Starved So That Millions Could Live* (9–12). Illus. 2006, Free Press $26.00 (0-7432-7030-4). 304pp. The fascinating story of 36 conscientious objectors who took part in research at the end of World War II into the effects of lengthy starvation on the human body. (Rev: BL 3/15/06)

1726 Walker, Stephen. *Shockwave: Countdown to Hiroshima* (9–12). 2005, HarperCollins $26.95 (0-06-074284-4). 384pp. A gripping account of the events that led from the first atomic bomb test on

July 16, 1945, to the attack on Hiroshima three weeks later. (Rev: BL 7/05) [623.4]

Modern World History (1945–)

1727 Carlisle, Rodney P. *Iraq War* (7–10). Illus. 2005, Facts on File $35.00 (0-8160-5627-7). 176pp. Information on Iraq's history is paired with discussion of September 11 and the 2003 military incursion into Iraq. (Rev: BL 2/15/05; SLJ 4/05) [956.7044]

1728 Carlisle, Rodney P. *Persian Gulf War* (9–12). Series: America at War. 2003, Facts on File $35.00 (0-8160-4942-4). 160pp. A look at the background to this 1991 conflict, the fighting that took place, and the decision to leave Saddam Hussein in power. (Rev: SLJ 2/04) [956.7]

1729 Feuer, Alan. *Over There: From the Bronx to Baghdad: Two Months in the Life of a Reluctant Reporter* (9–12). 2005, Counterpoint $24.00 (1-58243-327-5). 304pp. A perceptive, personal account by a *New York Times* reporter of the 2003 invasion of Iraq; for mature teens. (Rev: BL 4/1/05) [956.7044]

1730 Isserman, Maurice. *Korean War.* Rev. ed. (9–12). Series: America at War. 2003, Facts on File $35.00 (0-8160-4939-4). 146pp. A look at the background to this conflict, the fighting that took place, and the aftermath. (Rev: SLJ 2/04) [951.904]

1731 Koopman, John. *McCoy's Marines: Darkside to Baghdad* (11–12). Illus. 2005, Zenith $24.95 (0-7603-2088-8). 286pp. Koopman, a *San Francisco Chronicle* reporter and marine veteran, was embedded with a U.S. Marine Corps battalion during the Iraq War; for mature teens. (Rev: BL 3/1/05) [956.7]

1732 Nakaya, Andrea C., ed. *Iraq* (8–12). Series: Current Controversies. 2004, Gale LB $21.96 (0-7377-2210-X); paper $14.96 (0-7377-2211-8). 202pp. Statements by key U.S. figures including President Bush and Colin Powell are included in this survey of opinions about the Iraq war. (Rev: SLJ 12/04; VOYA 6/05) [956]

1733 Sherman, Josepha. *The Cold War* (6–12). Illus. Series: Chronicle of America's Wars. 2003, Lerner LB $27.93 (0-8225-0150-3). 96pp. The half-century standoff between the United States and the Soviet Union is briefly chronicled, with coverage of the Korean and Vietnam wars, the Cuban Missile Crisis, and the Soviet invasion of Afghanistan. (Rev: BL 4/1/04) [909.82]

1734 Spinner, Jackie, and Jenny Spinner. *Tell Them I Didn't Cry: A Young Journalist's Story of Joy, Loss, and Survival in Iraq* (11–12). 2006, Scribner $23.00 (0-7432-8853-X). 288pp. Jackie Spinner's account of the myriad emotions she felt while covering the war in Iraq for nine months are paired with the fears of her sister Jenny back in Virginia; for older teens. (Rev: BL 2/15/06) [956.7044]

1735 Tucker, Mike. *Among Warriors in Iraq: True Grit, Special Ops, and Raiding in Mosul and Fallujah* (11–12). 2005, Lyons paper $16.95 (1-59228-732-8). 256pp. A former marine, now a war correspondent, sheds light on the bloody insurgency that followed the campaign to seize control of Iraq; for mature teens. (Rev: BL 5/1/05) [955.7]

1736 Wright, Evan. *Generation Kill: Devil Dogs, Iceman, Captain America, and the New Face of American War* (11–12). Illus. 2004, Penguin $24.95 (0-399-15193-1). 320pp. Wright, a contributing editor to *Rolling Stone* magazine, offers a close-up look at the 2003 invasion of Iraq through the eyes of a platoon of First Reconnaissance Battalion marines; for mature readers. (Rev: BL 6/1–15/04) [970.7]

Geographical Regions

Africa

General and Miscellaneous

1737 Bangs, Richard, and Pasquale Scaturro. *Mystery of the Nile: The Epic Story of the First Descent of the World's Deadliest River* (8–12). Illus. 2005, Penguin $25.95 (0-399-15262-8). 358pp. Rapids, crocodiles, sandstorms, and armed guerrillas were only some of the perils encountered during this trip down the Nile from the highlands of Ethiopia to the Mediterranean. (Rev: BL 2/1/05; SLJ 8/05) [916.204]

1738 Beckwith, Carol, and Angela Fisher. *Faces of Africa: Thirty Years of Photography* (8–12). Illus. 2004, National Geographic $35.00 (0-7922-6830-X). 252pp. Eye-catching photographs document the traditional life of diverse African peoples. (Rev: BL 9/1/04) [305.896]

1739 Habeeb, Mark W. *Africa: Facts and Figures* (7–10). Illus. Series: Continent in the Balance: Africa. 2005, Mason Crest LB $21.95 (1-59084-817-9). 80pp. An excellent overview of the continent, including its natural features, climate, cultural diversity, history, and economy. (Rev: BL 4/1/05*) [960]

1740 Holmes, Martha, et al. *Nile* (7–12). Illus. 2004, BBC $35.00 (0-563-48713-5). 168pp. From the BBC, this is a richly illustrated guide to the history and geology of the world's longest river. (Rev: BL 11/1/04) [902]

Central and Eastern Africa

1741 Beard, Peter. *Zara's Tales: Perilous Escapades in Equatorial Africa* (8–12). Illus. 2004, Knopf $26.95 (0-679-42659-0). 176pp. In this compelling memoir, Beard talks about his many encounters — some life-threatening — with the animals of East Africa. (Rev: BL 10/15/04) [967.70]

1742 Deng, Alephonsion, et al. *They Poured Fire on Us from the Sky: The True Story of Three Lost Boys from Sudan* (11–12). 2005, PublicAffairs $25.00 (1-58648-269-6). 336pp. Three young men recount the horrors of the civil war that forced them to flee their homelands in southern Sudan and seek refuge in America; for mature readers. (Rev: BL 4/15/05) [962.404]

1743 Fisanick, Christina, ed. *The Rwanda Genocide* (9–12). Series: At Issue in History. 2004, Gale LB $28.70 (0-7377-1985-0); paper $19.95 (0-7377-1986-9). 141pp. The deaths of an estimated 800,000 Rwandans in the mid-1990s are the topic of essays that present different points of view on the causes, the global reaction, and the measures taken to rebuild the country. (Rev: SLJ 12/04) [967]

1744 *History of Central Africa* (7–12). Illus. Series: History of Africa. 2003, Facts on File $30.00 (0-8160-5064-3). 112pp. A historical overview of the region that includes information on the Atlantic slave trade and on European colonial rule. Also use *History of East Africa* (2003). (Rev: SLJ 1/04) [967]

1745 Jansen, Hanna. *Over a Thousand Hills I Walk with You* (7–10). Trans. by Elizabeth D. Crawford. 2006, Carolrhoda $16.95 (1-57505-927-4). 344pp. The heartbreaking story of 8-year-old Jeanne, the only member of her family to survive the Rwandan genocide of 1994, is told by the girl's adoptive mother. (Rev: BL 4/1/06*) [833]

1746 Koopmans, Andy. *Rwanda* (7–10). Illus. Series: Africa. 2005, Mason Crest LB $21.95 (1-59084-812-8). 87pp. Covers the geography, history, politics, government, economy, people, and culture of Rwanda, providing a map, flag, recipes, glossary, timeline, and colorful photographs. (Rev: SLJ 3/05) [967.571]

1747 MacDonald, Joan Vos. *Tanzania* (7–10). Illus. Series: Africa. 2005, Mason Crest LB $21.95 (1-59084-813-6). 87pp. Covers the geography, history, politics, government, economy, people, and culture of Tanzania, providing a map, flag, recipes, glossary, timeline, and colorful photographs. (Rev: SLJ 3/05; VOYA 8/04) [967.8]

North Africa

1748 Benanav, Michael. *Men of Salt: Across the Sahara with the Caravan of White Gold* (11–12). 2006, Lyons $23.95 (1-59228-772-7). 256pp. Benanav writes about his experiences traveling with salt miners who cross the Sahara by camel. (Rev: BL 12/1/05) [916.604]

Southern Africa

1749 Beecroft, Simon. *The Release of Nelson Mandela* (6–12). Illus. Series: Days that Changed the World. 2004, World Almanac LB $21.95 (0-8368-5571-X); paper $11.95 (0-8368-5578-7). 48pp. The significance of Mandela's release after 27 years of imprisonment is made clear through the explanation of the struggle against apartheid, with discussion of the progress South Africa has made since then. (Rev: BL 4/1/04; SLJ 7/04) [618.1]

1750 Downing, David. *Apartheid in South Africa* (7–10). Illus. Series: Witness to History. 2004, Heinemann $20.70 (1-4034-4870-1). 60pp. This brief historical survey draws on primary sources — including newspaper articles and full-color photographs — to trace apartheid's rise and fall and its impact on both the country's black and white communities. (Rev: BL 1/05) [323.168]

1751 Wooten, Jim. *We Are All the Same: A Story of a Boy's Courage and a Mother's Love* (8–12). 2004, Penguin $19.95 (1-59420-028-9). 244pp. ABC News correspondent Wooten writes movingly of Nkosi Johnson, a young South African boy born with AIDS, and his white foster mother and how together they fought the disease and the South African government's failure to acknowledge the magnitude of the AIDS problem. (Rev: BL 9/1/04) [362.196]

West Africa

1752 Kryza, Frank T. *The Race for Timbuktu: In Search of Africa's City of Gold* (10–12). Illus. 2006, Ecco $24.95 (0-06-056064-9). 352pp. The exciting story of Alexander Gordon Laing's 19th-century expedition to find the lost city of Timbuktu. (Rev: BL 12/1/05) [966.23]

1753 Walker, Ida. *Nigeria* (7–10). Illus. Series: Africa. 2005, Mason Crest LB $21.95 (1-59084-811-X). 79pp. Covers the geography, history, politics, government, economy, people, and culture of Nigeria, providing a map, flag, recipes, glossary, timeline, and colorful photographs. (Rev: SLJ 3/05) [966.9]

Asia

General and Miscellaneous

1754 Hanks, Reuel R. *Central Asia: A Global Studies Handbook* (10–12). 2005, ABC-CLIO $55.00 (1-85109-656-6). 466pp. This useful guide combines narrative about the history, geography, culture, and economy of Uzbekistan, Kazakhstan, and Kyrgyzstan with a reference section listing events, organizations, and so forth. (Rev: SLJ 1/06)

1755 Kort, Michael. *Central Asian Republics* (7–12). Series: Nations in Transition. 2003, Facts on File $35.00 (0-8160-5074-0). 200pp. After a history of the region, each of the independent republics is introduced with discussion of the current challenges it faces; these include border disputes, poor environment, poor health care and quality of life, and government corruption. (Rev: SLJ 4/04)

China

1756 Hardy, Grant, and Anne Behnke Kinney. *The Establishment of the Han Empire and Imperial China* (10–12). Series: Greenwood Guides to Historic Events of the Ancient World. 2005, Greenwood LB $45.00 (0-313-32588-X). 170pp. The political, institutional, technological, and social aspects of the Han dynasty are discussed and placed in historical context. (Rev: SLJ 7/05) [951]

1757 Lovell, Julia. *The Great Wall: China Against the World, 1000 bc–2000 ad* (10–12). 2006, Grove $25.00 (0-8021-1814-3). 432pp. A history of the Chinese fortification and its continuing metaphorical existence as a barrier. (Rev: BL 3/1/06) [951]

1758 Schoppa, R. Keith. *Twentieth Century China: A History in Documents* (9–12). Series: Pages from History. 2004, Oxford LB $36.95 (0-19-514745-6). 222pp. Photographs, reproductions, cartoons, and posters add to the excerpts from primary sources that document the history of China during the 20th century. (Rev: SLJ 4/05) [951]

India, Pakistan, and Bangladesh

1759 Brown, Louise. *The Dancing Girls of Lahore: Selling Love and Saving Dreams in Pakistan's Ancient Pleasure District* (11–12). 2005, HarperCollins $23.95 (0-06-074042-6). 320pp. A gritty account of the life of three young girls growing up with their mother, drug-addicted father, and his second wife in the red-light district of Lahore, Pakistan; for mature teens. (Rev: BL 5/15/05) [306.74]

1760 Sinkler, Adrian. *Pakistan* (9–12). Series: Nations in Transition. 2004, Gale LB $22.96 (0-7377-1208-2). 127pp. Useful for report writers, this profile of Pakistan examines the country's geography, history, people, culture, religion, politics, and government. (Rev: SLJ 3/05) [954.9]

1761 Valliant, Doris. *Bangladesh* (8–12). Illus. Series: The Growth and Influence of Islam in the Nations of Asia and Central Asia. 2005, Mason Crest LB $25.95 (1-59084-879-9). 120pp. A well-illustrated look at Bangladesh and the importance of Islam in the country's history, politics, economy, and foreign relations. (Rev: SLJ 9/05) [954.9]

Other Asian Countries

1762 Boaz, John, ed. *The U.S. Attack on Afghanistan* (10–12). Illus. Series: At Issue in History. 2005, Gale LB $23.96 (0-7377-1983-4). 142pp. Essays present arguments for and against the United States' intervention in Afghanistan after September 11, 2001; a chronology and a foreword provide useful background information. (Rev: BL 9/15/05) [958.104]

1763 Einfeld, Jann, ed. *Afghanistan* (9–12). Series: Current Controversies. 2005, Gale LB $34.95 (0-7377-2470-6); paper $23.70 (0-7377-2471-4). 188pp. Essays dissect the current political situation in Afghanistan and offer some predictions for the future. (Rev: SLJ 7/05) [958.104]

1764 Emadi, Hafizullah. *Culture and Customs of Afghanistan* (9–12). Series: Culture and Customs of Asia. 2005, Greenwood $49.95 (0-313-33089-1). 252pp. An in-depth look at Afghanistan through history, with an emphasis on social customs and interesting material on family life and the role of women. (Rev: SLJ 1/06) [958.1]

1765 Hanson, Jennifer L. *Mongolia* (7–10). Series: Nations in Transition. 2003, Facts on File $35.00 (0-8160-5221-2). 152pp. A thorough review of Mongolia's history, geography, and culture, detailing the difficulties involved in making a transition to democracy. (Rev: SLJ 5/04; VOYA 6/04) [951]

1766 Jones, Ann. *Kabul in Winter: Life Without Peace in Afghanistan* (10–12). 2006, Holt $24.00 (0-80507-884-3). 288pp. In a fascinating look at life in post-Taliban Afghanistan, Jones describes her work in schools and prisons there and focuses on the subservient role of Afghani women. (Rev: BL 2/1/06) [958.104]

1767 Miller, Debra A. *North Korea* (6–12). Series: The World's Hot Spots. 2004, Gale LB $22.96 (0-7377-2294-0); paper $15.96 (0-7377-2295-9). 128pp. Reprinted essays, speeches, and news articles provide a fascinating — if somewhat one-sided

— overview of North Korea and its relations with the outside world. (Rev: BL 6/1–15/04; SLJ 7/04) [951.93]

1768 Otfinoski, Steven. *Afghanistan* (7–12). Series: Nations in Transition. 2003, Facts on File $35.00 (0-8160-5056-2). 130pp. A thorough overview of Afghanistan presenting the current political and security problems — including healthcare needs, opium trade, and reliance on foreign funding — as well as material on the country's history, geography, people, culture, and so forth. (Rev: SLJ 4/04; VOYA 6/04) [958.1]

1769 Stewart, Gail B. *Life Under the Taliban* (6–10). Series: The Way People Live. 2004, Gale LB $27.45 (1-59018-291-X). 112pp. A look at what life was like in Afghanistan under the repressive Taliban regime. (Rev: SLJ 1/05) [958.1]

1770 Whitehead, Kim. *Afghanistan* (8–12). Illus. Series: The Growth and Influence of Islam in the Nations of Asia and Central Asia. 2005, Mason Crest LB $25.95 (1-59084-833-0). 136pp. A well-illustrated look at Afghanistan and the importance of Islam in the country's history, politics, economy, and foreign relations. (Rev: SLJ 9/05) [958.104]

Australia and the Pacific Islands

1771 Nightingale, Neil, et al. *Wild Australasia* (9–12). Illus. 2003, Firefly $29.95 (1-55297-855-9). 240pp. From wombats and kiwi to rain forests and glaciers, this is an appealing and well-written overview of the nature, climate, and geography of Australia, New Zealand, and Papua New Guinea. (Rev: SLJ 6/04) [508.9]

1772 Vail, Martha, and John S. Bowman, eds. *Exploring the Pacific* (6–12). Illus. Series: Discovery and Exploration. 2005, Facts on File $40.00 (0-8160-5258-1). 162pp. Exploration in the Pacific, from early Polynesians onward and including such figures as Magellan and Cook, is the focus of this volume that contains clear, informative text plus maps, illustrations, and excerpts from primary sources. (Rev: SLJ 8/05) [973]

Europe

General and Miscellaneous

1773 Lace, William W. *The Vatican* (7–12). Series: Building History. 2004, Gale $27.45 (1-56006-843-4). The story behind the construction of Vatican City, the centerpiece of which is St. Peter's Basilica, is told in a richly illustrated text full of interesting facts and sidebars that add context. (Rev: BL 10/1/04) [945.6]

1774 Stafford, James. *The European Union: Facts and Figures* (8–11). Illus. Series: European Union. 2006, Mason Crest LB $21.95 (1-4222-0045-0). 88pp. A useful, information-packed guide to the European Union and its origins and goals. (Rev: BL 4/1/06) [641.242]

Eastern Europe and the Balkans

1775 King, David C. *Bosnia and Herzegovina* (7–10). Illus. Series: Cultures of the World. 2005, Benchmark LB $25.95 (0-7614-1853-9). 144pp. Explores the geography, history, people, culture, and lifestyles of Bosnia and Herzegovina. (Rev: SLJ 7/05) [949.7]

1776 Nichols, Jeremy, and Emilia Trembicka-Nichols. *Poland* (7–10). Series: Countries of the World. 2005, Facts on File LB $30.00 (0-8160-6005-3). 61pp. History, geography, culture, government, and economy are all covered in this attractive overview of Poland. (Rev: SLJ 1/06) [9.4.3]

1777 Otfinoski, Steven. *The Czech Republic* (7–12). Illus. Series: Nations in Transition. 2004, Facts on File $35.00 (0-8160-5083-X). 132pp. An updated edition that adds more recent events to the 1997 text about the history, people, culture, and government of the Czech Republic. (Rev: BL 12/1/04) [943.7105]

1778 Schuman, Michael A. *Bosnia and Herzegovina* (9–12). Series: Nations in Transition. 2003, Facts on File $35.00 (0-8160-5052-X). 152pp. After a section on the area's history through the recent civil war, Schuman looks at the contemporary situation, exploring the economy, culture, education, and way of life in Bosnia and Herzegovina. (Rev: SLJ 5/04) [949.7]

France

1779 Home, Alistair. *La Belle France: A Short History* (10–12). Illus. 2005, Knopf $30.00 (1-4000-4140-6). 544pp. This concise but comprehensive history traces France's development from the division of Gaul into three parts by Julius Caesar to the presidency of Jacques Chirac. (Rev: BL 7/05) [944]

Germany, Austria, and Switzerland

1780 Bartoletti, Susan Campbell. *Hitler Youth: Growing Up in Hitler's Shadow* (7–10). Illus. 2005, Scholastic $19.95 (0-439-35379-3). 176pp. This chilling look at the Hitler Youth movement, which at its peak boasted a membership of roughly 3.5 million boys and girls, includes excerpts from diaries, letters, oral histories, and the author's inter-

views with former members and resisters. (Rev: BL 4/15/05*; SLJ 6/05; VOYA 8/05) [943.086]

1781 Halleck, Elaine, ed. *Living in Nazi Germany* (8–12). Series: Exploring Cultural History. 2004, Gale LB $28.70 (0-7377-1732-7). First-person accounts excerpted from other works offer insight into life in Germany under the Nazis, from the point of view of those brutalized and of those who took part in the regime. (Rev: BL 8/04) [943.086]

Great Britain and Ireland

1782 Jocelyn, Marthe. *A Home for Foundlings* (7–10). Series: Lord Museum. 2005, Tundra paper $15.95 (0-88776-709-5). 128pp. A fascinating history of London's Foundling Hospital, which was opened in the 18th century to provide a home for babies whose mothers were unable to care for them and did not close until 1953. (Rev: BL 3/1/05; SLJ 6/05) [362.7]

1783 Rex, Richard. *The Tudors* (10–12). Illus. 2004, Tempus $35.00 (0-7524-2588-9). 254pp. An engaging history of the Tudors and their claim to the British throne. (Rev: BL 8/04) [942.05]

Russia and Other Former Soviet Republics

1784 Corrigan, Jim. *Kazakhstan* (8–12). Series: The Growth and Influence of Islam in the Nations of Asia and Central Asia. 2005, Mason Crest LB $25.95 (1-59084-882-9). 128pp. A well-illustrated look at Kazakhstan and the importance of Islam in the country's history, politics, economy, and foreign relations. (Rev: SLJ 9/05) [958]

1785 Eaton, Katherine B. *Daily Life in the Soviet Union* (11–12). Series: Daily Life Through History. 2004, Greenwood $49.95 (0-313-31628-7). 320pp. Explores what life was like in the Soviet Union, examining such topics as health care, education, economic system, class structure, and the arts. (Rev: SLJ 4/05) [947]

1786 Harmon, Daniel E. *Kyrgyzstan* (8–12). Illus. Series: The Growth and Influence of Islam in the Nations of Asia and Central Asia. 2005, Mason Crest LB $25.95 (1-59084-883-7). 120pp. A well-illustrated look at Kyrgyzstan and the importance of Islam in the country's history, politics, economy, and foreign relations. (Rev: SLJ 9/05)

1787 Otfinoski, Steven. *The Baltic Republics* (7–10). Series: Nations in Transition. 2004, Facts on File LB $35.00 (0-8160-5117-8). 182pp. Introduces the Baltic republics of Estonia, Latvia, and Lithuania, and the geography, history, people, culture, religious beliefs, and economy of each. (Rev: SLJ 1/05) [947]

1788 Robbins, Gerald. *Azerbaijan* (8–12). Series: The Growth and Influence of Islam in the Nations of Asia and Central Asia. 2005, Mason Crest LB $25.95 (1-59084-878-0). 128pp. A well-illustrated look at Azerbaijan and the importance of Islam in the country's history, politics, economy, and foreign relations. (Rev: SLJ 9/05) [947]

Middle East

General and Miscellaneous

1789 Halliday, Fred. *100 Myths About the Middle East* (9–12). 2005, Univ. of California $39.95 (0-520-24720-5); paper $12.95 (0-520-24721-3). 272pp. Debunks widely held misconceptions about the Middle East and its people. (Rev: BL 8/05) [956.04]

1790 Mahdi, Ali Akbar, ed. *Teen Life in the Middle East* (10–12). Series: Teen Life Around the World. 2003, Greenwood $55.00 (0-313-31893-X). 268pp. Separate articles describe a teen's typical day in 12 countries, looking at family, school, and social life, religion, sports, food, fashion, and so forth. (Rev: SLJ 6/04; VOYA 2/04) [305.23]

Egypt

1791 Beattie, Andrew. *Cairo: A Cultural History* (8–12). Series: Cityscapes. 2004, Oxford $15.00 (0-19-517892-0). 256pp. A cultural tour of Cairo, exploring the city's ancient past and pervasively Islamic present. (Rev: BL 11/15/04) [962]

Israel and Palestine

1792 Alger, Neil, ed. *The Palestinians and the Disputed Territories* (8–12). Series: The World's Hot Spots. 2004, Gale LB $22.96 (0-7377-1489-1); paper $15.96 (0-7377-1490-5). 144pp. Informative essays, articles, and analyses explore the history and current status of the Palestinians, emphasizing in particular the importance of Jerusalem and the role of other nations including the United States. (Rev: SLJ 6/04) [956.04]

1793 Gaughen, Shasta, ed. *The Arab-Israeli Conflict* (7–10). Series: Contemporary Issues Companion. 2004, Gale LB $43.15 (0-7377-1615-0); paper $28.75 (0-7377-1616-9). 160pp. After background on the long-running conflict, this volume provides opposing views about how to resolve the crisis and first-person stories of life amid turmoil. (Rev: SLJ 1/05) [956.04]

1794 Greenfeld, Howard. *A Promise Fulfilled: Theodor Herzl, Chaim Weizmann, David Ben-Gurion, and the Creation of the State of Israel* (7–10). Illus. 2005, Greenwillow LB $19.89 (0-06-051505-8). 144pp. This story of the creation of the state of Israel focuses on the contributions of three remarkable and very different men. (Rev: BL 4/15/05; SLJ 7/05) [320.54]

1795 Miller, Jennifer. *Inheriting the Holy Land: An American's Search for Hope in the Middle East* (9–12). 2005, Ballantine $24.95 (0-345-46924-0). 320pp. Miller, who has participated in the Seeds of Peace program that brings together young Israelis and Palestinians, voices her views and those of other young people on the prospects for peace. (Rev: BL 7/05; SLJ 2/06) [956.94]

1796 Rackers, Mark, ed. *The Arab-Israeli Conflict* (9–12). Series: Great Speeches in History. 2004, Gale LB $33.70 (0-7377-1649-5). 234pp. Speeches of key importance in the history of Israel and Palestine are introduced with historical and biographical information. (Rev: SLJ 12/04) [956]

1797 Reich, Bernard. *A Brief History of Israel* (9–12). Illus. Series: Brief History. 2004, Facts on File $45.00 (0-8160-5118-6); paper $19.95 (0-8160-5793-1). 368pp. Despite its title, this survey of Israeli history is sweeping in character, tracing the country's roots back to biblical times and forward to today's security problems. (Rev: BL 12/1/04) [956.940]

1798 *Three Wishes: Palestinian and Israeli Children Speak* (5–12). 2004, Groundwood $16.95 (0-88899-554-7). 144pp. In an evenhanded presentation that offers an introductory historical overview, 20 first-person accounts relate the experiences of Christian, Jewish, and Muslim young people during the ongoing conflict between Israelis and Palestinians. (Rev: BL 9/1/04*; SLJ 10/04) [956.04]

1799 Tolan, Sandy. *The Lemon Tree: An Arab, a Jew, and the Heart of the Middle East* (11–12). 2006, Bloomsbury $24.95 (1-58234-343-8). 368pp. The story of a stone house in Ramla, now part of Israel but once owned by Arabs, serves as an illustration of the ongoing Israeli-Palestinian conflict; for mature readers. (Rev: BL 4/1/06) [956.9]

Other Middle East Countries

1800 Bogdanos, Matthew, and William Patrick. *Thieves of Baghdad: One Marine's Passion for Ancient Civilizations and the Journey to Recover the World's Greatest Stolen Treasures* (9–12). Illus. 2005, Bloomsbury $25.95 (1-58234-645-3). 320pp. A riveting, behind-the-scenes look at the U.S. military investigation into the looting of Iraq's national museum in Baghdad following the U.S. invasion. (Rev: BL 11/15/05; SLJ 3/06) [956.704]

1801 Cinini, Mikko. *Iran* (8–12). Series: The World's Hot Spots. 2004, Gale LB $22.96 (0-7377-1723-8). 127pp. Discussion of the situation in Iran in the early 21st century is preceded by historical information. (Rev: SLJ 3/05) [955]

1802 Dudley, William, ed. *Iraq* (9–12). Series: Opposing Viewpoints. 2004, Gale LB $33.70 (0-7377-2286-X); paper $22.45 (0-7377-2287-8). 202pp. Speeches and articles by diverse contributors including Iraqis and Kurds give back-to-back pro and con viewpoints on U.S. intervention in Iraq, predictions for the future, and other topics of current interest. (Rev: SLJ 8/04) [956.7]

1803 Miller, Debra A. *Iraq* (6–12). Series: The World's Hot Spots. 2004, Gale LB $22.96 (0-7377-1813-7); paper $15.96 (0-7377-1814-5). 128pp. Reprinted essays, speeches, and news articles provide a fascinating overview of Iraq's history and the factors that precipitated the American-led invasion in 2003. (Rev: BL 6/1–15/04; SLJ 8/04) [956.704]

1804 Riverbend. *Baghdad Burning: Girl Blog from Iraq* (8–12). 2005, Feminist paper $14.95 (1-55861-489-3). 320pp. A young Iraqi blogger paints a grim picture of life in her country after the 2003 invasion of U.S. and allied forces. (Rev: BL 4/1/05) [956.7]

1805 Schaffer, David, ed. *Iraq* (10–12). Series: The History of Nations. 2003, Gale LB $34.95 (0-7377-1660-6); paper $22.45 (0-7377-1661-4). 240pp. For students researching the history of Mesopotamia and the region that is now Iraq, this collection of scholarly essays and excerpts will be useful. (Rev: SLJ 2/04) [956.7]

1806 Seierstad, Åsne. *A Hundred and One Days* (10–12). Trans. by Ingrid Christophersen. 2005, Basic Bks. $22.95 (0-465-07600-9). 336pp. Seierstad sheds light on what Iraqis were thinking in the days leading up to the 2003 invasion of their country. (Rev: BL 3/15/05; SLJ 7/05) [950.7]

1807 Sinkler, Adrian. *Iraq* (9–12). Series: Nations in Transition. 2006, Gale LB $28.70 (0-7377-3085-4). 128pp. Covers Iraq's history from 1932 through early 2005. (Rev: SLJ 2/06) [956.7]

North and South America (excluding the United States)

General and Miscellaneous

1808 Ackroyd, Peter. *Cities of Blood* (7–10). Illus. Series: Voyages Through Time. 2004, DK $19.99 (0-7566-0729-9); paper $9.95 (0-7566-0758-2). 144pp. In this colorful third installment of his award-winning series (after *The Beginning* and *Escape from Earth*), Ackroyd explores the surprisingly sophisticated pre-Columbian civilizations of the Olmecs, Aztecs, Mayas, and Incas. (Rev: BL 1/05; SLJ 3/05) [972]

1809 Cox, Caroline, and Ken Albala. *Opening Up North America, 1497–1800* (6–12). Series: Discovery and Exploration. 2005, Facts on File $40.00 (0-8160-5261-1). 196pp. Chronicles the arrival of Europeans in North America and their progression across the continent, with maps, illustrations, and excerpts from primary sources. (Rev: SLJ 8/05) [973]

1810 Mann, Charles C. *1491: New Revelations of the Americas Before Columbus* (10–12). Illus. 2005, Knopf $30.00 (1-4000-4006-X). 480pp. This eye-opening look at America before the arrival of Europeans finds a world far different from the one depicted in most history books. (Rev: BL 8/05) [970.01]

1811 Smith, Tom. *Discovery of the Americas, 1492–1800* (6–12). Illus. Series: Discovery and Exploration. 2005, Facts on File $40.00 (0-8160-5262-X). 206pp. European exploration of the New World is the focus of this volume that contains clear, informative text plus maps, illustrations, and excerpts from primary sources. (Rev: SLJ 8/05) [973]

North America

CANADA

1812 Garrington, Sally. *Canada* (7–10). Series: Countries of the World. 2005, Facts on File LB $30.00 (0-8160-6009-6). 61pp. History, geography, culture, government, and economy are all covered in this attractive overview of Canada. (Rev: SLJ 1/06) [971]

1813 Jenkins, McKay. *Bloody Falls of the Coppermine: Madness, Murder, and the Collision of Cultures in the Arctic, 1913* (10–12). 2005, Random $25.95 (0-375-50721-3). 278pp. This story of the 1913 murder of two Catholic missionaries by Eskimo hunters is a fascinating account illustrating tragic effects of basic misunderstandings between different cultures. (Rev: BL 12/15/04; SLJ 4/05) [364.152]

MEXICO

1814 Gall, Timothy L., and Susan Bevan Gall, eds. *Junior Worldmark Encyclopedia of the Mexican States* (7–12). Illus. 2004, Gale $58.00 (0-7876-9161-5). 336pp. This encyclopedia introduces readers to the 31 states of Mexico and its Federal District, providing facts and figures about the geography, history, people, government, and culture of each. (Rev: BL 12/15/04; SLJ 2/05) [972]

PUERTO RICO, CUBA, AND OTHER CARIBBEAN ISLANDS

1815 Carey, Charles W., Jr., ed. *Castro's Cuba* (7–12). Series: History Firsthand. 2004, Gale LB $33.70 (0-7377-1654-1); paper $22.45 (0-7377-1655-X). 205pp. Historical documents, interviews, and newspaper and magazine articles are used in this account of Castro's takeover in Cuba and developments since then. (Rev: SLJ 11/04) [972]

1816 Fisanick, Christina. *The Bay of Pigs* (6–12). Series: At Issue in History. 2004, Gale LB $22.96 (0-7377-1989-3); paper $15.96 (0-7377-1990-7). 112pp. The failed Bay of Pigs invasion is described in an introductory overview followed by a collection of essays, speeches, and editorials that provide diverse views about the event. (Rev: BL 9/1/04) [972.910]

1817 Sheehan, Sean, and Leslie Jermyn. *Cuba* (7–10). Illus. Series: Cultures of the World: Second Edition. 2005, Marshall Cavendish LB $25.95 (0-7614-1964-9). 144pp. A frank, balanced, and readable overview of Cuba's history, geography, economy, culture, and people. (Rev: BL 2/15/06) [972.91]

South America

1818 Fearns, Les, and Daisy Fearns. *Argentina* (7–10). Series: Countries of the World. 2005, Facts on File LB $30.00 (0-8160-6008-8). 61pp. History, geography, culture, government, and economy are all covered in this attractive overview of Argentina. (Rev: SLJ 1/06) [982]

1819 Higgins, James. *Lima: A Cultural History* (9–12). 2004, Oxford $15.00 (0-19-517890-4). 256pp. A cultural tour of Lima, Peru's largest city and home to many of the country's best-known writers. (Rev: BL 11/15/04) [985]

1820 Mittermeier, Russell A., et al. *Pantanal: South America's Wetland Jewel* (9–12). Photos by Theo Allofs. 2005, Firefly $35.00 (1-55407-090-2). 176pp. Striking color photographs of landscape and flora and fauna highlight this fascinating profile of South America's Pantanal, a vast wetlands network covering more than 80,000 square miles in the countries of Bolivia, Brazil, and Paraguay. (Rev: BL 10/1/05) [981.72]

1821 Somervill, Barbara A. *Empire of the Inca* (7–10). Illus. Series: Great Empires of the Past. 2004, Facts on File $30.00 (0-8160-5560-2). 128pp. In addition to covering the Inca civilization, Somerville draws connections from that ancient society to contemporary culture. (Rev: BL 2/1/05) [985]

Polar Regions

1822 Anderson, Harry S. *Exploring the Polar Regions* (8–11). Illus. Series: Discovery and Exploration. 2004, Facts on File $35.00 (0-8160-5259-X). 176pp. This analytical history of polar exploration looks at the motivations behind the expeditions as

well as the specifics of early and modern ventures into new terrain. (Rev: BL 1/05; SLJ 12/04) [910]

1823 Currie, Stephen. *Antarctica* (7–12). Illus. Series: Exploration and Discovery. 2004, Gale LB $21.96 (1-59018-495-5). 112pp. Currie examines early theories about what lay at the southern end of the Earth and chronicles the early-20th-century expeditions to learn more about the continent. (Rev: BL 10/15/04) [919.8]

1824 Fiennes, Ranulph. *Race to the Pole: Tragedy, Heroism, and Scott's Antarctic Quest* (8–12). 2004, Hyperion $27.95 (1-4013-0047-2). 480pp. Fiennes, a polar explorer himself, offers an in-depth account of Captain Robert Scott's ill-fated 1911–1912 expedition to the South Pole. (Rev: BL 9/15/04) [919.8]

1825 Henderson, Bruce. *True North: Peary, Cook, and the Race to the Pole* (8–12). Illus. 2005, Norton $24.95 (0-393-05791-7). 288pp. Who got to the North Pole first? Henderson offers evidence for the reader to mull over. (Rev: BL 1/1–15/05) [910]

1826 Legler, Gretchen. *On the Ice: An Intimate Portrait of Life at McMurdo Station, Antarctica* (11–12). 2005, Milkweed paper $15.95 (1-57131-282-X). 207pp. Legler combines a portrait of the spartan life of scientists stationed in Antarctica with an account of her own relationship with a woman named Ruth. (Rev: BL 11/1/05) [919]

1827 Wu, Norbert, and Jim Mastro. *Under Antarctic Ice: The Photographs of Norbert Wu* (8–12). Illus. 2004, Univ. of California $39.95 (0-520-23504-5). 192pp. Life beneath the ice of Antarctica is brilliantly captured in the photographs of Norbert Wu; with a useful introduction. (Rev: BL 10/15/04) [779]

United States

General History and Geography

1828 Bockenhauer, Mark H., and Stephen F. Cunha. *Our Fifty States* (4–10). Illus. 2004, National Geographic LB $45.90 (0-7922-6992-6). 239pp. Maps of the states are accompanied by basic facts, photographs, and archival reproductions of key historical events; also includes the U.S. territories. (Rev: SLJ 1/05) [973]

1829 Browne, Ray B., and Lawrence A. Kreiser. *The Civil War and Reconstruction* (9–12). Series: American Popular Culture Through History. 2003, Greenwood $50.00 (0-313-31325-3). 215pp. A fascinating exploration of the impact of the Civil War and the ensuing Reconstruction on popular culture in America, looking at topics including fashion, advertising, music, journalism, sports, travel, and transportation. (Rev: SLJ 4/04) [973]

1830 Edwards, Judith. *Abolitionists and Slave Resistance: Breaking the Chains of Slavery* (6–12). Series: Slavery in American History. 2004, Enslow LB $20.95 (0-7660-2155-6). 128pp. A well-written survey of the emergence and progress of the antislavery movement. (Rev: SLJ 8/04) [326]

1831 Grunwald, Lisa, and Stephen J. Adler, eds. *Women's Letters: America from the Revolutionary War to the Present* (10–12). Illus. 2005, Dial $35.00 (0-385-33553-9). 806pp. A fascinating collection of more than 400 letters documenting women's evolving views on everyday life and on key events and issues in American history. (Rev: BL 9/1/05; SLJ 1/06) [305.4]

1832 McNeese, Tim. *The Rise and Fall of American Slavery: Freedom Denied, Freedom Gained* (6–12). Illus. Series: Slavery in American History. 2004, Enslow LB $19.95 (0-7660-2156-4). 128pp. Traces the growth of the slave trade in the American colonies, as well as the rise of the abolition movement that later pushed for an end to slavery. (Rev: BL 9/1/04; SLJ 8/04) [97]

1833 Mintz, Steven. *Huck's Raft: A History of American Childhood* (11–12). Illus. 2004, Harvard $29.95 (0-674-01508-8). 480pp. Huckleberry Finn's presumed freedom to explore is shown as unusual in this examination of children's responsibilities across three centuries of American history. (Rev: BL 11/1/04) [305.23]

1834 Raphael, Ray. *Founding Myths: Stories That Hide Our Patriotic Past* (9–12). Illus. 2004, New Press $26.95 (1-56584-921-3). 368pp. Raphael debunks a number of widely disseminated myths about the early history of America. (Rev: BL 9/1/04; SLJ 1/05) [973.3]

1835 White, Shane, and Graham White. *The Sounds of Slavery: Discovering African American History Through Songs, Sermons, and Speech* (9–12). 2005, Beacon $29.95 (0-8070-5026-1). 234pp. The sounds of everyday life for America's slaves — the spirituals and sermons, field calls and work songs, and the cries of agony — are captured in this volume and the audio CD that accompanies it. (Rev: BL 2/15/05) [973]

1836 Worth, Richard. *Slave Life on the Plantation: Prisons Beneath the Sun* (6–12). Illus. Series: Slavery in American History. 2004, Enslow LB $19.95 (0-7660-2152-1). 128pp. A vivid portrait of what daily life was like for slaves laboring on the vast plantations of the American South. (Rev: BL 9/1/04; SLJ 12/04) [306.3]

1837 Worth, Richard. *The Slave Trade in America: Cruel Commerce* (6–12). Series: Slavery in American History. 2004, Enslow LB $20.95 (0-7660-2151-3). 128pp. The slave trade is traced back to its origins in the days of early Romans before a more detailed survey of the American slave trade in the

17th and 18th centuries, with attention to the social and economic aspects. (Rev: SLJ 8/04) [382]

Historical Periods

NATIVE AMERICANS

1838 Cornell, George L., and Gordon Henry. *Ojibwa* (8–12). Series: North American Indians Today. 2003, Mason Crest LB $22.95 (1-59084-673-7). 94pp. The contemporary status of Ojibwa Indians is emphasized in this volume that covers religion, government, and the arts. (Rev: SLJ 5/04) [973]

1839 Dando-Collins, Stephen. *Standing Bear Is a Person: The True Story of a Native American's Quest for Justice* (9–12). Illus. 2004, Da Capo $26.00 (0-306-81370-X). 272pp. Standing Bear, a chief of the Ponca Indians, fought in the late 19th century for his tribe's right to live on fertile land. (Rev: BL 12/15/04) [978.004]

1840 Keoke, Emory Dean, and Kay Marie Porterfield. *Trade, Transportation, and Warfare* (7–10). Illus. Series: American Indian Contributions to the World. 2005, Facts on File $35.00 (0-8160-5395-2). 160pp. Native American accomplishments in both North and South America in the realms of transportation, trade, sports, governance, and military strategy are among the aspects highlighted here. (Rev: BL 4/1/05; SLJ 6/05) [970.004]

1841 McIntosh, Kenneth. *Apache* (8–12). Series: North American Indians Today. 2003, Mason Crest LB $22.95 (1-59084-664-8). 94pp. The contemporary status of Apache Indians is emphasized in this volume that covers religion, government, and the arts. (Rev: SLJ 5/04) [973]

1842 McIntosh, Kenneth, and Marsha McIntosh. *Cheyenne* (8–12). Series: North American Indians Today. 2003, Mason Crest LB $22.95 (1-59084-666-4). 94pp. The contemporary status of Cheyenne Indians is emphasized in this volume that covers religion, government, and the arts. Also use *Iroquois* (2003). (Rev: SLJ 5/04) [973]

1843 McMaster, Gerald, and Clifford E. Trafzer, eds. *Native Universe: Voices of Indian America* (9–12). Illus. 2004, National Geographic $40.00 (0-7922-5994-7). 320pp. In three main sections — "Our Universe," "Our Peoples," and "Our Lives" — photographs and text document the diversity of Native American culture and history. (Rev: BL 8/04) [970.004]

COLONIAL PERIOD AND FRENCH AND INDIAN WARS

1844 Fowler, William. *Empires at War: The French and Indian War and the Struggle for North America, 1754–1763* (10–12). Illus. 2005, Walker $27.00 (0-8027-1411-0). 368pp. In addition to recounting the major events of the French and Indian War, this volume includes useful biographical sketches and a timeline. (Rev: BL 12/15/04) [973.2]

REVOLUTIONARY PERIOD AND THE YOUNG NATION (1775–1809)

1845 Aronson, Marc. *The Real Revolution: The Global Story of American Independence* (9–12). Illus. 2005, Clarion $20.00 (0-618-18179-2). 256pp. Was the American Revolution an isolated incident or connected to events elsewhere in the world? A thought-provoking, well-illustrated and well-documented analysis. (Rev: BL 9/15/05; SLJ 10/05*) [973.3]

1846 Chadwick, Bruce. *The First American Army: The Remarkable Story of George Washington and the Men Behind America's Fight for Freedom* (10–12). 2005, Sourcebooks $24.95 (1-4022-0506-6). 320pp. Drawing on first-person accounts from letters and journals, Chadwick looks at the American Revolution through the eyes of the boys and men who fought on the front lines. (Rev: BL 11/1/05) [973.3]

1847 McCullough, David. *1776* (8–12). Illus. 2005, Simon & Schuster $32.00 (0-7432-2671-2). 386pp. McCullough brings to life the key events of the year 1776 for George Washington and the new young nation. (Rev: SLJ 10/05) [973]

1848 Morton, Joseph C. *The American Revolution* (7–12). Series: Greenwood Guides to Historic Events, 1500–1900. 2003, Greenwood $45.00 (0-313-31792-5). 218pp. A thorough, text-dense overview of the events leading up to the war, the war itself, and its aftermath, with profiles of key individuals. (Rev: SLJ 7/04) [973.3]

1849 Murray, Aaron R. *American Revolution Battles and Leaders* (6–12). Illus. Series: Battles and Leaders. 2004, DK $19.99 (0-7894-9888-X); paper $12.99 (0-7894-9889-8). 96pp. A richly illustrated, easily accessed source of reliable information on the battles and key figures of the Revolution. (Rev: BL 4/1/04*) [973.3]

NINETEENTH CENTURY TO THE CIVIL WAR (1809–1861)

1850 Blight, David W., ed. *Passages to Freedom: The Underground Railroad in History and Memory* (8–12). Illus. 2004, Smithsonian $39.95 (1-58834-157-7). 256pp. Essays, photographs, and illustrations document the reality, rather than the myth, of the Underground Railroad; compiled on behalf of the National Underground Railroad Center in Cincinnati. (Rev: BL 7/04) [973.7]

1851 de Ramus, Betty. *Forbidden Fruit: Love Stories from the Underground and Beyond* (9–12). Illus. 2005, Atria $25.00 (0-7434-8263-8). 268pp.

Drawing on newspaper accounts, oral histories, slave narratives, census data, and unpublished memoirs, De Ramus tells 13 moving stories of love against the backdrop of American slavery. (Rev: BL 2/1/05) [973.7]

1852 Mills, Bronwyn. *U.S.-Mexican War*. Rev. ed. (9–12). Series: America at War. 2003, Facts on File $35.00 (0-8160-4932-7). 143pp. Informative and interesting, this account of the brief conflict and the key figures involved puts it into global historical context. (Rev: SLJ 1/04) [973.6]

1853 Schlesinger, Arthur M., Jr., ed. *The Election of 1860 and the Administration of Abraham Lincoln* (8–12). Series: Major Presidential Elections and the Administrations That Followed. 2003, Mason Crest LB $24.95 (1-59084-355-X). 128pp. A good source of speeches, quotations, and excerpts from public documents, with commentary, illustrations, and further reading. (Rev: SLJ 1/04) [973.7]

CIVIL WAR (1861–1865)

1854 Chaffin, Tom. *Sea of Gray: The Around-the-World Odyssey of the Confederate Raider Shenandoah* (10–12). Illus. 2006, Hill & Wang $25.00 (0-8090-9511-4). 400pp. The little-known Civil War story of the Confederate ship *Shenandoah* and its round-the-world voyage is recounted here. (Rev: BL 12/1/05) [973.7]

1855 Geary, Rick. *The Murder of Abraham Lincoln* (9–12). Illus. Series: A Treasury of Victorian Murder. 2005, NBM $15.95 (1-56163-425-5). 80pp. Volume seven of the Treasury of Victorian Murder series tackles one of the most infamous crimes of the period: the assassination of President Abraham Lincoln. (Rev: BL 6/1–15/05; SLJ 9/05; VOYA 10/05) [973.709]

1856 Lalicki, Tom. *Grierson's Raid: A Daring Cavalry Strike Through the Heart of the Confederacy* (7–12). 2004, Farrar $18.00 (0-374-32787-4). 208pp. Lalicki recounts Union Colonel Benjamin Grierson's daring 16-day raid through the state of Mississippi in 1863. (Rev: BL 8/04; HB 7–8/04; SLJ 6/04; VOYA 8/04) [973.7]

1857 Murray, Aaron R. *Civil War Battles and Leaders* (6–12). Illus. Series: Battles and Leaders. 2004, DK $19.99 (0-7894-9890-1); paper $12.99 (0-7894-9891-X). 96pp. A richly illustrated, easily accessed source of reliable information on the battles and key figures of the Civil War. (Rev: BL 4/1/04*) [973.7]

1858 Tackach, James, ed. *The Civil War* (9–12). Series: Turning Points in World History. 2004, Gale LB $26.96 (0-7377-1114-0). 186pp. The causes, battles, and aftermath of the Civil War are examined in a collection of essays by prominent historians; discussion questions and further readings add to this volume's usefulness. (Rev: SLJ 1/05) [973.7]

1859 Woodworth, Steven E., and Kenneth J. Winkle. *Oxford Atlas of the Civil War* (9–12). 2004, Oxford LB $85.00 (0-19-522131-1). 400pp. Dividing its coverage into five sections — one for each year of the war — this atlas covers the important battles plus many nonmilitary topics (population, economy, transportation, and so forth). (Rev: BL 7/05; SLJ 6/05) [910]

WESTWARD EXPANSION AND PIONEER LIFE

1860 Dary, David. *The Oregon Trail: An American Saga* (8–12). Illus. 2004, Knopf $35.00 (0-375-41399-5). 448pp. A sweeping and very readable history of the Oregon Trail, from its early-19th-century origins through a period of obscurity to its present importance. (Rev: BL 10/15/04) [978]

1861 Isserman, Maurice. *Across America: The Lewis and Clark Expedition* (6–10). Series: Discovery and Exploration. 2004, Facts on File $35.00 (0-8160-5256-5). 180pp. A detailed look at the expedition with clear, informative text plus photographs, illustrations, and excerpts from primary sources. (Rev: SLJ 12/04) [973]

1862 Isserman, Maurice. *Exploring North America, 1800–1900* (6–12). Series: Discovery and Exploration. 2005, Facts on File $40.00 (0-8160-5263-8). 198pp. Clear text and primary sources explain the 19th-century explorations of North America by John Fremont, John Wesley Powell, and others, and put them in historical and social context. (Rev: SLJ 8/05) [973]

1863 Rau, Margaret. *The Mail Must Go Through: The Story of the Pony Express* (7–10). Illus. Series: America's Moving Frontier. 2005, Morgan Reynolds LB $24.95 (1-931798-63-X). 176pp. A lively account of the exciting — but brief — history of the Pony Express. (Rev: BL 6/1–15/05; SLJ 10/05) [383]

RECONSTRUCTION TO WORLD WAR I (1865–1914)

1864 Bolden, Tonya. *Cause: Reconstruction America, 1863–1877* (8–11). Illus. 2005, Knopf LB $21.99 (0-375-92795-6). 128pp. Although the text is a little uneven, this is a useful, well-documented and well-illustrated survey of the turbulent years of Reconstruction and the massive challenges facing both the North and South. (Rev: BL 10/15/05; SLJ 11/05*; VOYA 12/05) [973.7]

1865 Dudley, William, ed. *Reconstruction* (9–12). Series: At Issue in History. 2003, Gale LB $28.70 (0-7377-1356-9); paper $19.95 (0-7377-1357-7). 122pp. Presents the debates that took place over how reconstruction of the infrastructure and institutions of the South should proceed after the Civil War. (Rev: SLJ 1/04) [973]

1866 Ferrell, Claudine L. *Reconstruction* (5–10). Series: Greenwood Guides to Historic Events, 1500–1900. 2003, Greenwood $45.00 (0-313-32062-4). 220pp. Covers key individuals involved in Reconstruction and the speeches, proclamations, and other primary documents that cast light on the events of the time. (Rev: SLJ 6/04) [973.8]

1867 Golay, Michael. *Spanish-American War.* Rev. ed. (9–12). Series: America at War. 2003, Facts on File $35.00 (0-8160-4935-1). 154pp. Informative and interesting, this account of the brief conflict and the key figures involved puts it into global historical context. (Rev: SLJ 1/04) [973.8]

1868 Vowell, Sarah. *Assassination Vacation* (8–12). Illus. 2005, Simon & Schuster $21.00 (0-7432-6003-1). 258pp. Author Sarah Vowell takes readers on a pilgrimage to historical sites related to the assassinations of Presidents Lincoln, Garfield, and McKinley. (Rev: SLJ 11/05)

BETWEEN THE WARS AND THE GREAT DEPRESSION (1918–1941)

1869 Brown, Lois. *Encyclopedia of the Harlem Literary Renaissance: The Essential Guide to the Lives and Works of the Harlem Renaissance Writers* (9–12). 2005, Facts on File $65.00 (0-8160-4967-X). 612pp. More than 800 alphabetically arranged entries cover writers and their works, events, educational and other institutions, awards and prizes, and so forth. (Rev: BL 2/15/06; SLJ 2/06) [700]

1870 Callan, Jim. *America in the 1930s* (7–10). Illus. Series: Decades of American History. 2005, Facts on File $35.00 (0-8160-5638-2). 128pp. Excellent information — especially for report writers — is hampered by poor design. (Rev: BL 1/1–15/06) [973.917]

1871 Egan, Timothy. *The Worst Hard Time: The Untold Story of Those Who Survived the Great American Dust Bowl* (10–12). Illus. 2006, Houghton $28.00 (0-618-34697-X). 320pp. The human toll of the dust storms that ravaged the southern Great Plains in the mid-1930s is brought into vivid focus. (Rev: BL 12/15/05) [978]

1872 Hill, Jeff. *Prohibition* (9–12). Illus. Series: Defining Moments. 2005, Omnigraphics $38.00 (0-7808-0768-5). 225pp. A detailed analysis of the years of Prohibition, with a collection of primary sources that shed further light on this period. (Rev: BL 5/1/05; SLJ 10/05) [363.4]

1873 Swisher, Clarice. *Women of the Roaring Twenties* (6–10). Illus. Series: Women in History. 2005, Gale LB $22.96 (1-59017-363-0). 112pp. Using primary sources, this readable volume looks at life for women from diverse backgrounds during the turbulent 1920s. (Rev: BL 2/15/06) [305.4]

1874 Yancey, Diane. *Life During the Dust Bowl* (7–12). Illus. Series: The Way People Live. 2004, Gale LB $27.45 (1-59018-265-0). 112pp. Black-and-white photographs and excerpts from oral histories add to the narrative overview to paint a vivid portrait of the devastation caused by the Great Plains dust storms of the 1930s. (Rev: BL 8/04; SLJ 8/04) [978]

1875 Zeitz, Joshua. *Flapper: A Madcap Story of Sex, Style, Celebrity, and the Women Who Made America Modern* (11–12). Illus. 2006, Crown $24.95 (1-4000-8053-3). 352pp. The carefree flappers of the roaring '20s — Zelda Fitzgerald, Coco Chanel, Clara Bow, Louise Brooks — are vividly portrayed against the backdrop of the Jazz Age. (Rev: BL 2/15/06) [813]

WORLD WAR II

1876 Brinkley, Douglas, ed. *The World War II Memorial: A Grateful Nation Remembers* (8–12). Illus. 2004, Smithsonian $39.95 (1-58834-210-7). 287pp. Published in conjunction with the dedication of the World War II Memorial in Washington, D.C., this striking coffee table book is loaded with photos and remembrances of the war and its lasting impact on America. (Rev: BL 9/1/04) [940.54]

1877 Esposito, John C. *Fire in the Grove: The Cocoanut Grove Tragedy and Its Aftermath* (10–12). 2005, Da Capo $24.00 (0-306-81423-4). 246pp. The story of the tragic fire that claimed nearly 500 lives in a Boston nightclub in 1942. (Rev: SLJ 3/06)

1878 Renner, Elmer, and Kenneth Birks. *Sea of Sharks: A Sailor's World War II Shipwreck Survival Story* (9–12). Illus. 2004, Naval Institute $28.95 (1-59114-714-X). 262pp. In this gripping World War II survival story, Renner tells how he and three crewmates survived the sinking of an American minesweeper in the Pacific. (Rev: BL 10/15/04) [940.54]

1879 Schneider, Dorothy, and Carl J. Schneider. *World War II: An Eyewitness History* (9–12). Series: Facts on File Library of American History. 2003, Facts on File $75.00 (0-8160-4484-8). 472pp. Firsthand accounts — letters, speeches, and quotations — illustrate civilian and military life for Americans before and during World War II; maps, profiles of key individuals, and excerpts from significant documents are included. (Rev: SLJ 2/04) [940.53]

POST WORLD WAR II UNITED STATES (1945–)

1880 Kallen, Stuart A. *The Kennedy Assassination* (9–12). Series: The Mystery Library. 2003, Gale LB $21.96 (1-59018-128-X). 112pp. Examines the doubts surrounding Kennedy's assassination that continue to exist to this day, with material on Lee

Harvey Oswald and Jack Ruby as well as on other suspects and contradictions that have never been fully resolved. (Rev: SLJ 2/04) [364.15]

1881 MacPherson, Malcolm. *Roberts Ridge: A Story of Courage and Sacrifice on Takur Ghar Mountain, Afghanistan* (11–12). 2005, Delacorte $25.00 (0-553-80363-8). 352pp. The gripping story of Navy SEALs' valiant — but ultimately unsuccessful — attempt to rescue one of their own who was left behind on an Afghani mountaintop; for mature teens. (Rev: BL 9/15/05) [958.104]

1882 Maus, Derek C., ed. *Living Under the Threat of Nuclear War* (7–10). Series: Living Through the Cold War. 2005, Gale LB $32.45 (0-7377-2130-8). 143pp. This title examines how Americans coped with the ever-present threat of nuclear war during the half-century-long Cold War. (Rev: SLJ 10/05) [973]

1883 Miles, Barry. *Hippie* (11–12). Illus. 2004, Sterling $24.95 (1-4027-1442-4). 384pp. For mature readers, this large-format photoessay captures the cultural upheaval of the 1960s. (Rev: BL 8/04) [305.568]

1884 Morrow, Lance. *The Best Year of Their Lives: Kennedy, Johnson, and Nixon in 1948: Learning the Secrets of Power* (11–12). 2005, Basic Bks. $26.00 (0-465-04723-8). 312pp. Morrow argues that separate 1948 events in the lives of Lyndon B. Johnson, John F. Kennedy, and Richard M. Nixon set the theme for their future political lives. (Rev: SLJ 9/05) [973]

1885 Olsen, Gregg. *The Deep Dark: Disaster and Redemption in America's Richest Silver Mine* (9–12). 2005, Crown $24.95 (0-609-61016-3). 336pp. The story of the 1972 Sunshine Mine disaster in Idaho, in which more than 90 died and others survived a week-long ordeal. (Rev: BL 1/1–15/05) [363.11]

1886 Pozner, Neal J., ed. *How Should the United States Withdraw from Iraq?* (10–12). Series: At Issue. 2004, Gale LB $21.96 (0-7377-2232-X); paper $14.96 (0-7377-2323-8). 80pp. Students preparing material on this controversial issue will find this a useful — although limited — collection of speeches and articles. (Rev: BL 2/1/05) [956.7044]

1887 Roleff, Tamara L., ed. *The Oklahoma City Bombing* (9–12). Series: History Firsthand. 2004, Gale LB $33.70 (0-7377-1658-4); paper $22.45 (0-7377-1659-2). 224pp. Court documents, speeches, letters, and eyewitness accounts tell the story of the bombing from the planning stage through the trial, execution, and building of a memorial. (Rev: SLJ 11/04) [364.16]

1888 Schlesinger, Arthur M., Jr., ed. *The Election of 1948 and the Administration of Harry S. Truman* (8–12). Series: Major Presidential Elections and the Administrations That Followed. 2003, Mason Crest

LB $24.95 (1-59084-360-6). 128pp. A good source of speeches, quotations, and excerpts from public documents, with commentary, illustrations, and further reading. Also use *The Election of 1912 and the Administration of Woodrow Wilson* and *The Election of 1960 and the Administration of John F. Kennedy* (both 2003). (Rev: SLJ 1/04) [973]

1889 Wicker, Tom. *Shooting Star: The Brief Arc of Joe McCarthy* (10–12). 2006, Harcourt $22.00 (0-15-101082-X). 224pp. A very readable and enlightening look back at the McCarthy era of the early 1950s and the Communist witch hunt started by the junior senator from Wisconsin. (Rev: BL 2/15/06) [973.921]

KOREAN, VIETNAM, AND GULF WARS

1890 Caputo, Philip. *10,000 Days of Thunder: A History of the Vietnam War* (7–10). Illus. 2005, Simon & Schuster $22.95 (0-689-86231-8). 128pp. In this sweeping overview of the Vietnam War, Caputo traces the fractured country's history from the beginnings of resistance to French colonial rule to the fall of Saigon and also assesses the conflict's enduring impact on Americans. (Rev: BL 10/1/05; SLJ 11/05*; VOYA 10/05) [959.704]

1891 Caputo, Philip. *13 Seconds: A Look Back at the Kent State Shootings* (9–12). 2005, Penguin $19.95 (1-59609-080-4). 208pp. Pulitzer Prize-winning author Philip Caputo searches for meaning in this review of the tragic 1970 shooting of four students at Kent State University. (Rev: BL 6/1–15/05) [378.771]

1892 Drez, Ronald J., and Douglas Brinkley. *Voices of Courage: The Battle for Khe Sanh, Vietnam* (10–12). Illus. 2005, Bulfinch $35.00 (0-8212-6196-7). 192pp. Recounts the bloody 1968 battle for control of the U.S. Marine Corps base at Khe Sanh in South Vietnam; for advanced history students. (Rev: BL 8/05) [959.704]

1893 Feldman, Ruth Tenzer. *The Korean War* (6–12). Illus. Series: Chronicle of America's Wars. 2003, Lerner LB $27.93 (0-8225-4716-3). 96pp. Explores events before, during, and after the Korean War and introduces the key individuals involved. (Rev: BL 4/1/04) [951.904]

Regions

MOUNTAIN AND PLAINS STATES

1894 Laskin, David. *The Children's Blizzard* (9–12). 2004, HarperCollins $24.95 (0-06-052075-2). 320pp. The personal impact of the fateful January 1888 blizzard is brought to life in this gripping look at how the storm affected five pioneer families in the upper Great Plains. (Rev: BL 10/15/04; SLJ 4/05) [978]

NORTHEASTERN AND MID-ATLANTIC STATES

1895 Berlin, Ira, and Leslie M. Harris, eds. *Slavery in New York* (10–12). Illus. 2005, New Press paper $22.50 (1-56584-997-3). 400pp. The little-known history of slavery in New York City is chronicled in this collection of essays by historians specializing in slavery and African American history. (Rev: BL 10/15/05) [974.7]

Philosophy and Religion

Philosophy

1896 Holbrook, Kate, et al., eds. *Global Values 101: A Short Course* (10–12). 2006, Beacon paper $14.00 (0-8070-0305-0). 256pp. The interviews in this volume — all originally conducted as part of a Harvard seminar on "Personal Choice and Global Transformation" — explore what individuals can do to help make the world a better place to live. (Rev: BL 1/1–15/06) [170]

1897 Papineau, David, ed. *Western Philosophy: An Illustrated Guide* (9–12). 2004, Oxford $35.00 (0-19-522143-5). 224pp. Plenty of illustrations and explanatory text boxes add to this challenging discussion of concepts and key figures in Western philosophy. (Rev: SLJ 4/05) [190]

1898 Stokes, Philip. *Philosophy: 100 Essential Thinkers* (10–12). 2003, Enchanted Lion $18.95 (1-59270-016-0). 218pp. Important philosophers are grouped chronologically within schools of thought, with material on each individual's contribution to the progress of that philosophy. (Rev: SLJ 2/04)

World Religions and Holidays

General and Miscellaneous

1899 Asma, Stephen T. *The Gods Drink Whiskey: Stumbling Toward Enlightenment in the Land of the Tattered Buddha* (9–12). 2005, HarperSanFrancisco $24.95 (0-06-072395-5). 256pp. Philosophy professor Stephen T. Asma recounts his spiritual journey to Cambodia to explore the historical roots of Theravada Buddhism. (Rev: BL 6/1–15/05) [294.3]

1900 Gaskins, Pearl Fuyo. *I Believe In . . .: Christian, Jewish, and Muslim Young People Speak About Their Faiths* (7–10). 2004, Cricket $18.95 (0-8126-2713-X). 208pp. Suitable for browsing, this is a collection of interviews with about 100 young adults from diverse religious backgrounds in the Chicago area. (Rev: BCCB 9/04; BL 10/1/04; HB 7–8/04) [200]

1901 Head, Tom, ed. *Religion and Education* (9–12). Series: At Issue: Religion. 2005, Gale LB $22.96 (0-7377-2743-8); paper $15.96 (0-7377-2744-6). 96pp. Thought-provoking essays and articles explore various aspects of the interplay between religion and education in America, including school prayer and the teaching of evolution. (Rev: BL 10/1/05) [379.2]

1902 Mason, Claire. *New Religious Movements: The Impact on Our Lives* (6–10). Series: 21st Century Debates. 2003, Raintree LB $28.56 (0-7398-6032-1). 64pp. Zen Buddhists, Hare Krishnas, Mormons, and Scientologists are all included in this discussion of non-mainstream religious movements and cults around the world. (Rev: SLJ 6/04)

1903 Taylor, Rodney L. *Confucianism* (9–12). Series: Religions of the World. 2004, Chelsea

House LB $26.95 (0-7910-7857-4). 151pp. As well as covering the history and beliefs of Confucianism, this volume looks at the traditions still being practiced today. (Rev: SLJ 9/04) [299]

1904 Williams, George. *Shinto* (11–12). Series: Religions of the World. 2004, Chelsea House LB $26.95 (0-7910-8097-8); paper $11.95 (0-7910-8355-1). 120pp. In this title from the Religions of the World series, author George Williams introduces readers to the history, beliefs, and practices of Shinto, the indigenous religion of Japan. (Rev: SLJ 4/05)

Christianity

1905 Connolly, Sean. *New Testament Miracles* (5–10). Series: Art Revelations. 2004, Enchanted Lion $18.95 (1-59270-012-8). 32pp. Presents brief retellings of 12 miracles performed by Jesus Christ, each illustrated by a well-known painting by an eminent artist, such as Rembrandt, El Greco, and Tintoretto. (Rev: SLJ 8/04) [226.7]

1906 Sweeney, Douglas A. *The American Evangelical Story: A History of the Movement* (10–12). Illus. 2005, Baker Academic paper $17.99 (1-8010-2658-X). 208pp. A readable, informative history of the evangelical movement in America. (Rev: BL 8/05) [277.3]

1907 Zoba, Wendy Murray. *The Beliefnet Guide to Evangelical Christianity* (10–12). 2005, Doubleday paper $9.95 (0-385-51452-2). 144pp. An interesting overview of the essential elements of evangelical Christianity and the major sects existing today and in history. (Rev: BL 5/15/05) [270.8]

Islam

1908 Carr, Melissa S. *Who Are the Muslims? Where Muslims Live, and How They Are Governed* (9–12). Series: Introducing Islam. 2004, Mason Crest LB $22.95 (1-59084-701-6). 120pp. A look at the widely diverse circumstances — geographic and cultural — in which Muslims live. (Rev: SLJ 10/04) [297]

1909 Dudley, William. *Islam* (8–12). Series: Opposing Viewpoints. 2004, Gale LB $26.96 (0-7377-2238-X); paper $17.96 (0-7377-2239-8). 203pp. Opposing perspectives are offered on wide-ranging topics including the compatibility of Islam with democratic ideals; the status of women; conflicts with Western values; and attitudes toward terrorism and violence. (Rev: BL 10/1/04; SLJ 12/04) [297.2]

1910 Egendorf, Laura K., ed. *Islam in America* (7–12). Series: At Issue. 2005, Gale LB $28.70 (0-7377-2727-6). 112pp. Essays cover topics including discrimination against Muslims, the growing popularity of the religion among Hispanic Americans, and the degree of support of terrorism. (Rev: SLJ 2/06) [297]

1911 Hassaballa, Hesham A., and Kabir Helminski. *The Beliefnet Guide to Islam* (9–12). Series: Beliefnet. 2006, Doubleday paper $9.95 (0-385-51454-9). 188pp. An excellent overview of Islam, explaining the five pillars of faith and presenting the historical context necessary to a full understanding. (Rev: BL 2/15/06) [297]

1912 Hodges, Rick. *What Muslims Think and How They Live* (9–12). Series: Introducing Islam. 2004, Mason Crest LB $22.95 (1-59084-702-4). 112pp. Muslim opinions on a wide range of topics are based on a Gallup poll. (Rev: SLJ 10/04) [297]

1913 Whitehead, Kim. *Islamic Fundamentalism* (9–12). Series: Introducing Islam. 2004, Mason Crest LB $22.95 (1-59084-703-2). 119pp. A look at the Islamic fundamentalism that arose in the 20th century, and the varying degrees of radicalism in such countries as Algeria, Indonesia, and Egypt. (Rev: SLJ 10/04) [297]

Judaism

1914 Ward, Elaine. *Old Testament Women* (5–10). Series: Art Revelations. 2004, Enchanted Lion $18.95 (1-59270-011-X). 32pp. Paintings by masters accompany stories about 18 women including Rachel, Ruth, and Bathsheba. (Rev: SLJ 8/04) [224]

Religious Cults

1915 Guest, Tim. *My Life in Orange: Growing Up with the Guru* (11–12). 2005, Harcourt paper $14.95 (0-15-603106-X). 320pp. British journalist Guest writes about a rootless childhood spent in various communes; for mature readers only. (Rev: BL 12/1/04) [299]

Society and the Individual

Government and Political Science

International Relations, Peace, and War

1916 Bixler, Mark. *The Lost Boys of Sudan: An American Story of the Refugee Experience* (8–12). Illus. 2005, Univ. of Georgia $24.95 (0-8203-2499-X). 288pp. Journalist Bixler tracks the progress of four young men — refugees who were part of the so-called Lost Boys of Sudan — as they adjust to their new lives in America. (Rev: BL 2/1/05) [962.404]

1917 Dalton, Dave. *Refugees and Asylum Seekers* (7–10). Illus. Series: People on the Move. 2005, Heinemann LB $21.95 (1-4034-6961-X). 56pp. A look at the plight of civilians who have been forced from their native lands by war or ethnic cleansing; a poor layout is offset by the personal stories. (Rev: BL 8/05; SLJ 12/05) [305.9]

1918 Gottfried, Ted. *The Fight for Peace: A History of Antiwar Movements in America* (8–11). Illus. Series: People's History. 2005, Twenty-First Century LB $26.60 (0-7613-2932-3). 136pp. Chronicles the history of American protest movements from the Civil War to the present. (Rev: BL 10/1/05; SLJ 11/05) [303.6]

1919 Lang, W. Patrick. *Intelligence: The Human Factor* (9–12). Series: Securing the Nation: Issues in American National Security Since 9/11. 2004, Chelsea House LB $22.95 (0-7910-7616-4). 100pp. From the Revolutionary War to today, this is an overview of methods of collecting and using information and the traits needed to become a successful spy. (Rev: SLJ 7/04)

1920 Moorehead, Caroline. *Human Cargo: A Journey Among Refugees* (11–12). 2005, Holt $26.00 (0-8050-7443-0). 288pp. After an overview of the plight of 20th-century refugees, the author details

individual cases of suffering; for mature teens. (Rev: BL 2/1/05) [305.9]

1921 Moran, Lindsay. *Blowing My Cover: My Life as a CIA Spy and Other Misadventures* (9–12). 2005, Penguin $23.95 (0-399-15239-3). 304pp. Moran writes about the disillusionment she experienced during her five years with the CIA; young readers will particularly enjoy the details of her interviews and early training. (Rev: BL 1/1–15/05) [327.1273]

1922 Owen, David. *Spies: The Undercover World of Secrets, Gadgets and Lies* (9–12). Illus. 2004, Firefly $19.95 (1-55297-795-1); paper $9.95 (1-55297-794-3). 128pp. This title covers all aspects of espionage, with information on codes and code breaking, various gadgets, the history of spying, case studies, and profiles of famous spies. (Rev: SLJ 10/04) [327.12]

1923 Torr, James D., ed. *U.S. Policy Toward Rogue Nations* (9–12). Series: At Issue. 2004, Gale LB $27.45 (0-7377-2196-0); paper $18.70 (0-7377-2197-9). 95pp. Authoritative articles that take different perspectives discuss topics including the invasion of Iraq, possible regime change in Syria and Iran, and strategies for dealing with North Korea. (Rev: SLJ 11/04)

United States Government and Institutions

General and Miscellaneous

1924 Leepson, Marc. *Flag: An American Biography* (9–12). Illus. 2005, St. Martin's $24.95 (0-312-32308-5). 336pp. Leepson distinguishes between truth and myths about the flag and its history. (Rev: BL 5/1/05) [929.9]

1925 McIntosh, Kenneth, and Marsha McIntosh. *When Religion and Politics Mix: How Matters of Faith Influence Political Policies* (7–10). Illus. Series: Religion and Modern Culture. 2006, Mason Crest LB $22.95 (1-59084-971-X). 112pp. Statistics from the 2004 election provide a basis for this overview of Americans' views on religion and politics. (Rev: BL 4/1/06) [201]

1926 Roberts, Sam. *Who We Are Now: The Changing Face of America in the Twentyfirst Century* (9–12). Illus. 2004, Holt $27.50 (0-8050-5555-0); paper $15.00 (0-8050-7080-X). 336pp. *New York Times* reporter Roberts uses data from the 2000 U.S. census to put a face on contemporary America. (Rev: BL 9/1/04) [973.931]

The Constitution

1927 Friedman, Ian C. *Freedom of Speech and the Press* (7–12). Series: American Rights. 2005, Facts on File $35.00 (0-8160-5662-5). 128pp. Issues relating to the freedoms of speech and the press — in the past, present, and future — are explored in this title. (Rev: SLJ 12/05)

1928 Head, Tom. *Freedom of Religion* (7–10). Illus. Series: American Rights. 2005, Facts on File $35.00 (0-8160-5664-1). 146pp. Examines the significance of freedom of religion as guaranteed by the First Amendment to the Constitution and provides an overview of the role played by religion in America's early history, the Scopes trial, and questions surrounding school prayer. (Rev: BL 10/15/05) [323.44]

1929 Johnson, Terry. *Legal Rights* (7–12). Series: American Rights. 2005, Facts on File $35.00 (0-8160-5665-X). 152pp. A look at the controversial issue of legal rights under the U.S. Constitution, with discussion of government initiatives since September 11, 2001. (Rev: SLJ 12/05)

1930 Zacharias, Gary, and Jared Zacharias, eds. *The Bill of Rights* (9–12). Series: At Issue in History. 2003, Gale LB $28.70 (0-7377-1425-5); paper $19.95 (0-7377-1426-3). 112pp. After an essay introducing the background to the Constitution, this volume provides correspondence and other primary documents concerning the need for a Bill of Rights plus articles and commentary discussing later developments. (Rev: SLJ 1/04) [342.73]

Federal Government, Its Agencies, and Public Administration

1931 DeParle, Jason. *American Dream: Three Women, Ten Kids, and a Nation's Drive to End Welfare* (10–12). 2004, Viking $25.95 (0-670-89275-0). 384pp. *New York Times* reporter DeParle examines how the 1996 welfare reform program

affected three African American welfare mothers and their children. (Rev: BL 9/15/04) [362.5]

1932 Esherick, Joan. *The FDA and Psychiatric Drugs: How a Drug Is Approved* (6–10). Illus. Series: Psychiatric Disorders: Drugs and Psychology for the Mind and Body. 2003, Mason Crest LB $24.95 (1-59084-578-1). 124pp. As well as a clear explanation of the drug approval process, this volume contains information on alternative medicines and an interesting look at how treatment of schizophrenia has advanced over time. (Rev: SLJ 5/04)

1933 Gerdes, Louise L., ed. *Espionage and Intelligence Gathering* (10–12). Series: Current Controversies. 2004, Gale LB $26.96 (0-7377-1581-2); paper $17.96 (0-7377-1582-0). 192pp. Thought-provoking articles examine the current state of intelligence gathering in the United States, changes that have taken place since September 11, 2001, and the threat to civil liberties of new security measures. (Rev: SLJ 11/04) [327.1273]

1934 Hiltzik, Michael A. *The Plot Against Social Security: How the Bush Plan Is Endangering Our Financial Future* (9–12). 2005, HarperCollins $24.95 (0-06-083465-X). 272pp. Hiltzik scrutinizes proposals to substitute private investment accounts for the existing Social Security program and finds them wanting. (Rev: BL 5/15/05) [368.4]

The Law and the Courts

1935 Bailey, John. *The Lost German Slave Girl: The Extraordinary True Story of the Slave Sally Miller and Her Fight for Freedom in Old New Orleans* (9–12). 2005, Atlantic Monthly $25.00 (0-87113-921-9). 288pp. History and a novel-like presentation are combined in this story of a 19th-century legal battle to determine whether a slave in New Orleans was actually the dark-skinned daughter of a German immigrant and thus entitled to her freedom. (Rev: BL 11/15/04; SLJ 3/05) [305.8]

1936 Bogira, Steve. *Courtroom 302: A Year Behind the Scenes in an American Criminal Courthouse* (11–12). 2005, Knopf $25.00 (0-679-43252-3). 401pp. A compelling behind-the-scenes look at America's criminal justice system, showing how everything from plea bargaining to the pressures on those who work within the system — including elected officials — has an impact on the outcomes of individual cases. (Rev: BL 3/1/05; SLJ 7/05) [345.773]

1937 Fireside, Bryna J. *The Trial of the Police Officers in the Shooting Death of Amadou Diallo: A Headline Court Case* (8–11). Illus. Series: Headline Court Cases. 2004, Enslow LB $19.95 (0-7660-2166-1). 128pp. Covers the trial of four New York City police officers for the 1999 shooting of West

African immigrant Amadou Diallo. (Rev: BL 2/1/05) [345.73]

1938 Fridell, Ron. *Capital Punishment* (8–12). Series: Open for Debate. 2003, Benchmark LB $25.95 (0-7614-1587-4). 144pp. Strong illustrations, graphs, and sidebars add to the narrative on the history of the death penalty, the arguments for and against, and ways to make the system more just and humane. (Rev: SLJ 3/04) [346.66]

1939 Gershman, Gary P. *Death Penalty on Trial: A Handbook with Cases, Laws, and Documents* (10–12). Series: On Trial. 2005, ABC-CLIO $55.00 (1-85109-606-X). 265pp. A balanced and thorough review of the history and current status of the controversial death penalty, with excerpts from key decisions, a glossary, a table of cases, and further reading. (Rev: SLJ 12/05)

1940 Gold, Susan Dudley. *Brown v. Board of Education: Separate But Equal?* (7–12). Series: Supreme Court Milestones. 2004, Benchmark LB $25.95 (0-7614-1842-3). 143pp. An overview of the groundbreaking decision, with information on the key individuals involved and on the legal process itself plus human-interest stories that add depth. (Rev: SLJ 1/05) [344.73]

1941 Gold, Susan Dudley. *The Pentagon Papers: National Security or the Right to Know* (7–12). Series: Supreme Court Milestones. 2004, Benchmark LB $25.95 (0-7614-1843-1). 144pp. An easily understood account of the events surrounding the Pentagon Papers case and the high court's decision that blocked the Nixon administration's efforts to keep the papers secret. (Rev: SLJ 1/05) [342.73]

1942 Hilldorfer, Joseph, and Robert Dugoni. *The Cyanide Canary* (11–12). 2004, Free Press $26.00 (0-7432-4652-7). 352pp. Environmental and judicial issues arise in this case in which a fertilizer plant worker was left severely brain damaged after being ordered to clean out a tank containing cyanide. (Rev: BL 8/04) [364.1]

1943 Junkin, Tim. *Bloodsworth: The True Story of the First Death Row Inmate Exonerated by DNA* (11–12). 2004, Algonquin $24.95 (1-56512-419-7). 304pp. This gripping real-life science thriller documents how DNA was used to exonerate Maryland death row inmate Kirk Bloodsworth, who was wrongly convicted of killing a 9-year-old girl. (Rev: BL 6/1–15/04) [364.6]

1944 Koopmans, Andy. *Leopold and Loeb: Teen Killers* (7–12). Series: Famous Trials. 2004, Gale LB $21.96 (1-59018-227-8). 112pp. The story of the famous trial of two privileged boys for the murder of a third, with details of Clarence Darrow's innovative defense strategy. (Rev: SLJ 6/04) [345.73]

1945 Kowalski, Kathiann M. *Lemon v. Kurtzman and the Separation of Church and State Debate*

(8–12). Series: Debating Supreme Court Decisions. 2005, Enslow LB $26.60 (0-7660-2391-5). 128pp. This well-documented title examines the Supreme Court's decision in Lemon v. Kurtzman and reviews its impact on the doctrine of separation of church and state. (Rev: SLJ 12/05)

1946 Kurtis, Bill. *The Death Penalty on Trial: Crisis in American Justice* (9–12). 2004, PublicAffairs $25.00 (1-58648-169-X). 192pp. Kurtis looks at the continuing debate over capital punishment and includes two case studies that illustrate many judicial system problems. (Rev: BL 9/15/04) [364.66]

1947 Telgen, Diane. *Brown v. Board of Education* (8–12). Series: Defining Moments. 2005, Omnigraphics LB $38.00 (0-7808-0775-8). 246pp. An accessible examination of the landmark Supreme Court decision on school segregation, including many interesting sidebar features and chronicling events before and after the ruling, up to the present day. (Rev: SLJ 12/05*)

1948 Torr, James D. *The Patriot Act* (7–12). Series: The Lucent Terrorism Library. 2005, Gale LB $28.70 (1-59018-774-1). 96pp. Torr explores the provisions of this controversial piece of legislation and looks at the ongoing criticisms about its threats to privacy and the Fourth Amendment. (Rev: SLJ 3/06) [345.73]

1949 Wecht, Cyril H., ed. *Crime Scene Investigation: Crack the Case with Real-Life Experts* (8–12). Illus. 2004, Reader's Digest $26.95 (0-7621-0540-2). 192pp. Fans of television's popular *CSI* series will be fascinated by this step-by-step examination of the crime scene investigation process. (Rev: SLJ 4/05)

1950 Weiner, Mark S. *Black Trials: Citizenship from the Beginnings of Slavery to the End of Caste* (9–12). 2004, Knopf $26.95 (0-375-40981-5). 448pp. Traces the evolution of race relations in America through an examination of 14 court cases that shaped the legal standing of African American citizens. (Rev: BL 10/1/04) [342.7308]

Politics

GENERAL AND MISCELLANEOUS

1951 Dreher, Rod. *Crunchy Cons: How Birkenstocked Burkeans, Gun-Loving Organic Gardeners, Evangelical Free-Range Farmers, Hip Homeschooling Mamas, Right-Wing Nature Lovers, and Their Diverse Tribe of Countercultural Conservatives Plan to Save America (or at Least the Republican Party)* (10–12). 2006, Crown Forum $24.00 (1-4000-5064-2). 256pp. Dreher introduces readers to the world of "crunchy cons," conservatives who rebel at the mainstream movement's lack of dedication to protecting our natural resources and living healthy. (Rev: BL 2/1/06) [320.52]

ELECTIONS

1952 Henderson, Harry. *Campaign and Election Reform* (9–12). Series: Library in a Book. 2004, Facts on File $45.00 (0-8160-5136-4). 316pp. From the financing of campaigns to the mechanics of elections, this informative volume examines precedents, existing and potential legal limitations, and the role of interest groups. (Rev: SLJ 6/04) [324.6]

1953 Marzilli, Alan. *Election Reform* (7–10). Series: Point/Counterpoint. 2003, Chelsea House LB $25.95 (0-7910-7698-9). 123pp. The thorny topics of voter registration, campaign contributions, and political advertising are discussed after an account of the November 2000 Florida recount. (Rev: SLJ 6/04) [324.6]

The Armed Forces

1954 Haley, James, ed. *Women in the Military* (9–12). Series: At Issue. 2005, Gale LB $27.45 (0-7377-2298-3); paper $18.70 (0-7377-2299-1). 94pp. Presents differing views about whether women should be involved in combat. (Rev: SLJ 1/05) [355]

1955 Haney, Eric L. *Inside Delta Force: The Story of America's Elite Counterterrorist Unit* (7–10). 2006, Delacorte LB $17.99 (0-385-90273-5). 192pp. Haney, one of the founding members of Delta Force, offers a fascinating look inside the U.S.

Army's elite counterterrorist unit. (Rev: BL 2/1/06; SLJ 3/06) [356]

1956 Henderson, Kristin. *While They're at War: The True Story of American Families on the Homefront* (10–12). 2006, Houghton $23.00 (0-618-55875-6). 336pp. The wife of a U.S. Navy chaplain looks at the lives of families of men and women serving in Afghanistan and Iraq. (Rev: BL 11/1/05) [956.7044]

1957 *Voices of War: Stories of Service from the Home Front and the Front Lines* (9–12). Illus. 2004, National Geographic $30.00 (0-7922-7838-0). 336pp. A close-up look at the horrors of war is provided by this collection of first-person accounts by 60 Americans — men and women, some very young — who served in the major conflicts of the 20th century; a product of the Veterans History Project. (Rev: BL 11/1/04) [355]

1958 Wiener, Tom. *Forever a Soldier: Unforgettable Stories of Wartime Service* (9–12). Illus. 2005, National Geographic $26.00 (0-7922-4189-4). 352pp. Drawn from the Library of Congress's vast Veterans History Project, this collection of firsthand accounts vividly conveys life on the front lines. (Rev: BL 11/1/05) [355]

1959 Williams, Kayla. *Love My Rifle More Than You: Young and Female in the U.S. Army* (11–12). Illus. 2005, Norton $24.95 (0-393-06098-5). 288pp. In this assertive, no-holds-barred memoir, Williams writes about what life was like for a female serving in the male-dominated military in Iraq; for mature teens. (Rev: BL 8/05) [355]

Citizenship and Civil Rights

General and Miscellaneous

1960 Carroll, Jamuna, ed. *Students Rights* (9–12). Series: Opposing Viewpoints. 2005, Gale LB $34.95 (0-7377-3088-9); paper $23.70 (0-7377-3089-7). 207pp. Essays explore both sides of the continuing debate over student rights regarding such issues as privacy, religion, dress codes, health, a high-quality education, and so forth. (Rev: SLJ 12/05)

1961 Ellis, Richard J. *To the Flag: The Unlikely History of the Pledge of Allegiance* (7–12). Illus. 2005, Univ. Press of Kansas $29.95 (0-7006-1372-2). 312pp. Traces the history of the Pledge of Allegiance and the flap over two words — "under God" — that were inserted into the pledge nearly 60 years after it was written. (Rev: BL 3/1/05) [323.6]

Civil and Human Rights

1962 Ball, Howard. *The U.S.A. Patriot Act of 2001: Balancing Civil Liberties and National Security: A Reference Handbook* (10–12). Series: Contemporary World Issues. 2004, ABC-CLIO $55.00 (1-85109-722-8). 265pp. An evenhanded overview of the controversy surrounding the U.S.A. Patriot Act and its curtailment of certain civil liberties in the interest of increasing national security. (Rev: SLJ 2/05)

1963 Bausum, Ann. *With Courage and Cloth: Winning the Fight for a Woman's Right to Vote* (6–12). 2004, National Geographic $32.90 (0-7922-6996-9). 112pp. A lively, well-illustrated text chronicles the history of the women's suffrage movement in America, focusing in particular on the period between 1913 and 1920 when the more militant National Women's Party, led by Alice Paul, stepped up pressure for women's right to vote. (Rev: BCCB 1/05; BL 10/15/04; SLJ 9/04) [324.6]

1964 Boyd, Herb. *We Shall Overcome: A Living History of the Civil Rights Struggle Told in Words, Pictures and the Voices of the Participants* (9–12). 2004, Sourcebooks $45.00 (1-4022-0213-X). 320pp. Covering the civil rights movement from the murder of Emmett Till in 1955 to Martin Luther King Jr.'s assassination in 1968, this volume highlights key events and individuals, using archival photographs, journalistic narrative, and the speeches and recollections included on the accompanying CDs. (Rev: BL 11/1/04; SLJ 12/04) [323.1196]

1965 Cleaver, Eldridge. *Target Zero: A Life in Writing* (11–12). Ed. by Kathleen Cleaver. Illus. 2006, Palgrave Macmillan $27.95 (1-4039-6237-5). 352pp. This collection of his writings chronicles Cleaver's transformation from black militant to born-again Christian and champion of the American capitalist system. (Rev: BL 12/15/05) [323]

1966 Etzioni, Amitai. *How Patriotic Is the Patriot Act? Freedom Versus Security in the Age of Terrorism* (9–12). 2004, Routledge $25.00 (0-415-95047-3). 224pp. How will the United States balance security concerns and the protection of individual rights? Etzoni tackles practical issues such as ID cards and threats to public health. (Rev: BL 11/15/04) [345.73]

1967 Frost-Knappman, Elizabeth, and Kathryn Cullen-DuPont. *Women's Suffrage in America: An Eyewitness History*. Rev. ed. (9–12). Illus. Series: Eyewitness History. 2005, Facts on File $75.00 (0-8160-5693-5). 496pp. This revised edition adds new images, maps, and letters to the many primary sources that offer insights into the women's suffrage movement. (Rev: SLJ 10/05) [324.6]

1968 Gay, Kathlyn. *Cultural Diversity: Conflicts and Challenges: The Ultimate Teen Guide* (7–12). Series: It Happened to Me. 2003, Scarecrow paper $25.95 (0-8108-4805-8). 121pp. Prejudice, stereotypes, and intolerance are among the topics discussed in this overview of the challenges faced and the possible solutions; teens' personal stories add immediacy. (Rev: SLJ 5/04; VOYA 4/04) [305.8]

1969 Hill, Jeff. *Women's Suffrage* (9–12). Series: Defining Moments. 2005, Omnigraphics $43.00 (0-7808-0776-6). 207pp. Covers the history of the movement, with profiles of key figures, excerpts from documents, and a discussion of the impact of passage of the 19th Amendment. (Rev: SLJ 3/06) [305.42]

1970 Hudson, David L., Jr. *Gay Rights* (8–12). Series: Point/Counterpoint. 2004, Chelsea House LB $25.95 (0-7910-8094-3). 114pp. Both sides of the heated debate over gay rights are addressed, including the peripheral issues of military service, rights in the workplace, gay marriage, and adoption rights. (Rev: SLJ 4/05) [305.9]

1971 Joshi, S. T. *In Her Place: A Documentary History of Prejudice Against Women* (9–12). 2006, Prometheus $28.00 (1-59102-380-7). 450pp. Joshi presents primary-source documentation of the antifeminist propaganda that was widely disseminated for generations. (Rev: BL 2/15/06) [305.42]

1972 McKissack, Patricia C., and Arlene Zarembka. *To Establish Justice: Citizenship and the Constitution* (6–10). Illus. 2004, Knopf LB $20.99 (0-679-99308-8). 160pp. Legal decisions regarding the civil rights of various minority groups — Native Americans, slaves, immigrants, women, students, gays and lesbians — are reviewed in light of the mainstream thinking of the time. (Rev: BL 10/15/04; SLJ 10/04; VOYA 10/04) [342.7]

1973 Mayer, Robert H. *The Civil Rights Act of 1964* (6–12). Series: At Issue in History. 2004, Gale LB $22.96 (0-7377-2304-1); paper $15.96 (0-7377-2305-X). 128pp. The landmark act is described in an introductory overview followed by a collection of essays, speeches, and editorials that provide diverse views about the legislation and its impact on race relations in the United States. (Rev: BL 9/1/04; SLJ 9/04) [342.73]

1974 Morrison, Toni. *Remember: The Journey to School Integration* (5–12). Illus. 2004, Houghton $18.00 (0-618-39740-X). 80pp. With striking archival photographs and a fictionalized narrative based on historical fact, this fascinating book explores the impact of the American struggle for civil rights on the children who were often at its center. (Rev: BL 4/15/04; SLJ 6/04) [379.2]

1975 Nakaya, Andrea C., ed. *Censorship* (7–12). Series: Opposing Viewpoints. 2005, Gale LB $34.95 (0-7377-2925-2); paper $23.70 (0-7377-

2926-0). 192pp. This new edition adds thoughtful essays on censorship and free speech as they relate to the press, telemarketing, electronic filtering, spam, and other issues. (Rev: SLJ 9/05) [363.3]

1976 Nakaya, Andrea C., ed. *Civil Liberties and War* (8–11). Illus. Series: Examining Issues Through Political Cartoons. 2005, Gale LB $21.96 (0-7377-2517-6). 78pp. A current hot-button issue — the suspension of civil liberties during wartime — is put into historical perspective in this volume with cartoons dating from the wars as far back as the Civil War. (Rev: BL 2/1/06) [323]

1977 Ojeda, Auriana, ed. *Civil Liberties* (9–12). Series: Opposing Viewpoints. 2004, Gale LB $33.70 (0-7377-1675-4); paper $22.45 (0-7377-1676-2). 204pp. Various perspectives on the curtailment of civil liberties are offered in this volume that explores issues including flag burning, ethnic profiling, public surveillance cameras, and child pornography. (Rev: SLJ 8/04; VOYA 4/05) [323.4]

1978 Steffens, Bradley. *The Free Speech Movement* (9–12). Series: American Social Movements. 2004, Gale LB $33.70 (0-7377-1156-6). 223pp. A good source of balanced opinions on various aspects of free speech and its impact on American life, including Internet filtering. (Rev: SLJ 2/05) [323.44]

1979 Yoshino, Kenji. *Covering: The Hidden Assault on Our Civil Rights* (11–12). 2006, Random $24.95 (0-375-50820-1). 304pp. Yale law professor Yoshino, who is gay, examines America's continuing reluctance to grant gay Americans equal status under the law. (Rev: BL 1/1–15/06) [342.7308]

Immigration

1980 Allport, Alan. *Immigration Policy* (9–12). Illus. Series: Point/Counterpoint. 2005, Chelsea House LB $26.95 (0-7910-7923-6). 126pp. An evenhanded review of hot-button immigration issues, including the challenges posed by widespread illegal immigration and whether the United States should adopt English as its official language. (Rev: BL 8/05; SLJ 9/05) [325.73]

1981 Aykroyd, Clarissa. *Refugees* (8–12). Series: The Changing Face of North America: Immigration Since 1965. 2004, Mason Crest LB $24.95 (1-59084-692-3). 112pp. An overview of the origins of refugees to the United States and Canada, the reasons for their flight from their home countries, and the process they must undergo on arrival. (Rev: SLJ 11/04)

1982 Gerdes, Louise L., ed. *Immigration* (10–12). Series: Current Controversies. 2005, Greenhaven $27.96 (0-7377-2779-9); paper $18.96 (0-7377-2780-2). 224pp. More than 30 essays cover such topics as illegal immigration, the treatment of immigrants, and the extent of the problem. (Rev: BL 8/05) [325.73]

1983 Outman, James L., and Lawrence W. Baker. *U.S. Immigration and Migration Primary Sources* (7–10). Series: Immigration and Migration Reference Library. 2004, Gale $60.00 (0-7876-7669-1). 232pp. Primary source documents — including articles, letters, and Supreme Court rulings — chronicle the history of immigration to and migration within America. (Rev: SLJ 2/05) [304.8]

1984 Sherman, Augustus F. *Augustus F. Sherman: Ellis Island Portraits, 1905–1920* (8–12). Illus. 2005, Aperture $40.00 (1-931788-60-X). 160pp. Moving photographs taken by an Ellis Island immigration clerk spotlight would-be immigrants — many of them young people — who were held for further interrogation. (Rev: BL 5/15/05) [779.9]

1985 Staeger, Rob. *Asylees* (8–12). Series: The Changing Face of North America: Immigration Since 1965. 2004, Mason Crest LB $24.95 (1-59084-685-0). 112pp. An overview of asylum seekers in the United States and Canada and the process they must undergo on arrival. Also use *Deported Aliens* (2004). (Rev: SLJ 11/04)

1986 Wills, Chuck. *Destination America: The People and Cultures That Created a Nation* (7–12). Illus. 2005, DK $35.00 (0-7566-1344-2). 284pp. A companion to the PBS series of the same name, this volume examines the waves of immigration that helped to shape the United States into the country it is today. (Rev: BL 12/1/05) [973]

Ethnic Groups and Prejudice

General and Miscellaneous

1987 Fountas, Angela Jane, ed. *Waking Up American: Coming of Age Biculturally; First-Generation Women Reflect on Identity* (9–12). 2005, Seal paper $15.95 (1-58005-136-7). 256pp. Young American women of bicultural heritage write candidly about what life is like for those caught between two different worlds. (Rev: BL 9/15/05) [305.48]

1988 Torr, James D., ed. *Race Relations* (10–12). Series: Opposing Viewpoints. 2005, Gale LB $34.95 (0-7377-2955-4); paper $23.70 (0-7377-2956-2). 208pp. Essays present both sides of diverse issues including interracial marriage, affirmative action, and reparations for slavery. (Rev: SLJ 11/05) [305.8]

African Americans

1989 Horton, James Oliver. *Landmarks of African American History* (8–12). Series: American Land-

marks. 2005, Oxford LB $30.00 (0-19-514118-0). 207pp. A tour of 13 historic sites that played a significant role in African American history, with good illustrations and maps. (Rev: SLJ 8/05) [973]

1990 Horton, James Oliver, and Lois E. Horton. *Slavery and the Making of America* (9–12). Illus. 2004, Oxford $35.00 (0-19-517903-X). 255pp. Chronicles the history of slavery in America and explores how the legacy of slavery has helped to shape the United States as we know it today, using the stories of well-known and unknown individuals. (Rev: BL 10/1/04; SLJ 2/05) [973]

1991 McWhorter, John. *Winning the Race: Beyond the Crisis in Black America* (11–12). 2006, Gotham $27.50 (1-592-40188-0). 432pp. McWhorter, author of *Losing the Race* (2000), says that African Americans must abandon their mindset of "therapeutic alienation" if they are to improve their prospects for the future. (Rev: BL 1/1–15/06) [305.896]

1992 Mosley, Walter. *Life Out of Context* (10–12). 2006, Thunder's Mouth $12.95 (1-56025-846-2). 112pp. Mosley calls on young African Americans to take responsibility for their destinies and those of other people of color around the globe. (Rev: BL 12/15/05) [305.8]

1993 Norrell, Robert J. *The House I Live In: Race in the American Century* (9–12). Illus. 2005, Oxford $30.00 (0-19-507345-2). 368pp. Historian Robert J. Norrell offers a scholarly survey of American race relations across the last 150 years. (Rev: BL 2/1/05) [305.8]

1994 Sharp, Anne Wallace. *A Dream Deferred: The Jim Crow Era* (7–10). Illus. Series: Lucent Library of Black History. 2005, Gale LB $22.96 (1-59018-700-8). 112pp. An overview of the impact of the Jim Crow laws that stretched from Reconstruction to the Supreme Court's decision in *Brown* v. *Board of Education* (1954). (Rev: BL 10/15/05) [323.1196]

1995 Summers, Barbara, ed. *Open the Unusual Door: True Life Stories of Challenge, Adventure, and Success by Black Americans* (8–11). 2005, Houghton paper $7.99 (0-618-58531-1). 224pp. Sixteen successful African Americans write about choices they made that changed the direction of their lives. (Rev: BL 1/1–15/06; SLJ 12/05) [920]

1996 Taylor, Yuval, ed. *Growing Up in Slavery: Stories of Young Slaves as Told by Themselves* (9–12). 2005, Lawrence Hill $22.95 (1-55652-548-6). 240pp. A searing portrait of slavery and its effects on the enslaved can be found in this collection of first-person accounts written by African Americans who spent the early part of their lives in bondage. (Rev: BL 2/1/05; SLJ 7/05) [306.3]

Asian Americans

1997 Martin, Jennifer C. *The Korean Americans* (10–12). Illus. Series: Immigrants in America. 2005, Gale LB $22.96 (1-59018-079-8). 112pp. Examines the pattern of Korean immigration to the United States, assimilation problems, and the contributions of notable Korean Americans. (Rev: BL 8/05) [973]

1998 Oppenheim, Joanne. *Dear Miss Breed: True Stories of the Japanese American Incarceration During World War II and a Librarian Who Made a Difference* (7–10). Illus. 2006, Scholastic $22.99 (0-439-56992-3). 288pp. An affecting portrait of a World War II children's librarian and the incarcerated young Japanese Americans who benefited from her commitment to her profession. (Rev: BL 1/1–15/06*; SLJ 3/06; VOYA 2/06) [940.53]

Hispanic Americans

1999 Acuna, Rodolfo F. *U.S. Latino Issues* (10–12). Series: Contemporary American Ethnic Issues. 2003, Greenwood $45.00 (0-313-32211-2). 213pp. Bilingual education, border politics, affirmative action, and services for undocumented immigrants are among the issues addressed here that affect the Latino population in the United States. (Rev: SLJ 6/04) [305.868]

2000 Tobar, Héctor. *Translation Nation: Defining a New American Identity in the Spanish Speaking United States* (8–12). 2005, Riverhead $24.95 (1-57322-305-0). 320pp. Tobar, a Pulitzer Prize-winning journalist, explores how the rapidly growing Spanish-speaking population is changing the face of America, presenting his own story (he was born in Los Angeles to Guatemalan immigrants) and the experiences and aspirations of many legal and illegal migrants. (Rev: BL 3/15/05) [305.868]

Other Ethnic Groups

2001 Schur, Joan Brodsky. *The Arabs* (8–11). Illus. Series: Coming to America. 2005, Gale LB $26.96 (0-7377-2148-0). 218pp. With profiles of several famous Arab Americans (including Ralph Nader and Naomi Shihab Nye), this title uses primary and secondary sources to present an overview of Arab Americans, their reasons for migrating, their social mores, and their adaptation to their new country. (Rev: BL 3/15/05; SLJ 3/05) [973]

2002 Verbrugge, Allen, ed. *Muslims in America* (9–12). Series: Contemporary Issues Companion. 2005, Gale LB $26.96 (0-7377-2315-7). A brief history of Muslims in America precedes essays presenting varying viewpoints on topics ranging from bias against Muslims following September 11 to issues facing Muslim women. (Rev: BL 8/05; SLJ 3/05) [305.6]

2003 Yaghmaian, Behzad. *Embracing the Infidel: Stories of Muslim Migrants on the Journey West* (10–12). Illus. 2005, Delacorte $24.00 (0-553-80393-X). 368pp. The stories of Muslim migrants to countries in the West are told in this compelling collection of first-person accounts excerpted from interviews conducted by the author. (Rev: BL 11/1/05) [305.6]

Forms of Dissent

2004 Katovsky, Bill. *Patriots Act: Voices of Dissent: An Oral History* (9–12). 2006, Lyons $22.95 (1-59228-816-2). 272pp. This collection of interviews with 20 Americans explores the relationship between patriotism and dissent, focusing particularly on how the latter has come to be viewed as disloyal and unpatriotic. (Rev: BL 2/15/06) [320.5]

178

Social Concerns and Problems

General and Miscellaneous

2005 Berger, Dan, et al., eds. *Letters from Young Activists: Today's Rebels Speak Out* (11–12). 2005, Thunder's Mouth paper $14.95 (1-56025-747-4). 288pp. This collection of essays by young activists addresses a wide array of social issues, including racism, immigration reform, homophobia, sexism, ecology, capital punishment, and peace. (Rev: BL 10/15/05) [322.4]

2006 Griffin, Starla. *Girl, 13: A Global Snapshot of Generation e* (6–12). 2005, Hylas paper $22.95 (1-59258-112-9). 239pp. Thirteen-year-olds around the world contributed to this volume, answering questions about their views of the world and writing essays about their lives and aspirations. (Rev: SLJ 2/06)

2007 Halpern, Jake. *Braving Home: Dispatches from the Underwater Town, the Lava-Side Inn, and Other Extreme Locales* (9–12). 2003, Houghton $23.00 (0-618-15548-1). 256pp. A look at people who choose to live in locations threatened by floods, hurricanes, volcanoes, and so forth. (Rev: SLJ 1/04) [973.9]

2008 Leland, John. *Hip: The History* (10–12). 2004, Ecco $26.95 (0-06-052817-6). 405pp. Prohibition, civil rights, and such individuals as Emerson and Thoreau all play a role in this study of hipness and how it emanates from sometimes unlikely subcultures. (Rev: BL 10/1/04; SLJ 3/05) [306]

2009 Schechter, Harold. *Savage Pastimes: A Cultural History of Violent Entertainment* (9–12). Illus. 2005, St. Martin's $24.95 (0-312-28276-1). 208pp. Schechter challenges the idea that today's popular entertainment is more violent than that of the past. (Rev: BL 2/1/05) [303.6]

2010 Shirk, Martha, and Gary Stangler. *On Their Own: What Happens to Kids When They Age out of the Foster Care System* (9–12). 2004, Westview $24.95 (0-8133-4180-9). 304pp. Explores the plight of young people who are forced out of the foster care system at the age of 18, whether they are ready to stand on their own or not. (Rev: BL 9/15/04) [362.73]

2011 Streissguth, Thomas. *Hate Crimes* (10–12). Series: Library in a Book. 2003, Facts on File $45.00 (0-8160-4879-7). 316pp. After describing hate crimes and their history, this volume presents easily understood information on legislation and court decisions plus short biographies of important individuals, a glossary, a research guide, and a list of relevant organizations. (Rev: SLJ 2/04) [364.15]

Environmental Issues

General and Miscellaneous

2012 Blatt, Harvey. *America's Environmental Report Card: Are We Making the Grade?* (8–12). Illus. 2004, MIT $27.95 (0-262-02572-8). 284pp. From global warming to water pollution, this volume looks at today's burning environmental issues and potential solutions. (Rev: BL 11/1/04) [363.7]

2013 Burdick, Alan. *Out of Eden: An Odyssey of Ecological Invasion* (10–12). 2005, Farrar $25.00 (0-374-21973-4); paper $14.00 (0-374-53043-2). 324pp. The disruption caused by animal and plant migrations to new environments — wild camels in Australia, snakes in Hawaii, for example — is the focus of this interesting exploration. (Rev: SLJ 1/06)

2014 Haley, James, ed. *Foreign Oil Dependence* (9–12). Series: At Issue. 2004, Gale LB $27.45 (0-

7377-2272-X); paper $18.70 (0-7377-2273-8). 93pp. Opposing perspectives are presented on topics including the state of the global oil supply, the dangers of dependence on Middle East oil, drilling in Alaska, and vehicle fuel economy standards. (Rev: SLJ 11/04) [333.8]

2015 Kovach, Robert, and Bill McGuire. *Firefly Guide to Global Hazards* (10–12). Illus. 2004, Firefly paper $14.95 (1-55297-815-X). 256pp. Covering various kinds of disaster — earthquakes, storms, disease, drought, avalanches, and so forth — this small, well-illustrated volume reviews the likelihood of incidents, the human contribution in terms of pollution, and the ways in which the impact can be mitigated. (Rev: SLJ 6/04; VOYA 6/04) [551]

2016 Reece, Erik. *Lost Mountain: A Year in the Vanishing Wilderness; Radical Strip Mining and the Devastation of Appalachia* (9–12). 2006, Riverhead $23.95 (1-59448-908-4). 240pp. An expose of the devastation of a portion of Appalachia by strip mining. (Rev: BL 2/1/06) [622]

2017 Weyler, Rex. *Greenpeace: How a Group of Journalists, Ecologists, and Visionaries Changed the World* (9–12). 2004, Rodale $24.95 (1-59486-106-4). 624pp. The fascinating story behind Greenpeace and its brand of highly active activism is told in rich detail by one of its founders. (Rev: BL 10/15/04) [333.72]

Pollution

2018 Cone, Maria. *Silent Snow: The Slow Poisoning of the Arctic* (9–12). 2005, Grove $24.00 (0-8021-1797-X). 240pp. The pollutants from the industrialized world that are harming the people and wildlife of the Arctic are detailed clearly here. (Rev: BL 4/15/05) [363.73]

2019 Wilson, Diane. *An Unreasonable Woman: A True Story of Shrimpers, Politicos, Polluters, and the Fight for Seadrift, Texas* (10–12). 2005, Chelsea Green $27.50 (1-931498-88-1). 400pp. Diane Wilson, a fourth-generation shrimper and mother of five, recounts her courageous battle to stop a giant plastics company from poisoning the coastal Texas county in which she lives. (Rev: BL 9/1/05) [639]

Waste Management

2020 Rogers, Heather. *Gone Tomorrow: The Hidden Life of Garbage* (9–12). 2005, New Press $23.95 (1-56584-879-9). 224pp. Sobering answers for all those who wonder what becomes of the vast quantities of household waste in America. (Rev: BL 10/15/05) [363.72]

2021 Royte, Elizabeth. *Garbage Land: On the Secret Trail of Trash* (9–12). 2005, Little, Brown $24.95 (0-316-73826-3). 304pp. Royte travels behind the scenes to find out what happens to the billions of tons of waste that Americans discard each year; her persistence elicits interesting facts and will be enlightening to students. (Rev: BL 6/1–15/05) [363.72]

Population Issues

General and Miscellaneous

2022 Atkin, S. Beth. *Gunstories: Life-Changing Experiences with Guns* (7–10). Illus. 2006, HarperCollins LB $17.89 (0-06-052660-2). 256pp. In first-person accounts, teenagers write about their very varied experiences with guns. (Rev: BL 1/1–15/06; SLJ 1/06) [363.33]

2023 Crooker, Constance Emerson. *Gun Control and Gun Rights* (9–12). Series: Historical Guides to Controversial Issues in America. 2003, Greenwood $50.00 (0-313-32174-4). 180pp. The arguments for and against gun control are clearly laid out, with statistics, quotations, notes, and a bibliography. (Rev: SLJ 2/04) [363.3]

2024 Currie, Elliott. *The Road to Whatever: Middle-Class Culture and the Crisis of Adolescence* (11–12). 2005, Holt $26.00 (0-8050-6763-9). 320pp. An examination of the growing malaise among white, middle-class adolescents in America; for mature teens. (Rev: BL 1/1–15/05) [305.235]

2025 Garbarino, James. *See Jane Hit: Why Girls Are Growing More Violent and What Can Be Done About It* (11–12). 2006, Penguin $25.95 (1-59420-075-0). 290pp. A thought-provoking study of the troubling increase in aggression on the part of American girls. (Rev: BL 12/1/05) [303.6]

2026 Gold, Susan Dudley. *Gun Control* (8–12). Series: Open for Debate. 2003, Benchmark LB $25.95 (0-7614-1584-X). 143pp. An evenhanded survey of the gun control controversy, discussing the Second Amendment, history of legislation, school shootings, and the activities of gun makers and dealers. (Rev: SLJ 3/04) [363.3]

2027 Haley, John, and Wendy Stein. *The Truth About Abuse* (9–12). Series: The Truth About. 2005, Facts on File $35.00 (0-8160-5297-2). 212pp. Explores various forms of abuse, including domestic violence, bullying, date rape, hazing, and child molestation, offering facts and figures and teens' own stories. (Rev: SLJ 9/05)

2028 Harrison, Kathy. *One Small Boat: The Story of a Little Girl, Lost Then Found* (10–12). 2006, Putnam $23.95 (I-58542-465-X). 224pp. The moving story of a foster child who suffered a severe speech impediment as well as eating disorders. (Rev: BL 3/15/06) [362.73]

2029 Kleinfield, Sonny. *His Oldest Friend: The Story of an Unlikely Bond* (9–12). 2005, Holt $24.00 (0-8050-7580-1). 288pp. The story of an unlikely friendship between a 93-year-old nursing home resident and a 20-year-old Hispanic volunteer. (Rev: BL 9/1/05) [305.26]

2030 Reef, Catherine. *Alone in the World: Orphans and Orphanages in America* (8–11). Illus. 2005, Clarion $18.00 (0-618-35670-3). 144pp. A history of orphanages in America from the early years of the 18th century through their decline in the early 1900s. (Rev: BL 4/1/05; SLJ 6/05; VOYA 10/05) [362.73]

Aging, Death, and Burial Practices

2031 Roach, Mary. *Spook: Science Tackles the Afterlife* (10–12). Illus. 2005, Norton $24.95 (0-393-05962-6). 310pp. With determination and humor, Roach investigates the possibility of an afterlife. (Rev: BL 9/1/05) [129]

Crime, Gangs, and Prisons

2032 Balkin, Karen F., ed. *Violence Against Women* (8–12). Series: Current Controversies. 2003, Gale LB $33.70 (0-7377-2041-7); paper $22.45 (0-7377-2042-5). 208pp. Contributors from many walks of life present differing viewpoints on the causes, nature, and extent of violence against women and what can be done to prevent it. (Rev: SLJ 6/04) [362.88]

2033 Barbour, Scott, ed. *Gangs* (8–12). Illus. Series: Introducing Issues with Opposing Viewpoints. 2005, Gale LB $32.45 (0-7377-3221-0). 128pp. Diverse opinions are presented on topics including the reasons why young people join gangs and measures that can be taken to reduce the violence. (Rev: SLJ 1/06) [364.1]

2034 Connelly, Michael. *Crime Beat: A Decade of Covering Cops and Killers* (11–12). 2006, Little, Brown $25.95 (0-316-15377-X). 288pp. Popular mystery novelist Connelly recounts 22 real-life crime stories that he covered during a decade as a crime reporter; for mature teens. (Rev: BL 4/1/06) [363.25]

2035 Delaney, Lucinda. *A Hunt for Justice: The True Story of a Woman Undercover Wildlife Agent* (9–12). 2006, Lyons $21.95 (1-59228-882-0). 288pp. A real-life thriller in which the author, a longtime agent with the U.S. Fish and Wildlife Service, undertakes an undercover mission to nab a big-time wildlife poacher in Alaska. (Rev: BL 2/15/06) [364.1]

2036 Dudley, William, and Louise L. Gerdes, eds. *Gangs* (8–12). Series: Opposing Viewpoints. 2005, Gale LB $34.95 (0-7377-2234-7); paper $23.70 (0-

7377-2235-5). 206pp. A look at the causes of gang behavior and what can be done to combat the alarming increase in violence. (Rev: SLJ 8/05) [364.1]

2037 Evans, Wanda, and James Dunn. *Trail of Blood: A Father, a Son and a Tell-Tale Crime Scene* (11–12). 2005, New Horizon $23.95 (0-88282-261-6). 320pp. This gripping whodunit blends the story of a father's six-year quest to find out what happened to his son with an overview of the forensic investigation that solved the case; for mature teens. (Rev: BL 3/1/05) [364]

2038 Ferro, Jeffrey. *Juvenile Crime* (10–12). Series: Library in a Book. 2003, Facts on File $45.00 (0-8160-5055-4). 316pp. After describing juvenile crime and its history, this volume presents easily understood information on legislation and court decisions plus short biographies of important individuals, a glossary, a research guide, and a list of relevant organizations. (Rev: SLJ 2/04) [364.36]

2039 Hubner, John. *Last Chance in Texas: The Redemption of Criminal Youth* (11–12). 2005, Random $25.95 (0-375-50809-0). 304pp. Hubner explores an innovative Texas program that is having success in turning juvenile offenders away from a life of crime; for mature teens. (Rev: BL 8/05; SLJ 2/06) [365]

2040 Innes, Brian. *Fakes and Forgeries: The True Crime Stories of History's Greatest Deceptions: The Criminals, the Scams, and the Victims* (9–12). 2005, Reader's Digest $26.95 (0-7621-0625-5). 256pp. Some of history's greatest deceptions — including a diary purported to have been written by Jack the Ripper and a young woman's claim that she is the long-missing Anastasia, daughter of Tsar Nicholas II — are described in accessible text with lots of illustrations, news clippings, biographical profiles, and so forth. (Rev: SLJ 12/05)

2041 Junger, Sebastian. *A Death in Belmont* (11–12). 2006, Norton $23.95 (0-393-05980-4). 288pp. A fascinating true crime story that also reveals early 1960s politics and race relations, centering on Junger's possible proximity (at the age of one) to the Boston Strangler on the day of a death in Belmont, Massachusetts; for mature teens. (Rev: BL 2/15/06) [364.152]

2042 Kleid, Neil, and Jake Allen. *Brownsville* (9–12). Illus. 2006, NBM $18.95 (1-56163-458-1). 208pp. This profile in graphic novel format of Allie Tannenbaum, a member of Murder Inc., offers an inside look at the world of organized crime and murder for hire. (Rev: BL 3/15/06; SLJ 7/06) [741.5]

2043 Mann, Robert, and Miryam Ehrlich Williamson. *Forensic Detective: How I Cracked the World's Toughest Cases* (11–12). 2006, Ballantine $24.95 (0-345-47941-6). 272pp. Forensic anthropologist Mann writes about some of the more puzzling cases of his career; for mature teens. (Rev: BL 3/15/06) [614]

2044 Nakaya, Andrea C., ed. *Juvenile Crime* (8–12). Series: Opposing Viewpoints. 2005, Gale LB $34.95 (0-7377-2945-7); paper $23.70 (0-7377-2946-5). 208pp. A collection of diverse opinions on the causes of juvenile crime and on ways to prevent it, to punish or treat offenders, and to improve the juvenile justice system. (Rev: SLJ 1/06) [364.9]

2045 Platt, Richard. *Forensics* (5–10). Illus. Series: Kingfisher Knowledge. 2005, Kingfisher paper $12.95 (0-7534-5862-4). 64pp. This introduction to the use of the forensic sciences in crime investigation is presented in short blocks of text that will make it appealing to reluctant readers. (Rev: SLJ 11/05) [363.2]

2046 Schroeder, Andreas. *Thieves!* (5–10). Series: True Stories from the Edge. 2005, Annick $18.95 (1-55037-933-X); paper $8.95 (1-55037-932-1). 164pp. Ten world-class crimes are described in compelling detail. (Rev: SLJ 3/06) [364]

2047 Simpson, Colton, and Ann Pearlman. *Inside the Crips: Life Inside L.A.'s Most Notorious Gang* (11–12). Illus. 2005, St. Martin's $24.95 (0-312-32929-6). 352pp. Simpson succeeded in extracting himself from the Crips gang, and here reveals what life is like for its members; for mature teens. (Rev: BL 8/05) [364.1]

2048 Torr, James D., ed. *Crime and Criminals* (9–12). Series: Opposing Viewpoints. 2004, Gale LB $33.70 (0-7377-2222-3); paper $22.45 (0-7377-2223-1). 208pp. Thought-provoking articles provide differing opinions on topics including gun control and racial profiling. (Rev: SLJ 11/04) [364.9]

2049 Yancey, Diane. *Murder* (7–10). Illus. Series: Inside the Crime Lab. 2006, Gale LB $24.96 (1-59018-619-2). 112pp. Readers learn how clues found at a murder scene are analyzed and interpreted to reconstruct what happened; there are references to famous cases, and sidebar features and photographs add interest. (Rev: BL 4/1/06) [363.25]

Poverty, Homelessness, and Hunger

2050 Erlbaum, Janice. *Girlbomb: A Halfway Homeless Memoir* (9–12). 2006, Villard $21.95 (1-4000-6422-8). 272pp. In this gritty memoir, Janice Erlbaum writes of her experiences as a teenager navigating the treacherous waters of the social welfare system. (Rev: BL 1/1–15/06) [362.74]

2051 Haugen, David M., and Matthew J. Box, eds. *Poverty* (8–11). Series: Social Issues Firsthand. 2005, Gale LB $22.96 (0-7377-2899-X). 108pp. Wide-ranging essays present the plight of those living in poverty as well as the thoughts of those who are determined to do something about the problem. (Rev: BL 10/15/05) [362.5]

2052 Murray, Charles. *In Our Hands: A Plan to Replace the Welfare State* (10–12). 2006, AEI $20.00 (0-8447-4223-6). 240pp. A fascinating proposal for replacing the American system of welfare. (Rev: BL 2/15/06) [361.6]

2053 Russell, Sharman Apt. *Hunger: An Unnatural History* (10–12). 2005, Basic Bks. $23.95 (0-465-07163-5). 288pp. Explores the physiological and psychological effects of hunger and documents famines and starvation that took place in the 20th century as well as looking at everyday hunger; for mature readers. (Rev: BL 9/1/05; SLJ 2/06) [363.8]

2054 Yankoski, Mike. *Under the Overpass: A Journey of Faith on the Streets of America* (10–12). 2005, Multnomah paper $11.99 (1-59052-402-0). 224pp. Mike Yankoski, who took a break from college to immerse himself in the world of the homeless, writes movingly about his experiences and the testing of his faith. (Rev: SLJ 7/05) [362.7]

Sex Roles

2055 Levy, Ariel. *Female Chauvinist Pigs: Women and the Rise of Raunch Culture* (11–12). 2005, Free Press $25.00 (0-7432-4989-5). 224pp. The author casts a jaundiced eye on the rising popularity of so-called raunch culture among young women; for mature teens. (Rev: BL 8/05) [305.42]

Social Action, Social Change, and Futurism

2056 Friedman, Thomas L. *The World Is Flat: A Brief History of the Twenty-First Century* (10–12). 2005, Farrar $27.50 (0-374-29288-4). 488pp. Foreign affairs expert Friedman argues persuasively that the dominant trend of the early 21st century is globalization and that the computer is the driving factor. (Rev: SLJ 11/05)

2057 Gay, Kathlyn. *Volunteering: The Ultimate Teen Guide* (8–12). Series: It Happened to Me. 2004, Scarecrow $32.50 (0-8108-4922-4). 127pp. This guide examines a wide range of volunteering opportunities for teenagers, from working with the elderly or the homeless to tutoring to building houses; real-life stories add interest. (Rev: SLJ 4/05; VOYA 4/05) [361.8]

2058 Goldman, Paula, ed. *Imagining Ourselves: Global Voices from a New Generation of Women* (9–12). Illus. 2006, New World Library paper $26.95 (1-57731-524-3). 240pp. Women from diverse walks of life around the world discuss their lives and how they differ from those of their mothers. (Rev: BL 2/15/06) [305.242]

2059 Halpin, Mikki. *It's Your World — If You Don't Like It, Change It: Activism for Teenagers* (7–12). 2004, Simon & Schuster paper $8.99 (0-689-87448-0). 304pp. Covering activism on a wide range of topics — the environment, war, gay rights, women's rights, and so forth — this is a useful guide, providing practical ideas and sensible cautions. (Rev: BL 12/15/04; SLJ 12/04) [305.23]

2060 Karnes, Frances A., and Kristen R. Stephens. *Empowered Girls: A Girl's Guide to Positive Activism, Volunteering, and Philanthropy* (6–12). 2005, Prufrock paper $14.95 (1-59363-163-4). 191pp. A helpful, information-packed guide that will motivate young people to volunteer. (Rev: SLJ 2/06; VOYA 4/06) [361.8]

2061 Marcovitz, Hal. *Teens and Volunteerism* (7–10). Series: The Gallup Youth Survey, Major Issues and Trends. 2005, Mason Crest LB $22.95 (1-59084-877-2). 112pp. An attractive volume documenting Gallup findings on teens' attitudes toward various forms of volunteerism including community service, military service, and activism. (Rev: SLJ 1/06) [361.8]

Social Customs and Holidays

2062 Bamberger, Michael. *Wonderland: A Year in the Life of an American High School* (9–12). 2004, Grove $24.00 (0-87113-917-0). 224pp. A year in the life of students at Pennsbury High School, a suburban Philadelphia school most notable for turning its annual prom into a genuine extravaganza. (Rev: BL 6/1–15/04) [305.235]

Terrorism

2063 Balkin, Karen F., ed. *The War on Terrorism* (7–12). Illus. Series: Opposing Viewpoints. 2004, Gale LB $33.70 (0-7377-2336-X); paper $22.45 (0-7377-2337-8). 206pp. The 28 essays in this collection present both sides of the ongoing debate over the Bush administration's measures to combat terrorism. (Rev: SLJ 3/05) [973.9]

2064 Brzezinski, Matthew. *Fortress America: On the Front Lines of Homeland Security — An Inside Look at the Coming Surveillance State* (10–12). 2004, Bantam $25.00 (0-553-80366-2). 256pp. An unsettling, candid assessment of America's homeland security in the wake of 9/11. (Rev: BL 8/04) [363.3]

2065 Dwyer, Jim, and Kevin Flynn. *102 Minutes: The Untold Story of the Fight to Survive Inside the Twin Towers* (9–12). 2005, Times Bks. $26.00 (0-8050-7682-4). 322pp. An unflinching account of the struggle for life within the twin towers of the World Trade Center in the 102 minutes between the impact of the first plane and the collapse of the second tower. (Rev: BL 11/15/04; SLJ 4/05) [974.7]

2066 Egendorf, Laura K., ed. *Terrorism* (10–12). Series: Opposing Viewpoints. 2004, Gale LB $33.70 (0-7377-2246-0); paper $22.45 (0-7377-2247-9). 204pp. A thought-provoking collection of essays that look at the many faces of terrorism and offer diverse views on what can be done to respond to this threat. (Rev: SLJ 2/05)

2067 Friedman, Lauri S., ed. *What Motivates Suicide Bombers?* (9–12). Series: At Issue. 2005, Gale LB $28.70 (0-7377-2320-3); paper $19.95 (0-7377-2321-1). 93pp. This collection of essays looks into the multiplicity of factors that motivate suicide bombers. (Rev: SLJ 4/05) [363.3]

2068 Houle, Michelle E., ed. *Terrorism* (9–12). Series: History of Issues. 2005, Gale LB $26.96 (0-7377-1909-5); paper $17.96 (0-7377-1910-9). 170pp. Various forms of terrorism are presented through primary documents and essays that offer historical and cultural context. (Rev: BL 4/1/05) [303.6]

2069 Katz, Samuel M. *Against All Odds: Counterterrorist Hostage Rescues* (6–12). Series: Terrorist Dossiers. 2004, Lerner LB $26.60 (0-8225-1567-9). 72pp. The notable hostage rescues by antiterrorist groups around the world covered here go back to the early 19th century. (Rev: SLJ 4/05; VOYA 6/05) [364.15]

2070 Katz, Samuel M. *Global Counterstrike: International Counterterrorism* (9–12). Series: Terrorist Dossiers. 2004, Lerner LB $26.60 (0-8225-1566-0). 72pp. Discusses various countries' strategies to protect their citizens and infrastructures from terrorist attacks. Also use *U.S. Counterstrike: American Counterterrorism* (2004). (Rev: SLJ 1/05) [364.1]

2071 Quin, Mary. *Kidnapped in Yemen: One Woman's Amazing Escape from Captivity* (11–12). 2005, Lyons $23.95 (1-59228-728-X). 258pp. In this gripping story of survival, former Xerox executive Mary Quin relives her 1998 kidnapping — along with other tourists — by terrorists in Yemen and her decision to quit her job and find out more about her kidnappers; for mature teens. (Rev: BL 5/15/05) [364.15]

2072 Ruschmann, Paul. *The War on Terror* (7–10). Series: Point/Counterpoint. 2005, Chelsea House LB $26.95 (0-7910-8091-9). 134pp. Offers opposing views on terrorism-related topics, including preemptive wars, the suspension of human rights, and anti-terror laws. (Rev: SLJ 9/05)

2073 Shostak, Arthur B., ed. *Defeating Terrorism: Developing Dreams* (9–12). Series: Defeating Terrorism/Developing Dreams. 2004, Chelsea House LB $22.95 (0-7910-7955-4). 185pp. Thought-provoking essays on the global situation post 9/11 examine the profound cultural divide between America and the Islamic world, as well as the role of media in reporting this clash of cultures. (Rev: BL 6/1–15/04) [956.7]

2074 Shostak, Arthur B., ed. *Trade Towers/War Clouds* (9–12). Illus. Series: Defeating Terrorism/Developing Dreams. 2004, Chelsea House LB $22.95 (0-7910-7956-2). 128pp. A look at the impact of the September 11 attacks — and of the subsequent invasion of Iraq — on American society. (Rev: BL 6/1–15/04; SLJ 11/04) [956.7]

2075 Woolf, Alex. *Terrorism: The Impact on Our Lives* (6–10). Series: 21st Century Debates. 2003, Raintree LB $28.56 (0-7398-6034-8). 64pp. From the terror of the French Revolution (when the word first appeared) to the activities of the IRA, Hamas, the PLO, the Tamil Tigers, Basque separatists (ETA), and al Qaeda, this is an overview of terrorism and how it affects us. (Rev: SLJ 6/04)

Economics and Business

General and Miscellaneous

2076 Frisch, Aaron. *The Story of Nike* (6–10). Series: Built for Success. 2003, Smart Apple Media LB $19.95 (1-58340-295-0). 48pp. Traces Nike's development from a small importer to a major internationally recognized brand, with details of successes and setbacks, celebrity endorsements, and advertising campaigns. (Rev: SLJ 7/04) [338.7]

2077 Richardson, Adele. *The Story of Disney* (6–10). Series: Built for Success. 2003, Smart Apple Media LB $19.95 (1-58340-291-8). 48pp. Traces Disney's development into the major internationally recognized brand it is today, with a biography of Walt Disney, a timeline of important events, discussion of Disney's influence on our lives, and mention of criticism of Disney's liberties with history. (Rev: SLJ 7/04) [384.8]

2078 Schiffman, Stephan. *The Young Entrepreneur's Guide to Business Terms* (7–12). Illus. 2003, Scholastic LB $38.00 (0-531-14665-0). 128pp. A useful, alphabetically arranged guide to business terms and concepts, with feature sidebars. (Rev: BL 1/1–15/04; SLJ 7/04) [650]

Labor Unions and Labor Problems

2079 Laughlin, Rosemary. *The Ludlow Massacre of 1913–1914* (9–12). Illus. Series: American Workers. 2006, Morgan Reynolds LB $26.95 (1-931798-86-9). 144pp. The story of the bitter coal mining strike that culminated in a deadly National Guard attack on a tent city erected by striking workers and their families in Ludlow, Colorado. (Rev: BL 4/1/06) [331.892]

Money and Trade

2080 January, Brendan. *Globalize It!* (8–12). Illus. 2003, Millbrook LB $26.90 (0-7613-2417-8). 144pp. The continuing advance of globalization and arguments for and against this phenomenon are thoughtfully examined in this accessible overview. (Rev: BL 1/1–15/04; SLJ 5/04) [337]

Marketing and Advertising

2081 Reichblum, Charles. *Dr. Knowledge Presents: Strange and Fascinating Facts About Famous Brands* (9–12). 2004, Black Dog & Leventhal paper $9.95 (1-57912-356-2). 304pp. Little-known stories behind some of the food industry's biggest brand names, including Wendy's, Betty Crocker, Spam, Heinz, and Uncle Ben; suitable for browsing but less useful for research. (Rev: SLJ 3/05)

Guidance and Personal Development

Education and Schools

General and Miscellaneous

2082 Bluestein, Jane, and Eric D. Katz. *High School's Not Forever* (8–12). Illus. 2005, Health Communications paper $12.95 (0-7573-0256-4). 302pp. High school students talk about their experiences in high school, covering a range of typical problems plus some of the joys of those years. (Rev: SLJ 1/06) [373.18]

2083 Brown, Oral Lee, and Caille Millner. *The Promise: How One Woman Made Good on Her Extraordinary Pact to Send a Classroom of First Graders to College* (9–12). 2005, Doubleday $22.95 (0-385-51147-7). 288pp. The inspiring story of Oral Lee Brown's adoption of a first-grade class and her success in sending most of them to college. (Rev: BL 2/1/05) [370]

2084 Jacobs, Joanne. *Our School: The Inspiring Story of Two Teachers, One Big Idea, and the School That Beat the Odds* (11–12). 2005, Palgrave Macmillan $24.95 (1-4039-7023-8). 256pp. The remarkable success story of Downtown College Prep, a San Jose (CA) charter school that has transformed the lives of its mostly Hispanic American student body. (Rev: BL 12/1/05) [371.01]

2085 Llewellyn, Grace, ed. *Real Lives: Eleven Teenagers Who Don't Go to School Tell Their Own Stories*. 2nd ed. (9–12). 2005, Lowry paper $18.00 (0-9629591-2-X). 320pp. In the first edition of this book, 11 teens explained why they and their families opted for homeschooling; this revision adds interesting details about what these individuals are doing today. (Rev: SLJ 11/05) [370]

2086 Medina, Loreta, ed. *Bilingual Education* (10–12). Series: At Issue. 2004, Gale LB $27.45 (0-7377-1605-3); paper $18.70 (0-7377-1606-1). 79pp. Arguments for and against bilingual education are presented in a collection of previously published articles. (Rev: SLJ 7/04) [370.1]

2087 Pletka, Bob. *My So-Called Digital Life: 2,000 Teenagers, 300 Cameras, and 30 Days to Document Their World* (9–12). Illus. 2005, Santa Monica paper $24.95 (1-59580-005-0). 176pp. The day-to-day lives of typical California high school teens are captured in this collection of students' photos and essays. (Rev: BL 11/15/05; VOYA 2/06) [779]

Development of Academic Skills

Tests and Test Taking

2088 Bardin, Matt, and Susan Fine. *Zen in the Art of the SAT: How to Think, Focus, and Achieve Your Highest Score* (9–12). 2005, Houghton paper $7.99 (0-618-57488-3). 240pp. The principles of Zen Buddhism are recommended as an efficient way to reduce anxiety and increase focus when under pressure. (Rev: BL 9/1/05; SLJ 11/05) [378.1]

Academic Guidance

Colleges and Universities

2089 Cohen, Harlan. *The Naked Roommate: And 100 Other Issues You Might Run Into in College* (11–12). 2005, Sourcebooks paper $14.95 (1-4022-0337-3). 374pp. This tongue-in-cheek look at college life covers everything from homesickness and laundry to roommates, alcohol, and sex. (Rev: SLJ 4/05) [378.1]

2090 Fox, Gunnar. *Kick Ass in College: A Guerrilla Guide to College Success* (9–12). Illus. 2005, Kick Ass Media paper $16.95 (0-9762928-2-3). 248pp. Sound advice for prospective college students, with personal anecdotes and tips on extracurricular activities. (Rev: BL 10/1/05) [378.1]

2091 Hutchin, Megan, et al. *Choose the Right College and Get Accepted!* (10–12). Series: Students Helping Students. 2003, Natavi Guides paper $12.95 (0-9719392-9-2). 252pp. Covering such topics as essays, tests, and campus visits, and financial aid, this helpful guide includes advice from admissions deans and many quotations from college students and recent grads. (Rev: SLJ 2/04) [378]

2092 Matthews, Arlene. *Getting in Without Freaking Out: The Official College Admissions Guide for Overwhelmed Parents* (10–12). 2006, Three Rivers paper $13.95 (1-4000-9841-6). 256pp. College-bound teens will find this advice salutary. (Rev: BL 1/1–15/06) [378.1]

2093 *Navigating Your Freshman Year: How to Make the Leap to College Life — and Land on Your Feet* (10–12). Series: Students Helping Students. 2005, Prentice Hall paper $12.95 (0-7352-0392-X). 176pp. Written and edited by current and former college students, this volume offers helpful, if overly upbeat, advice to incoming freshmen. (Rev: BL 6/1–15/05; VOYA 10/05) [378.1]

2094 Princeton Review Staff. *Eye on Apply: Six True Stories of College Admissions* (10–12). 2004, Random paper $15.95 (0-375-76426-7). 242pp. In their online journal postings, six high school students reveal their college application experiences. (Rev: SLJ 3/05)

2095 Williams, Juan, and Dwayne Ashley. *I'll Find a Way or Make One: A Tribute to Historically Black Colleges and Universities* (10–12). Illus. 2004, HarperCollins $35.00 (0-06-009453-2). 448pp. A history of America's historically black colleges and universities, the reasons for their establishment, and their contributions and best-known graduates. (Rev: BL 10/15/04) [378.73]

Scholarships and Financial Aid

2096 Karnes, Frances A., and Tracy L. Riley. *Competitions for Talented Kids: Win Scholarships, Big Prize Money, and Recognition* (7–10). 2005, Prufrock paper $17.95 (1-59363-156-1). 295pp. More than 140 competitions covering a number of academic subjects, the performing arts, and leadership are listed alphabetically, with brief advice on entering these contests. (Rev: BL 12/1/05) [371.95]

2097 Wheeler, Dion. *The Sports Scholarships Insider's Guide: Getting Money for College at Any Division* (11–12). 2005, Sourcebooks paper $14.95 (1-4022-0376-4). 347pp. A practical guide to sports scholarships and the recruiting process. (Rev: SLJ 6/05) [378.1]

Careers and Occupational Guidance

Careers

General and Miscellaneous

2098 Ballard, Chris. *The Butterfly Hunter: Adventures of People Who Found Their True Calling Way Off the Beaten Path* (9–12). 2006, Broadway $23.95 (0-7679-1868-1). 272pp. Describes the occupations of ten men and women who are totally happy in their jobs. (Rev: BL 2/1/06) [650.92]

2099 Cefrey, Holly. *Archaeologists: Life Digging Up Artifacts* (5–10). Series: Extreme Careers. 2004, Rosen LB $19.95 (0-8239-3963-4). 64pp. This is an introduction to the field of archeology, its problems, its opportunities, and its rewards. (Rev: BL 5/15/04) [930]

2100 *Coaches and Fitness Professionals* (9–12). Series: Careers in Focus. 2004, Facts on File $22.95 (0-8160-5548-3). 188pp. An excellent overview of jobs in the fields of physical education and fitness training; in addition to coaching positions, the guide considers jobs in yoga instruction, motivational speaking, and diet / fitness writing. (Rev: BL 7/04; SLJ 11/04) [796]

2101 Colbert, Judy. *Career Opportunities in the Travel Industry* (8–12). Series: Career Opportunities. 2004, Ferguson $49.50 (0-8160-4864-9). 246pp. A quick overview of the wide number of opportunities in the travel industry, providing an outline of duties, salary ranges, employment outlook, required education and training, and so forth. (Rev: SLJ 7/04) [331.7]

2102 *Communication Skills.* 2nd ed. (9–12). Series: Career Skills Library. 2004, Ferguson $21.95 (0-8160-5517-3). 138pp. Examines the importance of communications in the workplace and offers practical advice on public speaking, written communications, and team building; quizzes and problem-solving exercises add interest. (Rev: SLJ 1/05) [384]

2103 Coon, Nora E. *Teen Dream Jobs: How to Find the Job You Really Want Now!* (8–12). 2004, Beyond Words paper $9.95 (1-58270-093-1). 132pp. Written by a teen, this is a reader-friendly guide that refers teens to online career-choice quizzes, gives advice on job-finding activities, and suggests possible careers and ways to enter them. (Rev: SLJ 6/04)

2104 Freedman, Samuel G. *Letters to a Young Journalist* (10–12). 2006, Basic Bks. $22.95 (0-465-02455-6). 224pp. Freedman, a Columbia University journalism professor and former reporter for the *New York Times*, offers an unflinching appraisal of American journalism over the last several decades. (Rev: BL 3/1/06) [070.4]

2105 Greenberger, Robert. *Cool Careers Without College for People Who Love to Drive* (8–12). Series: Cool Careers Without College. 2004, Rosen LB $30.60 (0-8239-3786-0). 144pp. Benefits and disadvantages of this kind of work, education and training, salary outlook, and a description of on-the-job activities are provided for a number of career choices, both working for others and as an entrepreneur. (Rev: SLJ 5/04)

2106 Hinton, Kerry. *Cool Careers Without College for People Who Love Food* (8–12). Series: Cool Careers Without College. 2004, Rosen LB $30.60 (0-8239-3787-9). 144pp. Benefits and disadvantages of this kind of work, education and training, salary outlook, and a description of on-the-job activities are provided for a number of career choices, both working for others and as an entrepreneur. (Rev: SLJ 5/04)

2107 McAlpine, Margaret. *Working in the Fashion Industry* (6–12). Series: My Future Career. 2005, Gareth Stevens LB $26.00 (0-8368-4774-1). 64pp. Seven careers in the field of fashion are highlighted with plenty of good photographs, explanations of a typical day's activities, and "Good Points and Bad Points." (Rev: SLJ 1/06)

2108 McAlpine, Margaret. *Working in the Food Industry* (6–12). Series: My Future Career. 2005, Gareth Stevens LB $26.00 (0-8368-4776-8). 64pp. Seven careers in the food industry are highlighted with plenty of good photographs, explanations of a typical day's activities, and "Good Points and Bad Points." (Rev: SLJ 1/06)

2109 McAlpine, Margaret. *Working with Animals* (6–10). Series: My Future Career. 2005, Gareth Stevens LB $26.00 (0-8368-4240-5). 64pp. In addition to describing various jobs working with animals, McAlpine discusses the best personality type for each task and provides a detailed breakdown of a typical day. (Rev: SLJ 3/05) [636]

2110 McAlpine, Margaret. *Working with Children* (6–10). Series: My Future Career. 2005, Gareth Stevens LB $26.00 (0-8368-4241-3). 64pp. In addition to describing various jobs working with children, McAlpine discusses the best personality type for each one and provides a detailed breakdown of a typical day. (Rev: SLJ 3/05) [362.7]

2111 Paquette, Penny Hutchins. *Apprenticeship: The Ultimate Teen Guide* (9–12). Series: It Happened to Me. 2005, Scarecrow $42.00 (0-8108-4945-3). 373pp. A history of apprenticeship is followed by chapters on fields where apprenticeships are common — construction, entertainment, security services, and so forth — and details of what is involved, potential salaries, and outlook for growth; brief real-life stories appear throughout. (Rev: SLJ 2/06)

2112 *Professional Ethics and Etiquette*. 2nd ed. (9–12). Series: Career Skills Library. 2004, Ferguson $21.95 (0-8160-5523-8). 138pp. Practical and well-presented advice on how to behave in the business world is accompanied by quizzes and real-life examples. (Rev: SLJ 1/05) [395]

2113 Reeves, Diane Lindsey, and Gail Karlitz. *Career Ideas for Teens in Architecture and Construction* (8–12). Illus. Series: Career Ideas for Teens. 2005, Ferguson $40.00 (0-8160-5289-1). 170pp. In addition to details of education requirements, salaries, and so forth, this attractive guide offers interview tips, advice from "real people," and questionnaires. (Rev: SLJ 2/06)

2114 Rosenberg, Aaron. *Cryptologists: Life Making and Breaking Codes* (5–10). Series: Extreme Careers. 2004, Rosen LB $19.95 (0-8239-3965-0). 64pp. After some background material on the histo-

ry of codes, this volume discusses career opportunities as a cryptologist. (Rev: BL 5/15/04; SLJ 5/90) [410]

2115 Webster, Harriet. *Cool Careers Without College for People Who Love to Work with Children* (8–12). Series: Cool Careers Without College. 2004, Rosen LB $30.60 (0-8239-3792-5). 144pp. Benefits and disadvantages of this kind of work, education and training, salary outlook, and a description of on-the-job activities are provided for a number of career choices, both working for others and as an entrepreneur. (Rev: SLJ 5/04)

2116 Whynott, Douglas. *A Country Practice: Scenes from the Veterinary Life* (7–10). 2004, Farrar $24.00 (0-86547-647-0). 290pp. Covering all aspects of veterinary practice — including finances, staff, and bedside manner — this is an intriguing account of a year in the life of a veterinarian who treats both domestic pets and farm animals. (Rev: BL 11/1/04) [636.089]

Arts, Entertainment, and Sports

2117 *Art* (9–12). Series: Careers in Focus. 2004, Facts on File $22.95 (0-8160-5547-5). 187pp. A look at the wide diversity of career possibilities in the art field — from art and antique dealers to museum curators — with descriptions of duties, salaries, outlook, and so forth. (Rev: BL 7/04; SLJ 11/04) [702]

2118 *Design*. 2nd ed. (7–12). Series: Careers in Focus. 2005, Ferguson $22.95 (0-8160-5865-2). 188pp. Describes careers in the broad field of design — Including architects, fashion designers, exhibit designers, industrial designers, and toy and game designers. (Rev: SLJ 12/05)

2119 *Film* (9–12). Illus. Series: Discovering Careers for Your Future. 2005, Facts on File $19.95 (0-8160-5569-6). 92pp. A frank look at the not-always-glamorous film world and the careers available there, with material on education and training, salary ranges, and job outlook. (Rev: BL 3/15/05; SLJ 4/05) [791.43]

2120 McAlpine, Margaret. *Working in Film and Television* (6–10). Series: My Future Career. 2005, Gareth Stevens LB $26.00 (0-8368-4237-5). 64pp. In addition to describing various jobs in the film and television world, McAlpine discusses the best personality type for each one and provides a detailed breakdown of a typical day. (Rev: SLJ 3/05) [791.43]

2121 McAlpine, Margaret. *Working in Music and Dance* (6–12). Series: My Future Career. 2005, Gareth Stevens LB $26.00 (0-8368-4777-6). 64pp. Seven careers in the fields of music and dance are highlighted with plenty of good photographs, explanations of a typical day's activities, and "Good Points and Bad Points." (Rev: SLJ 1/06)

2122 *Music* (6–12). 2004, Ferguson LB $22.95 (0-8160-5555-6). 218pp. Describes careers in music, with information on qualifications, working conditions, salaries, opportunities, rewards, and methods of exploring and entering the field. (Rev: SLJ 1/05) [780]

2123 *Sports*. 3rd ed. (9–12). Series: Careers in Focus. 2003, Ferguson LB $22.95 (0-8160-5486-X). 204pp. After a general and historical overview, more than 20 careers are described, covering the nature of the job, educational requirements, rewards, salaries, working conditions, and how to get into the field. (Rev: SLJ 5/04)

Business

2124 *Advertising and Marketing* (9–12). 2003, Ferguson LB $22.95 (0-8160-5482-7). 188pp. A thorough description of jobs in these fields, covering educational requirements, working conditions, current salaries and future outlook, and so forth. (Rev: SLJ 6/04)

2125 Giles, M. J. *Young Adult's Guide to a Business Career* (8–12). Illus. 2004, Business Bks. $14.95 (0-9723714-3-5). 115pp. Full of useful tips, this guide describes more than 25 occupations in business and finance, giving details of benefits and drawbacks, salaries, educational requirements, and so forth. (Rev: SLJ 7/04) [331.7]

2126 Thomason-Carroll, Kristi L. *Young Adult's Guide to Business Communications* (8–12). Illus. 2004, Business Bks. $14.95 (0-9723714-4-3). 124pp. Full of useful tips, this guide describes the basics required for a job in the business world, including telephone skills, the ability to communicate clearly by letter and e-mail, and proper behavior during meetings. (Rev: SLJ 7/04) [651.7]

Education and Librarianship

2127 *Education*. 2nd ed. (9–12). Series: Careers in Focus. 2003, Ferguson LB $22.95 (0-8160-5485-1). 188pp. After a general overview and a history of education as an occupation, 20 top careers are described, covering the nature of the job, educational requirements, rewards, salaries, working conditions, and how to get into the field. (Rev: SLJ 5/04)

2128 Reeves, Diane Lindsey, and Gail Karlitz. *Career Ideas for Teens in Education and Training* (8–12). Illus. Series: Career Ideas for Teens. 2005, Ferguson $40.00 (0-8160-5295-6). 183pp. In addition to details of education requirements, salaries, and so forth, this attractive guide offers interview tips, advice from "real people," and questionnaires. (Rev: SLJ 2/06)

Law, Police, and Other Society-Oriented Careers

2129 Ackerman, Thomas H. *FBI Careers: The Ultimate Guide to Landing a Job as One of America's Finest*. 2nd ed. (9–12). Illus. 2005, JIST paper $19.95 (1-59357-237-9). 333pp. Good advice on applying to work at the FBI and descriptions of various positions are accompanied by a history of the organization plus an outline of its structure. (Rev: SLJ 2/06)

2130 Craig, Emily. *Teasing Secrets from the Dead: My Investigations at America's Most Infamous Crime Scenes* (11–12). 2004, Crown $24.95 (1-4000-4922-9). 288pp. Craig describes her work as a forensic anthropologist, imparting technical information and insight into interpersonal relations in the process; for mature readers. (Rev: BL 8/04) [363.25]

2131 Hallcox, Jarrett, and Amy Welch. *Bodies We've Buried: Inside the National Forensic Academy, the World's Top CSI Training School* (10–12). Illus. 2006, Berkley $24.95 (0-425-20752-8). 304pp. An introduction to forensic science and the national academy's now-very-popular 10-week program. (Rev: BL 1/1–15/06) [363.25]

2132 Murdico, Suzanne J. *Bomb Squad Experts: Life Defusing Explosive Devices* (5–10). Series: Extreme Careers. 2004, Rosen LB $19.95 (0-8239-3968-5). 64pp. A look at the career opportunities in bomb squads, with material on training, salaries, and working conditions. (Rev: BL 5/15/04) [363]

2133 Murdico, Suzanne J. *Forensic Scientists: Life Investigating Sudden Death* (5–12). Series: Extreme Careers. 2004, Rosen LB $19.95 (0-8239-3966-9). 64pp. A look at this rapidly growing science and the career opportunities offered. (Rev: BL 5/15/04) [363.2]

2134 Temple, John. *Deadhouse: Life in a Coroner's Office* (9–12). 2005, Univ. Press of Mississippi $28.00 (1-57806-743-X). 192pp. The experiences of two young interns add to this look at the workings of the Allegheny County Coroner's Office, which serves the city of Pittsburgh and its suburbs. (Rev: BL 4/15/05) [614.1]

Medicine and Health

2135 *Alternative Health Care* (9–12). 2003, Ferguson LB $22.95 (0-8160-5483-5). 220pp. A thorough description of jobs in this field, covering educational requirements, working conditions, current salaries and future outlook, and so forth. (Rev: SLJ 6/04)

2136 Reeves, Diane Lindsey, and Gail Karlitz. *Career Ideas for Teens in Health Science* (7–12). Illus. Series: Career Ideas for Teens. 2005, Ferguson $40.00 (0-8160-5290-5). 184pp. In addition to details of education requirements, salaries, and so forth, this attractive guide offers interview tips, advice from "real people," and questionnaires. (Rev: SLJ 2/06) [610.69]

Science and Engineering

2137 Echaore-Mcdavid, Susan. *Career Opportunities in Science* (9–12). 2003, Facts on File $49.50 (0-8160-4905-X). 306pp. More than 80 careers in the sciences (including those in business and education) are profiled, with material on duties, job titles, salary, job outlook, education and training, and any special skills or character traits needed. (Rev: SLJ 2/04) [509]

Technical and Industrial Careers

2138 Cassedy, Patrice. *Computer Technology* (7–10). Series: Careers for the Twenty-First Century. 2004, Gale LB $27.45 (1-56006-896-5). 112pp. Helpful information about work environment and job satisfaction accompanies the usual material on salary, career prospects, and so forth; the format has less appeal. (Rev: SLJ 11/04) [005]

2139 *Computer and Video Game Design* (7–12). Series: Careers in Focus. 2005, Ferguson $22.95 (0-8160-5850-4). 188pp. Describes the tasks of artists and animators, game designers, packaging designers, technical support specialists, and video game testers. (Rev: SLJ 12/05)

2140 *Computers*. 4th ed. (6–12). Series: Careers in Focus. 2004, Ferguson LB $22.95 (0-8160-5552-1).

188pp. Describes careers in the computer field, with information on qualifications, working conditions, salaries, opportunities, rewards, and methods of exploring and entering the field; a helpful feature is a list of acronyms and identification numbers used in government career indexes. (Rev: SLJ 1/05) [004]

2141 Gerardi, Dave, and Peter Suciu. *Careers in the Computer Game Industry* (6–12). Illus. Series: Careers in the New Economy. 2005, Rosen LB $31.95 (1-4042-0252-8). 144pp. The authors review a wide array of job opportunities in the computer game industry, including designers, testers, graphic artists, animators, and programmers. (Rev: SLJ 10/05) [331.7]

2142 Henderson, Harry. *Career Opportunities in Computers and Cyberspace*. 2nd ed. (8–12). Series: Career Opportunities. 2004, Ferguson $49.50 (0-8160-5094-5). 241pp. A quick overview of the wide number of opportunities in such fields as programming and software development, information systems management, and information science, providing an outline of duties, salary ranges, employment outlook, required education and training, and so forth. (Rev: SLJ 7/04) [004]

2143 McAlpine, Margaret. *Working with Computers* (6–10). Series: My Future Career. 2005, Gareth Stevens LB $26.00 (0-8368-4242-1). 64pp. In addition to describing various jobs working with computers, McAlpine discusses the best personality type for each one and provides a detailed breakdown of a typical day. (Rev: SLJ 3/05) [004]

Personal Finances

Money Management

2144 Deering, Kathryn R., ed. *Cash and Credit Information for Teens* (9–12). Series: Teen Finance. 2005, Omnigraphics LB $58.00 (0-7808-0780-4). 407pp. This title contains a wealth of practical advice to help teenagers make sound decisions on matters of cash management and credit use. (Rev: BL 10/15/05; SLJ 3/06) [332.024]

2145 Deering, Kathryn R. *Savings and Investment Information for Teens: Tips for a Successful Financial Life* (9–12). Series: Teen Finance. 2005, Omnigraphics LB $65.00 (0-7808-0781-2). 370pp. Budgets, bank accounts, investment strategies, and the stock market are all explained in clear language. (Rev: SLJ 1/06) [332]

2146 Fowles, Debby. *1000 Best Smart Money Secrets for Students* (10–12). 2005, Sourcebooks paper $12.95 (1-4022-0548-1). 338pp. Practical tips for saving, earning, and managing money; aimed at prospective college students. (Rev: SLJ 12/05)

Health and the Human Body

Aging and Death

2147 Marzilli, Alan. *Physician-Assisted Suicide* (7–12). Series: Point/Counterpoint. 2003, Chelsea House LB $25.95 (0-7910-7485-4). 112pp. The arguments for and against the right to choose how and when to die, whether medical advice should be necessary, and the implications of medical intervention are all discussed with reference to federal and state laws and court cases. (Rev: SLJ 4/04) [179]

Alcohol, Drugs, and Smoking

2148 Balkin, Karen F., ed. *Club Drugs* (9–12). Series: At Issue. 2004, Gale LB $27.45 (0-7377-1607-X); paper $18.70 (0-7377-1608-8). 96pp. Ten previously published articles offer a variety of views on the growing popularity of club drugs and what, if anything, should be done to control their use. (Rev: SLJ 7/05) [362.2]

2149 Booth, Martin. *Cannabis* (9–12). 2004, St. Martin's $24.95 (0-312-32220-8). 368pp. An even-handed examination of the history of cannabis, the global trade in marijuana and hashish, references to the drug and its use by artists, laws banning its use, and so forth. (Rev: BL 6/1–15/04) [362.]

2150 Elliot-Wright, Susan. *Heroin* (8–10). Series: Health Issues. 2004, Raintree LB $32.79 (0-7398-6894-2). 64pp. This slim volume provides a concise history of heroin and examines the drug's effects on users and its impact on society. (Rev: SLJ 3/05) [363.29]

2151 Fitzhugh, Karla. *Steroids* (7–10). Illus. Series: Health Issues. 2003, Raintree LB $28.56 (0-7398-6426-2). 64pp. An attractive, slim overview of

steroids and how they affect the body. (Rev: SLJ 5/04) [362.29]

2152 Fooks, Louie. *The Drug Trade: The Impact on Our Lives* (6–10). Series: 21st Century Debates. 2003, Raintree LB $28.56 (0-7398-6033-X). 64pp. Covers the types of illegal drugs being sold; the reasons why governments find it hard to control their growth/creation, distribution, and sale; the people who take these drugs; and the methods used to move them around the world. (Rev: SLJ 6/04) [362.2]

2153 Gottfried, Ted. *The Facts About Alcohol* (7–12). Series: Drugs. 2004, Benchmark LB $25.95 (0-7614-1805-9). 111pp. A history of alcohol use plus discussion of its effects on the body and impact on society. (Rev: SLJ 3/05) [613.8]

2154 Hyde, Margaret O., and John K. Setaro. *Smoking 101: An Overview for Teens* (7–12). 2005, Twenty-First Century LB $26.60 (0-7613-2835-1). 128pp. A nonjudgmental account of the physical effects of smoking, with information on tobacco advertising, the kinds of products marketed, and the industry both in the United States and around the world. (Rev: SLJ 1/06) [362.29]

2155 Isralowitz, Richard. *Drug Use* (9–12). Series: Contemporary World Issues. 2004, ABC-CLIO $50.00 (1-57607-708-X). 269pp. A concise overview of the key issues, facts, and controversies surrounding the use and abuse of harmful drugs — including alcohol, prescription medications, and illegal drugs — in the United States and abroad; with statistics and excerpts from various sources. (Rev: SLJ 10/04)

2156 Kittleson, Mark J., ed. *The Truth About Alcohol* (8–12). Series: Truth About. 2004, Facts on File $29.95 (0-8160-5298-0). 196pp. Discusses the effects and dangers of alcohol use, including binge drinking, alcoholism, unsafe sexual behavior, and impaired driving. (Rev: SLJ 4/05) [613.8]

2157 Lennard-Brown, Sarah. *Cocaine* (8–10). Series: Health Issues. 2004, Raintree LB $32.79 (0-7398-6893-4). 64pp. A look at the history of cocaine as well as the drug's effects on users and its impact on society. (Rev: SLJ 3/05) [362.29]

2158 Lennard-Brown, Sarah. *Marijuana* (8–10). Series: Health Issues. 2004, Raintree LB $32.79 (0-7398-6896-9). 64pp. Traces the history of marijuana and explores the drug's effects on users and on society. (Rev: SLJ 3/05) [362.29]

2159 Levert, Suzanne. *The Facts About Steroids* (7–12). Illus. Series: Drugs. 2004, Benchmark LB $25.95 (0-7614-1808-3). 96pp. Examines the effects of steroids on users, the health risks, and the laws governing steroid use. (Rev: SLJ 3/05) [362.29]

2160 Lookadoo, Justin. *The Dirt on Drugs: A Dateable Book* (6–10). Illus. Series: The Dirt. 2005, Reveil paper $9.99 (0-8007-5919-2). 112pp. A former Texas probation officer writes frankly about the dangers of drugs. (Rev: SLJ 7/05) [616.8]

2161 Menhard, Francha Roffe. *The Facts About Inhalants* (7–12). Series: Drugs. 2004, Benchmark LB $25.95 (0-7614-1809-1). 92pp. Explores the dangers associated with the use of inhalants. (Rev: SLJ 3/05) [362.29]

2162 Shannon, Joyce Brennfleck, ed. *Alcohol Information for Teens: Health Tips About Alcohol and Alcoholism* (7–12). Series: Teen Health. 2005, Omnigraphics $58.00 (0-7808-0741-3). 370pp. Authoritative information about the effects of alcohol on the mind and body and the dangers of alcohol dependency. (Rev: SLJ 7/05) [613.8]

2163 Sheen, Barbara. *Teen Alcoholism* (7–12). Illus. Series: Teen Issues. 2004, Gale LB $21.96 (1-59018-501-3). 112pp. This straightforward examination of teen alcoholism explores the individual and societal impact of the illness and offers a survey of possible treatment programs. (Rev: BL 7/04) [616.86]

2164 Smith, Lynn Marie. *Rolling Away: My Agony with Ecstasy* (11–12). 2005, Atria $24.00 (0-7434-9043-6). 304pp. Smith writes candidly about her struggles with substance abuse; for mature teens. (Rev: BL 5/1/05) [362.29]

2165 Zailckas, Koren. *Smashed: Story of a Drunken Girlhood* (11–12). 2005, Viking $21.95 (0-670-03376-6). 342pp. In this graphic memoir suitable for mature teens, Zailckas chronicles the downward spiral of her life that began with her first sip of alcohol at the age of 14. (Rev: BL 12/15/04) [616.8]

Bionics and Transplants

2166 Schwartz, Tina P. *Organ Transplants: A Survival Guide for the Entire Family: The Ultimate Teen Guide* (7–12). Illus. Series: It Happened to Me. 2005, Scarecrow $36.50 (0-8108-4924-0). 243pp. A clear explanation, in question-and-answer format, of the complex problems relating to medical transplants, with discussion of the hazards and the emotional upheaval to be expected. (Rev: SLJ 10/05) [617.9]

Diseases and Illnesses

2167 Balkin, Karen F., ed. *Food-Borne Illness* (7–12). Series: At Issue. 2004, Gale LB $28.70 (0-7377-1334-8); paper $19.95 (0-7377-1335-6). 80pp. A collection of previously published articles that examine the dangers of food-borne illness and what can be done to protect consumers. (Rev: SLJ 4/05) [615.9]

2168 Bellenir, Karen, ed. *Asthma Information for Teens: Health Tips About Managing Asthma and Related Concerns* (8–12). Illus. Series: Teen Health. 2005, Omnigraphics LB $58.00 (0-7808-0770-7). 386pp. Information-packed but readable, this volume covers all aspects of asthma. (Rev: SLJ 9/05) [616.2]

2169 Bryan, Jenny. *Asthma* (5–10). Illus. Series: Just the Facts. 2004, Heinemann LB $27.07 (1-4034-4599-0). 56pp. A well-organized explanation of asthma, illustrated with numerous color photographs and providing material on how air pollution and smoking are factors in causing or aggravating the disease. (Rev: SLJ 6/04) [616.2]

2170 Bryan, Jenny. *Diabetes* (5–10). Illus. Series: Just the Facts. 2004, Heinemann LB $27.07 (1-4034-4600-8). 56pp. An illustrated overview of the disease, including causes and treatments and the effects of diet and cultural factors. (Rev: SLJ 6/04) [616.4]

2171 Elliot-Wright, Susan. *Epilepsy* (7–10). Illus. Series: Health Issues. 2003, Raintree LB $28.56 (0-7398-6423-8). 64pp. An attractive, slim overview of epilepsy and how it affects the body and mind. (Rev: SLJ 5/04) [616.8]

2172 Landau, Elaine. *Alzheimer's Disease: A Forgotten Life* (7–10). Illus. Series: Health and Human Disease. 2006, Scholastic LB $26.00 (0-531-16755-0). 128pp. Symptoms, diagnosis, treatment, and prognosis are all covered here, plus a question-and-answer "ask the doctor" feature that adds pertinent information. (Rev: BL 12/1/05; SLJ 1/06) [616.8]

2173 Moran, Katherine J. *Diabetes: The Ultimate Teen Guide* (9–12). Illus. Series: It Happened to Me. 2004, Scarecrow $34.50 (0-8108-4806-6). 181pp. Management of diabetes is the main focus of this volume, which covers the basics of the disease and its symptoms, the importance of diet and exercise, and the types of insulin and delivery methods used today. (Rev: SLJ 8/04)

2174 Nakaya, Andrea C., ed. *Obesity* (8–12). Series: Opposing Viewpoints. 2005, Gale LB $23.70 (0-7377-3233-4). 203pp. The causes of the soaring rates of obesity are discussed from various viewpoints, as well as who is responsible and what can be done to reduce this health problem. (Rev: SLJ 1/06) [616.3]

2175 Oshinsky, David M. *Polio: An American Story* (9–12). Illus. 2005, Oxford $30.00 (0-19-515294-8). 432pp. The story of the 20th-century marshalling of political and scientific resources to combat the scourge of polio includes material — some not laudatory — on Roosevelt, Salk, and Sabin. (Rev: BL 3/15/05; SLJ 10/05) [614.5]

2176 Panno, Joseph. *Cancer: The Role of Genes, Lifestyle and Environment* (7–12). Illus. Series: The New Biology. 2004, Facts on File $35.00 (0-8160-4950-5). 162pp. In this title from the New Biology series, author Joseph Panno explores the role of genetics, lifestyle choices, and the environment in cancer. (Rev: SLJ 2/05; VOYA 8/04)

2177 Panno, Joseph. *Gene Therapy: Treating Disease by Repairing Genes* (7–12). Illus. Series: The New Biology. 2004, Facts on File $35.00 (0-8160-4948-3). 172pp. The hot-button topic of gene therapy and its implications for the future treatment of diseases and physical injuries are explored in this title from the New Biology series. (Rev: SLJ 2/05)

2178 Peters, Stephanie True. *The Battle Against Polio* (6–10). Illus. Series: Epidemic! 2004, Benchmark LB $29.93 (0-7614-1635-8). 80pp. The history of polio, the toll it took on young lives, and the ultimately successful search for a vaccine are related in a compelling presentation. (Rev: BL 12/15/04; SLJ 2/05) [614.54]

2179 Pierce, John R., and James V. Writer. *Yellow Jack: How Yellow Fever Ravaged America and Walter Reed Discovered Its Deadly Secrets* (9–12). Illus. 2005, Wiley $24.95 (0-471-47261-1). 272pp. The fascinating story of the battle against yellow fever — a disease that ravaged the Americas across three centuries. (Rev: BL 4/15/05) [614.5]

2180 Routh, Kristina. *Epilepsy* (5–10). Illus. Series: Just the Facts. 2004, Heinemann LB $27.07 (1-4034-4601-6). 56pp. An overview of epilepsy, with attention to its effect on individuals when it comes to driving, sports, education, and employment. (Rev: SLJ 6/04) [616.8]

2181 Saffer, Barbara. *Anthrax* (9–12). Series: Diseases and Disorders. 2004, Gale LB $21.96 (1-59018-405-X). 112pp. The history of anthrax outbreaks, development of vaccines, and potential use as a weapon are all discussed in clear narrative with black-and-white photographs. (Rev: SLJ 10/04) [616.9]

2182 Silverstein, Alvin, et al. *Cancer: Conquering a Deadly Disease* (8–12). Series: Twenty-First Century Medical Library. 2005, Twenty-First Century LB $27.93 (0-7613-2833-5). 121pp. Using case studies to introduce topics, this is a thorough exploration of new developments in the fight against cancer. (Rev: SLJ 3/06)

2183 Stewart, Gail B. *SARS* (9–12). Series: Diseases and Disorders. 2004, Gale LB $21.96 (1-59018-529-3). 112pp. The story of the SARS outbreak of 2003 and the economic and healthcare implications. (Rev: SLJ 10/04) [616.2]

2184 Tayman, John. *The Colony: The Harrowing True Story of the Exiles of Molokai* (9–12). Illus. 2006, Scribner $27.50 (0-7432-3300-X). 432pp. Excerpts from primary sources and affecting personal stories add to the immediacy of this history of the leper colony on the Hawaiian island of Molokai. (Rev: BL 11/1/05) [614.5]

2185 Williams, Mary E., ed. *Epidemics* (9–12). Series: Opposing Viewpoints. 2005, Gale $34.95 (0-7377-2282-7); paper $23.70 (0-7377-2283-5). 208pp. Explores various questions surrounding infectious diseases and how best to control their spread. (Rev: SLJ 7/05) [614.4]

Doctors, Hospitals, and Medicine

2186 Bardhan-Quallen, Sudipta. *Chemotherapy* (8–12). Illus. Series: Great Medical Discoveries. 2004, Gale LB $21.96 (1-56006-926-0). 128pp. An informative history of the use of chemotherapy to treat cancer, with discussion of its efficacy and side effects, and future improvements and alternatives. (Rev: SLJ 8/04)

2187 Collier, James Lincoln. *Vaccines* (6–10). Series: Great Inventions. 2003, Benchmark LB $25.95 (0-7614-1539-4). 127pp. As well as discussing the development and mechanism of vaccines themselves, this well-illustrated volume includes a survey of infectious diseases such as smallpox, cholera, diphtheria, influenza, and AIDS. (Rev: SLJ 3/04) [615]

2188 Davis, Sampson, et al. *We Beat the Street: How a Friendship Led to Success* (7–10). 2005, Dutton $16.99 (0-525-47407-2). 128pp. Draper recounts the inspiring story of three young men who grew up in a tough neighborhood of Newark, New

Jersey, escaped the mean streets of their childhood, and went on to become doctors. (Rev: BL 4/1/05; SLJ 5/05) [610]

2189 Facklam, Margery, et al. *Modern Medicines: The Discovery and Development of Healing Drugs* (7–12). Series: Science and Technology in Focus. 2004, Facts on File $29.95 (0-8160-4706-5). 208pp. This updated title traces the development of medications from ancient herbal remedies to today's powerful pharmaceuticals, discussing research and testing, the role of the FDA, and the economics of the pharmaceutical industry. (Rev: BL 8/04) [615]

2190 Naff, Clay Farris. *Vaccines* (10–12). Series: Exploring Science and Medical Discoveries. 2005, Gale LB $23.70 (0-7377-1970-2). The controversies surrounding the development of vaccines against infectious diseases and their use in mass inoculation programs are discussed in 26 in-depth essays. (Rev: BL 12/1/04; VOYA 12/05) [615]

Genetics

2191 Hamer, Dean H. *The God Gene: How Faith Is Hardwired into Our Genes* (10–12). 2004, Doubleday $25.95 (0-385-50058-0). 256pp. In this thought-provoking book, geneticist Hamer argues that human spirituality or the lack thereof is linked to a single gene. (Rev: BL 9/1/04) [200]

2192 Harris, Nancy. *Cloning* (9–12). Series: Exploring Science and Medical Discoveries. 2005, Gale LB $23.70 (0-7377-1966-4). The science and ethics of cloning are dissected in this thought-provoking title. (Rev: BL 12/1/04) [660.6]

2193 Kafka, Tina. *DNA on Trial* (6–12). Series: Overview. 2004, Gale LB $27.45 (1-59018-337-1). 112pp. Stories of DNA's use in solving criminal cases are accompanied by discussion of the technology's potential flaws and of the process involved in DNA testing. (Rev: SLJ 3/05) [614]

2194 Panno, Joseph. *Aging: Theories and Potential Therapies* (7–12). Illus. Series: The New Biology. 2004, Facts on File $35.00 (0-8160-4951-3). 157pp. In this title from the New Biology series, author Joseph Panno examines various theories about the aging process, as well as methods to stave off the depredations of age. (Rev: SLJ 2/05)

2195 Panno, Joseph. *Stem Cell Research: Medical Applications and Ethical Controversy* (9–12). Series: New Biology. 2004, Facts on File $35.00 (0-8160-4949-1). 178pp. A clear and scientifically detailed look at the potential uses of stem cells, the ethical issues surrounding their use, and the legal practices in the United States and Europe. (Rev: BL 1/1–15/05; SLJ 2/05) [616]

2196 Wade, Nicholas. *Before the Dawn: Recovering the Lost History of Our Ancestors* (10–12). Illus. 2006, Penguin $24.95 (1-59420-079-3). 312pp. Wade looks at what genetic research is revealing about our prehistoric origins and evolution as a species. (Rev: BL 4/1/06) [599.93]

2197 Yount, Lisa. *Biotechnology and Genetic Engineering.* Rev. ed. (8–12). Series: Library in a Book. 2004, Facts on File $45.00 (0-8160-5059-7). 316pp. An overview of genetic engineering and biotechnology, with chapters on scientific achievements, ethical concerns, court battles, health issues, and scientific problems. (Rev: SLJ 2/05) [303.48]

Grooming, Personal Appearance, and Dress

2198 Graydon, Shari. *In Your Face: The Culture of Beauty and You* (7–12). 2004, Annick paper $14.95 (1-55037-856-2). 176pp. Graydon offers commonsense advice and reassurance to teenagers who may feel overwhelmed by the seemingly ubiquitous message that beauty is all-important. (Rev: BL 12/15/04; SLJ 3/05) [391.6/3]

2199 Libal, Autumn. *Can I Change the Way I Look? A Teen's Guide to the Health Implications of Cosmetic Surgery, Makeovers, and Beyond* (7–12). Illus. Series: The Science of Health. 2005, Mason Crest LB $24.95 (1-59804-843-8). 128pp. Libal clearly lays out the pitfalls of obsessing about body image, as well as the risks involved in piercing, tattooing, eating disorders, cosmetic surgery, and even common cosmetic products. (Rev: SLJ 7/05) [613.4]

2200 Mason, Linda. *Teen Makeup: Looks to Match Your Every Mood* (6–12). Illus. 2004, Watson-Guptill paper $16.95 (0-8230-2980-8). 144pp. A photograph-filled how-to guide to the basics of skin care and makeup. (Rev: SLJ 11/04)

2201 Warrick, Leanne. *Hair Trix for Cool Chix: The Real Girl's Guide to Great Hair* (6–12). 2004, Watson-Guptill paper $9.95 (0-8230-2179-3). 96pp. From quizzes and practical tips to step-by-step directions for different styles and accessories, this is a reader-friendly guide to hair care. (Rev: SLJ 7/04) [391.5]

The Human Body

General and Miscellaneous

2202 Esherick, Joan. *Balancing Act: A Teen's Guide to Managing Stress* (9–12). Illus. Series: The Science of Health: Youth and Well-being. 2005, Mason Crest LB $24.95 (1-59084-853-5). 128pp. A look at the effects of stress on teens, outlining steps that can be taken to cope more effectively with the pressures of everyday life. Also in this series are *Dead on Their Feet: Teen Sleep Deprivation and Its Consequences* and *The Silent Cry: A Teen's Guide to Escaping Self-Injury and Suicide* (both 2005). (Rev: SLJ 6/05)

2203 McNally, Robert Aquinas, ed. *Skin Health Information for Teens: Health Tips About Dermatological Concerns and Skin Cancer Risks* (7–12). Illus. Series: Teen Health. 2003, Omnigraphics $58.00 (0-7808-0446-5). 429pp. Detailed information is provided on health problems and risks including acne, cosmetics, tanning, tattoos, and piercing. (Rev: SLJ 1/04; VOYA 2/04) [616.5]

2204 Rosen, Marvin. *Sleep and Dreaming* (6–12). Illus. Series: Gray Matter. 2005, Chelsea House LB $32.95 (0-7910-8639-9). 159pp. Snoring, sleepwalking, and night terrors are among the topics covered in this survey of our sleep processes and our dreams; Freudian and Jungian theories are also addressed. (Rev: SLJ 3/06) [616]

2205 Walker, Pam, and Elaine Wood. *The Endocrine System* (6–10). Illus. Series: Understanding the Human Body. 2003, Gale LB $27.45 (1-59018-333-9). 96pp. A clear survey of the structure and functions of the endocrine system, discussing the impact of disease and injury and the current and future medical technologies that can help. (Rev: SLJ 2/04) [612.4]

2206 Walker, Richard. *Firefly Guide to the Human Body* (10–12). 2004, Firefly paper $14.95 (1-55297-879-6). 192pp. Introductory material on the composition of the body is followed by information on each body system and a glossary defining parts of the body, diseases, and medical procedures; a small-format, well-illustrated guide. (Rev: SLJ 6/04; VOYA 6/04) [612]

2207 Wolman, David. *A Left-Hand Turn Around the World: Chasing the Mystery and Meaning of All Things Southpaw* (10–12). 2005, Da Capo $23.95 (0-306-81415-3). 256pp. Even readers who are right-handed will enjoy this tale of a proud southpaw's single-minded search for scientific proof that left-handedness is a sign of superior intellect. (Rev: BL 11/1/05) [152.3]

Brain and Nervous System

2208 Saab, Carl Y. *The Spinal Cord* (6–12). Illus. Series: Gray Matter. 2005, Chelsea House LB $32.95 (0-7910-8511-2). 93pp. Explores the importance of the spinal cord to the whole nervous system and the impact of disorders and injuries. (Rev: SLJ 3/06)

Musculoskeletal System

2209 Walker, Pam, and Elaine Wood. *The Skeletal and Muscular System* (6–10). Illus. Series: Understanding the Human Body. 2003, Gale LB $27.45 (1-59018-334-7). 96pp. A clear survey of the structure and functions of the skeleton and muscular system, discussing the impact of disease and injury and the current and future medical technologies that can help. (Rev: SLJ 2/04) [612.7]

Senses

2210 Chorost, Michael. *Rebuilt: How Becoming Part Computer Made Me More Human* (11–12). 2005, Houghton $24.00 (0-618-37829-4). 256pp. Chorost, hard of hearing since childhood and totally deaf since 2001, tells how a cochlear implant transformed his life, widening his social horizons; for mature teens. (Rev: BL 6/1–15/05) [617.8]

Hygiene and Physical Fitness

2211 Finestone, Jeanne. *A Girl's Guide to Yoga* (8–11). Illus. Series: Ener-Chi. 2004, Barrons paper $8.95 (0-7641-2839-6). 80pp. Guides readers through a complete hatha yoga session, pointing out the many benefits offered by the practice and illustrating the poses. (Rev: BL 1/1–15/05; VOYA 2/05) [613.7]

Mental Disorders and Emotional Problems

2212 Antonetta, Susanne. *A Mind Apart: Travels in a Neurodiverse World* (9–12). 2005, Putnam $24.95 (1-58542-382-3). 256pp. Antonetta's personal descriptions of her bipolar experiences add to the impact of her discussion of diverse neurological conditions. (Rev: BL 11/15/05) [616.89]

2213 Bonnice, Sherry, and Carolyn Hoard. *Drug Therapy and Cognitive Disorders* (6–10). Illus. Series: Psychiatric Disorders: Drugs and Psychology for the Mind and Body. 2003, Mason Crest LB $24.95 (1-59084-562-5). 126pp. Diagrams and charts reinforce the easily read text, which includes discussion of the nature of these disorders and how they are treated plus personal anecdotes from one of the authors. (Rev: SLJ 5/04)

2214 Falk, John. *Hello to All That: A Memoir of War, Zoloft, and Peace* (11–12). 2005, Holt $25.00 (0-8050-7218-7). 320pp. Falk interweaves details of his struggles with deep depression with stories of his attempt to establish himself as a correspondent in war-torn Bosnia; for mature teens. (Rev: BL 12/15/04) [616.85]

2215 Kittleson, Mark J., ed. *The Truth About Fear and Depression* (8–12). Series: Truth About. 2004, Facts on File $29.95 (0-8160-5301-4). 164pp. Anxiety and depression are the main focus of this user-friendly volume that describes the causes of these problems, their treatment, individual experiences, and ways to get help. (Rev: SLJ 4/05) [616.85]

2216 Libal, Autumn. *Runaway Train: Youth with Emotional Disturbance* (7–12). Illus. Series: Youth with Special Needs. 2004, Mason Crest LB $24.95 (1-59084-732-6). 127pp. The story of a disturbed high school student who resorts to cutting herself is combined with facts about the causes, symptoms, and treatment of severe emotional disturbance. (Rev: SLJ 12/04)

2217 Polis, Ben. *Only a Mother Could Love Him: My Life with and Triumph over ADD* (8–12). 2004, Ballantine $22.95 (0-345-47188-1). 208pp. Polis's story of his courageous struggle to overcome attention deficit disorder will resonate with many teens. (Rev: BL 12/1/04) [618.92]

2218 Siana, Jolene. *Go Ask Ogre: Letters from a Deathrock Cutter* (11–12). Illus. 2005, Process paper $18.95 (0-9760822-1-7). 192pp. Seventeen-year-old Siana's letters to a punk rocker named Ogre reveal her depression, her self-mutilation, drug and alcohol abuse, and also her creativity; resources for young people suffering similar problems are appended. (Rev: SLJ 1/06) [362.7]

Nutrition and Diet

2219 Collins, Tracy Brown, ed. *Fast Food* (9–12). Series: At Issue. 2004, Gale LB $27.45 (0-7377-2318-1); paper $18.70 (0-7377-2319-X). 91pp. This collection of previously published articles sheds light on both sides of the controversy over fast food and its impact on health. (Rev: SLJ 7/05) [613]

2220 De Pree, Julia K. *Body Story* (9–12). 2004, Swallow $24.95 (0-8040-1063-3); paper $13.95 (0-8040-1064-1). 154pp. A moving memoir of a battle with anorexia; for mature readers with some experience of such disorders. (Rev: BL 6/1–15/04) [362.196]

2221 Ingram, Scott. *Want Fries with That? Obesity and the Supersizing of America* (8–11). Illus. 2005, Scholastic LB $26.00 (0-531-16756-9). 128pp. Examines the relationship between America's burgeoning fast-food business and the country's obesity epidemic. (Rev: BL 11/15/05; SLJ 1/06) [362.196]

2222 Kittleson, Mark J., ed. *The Truth About Eating Disorders* (8–12). Series: Truth About. 2004, Facts on File $29.95 (0-8160-5300-6). 166pp. Causes, diagnosis, and treatment are all covered in this user-friendly guide that looks at emotions along with physical symptoms and does not neglect adolescent males with eating problems. (Rev: SLJ 4/05) [[616.85]

2223 Lawton, Sandra Augustyn, ed. *Eating Disorders Information for Teens: Health Tips About Anorexia, Bulimia, Binge Eating, and Other Eating Disorders* (7–12). Series: Teen Health. 2005, Omnigraphics $58.00 (0-7808-0783-9). 337pp. This title explores all aspects of eating disorders as well as such related topics as body image, nutrition, self-esteem, and athleticism. (Rev: SLJ 12/05; VOYA 4/06)

2224 Moore, Judith. *Fat Girl* (8–12). 2005, Penguin $21.95 (1-59463-009-7). 208pp. An affecting memoir that will resonate with teens and young adults who have struggled with weight problems. (Rev: BL 12/1/04) [362.196]

Reproduction and Child Care

2225 Brynie, Faith Hickman. *101 Questions About Reproduction: Or How 1 + 1 = 3 or 4 or More . . . .* (6–10). 2005, Twenty-First Century LB $27.90 (0-7613-2311-2). 176pp. Information on conception, pregnancy, childbirth, contraception (including a pill for males), abortion, reproductive disorders, and other issues of importance to teens is provided in a question-and-answer format with detailed black-and-white illustrations. (Rev: SLJ 1/06) [612]

2226 Fessler, Ann. *The Girls Who Went Away: The Hidden History of Women Who Surrendered Children for Adoption in the Decades Before Roe v. Wade* (11–12). 2006, Penguin $24.95 (1-59420-094-7). 322pp. Moving stories reveal the suffering of unwed mothers — many of them teenagers — who gave up their babies for adoption in the years before 1973. (Rev: BL 2/15/06) [362.82]

2227 Herring, Mark Y. *The Pro-Life/Choice Debate* (9–12). Series: Historical Guides to Controversial Issues in America. 2003, Greenwood $50.00 (0-313-31710-0). 200pp. A wide-ranging overview of abortion and society's past and present attitudes toward it, with details of key court decisions. (Rev: SLJ 2/04) [363.46]

2228 Kline, Barbara. *White House Nannies: True Tales from the Other Department of Homeland Security* (10–12). 2005, Tarcher $23.95 (1-58542-410-2). 238pp. Kline, founder of a childcare agency called White House Nannies, shares humorous behind-the-scenes stories that also impart wisdom on child care and running a business. (Rev: SLJ 9/05)

2229 MacDonald, Fiona. *The First "Test-Tube Baby"* (6–12). Illus. Series: Days that Changed the World. 2004, World Almanac LB $21.95 (0-8368-5567-1); paper $11.95 (0-8368-5574-4). 48pp. The science and ethics of in-vitro fertilization are explored in this overview of the 1978 birth of the world's first "test-tube baby." (Rev: BL 4/1/04; SLJ 7/04) [618.1]

2230 Page, Cristina. *How the Pro-Choice Movement Saved America: Sex, Virtue, and the Way We Live Now* (11–12). 2006, Basic Bks. $24.00 (0-465-05489-7). 256pp. Page outlines the history of the pro-choice movement and the current debates about reproductive rights. (Rev: BL 1/1–15/06) [344.041]

2231 Powers, Meghan, ed. *The Abortion Rights Movement* (8–11). Series: American Social Movements. 2006, Gale LB $27.96 (0-7377-1947-8). 176pp. This collection of 18 articles, speeches, first-person accounts, and interviews lays out the case for abortion. (Rev: BL 2/15/06) [363.46]

2232 Zach, Kim K. *Reproductive Technology* (10–12). Illus. Series: Great Medical Discoveries. 2004, Gale LB $27.45 (1-59018-344-4). 111pp. This volume explores the options available to infertile couples and the ethical issues associated with current and future technologies. (Rev: SLJ 7/04) [616.6]

Safety and First Aid

2233 Lee, Laura. *100 Most Dangerous Things in Everyday Life and What You Can Do About Them* (8–12). Illus. 2004, Broadway paper $12.95 (0-7679-1716-2). 240pp. The dangers posed by common, everyday objects are explored in accessible, often humorous text and are arranged alphabetically. (Rev: SLJ 1/05) [613.6]

Sex Education and Sexual Identity

2234 Bailey, Jacqui. *Sex, Puberty and All That Stuff: A Guide to Growing Up* (5–10). 2004, Barron's paper $12.95 (0-7641-2992-9). 112pp. In this comprehensive volume full of lighthearted illustrations, Bailey covers the wide range of changes that affect young people, emphasizing the individual's right to choose and the need to resist peer pressure. (Rev: SLJ 1/05) [613.9]

2235 Elliot-Wright, Susan. *Puberty* (7–10). Illus. Series: Health Issues. 2003, Raintree LB $28.56 (0-7398-6424-6). 64pp. An attractive, slim overview of puberty and how it affects the body and mind. (Rev: SLJ 5/04) [612]

2236 Kemp, Kristen. *Healthy Sexuality* (5–10). Illus. Series: Life Balance. 2004, Watts LB $19.50 (0-531-12336-7); paper $6.95 (0-531-16689-9). 80pp. Covering both boys and girls, this easy-to-understand volume looks at physical and emotional changes and provides practical tips on handling difficult decisions and confusing feelings. (Rev: BL 10/15/03; SLJ 4/05)

2237 Marcovitz, Hal. *Teens and Gay Issues* (7–10). Series: The Gallup Youth Survey, Major Issues and Trends. 2005, Mason Crest LB $22.95 (1-59084-873-X). 112pp. An attractive volume documenting Gallup findings on gay teens' attitudes toward coming out, homophobia, the nature/nurture debate, and gay marriage and adoption. (Rev: SLJ 1/06) [305.9]

2238 Rooney, Frances, ed. *Hear Me Out: True Stories of Teens Confronting Homophobia* (8–12). 2005, Second Story paper $9.95 (1-896764-87-8). 197pp. Young people who are volunteers in a Toronto organization called T.E.A.C.H. (Teens Educating and Confronting Homophobia) talk about prejudice they've experienced because of their sexual orientation. (Rev: BL 8/05; SLJ 5/05; VOYA 4/05) [306.76]

Sex Problems (Abuse, Harassment, etc.)

2239 Feuereisen, Patti, and Caroline Pincus. *Invisible Girls: The Truth About Sexual Abuse* (9–12). 2005, Seal paper $15.95 (1-58005-135-9). 233pp. The author, a psychotherapist, debunks myths about abuse, offers some case studies, and provides suggestions for preventing, reporting, and recovering from incest, rape, and other forms of abuse. (Rev: SLJ 11/05) [362.7]

2240 Howard-Barr, Elissa. *The Truth About Sexual Behavior and Unplanned Pregnancy* (10–12). Series: Truth About. 2005, Facts on File $35.00 (0-8160-5307-3). 182pp. A matter-of-fact, balanced, alphabetical discussion of sexual issues, with question-and-answer sections and first-person commentaries. (Rev: BL 9/15/05; SLJ 9/05) [306.7]

2241 Lehman, Carolyn. *Strong at the Heart: How It Feels to Heal from Sexual Abuse* (8–11). 2005, Farrar $16.00 (0-374-37282-9). 176pp. First-person accounts reveal the damage caused by sexual abuse and present strategies for healing. (Rev: BL 9/15/05; SLJ 11/05; VOYA 10/05) [362.76]

Human Development and Behavior

General and Miscellaneous

2242 Bernard, Emily, ed. *Some of My Best Friends: Writings on Interracial Friendships* (11–12). 2004, HarperCollins $23.95 (0-06-008276-3). 240pp. For older readers, this is a thought-provoking collection of essays on the joys and challenges of friendships between people of different racial and ethnic backgrounds. (Rev: BL 7/04) [302.3]

2243 Szalavitz, Maia. *Help at Any Cost: How the Troubled-Teen Industry Cons Parents and Hurts Kids* (11–12). 2006, Riverhead $25.95 (1-59448-910-6). 320pp. An exposé of the practices of programs that claim to help troubled teens, targeting such major players as Straight Incorporated, North Star, KIDS, and the World Wide Association of Specialty Programs; for mature teens. (Rev: BL 2/15/06) [362.74]

Psychology and Human Behavior

General and Miscellaneous

2244 Baskin, Julia, et al. *The Notebook Girls* (11–12). Illus. 2006, Warner $22.95 (0-446-57862-2). 256pp. Produced in journal format, with pasted-in photos, this fascinating volume is the creation of four contemporary teens — classmates at New York City's prestigious Stuyvesant High School — who shared a joint diary and confided in it the interesting aspects of their lives; for mature readers because of discussion of sex, drugs, and alcohol. (Rev: BL 3/15/06) [305.235]

2245 Gross, Michael Joseph. *Starstruck: When a Fan Gets Close to Fame* (8–12). 2005, Bloomsbury $23.95 (1-58234-316-0). 256pp. Gross explores the potent allure of celebrity and the fans who fall under its spell. (Rev: BL 3/1/05) [306.4]

2246 Headley, Maria Dahvana. *The Year of Yes* (10–12). 2006, Hyperion $22.95 (1-4013-0230-0). 288pp. In this engaging dating memoir, Headley tells how her decision to relax her standards finally led her to Mr. Right. (Rev: BL 1/1–15/06) [306.81]

2247 Hernández, Roger K. *Teens and Relationships* (7–10). Series: The Gallup Youth Survey, Major Issues and Trends. 2005, Mason Crest LB $22.95 (1-59084-875-6). 112pp. An attractive volume documenting Gallup findings on teens' attitudes toward parents, divorce, blended families, friendship, and dating the opposite sex. (Rev: SLJ 1/06)

2248 Marcus, David L. *What It Takes to Pull Me Through: Why Teenagers Get in Trouble and How Four of Them Got Out* (11–12). 2005, Houghton $25.00 (0-618-14545-1). 352pp. Marcus follows four troubled teens as they struggle along the road to recovery at a therapeutic boarding school; for mature readers. (Rev: BL 12/1/04) [352.7]

2249 Musgrave, Susan, ed. *Perfectly Secret: The Hidden Lives of Seven Teen Girls* (10–12). 2004, Annick $18.95 (1-55037-865-1); paper $8.95 (1-55037-864-3). 107pp. Seven women tell frank, autobiographical stories of dreadful secrets — about abuse, adultery, rape, self-mutilation, and alcoholism — that they kept when they were teens. (Rev: SLJ 12/04)

2250 Salerno, Steve. *SHAM: How the Self-Help Movement Made America Helpless* (9–12). 2005, Crown $24.95 (1-4000-5409-5). 272pp. An indictment of the self-help industry and its leading lights, among them Suze Orman, Drs. Laura and Phil, Tony Robbins, Marianne Williamson, and John Gray. (Rev: BL 6/1–15/05) [155.2]

2251 Slater, Lauren. *Blue Beyond Blue: Extraordinary Tales for Ordinary Dilemmas* (11–12). Illus.

2005, Norton $23.95 (0-393-05959-6). 224pp. Slater, a psychologist, explores the use of narrative psychotherapy as a way to help patients gain greater insight into their problems; the 16 original fairy tales included are symbol-filled stories of love, addiction, and so forth; for mature readers. (Rev: BL 6/1–15/05) [823]

2252 Thompson, Kristi Collier. *The Girls' Guide to Dreams* (7–12). 2003, Sterling paper $12.95 (1-4027-0032-6). 128pp. A light and accessible guide to the possible meanings of dreams. (Rev: SLJ 1/04) [154.6]

Emotions and Emotional Behavior

2253 Gootman, Marilyn E. *When a Friend Dies: A Book for Teens About Grieving and Healing*. Rev. ed. (6–12). Ed. by Pamela Espeland. 2005, Free Spirit paper $9.95 (1-57542-170-4). 118pp. An updated edition of a guide first published in 1994, this volume offers sound advice and reassurance for teenagers suffering the loss of a friend or peer, including quotes from bereaved teens. (Rev: SLJ 10/05) [155.9]

2254 Myers, Edward. *When Will I Stop Hurting? Teens, Loss, and Grief* (7–12). Series: It Happened to Me. 2004, Scarecrow $34.50 (0-8108-4921-6). 159pp. Firsthand accounts from teens add to this discussion of the stages of grief and of warning signs that should be monitored. (Rev: SLJ 11/04) [155.9]

Intelligence and Thinking

2255 McInerny, D. Q. *Being Logical: A Guide to Good Thinking* (10–12). Illus. 2004, Random $19.95 (1-4000-6171-7). 160pp. Essential reading for anyone interested in logic and reasoned thinking. (Rev: BL 8/04) [160]

Personal Guidance

2256 Behrendt, Greg, and Amiira Ruotola-Behrendt. *It's Called a Breakup Because It's Broken: The Smart Girl's Breakup Buddy* (11–12). 2005, Broadway $19.95 (0-7679-2185-2). 208pp. A lighthearted, positive guide to surviving the disappointment of a failed relationship, with practical tips, copies of letters seeking advice (with the authors' responses), and some case studies/horror stories; for mature teens. (Rev: BL 9/1/05) [158.2]

2257 Bradley, Michael J. *Yes, Your Parents Are Crazy! A Teen Survival Guide* (9–12). 2004, Harbor paper $14.95 (0-936197-48-X). 399pp. Dealing with parents is the focus of this teen-friendly book full of case histories of the challenges young people face

and advice on tackling societal inconsistencies. (Rev: SLJ 12/04; VOYA 2/05)

2258 Canfield, Jack, and Mark Victor Hansen, comps. *Chicken Soup for the Teenage Soul's The Real Deal: School: Cliques, Classes, Clubs and More* (7–12). Series: Chicken Soup for the Soul. 2005, Health Communications paper $12.95 (0-7573-0255-6). 292pp. Written for teenagers by teenagers, this collection of essays addresses many problems that confront high school students today. (Rev: SLJ 11/05)

2259 Chambers, Veronica. *The Joy of Doing Things Badly: A Girl's Guide to Love, Life, and Foolish Bravery* (9–12). 2006, Broadway $17.95 (0-385-51212-0). 240pp. In a collection of uplifting essays, Chambers writes about her triumphs and defeats and her refusal to let fear limit her approach to life. (Rev: BL 3/15/06) [646]

2260 Chopra, Deepak. *Teens Ask Deepak: All the Right Questions* (7–10). 2006, Simon & Schuster $12.95 (0-689-86218-0). 208pp. The popular spiritual guru turns his attention to teenage concerns — friendship, success, health, religion, and so forth. (Rev: BL 1/1–15/06; SLJ 1/06) [616]

2261 Desetta, Al. *The Courage to Be Yourself: True Stories by Teens About Cliques, Conflicts, and Overcoming Peer Pressure* (8–11). 2005, Free Spirit paper $13.95 (1-57542-185-2). 160pp. Teens from a wide variety of backgrounds offer personal accounts of how they overcame adversities such as bullying, cliques, prejudice, and peer pressure. (Rev: BL 2/1/06; VOYA 4/06) [305.235]

2262 Downs, Hugh. *Letter to a Great Grandson: A Message of Love, Advice, and Hope for the Future* (9–12). 2004, Scribner $15.95 (0-7432-4723-X). 128pp. Broadcast journalist Hugh Downs offers some valuable life lessons in this collection of letters written to provide counsel for his great-grandson at various stages of his development. (Rev: BL 6/1–15/04) [170]

2263 Drew, Naomi. *The Kids' Guide to Working Out Conflicts: How to Keep Cool, Stay Safe, and Get Along* (6–10). 2004, Free Spirit paper $13.95 (1-57542-150-X). 146pp. Misunderstandings, teasing, bullying, and sexual harassment are all discussed in this guide that includes scenarios and offers strategies for improving self-control plus many quotations from middle school students. (Rev: SLJ 9/04) [303.6]

2264 Gibbon, Andy. *Make College Yours: How to Leave Home, Make Your Place, and Build Relationships for Success* (9–12). 2003, Preston paper $17.95 (0-9740986-0-4). 104pp. Homesickness, roommates, long-distance relationships, dating, and drinking are covered in this guide to the social aspects of moving on from high school to college. (Rev: SLJ 3/04)

2265 *Girlsource: A Book by and for Young Women About Relationships, Rights, Futures, Bodies, Minds, and Souls* (10–12). Illus. 2003, Ten Speed paper $12.95 (1-58008-555-5). 96pp. Solid advice for teens on social, mental, and physical well-being, with checklists, quizzes, and quotations from teens. (Rev: SLJ 2/04; VOYA 2/04)

2266 Hughes, Lynne B. *You Are Not Alone: Teens Talk About Life After the Loss of a Parent* (9–12). 2005, Scholastic $16.99 (0-439-58590-2); paper $8.99 (0-439-58591-0). 192pp. The author, whose parents died when she was young and who is the founder of Comfort Zone Camp, a refuge for grieving children, explains the process of grieving with reference to the stories of individual teens. (Rev: BL 10/1/05; SLJ 1/06) [155.9]

2267 Lawson, Dorie McCullough. *Posterity: Letters of Great Americans to Their Children* (9–12). 2004, Doubleday $24.95 (0-385-50330-X). 316pp. Letters — from individuals who have made a significant contribution to the United States — offering advice to the next generation are collected in this thought-provoking volume. (Rev: SLJ 7/04) [973]

2268 O'Reilly, Bill, and Charles Flowers. *The O'Reilly Factor for Kids: A Survival Guide for America's Family* (9–12). 2004, HarperCollins $22.95 (0-06-054424-4). 208pp. Controversial talk show host Bill O'Reilly serves up advice for today's teenagers. (Rev: BL 8/04; SLJ 11/04) [646.7]

2269 Piquemal, Michel, and Melissa Daly. *When Life Stinks: How to Deal with Your Bad Moods, Blues, and Depression* (6–10). Series: Sunscreen. 2004, Abrams paper $9.95 (0-8109-4932-6). 112pp. Sensible advice for adolescents suffering from normal anxieties and frustrations and for those who need to recognize that their problems are more deep-seated and professional help is necessary. (Rev: SLJ 4/05) [616.85]

2270 Quindlen, Anna. *Being Perfect* (11–12). 2005, Random $12.95 (0-375-50549-0). 49pp. Quindlen urges readers to steer clear of the "perfection trap." (Rev: SLJ 6/05)

2271 Rutledge, Jill Zimmerman. *Dealing with the Stuff That Makes Life Tough: The 10 Things That Stress Girls Out and How to Cope with Them* (8–10). 2003, Contemporary paper $14.95 (0-07-142326-5). 228pp. Body image, boys, homosexuality, smoking and drinking, divorce — these and other sources of stress are addressed with sensible advice and helpful anecdotes. (Rev: SLJ 1/04)

2272 Tym, Kate, and Penny Worms. *Coping with Your Emotions: A Guide to Taking Control of Your*

Life (6–10). Illus. Series: Get Real. 2004, Raintree LB $29.93 (1-4109-0575-6). 48pp. The magazine-style layout, case studies, quizzes, photos, and advice will draw teens to this discussion of issues including depression, peer pressure, love interests, schoolwork, and teacher conflicts. Also use *School Survival: A Guide to Taking Control of Your Life* (2004). (Rev: SLJ 3/05) [646]

2273 Winkler, Kathleen. *Bullying: How to Deal with Taunting, Teasing, and Tormenting* (6–10). Series: Issues in Focus Today. 2005, Enslow $31.93 (0-7660-2355-9). 104pp. Including a chapter on girls who bully, this is an accessible look at the problem that draws on discussions with both teens and professionals. (Rev: SLJ 12/05)

Social Groups

Family and Family Problems

2274 Haugen, David M., and Matthew J. Box, eds. *Adoption* (8–12). Series: Social Issues Firsthand. 2005, Gale LB $28.70 (0-7377-2881-7). 108pp. Personal accounts from adoptees, birth parents, and adoptive parents give moving perspectives on the process of adoption; gay parents, transracial adoptions, custody battles, and the search for adoptees and birth parents are all covered. (Rev: SLJ 2/06) [362.7]

2275 Meyer, Don, ed. *The Sibling Slam Book: What It's Really Like to Have a Brother or Sister with Special Needs* (7–12). 2005, Woodbine paper $15.95 (1-890627-52-6). 152pp. Young people with special-needs siblings share their hopes, joys, fears, frustrations, and triumphs in this slam book. (Rev: SLJ 6/05)

2276 Musgrave, Susan, ed. *Certain Things About My Mother: Daughters Speak* (10–12). 2003, Annick $18.95 (1-55037-813-9); paper $7.95 (1-55037-812-0). 124pp. Seven adult daughters write about their memories — some good, some bad — of their relationships with their mothers as teens. (Rev: SLJ 3/04; VOYA 2/04) [306.874]

2277 Weinstein, Miriam. *The Surprising Power of Family Meals: How Eating Together Makes Us Smarter, Stronger, Healthier and Happier* (9–12). 2005, Steerforth $22.95 (1-58642-092-5). 272pp. Weinstein makes a strong argument for family meals, a practice she contends helps produce better-adjusted children. (Rev: BL 9/15/05) [306.85]

Physical and Applied Sciences

General and Miscellaneous

2278 Hakim, Joy. *The Story of Science: Newton at the Center* (7–10). Illus. Series: Smithsonian's Story of Science. 2005, Smithsonian $24.95 (1-58834-161-5). 480pp. In the second volume of the series, Hakim introduces readers to the discoveries of Copernicus, Galileo, Newton, and others. (Rev: BL 12/1/05; SLJ 12/05*; VOYA 2/05) [590]

2279 Leland, John. *Aliens in the Backyard: Plant and Animal Imports into America* (9–12). Illus. 2005, Univ. of South Carolina $29.95 (1-57003-582-2). 256pp. Non-indigenous species' good and bad effects on North America's environment are documented in this engaging look at history and science. (Rev: BL 8/05) [578.6]

2280 Lightman, Alan, ed. *The Best American Science Writing, 2005* (10–12). 2005, HarperPerennial paper $13.95 (0-06-072642-3). 320pp. Twenty-seven articles cover a wide array of science-related topics, including bioterrorism, life on Mars, bumblebees, human genome study, and the delicate relationship between humans and nature. (Rev: BL 9/1/05) [500]

2281 Lightman, Alan. *The Discoveries: Great Breakthroughs in 20th Century Science* (10–12). Illus. 2005, Pantheon $32.50 (0-375-42168-8). 592pp. From a century of revolutionary scientific discoveries, Lightman singles out 25 breakthrough achievements in such diverse disciplines as cosmology, molecular biology, and medicine and introduces the original documentation. (Rev: BL 10/15/05) [509]

2282 Pinker, Steven, and Tim Folger, eds. *The Best American Science and Nature Writing, 2004* (10–12).

2004, Houghton $27.50 (0-618-24697-5); paper $14.00 (0-618-24698-3). 240pp. An eclectic collection of science articles compiled from popular and specialized periodicals. (Rev: BL 10/1/04) [500]

2283 Spangenburg, Ray, and Diane Kit Moser. *The Birth of Science: Ancient Times to 1699.* Rev. ed. (6–10). Illus. Series: The History of Science. 2004, Facts on File $35.00 (0-8160-4851-7). 256pp. A survey of the development of scientific knowledge from ancient times through the seventeenth century, with brief profiles of major scientists plus discussion of discoveries that didn't pan out. Also use *The Rise of Reason: 1700–1799, The Age of Synthesis: 1800–1895, Modern Science: 1896–1945,* and *Science Frontiers: 1946 to the Present* (all 2004). (Rev: SLJ 12/04) [509]

2284 Weiner, Jonathan, and Tim Folger, eds. *The Best American Science and Nature Writing, 2005* (9–12). Series: Best American. 2005, Houghton $27.50 (0-618-27341-7); paper $14.00 (0-618-27343-3). 336pp. Twenty-five essays look at aspects of science and nature that are important to our technological, social, and political lives today. (Rev: BL 10/15/05) [500]

2285 Young, Michael, ed. *The Scientific Revolution* (10–12). Series: Turning Points in World History. 2005, Gale LB $27.96 (0-7377-2987-2). 240pp. A look at the roots and achievements of the "scientific revolution," covering such major figures as Copernicus, Galileo, Kepler, Boyle, and Newton. (Rev: BL 1/1–15/06) [509]

Astronomy and Space Science

General and Miscellaneous

2286 Brunier, Serge, and Anne-Marie Lagrange. *Great Observatories of the World* (9–12). Illus. 2005, Firefly $59.95 (1-55407-055-4). 240pp. A dramatic photographic tour of the great astronomical observatories of the world and outer space, with discussion of the technology and the value of the research done there. (Rev: BL 9/1/05) [522.1]

2287 Garlick, Mark A. *Astronomy: A Visual Guide* (8–12). Illus. 2004, Firefly $29.95 (1-55297-958-X). 304pp. An excellent, photo-filled guide to observing and understanding the nighttime sky. (Rev: BL 10/15/04) [522]

2288 Hope, Terry. *Spacecam: Photographing the Final Frontier from Apollo to Hubble* (6–12). Illus. 2005, F & W $24.99 (0-7153-2164-1). 256pp. Images captured from space — many never before published — offer fantastic views of Earth and beyond. (Rev: BL 12/15/05) [778.35]

2289 Levy, David A. *Deep Sky Objects: The Best and Brightest from Four Decades of Comet Chasing* (9–12). Illus. 2005, Prometheus paper $20.00 (1-59102-361-0). 206pp. A fascinating guide, organized by distance from earth and full of interesting personal and historical anecdotes, to the objects that may be confused with comets. (Rev: BL 11/15/05) [523.8]

2290 Moore, Patrick. *Guide to Stars and Planets*. Rev. ed. (9–12). Illus. 2005, Firefly paper $19.95 (1-55407-053-8). 256pp. An excellent guide that provides the basics of identifying celestial bodies, maps of constellations, and categories that can be viewed using binoculars and small telescopes. (Rev: BL 9/15/05) [523]

2291 Ward, Peter. *Life as We Do Not Know It: The NASA Search for (and Synthesis of) Alien Life* (9–12). Illus. 2005, Viking $25.95 (0-670-03458-4). 278pp. Peter Ward, the lead investigator in NASA-funded research into alien life forms, offers his thoughts about what forms of life might eventually be found elsewhere in the universe. (Rev: BL 10/15/05)

Astronautics and Space Exploration

2292 Carlisle, Rodney P. *Exploring Space* (6–10). Series: Discovery and Exploration. 2004, Facts on File $35.00 (0-8160-5265-4). 152pp. The motivations for exploring space are examined in clear, informative text plus photographs, illustrations, and excerpts from primary sources. (Rev: SLJ 12/04) [629.5]

2293 Pyle, Rod. *Destination Moon: The Apollo Missions in the Astronauts' Own Words* (9–12). Illus. 2005, HarperCollins $24.95 (0-06-087349-3). 192pp. With photographs and dialogue from the astronauts themselves, Pyle chronicles the story of the Apollo space program. (Rev: BL 11/15/05) [629.45]

Comets, Meteors, and Asteroids

2294 Koppes, Steven N. *Killer Rocks from Outer Space: Asteroids, Comets, and Meteorites* (7–10). Illus. 2003, Lerner LB $26.60 (0-8225-2861-4). 112pp. Koppes examines the science and history of planetary impacts by asteroids, comets, and meteorites and looks at steps being taken to protect the Earth from such impacts in the future. (Rev: BL 1/1–15/04; SLJ 3/04) [523.5]

2295 Miller, Ron. *Asteroids, Comets, and Meteors* (7–10). Illus. Series: Worlds Beyond. 2005, Twenty-First Century LB $27.93 (0-7613-2363-5). 80pp. Using color photographs, vivid paintings, and helpful diagrams, this title introduces readers to asteroids, comets, and meteors. (Rev: SLJ 12/05)

Stars

2296 Kerrod, Robin. *The Star Guide: Learn How to Read the Night Sky Star by Star.* 2nd ed. (8–12). Illus. 2005, Wiley $29.95 (0-471-70617-5). 160pp. This guide to identifying heavenly bodies is well organized for novices and includes a removable sky map. (Rev: BL 4/15/05) [523.8]

Sun and the Solar System

2297 Miller, Ron. *Mars* (7–10). Illus. Series: Worlds Beyond. 2005, Twenty-First Century LB $27.93 (0-7613-2362-7). 96pp. Introduces readers to the planet Mars in a blend of easy-to-understand narrative and colorful space photos. (Rev: SLJ 12/05)

2298 Sobel, Dava. *The Planets* (10–12). 2005, Viking $24.95 (0-670-03446-0). 262pp. Science, culture, mythology, and astrology are all blended in this interesting survey of the planets of our solar system. (Rev: BL 8/05; SLJ 2/06) [523.2]

2299 Spence, Pam. *Sun Observer's Guide* (7–12). Illus. 2004, Firefly paper $14.95 (1-55297-941-5). 160pp. A useful guide to the sun and the equipment that ensures safe observation of it. (Rev: BL 11/1/04) [522]

Universe

2300 Miller, Ron. *Stars and Galaxies* (7–10). Illus. Series: Worlds Beyond. 2005, Twenty-First Century LB $27.93 (0-7613-3466-1). 96pp. A comprehensive overview of the universe, discussing theories and facts about neighboring stars and distant galaxies alike, with wonderful NASA photos mixed with original art. (Rev: BL 12/1/05; SLJ 12/05) [523.8]

2301 Villard, Ray, and Lynette Cook. *Infinite Worlds: An Illustrated Voyage to Planets Beyond Our Sun* (8–12). Illus. 2005, Univ. of California $39.95 (0-520-23710-2). 252pp. Using known data, the author and illustrator speculate about the likely appearance of planets in other solar systems. (Rev: BL 6/1–15/05) [523.21]

Biological Sciences

General and Miscellaneous

2302 Haupt, Lyanda Lynn. *Pilgrim on the Great Bird Continent: The Importance of Everything and Other Lessons from Darwin's Lost Notebooks* (10–12). Illus. 2006, Little, Brown $24.95 (0-316-83664-8). 288pp. For students interested in Darwin and nature, this is an interesting observation of his voyage of discovery. (Rev: BL 3/1/06) [508]

2303 Panno, Joseph. *Animal Cloning: The Science of Nuclear Transfer* (7–12). Illus. Series: The New Biology. 2004, Facts on File $35.00 (0-8160-4947-5). 164pp. A look at the controversial issue of animal cloning and its scientific implications. (Rev: SLJ 2/05)

2304 Panno, Joseph. *The Cell: Evolution of the First Organism* (7–12). Illus. Series: The New Biology. 2004, Facts on File $35.00 (0-8160-4946-7). 186pp. Reviews theories about life's origin and examines such related topics as cell structure, cell cycle, genes, multi-cellular organisms, and neurons. (Rev: SLJ 2/05)

2305 Walker, Pam, and Elaine Wood. *Ecosystem Science Fair Projects Using Worms, Leaves, Crickets, and Other Stuff* (6–12). Illus. Series: Biology! Best Science Projects. 2005, Enslow LB $26.60 (0-7660-2367-2). 128pp. Biology science projects are clearly presented with background information necessary to full understanding of the underlying principles. (Rev: SLJ 7/05) [570]

Botany

Foods, Farms, and Ranches

GENERAL AND MISCELLANEOUS

2306 *Bound for Glory: America in Color, 1939–43* (8–12). Illus. 2004, Abrams $35.00 (0-8109-4348-4). 192pp. American farm life during the late 1930s and early 1940s is beautifully captured in these color photographs taken under the auspices of the Farm Security Administration, best known for earlier black-and-white collections. (Rev: BL 6/1–15/04) [779]

2307 Montgomery, M. R. *A Cow's Life: The Surprising History of Cattle and How the Black Angus Came to Be Home on the Range* (9–12). Illus. 2004, Walker $25.00 (0-8027-1414-5). 272pp. An entertaining evolutionary history of domesticated cattle. (Rev: BL 10/15/04) [636.2]

2308 Niman, Bill. *The Niman Ranch Cookbook: From Farm to Table with America's Finest Meats* (9–12). Illus. 2005, Ten Speed $35.00 (1-58008-520-2). 240pp. For readers interested in humane animal treatment and high-quality food, this is a fascinating account of modern farming practices. (Rev: BL 10/15/05) [641.3]

2309 Rosenblum, Mort. *Chocolate: A Bittersweet Saga of Dark and Light* (9–12). 2005, Farrar $24.00 (0-86547-635-7). 272pp. For an in-depth report, this volume offers history, statistics, important characters, and debate. (Rev: BL 2/1/05) [641.3]

Forestry and Trees

2310 Logan, William Bryant. *Oak: The Frame of Civilization* (9–12). Illus. 2005, Norton $24.95 (0-

393-04773-3). 320pp. An attractive and accessible history of the oak and its many contributions to human civilization. (Rev: BL 5/1/05) [634.7]

Zoology

General and Miscellaneous

2311 Wetherbee, Kris, and Rick Wetherbee. *Attracting Birds, Butterflies and Other Winged Wonders to Your Backyard* (8–12). Illus. 2005, Sterling $24.95 (1-57990-594-3). 178pp. From shelter to food and water, this guide provides many suggestions for gardeners and nature watchers. (Rev: BL 8/05) [598]

Amphibians and Reptiles

FROGS AND TOADS

2312 Behler, John, and Deborah Behler. *Frogs: A Chorus of Colors* (9–12). Illus. 2005, Sterling $19.95 (1-4027-2814-X). 160pp. An attractive and informative introduction to the diverse world of frogs, created to accompany a traveling exhibit. (Rev: BL 11/1/05) [597.89]

2313 Beltz, Ellin. *Frogs: Inside Their Remarkable World* (9–12). Illus. 2005, Firefly $34.95 (1-55297-869-9). 176pp. A bright and thorough introduction to frogs and the threats they face today, with information on frogs in literature and some interesting frog facts. (Rev: BL 1/1–15/06) [597.8]

TORTOISES AND TURTLES

2314 Chambers, Paul. *A Sheltered Life: The Unexpected History of the Giant Tortoise* (10–12). Illus. 2005, Oxford $28.00 (0-19-522396-9). 320pp. Chambers, a British scientist, provides an engaging account of the discovery of the giant tortoise and the attention paid to these animals over the past two centuries. (Rev: BL 10/15/05) [597.92]

2315 Nicholls, Henry. *Lonesome George: The Life and Loves of a Conservation Icon* (9–12). Illus. 2006, Macmillan $24.95 (1-4039-4576-4). 256pp. The sad tale of Lonesome George, the last known Galapagos giant tortoise, is a good introduction to the importance of conservation. (Rev: BL 4/1/06) [597.9]

2316 Spotila, James R. *Sea Turtles: A Complete Guide to Their Biology, Behavior, and Conservation* (9–12). Illus. 2004, Johns Hopkins paper $24.95 (0-8018-8007-6). 224pp. The need for conservation is a strong theme in this detailed but accessible guide to sea turtles. (Rev: BL 12/1/04) [597.92]

Animal Behavior

GENERAL AND MISCELLANEOUS

2317 Crump, Marty, and Alan Crump. *Headless Males Make Great Lovers and Other Unusual Natural Histories* (9–12). Illus. 2005, Univ. of Chicago $25.00 (0-226-12199-2). 207pp. Bizarre behavior within the animal kingdom is showcased by field biologist Marty Crump in this richly illustrated volume. (Rev: BL 11/1/05) [590]

2318 Masson, Jeffrey Moussaieff. *Raising the Peaceable Kingdom: What Animals Can Teach Us About the Social Origins of Tolerance and Friendship* (10–12). Illus. 2005, Ballantine $22.95 (0-345-46613-6). 192pp. A fascinating study of how young animals — a puppy, a kitten, two chickens, and two rats — interact with each other and a family of humans. (Rev: BL 9/1/05) [591.5]

COMMUNICATION

2319 Reynolds, Bonnie Jones, and Dawn E. Hayman. *If Only They Could Talk: The Miracles of Spring Farm* (10–12). Illus. 2005, Pocket paper $14.00 (0-7434-6486-9). 320pp. The story of New York's Spring Farm and its groundbreaking research into communications between species. (Rev: BL 10/15/05) [636.08]

Animal Species

BEARS

2320 Breiter, Matthias. *Bears: A Year in the Life* (9–12). Illus. 2005, Firefly $34.95 (1-55407-077-5). 176pp. Traces the lives of black, grizzly, and polar bears through a year, with cubs maturing and learning to hunt and socialize. (Rev: BL 9/15/05) [599.78]

2321 Fergus, Charles. *Bears* (10–12). Illus. 2005, Stackpole Bks. $19.95 (0-8117-3251-7). 128pp. Introduces readers to the three major bear species — black, grizzly, and polar — of North America, examining physical characteristics, social behavior, feeding behavior, habitat, hibernation, territoriality, and relations with humans. (Rev: BL 9/15/05) [599.78]

2322 Jans, Nick. *The Grizzly Maze: Timothy Treadwell's Fatal Obsession with Alaskan Bears* (9–12). 2005, Dutton $24.95 (0-525-94886-4). 272pp. Teens riveted by the story of the bear aficionados who were eaten by their subjects will also absorb information about grizzlies, the park service, and human-animal interactions. (Rev: BL 7/05; SLJ 12/05) [599.784]

CATS (LIONS, TIGERS, ETC.)

2323 Gamble, Cyndi. *Leopards: Natural History and Conservation* (7–10). Photos by Rodney Griffiths. Series: WorldLife Library. 2004, Voyageur paper $12.95 (0-89658-656-1). 48pp. Introduces readers to the three leopard species of the world, their habitats, and the threats they face. (Rev: SLJ 4/05) [599.74]

2324 Helfer, Ralph. *Zamba: The True Story of the Greatest Lion That Ever Lived* (9–12). Illus. 2005, HarperCollins $24.95 (0-06-076132-6). 272pp. The heartwarming story of Zamba, an orphaned lion cub raised to adulthood by the author and featured in many films, TV shows, and commercials. (Rev: BL 7/05; SLJ 1/06) [599.757]

2325 Matignon, Karine Lou. *Tiger, Tiger* (8–12). Illus. 2004, Thames & Hudson $40.00 (0-500-51193-4). 185pp. This informative, photo-filled volume uses *Two Brothers*, the film about two tiger siblings separated at birth, as the base for an exploration of tigers and the historic relationship between the big cats and humans. (Rev: BL 11/1/04) [599.7]

2326 Mills, Stephen. *Tiger* (8–12). Illus. 2004, Firefly paper $24.95 (1-55297-949-0). 168pp. For report writers and general interest, this is an excellent introduction to tigers, their behavior, and the threats they face. (Rev: BL 11/1/04) [599.756]

2327 Seidensticker, John, and Susan Lumpkin. *Cats: Smithsonian Answer Book* (8–12). Illus. 2004, Smithsonian $55.00 (1-58834-125-9); paper $24.95 (1-58834-126-7). 304pp. From the characteristics of the common tabby to the exotic puma, researchers and browsers will find a wealth of information in this book, which is arranged in question-and-answer format and includes many color photographs. (Rev: BL 10/1/04) [599.75]

COYOTES, FOXES, AND WOLVES

2328 Reid, Catherine. *Coyote: Seeking the Hunter in Our Midst* (10–12). 2004, Houghton $18.00 (0-618-32964-1). 192pp. Naturalist/poet Reid interweaves information about her own life with her research on the return of the coyote to eastern North America. (Rev: BL 9/15/04) [599.77]

2329 Smith, Douglas W., and Gary Ferguson. *Decade of the Wolf: Returning the Wild to Yellowstone* (9–12). Illus. 2005, Lyons $23.95 (1-59228-700-X). 240pp. Smith describes the ultimately successful reintroduction of wolves to the wild in Yellowstone National Park. (Rev: BL 4/15/05) [599.773]

DEER FAMILY

2330 Heuer, Karsten. *Being Caribou: Five Months on Foot with an Arctic Herd* (9–12). Illus. 2005, Mountaineers Books $24.95 (1-59485-010-0). 256pp. Heuer describes how he and his wife following the annual migration of a vast caribou herd to and from calving grounds in the Arctic National Wildlife Refuge — a refuge threatened by development. (Rev: BL 12/15/05) [599.65]

PANDAS

2331 Croke, Vicki Constantine. *The Lady and the Panda: The True Adventures of the First American Explorer to Bring Back China's Most Exotic Animal* (8–12). Illus. 2005, Random $25.95 (0-375-50783-3). 400pp. The unlikely story of Manhattan socialite Ruth Harkness, who successfully completed her late husband's expedition to capture and bring to America a live giant panda. (Rev: BL 5/1/05) [599.789]

Birds

GENERAL AND MISCELLANEOUS

2332 Gibson, Graeme. *The Bedside Book of Birds: An Avian Miscellany* (9–12). Illus. 2005, Doubleday $29.95 (0-385-51483-2). 352pp. Gibson, a Canadian novelist and avid birder, has compiled a rich selection of works touching on the relationship between humans and birds. (Rev: BL 10/15/05) [598]

BEHAVIOR

2333 Chu, Miyoko. *Songbird Journeys: Four Seasons in the Lives of Migratory Birds* (9–12). Illus. 2006, Walker $23.00 (0-8027-1468-4). 320pp. Ornithologist Chu follows songbirds from their winter territory in the American tropics to their spring and summer homes as far north as Canada and then back south again as the weather turns cooler. (Rev: BL 2/1/06) [598.252]

2334 Levy, Bob. *Club George: The Diary of a Central Park Bird Watcher* (10–12). Illus. 2006, St. Martin's $23.95 (0-312-34167-9). 384pp. A charismatic red-winged blackbird named George converted Levy into a bird lover. (Rev: BL 2/1/06) [598]

2335 Read, Marie. *Secret Lives of Common Birds: Enjoying Bird Behavior Through the Seasons* (8–12). Illus. 2005, Houghton paper $14.95 (0-618-55872-1). 96pp. Beautiful photographs and season-by-season discussion of bird behavior make this satisfying both for browsers and report writers. (Rev: BL 12/15/05) [598.15]

EAGLES, HAWKS, AND OTHER BIRDS OF PREY

2336 Nielsen, John. *Condor: To the Brink and Back — The Life and Times of One Giant Bird* (9–12). Illus. 2006, HarperCollins $25.95 (0-06-008862-1). 272pp. The inspiring story behind the recovery of the California condor from the brink of extinction. (Rev: BL 12/15/05) [598.9]

OWLS

2337 Berger, Cynthia, and Amelia Hansen. *Owls* (9–12). Illus. Series: Wild Guide. 2005, Stackpole Bks. paper $19.95 (0-8117-3213-0). 144pp. Introduces the members of the owl family, examining their physical characteristics, behavior, habitat, diet, and life cycle. (Rev: BL 8/05) [598.9]

Environmental Protection and Endangered and Extinct Species

2338 Dinerstein, Eric. *Tigerland and Other Unintended Science Destinations* (10–12). 2005, Island $25.95 (1-55963-578-9). 288pp. The chief scientist for the World Wildlife Fund writes about his wildlife expeditions to far-flung corners of the globe. (Rev: BL 9/15/05) [590.92]

2339 Ellis, Richard. *No Turning Back: The Life and Death of Animal Species* (9–12). Illus. 2004, HarperCollins $25.95 (0-06-055803-2). 432pp. A fascinating look at bird and mammal species that could face extinction unless drastic measures are taken to protect them. (Rev: BL 7/04) [576.8]

2340 Franke, Mary Ann. *To Save the Wild Bison: Life on the Edge in Yellowstone* (9–12). Illus. 2005, Univ. of Oklahoma $29.95 (0-8061-3683-9). 310pp. The bison of Yellowstone, the last true bison in the nation, are threatened by cattle farmers who fear contamination. (Rev: BL 9/15/05) [333.95]

Insects and Arachnids

GENERAL AND MISCELLANEOUS

2341 Attenborough, David. *Life in the Undergrowth* (9–12). Illus. 2006, Princeton $29.95 (0-691-12703-4). 288pp. In this companion volume to the Animal Planet TV series of the same name, Attenborough offers a close-up look at the world of invertebrates, including insects and spiders. (Rev: BL 2/15/06) [595.7]

2342 Waldbauer, Gilbert. *Insights from Insects: What Bad Bugs Can Teach Us* (8–12). Illus. 2005, Prometheus paper $18.00 (1-59102-277-0). 260pp. Friend or foe? Waldbauer profiles 20 insects that most humans consider pests and their roles in the natural world. (Rev: BL 3/15/05) [632]

BEES AND WASPS

2343 Bishop, Holley. *Robbing the Bees: A Biography of Honey — The Sweet Liquid Gold that Seduced the World* (9–12). Illus. 2005, Free Press $24.00 (0-7432-5021-4). 310pp. Bishop interweaves information on the history and science of beekeeping with details of her own novice efforts. (Rev: BL 3/1/05) [638]

2344 Buchmann, Stephen, and Banning Repplier. *Letters from the Hive: An Intimate History of Bees, Honey, and Humankind* (8–12). Illus. 2005, Bantam $24.00 (0-553-80375-1). 274pp. A natural history of bees is accompanied by discussion of their importance as pollinators, their relationship with humans, methods of cooking with honey, and the medicinal benefits of honey. (Rev: BL 4/1/05) [638]

BUTTERFLIES, MOTHS, AND CATERPILLARS

2345 Schappert, Phil. *The Last Monarch Butterfly: Conserving the Monarch Butterfly in a Brave New World* (8–12). Illus. 2004, Firefly paper $19.95 (1-55297-969-5). 114pp. The fascinating story of the monarch butterfly and its incredible migrations is told with an emphasis on the threats it faces. (Rev: BL 12/15/04) [595.78]

Marine and Freshwater Life

GENERAL AND MISCELLANEOUS

2346 Ellis, Richard. *Singing Whales, Flying Squid, and Swimming Cucumbers: The Discovery of Marine Life* (10–12). Illus. 2006, Lyons $24.95 (1-59228-842-1). 288pp. Ellis, a marine researcher at the American Museum of Natural History, chronicles some of the most exciting discoveries of marine life and looks at potential future exploitation. (Rev: BL 1/1–15/06) [578.77]

CORALS AND JELLYFISH

2347 Walker, Pam, and Elaine Wood. *The Coral Reef* (8–11). Illus. Series: Life in the Seas. 2005, Facts on File $35.00 (0-8160-5703-6). 140pp. An excellent introduction to the world's coral reefs, looking at how they were formed, the creatures that thrive within them, and the threats they face. (Rev: BL 1/1–15/06) [5/8.77]

SHARKS

2348 Carwardine, Mark. *Shark* (7–12). Illus. 2004, Firefly paper $24.95 (1-55297-948-2). 168pp. Report writers and shark fans will find material of interest here. (Rev: BL 11/1/04) [597.3]

2349 Casey, Susan. *The Devil's Teeth: A True Story of Obsession and Survival Among America's Great White Sharks* (8–12). Illus. 2005, Holt $25.00 (0-8050-7581-X). 304pp. An account of the annual gathering of great white sharks near the Farallon Islands, less than 30 miles west of San Francisco in the Pacific Ocean. (Rev: BL 6/1–15/05) [597.3]

WHALES, DOLPHINS, AND OTHER SEA MAMMALS

2350 Brower, Kenneth. *Freeing Keiko: The Journey of a Killer Whale from Free Willy to the Wild* (10–12). 2005, Gotham $26.00 (1-592-50147-3). 288pp. The true, controversial story of Keiko the whale, the model for the central character in the film *Free Willy.* (Rev: BL 11/15/05) [599.5]

2351 Simmonds, Mark. *Whales and Dolphins of the World* (8–12). Illus. 2005, MIT $29.95 (0-262-19519-4). 160pp. This photo-filled volume introduces readers to the cetaceans — whales, dolphins, and porpoises — and to their relationship with humans. (Rev: BL 3/15/05) [599.5]

Microscopes, Microbiology, and Biotechnology

2352 Rainis, Kenneth G. *Cell and Microbe Science Fair Projects Using Microscopes, Mold, and More* (6–12). Illus. Series: Biology! Best Science Projects. 2005, Enslow LB $26.60 (0-7660-2369-9). 128pp. This introduction to the study of cells and microbes contains step-by-step instructions for a number of related experiments and projects. (Rev: SLJ 9/05) [578]

Pets

GENERAL AND MISCELLANEOUS

2353 Montgomery, Sy. *The Good Good Pig: The Extraordinary Life of Christopher Hogwood* (9–12). 2006, Ballantine $21.95 (0-345-48137-2). 240pp. A pig named Christopher Hogwood, adopted by the author as a sickly piglet but recovering quickly to grow and become an excellent companion and local celebrity, is the focus of this warmhearted memoir. (Rev: BL 3/15/06) [636.4]

DOGS

2354 Bain, Terry. *You Are a Dog (Life Through the Eyes of Man's Best Friend)* (8–12). Illus. 2004, Harmony $16.00 (1-4000-5242-4). 159pp. A humorous dog's-eye view of the world. (Rev: SLJ 1/05) [636.7]

2355 Derr, Mark. *A Dog's History of America: How Our Best Friend Explored, Conquered, and Settled a Continent* (9–12). Illus. 2004, Farrar $25.00 (0-86547-631-4). 352pp. Dogs' roles in American society from the earliest days are documented using historical records and personal accounts. (Rev: BL 9/1/04) [636.7]

2356 *Dog Is My Co-Pilot: Great Writers on the World's Oldest Friendship* (10–12). 2003, Crown $25.00 (0-609-61086-4). 288pp. Essays and short stories by writers including Erica Jong and Alice Walker convey the importance of our relationships with our dogs. (Rev: SLJ 4/04)

2357 Foster, Ken. *The Dogs Who Found Me: What I've Learned from Pets Who Were Left Behind* (9–12). 2006, Lyons paper $12.95 (1-59228-749-2). 240pp. In this touching memoir, Foster writes about his relationships with a number of abandoned dogs that he took in over the years. (Rev: BL 2/1/06) [636.7]

2358 Gingold, Alfred. *Dog World: And the Humans Who Live There* (8–12). 2005, Broadway $24.00 (0-7679-1661-1). 256pp. A lighthearted look at the wonders of dog ownership. (Rev: BL 2/1/05) [636.7]

2359 Grogan, John. *Marley and Me: Life and Love with the World's Worst Dog* (9–12). 2005, Morrow $21.95 (0-06-081708-9). 288pp. Grogan tells how a Labrador retriever named Marley taught him important lessons about love and generally enriched his life. (Rev: BL 10/1/05) [636.752]

2360 Katz, Jon. *Katz on Dogs: A Commonsense Guide to Training and Living with Dogs* (10–12). Illus. 2005, Villard $24.95 (1-4000-6403-1). 256pp. The fourth in an interesting series of books about dogs, this volume lays out easy-to-follow guidelines for training dogs and for living with them successfully. (Rev: BL 9/1/05) [636.7]

2361 Konik, Michael. *Ella in Europe: An American Dog's International Adventures* (8–12). 2005, Delacorte $20.00 (0-385-33851-1). 302pp. Charming stories about travels through Europe with a great dog named Ella. (Rev: BL 12/15/04) [636.7]

2362 Rogers, Katharine M. *First Friend: A History of Dogs and Humans* (8–12). Illus. 2005, St. Martin's $24.95 (0-312-33188-6). 288pp. Examines the millennia-long relationship between dogs and humans; well-selected illustrations add to the coverage. (Rev: BL 8/05) [636.7]

HORSES

2363 Korda, Margaret, and Michael Korda. *Horse Housekeeping: Everything You Need to Know to Keep a Horse at Home* (9–12). 2005, HarperCollins $26.95 (0-06-057308-2). 224pp. You *can* keep a horse in your own backyard — given certain space and other strictures — is the message of this practical guide. (Rev: BL 11/1/05) [798.2]

2364 Roberts, Monty. *The Horses in My Life* (10–12). Illus. 2005, Trafalgar Square $29.95 (1-57076-323-6). 256pp. The author of *The Man Who Listens to Horses* writes about the most memorable horses in his lengthy career. (Rev: BL 9/1/05) [636.1]

2365 Stromberg, Tony. *Spirit Horses* (8–12). Illus. 2005, New World Library $40.00 (1-57731-499-9).

168pp. A photographic celebration of horses in a large-format album, accompanied by quotes from diverse sources. (Rev: BL 11/1/05) [636.1]

Zoos, Aquariums, and Animal Care

2366 Balliet, Gay L. *Lions and Tigers and Mares. . . Oh My!* (8–12). 2004, RDR paper $17.95 (1-57143-105-5). 336pp. In humorous, appealing text, the wife of a Pennsylvania veterinarian sheds new light on the day-to-day challenges facing a vet who treats large and exotic animals. (Rev: BL 9/15/04) [636.089]

2367 Brown, Bradford B. *While You're Here, Doc: Farmyard Adventures of a Maine Veterinarian* (8–12). 2006, Tilbury House paper $15.00 (0-88448-279-0). 192pp. Entertaining stories about life as a veterinarian in rural Maine. (Rev: BL 3/15/06) [636.0]

2368 Fisher, Lester E. *Dr. Fisher's Life on the Ark: Green Alligators, Bushman, and Other "Hare-Raising Tales" from America's Most Popular Zoo and Around the World* (9–12). Illus. 2004, Racom $26.95 (0-9704515-6-3). 254pp. The longtime director of Chicago's Lincoln Park Zoo recalls some of the more memorable experiences from his years with the zoo and his foreign expedition. (Rev: BL 9/1/04) [590.73]

2369 Maitre-Alain, Thierry, and Christian Piednoir. *Aquariums: The Complete Guide to Freshwater and Saltwater Aquariums* (8–12). Illus. 2006, Firefly $39.95 (1-55407-085-6). 288pp. A handsome, photo-filled guide to aquariums, with advice on water, equipment, selection of fish, and suitable plants. (Rev: BL 2/1/06) [639.34]

Chemistry

General and Miscellaneous

2370 Bown, Stephen R. *A Most Damnable Invention: Dynamite, Nitrates, and the Making of the Modern World* (10–12). Illus. 2005, St. Martin's $23.95 (0-312-32913-X). 272pp. Historian Bown chronicles Alfred Nobel's 19th-century invention of dynamite, a nitroglycerine-based explosive that is far safer to handle than nitroglycerine alone. (Rev: BL 10/15/05) [553.6]

2371 Gardner, Robert. *Chemistry Science Fair Projects Using Acids, Bases, Metals, Salts, and Inorganic Stuff* (7–10). Illus. Series: Chemistry! Best Science Projects. 2004, Enslow LB $26.60 (0-7660-2210-2). 128pp. Experiments and projects that explore various aspects of inorganic chemistry are presented with background information and safety tips. (Rev: SLJ 2/05) [540]

2372 Gardner, Robert. *Chemistry Science Fair Projects Using French Fries, Gumdrops, Soap, and Other Organic Stuff* (7–12). Illus. Series: Chemistry! Best Science Projects. 2004, Enslow LB $26.60 (0-7660-2211-0). 128pp. Progressively more complex experiments and projects explore various aspects of organic chemistry using everyday items. (Rev: SLJ 4/05) [540]

2373 Goodstein, Madeline. *Plastics and Polymers Science Fair Projects: Using Hair Gel, Soda Bottles, and Slimy Stuff* (7–12). Illus. Series: Chemistry! Best Science Projects. 2004, Enslow LB $20.95 (0-7660-2123-8). 128pp. Introduced by a discussion of the concept of polymers and a model of a hydrocarbon chain, subsequent projects build on this knowledge. (Rev: SLJ 7/04) [507]

2374 Goodstein, Madeline. *Water Science Fair Projects: Using Ice Cubes, Super Soakers, and Other Wet Stuff* (7–12). Illus. Series: Chemistry! Best Science Projects. 2004, Enslow LB $20.95 (0-7660-2124-6). 128pp. Projects that use everyday materials teach students about water and its properties. (Rev: SLJ 7/04)

2375 Miller, Ron. *The Elements: What You Really Want to Know* (7–12). 2005, Twenty-First Century LB $29.27 (0-7613-2794-0). 135pp. After historical information and profiles of key scientists, Miller provides information on each element in order of atomic number. (Rev: SLJ 3/06) [540]

Geology and Geography

Earth and Geology

2376 Bjornerud, Marcia. *Reading the Rocks: The Autobiography of the Earth* (10–12). 2005, Westview $26.00 (0-8133-4249-X). 256pp. The geologic history of the earth is presented in very readable narrative. (Rev: BL 3/15/05) [551.7]

2377 Fortey, Richard. *Earth: An Intimate History* (10–12). Illus. 2004, Knopf $30.00 (0-375-40626-3). 480pp. Paleontologist Fortey introduces readers to important geological sites around the world, explaining the significance of each. (Rev: BL 10/15/04) [551.7]

2378 Gardner, Robert. *Planet Earth Science Fair Projects Using the Moon, Stars, Beach Balls, Frisbees, and Other Far-Out Stuff* (6–12). Illus. Series: Earth Science! Best Science Projects. 2005, Enslow LB $26.60 (0-7660-2362-1). 128pp. Earth science projects are clearly presented with background information necessary to give full understanding of the underlying principles. (Rev: SLJ 7/05) [551]

2379 Macdougall, Doug. *Frozen Earth: The Once and Future Story of Ice Ages* (10–12). Illus. 2004, Univ. of California $24.95 (0-520-23922-9). 284pp. A fascinating presentation that combines information on ice ages — and the author's belief that the earth is currently cooling — with biographies of key scientists and the importance of geology in general. (Rev: BL 9/15/04) [551.7]

Physical Geography

Forests and Rain Forests

2380 Lowman, Margaret D., et al. *It's a Jungle Up There: More Tales from the Treetops* (9–12). 2006, Yale $27.50 (0-300-10863-X). 304pp. In addition to interesting descriptions of the rain forest canopy and the threats to its health, Lowman and her sons recount family adventures in wilderness areas around the globe. (Rev: BL 3/15/06) [509]

Ponds, Rivers, and Lakes

2381 Lambrecht, Bill. *Big Muddy Blues: True Tales and Twisted Politics Along Lewis and Clark's Missouri River* (8–12). Illus. 2005, St. Martin's $25.95 (0-312-32783-8). 352pp. An engaging history of the Missouri and what has happened to its natural flow in the 200 years since the river was first charted by Lewis and Clark. (Rev: BL 3/15/05) [331.91]

Rocks, Minerals, and Soil

2382 Coenraads, Robert R. *Rocks and Fossils: A Visual Guide* (9–12). Illus. 2005, Firefly $29.95 (1-55407-068-6). 304pp. Full of illustrations and photographs, this is an excellent overview of rocks, fossils, and geologic processes that will serve as a good resource for report writers. (Rev: BL 9/1/05) [552]

2383 Oldershaw, Cally. *Firefly Guide to Gems* (10–12). 2004, Firefly paper $14.95 (1-55297-814-1). 224pp. This small-format, well-illustrated guide to gemstones starts with background material and proceeds to a listing of gems by chemical composition. (Rev: SLJ 6/04; VOYA 6/04) [553.8]

2384 Staubach, Suzanne. *Clay: The History and Evolution of Humankind's Relationship with Earth's Most Primal Element* (9–12). Illus. 2005, Berkley $23.95 (0-425-20566-5). 304pp. Staubach examines the extraordinary role that clay has played in the building of civilization, from primitive pottery to construction material to porcelain and the semiconductors that are at the heart of today's technological innovations. (Rev: BL 11/15/05) [620.1]

Mathematics

General and Miscellaneous

2385 Arianrhod, Robyn. *Einstein's Heroes: Imagining the World Through the Language of Mathematics* (9–12). Illus. 2005, Oxford $28.00 (0-19-518370-3). 338pp. Australian mathematician Robyn Arianrhod chronicles the quest to make sense of the physical world, focusing on the contributions of Isaac Newton, Michael Faraday, and James Clerk Maxwell and how they paved the way for the work of Albert Einstein. (Rev: BL 6/1–15/05) [530.9]

Meteorology

General and Miscellaneous

2386 Cox, John D. *Climate Crash: Abrupt Climate Change and What It Means for Our Future* (10–12). 2005, Joseph Henry $27.95 (0-309-09312-0). 224pp. In easy-to-understand language, science/environment journalist Cox outlines the history of research into sudden climate change and explores how such changes might affect the future, cautioning that it may be too early to assess the impact of greenhouse gases. (Rev: BL 5/15/05) [551.79]

2387 de Villiers, Marq. *Windswept: The Story of Wind and Weather* (10–12). Illus. 2006, Walker $25.00 (0-8027-1469-2). 352pp. An interesting discussion of our understanding of wind over time, touching on ancient myths about winds, the discovery of the jet stream, and specific windstorms of note. (Rev: BL 3/15/06) [551.51]

2388 Flannery, Tim. *The Weather Makers: The History and Future Impact of Climate Change* (10–12). 2006, Grove $25.00 (0-87113-935-9). 320pp. In this compelling examination of humans' impact on the weather, Australian scientist Flannery sees a catastrophe in the making. (Rev: BL 1/1–15/06) [363.738]

2389 Fredston, Jill. *Snowstruck: In the Grip of Avalanches* (9–12). Illus. 2005, Harcourt $24.00 (0-15-101249-0). 352pp. Based on her research and search-and-rescue experience, avalanche expert Fredston examines the awesome force of these natural phenomena and the human toll they exact. (Rev: BL 10/1/05) [551.3]

Storms

2390 Cerveny, Randy. *Freaks of the Storm: From Flying Cows to Stealing Thunder* (8–12). Illus. 2006, Thunder's Mouth paper $16.95 (1-56025-801-2). 368pp. Cerveny chronicles bizarre weather phenomena — from fish falling from the sky to chickens plucked bare by hurricane winds — and extremes of heat, cold, rainfall, and so forth. (Rev: BL 12/1/05) [551.5]

2391 Emanuel, Kerry. *Divine Wind: The History and Science of Hurricanes* (11–12). Illus. 2005, Oxford $45.00 (0-19-514941-6). 304pp. Advanced students will appreciate this comprehensive discussion of the science of hurricanes and the references to relevant art and literature. (Rev: BL 12/1/05) [551.55]

2392 Svenvold, Mark. *Big Weather: Chasing Tornadoes in the Heart of America* (9–12). 2005, Holt $26.00 (0-8050-7646-8). 320pp. The lives and personalities of people who chase dangerous storms are captured here. (Rev: BL 4/15/05) [551.55]

Water

2393 Gosnell, Mariana. *Ice: The Nature, the History, and the Uses of an Astonishing Substance* (9–12). Illus. 2005, Knopf $30.00 (0-679-42608-6). 512pp. Gosnell, a former *Newsweek* reporter, explores the science, dangers, benefits, and cultural significance of ice. (Rev: BL 11/1/05) [551.3]

Weather

2394 Buckley, Bruce, et al. *Weather: A Visual Guide* (8–12). Illus. 2004, Firefly $29.95 (1-55297-957-1). 304pp. Full of color photographs and clear graphics, this informative volume explores the forces that generate weather and the impact of weather extremes. (Rev: BL 10/15/04; SLJ 12/04; VOYA 4/05) [551.5]

2395 Burt, Christopher C. *Extreme Weather: A Guide and Record Book* (8–12). Illus. 2004, Norton paper $24.95 (0-393-32658-6). 304pp. An overview of weather at its worst, this richly illustrated volume contains a wealth of meteorological data on extreme events, including heat, drought, cold, floods, thunderstorms, windstorms, tornadoes, and fog. (Rev: SLJ 2/05) [551.6]

2396 Douglas, Paul. *Restless Skies: The Ultimate Weather Book* (9–12). Illus. 2005, Sterling $24.95 (0-7607-6113-2). 256pp. A midwestern TV meteorologist offers sound advice for staying safe in all kinds of weather. (Rev: BL 1/1–15/06) [551.55]

2397 Reynolds, Ross. *Guide to Weather: A Practical Guide to Observing, Measuring and Understanding the Weather* (10–12). Illus. 2005, Firefly paper $19.95 (1-55407-110-0). 208pp. A detailed yet easy-to-understand guide to the atmospheric forces that create weather. (Rev: BL 9/15/05) [551.6]

Oceanography

General and Miscellaneous

2398 Hutchinson, Stephen, and Lawrence E. Hawkins. *Oceans: A Visual Guide* (8–12). Illus. 2005, Firefly $29.95 (1-55407-069-4). 304pp. With dramatic photographs and highly readable text, oceanographers Hutchinson and Hawkins introduce readers to the oceans of the world and the qualities that clearly distinguish one from the other. (Rev: BL 10/15/05; VOYA 4/06) [551.46]

Underwater Exploration and Sea Disasters

2399 Krauss, Erich. *Wave of Destruction: The Stories of Four Families and History's Deadliest Tsunami* (11–12). 2005, Rodale $24.95 (1-59486-378-4). 256pp. The enormity of the disaster caused by the December 2004 Indian Ocean tsunami is revealed in this look at how the catastrophe affected four families in the path of the deadly wave; for mature readers. (Rev: BL 12/1/05) [959.304]

Physics

General and Miscellaneous

2400 Bortz, Fred. *The Quark* (7–10). Illus. Series: The Library of Subatomic Particles. 2004, Rosen LB $26.50 (0-8239-4533-2). 64pp. Suitable for reluctant readers, this is a clear explanation of the quark, featuring large text and many color illustrations. Also recommended in this series are *The Proton*, *The Photon*, and *The Electron* (all 2004). (Rev: SLJ 10/04)

2401 Darling, David. *Teleportation: The Impossible Leap* (10–12). 2005, Wiley $24.95 (0-471-47095-3). 288pp. Is teleportation in our future? Darling reviews the theories behind it and the experiments now being undertaken. (Rev: BL 5/1/05) [537.5]

2402 Hawking, Stephen, and Leonard Mlodinow. *A Briefer History of Time* (9–12). Illus. 2005, Bantam $25.00 (0-553-80436-7). 176pp. More concise and accessible than the classic *A Brief History of Time* (1988), this explanation of the concept of a dynamic cosmos makes excellent reading, especially for physics students. (Rev: BL 7/05) [523.1]

2403 Kaku, Michio. *Parallel Worlds: A Journey Through Creation, Higher Dimensions, and the Future of the Cosmos* (11–12). Illus. 2004, Doubleday $27.50 (0-385-50986-3). 320pp. Physicist Kaku explores the theoretical possibility that parallel and/or multiple universes may exist. (Rev: BL 12/1/04) [523.1]

2404 Ouellette, Jennifer. *Black Bodies and Quantum Cats: Tales from the Annals of Physics* (11–12). Illus. 2005, Penguin paper $15.00 (0-14-303603-3). 312pp. In this collection of 50 articles, Ouellette examines a wide array of physics principles from the layperson's viewpoint. (Rev: BL 11/1/05) [530]

2405 Randall, Lisa. *Warped Passages: Unraveling the Mysteries of the Universe's Hidden Dimensions* (10–12). Illus. 2005, Ecco $27.95 (0-06-053108-8). 512pp. Randall explains recent findings in cosmology, particle physics, string theory, and super symmetry using easy-to-understand analogies. (Rev: BL 9/1/05) [530]

2406 Rigden, John S. *Einstein, 1905: The Standard of Greatness* (10–12). Illus. 2005, Harvard $21.95 (0-674-01544-4). 192pp. Physics professor Rigden helps readers to understand the science behind five key documents that Albert Einstein published in 1905. (Rev: BL 12/1/04; SLJ 7/05) [530.11]

2407 Robinson, Kim Stanley. *Fifty Degrees Below* (9–12). 2005, Bantam $25.00 (0-553-80312-3). 405pp. In this sequel to *Forty Signs of Rain* (2004), weather catastrophes attributable to global warming include the stalling of the Gulf Stream, frigid temperatures along the East Coast, and flooding. (Rev: SLJ 3/06)

2408 Sonneborn, Liz. *Forces in Nature: Understanding Gravitational, Electrical, and Magnetic Force* (7–12). Illus. Series: Library of Physics. 2005, Rosen LB $25.25 (1-4042-0332-X). 48pp. Explores a wide variety of forces, including gravitational, electrical, magnetic, and electromagnetic, using clear narrative with diagrams and photographs. (Rev: SLJ 12/05)

2409 Willett, Edward. *The Basics of Quantum Physics: Understanding the Photoelectric Effect and Line Spectra* (7–12). Illus. Series: Library of Physics. 2005, Rosen LB $25.25 (1-4042-0334-6). 48pp. Examines the nature of light and the atom, key elements in the study of quantum physics, using clear narrative with diagrams and photographs. (Rev: SLJ 12/05)

Energy and Motion

General and Miscellaneous

2410 Crosby, Alfred W. *Children of the Sun: A History of Humanity's Unappeasable Appetite for Energy* (10–12). Illus. 2006, Norton $23.95 (0-393-05935-9). 208pp. An overview of humankind's historical demands for energy and the outlook for the future. (Rev: BL 1/1–15/06) [333.79]

2411 Robinson, Andrew. *Einstein: A Hundred Years of Relativity* (9–12). Illus. 2005, Abrams $29.95 (0-8109-5923-2). 256pp. An attractive celebration of Einstein's life and work, this volume includes useful resources for reports. (Rev: BL 10/15/05) [530]

2412 Viegas, Jennifer. *Kinetic and Potential Energy: Understanding Changes Within Physical Systems* (7–12). Illus. Series: Library of Physics. 2005, Rosen LB $25.25 (1-4042-0333-8). 48pp. Examines the distinction between potential and kinetic energy, as well as momentum, mechanical energy, and the laws of energy, using clear narrative with diagrams and photographs. (Rev: SLJ 12/05)

Nuclear Energy

2413 Alexievich, Svetlana. *Voices from Chernobyl* (9–12). Trans. by Keith Gessen. 2005, Dalkey Archive $22.95 (1-56478-401-0). 240pp. First-person accounts make this a shocking and vivid portrait of the human costs of the 1986 nuclear catastrophe. (Rev: BL 5/15/05) [363.17]

2414 Lüsted, Marcia, and Greg Lusted. *A Nuclear Power Plant* (8–12). Illus. Series: Building History. 2005, Gale LB $27.45 (1-59018-392-4). 112pp. Explores the history of nuclear power generation and considers the arguments for and against the construction of more nuclear power plants in the United States and elsewhere. (Rev: SLJ 6/05) [333.792]

Magnetism and Electricity

2415 Bodanis, David. *Electric Universe: The Shocking True Story of Electricity* (8–12). 2005, Crown $24.00 (1-4000-4550-9). 320pp. The cast of characters involved in harnessing electricity are subjected to rigorous and entertaining scrutiny. (Rev: BL 2/1/05) [537]

Technology and Engineering

General Works and Miscellaneous Industries

2416 Crompton, Samuel Willard. *The Printing Press* (7–10). Series: Transforming Power of Technology. 2003, Chelsea House LB $22.95 (0-7910-7451-X). 120pp. This interesting volume explores the impact of the invention of the printing press on literacy and general social and economic conditions. (Rev: SLJ 6/04)

2417 Gurstelle, William. *Adventures from the Technology Underground: Catapults, Pulsejets, Rail Guns, Flamethrowers, Tesla Coils, Air Cannons, and the Garage Warriors Who Love Them* (10–12). Illus. 2006, Clarkson Potter $25.00 (1-4000-5028-0). 240pp. A fascinating tour of technology for teens entranced by such notions as flying cars and fighting robots. (Rev: BL 1/1–15/06) [608]

2418 Hambling, David. *Weapons Grade: How Modern Warfare Gave Birth to Our High-Tech World* (10–12). Illus. 2005, Carroll & Graf $25.00 (0-7867-1476-X). 416pp. An interesting look at how military technologies developed during World War II and the Cold War have been transformed to meet civilian needs. (Rev: BL 3/15/05) [338.47]

2419 Harrison, Ian. *The Book of Inventions* (8–12). Illus. 2004, National Geographic $30.00 (0-7922-8296-5). 288pp. A photo-filled review of some eclectic and entertaining inventions, including sliced bread and the lava lamp. (Rev: BL 12/1/04) [609]

2420 Sargent, Ted. *The Dance of Molecules: How Nanotechnology Is Changing Our Lives* (11–12). 2006, Thunder's Mouth $25.00 (1-56025-809-8). 256pp. Sargent explores the fascinating field of nanotechnology and offers a glimpse at how this type of molecular-level engineering is likely to shape the future of life on Earth. (Rev: BL 12/1/05) [620]

2421 Woodford, Chris, et al. *Cool Stuff and How It Works* (8–12). Illus. 2005, DK $24.99 (0-7566-1465-1). 256pp. The inner workings of products ranging from the digital camera to the microwave oven are explained in clear text with lots of bright, often high-tech illustrations. (Rev: BL 12/1/05) [600]

Clothing, Textiles, and Jewelry

2422 Bell, Alison. *Fearless Fashion* (6–10). Illus. 2005, Lobster paper $14.95 (1-894222-86-5). 64pp. From preppy to punk to goth to boho, this volume analyzes seven hot fashion trends, looks at trends in history, and gives tips on developing one's own style. (Rev: SLJ 3/05) [391]

Computers, Automation, and the Internet

2423 Billings, Charlene W., and Sean M. Grady. *Supercomputers: Charting the Future of Cybernetics.* Rev. ed. (8–12). Illus. Series: Science and Technology in Focus. 2004, Facts on File $29.95 (0-8160-4730-8). 228pp. This revised and expanded edition covers the history of computing devices from ancient clay tablets onward and looks forward to the future potential of optical and quantum computers. (Rev: SLJ 6/04) [004.1]

2424 German, Dave. *Dave Gorman's Googlewhack! Adventure* (8–12). Illus. 2004, Overlook $24.95 (1-58567-614-4). 352pp. Gorman, a British stand-up comic, writes about his global quest to find googlewhacks — two-word Google search queries that yield a single, solitary hit — in the process of which he successfully put off writing a contracted novel. (Rev: BL 9/15/04) [910.4]

2425 Gordon, Sherri Mabry. *Downloading Copyrighted Stuff from the Internet: Stealing or Fair Use?* (7–10). Illus. Series: Issues in Focus Today. 2005, Enslow LB $23.95 (0-7660-2164-5). 104pp. In concise, accessible text, Gordon defines fair use and copyright and examines issues involving downloading of text, music, games, and so forth. (Rev: BL 11/1/05; SLJ 11/05) [346.730]

2426 Hally, Mike. *Electronic Brains: Stories from the Dawn of the Computer Age* (10–12). 2005, Joseph Henry $27.95 (0-309-09630-8). 256pp. The birth of the computer age and the questions surrounding its parentage are explored in this fascinating volume that chronicles the achievements of computer pioneers in the United States, United Kingdom, Australia, and Soviet Union. (Rev: BL 10/15/05) [004]

2427 Herumin, Wendy. *Censorship on the Internet: From Filters to Freedom of Speech* (5 Up). Series: Issues in Focus. 2004, Enslow LB $20.95 (0-7660-1946-2). 128pp. A look at the various ways we restrict the free exchange of information over the Internet and the pros and cons of doing so. (Rev: SLJ 4/04) [303.48]

2428 Lindsay, Dave. *Dave's Quick 'n' Easy Web Pages 2: A Guide to Creating Multi-page Web Sites* (6–10). 2004, Erin paper $11.95 (0-9690609-9-8). 122pp. Readers with little prior knowledge will learn such techniques as creating frames and cascading style sheets as this straightforward title introduces concepts clearly with graphics and advice boxes. (Rev: SLJ 11/04) [005.7]

2429 Selfridge, Benjamin, and Peter Selfridge. *A Kid's Guide to Creating Web Pages for Home and School* (5–10). Illus. 2004, Chicago Review paper $19.95 (1-56976-180-9). 110pp. Simple instructions on creating Web pages using HTML are accompanied by helpful illustrations and sample finished pages. (Rev: SLJ 2/05) [005.7]

2430 Weber, Sandra. *The Internet* (7–10). Series: Transforming Power of Technology. 2003, Chelsea House LB $22.95 (0-7910-7449-8). 110pp. A look at the influence of the Internet on areas ranging from the economy to society to health care and at the implications for schools and libraries. (Rev: SLJ 6/04) [004.6]

Electronics

2431 Chaplin, Heather, and Aaron Ruby. *Smart-Bomb: Inside the $25 Billion Videogame Explosion* (10–12). 2005, Algonquin $24.95 (1-56512-346-8).

296pp. The birth and development of the video game industry are presented in a riveting text that profiles key figures and clearly explains their importance. (Rev: BL 9/15/05; SLJ 4/06) [338.4]

Transportation

General and Miscellaneous

2432 Welsch, Roger. *From Tinkering to Torquing: A Beginner's Guide to Tractors and Tools* (9–12). 2005, MBI $21.95 (0-7603-2082-9). 224pp. In this one-of-a-kind guide, Welsch blends advice for collectors and restorers of antique tractors with plenty of folksy anecdotes. (Rev: BL 12/15/05) [631.3]

Airplanes, Aeronautics, and Ballooning

2433 Cadbury, Deborah. *Space Race: The Epic Battle Between America and the Soviet Union for Dominion of Space* (9–12). Illus. 2006, HarperCollins $24.95 (0-06-084553-8). 384pp. In addition to clearly describing rocket evolution from World War II to the moon landings, this volume provides biographical information on rocket designers Wernher von Braun and Sergei Korolev. (Rev: BL 2/15/06) [629.409]

2434 Dick, Ron, and Dan Patterson. *Aviation Century: The Golden Age* (9–12). Illus. Series: Aviation Century. 2004, Firefly $39.95 (1-55046-409-4). 288pp. Chronicles the history of aviation from 1919 to 1939, profiling some of the period's best-known aviators, including Amelia Earhart, Charles Lindbergh, Billy Mitchell, and Eddie Rickenbacker. Also use *Aviation Century: World War II* (2004). (Rev: BL 12/1/04) [940.54]

2435 Edgerton, Clyde. *Solo: My Adventures in the Air* (10–12). 2005, Algonquin $23.95 (1-56512-426-X). 296pp. Novelist Clyde Edgerton writes engagingly of his lifelong love of planes and flying, and the service that earned him a Distinguished Flying Cross during the Vietnam War. (Rev: BL 9/1/05) [629.130]

Automobiles and Trucks

2436 Christensen, Lisa. *Clueless About Cars: An Easy Guide to Car Maintenance and Repair* (9–12). Illus. 2004, Firefly paper $14.95 (1-55297-975-X). 160pp. This friendly, easy-to-use guide explains a car's systems and supplies basic car maintenance advice, boxed tips, and useful checklists. (Rev: SLJ 12/04) [629]

2437 Edmonston, Phil, and Maureen Sawa. *Car Smarts: Hot Tips for the Car Crazy* (7–10). Illus. 2003, Tundra paper $15.95 (0-88776-646-3). 80pp.

Attractive and lively, this is a large-format compendium of facts and advice about cars — their history, how they work, and their purchase and maintenance. (Rev: BL 4/1/04; SLJ 7/04; VOYA 10/04) [629.222]

2438 Gravelle, Karen. *The Driving Book* (9–12). 2005, Walker $16.95 (0-8027-8933-1); paper $9.95 (0-8027-7706-6). 160pp. An excellent resource for new drivers, this straightforward guide addresses a wide range of important topics, including auto maintenance, driving in bad weather, road rage, the effects of legal and illegal drugs on driving ability, and what to do in an emergency. (Rev: BL 3/1/05; SLJ 5/05; VOYA 8/05) [629.28]

Ships and Boats

2439 Kurson, Robert. *Shadow Divers: The True Adventure of Two Americans Who Risked Everything to Solve One of the Last Mysteries of World War II* (9–12). 2004, Random $26.95 (0-375-50858-9). 400pp. This compelling story of two divers' discovery of the wreckage of a German U-boat in deep ocean waters off New Jersey contains fascinating details of their dangerous explorations. (Rev: SLJ 2/05) [940.54]

2440 Pollack, John. *Cork Boat* (10–12). 2004, Pantheon $21.00 (0-375-42257-9). 291pp. A former journalist and speechwriter, Pollack decided to build a boat from wine bottle corks and this is the surprisingly compelling story of his successful project, which culminated in a trip down a Portuguese river. (Rev: SLJ 4/04) [797.1]

Weapons, Submarines, and the Armed Forces

2441 Ermey, R. Lee. *Mail Call* (8–12). Illus. 2005, Hyperion paper $17.95 (1-4013-0779-5). 256pp.

History Channel personality offers facts and figures about military weaponry, modern warfare, and other military trivia. (Rev: BL 12/15/04) [355.009]

2442 Gurstelle, William. *The Art of the Catapult: Build Greek Ballistae, Roman Onagers, English Trebuchets, and More Ancient Artillery* (5 Up). Illus. 2004, Chicago Review paper $14.95 (1-55652-526-5). 172pp. Information on history, physics, and military tactics, plus step-by-step instructions for the construction of 10 working catapults. (Rev: SLJ 11/04) [623.4]

2443 Lefkowitz, Arthur. *Bushnell's Submarine: The Best Kept Secret of the American Revolution* (7–10). Illus. 2006, Scholastic $16.99 (0-439-74352-4). 144pp. The little-known story of the *Turtle*, America's first submarine, which was launched during the closing days of the American Revolution. (Rev: BL 2/15/06; SLJ 4/06) [973.3]

2444 Stout, Jay A. *Hammer from Above: Marine Air Combat over Iraq* (9–12). 2005, Presidio $25.95 (0-89141-865-2). 416pp. A former Marine Corps fighter pilot examines the crucial role played by marine aircraft in the launching of Operation Iraqi Freedom. (Rev: BL 12/15/05) [956.7044]

2445 Torr, James D., ed. *Weapons of Mass Destruction* (7–10). Series: Opposing Viewpoints. 2004, Gale LB $26.96 (0-7377-2250-9); paper $17.96 (0-7377-2251-7). 207pp. Terrorist attacks using nuclear or biological weapons, the threat from "rogue" nations, U.S. policies regarding its own weapons of mass destruction, and national defense are all discussed in essays introduced by focus questions. (Rev: SLJ 4/05) [355.02]

2446 Walker, Sally M. *Secrets of a Civil War Submarine: Solving the Mysteries of the H. L. Hunley* (7–10). Illus. 2005, Carolrhoda $17.95 (1-57505-830-8). 64pp. Walker chronicles the story of the Confederate submarine *H. L. Hunley* from its design and construction through its successful attack on the *USS Housatonic* in 1864 to its discovery on the bottom of Charleston Harbor in 1995. (Rev: BL 4/15/05*; SLJ 5/05) [973.7]

Recreation and Sports

Crafts, Hobbies, and Pastimes

General and Miscellaneous

2447 Bell, Alison. *Let's Party!* (6–10). Series: What's Your Style? 2005, Lobster paper $14.95 (1-894222-99-7). 64pp. Eight theme parties are suggested, complete with invitations, decorations, food, music, and so forth; particularly useful may be the tips on keeping parents at bay and dealing with crashers. (Rev: SLJ 3/06) [793.2]

2448 Cicale, Annie. *The Art and Craft of Hand Lettering: Techniques, Projects, Inspiration* (9–12). Illus. 2004, Sterling $24.95 (1-57990-403-3). 192pp. A practical guide to calligraphy, showing how the art can be used to put a personal imprint on various crafts. (Rev: BL 7/04) [745.6]

2449 Ledoux, Jeanee. *Abode à la Mode: 44 Projects for Hip Home Decor* (11–12). Illus. 2006, Sterling paper $14.95 (1-4027-1343-6). 176pp. Good, affordable decorating ideas for teens planning for shared apartments, dorm rooms, or simply small budgets. (Rev: BL 1/1–15/06) [747]

2450 Miller, Jill. *Fabrics and Florals: 100+ Ideas for "Dressing Up" Your Pages!* (9–12). Illus. 2005, Watson-Guptill paper $14.95 (0-8230-1637-4). 80pp. Miller presents many ideas for giving scrapbooks a personal touch. (Rev: BL 12/15/05) [745.593]

2451 Murillo, Kathy Cano. *The Crafty Diva's Lifestyle Makeover: Awesome Ideas to Spice Up Your Life!* (5–12). Illus. 2005, Watson-Guptill paper $12.95 (0-8230-1008-2). 144pp. The Crafty Diva is back with this collection of easy-to-follow instructions for 50 projects that cover everything from room makeovers to fashion accessories. (Rev: SLJ 9/05)

2452 Taylor, Terry. *Altered Art: Techniques for Creating Altered Books, Boxes, Cards and More* (8–12). 2004, Lark $19.95 (1-57990-550-1). 144pp. Terry Taylor provides a fascinating introduction into the world of altered art. (Rev: BL 12/15/04; SLJ 4/05)

2453 Winters, Eleanor. *Calligraphy for Kids* (6–12). 2004, Sterling $14.95 (1-4027-0664-2). 128pp. Information on basic tools and techniques and the importance of correct posture introduce calligraphy projects. (Rev: BL 12/15/04) [745.6/1]

American Historical Crafts

2454 Anderson, Maxine. *Great Civil War Projects You Can Build Yourself* (7–10). Illus. 2005, Nomad paper $16.95 (0-9749344-1-0). 160pp. Craft projects explore various aspects of life on the Civil War battlefield and home front — making cornbread, a pinhole camera, a rag doll, and so forth. (Rev: BL 11/1/05; SLJ 11/05) [745.5]

Clay Modeling and Ceramics

2455 Belcher, Judy. *Polymer Clay Creative Traditions: Techniques and Projects Inspired by the Fine and Decorative Arts* (8–12). Illus. 2006, Watson-Guptill paper $21.95 (0-8230-4065-8). 144pp. Step-by-step instructions for more than 30 items that can be crafted from polymer clay. (Rev: BL 12/15/05) [745.57]

Cooking

2456 Bayless, Rick, and Lanie Bayless. *Rick and Lanie's Excellent Kitchen Adventures* (7–12). Photos by Christopher Hirsheimer. 2004, Stewart, Tabori & Chang $29.95 (1-58479-331-7). 231pp. A culinary tour of the world, sampling recipes from almost every continent. (Rev: SLJ 1/05) [641.5]

2457 Behnke, Alison, and Ehramjian Vartkes. *Cooking the Middle Eastern Way* (7–10). Illus. Series: Easy Ethnic Menu Cookbooks. 2005, Lerner LB $25.26 (0-8225-1238-6). 72pp. An introduction to the basics of Middle East cooking plus a number of authentic recipes from the region. (Rev: BL 5/15/05) [641.5956]

2458 Carle, Megan, and Jill Carle. *Teens Cook: How to Cook What You Want to Eat* (7–12). 2004, Ten Speed paper $19.95 (1-58008-584-9). 146pp. A witty and practical cookbook that introduces varied recipes used by teenage siblings Megan and Jill Carle. (Rev: SLJ 10/04; VOYA 12/04) [641]

2459 DeBorde, Rob. *Fish on a First-Name Basis: How Fish Is Caught, Bought, Cleaned, Cooked, and Eaten* (10–12). Illus. 2006, St. Martin's $24.95 (0-312-34220-9). 224pp. A basic cookbook-cum-useful reference tool, this volume by a writer for the Food Network's *Good Eats* show is easy to digest. (Rev: BL 3/1/06) [641.6]

2460 Lagasse, Emeril. *Emeril's There's a Chef in My Family! Recipes to Get Everybody Cooking* (5–10). Photos by Quentin Bacon. 2004, HarperCollins $22.99 (0-06-000439-8). 209pp. Seventy-six recipes are presented with clear instructions that focus on the enjoyment of cooking. (Rev: SLJ 7/04) [641.5]

2461 Locricchio, Matthew. *The Cooking of Greece* (5–10). Photos by Jack McConnell. Illus. Series: Superchef. 2004, Benchmark LB $20.95 (0-7614-1729-X). 80pp. Recipes follow an informative overview of regional cuisines in Greece and the ingredients commonly used. (Rev: SLJ 4/05)

2462 Segan, Francine. *The Philosopher's Kitchen: Recipes from Ancient Greece and Rome for the Modern Cook* (8–12). 2004, Random $35.00 (1-4000-6099-0). 250pp. Food historian Segan updates recipes from ancient Greece and Rome to suit contemporary tastes and injects culture and context with quotes from Hippocrates, Aristotle, and others. (Rev: SLJ 1/05)

2463 Wolke, Robert L. *What Einstein Told His Cook: Further Adventures in Kitchen Science*, Vol.2 (8–12). Illus. 2005, Norton $25.95 (0-393-05963-7). 384pp. Frequently asked culinary questions are answered in this collection of essays on food and food preparation. (Rev: BL 3/15/05) [641.5]

Costume and Jewelry Making, Dress, and Fashion

2464 Bateman, Sharon. *Findings and Finishings: A Beadwork How-to-Book* (9–12). Illus. Series: Beadwork How-To. 2003, Interweave paper $21.95 (1-931499-40-3). 116pp. Projects ranging from simple earrings to complex pieces are presented in clear images and text along with a brief history of jewelry and discussion of tools and materials. (Rev: SLJ 4/04) [745.58]

2465 Haab, Sherri. *Designer Style Handbags: Techniques and Projects for Unique, Fun, and Elegant Designs from Classic to Retro* (7–12). Photos by Dan Haab. 2005, Watson-Guptill paper $19.95 (0-8230-1288-3). 128pp. Projects suitable for every skill level are accompanied by advice on choosing materials and include bags made from objects such as cigar boxes and candy tins as well as a variety of fabrics and yarns. (Rev: SLJ 1/06; VOYA 12/05) [646.4]

2466 Warrick, Leanne. *Style Trix for Cool Chix: Your One-Stop Guide to Finding the Perfect Look* (7–10). Photos by Shona Wood. Illus. 2005, Watson-Guptill paper $9.95 (0-8230-4940-X). 96pp. A useful collection of tips on shopping, color coordination, closet organization, accessories, and finding clothes that fit. (Rev: SLJ 8/05; VOYA 8/05) [391]

Drawing and Painting

2467 Chiarello, Mark, and Todd Klein. *The DC Comics Guide to Coloring and Lettering Comics* (9–12). Illus. 2004, Watson-Guptill paper $19.95 (0-8230-1030-9). 128pp. Step-by-step instructions for comic book coloring and lettering are accompanied by a look at their evolution. (Rev: BL 2/1/05) [741.5]

2468 Hart, Christopher. *Christopher Hart's Cartoon Studio* (8–12). 2003, Watson-Guptill paper $7.95 (0-8230-0624-7). 48pp. Hart introduces cartoon techniques such as drawing the same characters consistently from different angles. Also use *Christopher Hart's Animation Studio* (2003). (Rev: SLJ 1/04) [741.5]

2469 Jennings, Simon. *The New Artist's Manual: The Complete Guide to Painting and Drawing Materials and Techniques* (9–12). Illus. 2005, Chronicle paper $29.95 (0-8118-5124-9). 399pp. A comprehensive guide providing advice on everything from setting up a studio and selecting materials and equipment to the best techniques for various media, with lots of color photographs and step-by-step examples. (Rev: SLJ 3/06) [751]

2470 Miller, Steve, and Bryan Baugh. *Scared! How to Draw Fantastic Horror Comic Characters* (9–12). Illus. 2004, Watson-Guptill paper $19.95 (0-8230-1664-1). 144pp. A clear how-to guide, with historical information and profiles of successful practitioners. (Rev: BL 2/1/05) [741.5]

2471 Nagatomo, Haruno. *Draw Your Own Manga: Beyond the Basics* (7–12). Trans. from Japanese by Françoise White. 2005, Kodansha paper $19.95 (4-7700-2304-9). 111pp. Written and illustrated by Japanese manga artists, this is an entertaining yet professional guide to drawing in this style. (Rev: SLJ 9/05; VOYA 12/04) [741.5]

Gardening

2472 Klindienst, Patricia. *The Earth Knows My Name: Food, Culture, and Sustainability in the Gardens of Ethnic Americans* (8–12). Illus. 2006, Beacon $26.95 (0-8070-8562-6). 304pp. A tour of 15 American gardens that represent the culture and ethnicity of their immigrant designers. (Rev: BL 4/1/06) [635.09]

Kite Making and Flying

2473 Schmidt, Norman. *Best Ever Paper Kites* (10–12). Illus. 2003, Sterling paper $7.95 (1-895569-53-2). 96pp. Suitable for advanced kite builders, this account provides nearly 20 stunning designs plus discussion of kite history and aerodynamics. (Rev: SLJ 3/04) [629.133]

Paper Crafts

2474 Aimone, Katherine Duncan. *Artful Cards: 60 Fresh and Fabulous Designs* (8–12). Illus. 2005, Sterling $24.95 (1-57990-551-X). 144pp. Suggestions for creating a wide array of greeting cards, tags, and invitations are included in this easy-to-follow guide. (Rev: BL 12/15/05) [745.594]

2475 Nguyen, Duy. *Jungle Animal Origami* (4–12). 2003, Sterling $19.95 (1-4027-0777-0). 96pp. Best

suited for paper crafters with fairly advanced skills, this book by master artist Duy Nguyen offers instructions for creating a menagerie of origami animals. (Rev: BL 12/15/03; SLJ 3/04)

Photography, Video, and Film Making

2476 Bidner, Jenni. *The Kids' Guide to Digital Photography: How to Shoot, Save, Play with and Print Your Digital Photos* (7–10). Illus. 2004, Sterling $14.95 (1-57990-604-4). 96pp. A user-friendly guide to digital photography and the transfer of the results to the Web and other applications. (Rev: BL 1/1–15/05; SLJ 5/05) [775]

Sewing and Other Needle Crafts

2477 Carron, Cathy. *Hip Knit Hats: 40 Fabulous Designs* (9–12). Illus. 2005, Sterling $24.95 (1-57990-644-3). 144pp. Step-by-step instructions for knitting 40 fashionable hats; most patterns require double-pointed needles. (Rev: BL 12/15/05) [746.43]

2478 Eckman, Edie. *The Crochet Answer Book: Solutions to Every Problem You'll Ever Face, Answers to Every Question You'll Ever Ask* (7–12). Illus. 2005, Storey paper $12.95 (1-58017-598-8). 400pp. For novice crocheters, this is a well-organized and comprehensive guide. (Rev: BL 12/15/05) [746.43]

2479 Ivarsson, Anna-Stina Linden, et al. *Second-Time Cool: The Art of Chopping Up a Sweater* (7–10). Trans. by Maria Lundin. Illus. 2005, Annick $24.95 (1-55037-911-9); paper $12.95 (1-55037-910-0). 96pp. Adventurous clothes recycling for the ambitious teen with too much old wool lying around. (Rev: BL 1/1–15/06; SLJ 1/06) [646.4]

2480 Radcliffe, Margaret. *The Knitting Answer Book* (8–12). Illus. 2005, Storey paper $12.95 (1-58017-599-6). 400pp. This well-organized volume introduces newcomers to knitting and also provides expert guidance for longtime knitters. (Rev: BL 12/15/05) [746.43]

Mysteries, Curiosities, and Controversial Subjects

2481 Amberstone, Ruth Ann, and Wald Amberstone. *Tarot Tips: 78 Practical Techniques to Enhance Your Tarot Reading Skills* (10–12). Series: Special Topics in Tarot. 2003, Llewellyn paper $12.95 (0-7387-0216-1). 192pp. A light introduction to tarot cards and their interpretation that includes practical tips that will be of use to novice and advanced practitioners. (Rev: SLJ 5/04) [133.3]

2482 Baer, Gregory. *Life: The Odds (and How to Improve Them)* (10–12). Illus. 2003, Gotham $20.00 (1-592-40033-7). 252pp. An entertaining look at the odds of a wide variety of events — from the end of the world to getting into an Ivy League school — with background information on probability and how the odds were calculated. (Rev: SLJ 5/04) [519.2]

2483 Bobrick, Benson. *The Fated Sky* (10–12). Illus. 2005, Simon & Schuster $26.00 (0-7432-2482-5). 368pp. An interesting social and scientific history of astrology, the centuries-old study of the stars. (Rev: BL 11/15/05) [133.5]

2484 Boese, Alex. *Hippo Eats Dwarf: A Field Guide to Hoaxes and Other B.S* (9–12). Illus. 2006, Harcourt paper $14.00 (0-15-603083-7). 288pp. Phony celebrities, advertising disguised as news, and fraudulent sales pitches are only a few examples of the misinformation featured in this follow-up to *The Museum of Hoaxes* (2002). (Rev: BL 2/1/06) [001.9]

2485 Feldman, David, and Kassie Schwan. *Do Elephants Jump? An Imponderables Book* (8–12). Illus. Series: Imponderables. 2004, HarperCollins $19.95 (0-06-053913-5). 352pp. Why *do* elephants jump? Another intriguing — or unexpected — question is answered in this tenth installment in the attention-grabbing series. (Rev: BL 11/1/04) [031]

2486 Holt, David, and Bill Mooney, retel. *The Exploding Toilet: Modern Urban Legends* (7–12). 2004, August House $16.95 (0-87483-754-5); paper $6.95 (0-87483-715-4). 112pp. Amazing, often funny, shocking stories, many of which have appeared on the Internet. (Rev: SLJ 8/04) [398.2]

2487 Johnson, Julie Tallarad. *Teen Psychic: Exploring Your Intuitive Spiritual Powers* (8–12). 2003, Inner Traditions paper $14.95 (0-89281-094-7). 256pp. An introduction to investigating and developing one's intuitive powers, with quizzes, exercises, mediations, and many personal stories from teens. (Rev: BL 1/1–15/04; VOYA 4/04) [131]

2488 Plimmer, Martin, and Brian King. *Beyond Coincidence: Amazing Stories of Coincidence and the Mystery and Mathematics Behind Them* (9–12). 2006, St. Martin's $23.95 (0-312-34036-2). 288pp. A wonderful collection of coincidences of all kinds, plus discussion of the math or probability. (Rev: BL 12/15/05) [031.02]

2489 *Ripley's Believe It or Not! Planet Eccentric!* (6–12). 2005, Ripley $27.95 (1-893951-10-3). 256pp. Weird and wonderful facts in categories such as "Animal Antics" and "All-Consuming" are accompanied by eye-catching photographs. (Rev: SLJ 1/06) [031.02]

2490 Schott, Ben. *Schott's Original Miscellany* (9–12). Illus. 2003, Bloomsbury $14.95 (1-58234-349-7). 158pp. A wonderful source of trivia that is great for browsers and also has a useful index. (Rev: SLJ 1/04) [030]

2491 Shaw, Maria. *Maria Shaw's Book of Love: Horoscopes, Palmistry, Numbers, Candles, Gemstones and Colors* (8–12). Illus. 2005, Llewellyn paper $14.95 (0-7387-0545-4). 174pp. A lighthearted guide to unscientific methods of predicting the course of true love. (Rev: SLJ 2/05) [133.3]

2492 Van Praagh, James. *Looking Beyond: A Teen's Guide to the Spiritual World* (8–12). Illus. 2003, Simon & Schuster paper $12.00 (0-7432-2942-8). 160pp. Psychic Van Praagh tells teens what his contacts with the spirit world have taught him about the meaning of life and what we can do to make the most of it. (Rev: BL 1/1–15/04) [133.9]

Sports and Games

General and Miscellaneous

2493 Blumenthal, Karen. *Let Me Play: The Story of Title IX: The Law That Changed the Future of Girls in America* (6–10). Illus. 2005, Simon & Schuster $17.95 (0-689-85957-0). 160pp. Personal anecdotes, political cartoons, and profiles of female athletes add to the story of the 1972 passage of Title IX, which bans sex discrimination in U.S. schools. (Rev: BL 7/05; SLJ 7/05*) [796]

2494 Brisick, Jamie. *Have Board, Will Travel: The Definitive History of Surf, Skate, and Snow* (9–12). 2004, HarperCollins paper $19.95 (0-06-056359-1). 241pp. The sports of surfing, skateboarding, and snowboarding are portrayed in simple text and large, bright photographs that will attract reluctant readers. (Rev: SLJ 12/04)

2495 Cramer, Richard Ben, ed. *The Best American Sports Writing, 2004* (9–12). 2004, Houghton $27.50 (0-618-25134-0). 336pp. This anthology of the best in sports writing from 2004 brings you articles by such well-known authors as Mitch Albom, Ira Berkow, and Bob Ryan. (Rev: BL 11/1/04) [796]

2496 Davis, Joshua. *The Underdog: How I Survived the World's Most Outlandish Competitions* (9–12). Illus. 2005, Villard $21.95 (0-345-47658-1). 224pp. Arm wrestling and backward running are only two of the offbeat competitions Davis entered. (Rev: BL 9/1/05) [070.92]

2497 Duncan, Joyce D., ed. *Sport in American Culture: From Ali to X-Games* (9–12). 2004, ABC-CLIO $95.00 (1-57607-024-7). 479pp. Four hundred entries explore the cultural impact of sports on American society, covering such topics as sports apparel, scandals, civil rights issues, children's issues, and sports in literature, film, and humor. (Rev: BL 3/15/05; SLJ 6/05) [306.4]

2498 Glenn, Jim, and Carey Denton. *The Treasury of Family Games: Hundreds of Fun Games for All Ages, Complete with Rules and Strategies* (5–10). Illus. 2003, Reader's Digest $29.95 (0-7621-0431-7). 256pp. Games of every kind are simply explained and illustrated in this compendium, with material on their rules and their history. (Rev: SLJ 6/04) [793]

2499 Housewright, Ed. *Winning Track and Field for Girls* (7–12). 2003, Facts on File $35.00 (0-8160-5231-X). 188pp. A history of women's track is followed by specific information on sprints, hurdles, cross-country, triathlon, and so forth, with details of record holders and quotations from famous athletes; final chapters cover mental and physical preparation. (Rev: SLJ 6/04; VOYA 6/04) [796.42]

2500 Musiker, Liz Hartman. *The Smart Girl's Guide to Sports: A Hip Handbook for Women Who Don't Know a Slam Dunk from a Grand Slam* (9–12). 2005, Hudson Street $18.00 (1-59463-011-9). 316pp. A helpful guide to sports rules, legend, lingo, and traditions. (Rev: BL 9/1/05) [796]

2501 Porter, David L. *Winning Weight Training for Girls: Fitness and Conditioning for Sports* (7–12). 2003, Facts on File $35.00 (0-8160-5185-2). 205pp. The benefits of weight training for specific sports — basketball, softball, field hockey, and volleyball — are outlined following the basics of safe weight training. (Rev: SLJ 6/04) [613.7]

2502 Povich, Shirley, et al. *All Those Mornings . . . at the Post: The Twentieth Century in Sports from Famed Washington Post Columnist Shirley Povich* (9–12). 2005, PublicAffairs $27.50 (1-58648-315-3). 404pp. Selected columns by the longtime sportswriter document the evolution of organized sports in America during the 20th century. (Rev: SLJ 7/05) [796]

2503 Shannon, Joyce Brennfleck, ed. *Sports Injuries Information for Teens: Health Tips About Sports*

Injuries and Injury Prevention (8–12). Series: Teen Health. 2003, Omnigraphics $58.00 (0-7808-0447-3). 405pp. Basic information on sports injuries and treatment is provided in separate sections on such topics as emergency treatment, common injuries affecting teens, rehabilitation and physical therapy, injury prevention, and sports nutrition. (Rev: SLJ 7/04; VOYA 10/04) [617.1]

2504 Swissler, Becky. *Winning Lacrosse for Girls* (7–12). 2004, Facts on File $35.00 (0-8160-5183-6). 192pp. A clear and detailed introduction to the game of lacrosse, covering its history as well as individual skills and team dynamics. (Rev: SLJ 5/04) [796.34]

2505 Tomlinson, Joe, and Ed Leigh. *Extreme Sports: In Search of the Ultimate Thrill* (8–12). 2004, Firefly $19.95 (1-55297-992-X). 192pp. Explores the full spectrum of extreme sports — on land, in the air, and in or on the water. (Rev: SLJ 4/05; VOYA 10/05)

2506 Torr, James D., ed. *Professional Sports* (9–12). Series: Examining Pop Culture. 2003, Gale LB $26.96 (0-7377-1587-1); paper $17.96 (0-7377-1588-X). 192pp. Articles explore social and cultural aspects of sports — the popularity of extreme sports, the celebrity power of top athletes, chauvinism, and so forth. (Rev: SLJ 3/04)

Automobile Racing

2507 MacGregor, Jeff. *Sunday Money* (9–12). Illus. 2005, HarperCollins $25.95 (0-06-009471-0). 400pp. NASCAR history and details of key personalities are interwoven in this account of a year spent on the circuit. (Rev: BL 3/1/05) [796.72]

2508 Miller, Timothy, and Steve Milton. *NASCAR Now* (8–12). 2004, Firefly $19.95 (1-55297-829-X). 160pp. Covering the basics of maintenance, safety, and equipment as well as history, scoring, track features, and profiles of key individuals, this well-illustrated guide will suit novices and diehard fans. (Rev: SLJ 1/05) [796.72]

Baseball

2509 Bissinger, Buzz. *Three Nights in August: Strategy, Heartbreak, and Joy Inside the Heart of a Manager* (8–12). 2005, Houghton $25.00 (0-618-40544-5). 304pp. Bissinger dissects a three-game August 2003 series between baseball's St. Louis

Cardinals and Chicago Cubs. (Rev: BL 3/1/05) [796.357]

2510 Bryant, Howard. *Juicing the Game: Drugs, Power, and the Fight for the Soul of Major League Baseball* (8–12). 2005, Viking $24.95 (0-670-03445-2). 424pp. Traces the history of steroid use in professional baseball and the impact on the sport as a whole. (Rev: BL 7/05) [796.357]

2511 Carroll, Will. *The Juice: The Real Story of Baseball's Drug Problems* (9–12). 2005, Ivan R. Dee $24.95 (1-56663-668-X). 255pp. Carroll, a columnist for the online Baseball Prospectus, dissects the growing controversy over the use of performance enhancing drugs by professional baseball players. (Rev: SLJ 11/05)

2512 Rubin, Adam. *Pedro, Carlos, and Omar: A Season in the Big Apple with "Los Mets"* (9–12). 2006, Lyons $22.95 (1-59228-875-8). 240pp. Rubin explores Omar Minaya's first season as general manager of the New York Mets. (Rev: BL 3/15/06) [796.357]

2513 Simmons, Bill. *Now I Can Die in Peace: How ESPN's Sports Guy Found Salvation, with a Little Help from Buckner, Pedro, Shawshank and the 2004 Red Sox* (11–12). Illus. 2005, Hyperion $24.95 (1-933060-05-0). 352pp. The long and winding Red Sox road to a championship season in 2004 is described with humor and lots of authentically strong language; for mature teens. (Rev: BL 9/1/05) [796.357]

Basketball

2514 Austin, Dan. *True Fans: A Basketball Odyssey* (9–12). 2005, Lyons $19.95 (1-59228-779-4). 240pp. A bicycle road trip across the United States with basketball as a purpose (the Basketball Hall of Fame in Springfield, Massachusetts) and a unifying theme. (Rev: BL 9/1/05) [796.323]

2515 D'Orso, Michael. *Eagle Blue: A Team, a Tribe, and a High School Basketball Season in Arctic Alaska* (9–12). 2006, Bloomsbury $23.95 (1-58234-623-2). 336pp. D'Orso follows the fortunes of a successful high school basketball team in an isolated Alaska town over the course of the 2004–2005 season. (Rev: BL 3/1/06) [796.323]

2516 Feinstein, John. *Last Dance: Behind the Scenes at the Final Four* (10–12). Illus. 2006, Little, Brown $25.95 (0-316-16030-X). 320pp. A behind-the-scenes look at the NCAA's annual men's basketball tournament. (Rev: BL 1/1–15/06) [795.323]

2517 Klein, Leigh, and Matt Masiero, eds. *My Favorite Moves: Shooting Like the Stars* (6–12).

Series: Five Star Basketball. 2003, Wish paper $12.95 (1-930546-58-0). 137pp. Best for readers already familiar with the game, this drill book includes advice from five professional women players. Also use *My Favorite Moves: Making the Big Plays* (2003). (Rev: SLJ 1/04) [796.323]

2518 Lazenby, Roland. *The Show: The Inside Story of the Spectacular Los Angeles Lakers in the Words of Those Who Lived It* (8–12). Illus. 2006, McGraw-Hill $27.95 (0-07-143034-2). 544pp. This excellent volume traces the NBA team's fortunes from its inauspicious beginnings in Minneapolis in the early 1950s through its most recent string of championships. (Rev: BL 11/15/05) [796.323]

2519 Martindale, Wight. *Inside the Cage: A Season at West 4th Street's Legendary Tournament* (9–12). 2005, Simon & Schuster $22.95 (1-4169-0539-1). 304pp. Great street basketball takes place at a tiny court in New York City's Greenwich Village. (Rev: BL 7/05) [796.323]

2520 O'Connor, Ian. *The Jump: Sebastian Telfair and the High Stakes Business of High School Ball* (9–12). 2005, Rodale $23.95 (1-59486-107-2). 336pp. The harrowing journey of Sebastian Telfair from the high school basketball court to the heady atmosphere of the NBA, a story that shines a poor light on many. (Rev: BL 3/1/05) [796.323]

2521 Palmer, Chris. *Streetball: All the Ballers, Moves, Slams, and Shine* (8–12). Illus. 2004, Harper Resource paper $16.95 (0-06-072444-7). 224pp. A celebration of urban playground basketball and the talented young people who enjoy it. (Rev: BL 11/15/04) [796.323]

2522 Stewart, Mark. *The NBA Finals* (5–10). Series: Watts History of Sports. 2003, Watts LB $33.50 (0-531-11955-6). 95pp. National Basketball Association finals over more than half a century are detailed year by year, with ample information on the teams and the players. (Rev: SLJ 3/04) [797]

2523 Wertheim, L. Jon. *Transition Game: How Hoosiers Went Hip-Hop* (8–12). Illus. 2005, Penguin $23.95 (0-399-15250-4). 256pp. A look at how the game of basketball has changed over the past two decades. (Rev: BL 2/1/05) [796.323]

2524 Wojnarowski, Adrian. *The Miracle of St. Anthony: A Season with Coach Bob Hurley and Basketball's Most Improbable Dynasty* (9–12). 2005, Gotham $25.00 (1-592-40102-3). 384pp. Wojnarowski chronicles a championship season for the basketball team at a small high school in Jersey City, New Jersey. (Rev: BL 3/1/05) [796.323]

Bicycling, Motorcycling, etc.

2525 Sidwells, Chris. *Complete Bike Book* (8–12). Illus. 2005, DK paper $17.95 (0-7566-1427-9). 240pp. History, technology, training, and maintenance are all covered in this volume for all levels of riders that also includes a stunning section of color photographs. (Rev: BL 9/1/05) [796.6]

Chess, Checkers, and Other Board and Card Games

2526 Kushner, David. *Jonny Magic and the Card Shark Kids: How a Gang of Geeks Beat the Odds and Stormed Las Vegas* (9–12). Illus. 2005, Random $24.95 (1-4000-6407-4). 240pp. The game of Magic transformed Jon Finkel from an overweight computer game geek into the leader of a winning band of card sharks that took home $3.5 million in the World Series of Poker. (Rev: BL 9/1/05) [795.412]

Football

2527 Emmanuel, Greg. *The 100-Yard War: Inside the 100-Year-Old Michigan-Ohio State Football Rivalry* (9–12). 2004, Wiley $24.95 (0-471-67552-0). 288pp. Emmanuel explores the football rivalry between Ohio State University and the University of Michigan, still going strong after more than a century. (Rev: BL 9/1/04) [790.332]

2528 Feinstein, John. *Next Man Up: A Year Behind the Lines in the NFL* (9–12). Illus. 2005, Little, Brown $25.95 (0-316-00964-4). 502pp. A fascinating behind-the-scenes account of a difficult year in the life of the NFL's Baltimore Ravens. (Rev: BL 10/15/05) [796.332]

2529 McDonell, Chris, ed. *The Football Game I'll Never Forget: 100 NFL Stars' Stories* (8–12). Illus. 2004, Firefly paper $24.95 (1-55297-850-8). 224pp. One hundred football stars talk about the games they remember. (Rev: BL 9/1/04; VOYA 4/05) [796.332]

Ice Skating

2530 Jackson, Jon, and James Pereira. *On Edge: Backroom Dealing, Cocktail Scheming, Triple Axels, and How Top Skaters Get Screwed* (11–12).

2006, Thunder's Mouth $25.00 (1-56025-804-7). 320pp. For mature skaters and fans of skating, this is a rare behind-the-scenes look at the many problems associated with this popular sport. (Rev: BL 12/15/05) [796.91]

Olympic Games

2531 Coffey, Wayne. *The Boys of Winter: The Untold Story of a Coach, a Dream, and the 1980 U.S. Olympic Hockey Team* (8–12). Illus. 2005, Crown $23.95 (1-4000-4765-X). 320pp. In this inspiring look back at the 1980 Winter Olympics victory of the U.S. men's hockey team, sportswriter Coffey introduces readers to the players and coach who pulled off this miracle on ice. (Rev: BL 11/15/04; SLJ 5/05) [796.962]

2532 Macy, Sue. *Swifter, Higher, Stronger: A Photographic History of the Summer Olympics* (6–10). 2004, National Geographic $18.95 (0-7922-6667-6). 96pp. Full of photographs and fascinating trivia, this volume covers the history of the games through the Sydney Games of 2000 and discusses controversies, sportsmanship, and the opening up of the games to women. (Rev: BCCB 7–8/04; BL 7/04; SLJ 6/04) [796.4]

Running and Jogging

2533 Brant, John. *Duel in the Sun: Alberto Salazar, Dick Beardsley, and America's Greatest Marathon* (9–12). Illus. 2006, Rodale $22.95 (1-59486-262-1). 224pp. The story of the exciting 1982 Boston Marathon and the fates of the two runners who finished within seconds of each other. (Rev: BL 2/15/06) [796.42]

2534 Griffis, Molly Levite. *The Great American Bunion Derby* (5–10). 2003, Eakin $15.95 (1-57168-801-3); paper $9.95 (1-57168-810-2). 87pp. The story of a poor part-Cherokee farm boy who joined a marathon run across the United States in the late 1920s and won the $25,000 top prize. (Rev: BL 1/1–15/04; SLJ 3/04) [796.42]

Sailing, Boating, and Canoeing

2535 Heller, Peter. *Hell or High Water* (8–12). 2004, Rodale $24.95 (1-57954-872-5). 336pp. Heller chronicles the 2002 conquest of Tibet's Tsangpo River by an elite kayaking team and discusses the attractions of this dangerous sport. (Rev: BL 9/15/04) [797.122]

Skateboarding

2536 Badillo, Steve, and Doug Werner. *Skateboarding: Book of Tricks* (7–12). 2003, Tracks paper $12.95 (1-884654-19-3). 176pp. Basic and advanced moves are well illustrated in black-and-white photographs although Badillo is shown without protective gear. (Rev: SLJ 5/04) [796.2]

Soccer

2537 Stewart, Mark. *The World Cup* (5–10). Series: The Watts History of Sports. 2003, Watts LB $33.50 (0-531-11957-2). 96pp. An overview of the international soccer championship that takes place every four years, this volume, which will be useful for reports, starts with the 1930 games and includes information on teams and players. (Rev: SLJ 3/04) [796.3]

Surfing, Water Skiing, and Other Water Sports

2538 Lake, Sanoe, and Steven Jarrett. *Surfer Girl* (8–11). Illus. 2005, Little, Brown paper $12.99 (0-316-11015-9). 144pp. Designed especially for girls, this witty, easy-to-understand guide to surfing provides a brief history of the sport as well as helpful advice on equipment, techniques, and safety. (Rev: BCCB 7–8/05; BL 5/15/05; SLJ 7/05) [797.3]

Author Index

Authors are arranged alphabetically by last name. Authors' and joint authors' names are followed by book titles — which are also arranged alphabetically — and the text entry number. Book titles may refer to those that appear as a main entry or as an internal entry mentioned in the text. Fiction titles are indicated by (F) following the entry number.

Aaseng, Nathan. *Business Builders in Broadcasting*, 1443

Abbott, Stacey, ed. *Reading Angel*, 1665

Abrahams, Peter. *Down the Rabbit Hole*, 910(F)

Abu-Jaber, Diana. *The Language of Baklava*, 1324

Acampora, Paul. *Defining Dulcie*, 883(F)

Achebe, Chinua. *Collected Poems*, 1227

Acito, Marc. *How I Paid for College*, 217(F)

Ackerman, Thomas H. *FBI Careers*, 2129

Ackroyd, Peter. *Ancient Greece*, 1695
The Beginning, 1808
Cities of Blood, 1808
Escape from Earth, 1808

Acuna, Rodolfo F. *U.S. Latino Issues*, 1999

Adamowicz, Adam. *New Recruits*, 1616

Adams, Lorraine. *Harbor*, 376(F)

Adamson, Isaac. *Kinki Lullaby*, 911(F)

Addison, Paul. *Churchill*, 1526

Addonizio, Kim. *Little Beauties*, 11(F)

Adler, Stephen J. (jt. author). *Women's Letters*, 1831

Adlington, L. J. *The Diary of Pelly D*, 400(F)

Adoff, Jaime. *Jimi and Me*, 131(F)
Names Will Never Hurt Me, 377(F)

Ahern, Cecelia. *Rosie Dunne*, 995(F)

Aida, Yu. *Gunslinger Girl*, 551(F)

Aimone, Katherine Duncan. *Artful Cards*, 2474

Akane, Kazuki. *Heat Guy J*, 552(F)

Akane, Satelight (jt. author). *Heat Guy J*, 552(F)

Akbar, Said Hyder. *Come Back to Afghanistan*, 1542

Alarcón, Daniel. *War by Candlelight*, 1134(F)

Albala, Ken (jt. author). *Opening Up North America, 1497–1800*, 1809

Alcala, Alfredo (jt. author). *Spontaneous Generation*, 698(F)

Aldana, Patricia, ed. *Under the Spell of the Moon*, 1617

Aldrich, Lisa J. *Nikola Tesla and the Taming of Electricity*, 1478

Alegría, Malín. *Estrella's Quinceañera*, 113(F)

Alexievich, Svetlana. *Voices from Chernobyl*, 2413

Alger, Neil, ed. *The Palestinians and the Disputed Territories*, 1792

Allen, Jake (jt. author). *Brownsville*, 2042

Allen, M. E. *Gotta Get Some Bish Bash Bosh*, 218(F)

Allende, Isabel. *Zorro*, 781(F)

Allie, Scott, ed. *The Dark Horse Book of Witchcraft*, 554(F)

Allport, Alan. *Immigration Policy*, 1980

Almond, Steve. *The Evil B. B. Chow and Other Stories*, 1135(F)

Alphin, Elaine Marie. *The Perfect Shot*, 912(F)

Altman, Linda J. *Crimes and Criminals of the Holocaust*, 1712
Impact of the Holocaust, 1713

Altman, Steven-Elliot. *The Irregulars*, 913(F)

Alvarez, Julia. *Finding Miracles*, 114(F)

Amaki, Amalia K., ed. *A Century of African American Art*, 1629

Amateau, Gigi. *Claiming Georgia Tate*, 132(F)

Amberstone, Ruth Ann. *Tarot Tips*, 2481

Amberstone, Wald (jt. author). *Tarot Tips*, 2481

Amidon, Stephen. *Human Capital*, 133(F)

Amiry, Suad. *Sharon and My Mother-in-Law*, 1543

Amos, Tori. *Tori Amos*, 1363

Anaya, Rudolfo. *Serafina's Stories*, 773(F)

Anders, Gigi. *Jubana! The Awkwardly True and Dazzling Adventures of a Jewish Cubana Goddess*, 1544

Andersen, Hans Christian. *Fairy Tales*, 1232(F)

Andersen, Richard. *Arthur Miller*, 1348
Toni Morrison, 1350

Anderson, Catherine. *My Sunshine*, 996(F)

Anderson, Harry S. *Exploring the Polar Regions*, 1822

Anderson, Janet. *Modern Dance*, 1650

Anderson, Jodi Lynn. *Peaches*, 12(F)

Anderson, Kevin J. (jt. author). *The Battle of Corrin*, 1091(F)
Dune, 1091(F)
Prodigal Son, 859(F)

Anderson, Laurie Halse. *Prom*, 219(F)

Anderson, Maxine. *Great Civil War Projects You Can Build Yourself*, 2454

Angel, Jodi. *The History of Vegas*, 220(F)

Angelo, Bonnie. *First Families*, 1380

Anthony, Piers. *Currant Events*, 401(F)

Antieau, Kim. *Mercy, Unbound*, 199(F)

Antonetta, Susanne. *A Mind Apart*, 2212

Morpurgo, Michael. *Private Peaceful*, 817(F)

Morren, Ruth Axtell. *Wild Rose*, 1046(F)

Morris, Ian Macgregor. *Themistocles*, 1540

Morris, Mark, ed. *Cinema Macabre*, 1660

Morris, Mary McGarry. *The Lost Mother*, 807(F)

Morrison, Grant. *Kid Eternity*, 642(F)
Seven Soldiers of Victory, 641(F)
WE3, 643(F)

Morrison, John. *Cornel West*, 1441

Morrison, Toni. *Remember*, 1974

Morrow, Lance. *The Best Year of Their Lives*, 1884

Mortenson, Greg. *Three Cups of Tea*, 1580

Mortman, Doris. *Shades of Red*, 961(F)

Morton, Joseph C. *The American Revolution*, 1848

Morvan, Jean David. *Wake*, 1103(F)

Moser, Diane Kit (jt. author). *The Age of Synthesis*, 2283
The Birth of Science, 2283
Modern Science, 2283
The Rise of Reason, 2283
Science Frontiers, 2283

Moser, Laura (jt. author). *The Rise and Fall of a 10th Grade Social Climber*, 314(F)

Moses, Shelia P. *I, Dred Scott*, 785(F)

Mosher, Howard Frank. *Waiting for Teddy Williams*, 1128(F)

Mosley, Walter. *47*, 1104(F)
Life Out of Context, 1992

Moulton, Candy. *Chief Joseph*, 1425

Mowll, Joshua. *Operation Red Jericho*, 644(F)

Muckenhoupt, Margaret. *Dorothea Dix*, 1436

Mullane, Mike. *Riding Rockets*, 1475

Murakami, Maki. *Kanpai!* 645(F)

Murdico, Suzanne J. *Bomb Squad Experts*, 2132
Forensic Scientists, 2133

Murillo, Kathy Cano. *The Crafty Diva's Lifestyle Makeover*, 2451

Murphy, Rita. *Looking for Lucy Buick*, 174(F)

Murray, Aaron R. *American Revolution Battles and Leaders*, 1849
Civil War Battles and Leaders, 1857

Murray, Charles. *In Our Hands*, 2052

Murray, J. J. *Original Love*, 1047(F)

Murray, Yxta Maya. *The Queen Jade*, 5(F)

Musgrave, Susan, ed. *Certain Things About My Mother*, 2276
Perfectly Secret, 2249

Musiker, Liz Hartman. *The Smart Girl's Guide to Sports*, 2500

Myers, Anna. *Assassin*, 790(F)

Myers, Edward. *Ice*, 210(F)
When Will I Stop Hurting? 2254

Myers, Walter Dean. *Autobiography of My Dead Brother*, 124(F)
Voices from Harlem, 1217

Myracle, Lauren. *Rhymes with Witches*, 863(F)
ttfn, 321(F)
ttyl, 321(F)

Na, An. *Wait for Me*, 70(F)

Naden, Corinne J. *Lenin*, 1535

Naff, Clay Farris. *Vaccines*, 2190

Naff, Clay Farris, ed. *Evolution*, 1673

Nagatomo, Haruno. *Draw Your Own Manga*, 2471

Nakaya, Andrea C., ed. *Censorship*, 1975
Civil Liberties and War, 1976
Iraq, 1732
Juvenile Crime, 2044
Obesity, 2174

Nance, Kathleen. *Jigsaw*, 1048(F)

Napoli, Donna Jo. *Bound*, 1231(F)

Nardo, Don. *Ancient Philosophers*, 1508
Artistry in Stone, 1614
Arts, Leisure, and Entertainment, 1699
Arts, Leisure, and Sport in Ancient Egypt, 1693
Cleopatra, 1513
From Founding to Fall, 1699
A History of the Ancient Greeks, 1696
Mummies, Myth, and Magic, 1693
The Roman Army, 1699
A Roman Gladiator, 1700

Nathan, Melissa. *Persuading Annie*, 1049(F)

Naylor, Phyllis Reynolds. *Alice on Her Way*, 322(F)

Neale, Naomi. *Calendar Girl*, 1050(F)

Nelscott, Kris. *War at Home*, 962(F)

Nelson, Blake. *Prom Anonymous*, 71(F)
Rock Star, Superstar, 323(F)

Nelson, D.-L. *The Card*, 72(F)

Nelson, Marilyn. *Fortune's Bones*, 1218
A Wreath for Emmett Till, 1219

Nelson, R. A. *Teach Me*, 324(F)

Neufeld, Josh. *A Few Perfect Hours . . . and Other Stories from Southeast Asia and Central Europe*, 1581

Newcomb, Robert. *Savage Messiah*, 502(F)

Newman, Gerald. *A Student's Guide to John Steinbeck*, 1271

Newman, Kim (jt. author). *Horror*, 1255

Newman, Leslea. *Jailbait*, 325(F)

Newman, Sharan. *The Witch in the Well*, 722(F)

Nguyen, Dat. *Dat*, 1491

Nguyen, Duy. *Jungle Animal Origami*, 2475

Nicholls, Henry. *Lonesome George*, 2315

Nichols, Jeremy. *Poland*, 1776

Nicholson, Helen. *The Crusades*, 1705

Nicholson, Michael. *Mahatma Gandhi*, 1516

Nicieza, Fabian. *A Stake to the Heart*, 646(F)

Niederhoffer, Galt. *A Taxonomy of Barnacles*, 900(F)

Nields, Nerissa. *Plastic Angel*, 73(F)

Nielsen, John. *Condor*, 2336

Niffenegger, Audrey. *The Three Incestuous Sisters*, 503

Nightingale, Neil. *Wild Australasia*, 1771

Nightow, Yasuhiro. *Trigun Anime Manga*, 647(F)

Niles, Steve. *Last Train to Deadsville*, 648(F)

Nilsson, Per. *You and You and You*, 74(F)

Niman, Bill. *The Niman Ranch Cookbook*, 2308

Niven, Larry. *Building Harlequin's Moon*, 1105(F)

Nix, Garth. *Across the Wall*, 1162(F)

No, Yee-Jung. *Visitor*, 649(F)

Noel, Katharine. *Halfway House*, 211(F)

Noël, Alyson. *Art Geeks and Prom Queens*, 326(F)
Faking 19, 327(F)

Noël, Michel. *Good for Nothing*, 770(F)

Nolen-Weathington, Eri (jt. author). *Arthur Adams*, 1313

Norfleet, Celeste O. *The Fine Art of Love*, 1051(F)

Norman, Justin (jt. author). *Solstice*, 676(F)

Norrell, Robert J. *The House I Live In*, 1993

Norris, Chris (jt. author). *The Wu-Tang Manual*, 1645

Nothomb, Amelie. *The Book of Proper Names*, 328(F)

November, Deena (jt. author). *I Just Hope It's Lethal*, 1204

November, Sharyn, ed. *Firebirds Rising*, 1163(F)

Noyes, Alfred. *The Highwayman*, 1206

Noyes, Deborah. *Angel and Apostle*, 778(F)
Gothic! 864(F)

Nye, Naomi Shihab. *Going Going*, 394(F)
A Maze Me, 1199
You and Yours, 1200

Title Index

This index contains both main entry and internal titles cited in the entries. References are to entry numbers, not page numbers. All fiction titles are indicated by (F), following the entry number.

Subject/Grade Level Index

All entries are listed by subject and then according to grade level suitability (see the key at the foot of pages for grade level designations). Subjects are arranged alphabetically and subject heads may be subdivided into nonfiction (e.g., "Africa") and fiction (e.g. "Africa — Fiction"). References to entries are by entry number, not page number.

A

Abandoned children — Fiction
JS: 183 S–Adult: 251

Abolitionists
See also Slavery (U.S.)
JS: 1830, 1832

Abolitionists — Biography
JS: 1389

Abortion
JS: 2227, 2231 S–Adult: 1585, 2226, 2230

Abu-Jaber, Diana
JS: 1324

Academic guidance
JS: 2090

Acadia — Fiction
JS: 769

Accidents — Fiction
JS: 316 S–Adult: 136

Acting
JS: 1189, 1649

Acting — Fiction
JS: 23–24, 78, 291

Activism
JS: 2059 S–Adult: 2005

Activism — Fiction
JS: 394

Adams, Arthur
JS: 1313

Adoption
See also Foster care
JS: 2274 S–Adult: 1554, 2226

Adoption — Fiction
JS: 144, 161, 174, 182, 792

Adventure stories — Fiction
See also Mystery stories — Fiction
JS: 3, 6, 142, 644, 668, 676, 749, 804, 927, 941 S–Adult: 5, 781, 1077

Adventurers and explorers
JS: 1676, 1678, 1687, 1708, 1737, 1824 S–Adult: 1752

Adventurers and explorers — Biography
JS: 1303, 1306–7, 1530

***Adventures of Huckleberry Finn* — Fiction**
S–Adult: 786

Advertising
JS: 2081

Advertising — Careers
JS: 2124

Advertising — Fiction
S–Adult: 392

Afghanistan
JS: 1763–64, 1768–70 S: 1762 S–Adult: 1563, 1584, 1766, 1881

Afghanistan — Biography
JS: 1542

Afghanistan — Fiction
JS: 92, 397

Africa
See also specific countries and regions, e.g., East Africa
JS: 1739

Africa — Animals
JS: 1741

Africa — Biography
JS: 1505

Africa — Fiction
JS: 729–30, 1154

Africa — Folklore
JS: 1230

Africa — Peoples
JS: 1738

African Americans
JS: 1441 S–Adult: 1253, 1931, 1991, 2095

African Americans — Armed Forces
S–Adult: 1442

African Americans — Art
JS: 1310, 1629

African Americans — Biography
JS: 1214, 1316, 1329, 1339, 1343, 1350, 1368–69, 1386–88, 1390, 1392, 1394–96, 1398–99, 1438, 1488, 1494, 1505 S–Adult: 1374, 1393, 1442, 1598

African Americans — Civil rights
JS: 1950

African Americans — Fiction
JS: 104, 107, 123–24, 244, 537, 779, 812, 1013, 1154, 1457 S–Adult: 151, 201, 962, 1051

African Americans — History
JS: 1989, 1993–94

African Americans — Literature
S–Adult: 1137

African Americans — Poetry
JS: 1154, 1214, 1217, 1219 S–Adult: 1221

African Americans — Politics
S–Adult: 1992

African Americans — Women
JS: 1310 S–Adult: 1169

Aging
JS: 2194

JS = Junior High/Senior High;   S = Senior High;   S–Adult = Senior High/Adult

B

JS = Junior High/Senior High;   S = Senior High;   S–Adult = Senior High/Adult

JS = Junior High/Senior High;   S = Senior High;   S–Adult = Senior High/Adult

JS = Junior High/Senior High; S = Senior High; S–Adult = Senior High/Adult

JS = Junior High/Senior High;   S = Senior High;   S–Adult = Senior High/Adult

Cults — Biography
S–Adult: 1915

Cults — Fiction
JS: 15, 102

Cultural Revolution (China)
JS: 1608

Culture
JS: 2497 S–Adult: 1883

Curie, Marie
JS: 1460–61

Curiosities
JS: 2485, 2487, 2489

Cycling
See Bicycle racing; Bicycles

Czech Republic
JS: 1777

Czechoslovakia — Memoirs
JS: 1331

D

Dance
JS: 1650 S–Adult: 1651

Dance — Careers
JS: 2121

Dance — Fiction
JS: 345

Darwin, Charles
S–Adult: 1462, 1462, 2302

Darwin, Charles — Fiction
JS: 744

Date rape
See also Rape
JS: 2027

Dating (social)
JS: 2247 S–Adult: 1562, 2246, 2256

Dating (social) — Fiction
JS: 97, 235, 271, 330, 351, 369
S–Adult: 292

da Vinci, Leonardo — Fiction
S–Adult: 628, 747

**Deafness and the deaf —
Biography**
S–Adult: 2210

Death
S–Adult: 2031

Death — Fiction
JS: 131, 147, 159, 188, 193, 207, 236, 243, 248, 273, 300, 337, 550
S: 214 S–Adult: 41, 106, 176

Death penalty
JS: 1938, 1946 S: 1939
S–Adult: 1943

Deported aliens
JS: 1985

Depression, Great
S: 1558

Depression, Great — Fiction
JS: 804–6 S–Adult: 807

Depression (mental state)
JS: 1599, 2215, 2269
S–Adult: 2214, 2218

**Depression (mental state) —
Fiction**
JS: 171

Dery, Dominika
JS: 1331

Design
See also Clothing and dress;
Fashion design

Design — Careers
JS: 2118

Detectives — Fiction
See also Mystery stories — Fiction
JS: 567, 592

Diabetes
JS: 2170, 2173

Diaries
See also Journals
S–Adult: 1592, 2244

Diaries — Fiction
JS: 87, 191, 338, 768, 887, 902–3
S–Adult: 798

Dickens, Charles
JS: 1332 S–Adult: 1262

Dickinson, Emily
JS: 1281, 1333–34

Dictators — Biography
JS: 1521

Diderot, Denis
JS: 1529

Diet and dieting
JS: 2221

Dinesen, Isak
JS: 1335

Dinosaurs
JS: 1671

Dinosaurs — Humor
JS: 1244

Disabilities — Fiction
JS: 98

Disaster preparedness
S–Adult: 2064

Disasters
JS: 1885, 2007

Diseases and illness
See also Medicine; and specific
diseases, e.g., AIDS
JS: 2177, 2185, 2187
S–Adult: 1565

Diseases and illness — Fiction
JS: 814

Disfigurement — Fiction
S–Adult: 33

Disney, Walt
JS: 1379

Disney (firm)
JS: 2077

Divorce — Fiction
JS: 77, 346

Dix, Dorothea
JS: 1436

DNA
JS: 2193 S–Adult: 1943

DNA — Biography
JS: 1459

Doctors — Biography
JS: 2188

Dogs
See also Guide dogs
JS: 2354, 2357–59, 2361
S–Adult: 2356, 2360

Dogs — Fiction
S–Adult: 90

Dogs — History
JS: 2355, 2362

Dolphins
JS: 2351

Domestic violence — Fiction
JS: 164, 283 S–Adult: 150, 184

Dornstein, Ken
S–Adult: 1560

Dr. Seuss
S–Adult: 1621

Dracula **— Fiction**
S–Adult: 860

Dragons — Fiction
JS: 401, 441, 481, 489, 505, 539, 545, 549

Drake, Sir Francis
JS: 1530

Drawing and painting
See also Art; Crafts
JS: 1617, 2467, 2470–71
S–Adult: 1621, 1623

**Drawing and painting —
Biography**
JS: 1321

Dreams and dreaming
JS: 2204, 2252

**Dreams and dreaming —
Fiction**
S–Adult: 1032

Dred Scott Case — Fiction
JS: 785

JS = Junior High/Senior High;   S = Senior High;   S–Adult = Senior High/Adult

JS = Junior High/Senior High;   S = Senior High;   S–Adult = Senior High/Adult

JS = Junior High/Senior High;   S = Senior High;   S–Adult = Senior High/Adult

G

JS = Junior High/Senior High;   S = Senior High;   S–Adult = Senior High/Adult

H

JS = Junior High/Senior High;   S = Senior High;   S–Adult = Senior High/Adult

JS = Junior High/Senior High;   S = Senior High;   S–Adult = Senior High/Adult

JS = Junior High/Senior High;   S = Senior High;   S–Adult = Senior High/Adult

Lesbian mothers — Fiction
JS: 155, 178

Lesbians
See also Gay rights; Gay youth;
Homosexuality
S–Adult: 1826

Lesbians — Biography
S–Adult: 1547

Lesbians — Fiction
JS: 355 S–Adult: 665

Lester, Julius
JS: 1343

Letters
JS: 2267

Letters — Fiction
JS: 262, 370

Lewis, Sinclair — Criticism
S: 1266

Lewis and Clark Expedition
JS: 1861

**Lewis and Clark Expedition —
Fiction**
JS: 799

Librarians and librarianship
JS: 1998

Libya — Fiction
JS: 728

Lima (Peru)
JS: 1819

Lincoln, Abraham
JS: 1411–12, 1853

**Lincoln, Abraham —
Assassination**
JS: 1855

**Lincoln, Abraham —
Assassination — Fiction**
JS: 790

Lincoln, Abraham — Fiction
JS: 790

**Lindbergh, Charles A. —
Fiction**
S–Adult: 832

Lions
JS: 2324

**Literature — History and
criticism**
JS: 1254

**Literature — History and
criticism**
JS: 1255, 1260–61, 1270–71,
1273–74, 1276–77, 1281–82, 1336

Lithuania
JS: 1787

Little Crow
JS: 1429

Little Women **— Fiction**
JS: 788

Logic
S–Adult: 2255

London, England
JS: 1261

London, England — Fiction
JS: 67, 239, 374, 415, 740, 756
S: 309 S–Adult: 231

London, England — History
JS: 1782

Loneliness — Fiction
S–Adult: 33

Los Angeles — Fiction
JS: 28, 637 S–Adult: 1027

**Los Angeles Lakers (basketball
team)**
JS: 2518

Love — Fiction
JS: 296 S: 294, 555 S–Adult: 59,
240, 503

Love — Poetry
JS: 1196 S–Adult: 1216

Love — Memoirs
S–Adult: 1358

M

Macbeth **(play)**
JS: 1191

McCarthy, Joseph
S–Adult: 1889

McCourt, Frank
JS: 1344

Macdonald, Warren
JS: 1577

McGough, Matthew
JS: 1578

Mafia — Fiction
JS: 57

Magic and magicians — Fiction
JS: 415, 428, 461, 484, 493, 496,
502, 518, 523, 532, 694, 905
S–Adult: 948

Maine
JS: 2367

Mali
S–Adult: 1748

Mammals
See specific mammals, e.g., Bears

Mandan Indians — Fiction
JS: 777

Mandela, Nelson
JS: 1514, 1749

Manga
JS: 649, 2471 S: 551–52
S–Adult: 1623

Manga — Fiction
JS: 647

Manners
See Etiquette

Manzano, Juan Francisco
JS: 1345

Maps and globes
JS: 1685

**Marathon (race) — Boston
(MA)**
JS: 2533

Marie Antoinette
JS: 1536

Marijuana
JS: 2149, 2158

Marine Corps (U.S.)
JS: 2444 S–Adult: 1563

Marine life
See also Antarctic — Marine life;
Fish; and specific animals, e.g.,
Sharks
JS: 2347 S–Adult: 2346

Marketing — Careers
JS: 2124

Marketing — Memoirs
JS: 1566

Mars (planet)
JS: 2297

Marshall, George C.
JS: 1430

Martial arts — Fiction
S–Adult: 37

Martin, Jesse
JS: 1306

Mary, Queen of Scots
S–Adult: 1506

Massachusetts
S–Adult: 2041

Massachusetts — History
JS: 1701

Mathematics
JS: 2488

Mathematics — Biography
JS: 1479

Mathematics — History
JS: 2385

Mayan Indians
JS: 1808

Meat
JS: 2308

Media studies
JS: 2073

JS = Junior High/Senior High;   S = Senior High;   S–Adult = Senior High/Adult

JS = Junior High/Senior High;   S = Senior High;   S–Adult = Senior High/Adult

N

JS = Junior High/Senior High;   S = Senior High;   S–Adult = Senior High/Adult

JS = Junior High/Senior High;   S = Senior High;   S–Adult = Senior High/Adult

JS = Junior High/Senior High;   S = Senior High;   S–Adult = Senior High/Adult

Q

R

JS = Junior High/Senior High;   S = Senior High;   S–Adult = Senior High/Adult

JS = Junior High/Senior High;   S = Senior High;   S–Adult = Senior High/Adult

S

Saddam Hussein
See Hussein, Saddam

Safety
JS: 2233 S–Adult: 1942

Sagan, Carl
S–Adult: 1453

Saginor, Jennifer
JS: 1589

Salbi, Zainab
S–Adult: 1590

Salt
S–Adult: 1748

San Francisco — Fiction
JS: 238, 800 S–Adult: 928

Santa Claus — Fiction
JS: 581

Santiago, Esmeralda
S–Adult: 1358

Sarajevo — Fiction
S–Adult: 395

SARS
JS: 2183

Sartor, Margaret
S–Adult: 1592

Satire
S–Adult: 1296

Satrapi, Marjane
S–Adult: 1593

SATs — Fiction
JS: 34

Scandinavia
See also Norway; Vikings

Scandinavia — Mythology
JS: 1243

Scdoris, Rachel
JS: 1501

Scheeres, Julia
S–Adult: 1594

Scholarships
JS: 2096

Scholarships — Fiction
JS: 226

Schomaker, Annemarie Reuter
S–Adult: 1595

Schools
See also Boarding schools;
Education; High schools; Private
schools
JS: 2083, 2272

Schools — Fiction
JS: 52, 73, 88, 117, 250, 317, 324,
336, 775, 908 S–Adult: 85, 794

Schools — Segregation
JS: 1493, 1940, 1947, 1974

Schools — Violence — Fiction
JS: 377 S: 393

Science
See also branches of science, e.g.,
Chemistry
JS: 2284 S–Adult: 1453, 2280,
2282

Science — Biography
JS: 1444–45, 1449, 1451, 1455,
1460–61, 1467, 1472, 1480

Science — Careers
JS: 2137

**Science — Experiments and
projects**
See under specific branches of
science, e.g., Biology —
Experiments and projects

Science — History
JS: 1680, 2278, 2283 S: 2285
S–Adult: 2281

Science — Renaissance
JS: 2278

Science fairs
JS: 2305, 2352, 2371–72, 2378

Science fairs — Fiction
JS: 909

Science fiction
JS: 460, 565, 587–88, 1078,
1080–81, 1083–85, 1087–88,
1090–91, 1093–101, 1103–4, 1108,
1111–12, 1114, 1116–18, 1120, 1131,
1184 S: 899, 1119 S–Adult: 1077,
1079, 1082, 1086, 1089, 1092, 1102,
1105, 1107, 1109–10, 1113, 1115,
1139

Science fiction — Short stories
JS: 1163 S–Adult: 1140

Scotland — Biography
S–Adult: 1506

Scotland — Fiction
JS: 97, 147, 205, 750, 760–61, 898
S–Adult: 530, 916, 1029

Sea stories
S–Adult: 1541

Sea stories — Fiction
JS: 4

Sea turtles
JS: 2316

Seaton, Bill
JS: 1596

Seattle — Fiction
JS: 265

Segregation (U.S.) — Fiction
JS: 812

Self-help
JS: 2250

Self-image — Fiction
JS: 212, 218, 223, 331

Self-mutilation
S–Adult: 2218

Senate (U.S.)
JS: 1426

September 11, 2001
See also Terrorism
JS: 1466, 2065, 2074

September 11, 2001 — Fiction
JS: 389, 397 S–Adult: 84, 260, 384

Sex — Biography
JS: 1589

Sex — Fiction
JS: 74, 322, 324, 371, 888 S: 229,
284, 325, 353, 373 S–Adult: 198,
339, 347

Sex roles
JS: 2238 S–Adult: 2055

Sex roles — Fiction
JS: 249, 308

Sexual abstinence — Fiction
JS: 226

Sexual abuse
JS: 2239, 2241

Sexual abuse — Fiction
JS: 132 S–Adult: 257

Sexual behavior
S: 2240 S–Adult: 2230

Shackleton, Sir Ernest
JS: 1307

Shakespeare, William
JS: 1193–94, 1278–80

**Shakespeare, William —
Adaptations**
JS: 1192

Shakespeare, William — Fiction
JS: 762

Sharks
JS: 2348–49

Sherlock Holmes — Fiction
JS: 913

Shinto (religion)
S–Adult: 1904

Ships and boats
See also Shipwrecks
S–Adult: 2440

Ships and boats — History
JS: 1878 S–Adult: 1854

Shipwrecks
JS: 2439

Shoplifting — Fiction
JS: 76

JS = Junior High/Senior High; S = Senior High; S–Adult = Senior High/Adult

JS = Junior High/Senior High;   S = Senior High;   S–Adult = Senior High/Adult

T

JS = Junior High/Senior High; S = Senior High; S–Adult = Senior High/Adult

United States (1920s) — History
JS: 1873 S–Adult: 1875

United States (1930s) — History
JS: 1870

United States (1950s) — History
S–Adult: 1889

United States (1960s) — History
S–Adult: 1883

Universe
JS: 2291, 2300

Universities and colleges
S–Adult: 2097

Universities and colleges — Fiction
JS: 919

Urban legends
JS: 2486

USSR
See Soviet Union

Utah — Fiction
S–Adult: 816

Utopias
JS: 1094

Uzbekistan
S: 1754

V

Vacations — Fiction
S: 62

Vaccines
JS: 2175, 2178, 2187 S: 2190

Valentine's Day — Fiction
JS: 298

Vampires — Fiction
JS: 623, 646, 704, 843, 845, 848, 862, 871, 873–74, 876, 878 S: 678
S–Adult: 841, 875, 881

Van Buren, Martin
JS: 1414

Vatican City
JS: 1773

Vega, Marta Moreno
JS: 1602

Veterinarians
JS: 2366

Veterinarians — Biography
JS: 2367

Veterinarians — Careers
JS: 2116

Veterinarians — Fiction
S–Adult: 764

Victorian Age — Fiction
S–Adult: 741

Video games — Careers
JS: 2139, 2141

Video games — History
S–Adult: 2431

Vietnam War
JS: 1890, 1941 S–Adult: 1892

Vietnam War — Biography
S–Adult: 1341, 2435

Vietnam War — Fiction
JS: 836–37 S–Adult: 349, 839

Vietnam War — Protests
JS: 1891

Vietnamese Americans
JS: 1491

Vietnamese Americans — Memoirs
JS: 1603

Vikings — Fiction
JS: 711

Violence
See also Domestic violence;
   Schools — Violence; Teenagers
   — Violence
JS: 2027, 2032

Violence — Fiction
JS: 118, 143, 385, 399, 590

Violence — Mass media
JS: 2009

Virginia — Biography
S–Adult: 1435

von Braun, Wernher
JS: 2433

Vocabulary
JS: 142

Volunteerism
JS: 2057, 2060–61

W

Wagner, Richard
JS: 1362

Wales — Fiction
S–Adult: 149

Wales — History — Fiction
JS: 719

War
See also specific battles and wars,
   e.g., World War II
JS: 1679, 1917, 1976

War — Biography
JS: 1507

War — Children
JS: 1723

War — Fiction
JS: 79, 754

War — Memoirs
JS: 1958

War — Poetry
JS: 1198

War of the Roses — Fiction
JS: 748

Warhol, Andy
JS: 1322

Warner, Andrea
JS: 1603

Washington, DC
JS: 1876 S–Adult: 2228

Washington, DC — Fiction
JS: 39, 986

Washington, George
JS: 1415–16, 1847

Washington, Martha
JS: 1417

Washington (state) — Fiction
S–Adult: 40

Waste recycling
JS: 2020

Water
JS: 2374

Water sports
See specific sports, e.g., Surfing

Weapons
JS: 2441

Weapons of mass destruction
JS: 2445

Weather
See also Climate; and specific types
   of weather, e.g., Tornadoes
JS: 2390, 2394–96 S–Adult: 2397

Webber, Thomas L.
S–Adult: 1604

Weight control
JS: 2224

Weight problems — Fiction
JS: 204, 331

Weight training
JS: 2501

Weinstein, Lauren
JS: 1605

Weizmann, Chaim
JS: 1794

Welfare — United States
JS: 2050 S–Adult: 1931, 2052

West, Cornel
JS: 1441

West (U.S.)
See also Frontier life (U.S.)

West (U.S.) — Fiction
JS: 793 S–Adult: 29

JS = Junior High/Senior High;   S = Senior High;   S–Adult = Senior High/Adult

Y

Z

JS = Junior High/Senior High;   S = Senior High;   S–Adult = Senior High/Adult

About the Authors

JOHN T. GILLESPIE, renowned authority in children's literature, is the author of more than 30 books on collection development. In addition to the other volumes in the Best Books series (*Best Books for Children* and *Best Books for Middle School and Junior High Readers*), he is also the author of *Teenplots, Classic Teenplots, The Newbery Companion: Booktalk and Related Materials for Newbery Medal and Honor Books,* and *The Children's and Young Adult Literature Handbook: A Research and Reference Guide.*

CATHERINE BARR is the coauthor of other volumes in the Best Books series (*Best Books for Children* and *Best Books for Middle School and Junior High Readers*) and of *Popular Series Fiction for K–6 Readers, Popular Series Fiction for Middle School and Teen Readers*, and *High/Low Handbook: Best Books and Web Sites for Reluctant Teen Readers, 4th Edition.*